Drugs, Trafficking and Criminal Policy

The Scapegoat Strategy

Penny Green is Director of the Institute of Criminal Justice at the University of Southampton and a Senior Lecturer in Law. She is the author of *The Enemy Without: Policy and Class Consciousness in the Miners' Strike* (1990) and editor of *Drug Couriers: A New Perspective* (1996).

The **Waterside Press** Criminal Policy Series

Volume I

Transforming Criminal Policy

Volume II

Capital Punishment: Global Issues and Prospects

Volume III

Drugs, Trafficking and Criminal Policy: The Scapegoat Strategy

Volume IV

Criminal Justice and the Pursuit of Decency

In preparation (working titles)

The Scottish Criminal Justice Process

Golden Threads: Questions for the Law of Evidence

Drugs, Trafficking and Criminal Policy

The Scapegoat Strategy

Penny Green

Waterside Press Criminal Policy Series Volume III
Series Editor Andrew Rutherford

Drugs, Trafficking and Criminal Policy
The Scapegoat Strategy

Published 1998 by
WATERSIDE PRESS
Domum Road
Winchester SO23 9NN
Telephone or Fax 01962 855567
INTERNET 106025.1020@compuserve.com

ISBN Paperback 1 872 870 33 3

Cataloguing-in-Publication Data A catalogue record for this book can be obtained from the British Library

Waterside Press Criminal Policy Series Volume III

Printing and binding Antony Rowe Ltd, Chippenham.

Drugs, Trafficking and Criminal Policy

CONTENTS

CHAPTER

Glossary

ACPO	Association of Chief Police Officers
CDIU	Central Drugs and Immigration Unit
CELAD	European Community to Combat Drugs
CJPOA	Criminal Justice and Public Order Act 1994
CLO	Civil Liberties Organization (Nigeria)
DEA	Drug Enforcement Agency (US)
DTOA	Drug Trafficking Offences Act 1986
EDU	Europol Drugs Unit
EIS	Europol Information Service
EOD	European Observatory on Drugs
EU	European Union
FASTs	Flexible Anti-Smuggling Teams
FATF	Financial Action Task Force (Group of Seven's)
FBI	Federal Bureau of Investigation (US)
FCO	Foreign and Commonwealth Office
GSP	Generalised System of Preferences
IMF	International Monetary Fund
ISDD	Institute for the Study of Drug Dependence
MDMA	Methylenedioxymethamphetamine (Ecstasy)
MLATS	Mutual Legal Assistance Treaties
NCIS	National Criminal Intelligence Service
NDIU	National Drugs Intelligence Unit
NDLEA	National Drug Law Enforcement Agency (Nigeria)
PHARE	Drug related aid programme to Central and Eastern Europe
PSR	Pre- sentence Report
SAP	Structural Adjustment Programme
SCODA	Standing Conference on Drug Abuse
SIS	Schengen Information System
TACIS	Aid programme to the Commonwealth of Independent States
UNDCP	United Nations Drug Control Programme

Preface

This volume, the third to be published in the Waterside Press *Criminal Policy Series*, is especially timely in the contribution it offers to the debate taking place on both sides of the Atlantic as to how most sensibly to deal with illegal drugs. Focusing initially on the plight of foreign national drugs couriers, Penny Green explores the context of drug trafficking and its crucial place within international trade and the global economy. Demonising couriers, often desperate and tragic people from the poorest regions of the world, gets in the way of rational analysis and Dr Green insists that it is underlying geo-political issues which ultimately must be addressed.

Penny Green's study works well at various levels. She draws on a large sample of people imprisoned for trafficking and on the interviews she conducted within prisons in England and Wales. The impression of the drug courier which emerges is, in most instances, far from the image generated by the media or the day-to-day political discourse. By means of a case study of Nigeria, she also makes the link between the individual in a prison cell far from home and the complex configuration of economic and political interests. Dr Green's analysis leads her to conclude that contemporary policy must be freed from the 'scapegoat strategy' and be prepared to address such issues as developmental politics and Third World debt. This invaluable study will be of immediate interest to practitioners and policy-makers as well as to a wider readership frustrated by the narrow margins within which this issue is conventionally addressed.

Andrew Rutherford

July 1998

Acknowledgments

Many people provided their time and resources so as to make this book possible.

First, and most importantly, I want to thank all the imprisoned drug couriers who spent many hours talking with me about their experiences of drug trafficking and the circumstances which led them to prison. They form the central thread of the book's analysis and their testimonies are a powerful indictment of all that is wrong with international drug control. I hope that the book in some way exposes the injustices they face both as victims of the international drug trade and perhaps more significantly as victims of international drug control.

I was particularly fortunate in having the excellent research assistance of Rose Newman, Sharon Pickering and Sarah Rennie. I thank them for all their hard work and enthusiasm.

I would also like to thank, John Corkery at the Home Office for his valuable and patient statistical advice and reams of raw data; Nick Hammond and Rosemary Abernethey at the Middlesex Probation Service Foreign Nationals Unit for sharing vast knowledge of couriers and trafficking patterns; Bob Fairweather and his colleagues at the Foreign and Commonwealth Office; Frances Crook at the Howard League for first raising the problem of foreign couriers with me; Mike Grewcock for his witty cynicism; Melanie McFadyean for her insight and the prison and probation staff around the country who facilitated my prison visits.

The Institute for the Study of Drug Dependence Library was an important resource and my thanks go to the librarians whose assistance was invaluable.

Special thanks to Andrew Rutherford for his incisive editorial comments, and to my colleagues in the Law Faculty at Southampton University. I am grateful to the Faculty Research Committee and to the Howard League for Penal Reform which generously supported much of this research.

Finally, as always, my biggest thanks are to Bill Spence for his endless support and to Grace for the light she brings at the end of the working day.

Penny Green

July 1988

CHAPTER ONE

Introduction

Much has been written on the futile and destructive war that successive USA administrations have waged against the users and suppliers of illicit drugs. The militarisation of law enforcement, counter insurgency, political corruption, an expansion of organized crime and associated violence and wholesale assaults against Black and Hispanic domestic communities and Latin American coca-producing countries are just some of the consequences of that war. The results are bleak and growing bleaker and the problems associated with drugs and their prohibition have simply escalated (Gordon 1994; Nadleman 1993; Chomsky 1992; Scott and Marshall 1991; Reiman 1994). In terms of scale, the prohibition-driven drug crisis in the UK is relatively minor when compared with that which exists in the United States, but, as in the USA, it has fostered a punitive crime-control driven campaign underscored by the political rhetoric of national security, domestic order and alien threat. The assault against drugs has taken a number of forms in the UK since the inception (or construction) of the drugs 'problem' and has concentrated most punitively on the trafficking of proscribed drugs.

My research interest in drug trafficking was originally inspired by the plight of foreign national drug couriers—Third World people caught up in First World prisons, awaiting fates unknown—low-level drug players paying high level punishment prices. The stories that the couriers told took me well beyond the lives of the individual story-teller and into the realms of development politics and political economy. It became clear that any satisfactory analysis of how these people came to be where they were demanded an examination of both the geo-politics of the drug trade and the geo-politics of drug control. The plight of these couriers could not simply be understood within a framework of domestic criminal policy. Major issues of international political economy both sustain international drug trafficking and suppress any serious attempts to curb the trade. The cancellation of crippling IMF and World Bank loans for producer or transit countries is not contemplated and governments complicit in the trade are never seriously countered. Rather than tackle the root causes of problem drug use and the industry which has grown up around it, drug enforcement continues to 'mess about at the edges'. As with criminal policy more generally there is a focus on the individual agent as the source of the problem. Thus it is the drug baron who becomes the official target. But the real drug lords are

9

protected by wealth, power and weaponry, so there is a lowering of the target—but only in terms of practice not in terms of political rhetoric. The target is lowered and lowered until it settles upon those offenders most vulnerable to arrest. Thus the courier comes to centre stage in the war on drugs.

While the invisibility of the drug barons from the law and its agents is a truism in the popular perception of drug trafficking, its corollary— the visibility of the courier—is not. Low level players in the drugs trade continue to occupy the attention of the agents and ideologues of drug control despite an official public rhetoric which demonises the phantom baron. Perhaps the most important and at the same time most prosaic finding of my research is that the vast majority of those arrested, convicted and imprisoned for drug trafficking offences are unequivocally low level players, simply border conduits for drugs contraband. What seems to take place is a re-defining of what constitutes a 'serious' or 'major' drug offender—a process reinforced by Australian research which has shown that the definition of 'seriousness' applied by drug enforcement agents to drug offences is highly problematic, and in operational terms, 'specialist agencies tend to employ fluid measures of seriousness which blur the distinction between major and minor drug offender targets' (Green and Purnell 1995:35).

Within existing law and drug-control policy there is no real framework for drawing a distinction between low-level and high-level players, between for instance, sophisticated, powerful traffickers and naive, poor, unknowing couriers. One of the tasks of this book is to expose the official blurring of players in the drug trade—in foreign and domestic policy—and to examine why drug-control policy and enforcement continues to ignore the hierarchical distinctions which characterise the trade. It is possible to delineate a framework which distinguishes between the different roles and layers of involvement that drug markets offer 'employees', a framework which is capable of distinguishing low-level couriers from both intermediate and more powerful drug criminals. Dorn et al write of the 'fragmentary and fluid' nature of drug markets and isolated subcultural 'trading charities', 'sideliners', 'criminal diversifiers', criminal 'families', 'opportunistic irregulars' and 'retail specialists' (Dorn et al 1992:42). Maynard relies on a more rigid framework based on a hierarchical distribution of involvement defined by the weight of drugs traded (Maynard 1988:53).

In the Australian study noted above, the authors developed a typology based upon power and control—with street dealers, area distributors and Third World couriers on the bottom rungs of the 'seriousness' ladder and the heads of international networks and

10

financiers at the top (Green and Purnell 1996:100). Such frameworks would be of certain value to those policy makers and law enforcers committed to pursuing the major drug traffickers. In ideological terms, however, the distinctions outlined may be seen as providing complex and ambiguous public messages about the issue of illegal drugs.

There is nothing extraordinary about the structure of involvement in the drugs trade—illegality does little to alter the nature of capitalist hierarchy. If the drugs market was a licit market then we would equally be able to draw up a typology which would include—street traders, casual labourers, sales representatives, retailers, import/exporters, managers, corporate heads and financiers.

In terms of the distinctions which emerge between the traffickers interviewed for this book, there are four defining features—power, control, wealth and cognisance—which separate major from minor drug players. Only the 'professionals' or 'entrepreneurs' and the 'ailing bourgeoisie' described in *Chapter 5* displayed any real evidence of these traits. For the majority of imprisoned drug importers, power, control, wealth and cognisance were in serious deficit.

This book, attempts to offer an understanding about a particular group of drug traffickers, through an analysis of the political economy of British drug control policy and the role it plays for the state. The war on drugs in the UK is a more tepid war in every respect when compared with its progenitor, yet its dimensions are far reaching and remain rooted in the mimicry of USA strategy. Punitive law and order politics on crime, drugs and public order have, for almost two decades, characterised the tone of British criminal justice policy. As in the United States 'It has become as much the function of crime and illicit drug use to provide an opportunity for politically obligatory "get tough" postures as it is the role of recurring drug and crime wars to point the way toward solutions' (Gordon 1994:ix). This book seeks to explore why the war-on-drugs strategy survives by measuring some of the undeclared interests of that policy against the failures of the prohibitionist strategy. Those failures include the ready and increasing availability of illicit drugs despite a primarily supply-oriented control strategy; the spread of HIV among intravenous drug users; the overcrowding of our prisons, the continued lengthy imprisonment of impoverished Third World couriers, the failure to get close to the drug kings and queens; the hypocrisy inherent in the political support of the most dangerous yet legal drugs, tobacco and alcohol and the wilful neglect displayed by governments in addressing the economic and social misery experienced by many thousands of people in Britain's deprived communities.

The issue of domestic demand is never seriously pursued in policy terms. Rather than examine the root causes of poverty, urban deprivation, unemployment, homelessness and social misery, demand-focused policy orients itself almost entirely around drug education and the treatment of addicts. Demarcation lines have always been clearly drawn between the user and acceptable treatment-model reforming policies; and the traffickers of illicit drugs. For the latter—the drug importers, producers, suppliers and street dealers—there have been no non-punitive acceptable reforms. Except for the pioneering activities of isolated probation services,[1] the work of certain pressure groups[2] and even the efforts of unusually reformist prison staff[3] the punitive road would forge ahead without any commentary or critique at all. During the past decade and a half an increasingly repressive stance on drug trafficking has prevailed in the UK witnessed at all levels of the criminal justice process. Rather than presenting a beacon of light to inspire the reform process elsewhere British policy makers have forsaken past lessons and invested considerable resources into emulating the American war against drugs, apparently undeterred by its colossal failure.

Within a framework of British and international drug control this book offers a critical analysis of policy developments and trends and then concentrates its focus on one quite specific group of drug traffickers—those who carry drugs across borders. Despite their lowly status in the drug trade hierarchy couriers are the central target of customs border controls. In 1995 couriers convicted in Britain represented approximately nine per cent of all traffickers who were found guilty, cautioned or dealt with by compounding, but they represented 34 per cent of all traffickers sentenced to immediate custody. In addition, as is later documented, they suffer some of the harshest penalties inflicted by the criminal justice process. By focusing on this group of drug offenders I hope to draw out some of the central problematics of drug control policy. In doing so I hope to illustrate Nils Christie's basic proposition that offenders and in this case drug trafficking offenders 'are people, ordinary people, not a special breed, not bandits'. This is also, therefore, a book about ordinary people— ordinary people from Nigeria, from Colombia, from the Caribbean and from Britain, who were driven by the needs of personal and economic security to enter into (often at the lowest level) the international drug trade. Ordinary people who in many cases found themselves overwhelmed by the problems facing them and who agreed to carry drugs for rewards which they believed could potentially transform their lives. But for many of the subjects of this book the unimaginable happened, their lives were indeed transformed but in a direction which

12

led to increased not reduced misery. The course of action they took led these ordinary people to long terms of imprisonment very often in foreign jails, thousands of miles from family, friends and the unresolved problems which ultimately led them there.

The picture presented is not simply an attempt to dispel the lazy and ideological characterisation of drug couriers as 'ruthless traffickers in death' though it is certainly that. This study of drug couriers also, by necessity, became a study of the global divide between the developed north and the underdeveloped south. It is of the political economy of the international drug trade but with a specific emphasis on the way in which this political economy impacts on the relatively impoverished drug courier, and on the policies which criminalise him or her. With the use of biographies—the personal histories of those who have carried drugs across borders—and an understanding of the political economies from which they originate we can begin to understand the specific impact that the dynamic of underdevelopment has on those who are recruited for the high-risk, low-grade transport work of the drug trade.

As well as highlighting the impact of British criminal justice strategies on drug traffickers this book also examines the dialectical way in which drug production in the Third World has influenced the criminal justice system in the developed world. I argue that couriers cannot be understood in terms of traditional or even liberal criminological perspectives which take as their starting point the criminal event and the criminality of the courier. Drug trafficking is a phenomena intimately connected with issues of political economy, underdevelopment and Third World economic exploitation. The implications for drug control policy from this perspective are clear and point very firmly away from traditional models of crime control.

The chapters which follow chart the political and economic underpinnings of drug control policy and practice in the UK and within Europe through the 1980s and 1990s. Within that broader context the focus is on the impact of one select group of drug offenders—drug importers. The book begins by locating Britain's place on the international drug control map, first with an examination of Britain in the new Europe and the general moves to harmonise European drug control and second by charting British drug control's relationship with foreign policy. The next two chapters outline the 'geo-political' nature of drug control and locate the international drugs trade within that framework. *Chapter 4* provides a substantive geo-political case-study of Nigeria, an important drug transit country, whose citizens, during the late 1980s and 1990s, were over represented in British jails convicted of drug importation. In that chapter the impact of British drug control on a developing African country offers an illuminating example of the

13

relationship between global politics and the internationalisation of drug control. We hear the voices of imprisoned Nigerian traffickers offering their perspective and a new sense of understanding about the effects of economic, political and social upheaval on their involvement in the drug trade. This leads then to a qualitative study of a multi-national group of imprisoned drug couriers giving the lie to crass trafficking stereotypes. *Chapter 6* provides a brief history of drug-control policy in the UK charting the rise of the demon trafficker in political discourse. The emergence of the drug trafficker as a public enemy is essential to understanding the role of drug policy in shaping and spear-heading new and repressive law enforcement strategies. It is also essential to understanding why, in the face of the geo-political analysis offered earlier, the courier remains a central target in the war against drugs. The trends toward more punitive treatment of drug offenders in criminal justice and increasingly repressive drug enforcement legislation are analysed in terms of both Conservative and Labour policies. In *Chapter 7* I explore the nature of Britain's own war against drugs, documenting its fiscal costs, and relative failures. This chapter also examines the role of the police and customs in drug control and deals with the problematics of police versus government over the issue of decriminalisation, drug-related police corruption, drugs and the policing of black people as well as custom's policy and practice of targeting low-level players. Finally that chapter examines the punishment of drug traffickers and asks what the repressive punishment of this group of offenders contributes to drug control.

Underpinning each of the themes addressed in this book is the assumption that it is prohibition and not the drugs prohibited which is the central problem. This book, while not specifically addressing the legalisation debate, is nonetheless submitted as evidence of the necessity for a radical and informed change in drug control policy.

ENDNOTES

1 See in particular the excellent work of the Middlesex Area and Inner London Probation Services
2 See, e.g. the work of The Howard League, Women in Prison, Hibiscus and Save the Children Fund in the early 1990s
3 HMP Highpoint had a particularly progressive education department which catered very specifically for the needs of African prisoners most of whom had been convicted of the illegal importation of drugs. The Probation Department there organized meetings of African prisoners who were then able to petition the Home Office in respect of existing injustices faced by foreign national prisoners.

14

CHAPTER TWO

Britain, Europe and the World: European Union and the Drugs War

Britain's domestic drugs policies, and particularly those relating to drugs trafficking have always been informed by international (primarily American) concerns. Increasingly those policies will also come under the influence of political and economic decisions made in the European forum. This chapter examines the early years of drug enforcement in the European Union and the ideology which has shaped drug control policy particularly with reference to drug couriers who, by virtue of their existence, transgress border integrity. The Single European Act requires the removal of all frontier controls between the member states of the European Community, specifying that 'the internal market shall comprise an area without internal frontiers in which the free movement of goods, persons, services and capital is ensured in accordance with the provisions of this treaty' (article 8A SEA). Given the priority of 'borders' in any discussion on domestic and international drug control the abolition of internal frontiers raises an inevitable conflict between issues of national sovereignty and the notion of a unified drugs policy. Within the European Union drug policies have increasingly been incorporated into the wider political and security concerns of the Union. Six priority areas of action were outlined by the first two European plans as central to the strategy of repressing drug trafficking: the strengthening of drug controls at external borders; increased surveillance and cooperation *within* the European Community; the introduction of measures to prevent the illicit manufacture of drugs and the diversion of essential precursor chemicals; anti money-laundering measures; the reinforcement of existing drug trafficking laws and judicial systems; and the collation of statistical information. (European Commission 1994a: 39)

The advent of the single market and the new co-operative law enforcement strategies that are a product of that union are set to further reinforce the policies already in place which, as will be seen in later chapters, target the foreign drug courier as opposed to more significant players in the trade. While European Union is ostensibly about the relaxation of border controls between member states, those frontiers which are 'exposed' or adjacent to non-European countries are set to experience increased controls.[1]

Apart from increased external border control the new Europe will be specifically concerned with the introduction of some form of common restrictive visa policy for visiting nationals of 'third' countries and for

15

prospective immigrants; coast-line enforcement; uniform training for drug enforcement officers; a general harmonisation of drug trafficking legislation; operational guidelines for engaging in the 'hot pursuit' of drug traffickers and other criminals across internal borders; the establishment of national drugs intelligence units which will facilitate police and customs work; and 'an upgraded and common computerised system enabling the retrieval of information about international criminal profiles, trafficker types and methods of transport within seconds'. (Hopkinson 1991:17-18). The notion of a central European drug enforcement agency (Europol) to coordinate these was agreed upon at the July 1990 EC summit.

But the issue of relaxed border controls is somewhat illusory particularly in respect of the movement of 'non European' nationals across those borders—an issue pertinent to the drug couriers in my own research study. Drug traffickers have, it seems, become linked, in the lexicon of European policy, with illegal immigrants. The European union is interested in facilitating the movement of only certain kinds of labour—a position suitably reinforced by public representations of drug-smuggling, illegal, 'economic' immigrants. This is exemplified in the statement arising from the TREVI members' Programme of Action, 1990, which expressed their task as a 'synthesis of the arrangements . . . between police and security services in relation to terrorism, drug trafficking or any forms of crime including organized illegal immigration'.[2] The linked concerns of the European Commission are again clear when it warns of '. . . sources of instability leading to mass migration, fundamental extremism, terrorism, drugs and organized crime'. (European Commission, 1994b)

XENOPHOBIA AND THE DISPLACEMENT OF BLAME

Nicholas Dorn has argued that '. . . there is a tradition in Europe of describing drug traffickers in terms of foreign nationalities and, in particular, to equate *organized* trafficking and other criminality with nationalities outside the EU. This tendency is rife in the internal ministries and policing agencies of the EU member states, who effectively formulate pan-European trafficking policy'. (1996:251) This was made explicit by the Secretary General of Interpol who, when addressing a conference of British chief police officers claimed

> Most of the better established criminal organizations in Europe and elsewhere have very pronounced ethnic characteristics . . . we should also be concerned over the current resurgence of ethnic and national claims of some minorities in the world especially in many states emerging from communism as this may be giving rise to a more sinister element of drug trafficking. The common identity

16

of language and history, combined with political frustration, can bring together groups of individuals who may seek to commit criminal acts to further their goals. (Kendall 1994:7)[3]

Citing the ethnic Mafia in Russia, the American and Italian Cosa Nostra, the Chinese Triads, the Colombian cartels and the Turkish Mafia, Kendall went on to discuss drug trafficking in terms of a geo-political security threat. According to Dorn, in 1994 when the drugs intelligence units of member states were asked to conduct research into the nature of drug trafficking and organized crime in their respective countries 'foreign nationality' was apparently used as a criterion to determine whether crime or trafficking was 'organized'. He comments '. . . it seems fair to recognise the extent to which (a) xenophobia and (b) internal EU political conflicts and stalemates play their part in generating counter-productive levels of anxiety amongst European policy-makers and drug enforcement practitioners'. (1996:251) Blaming ethnic minorities is central to western strategies of drug control. In an analysis of drugs and foreign policy in post communist societies Lee and MacDonald situate the activities associated with drug trafficking unconditionally with the foreigner:

> Outside of Poland . . . amphetamine gangs operate through a kind of Polish pipeline, a broad network of resident Polish citizens or former Polish nationals . . . serve as critical links in the wholesale trade, taking delivery of drugs from Poland, storing them and reselling them to local distributors. The foreign connection is as important to Polish drug smuggling gangs as the estimated one million Colombians living in the United States are to the activities of the so-called Colombian cartels — or the two million Turks living in Europe are to Turkish heroin-smuggling families. (1994:196)

In the UK the same overriding concern with national criminal stereotypes is very much at work. The Home Affairs Committee Third Report on 'Organized Crime' illustrates the extent of these prejudices. Having 'established' that much of organized crime is 'ethnically' based it went on to suggest that ethnic groups '. . . whether from Italy, China, Turkey, Jamaica, Colombia or elsewhere—frequently had a network of family or cultural connections enabling links to be established across continents with ease.' Citing evidence from the Home Office which suggests that indigenous or domestic groups in the UK lack the sophistication and level of organization to fit the definition of organized crime the report returned to its ethnic group focus claiming that 'Many of these (and all of those just listed) had footholds and enterprises in the UK' (HOC 1995:xii-xiii). A secret dossier prepared by the National Criminal Intelligence Service (NCIS) for the home secretary in May 1997 discusses the threat of organized crime in the UK primarily in terms of ethnic gangs and again

17

fosters the notion of the foreigner as dangerous, with claims, for example, that South American cocaine dealers operate their drug trafficking trade under restaurant and tapas bar fronts.[4] In keeping with the theme of xenophobia the Foreign and Commonwealth Office note concern

. . . at the apparent involvement of West African crime networks in the international drugs trade. Traffickers smuggle Asian heroin to North America and Europe and South American cocaine to South Africa, Nigeria and Europe. In addition cannabis, which is the only illicit drug extensively grown in the region is shipped to Europe. (FCO personal communication, March 1997)

What this means in policy terms is a drug control strategy informed, not primarily by the nature of the drugs to be controlled, but rather by ethnic populations and Third World states which Western nations perceive as somehow politically, ideologically or militarily threatening. Traffickers from the target groups are therefore at greater risk of apprehension, not so much for the drug they carry but for the security threat their nationality is perceived to carry. How else can we explain the targeting, of two regions whose predominant cultivated drug is cannabis. The European Council has identified the fight against trafficking in illegal drugs as an area suitable for common action under CFSP (Common Foreign and Security Policy) and has identified the MAGHREB[5] and the Middle East as priority regions in that context. (European Commission 1994a:v)

The rise of Islamic fundamentalism and the economic and political insecurity of both the countries of the MAGHREB and those of the Middle East offer a much more plausible means of understanding the priority afforded these regions in terms of European drug control than elevating Western concerns over cannabis. Drug control is therefore a proxy for another much broader and politically sensitive form of people control—the control of the free movement of certain people from certain countries in the face of the increased prospect of the free movement of people within Europe.

A similar situation is reflected throughout the European Union. In Germany neo-Nazi groups and the new right-wing political parties have exploited the supposed relationship between drug trafficking and foreign nationals. Asylum seekers as a result are charged with posing a serious threat to the safety of the German public in an effort to further restrict immigration controls. Hans-Jorg Albrecht reports that some 40 per cent of newspaper articles about foreigners in Germany made reference to the criminal activities (largely drug trafficking) of those foreigners. Such is the political fusion taking place between the two in Germany that Albrecht writes 'Overall, ethnic minorities and drug traffickers are being increasingly linked in a manner which hinders independent analysis of either phenomenon'(1996:62)

EUROPEAN COOPERATION?

A perusal of the literature on European drugs policy, conventions and the fora for their determination leaves one reeling under the weight of bureaucratic excess and multiplicity. One is minded to borrow, with a little adaptation, Nils Christie's '*drug*-control as industry' analysis in order to understand what appears to have quickly become a self-serving job-creation bureaucracy. In practical terms, 'The plethora of national, international and global agencies involved in different aspects of drug control is a recipe for confusion, duplication of effort and inter-agency rivalries'. (Seward 1993:3)

The European approach to the control of international drug trafficking has involved a deluge of treaties, agreements, conventions and memoranda of understanding as well as an abundance of European and international bodies (see below). In 1987 The European Community took a decision in principle to be part of the UN conference on drug trafficking in Vienna—a new and apparently more 'outward-looking' departure based on the desire to engage in dialogue with partner countries, 'on national and regional policies to combat drug production and consumption . . . in the more general context of the economic development of the producer countries and of their cooperation with the European Community'. (Commission Communication, cited in G Estievenart 1995:54)

The accepted inadequacy of domestic controls and their impact on drug trafficking has frequently been cited as justification for the development of wider European initiatives:

> The need for urgent EC action was underlined by an investigation conducted by the European Parliament into links between drugs and the spread of organized crime. After interviewing customs officers, police, bankers, politicians and lawyers, the MEP's concluded that existing policies had cut drugs traffic by less than 15% and that the organizations involved were growing "at an alarming rate".

The inquiry chaired by British Labour MEP David Bowe, also demanded a range of new measures, including a new European Drugs Intelligence Unit of police and customs officers working closely with Interpol in addition to the new agency'. (*The European*, 23 April 1992)

EC drugs policy cooperation only began in 1989 when the EC created CELAD (European Community to Combat Drugs) as a ministerial level funding body responsible for co-ordinating member state anti-trafficking programmes and work undertaken in EC fora. The European Programme for the Fight Against Drugs established five action areas in 1990: co-ordination of member states anti-drug policies, measures to stop drug trafficking, demand reduction, EC multilateral participation, and the creation of a European Observatory on Drugs (EOD) to monitor drug production, legislation, trafficking and demand (Hopkinson 1991:17). However, at many levels there remains a great lack of cooperation between member states as to the precise nature of law enforcement measures. Seward documents the international reluctance towards cooperation:

> Western Europe still shows entrenched resistance to transferring any real authority in drugs matters from national to European level. Italy recently proposed the establishment of a regional computerised drugs information system, the concept of which was endorsed by the UN. It took a year of negotiations to get ten countries plus Interpol around the table. Then four West European countries objected on the grounds that a regional system should be run by an international organization, not an individual country. The same countries, however, show little enthusiasm for the proposal that the system be run by Interpol. The process of international consultation will not become any easier when Europol has to be included. Indeed, the net result might be increased reliance on bilateral moves, with the claim that this is the only way to get things done quickly.

And further:

> The dismal results of the Balkan Route Working Group on database sharing encapsulates the problem. After twelve months' hard work, the Group agreed to establish one data base, accessible to police and customs alike. Unfortunately, the agreement has never been implemented. Lack of trust, inter-agency rivalries, especially between customs and police, and the absence of a clear political imperative proved stronger than the need to cooperate. (Seward 1993: 7-8)

In rhetoric at least, there are some measures of agreement at the level of European drugs policy, mostly with regard to the need to accord equal priority to policies of supply and demand reduction and the rejection of moves to decriminalise any drugs which are currently prohibited (the anti-libertarian stand has mostly been attributed to the AIDS epidemic and the progression of users from soft to hard drugs despite evidence to the contrary produced in The Netherlands). However, it is within the supply side of the equation in which European initiatives can be located. There is little, if any, debate on the underlying principles of anti-drugs policy. Rather, European developments focus on the effectiveness and co-ordination of law enforcement strategies through various conventions and bodies. Perhaps this is understandable considering that these are issues on which international cooperation is easier to achieve and where progress on a 'seen to be doing something' level is tangible—despite the far from successful indications emerging from such 'European' initiatives. However, the development of supra-national efforts against drug trafficking via changes emanating from the Maastricht Treaty, the Schengen Agreement, the TREVI Group, Europol, and the Council of Europe's Pompidou Group[6] etc may be understood as based upon exaggerated portrayals of the threat to society posed by the drug problem. As with anti-terrorist measures drug trafficking fosters a united political front which itself is sustained and developed by measures of publicly encouraged fear. The greater the implied threat, the greater the public fear, the easier the introduction of exceptional judicial and political measures to deal with the apparent problem.

Despite the claim by Seward that '. . . the current anti-drugs strategy . . . can hardly be called successful while all the indicators of drug use in Europe show an upward curve' (Seward 1993:4) the European drugs war has not been unsuccessful in ideological terms. The proliferation of European measures to tackle the drug problem has a reinforcing impact for member governments set on the punitive path. Every new initiative, agreement, treaty, or drug control agency raises the ideological profile and demonisation of drug trafficking and in doing so cushions the impact of increasingly repressive national measures directed against drug offenders within, or at the borders, of member states.

EUROPOL AND THE EUROPOL DRUGS UNIT

According to the 1994 government Green Paper, *Tackling Drugs Together*, Title IV of the Maastricht Treaty aims to enhance cooperation between governments tackling drug misuse. This cooperation is intended to extend to judicial, customs and police areas and includes the establishment of Europol—a non-operational convention for the exchange of information and intelligence. The underlying rationale for Europol was summed up by the House of Lords Select Committee on European Communities as follows: 'In the common struggle against international organized crime, the methods available to police forces seeking information were perceived as primitive. An effective response would require a modern computer based information system, with a central capacity for analysing intelligence'(HL 1995). As Tony Bunyan has pointed out, the ideology implicit in the creation of Europol 'links organized crime, drug trafficking, money laundering, terrorism and "illegal" immigration as posing a new "threat" to the stability of the EU' (1995). The powers demanded for Europol have been such that governments and European police chiefs have justified them on the grounds that Europol will *not* be an operational force (*Statewatch*, March 1997:2). One of the first initiatives of Europol, which is currently before European national parliaments for ratification has been the establishment of a drugs unit (EDU) concerned with intelligence on illegal drug trafficking and associated money laundering. There is some emphasis on the exchange of information on demand reduction in article 129, but this is certainly a secondary consideration. John Major threw all of his UK weight behind Europol in 1994 at the European Heads of Government Summit in Corfu where he proposed a plan to tackle drug-trafficking and other organized crime by increased intelligence gathering, strengthening the drugs work of Europol and the sharing of national expertise.

The Europol Drugs Unit (EDU) was formed in 1993 and was to be the first stage toward the creation of Europol. The EDU is, again in theory, a non-operational unit for the exchange and analysis of drug-trafficking intelligence. Its purpose is to assist the co-ordination of law enforcement activities between member states, reporting to a National Criminal Intelligence Service in each of the member states (Bruggeman 1994). Since 1993, however, the focus of the EDU has been substantially extended to include the illicit trafficking of radioactive and nuclear materials, crimes associated with clandestine immigration networks, illicit vehicle smuggling and organized crime's involvement in money laundering (*Statewatch*, March 1997:3). And the very nature of the Convention appears to be changing—from non-operational to explicitly operational. Recommendations tabled in the 'Action Plan to Combat Organized Crime' from a 'High Level Group' of European prosecutors '. . . would make Europol operational, give a wide definition of "organized crime", and create new bodies to co-ordinate judicial and prosecution policies' (*Statewatch*, March 1997:3). The expanded remit is to include powers which would enable Europol to play an active role in facilitating and carrying out specific investigations.

There has been a dispute between the major European powers over the role and control of Europol with Germany lobbying to build up Europol while France and the UK oppose such a development. *The Times* reported on the nature of the conflict at the end of 1994:

> France insists that national police officers attached to Europol must have access not only to standardised data pooled in Europol, but also more sensitive intelligence. The latest German proposal, backed by all its other partners, would restrict access to sensitive data except where Europol and national liaison officers attached to it, were directly involved. The German position reflects concerns that national police forces do not lose control of the security of their most delicate operations. Mr. Charles Pasqua, the hardline French interior minister, is determined to keep the Europol project firmly under national government control, and in general he has strong support from Britain and Spain . . . France and the UK also rule out German ambitions for Europol to develop an eventual operational cross-border role . . . Underlying these rows are sharp distinctions over the Maastricht Treaty's "Third

22

Particular" on cooperation in internal security affairs, which allots a still undefined role to EU institutions. The UK and France are against the majority view that the European Court of Justice should have an appeal and adjudication role, that the Court of Auditors should be responsible for Europol's accounts, and that the European Parliament should oversee the agency.' (*The Times*, 1 December 1994).

Europol is not the only intelligence system being developed to face the border concerns of the EU. One of the proposals arising out of the Schengen Convention was for the development of a comprehensive information scheme and the establishment of a pan-European drugs intelligence organization. As Thomas Mathiesen (1998) reports, the Schengen Information System (SIS) currently involves nine EU countries and in September 1995 held four million records (Mathieson 1998). Following the ratification of the External Borders Convention the plan is that SIS will become more broad based and will cover all 15 European states. The development of the Europol Information System (EIS) expands even further the network of European intelligence data bases. EIS will work cooperatively with Europol, dealing with non-organized forms of low level crime, holding data on policing, crime, immigration and public order issues. (Bunyan 1993:176; Mathiesen 1998)

MAASTRICHT AND CRIMINAL JUSTICE

Nicholas Dorn has argued that the Maastricht Treaty is broader and potentially more wide-ranging in terms of criminal justice than it appears:

> . . . The Treaty contains a carefully worded Criminal Justice and Home Affairs section which consolidates existing trends in European and juridical cooperation in Europe, agrees the setting up of Europol, and anticipates harmonisation of legislation in certain (unspecified) areas of civil and criminal law. . . . Certainly, the law enforcement aspects will continue to be put into operation by EC Member States — even if political sentiments in some countries prevent early ratification of the Treaty as a whole. Ironically, perhaps, we may conceivably end up with harmonisation on law enforcement before we get economic, monetary or political union — in advance of democratization of the European institutions to which law-making and enforcement might be made accountable. (Dorn, 1993:98)

Moves towards harmonisation are viewed by conservative commentators as unacceptably slow. They cite the current broad band of penalties across the member states as evidence of this failure. The Netherlands, for example, operates the most liberal of European policies with the possession of up to 60 grams of cannabis legalised, while any amounts over this limit can incur a prison sentence up to two years and a fine. Italy

23

abolished the obligatory penal sentence attached to the possession of drugs in 1993 leaving it to the discretion of the judge to decide the sentence on those possessing cannabis above the legal limit. Ireland fines those in possession of cannabis up to £IR250 and a 12 month prison term. Germany has decriminalised the possession of small amounts of cannabis, but larger amounts can lead to a prison sentence of between one and 15 years. France makes no distinction between soft and hard drugs with the possession of cannabis drawing a sentence of between two and ten years.

While there are certainly disparities in criminal and sentencing policies within the European Union there is, however a more powerful *unifying* trend which may not find identification at the level of supra European control but which underpins all major national policy developments in relation to the control of illegal drugs, and that is increasing repression. A review of drug policies in European countries over the 1980s reveals a harmonising tendency toward increasing repression (Albrecht and van Kalmthout 1989). The Netherlands, long heralded as a progressive beacon for its liberal drug policies, exemplifies the current trend toward more punitive enforcement and punishment regimes.

In 1989 Anton van Kalmthout predicted the scenario now facing the liberal agenda:

> Instead of enlarging the policy of normalisation and cultural integration of drug consumption, the Dutch government seems to conform, in an increasing degree, to the agreement made within the framework of the United Nations and the Council of Europe for harmonisation of the legislation on drugs and for cooperation in the field of investigation, prosecution and punishment of drug crimes. The consequence is that the Dutch government, in the wake of other West European countries, stands increasingly under pressure to give up its pragmatic policy and to join the international repressive approach. (van Kalmthout 1989:277)

The Dutch government now intends to implement a 50 per cent reduction in the number of coffee-shops which are permitted to sell cannabis. In addition it is proposed to introduce compulsory detention for addicts who have committed offences which may not otherwise carry a sentence of imprisonment. (*The Independent*, 25 September 1995) It seems clear that under the influence of international conventions and the direction of US policy diktats a unified punitive drug control strategy will emerge in Europe as the century draws to a close. Despite inter-agency rivalries between policing and customs bodies and the divisive issues of national versus European sovereignty in the sphere of crime control, prohibition informed drug enforcement seems set to continue along the supply-oriented road equipped with increasingly sophisticated and repressive measures of surveillance, control and punishment.

Drug trafficking and its umbrella genre, organized crime, are thus facilitating new and increasingly powerful enforcement and intelligence mechanisms in the European sector.[7] As with anti-terrorist enforcement strategies in the UK domestic sphere,[8] these mechanisms will be readily transferable to other potential areas of enforcement interest and it is likely that we shall see an increasingly unified and normalised set of repressive investigative and intelligence gathering strategies in European criminal justice, deriving primarily from the free and willing hand assigned by political and judicial authorities to drug control.

EUROPEAN UNION, POLICING AND CUSTOMS

There seem to be two areas of official concern in the debate centred on policing; firstly, whether policing should move towards a supranational structure or remain at a national level with increased cooperation at an international level and, secondly, the nature of the relationship between customs and the police. What does not occupy the discussions of European bureaucrats, however, is the powerful role that the United States has played (and continues to play) in fashioning European drug control strategies, a theme I will return to.

The move towards national police forces (for those member states which rely on regionalised policing rather than a national force) is seen, from a European perspective, as both necessary and inevitable despite the reluctance of regional and local forces to relinquish powers. The focus of this move is portrayed as a pragmatic one—the practicalities of improving police cooperation in order to gain a 'good result' are argued to be facilitated by cooperating national forces. Added to this, cooperation between customs and police, with its far from harmonious history, poses further problems at both national and European levels. Both situations present difficulties due to the lack of equivalence between nations of the enforcement powers of both police and customs. Along with the German federal system which has 22 joint police and customs task forces, England and Wales (with its 43 regional police forces and distinct customs agency) is seen to be actively moving toward a national policing identity in the form of the current National Criminal Intelligence Service (NCIS) which is staffed by both police and customs officers.

Evaluating the impact of joint agency work is difficult but it seems to be generally accepted that it has been relatively successful (when measured by the numbers and quantities of seizures) and is seen as an essential element in national cooperation. There are some indications that such inter agency cooperation only proves fruitful when the roles of forces are carefully and clearly understood.

The national versus supranational policing debate has steered well clear of any philosophical issues of what is at stake beyond the pragmatic advantages or disadvantages of cooperation at the two levels. Advocates of the supranational approach cite the inefficiencies and the practical operational limitations which enforcement efforts are subjected to when there is no single body which overrides the differences between nations, while advocates of the national level offer an increased level of international cooperation arguing that a supranational force will only add to the demarcation disputes between various forces. Moves toward a supranational European force, ie Europol, have faltered somewhat in light of the very severe co-ordination problems embodied in the American equivalent, the FBI but its future is secured.

Highlighting the difficulties for forces operating at different levels Robertson's study on border controls concluded that:

> . . . although each agency could give arguments for and against particular controls it was rare that any nation could provide an objective evaluation of the role that each played within the overall strategy. Arrangements had developed independently of each other and reflected many factors other than effectiveness. Politics, budgets, rivalries, accidents, and different environments had all played a part in the evolution of controls. Coherence, integration and co-ordination were often described as being based on cooperation and mutual respect, which is to say, they were based on no system at all! (Robertson 1991: 68).

Evidence from the 1993 Wilton Park debate on 'Combating Drugs Trafficking and Abuse: the Challenge to Europe' aptly illustrates Robertson's argument and points to operational difficulties ahead:

> The dismal results of the Balkan Route Working Group on database sharing encapsulates the problem . . . Lack of trust, inter-agency rivalries, especially between customs and the police, and the absence of a clear political imperative proved stronger than the need to co-operate (Seward 1993:8).

With Europeanisation we are also likely to see an increase in the influence of market forces on drug enforcement. The single market creates the conditions for intra-European competition between policing, intelligence and customs agencies for drug control 'business'. Competition is expected not only between agencies from different countries but from within national enforcement agencies themselves—between, for example, cost units within a police force. (Dorn 1993:105) This position is reinforced by the general assessment of national enforcement agencies:

> The level of West European inertia is particularly disturbing as it hints at a more entrenched reluctance to share intelligence . . . Many agencies perceive

their advantage best served by hoarding rather than disseminating information. (Seward 1993:8)

That the single market provides a particularly favourable environment for the development of 'contract culture' within potentially competing agencies of social administration and control has long-term implications for the future direction and nature of European social control.

Geographically, the United Kingdom is in a unique position with regard to external checks on immigration, terrorism and drug trafficking. Making the most of its island(s) status the UK has insisted on retaining its sovereignty over border controls appealing to articles 13-19 which state:

> . . . nothing in these provisions shall affect the right of the Member States to take such measures as they consider necessary for the purpose of controlling immigration from third countries and to combat terrorism, crime, the traffic in drugs and illicit trading in works of art and antiques . . .

The Conservative government had been under constant pressure from other EC countries to fall in line with an 'open frontiers' policy but made it clear that it would retain its own national border checks to deter smugglers and terrorists. As a result the work of British Customs and Excise officers was not, for example, to be relaxed and remained organized around drug control. Douglas Hogg, under secretary at the Home Office made clear to the House of Commons in June 1989:

> . . . by treaty and by statute . . . we have retained the right to maintain at the ports of entry such controls as we deem necessary to prevent the importation of drugs and other criminal articles.[9]

The reluctance of the British to remove frontier controls can best be understood by reference to its siege-like historical control of immigration and terrorism, as well as drug trafficking.[10] The UK receives a large proportion of its visitors through EC countries and the state operates on the logic that any weakness in processing EC nationals opens up the system to 'exploitation' by those seeking illegal immigration, asylum or refugee status in the UK.

Rather than any perceived weakening in border control the coming into existence of the new Europe is enveloped in increased security concerns and technologies. It is not only external borders which will remain to some extent 'fortified'. As Jenkins rightly foresees, '. . . in order to compensate for the disappearance of internal frontier controls an exchange of information between police and security authorities is indispensable'.[11] The TREVI Group (and specifically TREVI 30, the Schengen Agreement, the K4 Coordinating Committee and Europol) have all developed with this purpose in mind.[12]

The increased use of intelligence and the intelligence services in border control is to be an inevitable product of the union:

> Tracking the movements of major criminals is an important objective of frontier controls. Any weakness in one nation's ability to track their movements will be fully exploited and will undermine the information sharing system which, as we shall see, has become such an important part of this new strategy. (Robertson 1991:76)

Prior to the advent of the single market the primary input made by HM Customs and Excise to EU and international cooperation had been via the 36 Drugs Liaison Officers, of which 28 are customs staff, situated at various locations around the world. According to HM Customs and Excise *Annual Report* for 1995, 'These officers, together with our Operational Intelligence Teams, provided information to our colleagues abroad, which led to 130 arrests and seizures of 1,778 kg of cannabis and 2,413 kg of cocaine and 298 kg of heroin'. (1995: 32).

In the UK, Customs and Excise have used the coming of the single market to further their current strategies of focusing on individuals. In its 1995 *Annual Report* the Board further notes:

> Although the Single Market has brought new freedom for travellers and business, our aim has been to avoid creating new opportunities for smugglers. With the introduction of new controls at the airports and ferry ports to detect and deter the importation of prohibited and restricted goods, the majority of EU passengers and freight can now be moved between Member States unimpeded. We maintained our effectiveness by targeting anti-smuggling checks on high risk traffic, using intelligence and risk assessment. (1995: 33)

THE EXPANSION OF EUROPE: AND OF WESTERN DRUG CONTROL

The desire for membership of the European Union by countries physically adjacent will in part ensure the expansion of western drug enforcement strategies. Any country seeking EU candidature must develop policing agencies, legal systems and political structures which are compatible with the models employed in democratic Europe, and increasingly with America. For those countries eligible for membership—Poland, Hungary, Romania, Bulgaria, the Czech and Slovak Republics—the EU has instituted programmes designed to facilitate 'democratisation'. The PHARE programme on drugs, for example, involved the development of such legal and administrative structures in Central and Eastern Europe as well as providing assistance with precursor monitoring, drug demand reduction, anti-money laundering mechanisms and the creation of drug information systems. It is likely that a similar strategy will be employed under the TACIS programme given EU concern over the role of the Commonwealth of Independent States in the manufacture of precursor chemicals.[13]

ENDNOTES

1. The reinforcement of external borders was identified by the first two European Plans as the first of the six priority areas for joint action to combat drug trafficking (European Commission 1994a: 39)
2. Cited in Bunyan T, *Statewatching the New Europe*, 1993, p. 21
3. Speaking on Drugs and Criminality at the Association of Chief Police Officers' National Drugs Conference held in Wakefield 8-10 June 1994
4. 'An Outline Assessment of the Threat and Impact by Organized/Enterprise Crime Upon United Kingdom Interests', NCIS, 1997, cited in *The Observer*, 1 June 1997
5. The MAGHREB is a term denoting the group of North African countries including Morroco, Algeria and Tunisia linked specifically by language
6. **Pompidou Group** The Council of Europe's Pompidou Group is the primary forum for developing wider cooperation on drugs matters in Europe. The UK chaired the group from 1984-1990 and is currently encouraging the active participation of former communist countries.

TREVI (Terrorism, Radicalism, Extremism, Violence, International) Since 1976, members of the TREVI group meet every six months and consist of ministers, civil servants and senior police officers of EC member states. One of four working parties look at serious crime and drug trafficking. The 1990 meeting issued a Programme of Action which included calls for intensification of regular and permanent updating of detailed information relating to drug trafficking, appointment of drug liaison officers by police forces, creation of national drugs intelligence units, encouragement of debate on the need for a European drugs intelligence unit and for a common police Europol Information System. The group is the lead entity on EC terrorism concerns. The US is an invited observer at TREVI meetings.

Schengen Convention France, Germany, Luxembourg, Holland and Belgium drew up the Schengen Convention in 1985 focusing on the eventuation of a frontier-free Europe and the need for enhanced police cooperation and information exchange to that end. It remains the foremost model of a Europe wide attempt at policing. After the five initial members signed on in 1990 (which abolished frontier controls), Italy, Spain and Portugal subsequently signed as did Greece in 1993. The only countries who are not party to the Convention are the Republic of Ireland, Denmark and the United Kingdom. The Schengen Convention, with regard to drugs, requires parties to be signatories to UN drug conventions (if they were not already so), and provides for a permanent working party to examine common problems. Legal responses to drug trafficking, including the confiscation of profits, are obligatory. In tackling the issue of 'monitored' deliveries, article 73 obliges countries to do this only to the extent that it remains in accordance with the individual country's constitution and law. This recognises the problematic nature, or at least sensitivity, of this issue but stops short of addressing the fundamental encroachment of civil liberties of this response. The information system which the Convention subscribes to was set up in 1993 and was proposed not to exchange intelligence and be subject to the Council of Europe and other data protection provisions but provide only an information exchange system between police forces.

Interpol The International Police Organization is a global organization with 160 member countries with particular interest in Europe due to an estimated 80% of its work being in the region. The European Secretariat is based in Lyons. The UK office was to be integrated within NCIS based at New Scotland Yard. It is a non-operational police force being used as a communication channel for police information and intelligence. The late 1980s saw the updating of the computer network and the introduction of the Criminal Information System which includes a drug seizures data base and an automated system to speed the retrieval of images, photographs, fingerprints etc. from electronic archives.

Working closely with Interpol is the EC wide drugs agency, known as the **European Drugs Monitoring Centre,** which provides governments with an accurate picture of the true scale of drugs problems facing the Community. Its main tasks include finding ways to reduce the demand for drugs, encouraging international cooperation, cutting off supplies and providing an accurate analysis of the economics of Europe's drug trade.

7 Drug trafficking has, for instance, been used to justify the sharing of information through the TREVI Group and Europol (Hebenton and Thomas 1992)

8 See Paddy Hillyard, 'The Normalisation of Special Powers', in Scraton, P (ed.), *Law, Order and the Authoritarian State,* Milton Keynes: Open University Press, 1987

9 Dorn, N and N South, 'Drugs, Crime and Law Enforcement: Some Issues For Europe' in Heidensohn F and M Farrell (eds.), *Crime in Europe,* Routledge: London, 1991

10 See e.g. Paddy Hillyard, *Suspect Community,* Pluto Press , 1988; Frances Webber, *Crimes of Arrival: Immigrants and Asylum Seekers in the New Europe,* Paper presented at the 23rd annual conference of the European group for the study of deviance and social control, Crossmaglen, September 1995

11 Jenkins, J, 'Foreign Exchange', *New Statesman and Society,* 28 July 1989:12

12 See T Bunyan, 'TREVI, Europol and the European State', in *Statewatching the New Europe,* Tony Bunyan (ed.), Statewatch: London, 1993

13 Communication from the Commission to the Council and the European Parliament on a European Union action plan to combat drugs, 1995-1999, COM (94) 234, Final, Brussels.

CHAPTER THREE

Foreign Policy as Drugs Policy: The Americanisation of Drug Control

Drug trafficking and traffickers can only be understood in the context of the international trade in illegal drugs. The same is true for drug trafficking control. No serious analysis of drug trafficking policy can limit its parameters to a consideration of criminal policy alone. The role of foreign policy has, since the Opium Wars, been a crucial feature in the construction and control of the movement of illicit drugs.[1] This chapter briefly outlines the relationship between American foreign policy and drug enforcement policy and then moves to an analysis of Britain's international drug control strategy in the wider context of the European Union.

Within western foreign policy there has been an elevation of criminal concerns particularly since the dissolution of the Soviet Union and the ending of the Cold War. According to the eminent political scientist Ethan Nadleman 'Never before have US foreign policy and US criminal justice been so deeply entangled'. (Nadleman 1993:xiii) Despite accounting for only around five per cent of total US Federal expenditure drug control programmes in foreign countries have been an essential pillar in the ideology of US domestic drug enforcement and in the framing of US foreign policy. As Peter Reuter notes, drug control has, for the past 25 years or so been central to United States relationships with a number of drug producing countries namely Peru, Colombia, Bolivia, Turkey, Mexico and Pakistan (1994:209).

As the spurious threat of Communism and its 'danger' to the North evaporated in South America, US aid to those countries became increasingly concentrated on efforts to reduce the export of cocaine to the US. The main focus of international cooperation has been on law enforcement and interdiction measures to disrupt drug supply routes. During the 1980s foreign aid and debt re-financing in the developing world became increasingly tied to compliance with United States drug control policy.

In 1983 Congress passed the Gilman-Hawkins Amendment which suspended all economic aid to countries which did not fully cooperate with US drug control policy (del Olmo 1996:36). The 1984 *National Strategy for Prevention of Drug Abuse and Drug Trafficking: '. . .* calls for US decisions on foreign aid and other matters, such as re-financing of debt, to be tied to the willingness of the recipient country to execute vigorous enforcement programs against narcotic traffickers'. [2]

In October 1986 the process of *certification* came into effect with the approval of the Anti-Drug Abuse Act. Accordingly,

> ... If the President fails to certify a country, or if the Congress disapproves a certification, the United States must withhold most economic and military assistance, along with support for World Bank and other loans.[3]

And with the introduction of the 1990 International Narcotics Control Act the President is required to

> determine that each country receiving aid is providing acceptable counter-narcotics cooperation, that its human rights practices meet international standards and that the civilian government prevails over the security forces. (Hopkinson 1991:18)

In addition, the signing of military aid agreements and reducing coca production is a pre-condition for Latin American aid recipients.

The intent remained the same in the 1991 'National Drug Control Policy'. Though seemingly less invasive than earlier strategies, it required:

> the political commitment of drug producer and transit countries to strengthen their laws, legal institutions, and programs to prosecute, punish, and where appropriate, extradite drug traffickers and money launderers; increased law enforcement effectiveness from producer and transit countries; [and the] provision of economic assistance for crop eradication in producer countries.[4]

In 1994, with the publication of the State Department's annual global survey of drug cultivation and trafficking, Nigeria, Burma, Iran and Syria were found not to be 'fully cooperating' with Washington's anti-drug efforts. Nigeria, for example, was penalised by having two US aid programmes, totalling $12 million, cut until its drug enforcement record was seen by US officials to improve.

SOFT CERTIFICATION: THE EUROPEAN WAY

Britain and the rest of Europe have not been immune to the conflation of foreign and drugs policies characteristic of US international relations. The United Nations International Drug Control Programme (UNDCP) co-ordinates international responses to drug control and commands a budget of around $100 million. Britain is the third largest donor to the programme. Its concerns are to initiate projects related to crop eradication, alternative development, improved law enforcement, demand reduction, legislative assistance and institution-building.[5]

Geographical Region	1993/94	1994/95
Latin America	1,724,000	518,000
Caribbean	120,000	1,000,000
SW Asia	150,000	1,690,000
SE Asia and Pacific	689,000	240,000
Balkans, FSU, East Europe	2,014,5000	1,208,000
Africa	184,000	50,000
Total	**4,883,500**	**4,686,000**

Table 1: UK Donations (£'s) by Country to the UNDCP

Source: Drugs and International Crime and Terrorism Department, Foreign and Commonwealth Office 1995

The UK provides drug-related assistance to the UNDCP via three bodies: the Home Office, the Overseas Development Administration and the Foreign and Commonwealth Office. The three bodies confer annually to ensure that there is no duplication or overlap of programmes. The distribution of funds is primarily supply-oriented:

> HO funds are used for projects in drug producer and transit countries with a view to preventing the flow of drugs to the UK. ODA's programme concentrates on alternative development and demand reduction, and FCO funds a variety of projects to meet drugs related and foreign policy objectives (FCO 1995).

There is evidence to suggest that while the UK's small (in real terms) contribution to the UNDCP has remained relatively static in recent years there has been an increasing tendency to spread the aid more thinly across an increasing number of countries and into an increasing number of projects. Thus while in 1995 the UK could point to its financial support of 22 projects in 17 different countries, in 1994 the money was spread across 13 projects in only eight different countries.[6] It seems that while financial support is progressively less substantial the government has *appeared* to play had a more active role in international drug control. Symbolism remains a central pillar in the war against drugs.[7]

33

As *Table* 2 illustrates UK expenditure on international drug control remained reasonably static in the early 1990s but dropped to £9.1 million in the fiscal year 1995/96.

	1992/3	1993/4	1994/5	1995/6
ODA	1.8	3.7	4.0	2.3
Home Office	5.6	4.9	2.7	3.3
FCO	2.8	1.0	3.5	3.5
Total (£million)	10.2	9.6	10.2	9.1

Table 2: UK Assistance (£'s) in the Drugs Sector by Agency

Source: Personal communication with the Foreign and Commonwealth Office (March 1997)

While Britain does not have a formal certification process of the kind employed by the USA it nonetheless operates an informal strategy linking aid to a country's drug control performance. According to the Drugs and International Crime Department of the Foreign and Commonwealth Office, 'We do . . . closely monitor drug related performance and of course the impact of any assistance we provide. The performance of countries on drugs control is one of the criteria used in determining aid allocation' (personal communication: January 1997). In August 1995 Michael Howard, while visiting a UNDCP alternative development project in Bolivia was reportedly upset to discover that illicit coca leaves were under cultivation nearby, 'apparently with impunity'. Upon his return to the UK and in his subsequent report to the prime minister he 'expressed his strongly held views, that before further investment was made in this type of development, undertakings should be obtained from the government concerned that tough enforcement action would be taken against drugs producers and traffickers'.[8]

The European approach to some degree approximates certification. According to the European Commission clauses on the 'fight against drugs' and on 'the fight against money laundering' must now be routinely included in any external agreement the EC enters into with third countries, 'not only to provide a basis for the cooperation but also to develop the political dialogue'. (1994a:21) Further, and perhaps more tellingly,

The political dialogue, the international commitments entered into by third countries on drugs questions, and the amounts of aid available, must be exploited so as to make third countries accept the fight against drugs as a priority aspect of the Union's cooperation activity. (1994a:23)

If third countries remain uncooperative—or as the European Commission puts it—if they *'maintain a resolutely negative attitude'* then any envisaged cooperation between Europe and the third country may be reviewed or suspended. It is clear from the European Plan that available aid is indeed conditional on a third country's compliance with western drug wars.

Region	1993/94	1994/95
Latin America	3,024,718	1,970 074
Caribbean	1,787,610	3,201,820
South West Asia	239,423	1,783,772
SE Asia & Pacific	1,039,929	501,309
Balkans/FSU/		
Eastern Europe	2,492,698	1,634,230
Africa	812,422	1,003,078
Near & Middle East	54,514	151,772
South Europe	76,217	216,486
Other	66 000	26 575
Total	9,593,531	10,489.116

Table 3: Total UK Drug Related Aid Assistance by Country (£'s) 1993/94 and 1994/5

Source: Foreign and Commonwealth Office[9]

Between 1991 and 1995 Britain committed around £37 million for overseas drug-related assistance with a stated emphasis on countries within the 'Balkan Route' along which opiates from South West Asia travel to European markets. (Home Office 1995:42) Drugs in the Caribbean have, since 1995, become the focus of an EU initiative. Following the investigation by an EU drugs expert study team of 'gaps and weaknesses' in the region's capacity to combat drugs, a set of predominantly supply-oriented proposals was announced including the introduction of a secure communications network, the establishment of sub-regional coastguards, the development and harmonisation of anti-drugs legislation and a regional prosecutorial cadre, an increased presence for the Caribbean Financial Action Task Force and lastly (and apparently leastly) the development of more effective demand reduction programmes.[10] The Caribbean countries have received the greatest UK financial assistance for drug control in recent years. Investment in drug control in the Caribbean is justified primarily because the region is seen by the Foreign and Commonwealth Office as a transit point for cocaine headed for the European market and because the UK has certain obligations to the Independent Territories in the region. Perhaps, however, the most powerful reason lies in the assessment that drugs represent the greatest threat to political stability in the Caribbean. According to an unpublished FCO report on the findings of an EU study team,

> . . . the problems associated with drugs and drug trafficking pose the greatest threat to the stability and economic and social development of the Caribbean and are now undermining democracy there . . . the corruption from drugs is affecting every level of society, and threatening to destroy the institutions needed to sustain democracy.[11]

As del Olmo (1996) and others have remarked, geo-politics and transnational economic concerns have become the international driving force behind drug control strategies in the late twentieth century.

Nigeria, for example, is recognised as an important drug transit zone yet, somewhat surprisingly (see *Chapter 4*), it has not been recognised as central to the UK drug-aid programme. Between 1990 and 1994 Nigeria received only £65,467, of which the bulk (£50,000) represented a 1993 contribution to the UNDCP Demand Reduction Project. [12]

If we examine the case of Burma it can be seen how hollow the political rhetoric surrounding the war on drugs is and how shallow official concerns for those whose lives are damaged within the drugs market. Burma, ruled by a ruthless and repressive military dictatorship, is currently the world's largest supplier of opium and heroin. According to Robert Gelbard, assistant United States secretary of state for narcotics, the drug trade is entrenched in Burma's economic life' (cited in *The Observer*, 2 February 1997). All the evidence suggests that Burma in the 1990s has become a narco-capitalist dictatorship. Combined with its appalling record of human rights violations and the economic misery the junta has heaped upon thousands of its inhabitants, Burma is a country that might rightfully be targeted in Britain's war against the 'trade in misery and despair'. Yet Britain's contribution of drug-related aid to South East Asia has decreased in recent years and in 1994/5 stood at only £501,309, with £100,000 of that figure allocated to a UNDCP drug control project in Burma. In the previous year the Home Office provided £407,000 for a Burma/Thailand border strengthening project and £282,000 for a UNDCP project to tighten the control of precursor chemicals there. The supply-orientation of this aid renders the projects insignificant in terms of international drug control and does nothing to address the sources of poverty and corruption in Burma which foster the black market. The Foreign Office's drug-control contribution to Burma was only £7,000 in 1996/97, apparently a consequence of the influence of EU sanctions against Burma, sanctions which Britain resisted under the Conservative administration. Both Britain and France refused to support European Union trade sanctions against the junta in the mid-1990s. France was concerned not to disrupt the $1.2 billion contract that its oil corporation Total had with the junta to build a pipeline across Burma; Britain, it seemed, was more generally concerned to protect potential trade routes in the region.

There is a great deal of bureaucracy and political posturing involved in drug-related aid contributions within the international community. But there is no evidence that the projects, schemes and paltry sums donated are anything more than window dressing for governments wishing to demonstrate their commitment to the international war effort. The introduction to a government paper detailing the UK's involvement in international drug control begins: 'Despite the counter narcotics efforts of the international community, production, trafficking and consumption of illicit drugs worsened in 1993/94 and 1994/95'. [13]

The governments of producer and transit countries are not without self interest in the drug-related aid bonanza. They too have 'problem' populations and the assistance from western sources is a means of strengthening state control over the population as a whole. As Nadleman observes:

> On the broader level, governments have an interest in maintaining the semblance of a legal order presided over by the central government. On a more focused level, governments have an interest in preventing any individual or group from attaining such power that it can challenge, or even appear to challenge, governmental authority within any portion of the national territory. On occasion, such individuals or groups are politically or ideologically motivated and traffic in drugs to gain revenues with which to buy weapons and support. (1985:89)

AMERICA: THE DRUG CONTROL MASTER

Despite the internal European debates over issues of national versus supranational sovereignty one thing is clear and that is the overall 'Americanisation' of European and British drug enforcement. Nadleman astutely assesses this process:

37

The notion of "Americanisation" applies most accurately to the changes demanded and incited by the Americans. With respect to some, evidence of the DEA's active hand is readily apparent and actively acknowledged by the Europeans: the creation of specialised drug enforcement units in major police agencies; the initial adoption of DEA-style undercover tactics and the subsequent training of European police in a variety of DEA-style techniques; the notion of "flipping" informants;[14] and the enactment of legislation authorising the forfeiture of drug traffickers' assets. But the notion of "Americanisation" can also be understood more passively as including changes in European drug enforcement caused not only by American pressures, incitements and training but also those changes shaped by the experience gained in working with the US drug enforcement agents, by the models and examples suggested by the DEA's own history and *modus operandi*, and by the popularisation through fiction and non-fiction media of the American approach to drug enforcement. (Nadleman 1993:194)

The kind of US pressure described by Nadleman above surfaces very clearly in relation to the structural changes taking place in Europe post-1992. Washington displayed acute Cold War paranoia as the plans for European unification unfolded:

Europe's well publicised march toward a single economic market in 1992 and a borderless Europe has created concerns in the United States about the potential impact of the Single European Act on increasing terrorism and drugs trafficking in the European Community as well as the movement of terrorists and drugs from Europe to the United States . . . The US government should continue to carefully monitor this evolving 1992 security structure. (House Foreign Affairs Committee, cited by Solomon and Jenkins 1990:15)

The House Foreign Affairs Committee has, as a result, urged EC member countries to prioritise the supply oriented strategies of money laundering controls, controlled deliveries, the targeting of major traffickers, the monitoring of precursor chemicals and cross border surveillance. In addition they call for the dissemination of European trafficking intelligence (1990:21). Imbued with parochial nationalism the House Committee argues that the implementation of the American approach to drug control is essential because '. . . decisions made by the EC concerning the control of terrorists, drug traffickers and criminals in the European Economic Community of 1992 will have a direct impact on Americans both in Europe and in the United States' (1990:21).

In an operational sense it is apparent that in terms of international cooperation the US has made very few concessions while demanding much from its 'partners'.

MUTUAL LEGAL ASSISTANCE TREATIES

International Mutual Legal Assistance Treaties (MLATS) are agreements between countries which attempt to overcome national legal impediments in the process of international evidence gathering. They have also been a means by which America has encouraged a uniformity (along US lines) of legislation, law enforcement and specifically drug law enforcement.

The UK has been active in promoting International Mutual Legal Assistance Treaties, primarily to assist the extradition of drug traffickers and to aid in investigations pursuant to the confiscation of the proceeds of drug trafficking (Levi 1991:287-295).

While MLATS at one important level are about attempting to reconcile different national legal systems in the pursuit of evidence, according to Nadleman they:

> . . . must be understood in the context of the bilateral conflicts generated by US efforts to obtain evidence unilaterally, efforts designed both to obtain evidence in individual investigations and prosecutions and to pressure foreign governments more generally to be more accommodating to US law enforcement needs. Indeed, the principal incentive for many foreign governments to negotiate MLATS with the United States was, and remains the desire to curtail the resort by US prosecutors, police agents and the courts to unilateral, extraterritorial means of collecting evidence from abroad (Nadleman 1993:315).

The operation of attempting to surmount the tensions involved when two legal systems interact has been '. . . one in which the US has made modest accommodations to foreign legal systems and foreign authorities have made much greater accommodations to US demands' (1993:315). In the process the US has applied coercive 'inducements' in order to secure compliance and has instituted not only bilateral treaties but also demanded unilateral measures and multilateral agreements.

Americanisation has occurred at a much broader policy-determining level as well. In fact the very framing of the international 'drug problem' is a product of US design. The example of Europe's treatment of cocaine and the countries which produce it is illustrative. Geography and an absence of strategic interest combined with the intense US counter narcotics activity in the region should impose certain limits on Europe's involvement in Latin America.

EUROPE AND THE ANDES: A SYMBOLIC FRONT

European drug control intervention in the coca producing countries of South America is influenced at the broadest level by US policy in the region. The cocaine scare exported to Europe by US drug officials in the late 1980s has resulted in European external drug strategies concentrating attention on the coca producing countries of Colombia, Peru and Bolivia despite the absence of a major cocaine crisis in Europe. The European Plan to Combat Drugs outlined by the Council of Europe in 1990 (and revised in 1992) is a strategy to combat drug demand and drug trafficking with an increased emphasis on international cooperation. Focusing on the plan's outline for international action, priority was to be given to 'cooperation in the fight against drugs . . . in terms of trade and development policy'. In terms of its external remit it is a *development* based strategy (but as we shall see largely symbolically so) rather than the *security* dominated strategy employed by the United States. In theory it supports the general economic development of countries heavily reliant on drug cultivation, and specifically the replacement of drug crops with licit alternatives. Special trade preferences (through the Generalised System of Preferences) were instituted in 1991 with the coca producing states. Tariff reductions are not conditional, in the American sense, on a country's compliance with crop substitution but an element of economic compliance is heavily weighted in the Commission's proposal that '. . . in the context of the GSP that the special arrangements aimed at the fight against drugs should be continued, *provided the countries concerned for their part continue their efforts to combat drugs and some results are achieved'*. (1994:21) (emphasis supplied)

For a country like Colombia the European GSP measures have meant a reduction in the application of tariffs from over 90 per cent of its exports to less than 10 per cent (Dorn 1996:260). In theory this may sound a potentially effective way of improving legitimate trade, encouraging a move (in drug producing countries) from illicit to licit production and thereby enhancing the circulation of legitimate finance into the economy. Calls for member states to reach international agreements on the fixing of basic commodity prices have, however, been far from successful. Ann Mennens, an independent consultant to the European Community, argues that the reality is that the EC has not improved commodity prices and cites the example of the price of coffee which lunged to half its 1981 price in 1982. (Mennens 1993:28) But there are other more fundamental reasons why the European plan will not succeed. Giant agri-businesses currently monopolise agricultural exports and it is impossible to expect peasant-based production (of commodities other than coca) to compete. It is big agri-business which stands to benefit from the special trade preferences offered by Europe. It is also true that Colombia has been best able to take advantage of the trade preferences despite producing only a quarter of the coca in the Andean region. There is another structural impediment and that concerns the experience of a generalised fall in commodity prices so that peasant farmers are faced with competition from increasingly cheap imported produce (Atkins 1993:22-23). The greatest impediment to 'success', however, lies in what Susan George describes as the 'debt-drug' link. Bolivia, producing one third of the world's coca, spends almost half of its export income on servicing IMF debt. Many economists argue that it is only Colombia's huge drug revenue (in the region of $2.5 billion)[15] that enables it to sustain its heavy debt burden and to remain financially more buoyant than Peru or Bolivia. Without cocaine profits Colombia would sink under the weight of its foreign debt obligations. The Peruvian economy is equally dependant upon coca. According to Susan George, 'the value of coca production is probably equal to the combined value of all the rest of Peru's agricultural production' (George 1992:46). For George, the essential first step toward solving the crisis cannot be circumvented:

> The International Monetary Fund must cease to impose policies which today make it, with or without its knowledge and consent, an accessory before and after the fact to the crimes of the cocaine outlaws. (George 1992:39)

In the 1990s the Andean countries highlighted one of the hypocrisies central to Western drug control—the imbalance between the control of plant drugs and that of chemical precursors required for drug refinement. The vast majority of precursors are manufactured in the West and without them the potency of coca, in particular, is massively reduced. As Dorn (1996) points out the developed countries offered little resistance to calls by the West for increased controls on the manufacture and movement of precursor chemicals (1996:245)

The European Community has one budget (North South Cooperation Programme in the context of the Campaign Against Drug Abuse) which is specifically targeted toward drug-related aid for drug-producing and transit countries. With miniscule funds at its disposal[16] the programme's role in supporting developing countries to reduce both production and demand for illegal drugs is symbolic only, especially given that in its first five years almost 50 per cent of its disbursements went to Latin America with 35 per cent going to Asia and 6 per cent to the Caribbean.

As Ann Mennens has claimed

> ... it is remarkable that so much of the EC assistance to producer countries goes to Latin America rather than to Asia, although the main drug consuming problem in the EC is heroin consumption: and the heroin comes largely from Asia. (Mennens 1994:30)

The European Community has other technical and financial aid budgets which are better financed. The Lome Convention, for example, which exists between Europe and 69 former African, Caribbean and Pacific colonies also provides trade preferences with the Convention countries so that EU tariffs on imports are greatly reduced.[17] As with the Generalised System of Preferences the impact of the Lome Convention is likely to be symbolic rather than pragmatic.

Unless Europe is prepared to seriously address the foreign debt crisis facing producer and transit countries and unless it is prepared to invest in the creation of jobs for the millions throughout the world who depend upon the drug economy then it seems inevitable that the European drug war will remain one of attrition.

THE BALKANS/EASTERN EUROPE AND THE FORMER SOVIET UNION

The issue of Europe's extended borders has highlighted the xenophobia so implicit in western drug control discourse. In a summary of the Wilton Park conference on drugs and the challenge to Europe Valerie Seward writes:

> West European frontier controls have been weakened by the dismantling of the Iron Curtain and *made porous by the unceasing flood of refugees and asylum seekers . . . a fateful connection between refugees and drugs trafficking has already been established, with most eastern countries equating greater drugs use and trafficking with the influx of foreign nationals* (Seward 1993) (Emphasis supplied).

Quite where the 'fateful connection' between drug trafficking and refugees has been 'established' is unreported but this fabricated conceptualisation of Europe as pure but for the presence of the wicked foreigner underpins the Union's whole approach to drug control.[18]

The Wilton Park Conference illustrates the flexible definition of the 'foreigner' in relation to border-line European states. The sanctity of European national identity—as free from the mantle of 'trafficking nation'—is not only preserved but extended to countries soon to be members of the Union so that they too may be represented as the victims of foreign corrupters. In Poland it is the 1,200 Colombian visitors on tourist visas who are portrayed as responsible for a dramatic rise in reported drug use and drug trafficking; in Bulgaria trafficking is carried out by 'foreign residents and transients from Iran, Middle Eastern states and Nigeria'; and in Romania the increased incidence of drug use and smuggling since the revolution is attributed to the country's 20,000 foreign nationals (Seward 1993:10-11).

The Europol Drugs Unit (EDU) is central to the ideological fusion taking place between drug and people trafficking. In its annual report for 1996 the EDU makes special reference to its project on 'clandestine immigration networks'. The project, known as the Balkan Route Project (implying more than a linguistic link with drug trafficking) focuses on 'clandestine immigration networks involving Turkish national and Turkish organisations' (EDU 1997). The report goes on to discuss the development of *operational* projects in respect of the 'clandestine immigrants', a timely reminder of the coming character of Europol. In 1996 the EDU was involved in a strategic analysis of *Drug Trafficking Activities by Turkish Criminal Organizations from an EU Perspective* with the Customs Cooperation Council. It is highly unlikely that the 'clandestine immigration networks' project is independent of Joint Action to combat drug smuggling along the Balkan Route. Here very forcefully the link between drug smuggling and illegal immigration has been forged in the official lexicon.

In 1991 it was claimed that between 70 and 80 per cent of the heroin consumed in Europe travelled from South West Asia along the Balkan Route, through Turkey, and the former Yugoslavia (until the civil war forced a close to that route), then from Istanbul through Bulgaria and Romania, or from Turkey through Greece and Macedonia to Italy (Hopkinson 1991:11). By 1993, however, official sources were questioning whether or not the Balkan Route still existed and were expressing their fears about the potential new threat to Western Europe posed by the Confederation of Independent Sates (particularly the Ukraine and the Baltic States), central Europe and Russia. The whole discourse around western European drug control is framed by notions of an alien threat, whether it be the source countries of Asia and Latin America or the transit countries of the Mediterranean, the Balkans, Africa or Russia and the former Eastern bloc. Policy-makers at both national and European Union level operate on the basis that the European drug problem is primarily an imported one which bears little domestic analysis and thus we find an obsessive concern within enforcement agencies and policy forums with any route changes in the trafficking of drugs.

ENDNOTES

1. See *Chapter 6* for a brief outline of the 'Opium Wars'
2. *Drug Abuse Policy,* The White House, National strategy for the prevention of drug abuse and drug trafficking, US Government Printing Office, Washington DC, 1984:11
3. The White House, *National Drugs Control Strategy,* US Government Printing Office, Washirgton DC, 1989, pp. 68-69.
4. Office of National Drug Control Policy (Executive Office of the President), *National Drug Control Policy,* US Government Printing Office, Washington DC, 1991
5. Foreigr and Commonwealth Office, *Background Brief,* March 1995:5
6. Figures from 'UK Involvement in International Anti-drug Developments in 1993/94 and 1994/5', produced by the Drugs, International Crime and Terrorism Department of the Foreign and Commonwealth Office, 1995
7. The Foreign and Commonwealth Office, has, since 1990, funded the training of some 2,000 overseas law enforcement officers by UK Customs and Excise officials. The Overseas Development Administration has also provided funding, through its aid programme, for the training of customs officials, police and drug enforcement groups. (Home Office 1995:43)
8. Unpublished Home Office (C5) document, 'UK Drug Related Assistance Overseas' 1995
9. Unpublished FCO Office Background Briefing paper 'UK Involvement in International Anti-drug Developments in 1993/4' — not quoted as an expression of government policy
10. Unpublished FCO Background Briefing document, 'The Problem of Drugs in the Caribbean: a European Union Initiative', September 1996 — not quoted as an expression of government policy
11. Ibid, 1996:3; Personal communication, Kevin Lyne, Caribbean desk, Foreign and Commonwealth Office, 29 May 1997
12. *Drug Related Aid to Nigeria provided by the UK*
    1991:
    (£5,000) Forensic lab equipment in Oshodi
    (£38,000) 'Drug Law Enforcement' training course
    1992:
    (£228) Attachment of an NDLEA officer to HM Customs Investigation Division
    (£4,000) Spare parts for forensic laboratory at Oshodi
    (£239) Supply of 30 radios for the customs service
    1993:
    (£28,000) 'In-country Drug Law Enforcement Training Course' for 18 NDLEA officers
    (£50,000) Contribution to UNDCP 'Demand Reduction' project
13. 'UK Involvement in International Anti-Drug Developments in 1993/4 and 1994/5'
14. This practice involves offering immunity or reduced charges to known drug dealers in order to 'flip' them into becoming informants. This practice was approved by the US courts during the era of prohibition
15. Humberto Campodonico, cited in George, 1992:52
16. Its budget in 1992 was only ECU10 million
17. The Lome Convention also provides for additional aid to assist in the funding of demand-reduction and regional anti-trafficking programmes
18. *The Wilton Park Paper 65* cites the 'fact' that 90% of all drug arrests involve asylum seekers as evidence of this claim. No reference is provided for the figure given and no allowance made for the possibility of the racist policing of drug offenders.

CHAPTER FOUR

Nigeria and the Politics of Drug Control

The official criminology and criminal policy of drug trafficking is circumscribed by singular concerns with enforcement strategies, drug baron demonology, border security and supply eradication. From this perspective the twinned issues of Third World development strategies and the social and economic conditions of life which lie behind the demand for illegal drugs in the industrialised west are seen as irrelevant to the positivistic task at hand (Taylor 1992). This chapter will concern itself with just one of these 'first order' issues in the jigsaw of the international drug trade—Third World development strategies. The focus will be on Nigeria, an important locus in the international drug market despite the fact that it is essentially a non-producer country.

Only by examining the political economy of this African giant can we begin to understand its apparent disproportionate involvement in the drugs trade and more specifically why British prisons have been home to so many Africans convicted of drug importation.[1]

This chapter links the political and economic condition of Nigeria directly to one aspect of the illegal drugs problem in the UK—drug importation and criminal justice. While a great many excellent analyses exist of the relationship between the US war on drugs and the political economies of Latin American producer countries (del Olmo 1991, 1996; Perl 1994; Johns 1991, 1992; Hermann 1991; Epstein 1990; George 1992; Scott and Marshall 1991) no similar analyses have been applied to Britain's war on drugs and the developing countries targeted in that war.

Certainly Britain's relationship with the producer countries of Latin America and Central and East Asia has not been so intimate and interventionist as the relationships successive US governments have initiated in those countries. But Britain has its own 'South America' and without an understanding of the dynamics of the relationship between the two countries and without an analysis of the political economy of post-colonial Nigeria, British criminal policy in relation to drug trafficking is doomed to failure. Major political reform and economic recovery are the only means by which Nigeria's involvement in the drugs market can hope to decline.

NIGERIANS AND DRUG TRAFFICKING

Nigerians now turn up in almost every major heroin seizure around the world. The country has earned such a reputation for drug smuggling that its citizens travelling abroad, regardless of credentials, must routinely undergo humiliating body searches. (*Time*, 18 April 1994)

Nigerians have assumed a perhaps surprisingly significant role in the international illicit drugs trade, emerging in the 1980s as an important transit country (Nadleman 1993). Apart from a small amount of cannabis cultivated domestically, Nigeria is not a producer of opium or cocaine. Yet Nigerians are over-represented in arrest and prison statistics in countries throughout the world (see particularly the UK, Netherlands, Thailand and the USA). Figures from Interpol indicate the increase in the number of Nigerians arrested abroad for drug trafficking as being from 1,261 in 1979 to 2,034 in 1988. Between 1979 and 1988, 14,883 Nigerian traffickers were arrested importing illegal drugs worldwide with the majority of arrests taking place in Britain, the United States and Saudi Arabia (Obot 1992:484). In May 1992, before the US Senate Committee on Foreign Relations, Melvyn Levitsky, assistant secretary, Bureau of International Narcotic Matters declared that 'Nigerian traffickers and their surrogates account for most of the heroin seized at US airports'. He claimed that in 1991, 31 per cent of 756 heroin seizures at airports involved Nigerian nationals and 11 per cent involved other Africans, likely to have been recruited by Nigerian networks At New York's JFK Airport, '48 per cent of all heroin seizures in Fiscal Year 1991 involved Nigerians directly. If Nigerian controlled couriers of other nationalities were included, the number would be nearly 60 per cent' (Committee on Foreign Relations, US Senate 1992). In 1995 the US assistant secretary of state for international narcotics, Robert Gelbard, testified to Congress on the 'ubiquitous reach' of Nigerian drug traffickers who were, he argued, amongst the world's most sophisticated and finely tuned transhipment, money moving and document-forging organizations. According to Gelbard's testimony Nigeria's role in the international drugs trade is a critical one, 'With a worldwide reputation for running large-scale effective and efficient operations, they are sought out by both Asian and Latin American producers' (*The Observer*, 28 January 1996).

In the UK approximately 30 per cent (268 out of the author's total sample of 900) of all imprisoned drug importers in the early 1990s were Nigerian nationals (Green 1991). In 1990 there were 404 Nigerian nationals serving sentences for drug offences in the UK. That figure was, however, to decline significantly in following years (from 316 in 1991 to 106 in 1994 and 113 in 1995).[2]

This general acknowledgement of Nigerian involvement in international drug trafficking must, however, be qualified in one important respect. When the arrest and seizure statistics are examined it is clear that the vast majority of those Nigerian couriers arrested and convicted of drug trafficking are carrying small amounts of the drug. According to Isidore Obot, 'While many are arrested for trafficking, few of them transport more than 1 kilogram of cocaine or heroin at a time. Even when Nigeria was ranked third in terms of the number of its citizens arrested for trafficking, the quantity of drugs seized was less than the quantity seized from citizens of a country ranked thirteenth' (1992:485). In my interviews with 38 Nigerian couriers only two people, both women, had imported class A drugs weighing in the region of one kilogram. The majority (29) had imported amounts of between 100 grams and 500 grams with an average consignment weighing 400 grams. The evidence from the sample supports the earlier contention that those Nigerian couriers who are convicted and imprisoned for drug trafficking offences in Britain have imported only relatively small amounts of class A drugs and that they are, therefore, only minor players in the trade. The range of sentences (with an average of almost six years) however, illustrates a scale of punishment of considerable severity not commensurate with the lowly status accorded the courier.

The involvement of Nigeria in the drug trade appears to have emerged in the late 1970s and reached a peak toward the end of the 1980s. During the early 1970s very few Nigerians featured in British drug crime statistics. Those who did were largely small scale importers of cannabis. Throughout the 1980s, however, increasingly large numbers of Nigerians were arrested in Britain for the illegal importation of heroin. The heroin originated in the producer countries of Thailand, Laos, Burma, Pakistan and Iran and arrived in Nigeria as a transit stage before wider distribution in Europe and America. It seems that by the mid 1980s Nigerians were taking a major organizational role in the drug distribution process and Nigeria, for a number of economic, political and structural reasons discussed below, had become a major transit destination for illegal drugs. During the mid-late 1980s Nigerian drug entrepreneurs began establishing networks for the distribution of heroin in Europe and North America, in particular, Britain, The Netherlands, Italy, Spain, the USA and Canada. More recent evidence also suggests a major foothold in South Africa.[3] In 1995 the US lobby group Trans Africa asserted that Nigeria was responsible for 80 per cent of the heroin smuggled into the United States. This was a particularly stinging accusation, undermining as it did the campaign by Nigeria's military ruler General Sani Abacha to have Nigeria removed from Washington's list of countries considered safe havens for drug traffickers (*The Guardian*, 21 July 1995).

According to Melvyn Levitsky of the Bureau of International Narcotics Matters:

> ... The Nigerian trafficking organizations are more loosely organized than their Latin American counterparts, and therefore more difficult to penetrate. There are no clear hierarchies and no unambiguous chains of command. Nonetheless, these are sophisticated organizations capable of quickly adapting to changes in US law enforcement activities. As more law enforcement attention has been directed toward Nigerian nationals, they have begun to recruit other African nationals, Americans, Europeans and Asians as couriers. (1992)

By the late 1980s the North American market for cocaine was approaching saturation and the Colombian drug cartels, seeking the development of new drug markets in Europe, began establishing links with West Africa. For a number of years South America and West Africa had been linked by air routes. Equally important, Nigeria's strong connections to the global economy have ensured that Nigeria is served by more international airlines than most other countries in sub-Saharan Africa. These routes were now exploited for the purpose of smuggling cocaine as well as the continuing trade in heroin. Enforcement statistics indicate that in the late 1980s and early 1990s the traffic in cocaine from South America via Nigeria into Europe and North America increased significantly—concomitantly so did the number of arrests of Nigerian drug couriers abroad.

Evidence from the Prison Service and the Foreign Nationals Unit at Middlesex Probation Service reveals that the numbers of Nigerian couriers arrested and imprisoned in the UK began declining significantly from 1992. The Foreign Nationals Unit, which collects data on all drug importers arrested at Heathrow airport, reported a concomitant rise in the number of South and East African couriers. According to Nick Hammond, senior probation officer with the unit,

> The change we're seeing is a cosmetic change—as Nigerians became increasingly targeted and arrested, their use as couriers became less profitable—in 1992/1993 while the numbers of Nigerian couriers declined, there was a major increase in the number of Ghanaians arrested, the drug organizers simply crossed the border to recruit couriers who wouldn't arouse suspicions in quite the same way as Nigerians.[4]

Despite this reduction in the number of Nigerians involved in the British criminal justice process their use as a case-study remains illuminating. Nigerian involvement in international drug trafficking continues apace and hundreds of Nigerian couriers are still serving long prison sentences in foreign jails. The organization of drug trafficking is an immensely fluid and reflexive business—trade routes adapt to enforcement changes, couriers from one nation may be easily dispensable once identified as a risk and others readily recruitable from a range of developing countries.

Mike Davis in describing the crack cocaine peddling of the LA 'proletarian capitalists', the Crips, presciently likens them to former corrupt African rulers who were prepared to sell a class of their own people into slavery. Davis writes: 'In an age of narco-imperialism they have become modern analogues to the "gunpowder states" of West Africa, those selfish rogue chieftaincies who were middlemen in the eighteenth-century slave-trade, prospering whilst the rest of Africa bled'. (1990:310)[5] This analogy fits not only the 'outlaw proletarians' of LA's gang-land but also that entrepreneurial class of West African capitalist 150 years on. Not only are the addicted poor the victims of this crass entrepreneurialism but so too are the couriers—sacrificial lambs on the world market altar.

THE IMPOVERISATION OF NIGERIA

Nigeria's dramatic economic decline, its political instability, endemic corruption and its commitment to the IMF's Structural Adjustment Programme are essential components in understanding its role in international drug trafficking.

In 1985 Nigeria was one of the wealthiest countries in Africa, classified by the IMF as a 'middle income country', with an annual income per person of US$1200. By 1991 per capita income had fallen to US$250 and it was now classified as the world's thirteenth poorest nation. With a population in the region of 88.5 million and an annual population growth of 3.3 per cent the problems of Nigeria's poor have been exacerbated by the introduction of the IMF and World Bank's Structural Adjustment Program. Struggle and despair characterise the lives of millions. Life expectancy for men is just 49 years and for women 53; infant mortality rates are appallingly high at 110 per 1,000 live births; and maternal mortality stands at 15 per 1,000 live births (Joshua 1996:24).

Since gaining independence in 1961 Nigeria has experienced only ten years of civilian rule. Successive military regimes have resulted in wide scale political repression and abuses of human rights (including

49

the withdrawal of *habeus corpus*) and the detention of political opponents. In June 1993, as part of the declared transition to democracy, presidential elections were held. Deemed free and fair by international observers early results indicated a clear victory for the leader of the Social Democratic Party, Chief Moshood Kashimawo Olawale Abiola. The official results were, however, never announced and eleven days later the military's ruling body, the National Defence and Security Council (NDSC) declared the election null and void. General Babangida was re-installed by the military as the President and Chief Abiola imprisoned. Following domestic and international pressure Babangida was forced to step down and an interim government (Interim National Government) led by Chief Ernest Shonekan was installed. Beset by problems it lasted only until November when its sole military member, General Sani Abacha assumed the reins of power and reinstated military rule. Britain's response was a tepid partial withdrawal of assistance to the regime, including the withdrawal of the British Military Advisory Team from Nigeria; suspension of assistance to Nigeria's War College; suspension of British visa facilities for members of the military, security and intelligence services; and a moratorium on the future programme of bilateral aid projects. But as a 1995 *The Guardian* report exposed, Britain continued to supply the Nigerian military regime with arms, despite assurances from government ministers that the 1993 embargo on 'lethal equipment' was being complied with (21 July 1995). And as the Foreign and Commonwealth Office reported:

> Despite the suspension of high-level ministerial visits between the two countries, Britain continues to engage in dialogue with the government of President Abacha. Britain has not pressed for the adoption of any particular style of democracy, nor has she tried to devise or broker solutions to Nigeria's political problems ... [6]

Diplomatic relations were restored following the death of Sani Abacha in June 1998 and with the commencement of negotiations between Nigeria's new military leader, General Abdulsalam Abubakar and the imprisoned Moshood Abiola over the conditions for restoration of civilian rule.

COLONIALISM AND THE NIGERIAN ECONOMIC CRISIS

An examination of the post-colonial economic and political development of Nigeria, coupled with its strategic geographical location, sheds considerable light on some of Britain's own criminal justice dilemmas. According to Nigerian political analyst Julius Ihonvbere:

> The Nigerian social formation is in a very deep crisis. Military rule has not only suffocated civil society but has also entrenched a culture of repression, corruption, privatisation of public office, official irresponsibility, arrogance and non-accountability to the public . . . Crime, corruption, waste, the use of public facilities and positions to advance personal interests, prostitution, and alienation from the state, its agents and agencies, have never been higher in the political history of Nigeria. (Ihonvbere 1994:1)

For Julius Ihonvbere this parlous state of affairs is a direct result of the history of Nigeria's experience of colonialism. The role of Britain, as with all colonial powers, was never to foster the domestic development of the countries it colonised, but rather the colonies represented vital new markets and a source of raw materials to be harnessed and developed in the interests of metropolitan capital. Underdevelopment was positively encouraged. The colonisers exerted a monopolistic control of trade which led to the emergence of an international division of labour in which the colony was encouraged to produce specific primary products for export to Britain, and to use its earnings therefrom in the purchase of British manufactured goods. Since colonial trade encouraged mainly private production and the use of unskilled labour the development of productive forces and internally generated industrialisation were discouraged. The emphasis was on the production of mineral and agricultural primary products for export so that indigenous economic activities, like the brewing of beer in Southern Nigeria or the smelting of tin in the north were prohibited under colonial law (Ahire 1991).

Traditional criminology has based its forays into the developing world on modernisation theory—focusing largely on street crime and theorising it in terms of a variety of criminological explanations which focus on the individual or on the immediate social context of the actor. According to this perspective, crime is a function of the development of modern society and the concomitant moral deregulation that is associated with modernisation.[7]

Dependency theorists by contrast, argue that the so-called retarded development of the Third World is due not to its lack of incorporation into the capitalist system but rather to its links with the capitalist system. According to the dependency theorists, the underdevelopment of the Third World began with European colonisation. Underdevelopment resulted because European imperialism only drew part of Third World economies into their world system—the parts which primarily served the economic interests of European capital. So a situation is created whereby the economies of certain countries are conditioned by the development and expansion of other countries, to which the former are subjugated.[8]

Consequently ' . . . decades of colonialism left Nigeria a severely backward, underdeveloped, distorted, disarticulated, dependent and poverty-stricken formation'. (Ihonvbere 1994:9-10)

NIGERIA'S RULING ELITE: ECONOMIC MISMANAGEMENT, CORRUPTION AND THE DRUGS TRADE

Important to our understanding of Nigeria's role in drug trafficking today is an analysis of the ruling elite and its political and economic management. Many of the imprisoned Nigerian couriers implicated their own military and political rulers in the trade for which they were being punished. This is supported by the testimony of Robert Gelbard, US assistant secretary of state for international narcotics matters who declared that the Nigerians involved in the drug networks were not 'random mules' or 'freelancers' but 'people working for very organized groups, which we have felt is with the protection of government officials' (*The Guardian*, 6 April 1994). Again Ihonvbere argues that the roots of understanding are to be found in the early experience of colonisation:

Colonialism had not come to Nigeria to create competitors for itself . . . its goal was the creation of an adjunct and dependent dominant elite that was to contribute to its surplus extraction in the colonised society. (1994:10)

When political independence came, in 1960, decades of colonial rule had left Nigeria under the control of an emasculated ruling class who inherited from the British a weak and disorganized infrastructure of administrative and industrial reforms. It was also a ruling class fully incorporated into the service of foreign capital and dependent on that capital. According to Ihonvbere the Nigerian bourgeoisie, while having made considerable superficial gains in the past 35 years—as a class it has grown, its relations with foreign capital have been strengthened, and political and economic restructuring have made certain individuals and their families wealthy—remains 'an underdeveloped, dependant, corrupt, unproductive, undisciplined, unpatriotic, wasteful, and highly factionalized elite in charge of a dependent economy and an unstable state'. (1994:10)

52

The 1970s witnessed a massive oil boom which left Nigeria financially independent in the international system. Between 1970 and 1979 oil production increased from 2.1 million barrels per day to a peak of 2.4 million barrels per day. At the peak of the boom, oil revenue constituted around 73 per cent of total revenue collected by the Nigerian government.[9]

Yet by the time the boom collapsed in 1983 the Nigerian newspaper *The Guardian* reported '. . . this year, all is quiet and sober. Economic hardship increasing almost daily in ugly dimensions, has taken all calculations to shreds, leaving pockets empty, markets deserted . . . This is the legacy of the economic crisis and the Nigerian twins: government mismanagement and corruption' (cited in Ihonvbere 1994: 24). The government consistently spent more than it earned and by the end of the 1970s it was forced to raise its first massive loan from a consortium of international banks

From a peak of N13,632 million in 1980, the value of oil exports declined to N8,583.8 million in 1982. Despite collecting more oil revenues than at any other time in its history (totalling over N43.6 billion in the years of civilian administration 1970-1983) the economy lurched into decline. According to F R A Marhino, Nigeria accrued '. . . more domestic and foreign debts in the four years of the same civilian administration than the cumulative debt ever owed before it . . . the administration spent more than 200 per cent more money than this country had ever spent from the time of its independence'.[10] Essentially the economy had been grossly mismanaged with domestic agriculture and manufacturing allowed to decline at the expense of foreign imports and with oil revenue spent on the importation of various consumer goods, capital goods, rice, and other agricultural produce which could have been profitably cultivated or produced in Nigeria. Waste and corruption characterised the way in which oil revenues were spent by the administration and prostitution, drug dealing and foreign currency speculation flourished in this climate of extravagance amongst the ruling elite.

> The most predominant route to wealth is corruption, politics, drug pushing, sinecure political appointments, currency trafficking, import-export activities, real estate, and fronting for powerful transnational interests. (Ihonvbere 1994:10)

According to one expert on the Nigerian political economy:

> Even if the scale of corruption was no greater than before, it was more visible . . . What people got was not performance but arrogance, displays of wealth that were stupidly insensitive to the economic realities of recession,

scarcity and suffering. Naira were sprayed around at social functions and donated to political causes by ministers and legislators in amounts that exceeded and often dwarfed their legitimate annual incomes. Draped in gold and magnificent dress, they assumed the bearing of aristocracy, and became considerably more distant from the people . . . The disastrous decline in Nigeria's oil income meant that every naira stolen or wasted sank the country further into debt and depression. (Diamond 1984:907-8)[11]

The civilian Shagari government was overthrown by a military coup in 1983. While the new regime 'inherited a bleeding economy and a society plagued by alienation, frustration, cynicism and massive opposition to the state' (Ihonvbere 1994:25) its own strategy of political management relied on political repression. Large numbers of dissidents were jailed and discussions on Nigeria's political future were banned.

It is important to outline the regime's economic strategy for recovery because, as will become evident later, it provides essential background for understanding the statements made by imprisoned Nigerian couriers.

Some of the basic components of the 1984 budget most relevant to an appreciation of the conditions which have fostered Nigerian drug trafficking are outlined by Julius Ihonvbere:

1. Rapid repayment of external loans in order to restore the country's credit worthiness;

2. A high rate of repayment of internal debts to placate local investors and contractors;

3. An increase in the rate and volume of internal revenue raised through taxes, levies, tolls, and fees;

4. Overall reduction in public expenditure, particularly on social services like education and health;

5. A freeze on wages and salaries and a reduction in the total amount paid as wages through the drastic reduction of allowances;

6. Large scale reduction of the labour force in the public service

7. Close monitoring and taxing of the economic activities of petty traders and other self-employed;

8. Expanded incentives to foreign investors;

9. Encouragement of wide-scale private investment in agriculture; and

10. Strict foreign exchange control in order to build up foreign reserves and encourage foreign investment. (1994:26)

The Nigerian economy has thus created fertile ground for the growth, largely among the petty bourgeoisie, of extra-legal activities which might alleviate the impact of the austerity programme. Aided by lax banking regulations, a heavy reliance on cash-based transactions, a large black market and the almost institutionalised corruption outlined above the drug trade has flourished. Nigeria's movement toward a more market-oriented economy, a move encouraged by Britain and the US, creates even further opportunities for trafficking and money laundering.

SMUGGLING AND THE TRADING TRADITION

The first impression of a visitor to Nigeria is of teeming markets selling everything from soap to engines . . . Trade (and transport) have deep and extensive roots in Nigeria's history and culture. (*The Economist* 1984:27)

Side by side with the conventional market place, however, lies 'an enormous parallel market' which is both powerful and ubiquitous.

Trading, both licit and illicit, is central to the economic and cultural identity of Nigeria and must be properly accounted for in any analysis of drug trafficking within the region. In the early 1980s, when output slumped and Nigeria lurched into crisis, many skilled and tertiary educated men and women, threatened by massive public sector wage cuts and possible redundancy, chose to move into the informal trading sector.

In the early 1980s illicit trading and smuggling were estimated to constitute as much as 25 per cent of all economic activity in the country. (*The Economist*, 1984:29)

Contraband passes the frontier with impunity in both directions (fuel, fertiliser and wheat leaving Nigeria, against cigarettes coming in). Periodic campaigns are launched to prevent illegal traffic (particularly of fuel and fertilizer), but the federal government is simply incapable of instilling civic responsibility in the face of such large potential profits . . . Estimates of unrecorded cross-border smuggling vary widely (by its nature there are no statistics), but a recent flurry of studies and surveys indicate that a tenfold multiplication of Nigeria's non-oil exports would still be a conservative guess. Whether they like it or not, for as long as monetary policies stay so far apart and price differentials remain, Nigeria's neighbours have little alternative but to suffer the effects of private sector regionalisation (Duncan James 1993:98-99)[12]

In 1980 gross profits for Nigerian companies declined by 3.9 per cent. The Central Bank of Nigeria cited smuggling and the activities of street traders as the primary cause of the decline. According to *The Economist,* 'The largest textile producer, Nigerian Textile Mills, claims that smuggled goods account for 60 per cent of demand for cloth. As a result, in a five month period, two major textile factories closed down in 1980 with the loss of 5,000 jobs (1984:19) The government's use of import restrictions to control trade in this period considerably facilitated smuggling. Before the advent of exchange rate controls *The Economist* noted,

> . . . the uncompetitiveness of many domestic industries in terms of quality as well as price, sophisticated urban consumers, and long-established trading traditions would make smuggling a continuing problem even if the naira were devalued. (1984:19)

PAIN AND POWER FROM THE WORLD BANK

In August 1985 the regime was overthrown by a *coup d'état* led by General Ibrahim Babangida. Against a background of declining oil revenues, rocketing inflation and food shortages the new regime embraced the Structural Adjustment Programmme (SAP) thrust upon it by the World Bank and the International Monetary Fund. IMF structural adjustment programmes aim to restore a positive balance of payments in order that the debtor country can then repay Northern governments, commercial banks and other lending institutions. Essentially a Structural Adjustment loan means the initiation of severe austerity programmes so that hard currency can be accumulated for repayment purposes.

> Only when debt service obligations can be substantially met does the IMF consider the debtor country free to pursue other objectives. The debtor has no choice but to heed the Fund's advice, since without its "seal of approval", no other source will provide loans, not even short-term trade credits (Susan George 1992:2)

SAP loans are characterised by an accompanying privatisation of public corporations, massive public sector job cuts, promotion of export industries to earn foreign exchange, of imports, the removal of trade barriers, the elimination or drastic reduction in social welfare, agriculture and food staple subsidies, high interest rates and restrictive monetary policies, and a reduction in real wages, particularly for the

56

already low paid. (George and Sabelli 1994:18-19). The Babangida regime, however, did not take the IMF loan (because of widespread opposition within Nigeria) but it did implement all of the conditions of the IMF SAP package. For ordinary Nigerians the price was a high one:

> SAP has meant a curse to a majority of Nigerians. It is a string of worries to the low income earners and those who earn nothing. The crisis deepens at the turn of each day. Hapless individuals are at their wits ends, pitted against the efforts of government's self-inflicted devaluation of the national currency the naira. The eroded naira has brought in its wake teeming crowds at the city's bus stops . . . exorbitant transport fares; a bothersome trend of graduate unemployment . . . and an elusive health-care delivery system. [13]

The Babangida regime introduced a period of 'economic emergency' from October 1985 which was to last 15 months. All workers suffered pay cuts, the importation of rice, wheat malt and maize was banned, a levy of 30 per cent was placed on all other imports, the currency was devalued by 80 per cent, the wage freeze was extended and the 80 per cent petroleum subsidy was removed.[14] Foreign debt more than doubled from 1986 to 1991 soaring from $18 million to $37 million. It now exceeds the country's Gross Domestic Product of US$30 million. The ruling elite remained untouched by the austerity measures, unreliant as they were on wages and salaries.

The impact of SAP has been uneven. The vast majority of urban dwellers (35 per cent of the total population) have experienced shrinking incomes and an escalating cost of living. The value of the naira has depreciated from parity with the pound in 1985 to a value less than five pence in 1992. There has been a massive public expenditure squeeze with attendant cuts in public service provision of health care and education as well as mass redundancies. For those living in rural areas (66 per cent) the impact has been a little more variable and some have seen real incomes grow. But the price of domestic goods and services sky-rocketed—between 1985 and the end of 1991 consumer prices had increased by 230 per cent and by an estimated 57 per cent in 1992. (Duncan James 1993:71) World Bank figures show that standards of living in Nigeria are now lower than they were in the 1950s. The World Bank has argued that the economic crisis of the 1980s was so severe that it essentially cancelled out the progress of the previous 20 years. According to the OECD Nigeria suffered the world's worst rate of decline in the 1980s.

In a move which could only worsen the economic crisis, US President Bill Clinton (acting on a global annual survey of drug cultivation and trafficking) cut two aid programmes, worth in the region of $12 million to Nigeria until the country's drug enforcement record was seen to improve (*Time*, 18 April 1994).

In many respects the rise and fall of Nigeria's economic fortunes conform to the material conditions which in sociological terms give rise to a state of anomie (see below).

Many of those interviewed were unemployed or had experienced unemployment in the preceding years. While official statistics reveal an unbelievable unemployment rate of two per cent, the Nigerian Labour Congress argues that the true figure is much greater with around 40 per cent of the industrial workforce having lost their jobs in the 1980s. (EIU 1996:8)

Many of the drug couriers I interviewed were representative of those whose lives have been most affected by the dramatic dislocation in Nigeria's economic fortunes. Their role in drug trafficking took place in this period of drastic economic decline.

> Drug trafficking in typical gang-style boomed in Nigeria with structural adjustment. Nigeria has become a major actor in the international drug business. All over Europe and North America hundreds of Nigerians are in jail for various drug-related offences as the young, unable to find work and caught in the paradoxically ostentatious life-styles of military leaders, and the new rich take to extra-legal means of accumulation. (Ihonvbere, 1994:132-133)

At the end of 1989 there were 1,576 Nigerians in jails around the world for drug-related offences. At the end of 1990 there were 527 Nigerians in British prisons (non-immigration cases) and of these 444 were held on drugs charges. By the end of 1995 the number of imprisoned Nigerians (non-immigration cases) had dropped to 204.[15]

The impact of what Amnesty International has described as 'one of the most serious human rights crises in the past 34 years' on drug trafficking is not considered in any depth because the interviews were conducted prior to the assumption of power by Sani Abacha's regime.[16] Suffice to say that the conditions which have fostered the widespread and state-sponsored abuses of human rights documented by Amnesty International in the 1990s are deep rooted and are also contributory to the drug trafficking crisis. Certainly since 1993, and the regime's use of arbitrary detention, mass arrests, extra-judicial killings and the routine harassment of pro-democracy groups there was an evident, and quite dramatic decline in the number of Nigerians arrested and imprisoned in the UK for drug smuggling. The increase in political repression may have had an impact in terms of covering the activities of sections of the population but it is also likely that other factors, inherent to the organization of international drug markets, and narcotics enforcement strategies have played a more significant role.

DRUG-RELATED CORRUPTION AND THE NIGERIAN STATE

Without the criminalisation of the international markets for cannabis, heroin and cocaine the necessity and opportunities for the corruption of public officials would be massively reduced. Similarly if the international war on drugs had been successful in curtailing consumer demand the room and scope for corruption in already fertile countries, like Nigeria, would be far less. Writing on corruption in Latin America and the Caribbean Ethan Nadleman has argued:

> Drug-related corruption can thus be seen as a consequence of the tensions between the two demands emanating from the United States: the US government's demand that Latin American and Caribbean governments criminalise the drug markets and enforce the laws aimed at their suppression; and the demand of American consumers for the psychoactive substances produced and exported by those countries . . . Indeed given the relative paucity of legitimate sources of wealth and employment, the anti-drug laws have been largely incapable of deterring people from taking advantage of the only significant economic opportunity available to them. From this perspective, drug-related corruption can be seen as the inevitable consequence of trying to repress a highly dynamic and economically significant market. (Nadleman 1993:255-6)

This is an important analysis in terms of understanding the limits of attainable drug reform.

Political and economic corruption in Nigeria, as we have seen, pre-dates the development of the international drugs trade. Its existence, however, has ensured a fertile environment for Nigerian involvement in the new industry.

Laurie Joshua has argued that

> The high numbers of Nigerian men and women in British prisons, and the number of children of convicted women accommodated by social services departments, would not be at the current levels without the connivance of "powerful interests" in Nigeria . . . Allegations of the involvement of top military officers and other so-called businessmen in the drug business have never been denied. Rather apprehended couriers usually die in mysterious circumstances. (1996:133)

Allegations of Nigerian official involvement in the drugs trade continue to be made in the African press. In the late 1980s a former Nigerian senator, Chief Adegoke, was jailed in the US for his role in smuggling over five kilograms of heroin (*Newswatch*, 11 December 1989). The case of Gloria Okon is cited frequently. After her arrest in Nigeria for drug trafficking she promised to reveal the names of the organizers she knew but was found dead in her cell a few weeks later. Powerful forces were claimed to be responsible for her death.

Some Nigerian commentators claim that Nigeria's 'notoriety' as a major player in global drug trafficking only came into being with the advent of structural adjustment, the rule of Babangida and the related devaluation of the naira. Then it is claimed, '. . . a general mood of distrust, suspicion, anger, disillusionment, and cynicism has taken over from what was once an active, ebullient innovative, creative, and productive society'.[17]

Nigeria's former head of state general Olusegun Obasanjo (detained in 1995 following a secret trial for allegedly plotting to overthrow the Abacha regime) has declared :

> . . . if Nigerians are not harried as cocaine traffickers, they are being chased for banking and financial frauds . . . corruption exists almost in every society. But in Nigeria and particularly since the advent of SAP, it has become uncontrolled and uncontrollably pervasive. Anything and anybody can now ' be settled'. Inside and outside Nigeria, people talk of corruption in Nigeria as if it is legalised or as a "way of life".[18]

Clement Nwankwo, secretary of the Civil Liberties Organization (CLO), has argued that reducing corruption in government is an essential pre-condition for tackling the problem of Nigerian drug trafficking: 'This is because drug trafficking is a reaction to the way a certain class of Nigerians live. Nigerian government officials do not hesitate to flaunt corruptly acquired wealth across the face of everybody'. (*Newswatch*, 11 December 1989)

In December 1989 the National Drug Law Enforcement Agency (NDLEA) was established as part of the Babangida regime's response to international pressure to curb Nigeria's increasing role in the international drugs trade. Designed in the mould of the American Drug Enforcement Agency it received US assistance for law enforcement equipment and training. Under the leadership of Fidelis Oyakhilome (until his suspension on corruption charges in 1991) the NDLEA embarked on a war designed to improve Nigeria's standing internationally. The NDLEA has, as have its international counterparts, been plagued by internal corruption. In a review of Nigeria's drug-

60

control 'performance' *vis-à-vis* US certification criteria, Levitsky noted that 'Corruption . . . is a serious problem limiting the effectiveness of counter narcotics enforcement. In May the federal military government enacted a law making drug offences non-bailable. Nonetheless the unauthorized release of drug suspects from police custody has continued' (1992:8) On coming to office in 1994, Oyakhilome's successor, Major General Musa Bamaiyi dismissed all 106 narcotic agents stationed at Murtala Mohammed International Airport, Ikeja on grounds of corruption and malpractice.[19] In 1994 *Time Magazine* reported the following:

> After years of ineptitude, and corruption, Nigeria's drug enforcement authorities wanted to get this one right. Last December they pulled off Africa's biggest narcotics haul ever, seizing more than $900 million worth of high-grade heroin as it entered the country from Thailand, en route to Europe and the US. To publicise their coup, the National Drug Law Enforcement Agency scheduled a televised bonfire in Lagos. But two days before the burning a judge examining the evidence discovered six 0.4 kg bags missing. The next day four more bags disappeared. The purloined powder, worth $13 million, has yet to be recovered. Worse, no drug kingpin involved in the deal was apprehended.[20]

An Economist Intelligence Unit Report published in the same year reported that:

> Already possessing a very poor record internationally for drug smuggling, Nigeria's reputation has received a further knock after investigation of the National Drug Law Enforcement Agency (NDLEA). The chairman of a six-member task force set up recently to sanitise the NDLEA is said to have uncovered a long list of illicit deals between officials of the agency and those suspected of drug smuggling. He noted that this type of collusion and the consequent failure to clamp down on the drugs trade jeopardised Nigeria's interests in the international community. The task force was formed in February after part of a large seizure of heroin subsequently went missing while in the custody of the NDLEA.[21]

And in June 1996 *West Africa* reported that some 488 staff at the NDLEA were dismissed for aiding and abetting drug traffickers (with 20 of them facing prosecution).

In response to the alleged use of false Nigerian passports by other West African nationals the Nigerian Federal Ministry of Internal Affairs redesigned the Nigerian passport, thereby invalidating all passports issued before April 1990.[22] For their part the British High Commission in Lagos, as part of an attempt to reduce visa applications from potential drug traffickers, increased the fees for visa processing by over 1,000 per cent. [23]

In June and July of 1990 the NDLEA introduced screening and clearance as a pre-condition for Nigerians seeking travel visas to the drug producing countries of East and Central Asia and Latin America. According to the former Chairman of the NDLEA, '. . . as many as a hundred applications are received daily but by the time the applicants fill in our screening forms and are subjected to some interview, a good many of them do not turn up again'. (*The African Guardian*, 23 July 1990)

As part of the 'war on drugs' strategy the NDLEA introduced the notion of public shaming into the punishment arena. The publication in the national press of the names and photographs of Nigerians imprisoned abroad was predicated on the belief that 'Nigerians ought to know who amongst them is responsible for tarnishing the country's image abroad and in addition to make guardians, who on seeing the faces of their children in the papers check other children from engaging in drug trafficking'. (*The African Guardian*, 23 July 1990).

In 1990 the NDLEA made trans-border trafficking, and with it the courier its specific focus. According to Oyakhilome such an orientation was necessary because '. . . the image of the country is very much at stake and . . . the agency feels that if it can stop drugs from coming into the country, we will be able to stop the amount available for internal distribution and consumption'.[24] The cosmetic concern with image by the country's corrupt ruling elite led to increasingly repressive measures directed against the carriers of drugs. Decree 33 of 1990, effective from October 10 of that year placed all Nigerians arrested abroad for drug offences in a situation of double jeopardy. Effectively it allows for the immediate re-arrest and re-prosecution of Nigerians convicted abroad once they have served their sentence and have returned home to Nigeria. The justification for this punitive form of double punishment essentially appears to be concerned with redressing the very tarnished image of Nigeria within the international community—the victims of this double jeopardy are effectively being tried for bringing '. . . the name of Nigeria into disrepute' (NDLEA 1990, Decree No. 33 of 1990). While it is unclear whether or not re-prosecutions have taken place, the regime has made it plain that the legislation is to be enforced. Commenting on the arrival of 179 deported Nigerians in Lagos (having served their sentences for drug smuggling abroad), Bamaiyi confirmed that the deportees would remain in detention and would be charged with tarnishing Nigeria's image under Decree 33 (*The Vanguard*, 6 May 1995).

The courier is here the scapegoat for all the corruption, greed, economic waste and social despair engendered by the regime. And, as is so often the case with scapegoats, they exist in plentiful supply, a fact recognised by the US State Department:

> The major drug traffickers in Nigeria never touch the drugs, or are involved in the actual transfer of money . . . There are thousands and thousands of couriers. You can arrest couriers from now until kingdom come and there will be other couriers to take their place. (Levitsky 1992:6)

Decree No. 20 of 1984 introduced the death penalty for drug trafficking. There was, however, a massive public outcry following the executions by firing squad in 1985 of three young men convicted of drug trafficking at the Kiri Kiri Prisons. Nobel laureate Wole Soyinka called the executions 'murder' but the then minister of justice and attorney general Chike Ofodile and the regimes 'number two man' major general Tunde Idiagbon declared that the executions would continue: 'A uniquely Nigerian solution is necessary to curb the get-rich-quick mania that encourages serious crimes' Idiagbon declared. The Buhari regime was, however, toppled four months later and when General Babangida took power in August 1985 he abolished the death sentence for drug trafficking and commuted existing sentences of death to terms of imprisonment. (*Newswatch*, 11 December 1989) The execution of drug traffickers is however back on the agenda with the current head of the NDLEA, major general Musa Bamaiyi a keen exponent of its virtues. The move toward the reintroduction of the death penalty for traffickers may be tempered by the international expressions of outrage over the executions of human rights activist Ken Saro-Wiwa and his eight colleagues in November 1995. Bamaiyi is a veteran of the Nigerian Civil War and was the North sector commander of UNPROFOR in the former Yugoslavia between 1992 and 1993. Prior to his role in heading Nigeria's war on drugs he was Commander for Training and Doctrine for the Nigerian Army.[25]

In 1996 the NDLEA introduced a policy of inspecting and vetting all exports in the search for concealed drugs, measures unrealisitic in practical terms, but designed to 'serve notice to the international community that Nigeria is taking seriously the worldwide campaign against drug trafficking'.[26]

IN THEIR OWN WORDS: NIGERIAN COURIERS SPEAK

Such is the state of life for many Nigerians that a British probation service official visiting Nigeria on a fact-finding mission in 1992 was prompted to comment:

I understand why there are so many Nigerians arrested in Britain for drug trafficking; what I don't understand is why there aren't more.[27]

Given the parlous state of Nigeria's political economy, the economic hardship experienced by so many, and the culture of corruption which ensures large-scale trafficking a relatively easy passage, it is indeed not difficult to understand why a considerable number of Nigerian men and women risk the many dangers of drug smuggling. According to Hammond and Walters:

> It was not difficult to see that for many Nigerians life was a constant struggle to earn enough to feed, clothe and house the immediate family, let alone meet the very real responsibilities and expectations of the extended family. Given the economic circumstances and general living standards we saw there was no difficulty (from a "western" perspective) in accepting that the main motivation is economic necessity. (1992:12)

This perception corroborated my earlier findings derived from a preliminary analysis of interviews with Nigerian couriers conducted in the early 1990s. (Green 1991; 1996)

A closer investigation of the perceptions of Nigerian couriers, however, provides much more than a poverty justification for the offence. It illuminates the human experience of living in a period of economic and political anomie and an insight into the range of 'choices' faced by those most affected.

Changing fortunes: poverty revisited

> In here you will find a lot of us who tasted life. Ten years ago there were no Nigerians in prison here, our lives were good — we didn't have to resort to drug dealing. (Peter, 37)

The majority of the imprisoned Nigerians interviewed, both men and women, had enjoyed well paid jobs, often professional careers, and a reasonable standard of living before the period of economic crisis. They were not typically of the rural poor though many had been born and grown up in rural villages before moving to cities and towns. Many were educated at tertiary level and had assumed careers which once would have guaranteed them comfortable life-styles. There were dentists, air traffic controllers, a former professional sportsman, accountants, airline employees, electrical installation contractors and civil servants. Very few now worked in the professions for which they had been trained citing redundancy, dismissal, lack of employment opportunities, discrimination and unsustainable public sector wage levels as the reason. In most cases these individuals had turned to trading as a means of making a living. The range of commodities traded was wide, including cosmetics, jewellery, spare-parts, stationary, electrical goods, brake fluid, PVC sheeting, computer cables and textiles. The colonial links with Britain and the long established trade route between the two countries (Britain remains Nigeria's largest overseas supplier) combined with Nigeria's own lack of a developed manufacturing sector has meant that many traders must purchase their goods from the UK. (*The Economist*, 1984:19) The oil rich years also saw significant numbers of Nigerians educated in British and US universities and colleges so that many young middle class Nigerians had the opportunity to develop potential business connections in their years abroad.

Oleka spent four years studying economics in Bridgeport, Connecticut but returned to Nigeria as the economy plunged into crisis:

> There were no jobs for many people with degrees when I came back to Nigeria so I got into the import business. The devaluation of the naira in 1986 led to my troubles. It was very difficult to buy goods, it affected the middle and lower classes especially in terms of job losses — and it particularly hit the small business people. Trading became no longer profitable. I lost capital with the devaluation. Before devaluation I used to earn N20,000, after devaluation, N5,000. It wasn't enough to buy a container on a ship . . . When things are very hard, when a doctor can't get a job, when there is no welfare — if you don't have it you don't have it — that's the way it goes in Nigeria . . . that's why since 1986 more decent Nigerians have been involved in drug trafficking . . . doctors go in for it for £1,000. Can you imagine it !

The following comments reinforce a general perception voiced by Nigerian inmates about the conditions of life experienced in Nigeria in the late 1980s:

> The gap between rich and poor is enormous. There is no hope, if I don't do drug business, of ever breaking out of being poor . . . that's why a lot of us are taking this risk — we know if we are caught we'll go to jail, but how long can we live poor? (Peter, 37, remanded in custody for the importation of 190 grams of heroin)

> People here [in Britain] don't understand what "hard life " means . . . where you can't afford one square meal a day, to pay the rent, to change your socks . . . with no sign of recovery. (Emmanuel, 38, former athlete)

65

I met a man at a friend's party, a businessman who imported spare-parts. He told me "You have to do something about your life" — I had lost my flat and I was squatting in a church in Lagos. I was very down, my mother was very sick. I trusted him. He told me he wanted to help me set up a flat and that if I took drugs to the UK then he could do that. (Liza, 28, serving six years for heroin importation)

Anomie and alienation: expectations and reality

In the context of Nigeria's economic decline from being oil rich in the 1970s to the world's thirteenth poorest nation by the end of the 1980s many of the interviewees revealed a general sense of insecurity and despair independent of their prison experience. The experience of many Nigerians provides a powerful empirical case-study to support the theories of 'anomie' articulated by both Durkheim and later the American sociologist, Robert Merton. At its core, anomie theory explores the disjunction between social goals and the means afforded by the social structure for the attainment of those goals. Mass consumption driven by mass production and distribution is central to economic growth under industrial capitalism. Consumption and the desire to consume is central to the momentum of the economy. However, when the cultivation of the desire to consume is coupled with an inability on the part of the political economy to satisfy that desire then the conditions are ripe for the rise of anomic deviation. 'For Durkheim, deregulation led to infinite aspirations; for Merton infinite aspirations led to deregulation. The result for both was the same: high rates of deviation'. (Downes and Rock 1988:121).

According to the *Economist* special report on Nigeria:

. . . the boom had made people used to money and the good things it can buy from abroad — bread and rice and radio-sets, cheap motor pumps to get water from the well, neat but tinny motor-buses that made even the poorest people mobile for a few coppers. (1986:4)

For the educated and better off the clash between the expectations formed in the oil rich years and the reality of economic decline finds its expression in comments like the following:

I'm 37 years old, I've been working all my life and I can't afford a Skoda. (Peter)

The country is in a mess politically, socially and economically; Nigerians are traditionally traders yet they are not permitted to import rice, stock-feed, wheat etc — all of that is controlled by the government . . . every avenue of survival is blocked by the government . . . the only avenue left is drugs . . . drugs are just another commodity. (Oleka)

66

For others the world had been turned on its head:

> I knew the risks involved, I knew that the whole world is against drug trafficking but you get to the stage where you don't care anymore. I became a courier for somebody that I know. If circumstances were different and I had a job, I would have been his boss, but instead I end up carrying the drugs for him. (Benjaman)

Sense of criminality

For the rational observer the issues of 'criminality' and 'criminal responsibility', so central (and inherently problematic) to British criminal justice policy, lose much of their power when applied to the activities of Third World couriers acting, for whatever personal reasons, from a base of national economic misery and social despair. Many couriers talked of being faced with no other option, of pressure on 'the common man', of life without a future, and implied that to carry drugs was the lesser of two evils.

> My father became very ill with a stroke in 1986 and I couldn't even afford to buy the drugs prescribed for him, and I'm the only son. My sisters helped but the bitterness creeps in that you can't take on the responsibilities you should. You are up against the wall. We don't come from a country where you walk into a bank with a good proposal to set up a business unless you are from the ruling elite . . . my orientation has never been criminal, I still don't have criminal tendencies. (Chris, 29, serving five years for importing 500 grams of heroin)

In the 1990s 'shame' became briefly fashionable as an alternative form of punishment within western criminological circles.[28] Its operation in countries like China and Nigeria where it travels comfortably alongside state repression should caution liberal western academics against its adoption as an 'alternative' means of punishment. Shame, as successive military regimes have acknowledged in their own 'war' against drug traffickers is a powerful instrument of social coercion in Nigeria. Many of the couriers interviewed expressed a sense of shame at their plight. More often their concern was for families at home in Nigeria who provide the real target for the public humiliation of drug couriers. Some as we noted earlier were choosing not to inform their families of their imprisonment preferring instead to create an impression of desertion or of unforseen opportunity which will detain them abroad for a number of years. Women in particular expressed a fear of rejection by husbands and families. Yet at the same time shame was given perspective in the majority of cases by the elevation of material circumstance over 'criminal intention' as the motive for the offence. 'People are not interested in drugs business when they have something to eat . . . I told the judge "If you were in my shoes you would have done it too"'. (Sasa, 39)

In some cases theft was seen as a worse crime:

I don't want to steal — that's what really pushed me into drugs (Peter, 37)

Several of the couriers referred to a religious commitment which they argued made their burden of shame all the more unbearable. Eke Obasi, a former Apostolic Church deacon declared:

I personally hate drugs, I don't drink or smoke — its just appalling that I should get myself involved in something I hate so much.

Another courier reported in a confused fashion her feelings in terms of religion:

I am very anti-drugs because of what it does to people and because of my religious background. I think the devil wanted to use me. I thank God for being here [in prison] — its another experience.

For some, the observation of drug addiction in British prisons had a powerful impact and, in theory at least, created a new consciousness:

In Holloway I saw what drugs could do — I swear to God if I'd known what people look like after taking heroin I'd never have carried it . . . because I'm a mother. (Cora, 37)

The normalisation of criminal activity

In the context of crime and corruption, political repression and social anomie the decision to traffic in illegal drugs becomes one which conforms to, or is not necessarily at odds with, 'accepted' strategies of survival. As one 36 year old Ibo trader explained, 'You cannot get anywhere in Nigeria without getting immersed in graft and bribery, all this rubbish'.

When bribery and corruption are rewarded and nepotism is the surest means of advancement; when operating on the black market has become accepted business practice and in many cases the only means by which small businesses can survive; when transgressing the law and evading customs duty is part of everyday business practice; when education and hard work are not rewarded (or not perceived as rewarded); when existence assumes the mantle of struggle in an environment where corruption is a dominant path to upward social mobility, then the leap to smuggling a commodity which is, in itself, prohibited seems not so great, seems less unacceptable than it might in

68

other material circumstances. All this is especially so given that in 1985 rice, maize, wheat and other imported food-stuffs were theoretically banned, ostensibly to support prices for Nigerian producers. Heroin, cocaine and cannabis might thus seem less outside the margins in the context of so many other prohibited imported commodities.

The interviews revealed a strong sense of the 'normalisation' of the criminal. Criminal offences of the highest order (murder, corruption, theft and drug trafficking) were seen to be conducted by members of the ruling elite, their families and senior state and military officials. Many of the Nigerian couriers referred to alleged criminal involvement by the ruling elite:

> Its not just ordinary Nigerians who are involved in drug trafficking ... the government is involved — the army's chief of staff is known to be involved ... the Alhadji's, the Muslims who have been to Mecca, made the drug contacts in Mecca. The drugs came, originally, in the diplomatic bags — none of them have been caught. The richest family in Nigeria were caught in 1985 before it was rampant. Highly influential people, who go to Pakistan on pilgrimage, bring drugs from Pakistan — they bring it by air. (Oleka , US educated trader serving eight years)

According to one newly graduated but unemployed courier:

> Over one million graduates are out of work. They have to eat and are brought up to steal and to beg. If someone offers you money to do something you'll do it. Nigerians see drugs as a commercial venture, and with the mess the country is in they have to survive somehow.

Another male courier articulated a widely held belief among Nigerian prisoners (and particularly those of Ibo origin) that education was a value no longer rewarded by that society:

> In Nigeria you don't have to be very intelligent to get on, you need to lace people's boots. (Sasa)

To evade customs duty, of itself, was not seen by those interviewed as a criminal act. Given the austerity measures, and the introduction of the very high import duties and taxes in the mid-1980s evading customs duty was regarded as very much a feature of the trading world. Of the 35 Nigerians interviewed only 15 acknowledged that they had carried drugs. The other 25 claimed to have been duped into unwittingly smuggling drugs. Eight of these couriers claimed to have believed that the packages they had swallowed contained gold dust, mercury dust, precious gems or pharmaceuticals and the purpose of concealment was customs evasion. Whether or not these claims are true, whether or not the individual's suspicions were aroused, are largely irrelevant in the context of the wider political and economic picture. The uniform lack of allegiance to the corrupt ruling junta reinforced by the economic demise of so many ordinary people outshadows the issue of justificatory excuse.

Perceptions of the state
Nigerian, and particularly male, couriers blamed their government for creating the economic distress which had 'forced' so many of them into drug trafficking and implicated senior ministers in the management of drug trafficking organizations within the country (see above).

> Officially, the corrupt government will feign anger and say that they frown upon such things — they will say that I have brought shame on the country ... But they have done worse things. (Daniel, serving seven years)

The endemic nature of corruption in Nigeria is evident in the testimonies of the Nigerian couriers in respect of their relationship to criminal justice practitioners in both Nigeria and Britain.

> The same people who sell you foreign currency on the black market are the same people who arrest you for possession of foreign currency. (Sasa, 39, former accountant, then trader)

Many were also highly suspicious of their legal representation in the UK believing the lawyers assigned them to be in the employ of HM Customs and Excise. This perception was not assisted by the generally poor quality of the legal representation afforded the courier (see Green 1991; Hedges and Tarzi 1990; Hammond and Abernethey 1992). State officials and figures of authority were to a considerable degree perceived to be tarred with the brush of Nigerian experience.

Women, in spite of being highly suspicious of authority, tended to be less dismissive and to expect more assistance from their embassy than did their male counterparts, who uniformly rejected any contact with Nigerian officialdom for fear of later reprisals. Those who contacted the Nigerian High Commission concerning their plight, however, were told that their embassy could not involve itself because of the drug-related nature of the case.

> The government encourages these things [drug trafficking]. When you create difficulties for citizens, no work for people coming out of university then people will do anything to get money to live. (Peter, 29, remanded for the importation of 190 grams of heroin)

There were suggestions from some that if one didn't conform to the culture of bribery and corruption prosperity was unattainable:

> In my country everyone interprets things as a bribe. I couldn't stand the bribery — its wrong, I was getting into trouble with my attitudes to bribery. If I had taken bribes from people I would never have ended up here [prison]. I would have had plenty of money, everyone does it. (Sasa, 39, serving five years for importing 220 grams of heroin)

Ethnic identity

Nigeria is a tremendously ethnically diverse country with over 250 distinct ethnic groups, of which three are predominant. In the Muslim north live the 15 million Hausa-Fulani people; in the South-East the ten million predominantly Christian Ibo people, and the 12 million Yoruba are based largely in the South-West. Since 1966 the ruling elite have originated largely from the Muslim North. From among many of the Ibo interviewees came a charge of discrimination and prejudice against the ruling Hausa-Fulani and the implication that much of the economic hardship suffered by groups in the south (which lay behind the decision to smuggle drugs) was attributable to this discrimination. This is supported to some extent by human rights monitors:

> The Nigerian government . . . has perpetuated tensions between Christian I[g]bos and Muslim Hausa-Fulanis in the northern part of the country by engaging in practices that discriminate against non-indigens and failing to prosecute the perpetrators of abuses. (The Refugee Council, October 1995:35)

Similarly and coinciding with the experience of many of the Ibo couriers interviewed the Canadian Immigration and Refugee Board have written that: 'The rise of religious fundamentalism, particularly that of Islam, coupled with the manipulation of religious sentiment by elements of the political and economic elite . . . have all contributed to the escalation of a conflict that, until the mid-1980s, had not really posed a threat to the stability of the nation. (*Nigeria: Religion and Conflict,* 1993:18)

> The Ibo are more susceptible than any other tribe because of the poverty and the civil war. The fact that the Ibos here are all highly skilled is no accident. In the Ibo states you cannot get a job, this is also true for the Yoruba though they didn't fight on the side of the Biafran government. There is racism in Nigeria against the Ibo. Highly skilled Ibo cannot get public service jobs in the rest of Nigeria and that's why they end up in the private sector. (Ikwans, 33, retrenched civil servant turned trader)

In its 1986 annual survey of Nigeria *The Economist* noted that despite a desperate shortage of teachers in northern Nigeria, qualified Yoruba and Ibo teachers from the southern states were rejected in favour of unqualified Muslim teachers.

The case of C Iwedike reinforces the general sense of discrimination experienced by the Ibo interviewed. He graduated in 1984 with a degree in marketing from the University of Science and Technology in Port Harcourt. He then served his compulsory National Youth Service, a prerequisite for graduate employment, and from that point found himself unemployable:

> Thousands of unskilled people are employed. I don't want to sound tribalistic. In the northern part of the country there is less qualified manpower. We, in the south, are very educated . . . we are supposed to be eligible to work anywhere in the country, but if you are from the south you'll only get contract work in the north and then only until there is a northerner to do the job. I did my youth service in the north. If the southern quota is filled there is no way a southerner will be used to fill the northern quota.

Another tertiary qualified Nigerian commented in similar vein:

> It seems as though the austerity measures were imposed to put the Ibo out of business. (Matthew)

While perceptions of personal crisis were often framed within an analysis of tribal discrimination the root causes remain steadfastly economic and political. Sectarianism and bigotry frequently arise from the ashes of economic and political crisis. According to Duncan James:

> A regular visitor over the past decade cannot fail to observe a progressive polarisation dividing Muslim and non-Muslim communities, in particular, and by association, people of northern origin from their southern neighbours. In an atmosphere of mutual suspicion relatively insignificant incidents risk escalating into violent confrontations. Although such flare-ups are largely unpredictable, it can be said that their primary cause is neither ethnic nor religious but economic. The origin of virtually every incident can be traced to squabbles over market-stall allocation, jealousy over employment prospects, incised prices of basic commodities or arguments over land. (Duncan James 1993:17)

FOUR STORIES

A Trader's Story

Peter

Peter was on remand for the importation of 190 grams of heroin, wrapped up in 40 packages which he had swallowed. He is a Yoruba man in his late thirties married with a wife and five children. Unlike the majority of the Nigerian men interviewed Peter had left school early, at the age of 14 to work in the printing trade. Following a course of evening classes he became a self-employed electrical installation contractor:

> Generally business is not going well so I decided to import computer cables and accessories as well. For the past four years I've been shuttling between England and Nigeria, four or five times a year but I couldn't make a good business. The cost of the flights became higher and higher. I see my other colleagues making money and I wonder how — it seems I can't do business. They were in fact involved with drugs. When the naira was devalued, by around 20 per cent life became very hard for those of us traders. I needed the money to buy the cables, so that's how I got involved in drugs, trying to raise money to support my business. A friend introduced me to another person who deals in drugs and I purchased the drugs from this man. I couldn't pay for it all so he gave it to me on trust. I gave him N10,000 and the drugs were supposed to have cost N30,000. This dealer gave me the name of someone I was to meet in London. I was to meet her at her house but I was arrested by customs officers before I left the airport. Now I can't afford to pay the rent and the children cost N300 each to go to school . . .

> You know, my wife worked for Nigerian Airways for 12 years — she was retrenched two years ago, paid off with just £200. If I really wanted to deal drugs that was the time I would have done it, when my wife was flying for 12 years.

The entrepreneur's story

Fadojou

It is difficult to make any true assessment of the number of Nigerian couriers among the interviewees who played a more entrepreneurial/organizational role in the trafficking of drugs. It is reasonable to assert, and supported by a range of evidence, that the more powerful the trafficker the greater the distance they are able to place between themselves and the contraband. For that reason alone the vast majority of imprisoned couriers are just that—simply the carriers of the drugs. Some, however, are more cognisant and act independently as drug dealers, purchasing the drugs from their own finances from

73

established dealers in Lagos, transporting them and selling them on to personal contacts abroad. Only two of those interviewed appeared to fall into this category. The first was, by profession, a smuggler of ivory and other dutyable goods, and the other was a trader in motor spare-parts whose business was in trouble:

> It all comes down to money doesn't it? I'm a smuggler — I don't want to pay tax. I was doing quite fine with my business until my goods were confiscated. I was in hospital for a while, after a bad car crash, and I was expecting a shipment of goods from Italy. I was going to declare the goods in Nigeria and then take them to sell in southern Africa. Because I couldn't supervise the clearance I ended up being double-crossed by people I trusted. When I got out of hospital I went to Zimbabwe and Kenya to organize business [the smuggling of ivory] through Tanzania. I invested a lot of money in this deal and then I was arrested for smuggling ivory . . . The ivory was confiscated but because I had 'connections' I wasn't charged . . . I'm a smuggler but not a drug smuggler . . . after the ivory was confiscated I went to Malawi where a friend had just come back from London. He was talking about smuggling cannabis and he wanted me to arrange for some girls to transport the drugs . . . I had real misgivings but my friend was very persuasive . . . (Fadoju, serving five years for importing 25 kilos of cannabis)

The Duped

Comfort's story

In 1991 Comfort Fairly was sentenced to three and a half years for her part in the importation of 500 grams of heroin with an estimated street value of £36,000. Problems in Africa had brought her to Britain in 1985 and for a time she lived in Scotland with her British husband. When they separated she and her seven-year-old daughter moved to London. Unable to find work they were housed by Westminster Council first in a bed and breakfast hotel and then in a homeless unit in Westbourne Park. She found work in a nearby laundry and then sent for her eldest daughter who was still living in Africa. She was simultaneously re-united with her eldest daughter's father and life improved with the move to a three bedroomed maisonette. Following the birth of a third child, however, the relationship once more disintegrated and life took a serious turn for the worse:

> We were living on £52 per week from Social Security and life was really terrible — it was impossible to pay the bills. Then in November my handbag was stolen in an Oxfam shop — I got crisis money of £21 and it had to last all month. I went to see a Zambian friend and her Nigerian boyfriend to see if they could help me with some money. A friend of theirs in Belgrade wanted to import semi-precious stones into the country, if I picked up the

74

bag he would give me £1000. It was a chance, so I went to Belgrade and collected the suitcase. I didn't get any money but he bought the ticket. I went to a hotel where I met the Nigerian woman contact. I gave her my bag and the drugs were then concealed in it—I thought they were semi-precious stones, I really didn't think to look for drugs. I stayed in Belgrade for two days then caught the plane back to London. When I arrived at Heathrow, customs officers searched me and asked who packed my bags. They didn't find anything but they called me back as I started to walk away Then they strip-searched me and let me go. Nobody mentioned drugs though I thought that's what they must be looking for, but there was no way I was carrying them. I had nothing to fear. I was nearly home, the bus was just about to leave the airport, when two men ran up the stairs and arrested me.

It was so out of character for me —even now I can't believe it. Its been like walking into the unknown.

Many of the Nigerian couriers interviewed claimed to have been unwittingly involved in smuggling operations, as the following case-study illustrates.

Agnes's story
Agnes is typical of a considerable number of Nigerian female couriers in that she claims to know nothing of the drugs that were found in luggage by customs officers upon arrival in the UK. At the time of her arrest Agnes was running her own hairdressing salon. She employed a number of people and was economically 'fairly comfortable'. When her plans to travel to the UK to buy cosmetics and hair-products for her business were disrupted by financial concerns she was offered help from a cousin who had been helped considerably over the years by Agnes's own family. The offer of financial assistance, as Agnes saw it, was a way of recompensing her family. Her cousin was married to a wealthy businessman and Agnes had no reason to suspect an ulterior motive in the generous offer of help. As she was packing to leave, Agnes's cousin arrived with some small parcels that she wanted delivered to a friend in England. Agnes took the packages freely, happy to help the person who had made the trip possible. She didn't ask what was inside the packages and had no reason to be suspicious. The drugs, she was to discover, were concealed within the body lotion and talcum powder containers that had been packed by her cousin.

•   •   •

The telling of Comfort's and Agnes's stories is important for reasons other than simply exposing unscrupulousness within the international drugs trade. More significantly, it forces us to examine the links between the allegedly duped courier and the cognisant courier in order to determine the true nature of injustice. What we find, when we look at the life experiences and events surrounding the offence, for both categories, is a set of material circumstances which itself may be described as criminogenic and which operates in differential ways upon individuals.

If Agnes is telling the truth must we feel greater sympathy for her because she is innocent or are the life crises of cognisant drug couriers and the political, economic and cultural contexts in which they struggle equally worthy of our understanding? It is important that any analysis of drug couriers does not take as its focal starting point the claims made by so many couriers that they were tricked or duped into carrying drugs. There is no way, short of an international investigation to validate such claims (and that may be no guarantee of determining truth). Many of the trafficker narratives suggest a degree of naiveté; cases of trusting the wrong people, of not asking the right questions or of not wanting to know the whole truth, and cases of being victims of unscrupulous trickery. In some instances the naiveté is plainly genuine, in others it is more studied and less plausible. Given the prejudice, misinformation and hysteria which surround illegal drugs and their trade it is hardly surprising that couriers develop stories and strategies to counter the inevitable moral condemnation and severe penalties which envelop the commission of an offence.

There is little doubt that some couriers are unsuspecting, innocent pawns and that others may be less unsuspecting but driven to 'ignore' the obvious by pressing needs. But my argument is that an emphasis on these cases—cases where the courier unwittingly carried drugs—leads to a distorted and limited understanding of the phenomenon as a whole. It leads to a harsher condemnation of those who were not duped and who knew what they were doing. Our 'sympathy' and concern, especially in policy terms, should extend much wider than the individual victims of unscrupulous drug traders. It must include those who are seen to make the 'choice' of carrying drugs. The purpose of contextualising the courier narratives within the framework of Nigerian political and economic history is to provide the basis for a more informed and more widespread 'sympathy'. There must be a de-centring away from the individual and onto the set of material circumstances which gives rise to the actions of individuals. If we are serious about understanding and alleviating the problems associated with drug trafficking individuals are important, but only in relation to the insights they offer about the impact of external material forces. This is the pivotal value of the couriers' testimonies. Their accounts illuminate their own relative insignificance in the trade and the

76

centrality of understanding the role of international political economies in sustaining the drugs trade. Without this de-centring from the individual subject to the global subject, any attempt at drug control will remain sterile and without impact.

ENDNOTES

1   Leaving aside for the moment the issues of racism and discrimination within the British criminal justice process which cannot alone account for the current situation.
2   Middlesex Probation Service, Foreign Nationals Unit, 1996
3   Philip van Niekerk, *The Observer*, 28 January 1996
4   Nick Hammond, personal communication, October 1997
5   Mike Davis, *City of Quartz: Excavating the Future in Los Angeles*, Verso, 1990:310
6   Nigeria, *Background Brief*, Foreign and Commonwealth Office, August 1995
7   See, in particular, the influence of Durkheim—industrialisation and urbanisation release people from the traditional forms of social constraint but nothing replaces them; see also modernisation theorists: Clinard and Abbott, *Crime in Developing Countries*, John Wiley: New York, 1973; Shelley, L, *Crime and Modernisation*, Carbondale and Edwardsville: Southern Illinois University Press, 1981
8   Sumner, C, *Crime, Justice and Underdevelopment*, Macmillan: London, 1982; van Onselen, C, *Chibaro*, Pluto: London, 1976; Huggins, M, *From Slavery to Vagrancy in Brazil*, Rutgers University Press: New Brunswick, 1985
9   Federal Government of Nigeria, *The Blue Book*, cited in Y Bala Usman, *Nigeria Against the IMF: The Home Market Strategy*, Kaduna, Nigeria: Vanguard Publishers, 1986:15
10 F R A Marhino, 'Nigeria: A Regenerative Economy or a Vegetative Existence?', Lagos Nigeria: NNPC, n.d., 3, undated
11 L Diamond, 'Nigeria in Search of Democracy', *Foreign Affairs*, 62, Spring 1984, 907-8
12 EIU, 'Nigeria After the Generals?'
13 Ademola Oguntayo, Kunle Ajibade and Margaret Ereme, 'The Hard Times', *African Concord*, 3 September 1990, p. 46
14 'Nigeria from Riches to Rags', *Newswatch*, Lagos, Nigeria, 5 October 1985
15 Unpublished, Home Office, S2 Division; Middlesex Probation Service, Foreign Nationals Unit, March 1996
16 'Nigeria: Military Government Clampdown on Opposition', *Newswatch*, Lagos, Nigeria, 11 November 1994:1
17 Ihonvbere, ibid, 1994:133
18 'The Nigerian Society and the Third Republic', *The Guardian*, 14 March 1992
19 *West Africa*, 29 July-4 August 1996:1184
20 *Time*, 18 April 1994
21 Economist Intelligence Unit, *Country Report, Nigeria*, 2nd quarter 1994
22 'International Cooperation in Crime-Prevention and Criminal Justice for the Twenty-First Century: The Nigerian Perspective', The Nigerian National Paper, Eighth United Nations Congress on the Prevention of Crime and the Treatment of Offenders, Havana, Cuba, 1990
23 *West Africa*, 13-19 March 1995
24 Cited in *The African Guardian*, 23 July 1990
25 *West Africa*, 29 July-4 August 1996:1184
26 *West Africa*, 17-23 June 1996
27 Personal communication, 1993
28 See particularly the work of Australian criminologist John Braithwaite.

CHAPTER FIVE

Unsuitable Enemies

Nils Christie writes of 'suitable enemies'(1993), Diana Gordon of 'the dangerous classes' (1994) and Noam Chomsky of an alien 'menace' (1991). Each description relates to that population which has been targeted by the state for drug control. In the chapters to follow we shall see how UK drug enforcement agencies have targeted minor drug offenders, i.e. drug users and street dealers, in their drug control practice. When it comes to the more serious offence categories, that is those relating to drug trafficking a very similar picture emerges. If, as I would argue, the purpose of drug control is at some level to deflect attention from internal domestic problems and to create public demons, then the selected enemy should occupy a space outside *our* ordinary, every day experience. Chomsky suggests that in order not to disrupt political and economic balances the targeted public enemy should be both weak and vulnerable and preferably of colour, 'In short the menace should be situated in the Third World, whether abroad or in the inner city at home'. (1991:114) In the reality of drug-related criminal justice processing and punishment it is the courier, and most frequently the foreign courier, who is the primary subject.

One of the linguistic legacies of the 1980s was the transformation of 'drug trafficker' into an ideological cue, a shorthand reference encompassing the menace, evil, greed, depravity and corruption (moral, financial and political) required to ease the passage of repressive new anti-drug legislation and policies[1]. Few have argued for more lenient criminal justice strategies for drug offenders when faced with the moral opprobrium invoked by the *drug trafficker*. Use of the term has in recent decades triggered a sense of rage and raised unanimous demands for harsh and retributive punishment. Yet the vast majority of drug traffickers themselves, that is those who actually carry the drugs, are rarely evil, greedy, depraved or corrupting. They are, very often, ordinary people who find themselves in difficult times. This reality surfaces at every stage of the criminal justice process, from the policing of low level inner-city street dealers to the lengthy sentencing of drug 'mules'. Yet powerful forces ensure that this reality remains distorted and obscured.

This study focuses very particularly on drug couriers arrested at international points of entry. In many respects this focus was a research response to a growing recognition within criminal justice of a disturbing and unjust situation which had emerged in relation to foreign national

78

drug offenders in British prisons through the 1980s. In a wider sense it was prompted by the hypocrisy, bigotry and narrow mindedness which shrouds political and legal debate on illegal drugs and drug trafficking. Fortson makes the point that there also exists a group of drug runners largely ignored by research into drug couriers—namely couriers who transport drugs within the domestic market. He writes 'It is difficult to see why they should be excluded from the debate when in fact the role played by them will often be just as subordinate as in the case of their importing counterparts . . .' (Fortson 1996:91). A small proportion of the British couriers interviewed in the present study reported having acted as domestic couriers prior to their conviction as drug importers.[2] It is hoped that the emphasis on importers, the largest category of imprisoned drug traffickers, will illuminate many of the wider concerns and particularities associated with the consequences of drug prohibition.

This chapter is based on 70 case studies, supported by general biographical data gathered on a wider sample of 900 imprisoned drug importers and a range of secondary empirical sources.[3] The case studies are representative of those drug importers who were in British prisons in the early 1990s—primarily British, Nigerian, Colombian, West Indian Pakistani and Ghanaian men and women with a smattering of Americans and Europeans. This is a study of lives behind the stereotype.

WHO ARE THE TRAFFICKERS?

The research data on people convicted of drug importation and imprisoned in Britain continues to reinforce a set of characteristics which sharply challenge official stereotypes of drug traffickers and raise serious doubts as to the purpose of drug control.

Most, apart from British couriers, appeared to have had no experience with drugs until the offence and were essentially ignorant of the value and nature of the substances they had smuggled. They had little information of value to customs officers and could normally report only minor details about those who directly gave them the drugs. In the vast majority of cases couriers had no knowledge of the 'meeter' or 'greeter' to whom they were to hand over the drugs once they arrive in Britain. Providing useful information to Customs and Excise officers is one of the very few means by which mitigation is afforded by the courts. Faced with the very long sentences handed down to drug importers the courier has in many cases a powerful incentive in passing on intelligence. Interviews revealed that many couriers did indeed pass on what little they knew (except in those cases where death threats to family members had been made) but it was clear from discussions with customs officials that this information was of scant value in terms of understanding larger drug networks and only rarely did it manifest itself in attempts to mitigate sentence. Against the political and legislative landscape of punishment and vilification, outlined in earlier chapters, the reality of the drug courier poses uncomfortable questions for policy makers and practitioners.

Some demographics

Almost three quarters (72 per cent) of the sample of 900, imprisoned for the illegal importation of drugs, were foreign nationals and the majority of them were from the developing world. Africans accounted for 35 per cent of this population, with the largest national category being Nigerian (30 per cent of the total). British couriers represented 28 per cent of the population with Jamaican/West Indian couriers constituting 9 per cent, Colombian couriers 5.3 per cent, Pakistani couriers 5.1 per cent and Dutch couriers 3.3 per cent. These figures are broadly representative of the later findings of Abernethy and Hammond (1992) whose research on Crown Court cases revealed that of all importers arrested at Heathrow Airport, and committed to Isleworth Crown Court over an eight month period in 1991/92: 26 per cent were British; 12 per cent were Colombian; 24 per cent were Nigerian; and 4 per cent Pakistani (1992:36). The non-representation of Jamaicans in this sample reflects the fact that flights from the Caribbean did not land at Heathrow Airport but at Gatwick and hence fell under a different Crown Court jurisdiction.

The predominance of foreign national drug couriers in British prisons is now well documented (Tarzi and Hedges 1990; Green 1991; Abernethy and Hammond 1992; Cheney 1993; Maden et al 1992). The rest of Europe presents a similar picture (see Albrecht 1996; Tomasevski 1994). Combined with the more limited international evidence available on the nature of those imprisoned for drug trafficking offences in countries like the United States, South America and Australia (see Huling 1995; del Olmo 1995; Mukherjee 1981; Easteal 1992) the evidence appears to reinforce Chomsky's argument of the necessity for states to manufacture alien and vulnerable enemies. Evidence from the United States Drug Enforcement Agency suggests that in the early 1990s up to 200 couriers were arriving at US airports each day, mostly from Nigeria (*The Guardian*, November 1990). Tracy Huling's research on female drug importers arrested in New York reveals that these couriers, like their counterparts in British jails, were low level players, without prior convictions, suffering from varying degrees of poverty and personal despair. Apart from the few professionals interviewed, virtually all couriers reported that they were serving their first prison sentence. This

80

evidence is virtually impossible to corroborate for foreign nationals in the research process but is reinforced by the findings of Abernethy and Hammond (1992) and Richards *et al* (1995a:163).

Drug couriers are, the evidence suggests, rarely drug users. The majority of those interviewed, particularly those from rural Third World backgrounds, and those who originated from non-source countries (e.g. Nigeria) were relatively naive about drugs generally. They were also largely unaware of the implications of their involvement in the Western drug problem. Only one of those interviewed was addicted to a class A drug at the time of arrest and he was both a professional drug smuggler and a British national. Apart from a number of young British couriers who were involved in the 'rave' scene and who took drugs like Ecstasy on a social basis, and some of the professionals, for whom drugs were serious money, recreational drug use was not a feature of the average courier's experience nor was need for drugs ever cited as a reason for involvement in smuggling. This is reinforced by Pat Carlen's study of women involved in drugs crime. While seventeen of the 39 women she interviewed claimed to have at some time been addicted to glue, heroin or alcohol and nine had committed offences in order to supply their addictions the two who had convictions for drug importation were neither addicted to illegal drugs nor were they drug users of any significance. Like the couriers in the present study it was the opportunity of financial betterment which motivated their offences (Carlen 1988:24).

Imprisoned drug couriers were not particularly young—the average age being 35.7 years, with 67 per cent of the sample aged over 30 years. Half the sample were married or cohabiting, 42 per cent single and seven per cent widowed, separated or divorced. Marital status, however, does not seem to be a particularly useful determinant of parental responsibility. Interviews revealed that a majority of single couriers were also responsible for children or other dependents. Richards *et al* (1995) found in a study of drug importers imprisoned in Britain that foreign national men and women were considerably more likely to have dependent children living with them. This lends further support to the 'economic need' analysis in explaining the primary motivating factor behind foreign nationals' involvement in trafficking.

Unemployment figured strongly in many couriers' experience. Almost one third of the large sample were unemployed at the time of arrest and another 14 per cent (51 per cent women and 30 per cent men) were employed in menial jobs (cleaners, factory hands, agricultural labourers etc.). Almost 30 per cent were self-employed as traders or some other form of business enterprise, but if Nigerians are subtracted from the sample this percentage declines markedly. Very few couriers (less thar. 5 per cent) were professionally employed at the time of arrest, although a significant number of Nigerian men, and some Nigerian women had been professionally trained and employed prior to the Nigerian economic crisis of the mid 1980s. Perhaps surprisingly, only a very small percentage of couriers were employed by airlines, airports, or in the merchant navy—occupations which 'lend' themselves to drug trafficking; though, of course, this might very easily be explained by customs operational policies and trafficker profiles as well as the benefits of inside knowledge.

Considering the media and political attention devoted to the cocaine 'menace' in the late 1980s and early 1990s, police warnings of an imminent 'crack' epidemic and customs expressed concern over cocaine seizures it is perhaps surprising to note that only 5.3 per cent of the total were at the time Colombian nationals. Couriers from other South American countries were insignificant, a feature which may be explained by drug routes which use transit countries like Nigeria and the USA to distribute the drugs into smaller consignments before heading for final destinations.

Gender demographics

The evidence from this research (supported by Home Office and Prison Department Statistics[4]) suggests that approximately 80 per cent of all imprisoned couriers are men. Earlier estimates had placed the percentage of women considerably higher. Virtually all media and pressure group interest in couriers has been on women as more sympathetic subjects for public consumption. This focus continues to assist in a distorted perception of the nature of the gender balance for this offence. What *is* significant, however, is that female drug couriers account for approximately 20 per cent of the total UK female prison population, whilst male couriers account for only 4 per cent of the total male prison population. In Britain it was estimated that there were between 320 and 400 women serving sentences and on remand for the importation of drugs in January 1991 of whom 37.1 per cent were African, with 29.4 per cent of all the women from Nigeria (Green 1991:13). Extrapolating from those figures, Andrew Rutherford estimated a prison population of 350 women convicted of drugs importation in 1996 (1997:424).

The over-representation of black women in British prisons is largely (though not entirely) accounted for by a disproportionate number of women not ordinarily resident in the United Kingdom, and convicted of drug importation. A study conducted by Maden *et al*, of 25 per cent of the female prison population (randomly selected young offenders and adults) concluded that when women ordinarily resident overseas are excluded from the statistics the proportion of black British women (i.e. of African-Caribbean origin) falls from 20 per cent to 13 per cent. When this group is excluded from the total of female imprisoned drug offenders the percentage falls from 40 to 13. Black British women are therefore not over-represented among drug offenders in prison (1992:218).

Australian research similarly reveals that around a quarter of all women in Australian jails are migrants or foreign nationals with the number of overseas born women in Australian prisons rising from 81 in 1982 to 147 in 1990 (Easteal 1992). According to Patricia Easteal a disproportionate number of these women are drug importers. In America, Tracy Huling's research at the women's jail on Riker's Island, New York, documents what seems increasingly to be a universal set of characteristics identifying imprisoned drug couriers and particularly women: 'The women I spoke to', she writes,

> were of all colours, nationalities and ages, but there were some things they had in common. All lacked any involvement with the criminal justice system and all were terrified of the realities of life on Riker's Island. There were no career criminals looking forward to "three hots and a cot". Most were despondent and frightened for children left behind, sometimes thousands of miles and an ocean or two away. All had been charged with possession of four ounces or more of a narcotic drug, an A-1 felony in New York that carries a mandatory minimum prison sentence of 15 years to life. (1996:49)

Returning to the UK sample there were certain demographic differences between First and Third World imprisoned female couriers and between male and female couriers. Male drug couriers were on average slightly older than females with women averaging 33 years of age and men 37 years. Almost 50 per cent of the women were under 30 but only 12 of the 276 in the sample were under 21. By contrast 74 per cent of men were older than 30.

Women, as was shown above, were much more likely to have been unemployed before their arrest and more likely to be employed in menial or low status service occupations. Nineteen per cent of women compared with 12 per cent of men worked in menial and low-status service occupations while 24 per cent of both men and women stated their occupation as 'trader' or some other form of business person. Only 2.7 per cent of the women had professional careers or training while 5.3 per cent of the men were employed professionals just prior to arrest. As with male couriers, the interview data suggested strongly that even for those women working outside the home it was financial hardship which led to the offence.

The differences between men and women, however, were graphically over-ridden in most cases, by the fact that the act of carrying drugs promised all who took the risk the possibility of relief from what were described as untenable financial circumstances.

Women and the lure of the drugs trade

Leaving theft aside, drug trafficking has become the most significant indictable offence currently identifying imprisoned women.[5] Given the burgeoning of feminist criminology in the 1980s it is surprising how little research exists on the role of women in the drug trafficking trade and even more surprising the scant attention devoted to this very large proportion of convicted women in prison. According to US criminologist Tracy Huling, there is international evidence to suggest 'that women's participation in transporting narcotics across national borders increased dramatically to become significant during the past decade' (Huling 1995:58). Certainly Rosa del Olmo's review of research in Latin America appears to confirm this trend. Figures from the 1984 *Annual Report* of the National Police of Colombia revealed a reported increase in the participation of women in cocaine trafficking, from 148 in 1983 to 802 in 1984. The major increase was in their role as *mulas* or drug mules (del Olmo 1990:40). Throughout Latin America the same picture seems to have evolved:

> In the women's prison in the city of Cuenca, Ecuador, in July of 1987, there were 40 inmates, of whom 62 per cent were expecting to be tried for crimes established under Ecuador's Law of Control and Prosecution of Narcotics and Psychotropic Substances Traffic. In Guayaquil at that time, 40 per cent of those arriving to be interned at that city's women's prison were there for the same reason. In Rio de Janeiro 28 per cent of the inmates of the women's prison, and in Caracas 51 per cent of the women in the Women's Annex had also faced these special laws . . . . in the city of Los Teques, 43 per cent [of female prisoners were] serving time under the Organic Law of Narcotic and Psychotropic Substances'. (del Olmo 1990:40)

Del Olmo posits a thesis of economic necessity to explain the rise in the incidence of drug trafficking offending among Latin American women, i.e. that in periods of economic crisis women's financial needs (determined by familial needs) will be greater than those of men. With fewer legal employment opportunities available for both men and women in periods of recession and crisis women are driven more directly into illegal work and therefore, in certain countries, into the most prominent of such work, the illicit drugs trade (Del Olmo, 1990:42). Given their already subordinate status in society generally, it follows that these women will assume positions at the lowest levels of the trade, i.e. as drug mules or couriers. It is a thesis which translates

84

well to the West African predominance in British women's prisons in the late 1980s and 1990s and begins to explain the disproportionately high numbers of women from developing countries involved in the offence. It is also supported by Tracy Huling's findings in New York. Those women who admitted their guilt all 'presented evidence of hard times—a small business in danger of folding; a husband who left with the money and without the children—or of "duties" as the sister, daughter, or wife of a drug dealer'(1996:48-49). It is a thesis which is confirmed, again in the American context, by a US Department of Justice study. Conducted in 1993 on 90,000 Federal prisoners, the DOJ study found that the most pronounced difference between high level and low level players in the drugs trade is that low level players are disproportionately female and of foreign nationality (US Department of Justice 1994).

North-South ethnographies
The backgrounds and experiences of couriers are relatively diverse but their role in drug trafficking is generally characterised by a lack of any history of involvement with the drug trade or with the institutions of criminal justice. More specifically they are united by a uniform lack of organizational involvement in the trafficking of drugs and by a carefully controlled ignorance of what was happening and who was in charge. It is useful to divide the drug importer's experience into certain categories which may illuminate possible differences as well as highlighting any commonalities between them. Was there a uniformity of experience for couriers and professionals, for those from the Third World and those from the First World, for male and for females, for young and old? Was the offence, even at the operational level, mediated by demographics, culture, class and gender?

THE RECRUITMENT OF COURIERS

There is a familiar ring to the accounts that couriers offered about the way in which they were recruited to smuggle drugs, whether that recruitment took place wittingly or unwittingly. North and South stories of indebtedness abound—money lenders and loan sharks who had other means of encouraging debt repayment, wealthy relatives with parcels to be delivered, family acquaintances offering financial assistance, new boyfriends with presents of exciting holidays and old girlfriends with contacts and support. The analysis portrayed so consistently in the popular media of young women lured into the trade by the men in their lives is true only in part. Only rarely was real coercion employed, and those who acted under duress were very often in debt to those applying the duress. For many couriers who admitted to the offence the opportunity to run drugs was precisely that—a perceived *opportunity*—a chance to break out of a cycle of poverty, or a moment of economic crisis. An interview with one professional who recruited young Antipodean travellers revealed another scenario—of reasonably sophisticated young people who welcomed the opportunity of 'easy' money to finance the rest of their travels. There were none of these young people in my sample possibly because they did not conform to the typical courier profile and therefore were less likely to be targeted and detected.

Some of the couriers in this study were probably duped, some coerced, but most were driven by the hope that the drug run would put an end to the cycle of economic despair they were experiencing. There were other couriers, particularly those who protested their innocence and offered contradictory accounts of their 'framing', who were difficult to categorise in any way and about whom little can be said beyond a sometimes entertaining narrative.[6] There were very few of these cases in my sample.

Poverty as motive: the Third World experience

Curiously, accused and fugitives are always linked with the Third World. Rare indeed are prosecutions against drug traffickers or financial institutions of the industrialised world, which is precisely where most of the proceeds of drug trafficking are kept. (Campodonico 1996:231)

In the context of the massive profits amassed by the powerful in the illegal drugs trade, the potential earnings of couriers are derisory. Promises of sums between £300 and £1000 were most frequently cited although several British and American couriers anticipated considerably more. By far the most common experience was for couriers to be provided with an air ticket and basic expenses for the days they would be abroad, with only a promise of full payment upon successful completion of the delivery. Acceptance of such meagre terms, despite the risks involved, illustrates the level of desperation experienced by the majority of those carrying drugs across borders. In keeping with this finding the overwhelming majority of couriers interviewed (85 per cent) cited economic distress as the sole reason for their involvement in drug trafficking. This finding was also reinforced by the findings of Abernethy and Hammond. (1992:39) While for most of this group it was a general experience of economic hardship from which no escape was legitimately possible, a considerable number of couriers were driven by immediate, specific needs. One young Jamaican woman took the risk of a drugs run in order to finance plastic surgery for her burns-injured brother. She had been living with her mother (who through illness was unable to work) and aunt in the United States and had been unemployed for the four years prior to her arrest. Following her arrest she was convicted and sentenced to seven years imprisonment for the importation of one kilo of cocaine.

> I needed the money. My brother was attacked by a girl in the West Indies — she threw acid in his face causing terrible injury. The legal and medical fees ran into thousands and thousands of dollars and he had no way of raising the money. I knew some dealers so I decided to bring drugs over to England . . . I was aware of what I was doing and why I was doing it, so I don't really regret it but I probably would have thought twice if I'd realised the implications.

The debt collector

Many cited the build-up of debts which required immediate re-payment. A Puerto-Rican mother of two chronically ill children cited her family's recent eviction and a miserable existence in New York's ghetto shelters, while a Colombian man was desperate to feed and educate his children who were presently, he said, surviving on only one meal a day.

Loan sharks and money lenders featured very prominently in couriers' experiences. From Colombia to Nigeria and also to a significant extent in Britain, drug dealers, relying on couriers to transport their contraband, find money-lending a highly successful means of recruiting/coercing those in their debt into drug smuggling. Ignatius is a 45 year old Nigerian serving five years for the importation of 190 grams of cocaine:

> I had been out of work for five years. The Nigerian economy is very bad. I had to sell everything. Then my wife left me and I had seven children to care for on my own. I borrowed some money from a man for my children's school fees and when I could not pay it back he said I had to carry drugs for him. He threatened my children and said he would kidnap them if I didn't do it.

Elisa is a Colombian single parent caring for two teenage daughters. In the late 1980s her father died and she inherited his considerable debts:

> I couldn't pay them all and the house was going to be taken from us. A friend told me about a money lender and I borrowed money which I would repay in three months. But I couldn't sell the house and when the time was up the money lender threatened to kill both my daughters and my mother and to blow up the house. They said that the debt would be repaid if I took a suitcase filled with dollars to London, they said they wanted to avoid paying tax on it. I refused but every day he was on the phone. Then he

87

turned up with four armed men. They beat my mother and one of my daughters. I said I was going to call the police. "Do that", he said. "I will take you there myself and when you get back your family will be dead".

She finally broke down and agreed to carry the contraband which she discovered at Heathrow airport was not dollars but two kilos of cocaine.

Crisis, poverty, culture and drugs

More common and more powerful than the explicit threats of drug organizers, in their guise as money lenders or otherwise, was, however, the overriding/generalised pressure of poverty or relative poverty faced by those driven to smuggle drugs as couriers.

It is estimated that around 300,000 (approximately one per cent) of Colombians are employed at some level in the cocaine industry. Cocaine earns more foreign exchange for Colombia than any other commodity. According to a report to the US Congress in 1990[7], employment opportunities in the cocaine trade have provided means of economic mobility which simply do not exist in the legitimate employment sector. Comparative earnings are much higher and given that the Colombian government 'integrates' coca dollars into the economy reasonably directly there is a sense of the normal about involvement in this illicit industry.[8] The ten Colombian *mulas* interviewed were the victims of grinding poverty and, driven by economic desperation, took the most obvious and potentially most lucrative means available to the poor in Colombia. Maria, serving a ten year sentence for the importation of 2 kilograms of cocaine was given nothing but an air ticket and the promise of 500 pesos upon her successful completion of the drug run. At 26 she was a widow and the mother of three children, the eldest of whom was born when Maria, herself, was only 13 years old. When her husband died in a car accident, she was 21 and unable to support her children alone. She moved in with her mother but there was so little money that she was forced to give up her secondary school education and look for work: 'I felt "mad" when my husband died . . . too much responsibility for me, school, rent, food, everything . . . I'm in prison for money'. Maria like so many other couriers was in prison because of her poverty. A surprisingly high proportion of Third World couriers cited the death or desertion of a bread-winning spouse as a precipitating factor behind their involvement in drug trafficking.

Paco left school when he was nine years old and worked intermittently mostly in the transport industry: 'Sometimes there would be work, sometimes not'. The wages he received were irregular and inadequate and they would frequently be spent on the same day he received them. Separated from his wife and three children a portion of anything he earned he sent to them, the rest barely covered survival.

Antonio is a 36-year-old Colombian, sentenced to six years imprisonment for the importation of 700 grams of cocaine. He had left school at 15 and was unemployed at the time of his arrest, although he was trying to sell jewellery he had made himself. Married with four children, he and his family (none of whom were working) were living in poverty with his mother in a village.

> I had many debts to pay off in my village so I visited family in Bogota and they gave me some gold statues which I was to sell in Venezuela to start me off. I was going to live in Venezuela for a few months to earn enough money to pay off my debts. But in a coffee house in Bogota I started talking to a man about my debt problems and he told me the solution to my problems was carrying drugs to England, that it was easy and the police would give me no trouble. He said that he would pay off all my debts when I got back. I was given $1,000, then I went to an apartment and was told to swallow 55 packets of cocaine. I wasn't worried, I just thought about the money sorting out my debts.

Other political and cultural considerations must also be accounted for in individual explanations of the drug trafficking phenomena. According to a Bolivian journalist, himself serving a sentence of eight years for cocaine smuggling,

> My country is involved from the presidential palace to the last peasant . . . economically we don't produce anything else but cocaine. It is a known situation even if the government claims to be fighting drugs, that if they cut out cocaine production the economy would collapse. There is no perception of the 'illegality' of drugs in Bolivia, they are recognised as crucial to the country's economic structure. Ordinary Bolivian's view it simply as their work to plant it, collect it etc. Its really their way of life. (Luis, 35)

Luis is also a reminder that not all Latin American couriers are hapless peasants. While describing his financial circumstances as 'catastrophic, chaotic and apocalyptic . . . also a description of the Latin American economy' he was not a victim of the grinding poverty faced by so many in his country. Instead he came from a middle class background and had studied at universities in Brazil and Germany. Prior to his conviction he had been working in Argentina and Greece as an interpreter for a tourist agency and as a free-lance journalist. His opportunities and earning power were considerably better in Greece but his visa situation was insecure. After six months in the country he was arrested as an illegal immigrant and required to leave. During his time in Greece, however, he met a Colombian who asked him to travel to Argentina to collect a consignment of cocaine and bring it to Greece.

Luis was provided with a false Spanish passport and paid $5,000 in advance (a further $10,000 to be paid on return). He flew to Cordoba in Argentina where he was met by a man who furnished him with a double fronted suitcase filled with 3.2 kilograms of cocaine.

> My return flight to Athens was routed via Zurich but a state of emergency was declared in Argentina so I was forced onto an earlier flight which was routed via London — I had no intention of going to the UK.

As we saw in the previous chapter the testimonies provided by the many Nigerians interviewed reveal the scale of impact that economic crisis combined with corrupt political leadership can have on the nature of the illicit drugs industry. It also illustrates the individual opportunities that can arise from that industry for those struggling on the economic margins.

Luke is a 29-year-old Nigerian Ibo with two children serving a four and a half year sentence for smuggling 200 grams of heroin (street value £17,000) packed in false bottomed shoes. He was to be paid £2,000 pounds for his role in the importation.

> Thousands of skilled people in Nigeria are unemployed. I graduated in 1984 with a degree in marketing, did my compulsory National Youth Service and have been unemployed since 1985. I met my partner in college, she got pregnant and dropped out. Then my father became very ill with a stroke in 1986 and I couldn't even afford to buy any of the drugs prescribed for him. My sister helped but I'm the only son and the bitterness creeps in when you can't take on the responsibilities you should. So I walked the street for three years without a job. You are up against the wall. We don't come from a country where you walk into a bank with a good proposal to set up a business unless you come from the ruling elite. I knew the risks involved, I knew the whole world was against it but you get to the stage where you don't care any more. I was looking for money and was introduced by friends to this man who offered a conditional loan; conditional on running drugs. He didn't threaten or force me — he didn't have to, I was against the wall. When you are in such a situation . . . my orientation has never been criminal, I still don't have criminal tendencies.

Weighing up the hazards

For couriers from the Third World the experience of the drug run held little excitement or pleasure. Rather it was fraught with unknown dangers, fear, bewilderment and sometimes overwhelming anxiety.

In the early 1990s there were at least five documented deaths of drug couriers in the UK. The deaths resulted from the dangerous form of internal concealment employed by drug dealers particularly in Nigeria. The risks to the health of the courier are enormous and it was clear from interviews that the danger inherent in swallowing packages of class A drugs was a largely unknown one for the courier. In September 1992 *The Guardian* reported the case of a Nigerian woman who died following a massive overdose of cocaine when two of the 84 packages which she had swallowed burst in her stomach.

> Clara Ayemwenre, aged 47, collapsed on Sunday on her way through Terminal Three, before reaching immigration. She was rushed to Ashford Hospital, in Surrey, where surgeons operated to remove the packages, but found that two were empty and had passed into her system . . . A Customs spokesman said the packages were amateurish in their construction and contained in total about half a kilo of the drug . . . The packages were mainly sticky tape around the drugs which, if proved to be cocaine, is worth £40,000 on London streets . . . every day there's somebody coming through. Eighty-four packages is a lot, but 184 have been found. (*The Guardian* 23 July 1992)

On average those couriers who carried drugs concealed in this way swallowed between 70 and 100 packages or condoms filled with either heroin or cocaine. It may take up to two days for all the drugs to be ingested, vomiting can occur and couriers are forced to take pills which induce constipation in order that the consignment remains where it is for the duration of the journey. In interviews couriers rarely commented on this life-threatening practice except to describe the slow and awkward process of ingestion. Very few indicated that they appreciated the dangers of swallowing potentially lethal heroin or cocaine.

'Emmanuel' swallowed 90 packets containing heroin:

> I could have died — at the time I didn't know it was drugs, he told me it was snuff but at the time I believed it was gold because I knew he would want to get into the gold smuggling racket. There was a stage when I was swallowing those packages when I started vomiting and I say "Man I don't think I can take any more". At that stage he said he would kill me and my family if I stopped now.

Many couriers, however, referred to the psychological processes involved in arriving at the decision to become involved in trafficking. For some there was little financial scope for reflection but all had to deal with moral anxieties, fear and trepidation.

North and South very often converge in the fate of a drug courier. American couriers may lead a Third World existence living in a New York project. Often of Hispanic or African descent their financial need is every bit as heavy as their Third World counterparts. Twenty-eight year old Rosa is an intelligent, highly articulate Puerto Rican American. One of 12 children from a very poor family her life had been a tragic one. At age 12 her mother committed suicide, and her natural father had disappeared some years before. Her Colombian husband was at the time of her arrest serving a three year sentence for firearms possession in a New York prison and her two chronically asthmatic children were being cared for by her sister. Without state welfare support and with her husband in jail Rosa had been unable to fight her family's eviction and for the months leading up to the offence she had been sleeping in shelters with the children.

For Rosa and so many like her weighing up the hazards of a drug run against the possible life enhancing returns was not a dilemma of unbalanced proportions. Against an existence blighted by poverty and despair for one's family the risks embodied in drug trafficking are often calculated as worth running.

Society condemns its poor and then condemns them again for trying to escape poverty through the only trade which offers them opportunities of financial mobility.

BRITISH COURIERS

British couriers share many of the characteristics of their overseas counterparts and the purpose of analysing them as a distinct group is simply to assist in identifying those features which may be locally informed from those which are common across international borders and which appear to generally characterise the lives and experiences of the imprisoned drug couriers. The other reason for spending time on exploring them as separate group is that to date there has been no research conducted on them despite the fact that it is estimated that around 30 per cent of imprisoned drug importers are of British nationality.

From the limited number of interviews conducted with British couriers it is possible to distinguish three basic categories into which they fall; self employed entrepreneurs, or professionals (five interviewed), couriers who for reasons of economic distress or external pressure agreed to carry drugs to resolve particular financial problems (seven interviewed) and the very young who see it as part of an exciting life-style and/or a means to another, better way of life (six interviewed). Ten of the 18 British couriers interviewed were themselves recreational drug users. For the young it was the 'dance' drugs LSD and Ecstasy, and cannabis which were popular. For the older and professional traffickers it was 'a line of coke now and then', and cannabis. Heroin was vehemently rejected by all but the one addicted trafficker.

Several (six) of the British women interviewed were between the ages of 17 and 21 at the time of their arrest. In some respects it was their youth and gender that appeared to have created or at least compounded existing problems.

Young girls and bad guys

There is a form of trafficking experience, well publicised (at least in young womens' magazines), which is mediated very specifically by gender and youth and that is the case of the young woman drawn into trafficking by shady men—boyfriends, landlords, distant cousins or loan sharks.

One young woman, only 16 at the time of her arrest, was enticed to America, by a man she met in South London, under the pretext of a potential modelling contract: 'I was 16, I just didn't think. I thought great!' The modelling never materialised and instead she returned to England ten days later, frightened, disillusioned and wearing 500 grams of cocaine strapped to her body. She had experienced violence and threats whilst in New York and was clearly disoriented by fear, her dashed expectations and recognition of her own naiveté:

My friend said that she had carried drugs herself as I was pretty nervous about it. She said that girls would come to her flat, stay the night and go back the next day. She made it seem all so straightforward and she seemed to be doing OK for herself. She had a beautiful place and nice things. I said "OK" and my friend then took over all the arrangements and everything was set within a week—I didn't speak to anyone myself. That week I started to get really scared but I had nowhere else to go and I was afraid that if I bottled out this woman wouldn't let me stay with her any longer.

On the Saturday night I was told I was going the following day and a woman arrived in a taxi from Birmingham with the ticket and £80. She stayed about 15 minutes and told me I'd be met by a man but she didn't know who. The next day I flew to New York and as I was leaving the arrivals hall a man winked at me. He took me to a motel in the Bronx and said he'd be back in the morning. I was terrified as it was a really nasty place full of drug users and other shady characters. The guy came back the next day and told me I could go out but not too far, not that I wanted to. It was very rough. I was miserable and frightened and on the third day I made a reverse charges call to my friend in London and told her I wanted to get out of there. That day they collected me and took me to a house where there were twelve guys, "Yardies", all smoking weed. They all had guns which they took off when they came into the house. I had a nice bedroom but I was so terrified that I bolted it shut every night. They wouldn't let me out as they didn't want me to know where I was. I couldn't use the phone and I was so scared that I didn't even ask them for something to eat. I wished I'd never asked to leave the hotel. On my tenth day in New York they told me I was going home that night. They drove me to buy some clothes. They took out all the metal fastenings and they gave me a girdle to wear with the packet of drugs fixed to the inside of the upper leg. They drove me to Newark airport and I was so relieved to be away from them all I just hated them. (Clare, 18, serving four years for importation of 610 grammes of cocaine)

Kim's experience was quite different. Persuaded by her landlord to run drugs she was presented with a ticket to Granada, given £400 spending money and driven to the airport by a friend of the landlord. In Granada she was met by her landlord who had travelled with his brother two days earlier. She stayed in the Caribbean for a month and had a 'lovely' time, sailing, water-skiing, partying and meeting new people. She was never left alone and liked and trusted the people she was with. 'They were brilliant, or that's what I thought, and we had real fun'. One week before she was due to leave the parcels were delivered to the landlord's apartment but she didn't see what was inside them. She was fitted up with the drugs by trying on different outfits. The landlord and his friend walked around the island with her to ensure that the drugs were appropriately concealed. When it was clear no-one could detect the drugs on her, Kim was even more convinced that everything would run smoothly. The drugs were then hidden until the time for her departure arrived. Wearing light summer clothes and with three parcels of cocaine (926 grams) taped to her body she boarded the plane to London confident that she would not arouse the suspicion of customs officers. Her landlord was to follow one week later.

Tracy too had a months holiday in the Caribbean staying with her former boyfriend's family who were themselves direct producers of cannabis. Tracy was shown the cannabis growing and the processes of picking and drying. Two days before she was due to leave for England she was taken, along with her 'minder', to a local senior police officer for the purpose of 'paying their way out' of the country. This was her second drugs run but this time her relationship with her boyfriend had ended and she had entered into a business arrangement with his family, an arrangement which promised to be considerably more lucrative than that which she had with her boyfriend. She and her co-defendant were arrested by customs officers with five kilograms of cannabis taped to their bodies.

Jen, now serving a nine year sentence was unemployed and studying fashion design part-time when she was arrested. A single parent of two young children, her boyfriend of four months had suddenly offered her a holiday in Antigua.

94

He offered on the Friday and we left on the Monday for a week. A couple of hours before we were due to fly home he told me I had to carry some drug parcels in my case. When I said no I didn't want to he said he'd beat me up and leave me out there. I was really scared and I just felt I had no choice — my kids were back home waiting for me.

The packages containing 7.52 grams of cocaine were discovered during a customs search when she arrived at London's Heathrow airport.

Dance, drugs and debt

Something which does appear to be a feature unique to the British and American samples is the 'lifestyle driven' offence. This was more true of the young courier and, in that sense, is therefore, relatively unusual even among British drug importers as an overall category.

Trish was 22. In some ways she was unrepresentative of the couriers in prison. She was young, single and had no children. But like the majority she was in prison for her first drug importing offence and like the majority it was financial problems which led her there:

I was a qualified chef at Gatwick Airport but working seven days a week from 2 pm until 10 pm or 7 pm until 3 am. I had no social life so I resigned but then I was unemployed for seven months. Catching up on lost time I went "wild" every night — raving. But the bills started piling up, I owed rent, telephone, gas, and electric so I borrowed money from a loan shark and that's how I ended up here.

Trish asked two of her friends to go with her to Spain to help her and together they smuggled 29 kilos of cannabis into Britain. This was her first such experience and though quite 'worldly' and familiar with recreational drugs through the 'rave' scene she knew of no-one who had acted as a drug courier. Like most couriers her role and knowledge relating to that role was limited to the business of receiving, carrying, travelling with and handing over the drugs once in London. Couriers are, in the majority of cases, ignorant of the nature and value of their consignments. One young courier reflected:

I'm so glad it wasn't heroin or cocaine — I could have got seven years. I didn't know what it was, just that it was "gear", it could easily have been heroin or cocaine. I didn't know the consequences, I wasn't even thinking. I just wanted to pay the geezer back his money.

Lizzie was living on social security when she was arrested, having dropped out of college after becoming heavily involved in the rave scene:

95

I hadn't been involved in drugs before — I'd even given a talk on drugs as part of my O-Levels. But when I got involved in the Acid House scene I started taking acid and Ecstasy. I didn't see anything wrong with taking these drugs and they filled you with love — it was much better than drinking alcohol. The scene was anti-establishment and it felt like we were "children of the revolution" sort of thing. I moved in with my boyfriend. He was 32 and a dealer on the "scene". It was exciting — the fast cars and the money. My boyfriend was involved in importing, distributing and selling. I started selling at parties to finance my own drug-taking and then graduated to being an internal courier taking drugs on the train to London and Scotland. It was easy money for just sitting in a train and I always worked for my boyfriend. I guess I did it for five or six months and used the money for drugs and spent it on more and better nights out with my boyfriend.

Lizzie then offered to go to Amsterdam to pick up some Acid for her boyfriend. When he was arrested she went 'on the run' for two weeks but then turned herself in to the police unable to live with the anxiety.

Drugs and the poverty-trap

Kim was 20 when she was arrested and convicted for the importation of almost a kilo of cocaine. Kim's background is more in keeping with the lives of women caught in the poverty-crime trap described so well by Pat Carlen (1988). Originally from Nottingham, she had been working as a prostitute for two and a half years. She had one previous conviction for which she was held on remand for a week and sentenced to 120 hours community service. Not a drug user she was unfamiliar with British drug laws and was persuaded by the lure of easy money when her Jamaican landlord raised it.

He said that customs were only interested in Jamaicans and Americans — mainly black people and would not be concerned with a young white English girl. He said that if the customs looked at my passport and saw that I was in my twenties and was a mother then they'd think I wouldn't risk such a thing. All I'd have to do was to look them straight in the eye.

From the few cases of young female couriers cited here it would seem that some of the attractions of youth lifestyle, combined with the existence and pressure from boyfriends and other more powerful men in their lives (loan sharks, landlords, for example) involvement in the drug scene, economic need, lack of experience, lack of resources and relative powerlessness were instrumental in their recruitment into the drugs trade.

Trish found herself coerced in very much the same way as her Third World counterparts:

> Things were very bad . . . bills started piling up. I owed rent, telephone, gas, electric . . . I got mixed up with a loan shark and that's how I ended up here. I borrowed money from this loan shark, who I knew nothing about. When I couldn't pay it back in time that's when he came down heavy on me. Three of them came round to my house; he beat me up a couple of times and then demanded interest on the £1,000 he had loaned me. He wanted me to go to Spain and bring back drugs — that was his "interest".

Clare was 17, pregnant and desperate when the opportunity to smuggle drugs was presented to her. Too worried to tell her mother, an educational psychologist, of her pregnancy, she dropped out of college, where she was studying for her A-levels, and went to London to find a job to pay for an abortion. She stayed with a friend and looked after her daughter to earn her keep while she looked for a job. The friend, it transpired was involved in smuggling drugs to Europe from the United States.

> At nine weeks I was getting desperate as I was under the impression that I couldn't have an abortion after 12 weeks. My friend said I could earn some fast money by bringing a parcel back from New York and at the same time I could have a bit of a holiday. She said she'd done it herself and that girls came and stayed overnight at the flat and would then go back the next day. I said I'd do it and within a few days it was all arranged. By this time I was getting really afraid, I'd just seen a programme on TV about women in prison for doing just this, but I decided to go through with it because I had nowhere else to go and I was afraid that if I bottled out this woman wouldn't let me live there any more.

The older British courier (apart from the professionals described below) uniformly reported that it was poverty or a combination of deteriorating economic circumstances and the opportunity to raise money offered by friends or acquaintances which prompted their involvement in drug trafficking. The following example is not untypical of the combination of need and opportunity. Mandy, in her mid-forties, had successfully managed a sales office until 1990 when she was diagnosed with cancer. Following major surgery she was unable to return immediately to work and the company she worked for asked her to take redundancy. Her sickness benefits were delayed for several months, the bank began placing pressure on her to repay her overdraft and her illness had left her feeling weak and depressed:

> . . . then out of the blue I ran into a man I knew a little in the High Road. This was really my first trip out since my surgery and we had coffee. This

man had been an acquaintance for many years, he always seemed decent and respectable, wore a suit and tie, seemed to have lots of money. This was on a Saturday. By Monday I was on the boat to Amsterdam.

THE PROFESSIONALS

Those couriers qualifying as self-employed entrepreneurs or professional drug importers were statistically and by their own admission a small minority of imprisoned couriers. They tended to be British and their social, occupational and economic circumstances distinguished them from the majority of those imprisoned for similar offences. Criminalisation makes drug trafficking highly profitable but risky. The professionals were corporate philosophers, accepting prison as an unfortunate but in-built occupational hazard. Three of the five acknowledged previous convictions for drug importation, manufacture or supply and one other for additional offences including fraud and receiving. They employed their own private lawyers as Toby colourfully illustrated—'A private drug smuggling lawyer, not the family one, a lawyer for every occasion—if you lead a double life you need to live in a duplex'. Each had also made contingency arrangements to protect their assets and to provide for their families in the event of their detention—an act which sharply distinguished them from the majority of their imprisoned peers whose bewildered families were left abruptly with neither support nor explanation. Some of the professionals were directly involved in the transportation of the drugs they were smuggling while others employed couriers. Each reported that they had used drugs socially and one was a registered addict. All but one claimed to employ a certain kind of drug smugglers morality which involved keeping ones hands clean of heroin. 'As a father I couldn't bring myself to smuggle heroin' was a uniform refrain.

Rex was 51 and married with three young children. He was an entrepreneur dealing in licit and illicit commodities. In many respects he conformed to the Arthur Daley image of a businessman on the fringes of the law: 'Well, I used to own a night club but now I'm in the motor trade—only Rollers and Porches, know what I mean.' He received a six year sentence for the importation of ten kilos of amphetamines with an estimated street value of £700,000.

For Rex drugs were simply another commodity and his involvement in their importation and distribution in Britain was simply an extension of existing business interests and networks. He was an experienced smuggler and had been involved in the importation of very large quantities of class A and class B drugs though never, he was adamant in pointing out, with heroin. He became involved in drug smuggling in the early 1980s when introduced to the idea by a business colleague in Spain. It proved a highly lucrative "sideline". 'Its easy money and what makes drugs so different from other commodities?' He didn't diversify because of immediate economic need or financial problems. 'I earn a couple of grand a week straight, I don't know why I get involved!'

On couriers generally he commented

> Prison is a breeding ground for people like me. You meet Colombians who can get you all the coke you want, you make contacts in here but the majority in here (prison) are just couriers, there are only a few like me.

Jack was also unrepresentative of those couriers who find themselves in prison. He was until his arrest a 'successful' smuggler with no previous drug related convictions. Reportedly involved on 30 previous drug runs Jack was apprehended on this occasion for an earlier traffic violation while carrying 2.2 kilos of amphetamines taped to his body. Jack was unlucky:

> When I come through customs I wear my uniform and I have a customs pass which exempts me from being customs searched. Unfortunately this time I didn't get arrested on suspicion of drugs, I got arrested for drinking and driving while banned, which was 18 months old as I'd been away at sea that long. I cleared customs then immigration officers came and arrested me on the train for London—it was very unlucky really, and then they searched me.

Jack, unusual even among the British couriers in prison, was a registered addict at the time of his arrest and offered a candid explanation of his involvement. He ran drugs to support his own drug habit, had no moral compunction with smuggling and his side-lining was feasible because his occupation largely protected him from the risk of exposure.

> I did it for the money, at the end of the day its money. I can earn £35,000 working for most companies and if I work for the Emirate states I'm talking double that and its tax free. But it takes me 12 months to earn £35,000 that way and I can earn it in six minutes coming through customs with drugs.

The professionals were driven by exactly the same motivation as any business entrepreneur dealing in legitimate commodities—large profit margins and quick returns. For Jack, bringing drugs across borders was a very lucrative sideline which dove-tailed neatly with his profession:

Wherever you go in the world being a merchant seaman you were always approached—I've smuggled heroin, cocaine, diamonds. The first thing I smuggled was diamonds from Sierra Leone. Once I'd smuggled the diamonds then the South Americans I delivered them in Amsterdam trusted me enough and from then on I used to contract run—taking US dollars out to South America, bringing back cocaine.

Without his legitimate employment drug smuggling would have been, for Jack, a much more hazardous affair. As it was it gave him confidence and allowed him to sustain his addiction with comparatively few risks. His accidental arrest for drug smuggling was 'unfortunate' if not manageable.

Jen lives in a council house and describes her economic situation as 'not all that good, not all that bad'. Unemployed at the time of her arrest, she had been a factory worker and had most recently been involved in a government training scheme teaching sewing and then as a fabric and textiles tutor on a council run scheme for the black community. She was certainly not 'big league' but earned a reasonable supplementary income from the importation of cannabis from the West Indies. Like the other entrepreneurs she approached her sentence with the resignation of one who accepts inconvenient but sometimes unavoidable occupational hazards. 'I don't see any problem with what I carry, its not wrong, it does no harm and its a risk I have to take. Its a job and I don't see any problem with the product'.

Apart from Jen each of the entrepreneurs described their economic situation as healthy. 'I'm a drug smuggler, you expect me to have plenty of money don't you', reported Toby a 36-year-old self-confessed smuggler who used his commercial pilot occupation and considerable resources for the lucrative sideline. Each of the five had cushioned themselves financially from the impact of detection and imprisonment. Only Rex had been subject to a confiscation order (made under the Drug Trafficking Offences Act 1986) in which an order for £160,000 was made and several of his luxury vehicles were confiscated. Most of his assets were, however, safely secured. As Jack who had evaded a confiscation order explained,

I'm quite clued up on confiscation, one of the ways is to put everything in your children's names and the other way is to have a safety deposit box which no one can get access to.

Toby too, despite his seven year sentence for the importation of 1/4 ton of cannabis, 'still managed to keep the money'.

Professionals bought their drugs from dealers in Amsterdam, the Caribbean. Spain or other transit destinations. Sometimes they used couriers or in some cases brought in the contraband personally. Each dealt with only two or three contacts—one at source and one at each major point of delivery. The same contacts were used for each consignment. Jack paid £1000 for two kilogrammes of amphetamines in Amsterdam and estimated that he would have sold them in Britain to his contact for £20,000.

For Rex, an experienced smuggler, involved in the importation of very large quantities of narcotics, drug smuggling was intimately tied to his 'legitimate' import business. He first began importing drugs in the early 1980s when a business contact in Spain approached him. He is currently serving six years for the importation of ten kilogrammes of amphetamines which were smuggled in with a shipment of Spanish tiles. He was not involved in accompanying the consignment from Spain, nor in meeting it but was arrested at his Bristol home on the basis of criminal intelligence which placed him as the organizer.

Jen always carried her own drugs in—she 'felt safer' that way, in control and not subject to the mistakes, or anxieties of others. While it is impossible to generalise it does seem that individual control is a central requirement for the professionals—another feature which distinguishes them from couriers for whom all control is relinquished.

Toby, every inch the public school boy who never quite grew up and never quite said goodbye to the swinging sixties, was a commercial pilot. He flew BA planes to the oil rigs and once flew goods consignments for the police. He also had a long history of involvement in the drug culture. Fifteen years earlier he had served 18 months of a prison sentence for the manufacture of amphetamine sulphate, the possession and supply of cocaine and LSD as well as cannabis. He had, by his own admission, led a relatively successful 'double life' for many years flying commercial aircraft and smuggling cannabis.

The professionals then are themselves a relatively mixed bunch. Career criminals, business sideliners, and those for whom drugs occupy a large part of their lives and for whom trafficking is merely a 'salaried' extension of that existence. The illegal nature of the commodities in which they trade ensures high levels of profitability and with it career motivation. The risks of detection are accepted by this group to be an inevitable if unpleasant component which, for the most part, can be avoided, if adequate care is taken.

Drugs and the ailing bourgeoisie

Several 'entrepreneurial' couriers fell into another category, that of wealthy business people whose involvement in drug smuggling was a 'desperate' measure to preserve a life of privilege and material comfort. Unlike the 'professionals', drug smuggling was not a career for these individuals but offered a potential 'quick fix' to a personal economic crisis.

Imran is an upper middle-class Pakistani businessman with a law degree. Convicted of the importation of 1200 grams of heroin (with a street value in the region of £120,000) he received a five year prison sentence. Married, with two children he was living in the Middle East returning to visit his family in Pakistan once a month. In the mid-1980s his company suffered severe economic losses and creditors began applying pressure for payment.

> Up to today I have never even seen drugs and only in the greatest hardship did I take a bad decision — it was the easiest and the quickest way. The local Dubai bank was pressing me. If I paid the bank around $5,000 they would have let me run another year. So, at the same time I started a building maintenance company and I appointed an engineer who was to get fast money and put it in the bank to keep my other company going; it wasn't set up as a long term business, but it failed in two years. The manager of a company I do business with knew my position and he wanted to help. He said trafficking in drugs was a sure way to make money. There are so many people involved in drugs in Pakistan, its not difficult to organize.

Pasha's experience most closely resembles that of Imran's above. She too was a successful, university educated business woman who smuggled drugs to service debts accrued in the course of operating legitimate businesses, in her case, two London restaurants.

> I've never seen poverty — I simply took a wrong decision under pressure . . . While I was in India in 1987 my house-maid in London phoned and said that the bailiffs had been and had put a lock on the door of my home. I contacted my solicitor in London and discovered that my husband [and business partner] had borrowed money and not repaid it . . . I was desperate. One of my old school friends said she had a friend in the import-export business who could help me. I understood it must be illegal and I knew it was drugs. I was offered £10,000 but needed more so initially I refused to take the heroin, but three hours before the flight I changed my mind. The men who gave me the drugs were extremely sweet and kind, so kind to the children . . . I passed through the red channel to declare jewellery as I always do and I paid the duty. I wasn't at all worried. I felt "its as if I'm doing nothing at all". (Pasha 44, serving 12 years)

It is the experience of wealth and control over their lives, as well as the level of cognisance at their involvement in the offence which distinguishes these business people so sharply from the majority of drug couriers. As they saw it they too were operating from untenable financial crises but it is clear that their acts were more considered and less desperate than many of those interviewed. The drug trade offers possibilities to all social classes but as with all such ventures it is the poor who run the greatest risk of detection and punishment—the elite, the wealthy and the powerful enjoy an array of financial and judicial protections which only rarely, as in the cases of Imran and Pasha, breakdown.

Professionals on couriers

Each of the self-employed distinguished themselves from those they described as 'couriers' or 'mules', that is, from the majority who share their offence category. The entrepreneurs were quick to highlight their professionalism as against the naiveté of the courier. Jack, while often carrying drugs himself also uses couriers regularly: 'British subjects or Australian and New Zealand people . . . they're travelling in Europe, they need money and they see an easy chance to make it'.

Describing fellow inmates arrested for illegal importation, Rex acknowledged that 'The majority in here are couriers but there are a few like me'.

Jen was convinced that the majority of imprisoned female drug importers, unlike herself, had never acted as couriers before and that they were generally ignorant of the punishment consequences as evidenced by the class of drug they carried. 'I would never take the risk of carrying coke, knowing the stupid sentences that they're getting. There's no way I am doing six years, ten years, eleven or 12 for the pittance that they are being paid to bring in drugs, no way'. Again alluding to the naiveté of the majority of couriers, Jack who himself had imported drugs on more than 30 occasions before his arrest, talked of the 'Kamikaze couriers' recruited by entrepreneurs like himself: 'They will have five on one ferry all carrying drugs so that the chances are that even if two get caught three will get through'.

Toby reported that he had never used couriers for other reasons unusual among the entrepreneurs. 'It would never interest me—smuggling without a measure of excitement . . . its a wonderful life if you don't get caught, navigating by moonlight over the wave crests'.

Each of the characteristics which define the self-employed drug smuggler also serve to distinguish them from the couriers—cognisance and control, financial well being, acceptance of the sentence as a serious inconvenience but a price generally worth paying, experience in the trade, the private legal resources which result from money and knowledge and a personal use of drugs.

Their acceptance of prison as 'a price to pay' distinguishes professionals quite markedly from the confusion, fear and bewilderment which the majority of couriers experience upon arrest, sentence and imprisonment.

Probably the greatest indictment of criminal justice and drug control is summed up by entrepreneur, Toby who found the system, despite the inconvenience of being caught up in it, to his favour:

> I did like it that there wasn't a separate charge for someone who goes all out to beat the system (like me) and those who chance everything from somewhere like Nigeria.

Jen proffered a much more sympathetic and less egocentric portrayal of the plight of her fellow inmates:

> The length of sentences are crazy . . . and somebody who is literally just a courier — its not actually their drugs, they're not the ones who were going to be making thousands and thousands of pounds out of it, and yet they are sitting here in prison doing so many years. They have little children at home and they don't know the system.

Ultimately Toby and Jen are drawing the same allusion—the courier, less knowing, less 'criminal', largely resourceless and very vulnerable suffers disproportionately from state drug control. The laws more aptly designed to control the 'criminality' of professional smugglers are perceived as orchestrated to control an altogether different population of offenders.

SOCIAL MARGINALISATION AND DRUG TRAFFICKING

As we have seen, the majority of couriers interviewed were already marginalised by poverty or economic hardship. The offence of drug trafficking was for most, however, to take them to new extremes of social isolation. This was especially true for those who found themselves confronted by the 'moral high ground' righteously occupied by customs officers, lawyers, prison officers and prison doctors. Several couriers referred to derogatory remarks made to them in respect of the nature of their offence. Seventeen year-old Clare suffered considerably from such remarks made by a prison doctor during gynaecological consultations. A Puerto Rican American, overcome with anxiety about her chronically asthmatic children in New York was told by a customs officer 'Why should we care about your kids, you don't think about ours'.

104

One Nigerian man who received a five year sentence reported being told by the barrister, whom he met just two minutes before the trial, 'I don't like defending drug dealers, because my child might die'. Another Nigerian, also serving five years claimed how in his case the barrister reinforced the judge's own prejudices about drugs: 'He was just messing around, he got the judge annoyed saying how serious the offence was and how drugs kill our children'.

Kim serving ten years, felt her life had been destroyed by her involvement in trafficking. Previously close to her family, she believed the estrangement and emotional wreckage she now experienced was due primarily to the fact that her offence had been one of drug trafficking, a fact her family had been unable to reconcile.

According to Pat Carlen, crime committed by already marginalised people further exacerbates their marginalisation. This she argues, is especially true for women who are 'usually made to carry a bigger load of guilt and bear a heavier burden of shame than male criminals' (1988:45). When the offence is such that it evokes a set of carefully manipulated fears and outrages (albeit based on ignorance and political expediency), as is the case with drug trafficking, then that shame and guilt is all the deeper. The interviews made clear that men were equally vulnerable to this sense of shame and social exclusion.

For the many Nigerians convicted of drug importation the experience and consequences of shame were far more damaging. The use of shame as discussed earlier, in *Chapter 4* is an integral component in the Nigerian state's armoury of social control. The Nigerian Drug Law Enforcement Agency (NDLEA) regularly release the names and photographs of Nigerians convicted abroad of drug smuggling. The national press, under headlines entitled *The Ugly Nigerians* and *Register of Shame*, print the names and photographs of Nigerian drug importers serving prison sentences abroad. The underlying rationale is that public exposure of this kind will automatically bring public shame and humiliation to the offenders and significantly to their families and will, as a result, act as a general deterrent to other Nigerians contemplating drug smuggling. In addition, the NDLEA maintains that graphic publication of these details may serve to inform the unwitting families of couriers whose 'shameful' circumstances have been concealed. The interviews certainly revealed an increased reticence on the part of Nigerian couriers to inform their families of their arrest and imprisonment and an almost unanimous unwillingness to communicate with representatives from the Nigerian High Commission for fear of public exposure. A small percentage wrote to waiting dependants saying they had enrolled in four year degree courses in Britain and would only be able to return upon completion.

Unlike most other drug offenders drug couriers rarely appear to be part of a 'drug scene' or subculture—their acts of trafficking are isolated ones, hidden from friends and family. Because they are generally not users themselves they know little of the world that drug users and dealers inhabit and are therefore, at one level, even more alone and marginalised by their involvement in the drug trade. Compounding this sense of isolation is the stigma commonly associated with trafficking—a crime more socially shameful than possession and the majority of other drug offences, it is the subject of general moral opprobrium.

For the professionals, there was no sense of shame or diminished social status, rather a resigned and impatient acceptance that prison was interrupting a lucrative and not at all demeaning career in commodity exchange.

ENDNOTES

[1] See, in particular, the Controlled Drugs (Penalties) Act 1995; Drug Trafficking Offences Act 1986; the consolidating Drug Trafficking Act 1994; Criminal Justice and Public Order Act 1994; Crime (Sentences) Act 1997

[2] The author attempted to gain further admission into a range of prisons in order to interview domestic couriers but was denied access by the Home Office

[3] This chapter is based on the data derived from two prison population samples. The first was derived from returns from 36 prisons documenting demographic details of 900 inmates sentenced for the illegal importation of drugs. The second sample involved in depth interviews with 70 imprisoned drug couriers in English prisons. The gender balance in the interview sample corresponded to the existing ratio of male to female convictions for this offence. The interviews took place between 1991 and 1994

[4] Home Office 1989, *Prison Statistics in England and Wales*, CM1221

[5] *Prison Statistics England and Wales 1995*

[6] For example, Carmen always proclaimed her innocence attributing her arrest to anti-Colombian prejudice and revenge. She is in her mid-thirties and claims to have her own criminal law practice in Bogota. She is serving a ten year sentence for the importation of 500 grams of cocaine which was concealed inside a handbag which she claims was given to her by her former chauffeur as a conciliatory gesture following a disagreement over money he apparantly owed her. As she said, 'He knew me well and was aware of the colours I prefer to wear so he knew I would use the wine coloured bag and he knew I would take it on my trip to Britain'. She believes that the drugs were planted in the bag when he gave it to her some weeks before her trip and claims he did it for revenge, a technique not uncommon, she claimed, in Colombia. She also claims that her ex-chauffeur is now a customs officer in Colombia and that she saw him walking around the airport on the day of her flight — she believes he tipped off British customs officers in London

[7] Peter Andreas, 'Peru's Addiction to Coca Dollars', 1990 Draft and Committee note 2, p. 81

[8] As Susan George reports: 'Colombia integrates drug dollars into the national economy in a straightforward way. Many of them go through the so-called "left window" — the Central bank's *ventanilla siniestra* which happily accepts dollars no questions asked. This *ventanilla* is not exactly a teller's window where you queue, but it is a policy. The government long ago decided that dubious dollars might as well be put to the good of the nation and spur economic activity — legal or not'. (1992:53).

CHAPTER SIX

The Trafficker is Born: A Recent History of British Drug Control

The previous two chapters offered insights into one important group of drug traffickers, the importers. With this knowledge, and within the framework of the international drug trade, and its control, the development of British drugs policy becomes more intelligible. With a clearer vision of who the importers are, as drug-control 'subjects', we are better able to analyse the ideological, political and punitive developments which have charted the rise of the 'demon' drug trafficker in British policy.

The criminalisation of drug trafficking is a relatively recent phenomenon, yet the offence now carries with it the most punitive of all maximum sentences—life imprisonment. How did the trading in drugs move from a situation of relative freedom in which use and supply were relatively unrestricted, to a situation of widescale prohibition, breach of which leads to draconian sanctions? The history of British drug policy is well documented (see, especially, the excellent accounts by Berridge and Edwards 1981; Berridge 1984; Bean 1974) but it is documented largely from the perspective of drug use and the ability of the medical and pharmaceutical professions to supply. What follows is an attempt to understand the evolution of the trafficker in British drugs control discourse because in every sense the 'trafficker' now embodies the punitive consensus and has become the ideological cue for the defence of the war on drugs.

The use of what are now proscribed drugs was relatively commonplace in Victorian Britain. Opiates and their derivatives as well as cannabis were widely used as medical treatments, for pleasure, and for their power to anaesthetise the poverty and misery that many nineteenth century workers experienced. According to the assessment of Berridge and Edwards (1987) opiates were used in far greater quantities and across a wider section of the population in the nineteenth century compared with late twentieth century Britain. In fact the 1894 Royal Commission on Opium recommended that the Indo-Chinese trade in opium should continue as neither controlled nor regular use of the drug was harmful. It was of course in Britain's economic interest to maintain this position. We are used now, in the mid-1990s, to conceiving of wars *against* drugs. A war *for* drugs is completely outside the parameters of the drugs discourse in the late twentieth century. But in 1839 and again in 1856 Britain had waged war against China in order to force it to lift its prohibition against opium. Britain recognised the enormous market potential which China presented if opium could be freely exported there. The colloquially named 'Opium Wars' were fought and won in order to force a reluctant China to legalise importation, thereby opening up a potentially vast market for Britain's East India Company. British colonialism in India was in fact to be considerably sustained by its trade in opium with China which 'provided roughly one seventh of the total revenue for British India' (Adams 1972: 366). According to Adams

> Opium not only became a bulwark of the tax base of colonial India, during much of the nineteenth century it served as the economic pivot around which the whole China trade revolved. (1972:367)

Trafficking in opiates was then, in relatively recent history, an activity to be promoted for economic and political ends. Unsurprisingly this drive to foster new markets and to internationalise the Asian drug trade initiated by Britain took place very largely outside its own domestic and cultural domain. There was general disapproval of non-medicinal opium use in Britain and the trade was seen very much in terms of foreign competition and foreign consumption—only to be promoted abroad. Warren Hastings as governor of Bengal declared in 1772 that opium was a 'pernicious article of luxury, which ought not to be permitted but for purposes of foreign commerce only', while one of his successors, commenting on the strategy to push Bengali opium production to the limits of the market, declared 'The sole and exclusive object of it is to secure to ourselves the whole supply by preventing Foreigners from participating in a trade of which at present they enjoy no inconsiderable share'. (cited in Adams 1972: 366, 367)

   Illegal drug controls in Britain did not emerge in any structured sense until the First World War when regulation 40B (made pursuant to the Defence of the Realm Act) was invoked to control the recreational use of cocaine by British troops and prostitutes. Regulation 40B made it an offence for anyone except medical professionals to possess cocaine. Such was the concern over cocaine use diminishing the efficiency of British soldiers that in February 1916 a former soldier and a London prostitute were convicted and sentenced to six months imprisonment for selling cocaine to Canadian troops stationed at Folkestone (Berridge 1984:20). This case and a media scare campaign over drug use increased demands for control and strengthened the Home Office's stake in the power battle it was currently waging with the Department of Health for ultimate drugs policy responsibility. Home Office under secretary, Sir Malcolm Delevingne forcefully laid claim to drug control by arguing:

The matter is very largely a police matter . . . the enforcement of the regulations has in the main to be undertaken by the police, and there would be considerable objections to its being transferred to another Department which is not on close relations with the police . . . (cited in Berridge 1984:23).

With the Dangerous Drugs Act 1920 we see the Home Office attempting to emulate the American penal approach to drug control by proposing penalties for both addicts and prescribing doctors. It was Britain's response to the first international attempt to control the opium trade, the International Opium Convention, which was agreed in 1912 in the Hague. The Act made it an offence to import, distribute or possess morphine, heroin and cocaine with maximum penalties of a £200 fine or six months imprisonment for a first offence. The courts embraced their new powers by sentencing almost all addicts brought before them to prison. At the same time there were Parliamentary calls for the harsh treatment of traffickers, with some of the more rabid MPs calling for flogging. Colonel Burn MP declared that 'These aliens are frightened by nothing else' (Berridge 1984:24).

Three years later, again partially in response to directions taken in United States' policy (specifically the Harrison Act), the Dangerous Drugs (Amendment) Act 1923 was passed. Police were given increased powers of search and the courts could now impose higher fines and longer sentences. This move towards a penal strategy was tempered only slightly by the victory of the medical profession in defeating Home Office attempts to restrict possession of scheduled drugs to only those doctors in 'actual practice'. In a sense, this Act marks another stage in the conflict which was to smoulder in drugs policy throughout the twentieth century in the UK—that between the medical profession which focused on the user and conceived of the issue (or more specifically part of the issue) in medical terms, and between the Home Office which constructed drug use and its attendant activities in criminal and penal terms. It is important, however, to note that the frequently posited dichotomy between the medical and penal models is much overdrawn, and by 1922 the control model was very firmly implanted for many drug offences (Berridge 1984; Smart 1984; Rutherford and Green 1988). Maintenance prescribing (i.e., the licit prescribing of heroin by doctors to registered addicts in maintenance doses)—the centrepiece of the 'British Treatment System'—only applied to heroin and other opiates. The use of other illicit drugs was always dealt with punitively (Berridge 1984:384). In addition the medicalisation of drug addiction (heroin addiction) provided the foundation for the later punitive conception of all illicit drug use. As Smart has argued, 'the identification of a physical "disease" was an essential element in the

109

transformation of an individual evil into a "scientifically" identified threat to the social fabric'. (1984:35)

In later years when considerable numbers of working class youths, influenced by the ideas of the counter-culture and the 1960s critique of capitalist society (and the work ethic it embodied for the working class) began to use and experiment with drugs it was the criminal justice system which was harnessed to shore up the 'social fabric' not the medical fraternity. Much of the faith and admiration in the 'British system' was therefore slightly misplaced but understandable in terms of its limited applications and also in terms of the nightmarish contrast that US drug control was beginning to present. Drug addiction could be treated as a medical concern between addict and doctor for as long as the population of addicts remained small (in the mid-1920s the number of registered addicts was approximately 600), middle class and predominantly female.

Class is central to understanding the dynamics of drug control strategies both against users and against traffickers. It is a truism that in the late twentieth century the cocaine users and their providers among Britain's rich and powerful are not policed or punished in the way that estate dwellers in Hackney, Brixton or Toxteth are policed and punished over illicit drugs. Class was equally an issue when drugs were first considered a concern of the policy makers. The repressive approach to drug control pursued between 1916-24 was abandoned primarily because drug use was minimal in this era and very importantly it was rare within the working class. In the 1920s the state could afford for the medical profession to be hegemonic in the conceptualisation of drug control; by the late 1960s it could not.

The dominance of the medical profession was reinforced by the findings of the Interdepartmental Committee on Morphine and Heroin Addiction (the Rolleston Committee). The committee concluded that addiction was an illness and only in exceptional cases a 'mere form of vicious indulgence' thereby confirming the need for treatment which attempted to withdraw an addict from the source of his or her addiction by a gradual reduction in heroin by prescription. However, there is evidence to suggest that a parallel and punitive approach continued to exist experienced only by the poor. While the evidence submitted and accepted by the committee made clear the overwhelming value, safety and medical benefit of gradual withdrawal, 'abrupt or rapid' withdrawal was strongly advocated by prison medical officers who claimed the approach produced 'no deleterious effects' (1926:15 para 39). The sympathy extended to middle-class addicts by their medical practitioners was not similarly extended to working class prisoners by those in their medical charge. There is only one mention in the Rolleston

110

Report of drug suppliers other than medical practitioners and as is clear from the following quote the individual addict and the medical practitioner were the only protagonists of concern in the mid 1920s. Rolleston reports:

> Although sources of illegitimate supply exist, it appears that those who might, in other circumstances, have obtained the drugs from non-medical sources are usually lacking in the determination and ingenuity necessary for overcoming the obstacles which the law now places in their way (1926: para 24)

The issue of drug abuse at the time was not only a relatively isolated and insignificant one but also a diminishing one. As reported by Rolleston there was a general belief that the Dangerous Drugs Acts 1920, 1923 and 1925 had resulted in addicts placing themselves in the care of the medical profession for potentially curative treatment and fewer new addicts being created because it was no longer possible for people to obtain morphine from pharmacies in order to treat their own ailments. (1926: para 24)

As the only 'traffickers' of significance were medical practitioners and with the Rolleston Committee composed entirely of medical practitioners, it is unsurprising that the committee's recommendations sought to reduce court and penal intervention, instead replacing them with medical tribunals to consider the consequences of medical practitioner breach of the law. Previously a doctor could lose the right to possess or supply drugs (at the intervention of the home secretary) only after a conviction in the then police court. The Rolleston Committee therefore recommended the establishment of a Medical Tribunal, to review breaches of the dangerous drugs laws :

> ... without recourse to those penalties of fine and imprisonment which the magistrates have the power to inflict ... consideration must be given to the public odium of a criminal trial and conviction which is specially felt when the prosecution takes place in the district in which the doctor practices. (para 67)

The Rolleston Committee's main recommendation, that a prescription of a proscribed drug shall only be given by a duly qualified medical practitioner for the purpose of medical treatment (and this could mean the administration of diminishing quantities of heroin or morphine to an addict in the process of gradual withdrawal) reinforced the established role of the medical profession in British drugs policy for the next 40 years (Rutherford and Green 1988: 385). In addition the underlying philosophy of the report—that addiction was a disease

111

requiring treatment and not an inherent wickedness demanding punishment—also held sway in policy circles until the late 1960s.

By 1959 an increase in the number of notified addicts and changing patterns in narcotic consumption, alerted the government to a potential problem and the interdepartmental Brain Committee was convened to re-examine drug misuse. Numbers of notified addicts remained very low (454 in 1960, a lower figure than the 620 of the depressed 1930s) and there appeared to be a new kind of user—young working class and consuming for pleasure not therapy. The Brain Committee however essentially reinforced the Rolleston approach that the conditions of minimal drug addiction required no new controls. Five years later, in July 1964, the committee was reconvened apparently under pressure from a greater rate of increase in the number of known heroin addicts (in 1964 the number of notified addicts had risen to 753). The increase was however regarded as very small in official circles and attributed almost entirely to the enforcement of the legislation on dangerous drugs. Arguably more influential in the decision to reconvene the committee was the changing public profile that drug users were now beginning to have. No longer the sick, helpless victims of uncontrollable cravings, drug users were fast becoming media pariahs as representative of 'unrepentant youth subcultures' challenging the social order (Whitaker 1987:41). Young people were beginning to extol the hedonistic virtues of drug use. Nonetheless, addiction remained 'an expression of mental disorder rather than a form of criminal behaviour' in the eyes of the committee and compulsory committal to treatment centres or any other coercive forms were rejected as inappropriate (1965, paras 27 and 28).

The mood in relation to illegal drugs was changing but still quite slowly at this stage. It is interesting to note, as Whitaker does, that the definition of an addict moved from 'an expression of mental disorder' in the first report to 'a sick person provided he does not resort to criminal acts' in the second report (1987:41). What can we say about the emergence of the trafficker at this stage? It appears that the criminalisation of the drug user preceded and indeed paved the way ideologically for the later criminalisation and demonisation of the dealer/trafficker. While drug suppliers remained within the bounds of the medical profession, protected from the vagaries of the black market, the problem could be constructed as one of individual pathology in the case of the addict, or professional misconduct in the case of the supplier. The development of the punitive, penal response to drug supply developed renewed strength as youth culture and the protest movements of the later 1960s parallel the increase in the use of illicit drugs for pleasure and experimentation. The Drugs (Prevention of

Misuse) Act 1964 outlawed the possession, production and supply of amphetamines (modified in 1966 to include LSD). At the very time that medico-centrism was achieving notoriety, and in some circles acclaim, the forces of punitive control were at work expanding and strengthening the criminal law and its sanctions. The medical profession was less relevant in control terms to the form of drug consumption based on youth pleasure and rebellion. The hidden threat to labour markets—of a generation potentially lost to the capitalist work ethic— was now the fear which underlay the development of more widespread penal responses to drug control.

The second Brain Committee recommended treatment centres for addicts which it hoped would restrict the supply of heroin, other opiates and cocaine. Significantly it also recommended that only doctors working within these treatment centres should be given the authority to prescribe and administer heroin and cocaine to addicts thus considerably curtailing the generalised power of the medical profession in this respect. The committee further recommended that it should be a statutory offence for other doctors to prescribe heroin and cocaine to addicts and that breaches of the statute should be dealt with by the General Medical Council (1965, paras 26, 31 and 35).

With passing of the Dangerous Drugs Act 1967 these recommendations were given force and for the first time doctors were required to notify the Home Office of all suspected addicts complete with full personal particulars. The 1967 Act is important in a number of respects but for present purposes, in following the trajectory of the evolution of the drug trafficker, it strengthened police powers of search and seizure and police were now provided with the power to search and detain, without warrant, those people police officers suspected of being in possession of an illegal drug. (Rutherford and Green 1989:387) Heavier sentences were also provided for and it was evident that illegal drugs had now assumed the status of a problem of 'special magnitude'. There followed little movement in illegal drugs legislation until the Misuse of Drugs Act 1971. This statute represented a clear break from the medico-centric approach to drugs policy which had been favoured in the 1950s and 1960s. It is clear from the foregoing discussion, however, that it was not quite the watershed leap from medical to penal control that is sometimes presented. Criminalisation represented less a fundamental break with past practice than an increasingly singular commitment to an ideology which had less fervently underpinned previous drug control-oriented strategies.

The Misuse of Drugs Act 1971 represented a total commitment to crime control policy and a punitive approach to the treatment of drug offenders. Its purpose was to regulate the use and distribution of

113

controlled drugs and 'to back up an administrative framework with an array of criminal offences'. (Fortson 1995)

> The treatment of addicts was barely an issue, criminalisation was to be rigorously pursued as the main means of stemming what was now becoming to be more widely considered as a threat of frightening proportions'. (Rutherford and Green 1989:387)

The 1971 Act distinguished between the possession and trafficking of drugs. Trafficking in class A drugs now carried a maximum penalty of 14 years' imprisonment, while possession of heroin carried a reduced maximum penalty of seven years. The ideological distinction between the two emerged in debates in the 1960s. As Dorn *et al* (1991) point out, drug users are described as typically weak personalities, living in deprived environments, misled by wayward peers or unscrupulous pushers. Theirs was a medical/psychological problem requiring treatment or counselling. Drug pushers/dealers/suppliers on the other hand, occupied a very different ideological terrain, typically described as evil, cold-blooded, ruthless murderers with a complete disdain for human life. While drug use was relatively small scale it was possible for the medico-centric approach to develop Drug Dependency Clinics which after 1968 provided registered addicts with prescriptions for opiates. The idea behind the 'British system' was that by legally providing heroin to addicts the black market could not only be circumvented but largely inhibited. The approach had much support, particularly from progressive American criminologists concerned to change the doomed direction of US policy, but as several commentators have pointed out the medico-centric approach did not replace or obviate the role of crime control strategies, which had co-existed throughout, but which were largely subsumed in a public discourse which highlighted the gentler more rational approach embodied in the British system.[1] Throughout the existence of the Drug Dependency Clinics the criminal justice process was busy criminalising the users and suppliers of illicit drugs. The non-medical possession or supply of opiates was strictly prohibited and enforced by the law. The rehabilitation and treatment orientation of the medico-centric debates, paralleled the policing, court sanctions and penalisation which was taking place on the streets.

In this period the primary supplier of drugs was the clinic, representing an oasis of progress and rationality, albeit within a control framework. The street level pusher, however, was in the process of being demonised, constructed in the media as preoccupied with corrupting and debauching the young and innocent (seedy characters hanging around school gates), desiring only to create new addicts in

114

order that their own cravings for drugs be satisfied. The pusher, as the real villain, provides the space in British drugs policy for a bifurcation strategy—sympathy in the form of the treatment/counselling approach for addicts (but not for hedonistic pleasure seekers indulging on a casual basis) and punitive criminal justice strategies for drug traders. Mike Collinson has argued that the lines drawn between the 'deserving' addict and the 'undeserving' dealer are far murkier than the criminal justice process allows. During the 1980s when medical practitioners and drug counsellors were encouraging addicts 'to come forward, be counted, receive relevant harm reduction information . . . [and] where appropriate seek treatment', an increasing number of drug users were being processed through the criminal justice system (Collinson 1993:384). The danger of being caught in the criminal justice net for these users was that despite qualifying for 'victim status' outside, once inside the system that status immediately disappeared and the logic of punishment took over. For drug importers and traffickers more generally, there is no grey area where sympathy might conflict with certain punishment. Their condition is outside the historic remit of the medical profession and as such no conflict has surrounded policy making in respect of their disposal.

As Gerry Stimson has argued, the medico-centric framework (with the addict at centre), within which drug markets have historically been discussed, has often blinkered our understanding of the central issues.

> There has always been an alternative model of the drug user, even if it received less attention. This saw the user (or technically, illegal possessor) as a criminal. Whilst professional debate has been about treatment and rehabilitation (the addict as patient), this country has in fact continued a vigorous legal and penal approach to drugs (the addict as criminal). (Stimson 1987:38)

This is the thread which enables us to understand the punitive measures of the 1980s onwards, not as a major shift toward repression but as a relatively natural progression within the framework of prohibition.

THE TRAFFICKER AS PARIAH

The notion of the trafficker emerges in its fully fledged demonic cloak during the 'law and order' informed 1980s. Never before had issues relating to crime and public order been so politicised and drug control was to be no exception. Here, at the same time that striking coal miners were being labelled by prime minister Margaret Thatcher as the *enemy within*, drug traffickers were presented as the *external* threat, posing a danger to society hitherto reserved only for terrorists. As in America there was a sense in which drug trafficking represented a threat to national security, to the very social fabric.

In its original draft, the Misuse of Drugs Act 1971 did not distinguish between classes of drug so that the maximum term of imprisonment for trafficking in both class A and class B drugs was the same—14 years. But as the value of imported consignments of class A drugs increased, British sentences appeared more lenient in the international arena. International pressure urged a more punitive sentencing strategy in order to prevent the targeting of Britain as an easy destination for drug importers (Fortson 1996). In 1985 therefore, the Controlled Drugs (Penalties) Act raised the maximum sentence for drug trafficking to life imprisonment. The drug trafficker, linked ideologically and punitively with the terrorist, becomes a pariah by the mid-1980s.

A particular feature of drug policy in the 1980s was the divergence which took place between national and local priorities. The central role of specialist drug services was effectively diminished when the Advisory Council on the Misuse of Drugs recommended in 1982 that work with drug users should now concentrate on the problems arising from drug use rather than on diagnosis and treatment which it was argued should be restricted to addicts. When, two years later, the Advisory Council published a second report on 'prevention' the national priorities became clearer. Concern now focused on reducing the risk of an individual engaging in drug use and with reducing the harm associated with that use. Community services, supported by specialist drug services and funded and directed by central government, were to carry out the policy. While the Advisory Council was promoting this community based response to drug misuse, the Home Office was pursuing a punitive policy of penal sanctions, increased law enforcement and supply oriented interdiction. The apparent contradiction is summed up by David Turner:

At a political level, the government was determined to reduce the role of the state, to place greater responsibility on individuals and on local decisions rather than on central intervention. At the same time, it was subject to considerable national and international pressure to take action on drugs. To maintain this position, it developed an approach in which prevention, treatment and rehabilitation were the responsibilities of local and regional authorities, with additional funds provided by the central government, while the direct role of government was in strengthening international activity and attacking the supply of drugs through, for instance, introducing additional penalties for drug offences. The inevitable consequence was that the language of the government and its actions became increasingly separated from the reality of practice at local and regional levels. (Turner 1991:182-183)

The 1980s saw the overt politicisation of illegal drugs and their control. The government's strategy document *Tackling Drug Misuse* (first published in 1985 and again in 1988) embodied this politicisation. Primacy in both political and economic terms was given to enforcement, underlined by a commitment to the reduction of 'illicit production and trafficking of drugs'. As part of that politicisation Stimson documents the replacement of 'experts' as the dominant force in the arena of drugs policy discussions by government and Parliamentary officials. Experts today he argues appear to have very little impact unless they sustain dominant political strategies.

In the late 1980s the government proposed to attack drug misuse on five fronts:

- reducing supplies from abroad
- making enforcement even more effective
- maintaining effective deterrents and tight domestic controls
- developing prevention
- improving treatment and rehabilitation.

Even before full implementation of the strategy it was clear that treatment and prevention were of secondary concern. The approach on the issue of demand was simply to discourage 'those who are not misusing drugs from doing so . . . [and] helping those who are already misusing to stop doing so'. (Home Office 1988:7) Nowhere was there an attempt to deal with the structural economic and social causes of drug misuse nor any consideration given to differential drug use by users and 'misusers'. By contrast, the strategy to reduce supply was clearly the overriding priority. It included:

- supporting international efforts to curb the production and trafficking of drugs
- strengthening customs and police enforcement
- tightening the controls on drugs produced and prescribed in this country so that there is no 'leakage' to the market
- deterring drug traffickers and dealers by high maximum penalties and by depriving them of the proceeds of their crimes.

It was this strategy and the increased resources it brought to all levels of enforcement and supply control which heralded the draconian Drug Trafficking Offences Act 1986 (DTOA).

117

The DTOA represented a further response to the increasingly punitive lead offered by the United States. David Mellor (then a Home Office minister and chair of the Interdepartmental Ministerial Group on Drug Misuse) instigated the publication of a report by the House of Commons Select Committee on Home Affairs which was strongly informed by a desire to emulate the American war on drugs. The report whose sources remained confidential argued that 'unless immediate and effective action is taken Britain and Europe stand to inherit the American drug problem in less than five years'. This unfounded scare-mongering was accompanied by recommendations to meet

> ... the ruthlessness of the big drug dealers ... by equally ruthless penalties once they are caught, tried and convicted ... the American practice, which we unhesitatingly support, is to give the courts draconian powers in both civil and criminal law to strip dealers of all the assets acquired from their dealings in drugs. (Home Affairs Committee 1985:6)

Its central provision, creating the power for the courts to order the confiscation of goods and monies believed to be the proceeds of drug trafficking, effectively introduced an additional punishment for those trafficking in drugs. Despite the recommendations of the Hodgson Committee[2] that confiscation orders be used to reduce terms of imprisonment and only be applied in circumstances where the drugs in question had a street value in excess of at least £100,000, the Act's double punishment provisions were enthusiastically endorsed by both political parties.(Hodgson 1984:36; Rutherford and Green 1989: 394-399). The Drug Trafficking Act 1994 substantially increased the punishment component so that the serving of a default sentence no longer expunged the existing confiscation order.

Despite the public display of state strength embodied in the introduction of confiscation powers even supporters of tougher measures recognised the impotency of such measures:

> The amounts of assets confiscated remain marginal in relation to even the most conservative estimates of the global turnover in drugs, and there is doubt whether the most stringent anti-money laundering provisions will substantially improve the confiscation ratio. (Seward 1993:26)

MONEY LAUNDERING

In the UK, the Drug Trafficking Offences Act 1986 was the first real product of the newly expressed US concern over the financial proceeds of the international drug trade, and represented, at least in theory, a strategy to direct drug enforcement at the higher echelons within the

118

trade. It established precedents for 'the erosion of banking confidentiality' and introduced 'suspicion' (of funds being the proceeds of drug trafficking) as a sufficient ground for applying for a confiscation order. As discussed later, the DTOA also reversed the traditional burden of proof so that—rather than the prosecution having to prove that the funds were the proceeds of trafficking—now the defendant must prove that they were not. Several commentators have observed that 'hot' drug money is pursued much more vigorously than the profits of other illicit financial enterprises.[3] This is largely a result of what Nigel South calls '. . . the easy rhetoric that can justify virtually anything in relation to drugs law enforcement' and the ready identification of the culprits as criminal 'foreign corruptors' (South 1997:4-5)

In 1989 the forerunner of NCIS, the National Drugs Intelligence Unit giving evidence to the Home Affairs Committee stated '. . . there must be a vast amount of money circulating within the legitimate banking system that is drug related (NDIU 1989:116). According to the Group of Seven's Financial Action Task Force (FATF) an estimated £43 billion was being laundered through Western banks in 1990 (Taylor 1991:122). The emphasis on pursuing the financial gains of drug trafficking as diligently as the traffickers themselves was a new development and as with all British developments in drug control it followed a major tactical change adopted by the US DEA in the 1980s. As Rosa Del Olmo points out it was the recognition by the DEA of the enormous flight of drug capital which was taking place from the US (to foreign banks for laundering before recirculation as legitimate currency in the US economy) which prompted the change in policy direction toward the economics of the trade (del Olmo 1996:34). The economics of drug trafficking suddenly took on a global importance:

> The public health aspects of cocaine are no longer considered grave, even though morbidity and mortality from cocaine are on the rise. It is the disorganizing aspects of billions of coca dollars in the producing and consuming nations that produces a level of corruption, violence, and demoralisation that harms us all. (Sidney Cohen, 'Cocaine: The Bottom Line', The American Council for Drug Education, Washington DC, 1985:8)

The internationalisation of drug control was now more central to the development of US policy than ever.

The law in relation to money laundering is now set out in the consolidating Drug Trafficking Act 1994. The Act has four separate offences all of which carry harsh penalties and cover a wide range of actions including professional relationships which would otherwise be subject to confidentiality (there is a specific exception for privilege).[4]

The offences all impose a duty on a third party who has knowledge regarding money laundering to report such offences to the police. Failure to report without a reasonable excuse is an offence, although an employee need only notify the relevant supervisor as per his or her employer's money laundering protocol. So far, however, in keeping with the enforcement practices of drug trafficking more generally,

> the accused and fugitives are always linked with the Third World. Rare indeed are prosecutions against drug traffickers or financial institutions of the industrialised world, which is precisely where most of the proceeds of drug trafficking are kept. (Campodonico 1996:231)

Humberto Campodonico reveals the existence of a 'double discourse' in official analyses of money laundering and its control in the drug producing countries. On the one hand while Western governments, the United States in particular, demand the adoption by drug producing nations of a range of neo-liberal economic policies which it is argued will curb money laundering (while at the same time demanding their compliance with Western drug control models), multi-national corporations are, on the other hand, exerting pressure to ensure that fiscal policy encourages the free movement of international capital (1996:231). Liberalisation of banking systems and export led economic models have, Campodonico argues, merely encouraged the laundering of 'narco-dollars'. Free movement of currencies between drug-producing nations and the rest of the world as a result of policies which lift banking restrictions mean that foreign currencies can be deposited without regard to their origin in countries such as Peru. The increased supply of foreign currency as a result of external trade leads to its over-valuation making imports cheaper and exports more expensive thus encouraging the 'legalised' circulation of drug trafficking finance (1996:234). Writing about Peru, Campodonico highlights the central irony inherent in Western money laundering controls:

> . . . the neo-liberal economic reforms have contributed to the increase of narco-dollars in the national economy and to the cultivation of coca. This conditionality lays upon Peru the responsibility to stop coca cultivation, whilst at the same time denying her the possibility of doing so. (1996:240)

It took five years and enormous resources to trace and confiscate just $14 million which had been laundered through the Bank of Credit and Commerce International. The control of money laundering is seen by the policy makers themselves as a Sisyphean task. Despite an optimism that the task will become easier their aims remain conservative as is evident from the Wilton Park Papers:

The aim of tighter controls is eventually to capture around five per cent of laundered money, enough to act as a deterrent to would-be launderers not to use the international financial system, thereby making it harder for traffickers to disguise their ill-gotten gains. (Hopkinson 1991:37)

Measures to curb the laundering of 'dirty' drugs money will inevitably be hampered by the contradictions of capitalism. Free market economics, the liberalisation of global banking, and the introduction of neo-liberal economic reforms in the developing world are all desired by the forces of international capital. The contradiction lies precisely here because the conditions which allow for the free movement of global capital are precisely the same as those which ease the passage for the laundering of illicit funds. Policy makers are in one important sense banging their heads against a brick wall.

While the big questions in relation to the international drug trade remain un-asked by the policy makers (primarily in relation to the cause and effect dialectic embodied in prohibition and the singular emphasis on law enforcement in drug control) there is little hope of cleaning up the dirty proceeds of the industry. South makes a salient point in relation to the international controls on the laundering of drug trafficking proceeds when he writes: 'The problem of laundering drug profits cannot, ultimately, be resolved unless there are no profits to launder'. (1997:9)

UK and European policy makers like their American counterparts before them, appear unwilling to address the big picture.

DRUGS POLICIES INTO THE 1990s

It was the Conservative government (1979-97) which dictated the punitive framework for drug control which was to carry Britain into the new millennium. Speaking at the ACPO drugs conference in Wakefield in 1994 Michael Howard, then home secretary, laid down, not for the first time, the basis of Conservative drugs policy:

This government has no intention of legalising any currently banned drug ... Drugs are harmful. They destroy people; they destroy families; they destroy the very fabric on which our society rests. (9 June 1994)

The outspoken commitment to prohibition by Michael Howard was a response to growing disquiet voiced by senior members of the judiciary and police that prohibition of certain drugs was counter-productive. In October 1993, Lord Woolf asked:

121

Should we not at least be considering whether it would be preferable for drugs, or at least some drugs, to be lawfully available in controlled circumstances so that it would be no longer necessary for addicts to commit crimes to feed their addiction? (*The Guardian*, 16 October 1993).

Earlier in the same year during the ACPO drugs conference in Preston, John Grieve, a Metropolitan Police commander argued that the time may have arrived 'to think the unthinkable . . . either we go to war on dealers across the globe or we have to come up with new options'. One of those options was the licensing of illegal drugs. Other senior police officers argued for legalisation as a strategy for removing the power bases of dealers and the drugs market from the underground economy. Decriminalisation was supported in various sections of the media with *The Guardian*, *The Economist*, *The Spectator*, *The Independent* and *The Times* all supporting it in some form. The arguments in favour of legalisation are well rehearsed—the black market would be undermined and the problems arising from inflated prices and the furtiveness of transactions would be eliminated; there would be less acquisitive crime and less need for women to work as prostitutes; fewer cases of intravenously transmitted HIV; police already practice forms of decriminalisation by merely cautioning certain users; prison overcrowding would be significantly reduced; profits from the market would benefit the Treasury and not the black marketeers and drug barons; and the inconsistent treatment of legal dangerous drugs, alcohol and tobacco would no longer offend rational sensibilities. But rather than engage with the disquiet voiced by the tentative advocates of reform, the Home Office reinforced its prohibition-led offensive against the marketeers and users of illegal drugs. And while, at the end of 1994, three ministries responsible for social policy—health, education and the minister responsible for co-ordinating policy agreed, in line with recommendations from the Drug Advisory Council, to re-orient their drugs policies away from enforcement toward prevention, Michael Howard instead led the Home Office yet further down the road of repressive enforcement. He announced a five-fold increase in maximum fines for cannabis users (from £500 to £2,500) and an instruction to the police to give offenders only one caution (*The Guardian*, 31 October 1995).

Tackling Drugs Together: A Strategy for England 1995-1998, the Conservative government's White Paper outlining the drugs strategy for England in the late twentieth century was simply a reiteration of pre-existing policy. Its Statement of Purpose, 'To take action by vigorous law enforcement and a new emphasis on education and prevention', might superficially have implied a changed emphasis in the direction of demand reduction but a closer reading of the body of the text reveals an undiluted and primary commitment to a punitive crime-control model. Prevention and treatment strategies became the domain of law enforcement, so that police forces were primary 'deliverers' of prevention initiatives.

The White Paper contained a reaffirmation of prohibition declaring that there would be no legalisation or decriminalisation of any currently controlled drug.

In early 1997, just weeks before its landslide defeat at the polls, the Conservative government succeeded in passing its final sentencing strategy for the punishment of traffickers of class A drugs. Section 2 Crime (Sentences) Act 1997 introduced mandatory sentences of 'at least seven years' for pe ople convicted of a class A trafficking offence where they have a history of two or more previous convictions for similar offences, unless exceptional circumstances justify the judge in ordering otherwise (1996:1; section 2(2)). Judges can avoid these mandatory sentences if, and only if, they would be 'unjust in all the circumstances'.

In addition, the 1997 Act abolishes automatic remission. These are the first proposed mandatory sentences for drug offences in the UK and are clearly in the mould of US sentencing strategies, though not yet repressive to the same degree.[5] According to a Human Rights Watch Report concerning disproportionate sentencing for New York drug offenders:

> Mandatory sentencing Laws for drug felonies and predicate offenders have increased the percentage of convicted offenders who receive prison sentences. As a consequence, the prison population has changed from one in which nine per cent were serving time for drug felonies (in 1980) to one today in which 34 per cent are drug felons (1997:12)

Drug trafficking, like terrorism before it, has become the harbinger for the expansion and normalisation of repression within criminal justice.

NEW 'HARD' LABOUR—OLD 'HARD' POLICIES

The advent of a new Labour government raised expectations of liberal reform, particularly as it followed almost two decades of Conservative rule. There has been little, however, in New Labour's policy pronouncements nor in its political ideology and practice which offers optimism for drug policy change.

At the second reading of the 1996 Crime (Sentences) Bill, the then Shadow home secretary, Jack Straw, declared his party's agreement with the Conservative government's efforts to increase the penalties facing drug traffickers:

As I have made clear repeatedly, there is no issue between us and the government on the Bill's overall aims of achieving clarity in sentencing, securing better public safety and ensuring tough sentences for repeat burglars and drug dealers. (4 November 1996:927)

Labour's endorsement of the Crime (Sentences) Bill was a culmination of the electoral 'tough on crime image' that New Labour has been so keen to cultivate. So concerned to distance itself from the suggestion of liberalism on the issue of crime in the pre-election period the Labour leadership in the House of Lords was prepared to abandon its own amendment (to restore judicial discretion not to pass the mandatory sentences, should they consider them unjust in particular cases).

In October 1995 Clare Short, shadow transport minister, upset what Stuart Hall would once have coined the 'Great Moving Right Show' of Tony Blair's New Labour. Short, during a televised interview with David Frost, called for a debate on cannabis decriminalisation, suggesting that in the light of the massive failure of drug control policies a commission charged with the remit of exploring the impact of cannabis decriminalisation should be set up. It was essentially an endorsement of a call made earlier by the Liberal Democrats for a Royal Commission into the issue. But the response of the Labour leadership could have been drafted by Conservative strategists and Clare Short was publicly rebuked for her outspoken, embarrassing and un-vetted views. A *Guardian* editorial summed up the Labour party's position on drugs policy as follows:

Labour's response has been just as pathetic. All serious debate has been ignored. Worse still it took a leaf out of the Tories's book and played the "soft on drugs" card against the Lib-Dem candidate in its disgraceful Littleborough and Saddleworth by-election campaign in the summer of 1996. Hence its deep embarrassment over Clare Short's endorsement of a Lib-Dem call for a Royal Commission. (*The Guardian,* 31 October 1995)

What the *Guardian* editorial failed to highlight was the electoral fit between Labour's position on drug control and the party's desire to outdo the Conservatives on what they saw as the electoral mileage embodied in hard-line law and order strategies.

In February 1994, the then shadow home secretary, Tony Blair made clear the party's electoral interest in drugs while reiterating Labour's opposition to any form of legalisation. Releasing the findings of a Labour study linking crime and drug costs, he argued that drug addicts were responsible for around half of the country's property crime. According to the Labour party figures he was speaking to, addicts steal approximately £2 billion per year to support their addictions, a crime

124

bill which he alleged cost every household around £114 per year in insurance and extra charges for goods. These figures are more than double such estimates arrived at by the Probation Service and other researchers and rely on a formula apparently first applied by Greater Manchester police to assess its own drug crime problem (Mills 1994). The emphasis Labour placed on street level drug crime and the inflated figures it carelessly used suggest a cynical political strategy to undercut the Conservatives own populist appeal to public fear of street crime.

Labour party policy in respect of drug misuse and drug trafficking has—during the course of the 1990s—become virtually indistinguishable from that of the former Conservative government. While rejecting the all out supply-driven war on drugs undertaken by the United States in the 1980s, Labour's demand-focused strategies were, however, overshadowed by the punitive rhetoric which corresponded with the 'tough on crime' image Labour had cultivated in the 1990s.

An examination of the three Labour party drug policy documents in the 1990s illustrates this particular shift. The 1991 *Drugs: A Consultation Document* was launched with a challenge to the Conservative government to tackle the urban decay, deprivation and unemployment of the inner cities[6] and did concentrate on demand reduction and harm minimisation. Particular attention was devoted to the link between drug misuse and socio-economic deprivation, drugs education and treatment. But as a *Guardian* report revealed many of the more progressive reforms advocated in the original consultation document were vetoed by the then shadow home secretary Roy Hattersley. As a result of leadership intervention Labour abandoned plans to discourage police from charging individuals in possession of small amounts of cannabis. In keeping with their developing policy on crime and law and order the Labour leadership did not want to be seen as 'soft on drugs'. And in keeping with this drive for electoral popularity the party also abandoned a policy to replace prosecution with cautioning for the possession of small quantities of controlled drugs. An earlier proposal which would have urged enforcement agencies to give greater priority to class A drugs was also deleted in the new look 'get tougher on drugs and street crime' image the party adopted. Also removed from the original consultation document were recommendations to review the harsh sentences handed down to 'naive' drug couriers or mules and the inclusion of information for prisoners on cleaning syringes to prevent the spread of HIV infection. These amendments say far more about Labour's political approach to the misuse of drugs than the remaining 'liberal' content of the emasculated document.

Labour's second policy document *Cutting the Lifeline: A Survey of Increases in Drug Use and Cuts in Provision* (1993), signalled the shift to a more supply-oriented approach again more in line with government strategy. With regard to drug traffickers and dealers it proposed that:

> Effective police and customs work is required to deal with the major importers and manufacturers, the distributors, and at street level with the dealers who can make life a misery for local people. Severe penalties are appropriate for those convicted of trafficking in drugs. (1993:7)

Where the 1991 consultative document differentiated between levels of trafficking, the 1993 document blurred any distinction between major and minor offences, paving the way for a full frontal assault on users and street dealers.

In 1991, Labour acknowledged the ideological hype which it considered distorted the debate surrounding illegal drug use: 'It is important, however, to keep drug misuse in perspective' the consultation document reported:

> The wide-scale use and abuse of legal substances such as alcohol and tobacco inflicts far more harm on individuals and society than illicit drugs . . . We need a calm non-sensational approach to policy development in this area and one which places these serious problems in context. (1991:1)

By 1996, no such contextualisation was in evidence. Instead New Labour had enthusiastically embraced every component of the hard line prohibition-determined drug control campaign. And they have gone further. In its 1996 policy document *Breaking the Vicious Circle: Labour's Proposals to Tackle Drug Related Crime*, Labour's commitment to a crack-down on minor drug offenders is made evident. If we examine just one proposal, that of breaking the link between drug addiction and crime, one of the central targets in Labour's war on drugs is now seen to be the user. In justifying this focus the report argues that

> The process of arrest, trial and sentencing offers a unique opportunity for society to intervene — to break the vicious circle and offer drug abuse treatment to a group of hard-core drug users who if left untreated will continue to impose a huge cost on themselves and the wider community. (1996:3)

This is very much in keeping with Labour home secretary, Jack Straw's general commitment to 'zero tolerance'—a right-wing American crime prevention initiative which essentially criminalises and repressively 'cleans up' the disorderly, the disruptive and the obstreperous (drunks, addicts, beggars, prostitutes, noisy youth, Straw's own squeegee merchants and the mentally disturbed) from community streets (Rutherford 1996:42).[7] Gone is the stated concern to address the root causes of drug addiction found in the 1991 Consultation Document:

> . . . the most severe problems of low level dealing and drug misuse are concentrated in areas of high socio-economic deprivation and unemployment. No government can hope to contain drug addiction unless it is prepared to tackle urban decay. (1991:2)

Instead compulsory treatment is promoted as the only way forward, 'Those who are made to enter treatment do as well as those who enter treatment voluntarily' (1996:5). For Labour individual responsibility has replaced social deprivation and urban decay and the drug user has become the central causal problematic for public policy:

> Whilst we must offer those who are addicted to hard drugs help in breaking their habit, those who are assisted also have a responsibility to show that they are sticking to their programme. Where a person's drug habit leads them to prey on those around them, to repeatedly steal from their neighbours, friends and relatives — then society has every right to step in and call a halt to the vicious circle of addiction and crime — for the offender's own good as well as society's. Too often offenders are allowed to deceive themselves and the courts. Often they say they have stopped using drugs, that they have stopped ripping off their neighbours when in fact they have done nothing of the sort. To that we say "OK. prove it. Prove you're committed to a new way of life, to going straight". (1996:3)

Jack Straw's response to the Conservative government's Crime (Sentences) Bill was singularly concerned with berating the secretary of state for not being tough enough in respect of the sentencing of drug dealers and domestic burglars, for failing to implement the proposed minimum sentences immediately and, in keeping with his party's commitment to an ill-defined notion of 'zero tolerance', he declared 'there is no strategy to deal with the plague of disorder on our streets which so undermines people's quality of life'. (HC 1996, col. 932)

In its 1997 pre-election manifesto, *New Labour Because Britain Deserves Better*, Labour made clear its commitment to continuing the Conservative's war against drugs at street level focusing in particular on 'the vicious circle of drugs and crime' which, in the wake of leading right-wing US political scientist, James Q Wilson, 'wrecks lives and threatens communities'. (1997:23) The policy implications for drug traffickers are, it would seem, clear. By embracing a policy of 'zero tolerance' for those who have not even necessarily broken the law, the Labour party has *de facto* committed itself to increasing the tariff for *real*

127

offences and particularly those offences which are 'undisputedly' serious enough to require mandatory minimum sentences.

The manifesto declared that upon a Labour victory at the polls the new government:

> will appoint an anti-drugs supremo to co-ordinate our battle against drugs across all government departments. The 'drug czar' will be a symbol of our commitment to tackle the modern menace of drugs in our communities. (1997:23)

Within three weeks of Labour coming to power, Ann Taylor, leader of the House was appointed by Labour to chair a high powered Cabinet committee 'to tackle the menace of drugs' and to seek the right 'supremo' to fill the job.[8] The home secretary also made clear that the appointment of a drugs czar would complement the Conservative administration's approach to drug control by 'build[ing] on arrangements established by the previous administration that had our firm support.' (*Hansard*, 19 May 1997:394). Keith Hellawell, former chief constable of West Yorkshire was appointed national drugs coordinator in October 1997 and holds the power to bring together all agencies involved in drug enforcement—police, customs, intelligence agencies, social services, prison and probation services as well as health boards and reports directly to the Cabinet sub-committee which includes the home secretary and the foreign secretary. This appointment, clearly moulded upon William Bennett, America's first 'Drug Czar' is likely to cement the process of criminalisation of both traffickers and of those for whom trafficking exists—'consumers'. Drug users under William Bennett became 'consumers', free-will purchasers, who were therefore forced to accept responsibility for the 'drug related chaos', and 'appalling, deepening crisis' that accompanies the trade.[9] A drug czar not only increases the political and symbolic significance of drug control but also adds to the entrenchment of drug enforcement bureaucracy. There is no reason to imagine the Labour government will not continue to draw 'inspiration' from American criminal justice and drug control strategies. The Blair government will, therefore, be mindful of the backlash against the Clinton regime's very tentative steps toward drug control reform in 1995 where a new emphasis on hard-core addicts, very minor cuts in interdiction funding and a moderate de-escalation in drug-war rhetoric brought a wave of Republican criticism which resulted in the failure of the proposed policy reform.[10] Evidence of this political sensitivity came in August 1997 when, following a public call from the chief constable of Bedfordshire for the introduction of American-style drugs courts, the Home Office responded immediately. George Howarth, Home Office minister with responsibility for drugs remarked, without any specifics, that the 'best principles' of American drugs courts would be introduced into the UK.[11]

Any major changes to drug control policy will require an enormous reappraisal of the ideology and practice of prohibition-driven drug enforcement. The powerful symbolism of the war on drugs will not easily be dismantled—'powerful and ruthless' drug lords; 'greedy and self-interested' traffickers; 'hopeless, criminal' users, and increasing quantities of dangerously addictive substances headed straight for the veins of Britain's youth—Tony Blair and Jack Straw have shown no inclination to embark on the challenge to dispel this misleading conventional wisdom. In June 1997 a Home Office minister told the Association of Chief Police Officers Drug Conference that *'any debate about legalisation or decriminalisation detracts from the strong message that drugs destroy lives'*. (*The Guardian*, 18 August 1997: emphasis supplied)

Within this policy orientation demand reduction, as well as supply reduction, is to be pursued via punitive law enforcement. The Labour government seems set, then, to follow in the steps of its Conservative predecessor.

ENDNOTES

[1] See, especially, Stimson 1987:38
[2] Established by the Howard League for Penal Reform to examine the scope of confiscation powers embodied in the Drug Trafficking (Offences) Act 1986
[3] See Barry Rider, 'Organized Crime and Money Laundering', 1991, MJIB; Nigel South 'On "Cooling Hot Money"': Transatlantic Trends in Drug-related Money Laundering and its Facilitation', 1997
http://www.alternatives.com/crime/SOUTH.HTML
[4] See sections 49-54 of the Act for the main provisions
[5] Drug offenders in New York State, e.g. face a minimum sentence of 15 years to life imprisonment for possessing four or more ounces of a narcotic drug, while possession of only two ounces carries a minimum of three years. (Huling, 1996: 49)
[6] *The Guardian*, 18 June 1991
[7] It was Jack Straw as Labour shadow home secretary who remarked on 'aggressive beggars and squeegee merchants'. See also the Labour Party's *A Quiet Life, Tough Action on Criminal Neighbours*, London, 1995
[8] Press Release, 'Ann Taylor to Oversee Anti-Drugs Effort', CAB, 9/97, 18 May 1997
[9] Cited in Noam Chomsky, *Deterring Democracy*, Vintage: London, 1992, p. 116
[10] Peter Reuter, Eva Bertram, Morris Blachman and Kenneth Sharpe, Paper delivered to the Annual Meeting of the American Society of Criminology, Boston, USA, November 1995
[11] The chief constable of Bedfordshire, Michael O'Byrne has called for the introduction of drug courts to counter what he saw as 'a lack of political will and a failing government drugs strategy', *The Guardian*, 18 August 1997. Mr. Howarth had in mind the oversight by the courts of drug treatment orders which were provided for in the Crime and Disorder Act 1998.

CHAPTER SEVEN

UK Drug Wars: Symbolic Success and Pragmatic Failure

There has been much discussion on the failure of the war on drugs particularly in terms of the US experience (Epstein 1988; del Olmo 1996; Gordon 1994). It is indeed true that drug production, trafficking and use have been largely undeterred by the supply-oriented attack. However, to see this only in terms of failure is essentially to accept the parameters laid down by those who argue in favour of prohibition, or at the very least of those who believe in a *drug* problem, rather than a drug *control* problem. To understand the war only as a failure is, it seems, to miss a central issue.

The war against drugs has, in many respects been a considerable political success in much the same way that anti-communism was an ideological success. Drugs, and the amorphous threat they are argued to pose, have been employed by Western governments to harness more general social fears, and it is in this respect that their success may be understood. With the ending of the Cold War in the late 1980s a vacuum was created in the armoury of public anxieties which governments traditionally foster to ameliorate the impact of potentially controversial political policy. The threat of drugs could be readily resurrected and re-defined in geo-political terms to capture some of the political flavour of the old Cold War fears; in a sense doubly necessary in Britain first with the temporary IRA cease-fire initiated in 1994 and the subsequent diminution of the terrorist threat which has accompanied the peace process in Northern Ireland.

In France, President Jaques Chirac had used the threat of drug importations from The Netherlands to win French support for opposition against the introduction of the Schengen Convention. This threat, coupled with the threat of terrorism was used by President Chirac for his own political ends to rally French support for the maintenance of internal border controls. Margaret Thatcher, in the final years of her administration, used the exaggerated threat of cocaine to similarly garner support for increased border controls within Europe, thereby augmenting her own Euro-sceptic political stance. Thus while failure sums up the results of the war on drugs, in terms of its *expressed* remit, the war's unexpressed or hidden *political* remit has been anything but a failure.

The war on drugs has also heralded legislative reform—repressive reforms, documented in *Chapter 6*, which would have been potentially controversial had they not been shrouded in the drug war mantle. Viewed from this perspective, a focus on low level players like drug couriers begins to make sense.

In many respects the war on drugs is more attractive than the Cold War ever was, despite President Clinton's declaration in February 1997 that demand reduction must now take centre stage in the national anti-drug campaign.[1] Primarily, as Nadleman documents, the war on drugs is, by comparison with the cold and other wars, a very cheap war. Drug enforcement has proven a very inexpensive means of what Noam Chomsky describes as 'population control'. Drug enforcement agencies have become increasingly powerful yet the cost to the states involved is, in a global sense, very small. According to Nadleman, the United States no longer wants to pay the high price for international hegemonisation through war. The internationalisation of drug control policy is much cheaper when compared with the military expenditure required for coerced co-operation (1993).

WHAT COST BRITAIN'S WAR? THE PRICE OF FAILURE

While critics of the American crusade against drugs can, with some level of accuracy, point to the relatively high fiscal cost of US drug control policies (and contrast that with the overwhelming lack of *apparent* success of those policies, and the relatively low state investment into social welfare) critics of British policy find it much more difficult to assess the scale of state investment in drug control. The few attempts at such estimates have focused primarily on resources granted to the two main drug enforcement agencies, HM Customs and Excise and the police service (Wagstaff and Maynard 1988; SCODA 1992; Sutton and Maynard 1994). Little attempt appears to have been made to build in the costs that are expended in terms of British military involvement in drug control nor in terms of the 'conditional' aid that Britain gives to certain developing countries involved in the supply of illicit drugs.

The Standing Conference on Drug Abuse (SCODA) estimates that £326.6 million is devoted to drug enforcement each year, that is, 68 per cent of total government expenditure on illegal drug policy (SCODA, 1992). The remaining 32 per cent (£153 million) is stretched to cover prevention and treatment. While the impact of this distribution has significantly undermined the provision of services for people with drug problems the enforcement war on drugs remains well funded.

The most recent available estimates on drug control expenditure are to be found in the Conservative government's 1995 White Paper,

Tackling Drugs Together. These estimates indicate that at least £526 million was spent on 'tackling drug misuse' in 1993-94. Broken down, £15 million was spent on international action; £209 million on police/customs enforcement and £137 million on deterrence/controls with the remaining £165 million expended on treatment/rehabilitation (£61 million) and prevention/education (£104 million) (1995:51).

Sutton and Maynard set out to provide an analysis of the cost-effectiveness of drug enforcement activity in Britain in 1994. Their data suggests that throughout the 1980s the annual expenditure, in real terms, by HM Customs and the police services for drug enforcement increased by 38 per cent and 74 per cent respectively (1994).

Can, then, the many millions spent on UK drug enforcement be justified in terms of obvious 'performance indicators'? Has, for example, the addiction rate declined, has drug availability declined, has the spread of disease via contaminated needles diminished, are there fewer drug-related crimes?

Perhaps the most obvious indicator in measuring the success of the enforcement led strategy is a measure of the scale of illicit drug use and acceptability. Illegal drugs remain popular with large numbers of the population. According to Home Office estimates three million people (six per cent of the population) consume illegal drugs in any given year, and over one third of 14 to 25-year-olds reported having used a drug. These figures may, however, be a considerable underestimate if we consider the findings of a 1995 study of 700 secondary school students in Leeds which conservatively extrapolated that at least two million British adolescents are illegal drug users. The report suggests that the availability of illicit drugs

is a normal part of the leisure-pleasure landscape . . . Over the next few years, and certainly in urban areas, non-drug trying adolescents will be a minority group. In one sense they will be the deviants . . . for many young people drug taking has become the norm. (Parker et al 1995:26)

It is important to note, however, that the research of Howard Parker and his colleagues does not distinguish between one-off users, casual users or more regular users and thus exaggerates the extent of 'normalisation'.

Problem drug use has also increased and continues to rise. The number of new addicts notified has risen between 16 and 21 per cent each year since 1990 so that in 1994 there were a total of 13,469 new addicts notified. The total number of addicts notified (including those renotified) in 1994 increased by 21 per cent to 33,952 (HOSB July 1995). Patterns of addiction have remained relatively unchanged. Of all drug addicts notified in 1989, 84 per cent were using heroin, 20 per cent

Methadone and six per cent cocaine. The ISDD estimated that between 74,000 and 112,000 people in the UK were dependent on opiates in 1989 (1990:9). By 1994, 66 per cent of addicts were using heroin, 46 per cent Methadone and nine per cent cocaine (HOSB: 1995:6-7). The decline in the proportion of heroin addicts may be balanced against the increased proportion of Methadone addicts and may be explained by the treatment of many heroin addicts with Methadone. The number of drug related deaths has also risen, from 1,280 in 1990 to 1,421 in 1992, most of which (between 74.5 and 80 per cent) were caused by overdoses related to the consumption of adulterated street heroin and other illicit drugs (White Paper 1995:40).

By the end of the 1980s the ISDD reported a reasonably stable drugs market, 'with heroin still important, cocaine increasing in availability but still of relatively minor concern, and the market dominated by cannabis and amphetamines. (South 1994:398)

Another obvious measure of the success or otherwise of enforcement, interdiction and drug seizures is the availability of illegal drugs on the street, their price and purity. Shapiro provides evidence to show that despite an increase in cocaine seizures the street value of cocaine remained constant (1991). While Shapiro posits that this might indicate a desire on the part of dealers to maintain an artificially high street price it is equally likely that paralleling increased seizures are increased imports of the drug. According to Release's National Drug Survey of 1994, there has been '. . . little change in the overall availability and price of street drugs in any parts of the country. This clearly indicates that supply interdiction efforts by police and customs are having little impact on the amount of drugs getting through to users' (1994). And an Australian study, conducted in the Australian Capital Territory, found that even when police had been successful in arresting several 'high level' traffickers there was no long-term effect on the availability of heroin to users. It was found by researchers that users gradually found new contacts to supply them (Bammer and Sengoz 1994).

If we add to these facts the evidence of wide scale police corruption (see below), the increasing violence which now accompanies much dealing on the black market (Power 1986:15-16), the crisis of prison overcrowding and the wide scale social misery which accompanies criminalisation then the failure of prohibition to prevent drug use and misuse is doubly manifest. It cannot be argued that prohibition-driven drug control has solved any of the problems widely attributed to drug use. That, however, as has already been argued, has never been the primary purpose of prohibition. It is evident that drug control policies are not concerned with the health, happiness, security and well being of users and non-users. By a whole range of indicators the evidence is incontrovertible—prohibition driven crime control strategies enormously amplify and in the majority of circumstances actually create the major social problems commonly associated with drug abuse (the spread of HIV; the existence of the black market; deaths resulting from overdoses and adulterated drugs, drug-related property offences, the growth of organized crime and so on).

THE SUPPLY FACTOR

Any reading of drug enforcement literature or government strategic policy in respect of drug control effectively takes the demand for illicit drugs as a given, a phenomena which is relatively intransigent and understood only as a response to supply. As O'Malley and Mugford write, demand 'is not seen as a phenomenon in its own right, but as a reflex of other authentic or real phenomena located elsewhere'. (1991:51) From this perspective then, the state is not required to seriously address the issues raised independently by demand. Research conducted by Bachman *et al* (1990) in the United States suggests that demand for certain illegal drugs—particularly cocaine and cocaine derivatives— appears to be declining. This decline is taking place in a market apparently saturated by these particular drugs, i.e. it is taking place quite independently of supply. Nonetheless from the early 1980s in America the problem of drugs was constructed as one of supply with the enemy cast very explicitly as external. Whatever the reasons for the decline in cocaine use the US administration have linked it to the results of the war against supply. The same emphasis on supply-oriented strategies is evident in Britain and the rest of Europe. Despite an official commitment to maintaining a balance between supply and demand reduction strategies, the evidence presented at the 1993 Wilton Park Conference, 'Combating Drugs Trafficking and Abuse' makes clear that no country seriously implements this approach to drugs policy. As Seward reports, 'supply reduction measures take the lion's share of resources' (1993:42). The war on drugs then has never been a war against the material conditions of life (poverty, unemployment, homelessness, powerlessness), which research strongly suggests, lead to the troubled use of illegal drugs. From the supply-oriented perspective there is no value in researching the whys and wherefores of problem drug use—drug abuse exists simply because drugs of abuse exist. To eliminate the source of production, to seize the drugs or the conduits of the drugs themselves continues to be the favoured strategy.

UK DRUG ENFORCEMENT

The recent history of British drug law enforcement and its organization has been well documented (Stimson 1987; Dorn *et al* 1992; South 1994). In this section I wish to raise some of the more problematic features of drug control in the UK.

The two state agencies with responsibility for drug enforcement are the police and HM Customs and Excise. Customs have primary responsibility for interdiction at national frontiers, police primarily within the borders of the UK. Conflict between the two agencies has at times been considerable, for the high status, high profile drug trafficking work. A 1988 report by Cindy Fazey, an independent consultant on drug misuse and former UN and Home Office drugs adviser, declared that 'Co-operation between the two services has deteriorated to the point where some police and some sections of Customs and Excise see each other as the enemy'. Fazey reported that many customs officers did not, in general, trust the police, especially the Metropolitan Police, and further that the overlap of duties between the services had created an 'intense rivalry'. In an effort to establish lines of demarcation the government laid down the following responsibilities:

> HM Customs and Excise have primary responsibility for preventing and detecting the illegal import and export of controlled drugs, the investigation of organizations and individuals engaged in international drugs smuggling, their prosecution and the identification of any proceeds of such crime. The police have a particular responsibility for dealing with offences of manufacture, supply and possession of drugs. (Home Office 1994)

Police and drug-trafficking
In 1994 there were an estimated 1,300 police officers employed in drug control. Each of the six Regional Crime Squads within England and Wales has a 'drugs wing' employing in total around 345 officers. In Northern Ireland the Royal Ulster Constabulary has a Drug Squad of around 20 officers and an estimated 60 per cent of Scotland's 85 strong Crime Squad's work is drug-related (Home Office 1994). The work of the drugs wings includes some international liaison over drug imports and surveillance operations targeting couriers, mid-level distributors and those users also engaged in small scale dealing (Dorn *et al* 1987:66).

From its establishment in 1973, through until 1985, the enforcement of drug control had been the responsibility of Scotland Yard's Central

Drugs and Illegal Immigration Intelligence Unit. The linking of drugs intelligence with immigration intelligence reflected a continuing association of drugs with alien suppliers. While this direct organizational relationship ended when the Central Drugs and Illegal Immigration Intelligence Unit was reorganized into the Central Drugs Intelligence Unit (CDIU) in 1984 drug trafficking remains, in the lexicon of the state, firmly located as an external evil conducted and sponsored by foreigners. As we saw in *Chapters* 2 and 3 the link between drug and immigration control has achieved a new pre-eminence with the advent of the European single market.

While servicing the whole of the UK the CDIU remained based within the Metropolitan Police, reflecting the view at the time that drugs were essentially a London problem (South 1994:410). In 1985, as a result of the government's policy document *Tackling Drug Misuse* and ACPO's 1985 Working Party on Drugs (the Broome Report) resources were made available for the establishment of a joint police/customs, National Drugs Intelligence Unit (NDIU) which would replace the old CDIU. The first director of the NDIU, Colin Hewett came with a pedigree which charted the way in which illegal drug trafficking was now to be seen. As former head of both Special Branch and the Anti-Terrorist Squad, Hewett's expertise in gathering intelligence was argued by the then home secretary, Leon Brittan, to be essential in the pursuit and apprehension of drug traffickers. Drug trafficking and terrorism became indelibly linked in the mid-1980s as the great external threats to the social fabric. Illicit drugs along with terrorism have provided the central pillars in political justifications for increased police centralisation and specialisation. And as Hebenton and Thomas argue:

Together they have coalesced into what is now referred to as 'proactive policing' — characterised by the targeting of specific criminal groups and reliance on information and intelligence gathering. (Hebenton and Thomas 1992:8)

The most recent domestic development within the organization of drugs intelligence has been the formation, in 1992, of the National Criminal Intelligence Service (NCIS). NCIS combines customs, police and Home Office personnel whose primary responsibility, amongst others, is to gather and analyse drugs intelligence which it then disseminates. There is an assumption that the target orientation of the NCIS Drug Division is the major trafficker. There are five regional offices of the NCIS and a Drugs Division employing a total of around 500 personnel (Home Office 1996). NCIS is set to play a foreground role in European drug control with its International Division managing a network of European drug liaison officers whose primary responsibility is one of intelligence gathering. Europol is already established at NCIS HQ while two NCIS officers are based in The Hague. These moves have taken place in anticipation of ministerial approval that Europol's HQ will be stationed there. The International Division is also home to the UK Bureau of Interpol thus providing NCIS with direct access to the 176 member countries of Interpol. Moves to place NCIS on a statutory footing were published in November 1996 with a new Police Bill. Instead of being under the control of the Home Office the Bill proposed that NCIS be accountable to a 'newly created service authority'.[2] The proposed autonomy of NCIS coupled with its extensive range of new powers raises particular civil libertarian concerns which have not been addressed and are unlikely to be satisfied by the creation of a 'service authority'. The more recent role of the intelligence services in the control of drug trafficking raises similar and more serious concerns. International drug control has offered MI5, Britain's internal and colonial counter-espionage and security service, and MI6, the secret service involved in intelligence gathering, espionage and destabilisation operations outside the UK and colonies, a new *raison d'etre*. The very existence of MI5 had been threatened by the demise of the Soviet threat and the historical process of decolonisation. In the immediate wake of the collapse of the Cold War, drug control offered the security services potentially gainful employment. According to a 1992 report by *Statewatch*, police chiefs expressed alarm at this possible extension of the security services' role (*Statewatch*, 1992:5). This new role was to be cemented in the first year of the Labour government. At the end of August 1997, the foreign secretary, Robin Cook, announced at a meeting in Kuala Lumpar that British intelligence and policing resources would now be re-focused in order to prioritise the pursuit of major drug traffickers. Drug trafficking would now, he reported, become a central concern of MI6.[3]

At the level of European Union the development of Europol is likely to have a significant impact on national strategies and in a dialectical sense NCIS and the intelligence services are offering a model for other European states which are currently moving toward centralised intelligence and information gathering authorities.

Policing pragmatics and political ideologues
In February 1994 home secretary Michael Howard unwittingly provoked police wrath when he unveiled his plans to increase fines for the possession of cannabis from £500 to £2,500. Amongst certain sections of the police force, however, this move caused consternation—a situation alluded to in *Chapter 6*. For a number of years, voices within police forces throughout the country had been expressing a certain

reluctance to pursue prohibitionist enforcement strategies in relation to cannabis offences. According to sergeant Gordon Payne the general feeling was not that drugs were no longer a danger to the community but that the present system of prohibition and punitive sanctions was 'unworkable' (*Police Review*, 28 February 1992). Police had experienced the bankruptcy of pursuing policies targeted at street level drug taking and dealing for some time. It was recognised that current 'prohibitions had been ignored', and that far from reducing the drug problem, present strategies 'may be contributing to the very growth in supply and use that we seek to reduce' (Ellison 1993:26). Home Office figures had revealed that 65 per cent of the £147 million spent on enforcing the drug laws in 1993 had been directed at cannabis use (*Hansard*, 31 January 1994). A *Police Review* editorial that year claimed that the increase in popularity of cannabis amongst the public had led, operationally, to 'the partial decriminalisation of cannabis possession through cautioning in most UK forces'. A review of the commentaries expressed in *Police Review*, particularly through the 1990s, reveals a growing disquiet amongst a section of the police. Most police critics concentrated on the unworkability of the present cannabis prohibitions but some went further:

> . . . the moral aspect of the law does not normally concern the police. Most of us would define a bad law as one as one which is unenforceable or which infringes personal liberty. A law which falls into both of these categories has little to commend it. (Gordon Payne, *Police Review*, 28 February 1992)

Changes in the law would not only improve police public relations, which were felt to be at risk because of drugs policing, but would also reduce the public dangers associated with drugs:

> . . . by decriminalising cannabis you would remove one of the great barriers between the police and young people and at the same time remove young people from the dangers that are implicit in having to go to dealers who want them to spend more money. (*Police Review*, 6 March 1992)

The use of cautioning for first-time drug offenders found in possession of small amounts of cannabis has increased dramatically over the past decade. In 1985 just 13 per cent of drug offenders received a caution ; by 1995 over 50 per cent of drug offenders were disposed of with a caution. In recent years many police forces have adopted a policy of cautioning first-time offenders in possession of small amounts of cannabis and other drugs.[4] Michael Howard's recommendations for tougher laws in relation to cannabis received criticism from a range of official sources beyond the police. The Liberal Democrats (the only major political party to develop a liberal drugs policy) claimed:

> the Home Office's own research shows that increased punishments are not an effective means of reducing crime . . . the police, however effective, cannot be relied upon to contain a problem of this scale by themselves. The result of Michael Howard's policy will be wasted money and wasted time. He should abandon his proposals and look again at what his own research is telling him. (Press Release, 25 February 1994)

Mike Gordon, director of Release suggested that no single British authority on drugs or law enforcement supported the notion that increasing penalties was a sensible means of dealing with the problem of growing drugs misuse (*The Guardian*, 15 February 1994). The vehemence with which the police attacked the government's proposals was considerable and clearly influenced by the attempts to undermine police organization and authority at the time. Police Federation spokesman, Mike Bennet declared the proposals 'absurd', claiming 'It would not make the problem go away, but would lead to more people going to prison because they could not pay their fines' (*The Guardian*, 14 May 1994). The government's actions were all the more counterproductive in light of the very different approach being adopted by the Scottish Office. They were also drafting new proposals on the cannabis issue but unlike the home secretary had decided to accept the advice offered by the experts. They were to introduce a system of fixed penalty fines of £25 for cases of simple cannabis possession. Offenders would be sent so called 'conditional offers' giving them the chance to avoid a court appearance and a potential criminal record by paying the simple £25 'fiscal fine' (*The Scotsman*, 8 February 1994). In this way criminal justice resources would be conserved and a large section of the population would remain uncriminalised.

The police revolt against Michael Howard's proposals was given legitimacy by the intervention of Keith Hellawell, chief constable for West Yorkshire (later to be appointed by the Labour government as its National Drugs Co-ordinator) who openly condemned the home secretary's recommendation and called for a wider debate on the cannabis issue. He argued that a lack of honesty about the more pleasurable effects of drugs had not only contributed to the overall ignorance of the general public about drugs but had itself contributed to the drug problem.

> The current policies are not working. We seize more drugs, we arrest more people, but when you look at the availability of drugs, the use of drugs, the crime committed because of and through people who use drugs, the

violence associated with drugs, its on the increase. It can't be working. (*The Guardian*, 23 May 1994)

The decriminalisation debate took centre stage for the police in June 1994 at ACPO's national drugs conference held in Wakefield, West Yorkshire. Here leading police figures spoke in favour of a relaxation of the laws relating to cannabis. Lord Mancroft presented the most forceful argument for legalisation in his controversial speech to the conference:

> . . . because the importation and supplying of drugs is illegal a huge black market has been created . . . like all black markets it is inextricably linked with crime. And because it is a black market the price is forced up to artificial heights . . . to buy drugs the consumer must pay more than he can afford . . . many of those who take drugs are obliged to resort to crime in order to pay the prices that the black market demands . . . by prohibiting drugs we have inadvertently, and unforeseeably, created the motivation behind a whole new area of crime. (1994)

Lord Mancroft's main argument centred around the evidence which suggests that drug prohibition has led to problems far greater than drug misuse and he proffered a solution which combined legalisation with government controlled sales outlets.

Michael Howard's contribution to the conference was characteristically uninformed. Ignoring the evidence and the mood of police dissatisfaction, Howard carefully ignored the central concerns raised at the conference:

> This government has no intention of legalising any currently banned drug. To do so would be bound to increase the human and social damage, especially that inflicted on the young. Drugs are harmful. They destroy people; they destroy families; they destroy the very fabric on which our society rests. (Home Office Press Release, 9 June 1994)

For political reasons, it seems, police dissatisfaction with the 'unworkable' drug laws quickly dissipated and the moment of potential change faded. The practice of cautioning to deal with offenders in possession of cannabis was now to be largely abandoned and the issue of new policy discussions to be dropped (*Police Review*, 17 June 1994). According to *Druglink* the *volte face* was a result of political pressure placed on senior officers to prevent them embarrassing the government. Junior officers were being told by senior ranks that the legalisation issue was now 'out of bounds' (July/August 1994:4). And so it has remained.

This liberalisation of police attitude was confined only to the operational sphere of cannabis use and is included here because it illustrates the level of political investment in drug prohibition even at the softest end of the offence scale.

DRUGS, POLICE AND CORRUPTION

The police play a very small role in the investigation and detection of our central interest, drug importers but play the central enforcement role against the generic category drug traffickers (which since 1995 has expanded to include the production of cannabis).

No discussion of drugs enforcement can ignore the issue of corruption. Corruption is endemic to the criminalisation of drugs—the cocktail of drugs illegality, the massive profits which this illegality ensures on the black market, police discretion and operational tactics combine to make police corruption a virtual inevitability in the drug market-place. (See also Kleiman 1989:30)

The policing of controlled drugs relies heavily on the use of informants. Dorn and South describe informants as '. . . very much the "bread and butter" of drug policing', with informant leads central to a number of drug operations (1992:135). Farrell illustrates how the use of informants not only encourages police corruption but also reinforces the very existence of the drugs trade:

> Sometimes the police just pay informers to carry on trading, occasionally setting up a deal which will give the police a 'result'. The informers themselves may have been caught dealing. They may be bribed with the possibility of a letter to the judge stressing their cooperation and a promise of a short sentence or bail. The young dealer may be threatened with being stitched up if cooperation is refused. The effect is straightforward. There is no reduction of the trade. Some dealers operate with a police licence and others are arrested, but the trade continues. (Farrell 1992:41)

The use of informants by police lends itself to fostering corrupt practices. As Cox *et al* relate:

> . . . A system had to be created whereby certain dealers were in effect licensed by the drug squad to deal without much fear of prosecution. In return for providing a number of their customers as "bodies" for the police, these favoured dealers could set up deals specially for the Drug Squad . . . The Home Office, once they discovered what was happening had a name for this technique. They called it re-cycling. (Cox *et al*, 1977:86-87)

Nevertheless both government and chief constables are seduced by the apparent impact that informants have on police clear-up rates and a privatised scheme of criminal rewards under which businesses provide

£1 million per year to pay informants who supply information to police about drugs was launched by Margaret Thatcher and the then home secretary, David Waddington in 1990. The scheme, known as Drug Command, was met with 'delight' by the Association of Chief Police Officers but with scepticism by David Turner, the director of the Standing Conference on Drug Abuse, who saw it primarily as an incentive to further corrupt police practices (*The Guardian*, 15 February 1990).

Yet according to research conducted by Dunnighan and Norris (1995) the 'success' and 'value for money' in using police informants has been exaggerated. The authors argue '. . . that not only does the practice of running informers often involve corner-cutting and breach of rules, but it also involves what many may view as ethical misconduct'. The research revealed a 'routine' failure by officers to tell the Crown Prosecution Service about the use of informers in cases which led to a prosecution—thereby hiding potentially tarnished information and miscarriages of justice.

Yet it is difficult to accurately assess the nature and scale of police corruption. The Police Complaints Authority which investigates *inter alia* alleged complaints of police corruption are prevented by law from releasing the details of their enquiries. Neither do they break down their annual statistics according to the nature of the complaint. It is thus impossible to determine how many complaints of drug related police corruption are lodged each year, how many of those complaints the authority found to be substantiated and what, if any, sanctions were recommended and applied to corrupt officers. The secrecy surrounding the investigation of police corruption ensures a climate in which corruption can continue publicly unchallenged. The case of Stoke Newington Police Force is illustrative. In 1992 Scotland Yard's Central Investigation Branch launched Operation Jackpot, one of Britain's largest ever police corruption probes. The investigation centred on North London's Stoke Newington police station. Long before the revelations of the 1990s broke in the national press, Stoke Newington police station had acquired a disturbing record of violence and misconduct. During the 1970s and 1980s the deaths of Asetta Sims, Michael Fereira, Colin Roach and Shiji Lapite, all in contested circumstances inside the station, marked local policing as dangerous and frightening particularly for the black population of this Hackney community. Michael Keith documents an internal Stoke Newington police report which declared 'Unfortunately Stoke Newington has a notoriety relating to incidents occurring within the station. Despite great efforts it has been difficult to allay the misguided fears of certain sections of the community' (1993:34). In 1983 Hackney Community

142

Action (a federation of 180 local organizations) initiated a 'break links' campaign urging the Hackney community to sever all official links with the local police until major reforms had been instituted. The strained relations between police and community provide the backdrop to the drugs corruption within the force which was exposed in the early 1990s. Combined with Hackney's economic decline to the status of poorest borough in London (Harrison 1983) the ground was ripe for widescale police corruption. By the early 1990s, according to one media report, 'Stoke Newington was gaining a reputation far and wide as a "bent nick"' (*Time Out*, 2 February 1994). Much of the corruption was alleged to be taking place in its drug squad. Allegations from the Hackney community of drug 'plants', fit-ups and police drug dealing abounded in the local press and 46 of its officers were eventually investigated during the three year Operation Jackpot. The central allegation investigated during Operation Jackpot was that an officer was receiving £1,000 per month from a woman who dealt in crack cocaine on his behalf. The same officer and others were also alleged to have planted drugs on suspects. In all, 22 complainants made 134 separate allegations naming 46 Stoke Newington police officers. Apart from the allegations of drugs dealing, there were 65 allegations of the planting of drugs and other evidence, 27 allegations of conspiracy to pervert the course of justice, 27 of theft and nine of assault. According to the Police Complaints Authority there were eleven specific allegations each against two officers, a further ten against another two, and eight against another officer. Another 18 officers faced between two and six allegations each while the remaining 22 officers faced one allegation each (*The Independent*, 1994:24). During the lengthy course of the inquiry eight officers were moved from Stoke Newington to other police stations and three were suspended. Of 90 cases where allegations against the police were made between December 1988 and November 1992, there were 12 successful appeals against conviction because of doubts raised about the reliability of evidence given by officers under investigation with a further 16 to be heard. (*The Independent*, 1994; *The Guardian*, July 1994). While journalists reported that the officer in charge of the inquiry, Detective Superintendent Russell was to recommend charges against ten of the officers involved in the corrupt practices in Hackney, the Crown Prosecution Service proceeded with only two. The charges, for alleged conspiracy to pervert the course of justice and perjury, related to only one of the hundreds of complaints made against Stoke Newington officers, the trial of Paul Noel for possession of cannabis resin with intent to supply. According to the press release issued by the Crown Prosecution service in July 1994, 'After careful consideration, and with the advice of Treasury Counsel, the CPS has

143

decided that there is insufficient evidence to support a realistic prospect of convicting any other officer for any criminal offence as a result of the investigation known as Operation Jackpot' (CPS, 1994). The Hackney Defence Association which dealt with 381 complaints against police officers from Hackney and Stoke Newington police stations and, by 1994, was supporting 83 civil actions against the Metropolitan police officers, called for a judicial inquiry. According to Graham Smith, secretary of the HDA,

> The inquiry seems to have had no effect on policing in Stoke Newington. We took 57 new complaints against the police last year. At the centre of this whole business is the drugs trade. They have not been policing it: they have been controlling the drugs market. (*The Guardian*, February 1994).

Given the lack of prosecutions and disciplinary action against corrupt officers in the case of Stoke Newington police station, police drugs corruption is unlikely to be curtailed by the findings of the Police Complaints Authority and the subsequent actions of the Crown Prosecution Service.

In October 1995 evidence began to emerge of further police malpractice in relation to drugs control in London. The extraordinary case of Eaton Green,[5] a Jamaican 'Yardie' turned Scotland Yard informant highlights the inherently fine line between police control of illegal drugs and police corruption. Green, on the run from a Jamaican murder charge, was first arrested in Britain in 1991 for a minor traffic offence. This initial contact with the Metropolitan Police was to result in his acting as an informant for Scotland Yard's intelligence specialists SO11. As Nick Davies reported for *The Guardian*, Green was

> not some casual squealer who occasionally traded his way out of trouble, but a full-time registered intelligence asset with his own code name, a top secret file, two specialist handlers and a two year history of supplying high-grade intelligence on the Yardies to the Metropolitan Police, the Home Office, Customs and Excise, the Jamaican government and the New York District Attorney (6 November 1995).

All the while however, Eaton Green sold crack cocaine in Brixton and Dalston, carried a gun which he frequently fired, was involved in armed robberies and imported his Yardie associates from Jamaica with the full knowledge and apparent tacit approval of Scotland Yard. Davies continued his investigative report, 'Green committed crimes; officers allowed him to get away with it. Green imported his associates; officers decided not to stop him'. When Nottinghamshire police arrested Green in 1994 for his involvement in a violent armed robbery, Scotland Yard

144

attempted to have the trial aborted and their source protected. Further it was discovered during the course of the trial that the first 86 intelligence reports filed by Green to Scotland Yard had been destroyed leaving less than half on file. It also emerged that two intelligence reports Green had filed on the Nottinghamshire robbery had been withheld by Scotland Yard from the investigating Nottinghamshire force.

The scale of drugs-related corruption is considerable and as David Downes has noted:

> The bottom line is . . . that drugs contaminate policing: by intensifying internal police conflicts, e.g. between specialised squads and beat police with local knowledge; by financing corrupter — corruptee relationships which surface on occasion as scandals that damage the police more generally; by seeming to legitimise questionable police tactics and strategies in the face of an elusive 'victimless' crime, and so on.' (Downes 1988:158) [6]

DRUGS AND THE POLICING OF BLACK PEOPLE

The policing of Britain's inner cities, certainly from the 1970s onwards has frequently been conducted at the interstices of drugs and race bigotry (Institute of Race Relations 1987; Solomos 1988; Keith 1993). In 1981 the inner city disturbances across the UK were not infrequently precipitated by the 'swamp' policing of largely black communities on the pretext of clearing an area of drug dealers (Institute of Race Relations 1987). In 1985 the riot on Tottenham's Broadwater Farm Estate was again in large part a response to intensive raids by the Metropolitan Police to weed out drug dealers (Rose 1992:51).

At the end of the 1980s, as we saw earlier, a new panic entered the media lexicon—crack cocaine—and with it an imported association between drugs and race. In April 1989, United States drug enforcement agents issued dire warnings to a receptive British government presaging a crack epidemic which would sweep the inner cities. The warnings were used to resource a national task force of police and customs officers, a task force which as we have already seen was to have only a limited life-span.

Dorn and South observe that drug trafficking in the UK was a predominantly white enterprise until the mid 1980s when 'race emerged as a recurrent motif in the debate on trafficking' (1992:44). Yet black communities living in the inner city areas of Britain's major cities had long experienced a form of differential drug-related policing (e.g. Notting Hill Gate during the 1970s; Brixton; Moss Side; Toxteth in the early 1980s; Tottenham's Broadwater Farm Estate and Hackney in the mid-1980s). With the advent of the late 1980s and the increasingly interventionist role of the United States DEA in British drugs policy some of the hyperbole associated with race and drugs acquired an imported flavour. The 'Yardies' provided the perfect medium for the intersection of a range of manufactured anxieties. *The Times* in February 1988 exemplified the media's response to the fears fostered by the police and American DEA officials with customary lack of evidence: 'Yardies, the criminal gangs which originated in Jamaica, could establish no-go areas in British cities as a cover for their increasing cocaine trafficking, a police assessment says' (8 February 1988). In 1991 Croydon police embarked on 'Operation Dalehouse', a 15 month inquiry into crack-related shootings and murders. The operation involved a team of 30 officers operating out of Thornton Heath police station. It was alleged that many were committed by Jamaican 'Yardies' who had entered Britain on false passports—260 arrests were made, 25 for murder and conspiracy to murder, 30 firearms seized and crack worth almost one million pounds confiscated. The majority of arrests were the result of a police policy of disruption, that is, disruption of an alleged drug/criminal network by widescale arrests peripheral to the major crimes targeted. This policy of widescale arrest and charge is designed simply to disrupt the central criminal activities of the group involved. Thus the offence list resulting from the Operation Dalehouse was dominated by relatively minor offences like car theft, cannabis possession, conspiracy to defraud, deception and handling charges.[7]

The Observer reported that 'The police and government strategy is in disarray, as evidence that the use of crack cocaine has become a national epidemic, responsible for a wave of violent crime . . .' (15 November 1992). Later in the same article the newspaper reported that 'The introduction to a Home Office study, *Crack and Cocaine in England and Wales*, published last week, claimed that there was "no evidence" that crack had reached "anything like epidemic proportions"'. This evidence, however, was not sufficient for reporters to change the alarmist tone of the piece.

Crack dominated the drugs news for some time in the late 1980s and early 1990s. The media accounts were contradictory. *The Observer* claimed in late 1992 that 'Across the country, black communities have been especially hard hit, bringing suggestions that racism lies behind the official disregard' (15 November 1992). Jason Bennetto, however, writing in 1991 for *The Independent on Sunday*, used research conducted in the London Borough of Lambeth to illustrate that policing strategies, and not a lack of concern about users and their communities, were informed by racial discrimination. According to the Lewisham study, conducted by researchers at Goldsmith's College, 95 per cent of people arrested for possessing crack cocaine were black despite the finding that the majority of crack users (55 per cent) in the south London borough were in fact white. The 1991 report noted that 'The most striking divergence between the police and other agencies is that, whereas 85 per cent of crack users seen by other agencies are white, 95 per cent of crack users arrested by the police are black'.[8] The Lewisham research provides yet more evidence of a policing strategy based on racially informed stereotypes of drug use and criminality. Racism, of course, is not simply a feature of domestic drug enforcement. At the level of border controls the issue of targeting couriers is intimately bound up in racial and cultural stereotypes. The predominance of black foreign national drug couriers incarcerated in British jails (described in other chapters) is testimony to an enforcement policy underpinned by an ethnically structured targeting strategy.

'Operation Academic' involved the smuggling of millions of pounds worth of cocaine into Britain. Four trials, five convictions and ten year sentences handed down to the three 'organizers' and six year sentences to the two Colombian couriers made for great copy. Hailed as a great coup for customs, with the smashing of an international drugs gang, it was widely touted as evidence of the success of British drug control strategies. But it also involved a very grave miscarriage of justice. Each of the three convicted 'organizers' was entirely innocent. Following two and half years in prison the Court of Appeal released one of the men and ordered a retrial for the other two. By the end of January 1995 they were all free men. This case is revealing on a number of grounds. The men convicted were all foreign nationals, a Colombian, a Greek-Zambian and a Trinidadian, the evidence against them was essentially circumstantial and customs gained more mileage than it lost as a result of the hype surrounding the original arrests. As Duncan Campbell reported:

> It would be possible to put the whole case down as an understandable if unfortunate error by Customs and Excise officers anxious to clamp down on the smuggling of a drug that could end up as "crack" on the streets of our inner cities. But it is part of something much deeper and more insidious. The men were described as a major international gang, the case received prominence as evidence of a victory won in the "war" on drugs. Preconceptions about Colombians and black people's involvement in drugs were reinforced. Operation Academic has to be seen in a wider context. (*The Guardian*, 2 February 1995)

In the 1990s 'illegal immigration' and asylum seeking have become important mediums through which the race-drug link is cemented in the official discourse. As noted earlier, in the context of European

Union and the array of treaties, agreements and conventions concerned with EU security, drug control has become indelibly linked with immigration control. Drug trafficking is the province of foreigners and in simple terms the security of Europe's external borders is threatened by both.

THE DRUG SEIZERS: HM CUSTOMS AND EXCISE

The linguistic association between customs and 'seizures' is now axiomatic. The role of customs is to *seize* drugs. There is something in the ideology surrounding illegal drugs which requires them (regardless of the quantity) to be *seized*. Other terms are inadequate in relaying the dramatic nature of drug detection and confiscation.

The three year strategy laid down in the Conservative government's 1995 White Paper for custom's drug enforcement is oriented around three tasks: the dismantling of major drug trafficking organizations; the detection and seizure of the financial assets of drug traffickers; and increasing the value of drugs prevented from entering the UK (1995:14).

During the 1990s the powers afforded to HM Customs and Excise for drug enforcement work were expanded by both the courts and by government. In 1990 the Court of Appeal ruled that customs officers had the power to seize airliners if they were known to be carrying illegal drugs. Three judges allowed the appeal by customs against a High Court decision that officers at Heathrow had acted unlawfully in 1987 by seizing an Air Canada aircraft following the discovery of cannabis on board (*Police Review*, 22 June 1990). And in 1991 Customs and Excise were given access to advance information on the movements and cargoes of international carriers under the Customs Transport Cooperation Initiative. UK customs officials have agreements with six major transport bodies including the Road Haulage Association and the General Council of British Shipping. Computerised records and travel routes are now available to customs officials. While Gillian Shephard, the then Treasury minister with responsibility for customs, argued that 'Such cooperation is crucial in helping to provide customs authorities with the information they need to target their checks more selectively' (*The Guardian*, 18 June 1991), the reality of customs targeting has been defined by an overarching operational emphasis on one drug, cannabis, and on the lowest level 'trafficker', the individual drug courier originating from the Third World. Of the total 7,949 seizures made by customs in 1996, 84 per cent (6,661 seizures) were for cannabis. Of the 79,923.074 kilogrammes of illegal drugs seized by customs in 1996

148

(excluding the 118,354 doses of LSD), a total of 76,689.4 kilogrammes (96 per cent) were of the class B drug cannabis.[9]

As Mike Goodman, director of Release argued in 1994:

> It is quite ridiculous for us to be wasting millions of pounds on drug enforcement measures most of which are directed against cannabis users and all of which are having little or no impact on either supply or demand. We should redirect our resources to local and national drug services who are targeting their work on the problematic users and who are desperately in need of more support. (Release 1994)

It is also important, from the perspective of criminal justice, to identify the nature of the average drug seizure. Apart from a few widely publicised exceptions, the majority of seizures of controlled drugs by HM Customs and Excise are for relatively small amounts. In 1994 customs made 399 cocaine seizures. Of these 26 were under one gram; 223 were between one gram and under 500 gram; 46 were over 500 grams and under one kilo; 78 over one and under 10 kilos. There were only seven seizures over 10 kilos; and three were over 100 kilos. A similar pattern emerges with heroin seizures. In 1994, customs made 148 heroin seizures. Nineteen were for amounts under one gram; 76 for amounts over one gram and under 500 grams; 10 for amounts over 500 gram and under one kilo; 33 for amounts over one kilo and under 10 kilos; and only seven heroin seizures over 10 kilos, and one seizure over 100kgs. [10]

By the 1990s the war on drugs had become the priority of Customs and Excise but it is difficult to determine with any precision how this prioritisation has been translated into operational terms. The Customs Directorate is a particularly secretive organization and reveals nothing which it considers bears on its *operational* work.[11]

In the early 1990s Customs and Excise had reviewed its policy in relation to 'frontier' work—its new strategy was now firmly to be 'based on protecting society against the threat of drugs and other prohibited items rather than worrying unduly about petty excess quantities of cigarettes and spirits ' (*Drugs Brief*, 1992). Throughout the 1980s customs officers developed profiles of the most likely drug smugglers (Home Affairs Committee 1985). The precise nature of these profiles remains obscure but interviews with customs officers suggest that nationality plays a determining role. What is clear, however, is that individuals from particular destinations have become increasingly vulnerable to stop and search practices at ports and airports. West Africans in particular are highlighted in custom's 1995-96 annual report as presenting a continuing problem. Courier 'profiles' are very important in determining the practices of customs officers at ports of entry. As the

Drugs Brief states 'seizures made in the day-to-day work at ports and airports depend much more on local development of risk assessment systems, supplemented by officers' experience and initiative in choosing the right passengers and freight consignments to check . . . ' According to the brief, 87 per cent of all heroin seized in 1989 was the result of acting on 'profiles' or 'cold finds'; the same method yielded 33 per cent of all cocaine seized.[12] The 1990s also saw an increasing emphasis placed on intelligence and advance targeting and in particular the development of flexible anti-smuggling teams—FASTs, as the former Secretary of State for the Home Office outlined in a written answer to Parliament:

> On the domestic front Her Majesty's Customs and Excise is extending its use of memoranda of understanding with trade organizations in order to improve the flow of drugs information and to assist organizations to develop security arrangements. The Department is also entering into a new training programme in 1992 to assist flexible anti-smuggling teams — FASTs — to make use of advance intelligence and advance targeting of drugs suspects. The implementation of the review of anti-smuggling controls continues with setting up of FASTs and co-operation between regional collections and their opposites in Europe through joint memoranda is being developed. In addition, research and development for enhanced scientific and technical aids continues to take place. (*Hansard*, 13 February 1992, 1581, col. 587)

Drugs Brief also confirms the emphasis which customs place on stopping individual passengers rather than freight, although officials would not reveal operational details. The vast majority of class A drug seizures are made from individual passengers. In terms of air travel, in 1989 customs seized 152 kilos of heroin and 114 kilos of cocaine respectively from air passengers while seizing only four and seven kilos respectively from air freight. The individual, it seems, is set to remain the primary target of customs detection operations.

But Britain's war on drugs is not to be conducted on an unlimited budget. Public sector cuts in the mid 1990s resulted in significant job losses within Customs and Excise. In December 1994, the Treasury announced that 4,000 Customs and Excise jobs were to be cut (from 25,000 to 21,000). This cut involved the loss of up to 600 anti-smuggling officers leading the Paymaster General to warn Jonathan Aitken,[13] then Chief Secretary to the Treasury in charge of public spending that 'Cuts of this order will be difficult to present in the context of the government's anti-drugs strategy' (*The Guardian*, 1 December 1994). These cuts may, in fact, be a tacit recognition that ever expanding resources pumped into enforcement have not produced any diminution of the trade and can therefore be safely curtailed. This is particularly the case if the agency experiencing the cuts can justify them without disrupting the ideology underpinning the war on drugs. A senior customs official argued that the cuts would not undermine the effectiveness of the service:

> We will be placing a greater emphasis on high risk and complex work, giving less priority to routine activity where the risks are lower and the results have been less . . . more emphasis would be placed on large seizures rather than smaller catches and on intelligence networks rather than on routine surveillance where risks are low. (*The Guardian*, 1 December 1994)

A greater emphasis is to be placed on investigation and intelligence functions with the establishment within Customs and Excise of a National Intelligence Division and a National Investigation Service.[14]

John Major told the House of Commons in November 1994, 'Whatever happens to the budgets . . . I can assure you that the battle against drugs will not suffer' (*The Guardian*, 1 December 1994). And to some degree he was right. American economist, Peter Reuter provides convincing evidence to suggest that in the United States an emphasis on interdiction and seizures will never have much impact on availability and price: '. . . even far greater success at interdicting drug shipments would have little effect on street prices because the overwhelming percentage of the final street value is added after shipments enter [the country]'. (1995)[15]

In September 1996 a further 250 job losses were announced from the custom's front line suggesting that current strategies and seizure rates were to a considerable extent independent of the more remotely placed officers or at least that the price of their sacrifice would be a small one. It seems that so long as the war rhetoric remains full bodied—in the big picture at least—a diminution of the officers at the 'front-line' is tacitly recognised as inconsequential. This rationalisation of human resources within Customs and Excise is a clear example of the trend which Andrew Rutherford describes as the 'cult of managerialism'. 'In the criminal justice arena', he writes, 'the new cult of managerialism serves to reinforce pragmatic expediency'. (1996:134)

The 'cult of managerialism' finds expression in the objectives and tasks laid down for HM Customs and Excise in the 1994 Green Paper, *Tackling Drugs Together*. In this document each enforcement agency is required by government to adhere to the same basic principles underlying drug control while instituting agency-specific performance targets and indicators. Each agency is to build strategic priorities for tackling drugs into its own financial and management planning process —the HM Customs and Excise Management Plan. The three year plan, from 1995 until 1998, was set out for HM Customs and Excise as follows:

Year One: 1995-96

HM Customs and Excise will consider what immediate changes it might wish to make in the light of the national drugs strategy and report findings to the Paymaster General by the end of June 1995. In particular, HM Customs and Excise will consider the deployment of resources, the training needs of its staff and its intelligence and risk-assessment strategies.

HM Customs and Excise will review its drugs operations to ensure that there is continued cooperation with the police service involving regular liaison, sharing of intelligence and planning joint operations.

HM Customs and Excise will draw up and implement an action plan to increase public awareness of its role in drugs enforcement . . .

HM Customs and Excise will set annual targets for the value of drugs prevented from entering the UK. These will be reviewed each year and published in the Department's annual Management Plan. The projected figures for the period 1994-95 to 1996-97 are:

- 1994-95:   £1,164 million
- 1995-96:   £1,364 million
- 1996-97:   £1,523 million.

Year Two: 1996-97 and Year Three: 1997-98

HM Customs and Excise will review its drugs operations, annual targets and other contribution to the national drugs strategy and make any changes necessary. (Green Paper, 1994: 43-54)

Managerialism is thus, both an ideology and a pragmatic means of delivering economic rationalism into a politically sensitive arena. It provides the means by which cuts can be made while at the same time reinforcing the 'integrity' of the anti-drugs mission. So long as the 'vernacular of demonisation'[16] remains central to drug control discourse the economic impact of the new managerialism is unlikely to have any impact on the supply of illegal drugs entering the UK.

When measuring the effectiveness of current drug policies or when attempting to win support for increased enforcement resources drug seizures are always held up as a definitive indicator of the state of the battle against drugs. High annual seizures by Customs and Excise lead either to claims that enforcement is winning the war or that the volume of drugs being imported is such that only greater investment of resources will enable the forces of law and order to reduce supply. Although embraced by government law enforcement agencies and the mass media as a barometer of drug control success, it is, even in official circles, widely acknowledged to be a very inadequate measure as on best estimates only around ten per cent of drug imports are ever intercepted (Sutton and Maynard 1994; Stimson 1987:49-50). In fact, if we examine custom's interception rates for heroin from 1979 until 1990 we see that the official estimation of interception rates range from as low as 3.3 per cent in 1980 to a maximum of 10.3 in 1985, with a mean rate of 6.1 per year (Sutton and Maynard 1994:23). The power of the 'seizure' is ideological—it evokes images of violence and struggle—the seized drugs a visible manifestation of potential lives saved. Customs officers at the front line are border protectors and saviours. In real terms, however, it is a superficial exercise which impacts only marginally on the illicit drugs market and a measure which should be treated with great caution in assessing success or failure.

Former detective chief superintendent Eddie Ellison, who headed Scotland Yard's drug squad until 1992, outlined what he saw as the real impact of increasing 'managerialism' on customs operations in an interview for *The Guardian*. In relation to custom's claims to have broken some 214 drug gangs he argued:

> A gang is in the eye of the man who is writing the report. Everyone is subject to performance measures these days ... the government — and that's all the parties — have to fudge the data. Seizures go up and success is claimed. If they go down, then its an indicator of a reduction in the supply chain and again we claim success. However the data is produced — because we're not actually very successful in reducing the level of misuse of drugs — we have to keep claiming success. (*The Guardian* 2, February 1995)

THE POLITICS OF DRUG PUNISHMENT

Why prevent smuggling when you can punish it — isn't that what jails are for. (Robert Sabbag 1976)

Over 7,000 people were given jail sentences in the UK in 1995 and a total of 93,631 were criminalised for drug offences (i.e. found guilty, cautioned or dealt with by compounding). Of that total, the vast majority (76,694 men and women) were criminalised for an offence involving cannabis. And in 1995 those drugs cases dealt with at court rose by ten per cent to 53,000 (HOSB 1996:15). Cannabis continues to occupy the enforcement and punitive concerns of British criminal justice. Unlawful possession of any drug remains by far the most common drugs offence with almost 90 per cent of all drug offenders found guilty or cautioned for it—and as Home Office statistics make clear the vast proportion of these offenders were in possession of cannabis (HOSB 1996:17).

Home Office statistics reveal a steady rise in the number of drug offenders sentenced to immediate custody since 1984, although the proportional use of custody for drug offences declined from 14 per cent to seven per cent between 1985 and 1995. The statistics also chart a steady increase in the length of sentence handed down by the courts. Between 1984 and 1994 average sentence length for drug offences increased from 18.8 months to 24.8 months. [17]

On 1 January 1996 the Conservative government announced the imminent introduction of heavier sentences for persistent drug dealers. Among its initial proposals was an automatic ten year sentence for a second offence in drug dealing or trafficking (*The Guardian*, 1 January 1996). Drug traffickers, sex offenders, domestic burglars and persistently violent criminals were to be the targets of this new severity. The Crime (Sentences) Act 1997 is a modified version of the government's original attempts at a harsher new sentencing strategy. The new law 'require[s] the court to impose a custodial sentence of at least seven years on people, aged 18 or above, who are convicted of a class A drug trafficking offence who have two or more convictions for similar offences, unless there are exceptional circumstances which justify not doing so'. (1996) The inclusion of drug traffickers with violent and sex offenders (as well as domestic burglars) is justified in terms of *'protecting the public'*. According to the then home secretary,

> Serious offenders cause harm, misery and distress to tens of thousands of victims every year. It is the duty of the government to do all that they can to protect the public from such offenders . . . to do all that they can to ensure that offenders will be properly punished. Those who persistently offend should know with certainty that they will face a stiff penalty if they offend again. (1996:col 911)

THE SENTENCING OF DRUG IMPORTERS: A CASE-STUDY

The example of drug importing offenders demonstrates the true nature of the new law. Given the research evidence which indicates that the vast majority of convicted drug importers are first-time offenders and given that as drug importers they are already subject to a very harsh sentencing tariff the new sentencing laws can be said to have little to do with 'protecting the public'. The new laws, while increasing the punitive nature of British criminal policy were also primarily about political posturing and vote securing in an election year.

The judiciary had already responded to repeated calls from the home secretary, Michael Howard, for more punitive sentencing with 'record' terms. In March 1997 eight men were sentenced to a total of 126 years by the High Court in Edinburgh for their role in a £10 million cannabis smuggling operation with sentences of 28 years, 24 years, 14 years, 12 years and ten years. (*The Guardian*, 14 March 1997). In August 1996 three Turkish Kurds and a Czech coach driver were sentenced at Southwark Crown Court for terms of 30, 26, 24, and 20 years for the importation of 198.5 kilos of heroin. Six months earlier two crack dealers were jailed for 14 years at Southwark Crown Court and in December 1995 a coach firm director was sentenced to 18 years at Maidstone Crown Court for the importation of £5 million of Ecstasy and £600,000 of amphetamines. In 1995 George Sansom and Coleman Mulkerrins were jailed for 30 years after convictions for the importation of 795 kilos of cocaine and accusations that they had masterminded the financial and marketing arrangements of the smuggling operation. Echoing the sentiments underpinning the home secretary's proposals for the sentencing of drug importers the judge in the trial declared that 'The defendant must be told in no uncertain terms—the courts will show no mercy' (*The Guardian*, 20 August 1996). Sentences for drug trafficking in large quantities have now converged with sentences handed down to IRA terrorists.[18] These sentences should also be seen in the light of the more general and increasingly punitive trend in the sentencing of drug offenders illustrated below.

As noted earlier the number of people sentenced to immediate custody in the UK for drug offences has increased dramatically, from 1,368 in 1979, when the Conservatives took power, to 6,566 in 1995. Sentencing in the same period reflected an increasing severity with the number of imprisoned drug offenders sentenced to over five years increasing from three per cent to ten per cent. *Table 1* illustrates the increase in the use of custody for drug offences between 1986 and 1995, an increase particularly pronounced since 1992; while *Table 2* charts the changes in the use of custody, between 1986 and 1995, for the offences of possession, drug trafficking and drug importation.

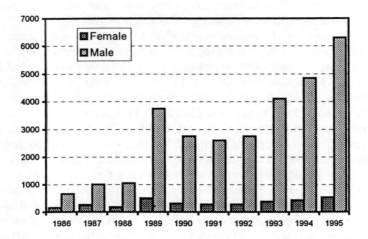

Table 1: Number of Drug Offenders Sentenced to Immediate Custody 1986-1995.
Source: Home Office unpublished statistics (1997)

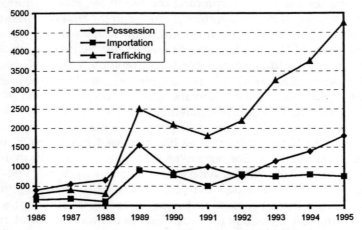

Table 2: UK Trends in the Use of Custody for Drug Offenders 1986-1995
Source: Home Office unpublished statistics (1997). Note: Drug Trafficking
includes unlawful import or export, unlawful production of drugs other
than cannabis (until 1995 then production of cannabis included), unlawful
supply and possession with intent to supply unlawfully.

In the ten years to the end of 1994 sentence lengths for drug offenders
also increased from 18.8 months to 24.8 months.[19] And it is drug
importers who have born the brunt of the new punitiveness—in 1979,
six per cent of drug importers were sentenced to terms of over five
years; by 1994 that figure had increased to 30 per cent and in 1995 it was

36 per cent.[20] The evidence presented in this study strongly suggests that the increased severity has been driven by the courts rather than by any changes in the nature of offending. The 1980s witnessed a series of increasingly repressive judicial and political measures related to the punishment of drug couriers, measures which in turn were reflected in the sentencing and imprisonment statistics of drug importers. In September 1982 Lord Lane in the leading case *Aramah*[21] established guidelines for the harsher sentencing of drug importers. He advised that for the importation of any amount of class A drug, a sentence should not be less than four years; for those trafficking in amounts to the value of £100,000 or more, the sentence should be seven years or more and for trafficking in amounts to the value of £1 million, sentences should fall between 12 and 14 years.

One year later in October 1983, the then home secretary, Leon Brittan, effectively increased the length of sentence served by severely restricting the right of parole for drug traffickers sentenced to more than five years. With the introduction of the Controlled Drugs (Penalties) Act 1985 the maximum penalty for trafficking in class A drugs was increased from 14 years to life. Life imprisonment was justified, it was argued by Lord Rodney, because it would '. . . reflect the revulsion society has for these parasites who trade in human misery'.[22] During the same debates Baroness Cox described traffickers as 'merchants of death' and '. . . despicable people who exploit and who profit handsomely from the misery of drug addiction'[23] and the Labour representative Robert Kilroy-Silk offered '. . . they are evil men and women who are making huge commercial profits out of the destruction of young lives'.[24]

In the second reading of the Crime (Sentences) Bill (now the Crime (Sentences) Act 1997) Richard Spring declared 'Drug trafficking is the greatest social evil of our generation' (Nov 1996:col. 991), while Toby Jessel demanded an amendment, 'so that seven years for a second offence of drug trafficking, as currently in the Bill—which is not enough because trafficking in drugs ruins so many lives—becomes a life sentence too' (Nov 1996: col. 992). Conservative MP for the Vale of Glamorgan, Walter Sweeney, declared:

> I am also delighted that traffickers in hard drugs will face a minimum of seven years' imprisonment. Drug barons who make vast profits out of human misery and loss of life should face the death penalty for a repeat conviction. The evil perpetrated by those people transcends in seriousness many offences of murder . . . '. (Nov 1996: col 971)

Lord Lane's views on the sentencing of drug couriers have been well documented (Green 1991,1996; Fortson 1996) but it is worth re-iterating them here. 'It is not difficult to understand', he declared in 1982, 'why in some parts of the world traffickers in heroin in any substantial quantity were sentenced to death and "executed"'. In light of the new maximum penalty of life imprisonment the sentencing guidelines were revised by Lord Lane in the case of *Bilinski* so that sentences suggested in *Aramah* of seven years and upwards where the value was £100,000, should be increased to ten years and upwards, and where the value of the smuggled drugs was in the region of £1 million then the tariff should rise to 14 years and upwards.[25]

Until 1994 the sentencing of class A drug importers was based on a tariff, determined by the estimated street value of the drugs imported. The centrality of street value in sentencing and its method of calculation raised serious problems which were systematically ignored by the courts. The first of those problems related to the uniquely nefarious status afforded to drug trafficking. What was it about this offence which required a distinct and pseudo-scientific sentencing tariff based on the purity and street value of the commodity involved? The second problem concerned the *mens rea* of the defendant. It would seem from the interview data that drug importers, in general, are completely ignorant about the purity and the wholesale/retail values of the drugs they import. These issues are irrelevant to their role as couriers. Why was it then that the courts used only this factor to determine the punishment of the courier? Why was it that ignorance on the part of the courier in respect of this central issue was explicitly ruled out as a mitigating factor by Lord Lane in *Aramah*? Couriers it seems were being held responsible for decisions, circumstances and issues outside their knowledge, experience and control. The final problem, of less theoretical significance but important for its impact on the sentencing process, was the crude, unreliable and unscientific estimation of street value and its uncritical acceptance in court.[26]

In June 1994 Lord Taylor, *Aranguren, Aroyewumi, Bioshogun, Littlefield and Gould*, significantly reinforced and strengthened the punitive sentencing strategy revised in *Bilinski*. The new case presented an opportunity for the courts to reassess the sentencing of drug couriers but rather than recognising the case for leniency Lord Taylor introduced revised sentencing yardsticks in which weight of drug rather than purity of drug became the central determinant of the sentencing tariff. If the street value of cocaine or heroin dropped because of plentiful supplies then, the court argued, sentences handed down would be lowered. To avoid the potential lowering of sentences the drug's estimated street value was abandoned in favour of its weight.

The new guidelines to be substituted for *Bilinski* in respect of class A drugs in powdered form were: 'Where the weight of the drugs at 100 per cent purity was of the order of 500 grams or more, sentences of ten years or upwards were appropriate. Where the weight at 100 per cent purity was of the order of five kilograms or more, sentences of 14 years and upwards were appropriate'. (*Aranguren and Others* (1994), 99 Cr. App. R. 347).

The court made its position on the morality of sentencing drug couriers clear by arguing that:

> Although making large profits from importing prohibited drugs was morally reprehensible, the main mischief to which the prohibitions were directed by Parliament was the widespread pushing of addictive drugs harmful to the community. It could not serve Parliament's purpose if the more drugs and therefore the lower the street price, the lower the level of sentencing.[27] (*Aranguren and Others*, supra)

With the class A drug Ecstasy which is sold in tablet rather than powdered form a similar approach is adopted. In *Warren and Beeley* the Court of Appeal decided that on the evidence that an average tablet of Ecstasy contains 100 mg. of the drug then 5,000 tablets would attract a sentence of ten years or more, and 50,000 tablets a sentence of 14 years or more (Fortson 1996:93).[28]

Sentencing guidelines for the importation of cannabis have always been determined by weight rather than street value. Amounts of herbal cannabis (or the equivalents in cannabis oil or resin) up to 20 kilograms lead to sentences of between 18 months and three years imprisonment; quantities over 20 kilograms will attract sentences of between three and six years while larger importations may result in sentences of around ten years. (*Aramah*). The reality is that large scale cannabis importation has drawn sentences in excess of 25 years (see the cases described above).

The most recent cases of drug trafficking illustrate that reform in the punishment of drug couriers will not, in the current climate, be initiated by the courts. The courts have responded to wider political and ideological pressures which have been exerted both nationally and more significantly, internationally. As Fortson has commented,

> . . . it would be idle to pretend that international pressure does not influence sentencing considerations where couriers are concerned . . . sentencing policy is linked with a series of conventions, treaties and agreements concerning both the creation of offences, and penalties, for drug offences, including simple possession. (1996:80)

Sentencing: the empirical evidence

Drug trafficking accounts for 72.04 per cent of all immediate custodial sentences handed down for drug offences. Drug importers constitute around 35 per cent of traffickers who receive sentences of immediate imprisonment.

According to the Home Office, 60 per cent of all illegal drug importers/exporters sentenced in 1994 received sentences of over two years and the average length of sentence was 50.7 months. This compares with an average sentence of 32.3 months for drug trafficking offences. The proportion of drug importers sentenced to terms of imprisonment of seven years or more is 16.1 per cent with only 13.7 per cent of those receiving a custodial sentence being sentenced to less than one year.[29] Drug importers fall, therefore, at the harsher end of the punishment spectrum.

The convicted drug importers represented in my larger study sample received average prison sentences of six years and four months. Seventy-five per cent of the couriers in that sample received sentences of over 4.5 years; only 7.7 per cent were sentenced to terms of imprisonment of under two years. Statistics do not reveal the class or street value of the drugs. In Abernethy and Hammond's smaller study of 149 individuals charged with drug importation offences at Isleworth Crown Court, 82 per cent were sentenced to immediate custody of whom 75 per cent were sentenced to prison terms in excess of four years. Because of the qualitative nature of their study they were able to determine that where cannabis importation was charged the average length of sentence was 23 months; for the importation of heroin the average sentence was five years and three months (average street value between £10-30,000) and for cocaine importation the average sentence was six years five months (average street value £70-100,000) (1992:44).

In my sample, British couriers received average sentences of six years, Nigerians 5.7 years, Jamaican/West Indians 6.1 years and Colombians 8.4 years. But the evidence from this study and from others[30] is that sentencing has little to do with nationality independent of the imported drug's street value. The case of 23 year old Sara Westwood is a useful illustration. White, upper middle class and convent educated, Sara acted as a courier for a cocaine smuggling operation and was jailed for 11 years in February 1997 for the importation of 2 kilograms of cocaine of an estimated value of £400,000. (*The Guardian*, 22 February 1997)

It was evident from the interviews that many couriers, and certainly the majority of foreign nationals, had not expected terms of imprisonment at all. Few of the men and women interviewed in the sub-sample appreciated the draconian nature of British drug penalties or the very long sentences that awaited them. Some had been informed by drug suppliers that the worst that could happen would be that the drugs would be confiscated and they would be deported home on the next available flight.

Gender, drugs and sentencing
Drug offences account for a considerably higher proportion of female imprisonment than they do for male imprisonment in the UK. It is, therefore, worthwhile examining separately the trends in female drug offending and imprisonment rates. At the beginning of the 1980s the proportion of female drug offenders was around 12 per cent. It dropped to nine per cent in 1991 but has been climbing slowly throughout the 1990s. (HOSB 1995) The proportion of female drug importers sentenced to immediate custody has also remained reasonably constant over the last decade (at about 50 per cent) with significant peaks in 1987, 1989 and 1993. *Table 3* reveals that in the UK, with the exception of drug importation, female involvement in all drug offences, including drug trafficking, has increased significantly over the past ten years.

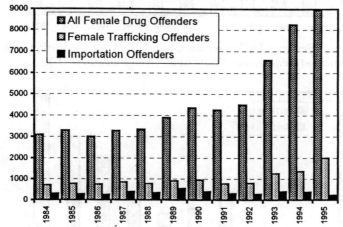

Table 3: UK Female Drug Offenders Found Guilty Cautioned or Dealt With by Compounding 1984-1985
Source: Extracted from Table S2.3, Home Office 1995. For the definition of 'drug trafficking', see the note to *Table 1.*

Why the number of female drug importers dropped so dramatically in 1995 is unclear but it is interesting to observe that female involvement in the offence has not followed the same pattern as female involvement in other offences within the category of drug trafficking. It is possible that the widespread media coverage given to couriers and particularly to female couriers has had some deterrent effect. Equally the drop may be the result of a temporary 'damage limitation' excercise by those employing the services of couriers.

The following *Tables 4, 5* and *6* illustrate the proportional use of custody for male and female drug offenders for the offence categories: possession, trafficking and importation. Importation offences are included in the larger category of trafficking.

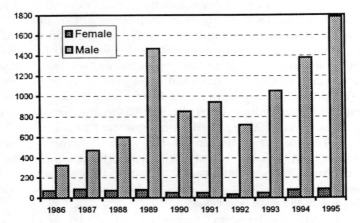

Table 4: Number Sentenced to Immediate Custody for Drug Possession 1986-1995
Source: Abstracted from Home Office unpublished statistics (1997).

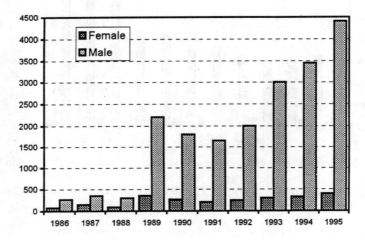

Table 5: Persons Sentenced to Immediate Custody for Drug Trafficking Offences 1986-1995
Source: Abstracted from Home Office unpublished statistics (1997). For the definition of 'drug trafficking', see the note to *Table 1.*

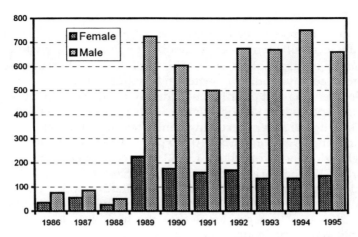

Table 6: Persons Sentenced to Immediate Custody for Offences of Illegal Drug
Importation 1986-1995
Source: Abstracted from Home Office unpublished statistics (1997)

The tables above reveal a number of very interesting trends as well as highlighting some important gender differentials. Most striking in the sentencing of both men and women is the increase in the use of custody for drug trafficking offences. Trafficking, as we have seen, expanded in definition from 1995, but this does not explain the rise in the use of custody for trafficking offences since the trend emerges much earlier, in the late 1980s. The proportion of drug traffickers (both male and female) sentenced to immediate custody has increased significantly since 1986. This is against a more general trend which shows a steady decline in the proportionate use of custody for drug offences over the same period.[31] Whilst the courts have reduced their proportional use of custodial disposals for minor offences, principally possession, they have reacted increasingly punitively toward trafficking offences (*Table 2*). The sentencing of drug importers reached its repressive peak in the years 1989-1992, and while this is true for both men and women it is reflected most strongly in the sentencing of women throughout this period, as *Table 5* illustrates. In 1992 drug importers represented 61 per cent of all female drug offenders sentenced to immediate custody. By 1995 that proportion had declined to 26 per cent, indicating a possible change in women's role/participation in drug trafficking but, equally likely, a harsher sentencing approach by the courts to the general category of drug trafficking offences. Since 1989 drug trafficking offences have accounted for around 70 per cent of female and 80 per cent of male drug-related custodial disposals.

In 1995, 510 women and 6,252 men, received sentences of immediate custody for drug offences. While 17.6 per cent of female offenders who received a custodial sentence were drug offenders only 12.5 per cent of men given sentences of immediate custody were convicted of drug offences.[32] The prohibition of drugs appears, therefore, to have a disproportionately significant impact on rates of female offending and punishment. This is even more pronounced when we look specifically at the offence of drug importation. Of the 510 female drug offenders receiving sentences of immediate custody in England and Wales in 1995, 410 (80 per cent) were convicted of drug trafficking offences, of whom 135 (33 per cent) were convicted drug importers. By comparison drug importers account for only 14.8 per cent of male drug traffickers sentenced to immediate custody. This evidence lends support to the thesis that women involved in drug trafficking tend to assume to a greater degree the high risk/low status roles exemplified by drug couriering.

In 1995 the average sentence length imposed on women (aged 21 and over) convicted of drug offences was 32 months. For female drug couriers the average sentence was much longer with 57.6 per cent serving sentences longer than two years and 27 per cent serving sentences in excess of five years. For male drug importers 66 per cent received sentences of over two years and 38 per cent sentences over five years.[33] Gender, in most instances of drug trafficking, appears to have relatively little impact on the sentencing practices of the courts although my own research supports the finding that women tend to be sentenced to periods slightly shorter than men of their own nationality. The sentencing of Nigerian women however contradicts this trend—they were punished more harshly than Nigerian men—on average receiving sentences ten months longer. This reversal of the general pattern might tentatively be explained by the courts' apparent impatience with those women who plead not guilty claiming that they have been duped into carrying drugs. Given the very small sample size it is impossible to generalise. However, six of the Nigerian women in the sub-sample were in this category; each of them received sentences over six years with two receiving sentences of ten and 12 years. The inclusion of these women in the Nigerian female sample may therefore contribute to a potentially inflated average sentence length. A more likely explanation, however, given that sentencing operates quite strictly according to the tariff, is that Nigerian women carried larger amounts of the drug they were involved in smuggling. Of the 28 Nigerians (14 men and 14 women) in the sample convicted of importing heroin this is certainly true. The average weight of drug men carried was 297 grams while the average weight of drug carried by women was 488 grams.

Where there's no room for mitigation

Unlike the court's treatment of most criminal offenders drug importers are offenders without personal backgrounds for the purpose of sentencing.

Potential mitigation of sentence has been a significant issue in highlighting the perceived injustices experienced by drug couriers, particularly foreign national drug importers. Social inquiry reports (SIRs)—which were replaced by pre-sentence reports (PSRs) with the implementation of the Criminal Justice Act 1991 in October 1992—were, at the time of the interviews conducted for this study, only prepared on defendants who were either British nationals or resident in Britain. Reports were not prepared on foreign nationals so that 72 per cent of the drug importers facing the very long sentences described above were denied the mitigation potential which might have arisen from an SIR or PSR. According to Fortson, 'the personal circumstances of the courier are unlikely to make a significant impact on sentence because deterrence, and not the reformation of the offender, is at the heart of the United Kingdom's sentencing strategy against drug-trafficking' (1996:79-80). In an experimental study of the impact of PSRs on foreign national drug offenders, Nick Hammond found that 'The value of PSRs if measured purely in terms of their impact on sentencing is marginal, given tariff sentencing'. (1994:3)

Between the implementation of the Criminal Justice Act 1991 in October 1992 and amendments contained in the Criminal Justice and Public Order Act 1994 (and implementation of the relevant provisions in February 1995) PSRs were required to be obtained and considered by the courts in most cases before imposing a custodial offence (except for offences which could only be tried on indictment). So for the first time PSRs were routinely prepared by probation services on foreign national drug offenders. Middlesex Probation Service, attuned to the injustices experienced by foreign national drug offenders, had introduced a pilot scheme in September 1991 to focus on pre-trial work with this hitherto neglected group. They continued their work after the introduction of the 1991 Act, under the auspices of the Foreign Nationals Unit working exclusively with foreign national drug importers arrested at Heathrow Airport. Their findings were important in that they highlighted the welfare benefits such reports could have while establishing their very limited value in influencing sentence length. According to the two case-workers running the unit,

The judges have indicated in comments during sentencing that they have found these reports of use and benefit. Defence barristers make reference to their contents when arguing for mitigation. Defendants now have the opportunity to have their own explanation and description of the offence, their background, and present personal circumstances available . . . Illegal importation of drugs inevitably results in a substantial custodial sentence. Nonetheless, the provision of pre-sentence reports is contributing towards greater understanding . . . of the background and motivation of drug smuggling. (Abernethy and Hammond 1996: 149-150)

The experiment was to be a brief one. In February 1995 the Criminal Justice and Public Order Act 1994 gave courts a discretion to dispense with a PSR when imposing sentence. Research conducted by Nick Hammond in 1994 to evaluate the likely impact of the change concluded:

As a group, foreign national offenders face exceptional difficulties within the criminal justice system. The value of PSRs, if measured purely in terms of their impact on sentencing, would possibly justify abandonment. However, criminal justice should not be "Treasury led". All defendants need to see and feel that justice has been done and the provision of the PSR made a contribution to this perception. (Hammond 1996:159)

The courts have generally ignored all potential mitigation excepting a plea of guilty in respect of this group of offenders. But even a plea of guilty may have little impact on final sentence.[34] Providing assistance to Customs and Excise may mitigate sentence but the evidence suggests that both forms of mitigation operate inconsistently. The fact that the courier may be able to provide drug enforcement officers with information relating to the chain of supply has impressed courts into including 'assistance' to customs and other investigating officers as a potential source of mitigation. But as Fortson suggests,

. . . it frequently happens that couriers are apprehended through surveillance techniques and intelligence reports, in circumstances where the line of supply is already established. In these cases, the courier is unlikely to be of much, or any, assistance to the authorities and the mere fact that a courier is *willing* to assist has far less clout as mitigation than valuable assistance actually given. (Fortson 1996:80)

A courier is more than likely to be a first-time offender, may be pregnant or accompanied by children, may be naive, or plainly impoverished, bewildered and remorseful. These factors, however, tend to operate negatively in drug trials. Ironically they harden and reinforce the severity of the judiciary in their war against this already exploited community. In the leading case *Aramah*, Lord Lane declared that,

The good character of the courier is of less importance than the good character of the defendant in other cases . . . the large scale operator looks for couriers of good character and for people of a sort which is likely to exercise the sympathy of the court if they are detected and arrested. Consequently one will frequently find students and sick and elderly people are used as couriers for two reasons: first of all they are vulnerable to suggestion and vulnerable to the offer of a quick profit, and secondly it is felt that the courts may be moved to misplace sympathy in their case. There are few, if any, occasions when anything other than an immediate custodial sentence is proper for this type of importation.[35]

Given the judicial support for Lord Lane's analysis, I have argued elsewhere (Green 1991) that PSRs are unlikely to be given serious consideration by a judge in the process of sentencing a courier. Recent research has revealed that judges are, however, willing to entertain considerable discounts of sentence but only in cases where the estimated street value was between £100,000 and one million pounds. For those importers of lesser amounts (the majority) there is virtually no flexibility extended and the four year minimum sentence for class A importation of 'any amount' is rigidly adhered to.[36] This is borne out in the case of *Imran,* cited below. Urbane and articulate, he felt his barrister made out an excellent case for mitigation on the basis that he came from a 'very respectable family'—references from Pakistan confirmed this and according to Imran 'really convinced the judge'. Both he and his barrister expected a ten year sentence. The rare occasions in which mitigation is accorded appear to be determined more by class than other sympathies. There are many cases in this study of Nigerian heroin importers pleading guilty to importing ten times less in quantity who are sentenced to between five and eight years. But class based mitigation operates inconsistently as evidenced by the case of the pregnant 23 year old, Sara Westwood cited above. In sentencing her to eleven years, Judge Oppenheimer told the defendant:

> You were a knowing courier of a comparatively large importation of a class A drug. You, like all your co-defendants, have taken part in a disgusting and terrible trade that all four of you knew before you committed the crime, causes destruction and death to other people . . . I have taken account in considering the sentence the circumstances in which your counsel says you were in at the time you were attracted into this trade. In particular I have considered your personal history, your background, the abusive relationships that you had before this offence was committed, and the depression you suffered.

Nonetheless it is difficult to imagine just how the judge accounted for Ms Westwood's personal circumstances at the point of sentence given its severity.

For most foreign national drug traffickers there is an added component of suffering in their punishment. They must serve their long prison sentences in relative isolation, in a country far from family and friends.

The vast majority of foreign national couriers will serve out their full sentence in Britain. While repatriation treaties exist between Britain and some countries (e.g. the USA and most European countries) there are no such treaties with the countries whose nationals make up the bulk of the imprisoned courier population (neither African, South American countries, Jamaica nor Pakistan share repatriation treaties with Britain).[37]

Confiscation: a double punishment

David Feldman has observed that the criminal law has been used 'increasingly rigorously against suppliers of drugs, in an attempt to make the trade unprofitable by confiscating the proceeds of trafficking'. (1991:26) The statistics on confiscation orders paid by convicted drug traffickers, however, suggest a different outcome from that of financially-induced deterrence.

With the introduction of the Drug Trafficking Offences Act 1986 (DTOA) confiscation powers were made available to courts. That Act was replaced by the Drug Trafficking Act 1994. The legislation specifies that the court leaves the confiscation order out of account when determining the appropriate sentence thus providing a new and additional punishment for those convicted of trafficking drugs. The Act reverses the traditional burden of proof so that the defendant must prove that any property in his or her possession at any time in the six years up until conviction was not the proceeds of drug trafficking. Any money or property received in connection with drug trafficking, and not simply profits or proceeds of the trade, is included in the court's assessment of the total value of trafficking assets. Existing powers of confiscation were substantially strengthened by the Criminal Justice Act 1993 which generalised confiscation proceedings to other crimes as well as drug trafficking offences.[38] Despite a small number of very large orders, confiscation orders are routinely applied against the bottom-end of drug trafficking defendants and there is no evidence to suggest that they have had any impact at all on the profits of large scale drug traffickers. Rather, as with the powerful and wealthy in other spheres of capitalist enterprise, major drug traffickers have few problems protecting and concealing their assets.

Contrary to the view expressed by the Audit Office, that 'Confiscation is not a form of punishment',[39] the Act provides heavy periods of additional imprisonment for failure to pay any amount exceeding £10,000. The legislation specifies that judges fix a further term of imprisonment to run consecutively if the defendant fails to satisfy the confiscation order. Under the DTOA 1986, serving a default sentence expunged the confiscation order. However, from February 1995 a confiscation order remains in force despite the serving of a default prison sentence. Since 1987 the number of confiscation orders applied by the courts has increased significantly, from 203 in 1987 to 1,562 in 1995. The emerging pattern, exemplified by the 1995 figures, is interesting. The vast majority of orders applied since 1987 are made for relatively insignificant sums. The 1995 figures on the 1,562 confiscation orders made by the Crown Court for that year reveal that 1,117 (71.5 per cent) were for amounts under £1,000, 224 (14.3 per cent) were for amounts between £1,000 and £3,000 and 120 (7.7 per cent) were for amounts between £3,000 and £10,000. Fifty six orders (3.6 per cent) were for amounts between £10,000 and £30,000 with only 25 (1.6 per cent) made for amounts in excess of £100,000 (Home Office 1996). While the total value of all confiscation orders made in 1995 exceeded £18 million the criminal statistics do not record the proportion of this amount actually recovered. If the original Hodgson Committee's proposals had been implemented less than two per cent of confiscation orders currently made would proceed, and prison sentences would be reduced rather than increased. Research conducted in Australia has demonstrated that drug enforcement agencies are largely incapable of distinguishing between minor and major drug offenders. (Green and Purnell 1996) The same inability is evident in the practices of British drug enforcement. The National Audit Office criticised the low levels of confiscation order proceeds in its 1996 report on the financial operation of H M Customs and Excise and urged the agency to place greater emphasis in identifying assets before applying for orders.[40] The confiscation figures and the findings of the National Audit Office reinforce our argument that it is those who are the lesser players and the most vulnerable within the drug trade who are routinely apprehended and castigated as traffickers. The consistency with which confiscation orders for relatively insignificant sums have been made against low level carriers of drugs undermines policy makers' stated intentions that confiscation orders are targeted at those who make immense profits from drug trafficking.

Those self-employed drug smugglers in the interview sample, who were in the position of organizing drug imports, each revealed that they were generally not subject to confiscation orders despite admitting to considerable wealth acquired as a result of trading in drugs. Each had taken precautions to ensure that their assets could not be traced to themselves. Despite capture, 'Toby', a British professional drug smuggler, 'still managed to keep the money' while 'Rex' the only self-employed drug smuggler in the sample to have had a confiscation order made against him (for the total sum of £160,000) had ensured that most of his assets were legally out of the court's reach.

Deportation: double double punishment

As with all matters 'criminal', policy concerns are not confined solely to the process of criminal justice. The global nature of the illegal drugs business and the internationalisation of its control have ensured that immigration policy has assumed a considerable role in the ideological and material control of drug trafficking (see *Chapter 2* for a fuller discussion on the relationship between drug and immigration control). The intervention of immigration law in respect of the punishment of drug importers has effectively increased the penalties for those classified as a 'foreign national'. As immigration lawyer, Alison Stanley has argued:

> . . . what is uncontestable is the fact that foreign nationals face a double punishment of expulsion from the UK at the end of their sentence. (Stanley 1996:113)

Section 3(6) Immigration Act 1971 specifies that a foreign national is liable for deportation if they do not meet certain strict citizenship criteria. And practice shows that foreign nationals will almost universally be recommended for deportation by the court if convicted of an imprisonable offence. European community citizens are subject to less stringent immigration controls and can only be deported on grounds of 'public policy, public health and public security'.[41] But as Alison Stanley has pointed out '. . . the international consensus surrounding the importers of controlled drugs places them squarely in the "public policy" exception and thus EC nationals can, and are, deported for all types of drug offences, other than simple possession'. (1996:114)

Data from the Immigration and Nationality Directorate show that between January 1994 and March 1997 there were 624 drug-related deportations.[42] This data unfortunately does not distinguish between types of drug offenders, nor are the statistics broken down in terms of nationality or gender.[43] It does, however, illustrate that for foreign national drug offenders and particularly foreign national drug importers, criminal justice sanctions are only part of the punishment. The status of the drugs offence, when committed by 'outsiders' in terms of public policy, appears to justify punishment above and beyond that which the criminal law lays down.

PROHIBITION AND THE CONSTRUCTION OF CRIME

Prohibition, by its very nature, produces 'criminals' and the criminalisation of drug users continues apace. There has been a dramatic rise in the number of people sentenced to immediate custody for drug offences over the past 15 years. Between 1979 and 1989 the number of people sentenced to immediate custody almost trebled, from 1,368 to 3,855. In 1992 the figure had dropped slightly to 3,400, but by 1995 it had risen to 7,086 (HOSB:1993,1996). The incidence of drug offences also rose dramatically throughout the 1980s and the 1990s. In 1982 a total of 20,356 people had been found guilty, cautioned or dealt with by compounding; by 1992 that figure had reached 48,927 (HOSB 1993). The 1992 figures were later revised by the Home Office, in order to reflect known under-recording, and published in the White Paper, *Tackling Drugs Together*. In the revised version, the 1992 figures soar to almost 62,000 and by 1995 the number of recorded drug offenders had reached 93,601. Drug control strategies have paralleled, if not contributed to, a continued rise in drug offending. Prohibitionist policies in the UK, as elsewhere, have contributed to a growing criminalisation of an increasingly significant section of the drug using population. British drugs control policy (compared with that employed in Australia) does not even pay lip service to prioritising drug enforcement against major drug offenders over minor drug offenders. Within the British enforcement lexicon the term *drug* appears simply to connote *major serious offence*. In fact by focusing on 'the safety of the community', as the former Conservative government's drugs strategy did, particularly in the context of the current political and criminal justice hostility to street crime, enforcement against low level street players was actively fostered. This will perhaps become even more evident given the Labour government's commitment to cracking down on 'disorder'.

ENDNOTES

[1] The 1997 National Drug Strategy (to cost $16 billion) has five goals – to educate American youth to say 'No' to drugs, alcohol and cigarettes; to reduce drug-related crime and violence; to reduce the health and social costs associated with drug use to 'shield America's air, land and sea frontiers from the drug threat' and to break 'foreign and domestic sources of supply'. National Drug Control Strategy, NCJ 163915, http://www.ncirs.org

[2] http://www.open.gov.uk.ncis

3 'Today Programme', BBC Radio 4, 28 August 1997

4 Home Office Statistical Bulletin: *Statistics of Drug Seizures and Offenders Dealt with in the United Kingdom*, 1995:15

5 Green was not the only 'exceptional' use of such an informant. Delroy Denton, convicted of the murder of a woman, was later to play a very similar role for the Metropolitan Police

6 Some examples of drug-related corruption in the UK include:

- In 1977, drug squad officers were found to have hijacked 1,200 lbs of cannabis (seized the previous year) on its way to confiscation, replacing it with another innoccuous substance. The haul was recorded as being destroyed and a number of drug squad officers then pressured market trader John Goss into selling the drugs. Goss was given an absolute discharge when the facts of the drug squad's involvement was accepted by Chelmsford Crown Court and eventually a detective chief inspector, a detective inspector and a detective constable were forced to resign following disciplinary hearings. A detective sergeant was imprisoned for his involvement (Morton 1993:160-161.

- Between 1982 and 1985 a group of Notting Hill police officers engaged in a series of corrupt practices under the auspices of 'Black Watch' — a vigilante group of racist police officers who harassed the local black population by physical intimidation, planting drugs, and false arrests and imprisonment (Keith 1986). In 1985, e.g., Vincent Lee was falsely arrested in Notting Hill and charged with possession of five bags of cannabis. Acquitted the following year, Lee was eventually awarded £3,500 in damages by the High Court for assault (police had hit him over the head with a truncheon), false imprisonment and malicious prosecution (police had originally planted the drugs on him).

- In February 1995 *The Guardian* reported the police practice of over estimating the street value of drugs seized for the purpose of securing convictions and lengthy sentences. Mathew Atha, an expert witness in drugs cases since 1991, with a background in drugs and chemical research, was giving evidence in a cannabis trial at Croydon Crown Court. Police had falsely claimed the value of the drugs to be £800,000 when in reality they were worth only £10,000. Because the police grossly overestimated the value of cannabis in this particular case the two defendants were denied bail as the value led the court to conclude that the drugs were produced for sale and not for personal use. Mathew Atha claimed that in every one of the 30 cases he had been involved in, the police estimate of the street value of the drugs had been too high (*The Guardian*, 4 February 1995). Overvaluations can lead to heavier prison sentences or long periods in jail on remand and it is not coincidental that the estimations of the police have always been overestimations.

- In October 1995, two Liverpool policewomen were jailed for 12 months after being convicted of possessing and supplying cannabis, amphetamines and Ecstasy (*The Times*, October 1995).

7 Personal communication: Detective Superintendent Brian Tompkins, South West Operational Command Unit, 1 October 1997

8 Pearson, G and Phillips S, *Drugs, People and Services In Lewisham*, Final Report of the Drug Information Project, Goldsmiths College: London, 1991

9 Similar figures are found in the Customs and Exise figures for 1995 where, of the 55650 kilogrammes of all illegal drugs seized, 52,516.5 kilogrammes (94%) were cannabis. (Customs and Excise Press Release, 1 May 1996)

10 Sources: Table S1.6 HO Statistics on the Misuse of Drugs—Supplementary Tables 1994

11 Personal Communication, J K Oxenford, Customs Directorate, March 1991

12 H M Customs and Excise, 1990 *Drugs Brief 1992: Frontier Checks and the Free Movement of People*

13 The since disgraced former Conservative Cabinet minister

14 HM Customs and Excise *Annual Report* 1995-96

15 Peter Reuter *et al*, Conference paper presented to the Annual Meeting of the American Society of Criminology, Boston, November 1995

16 Diana Gordon, 1994:184

17 Statistics of Drug Seizures and Offenders Dealt With, UK 1994

18 See for instance the case of Derek Doherty, convicted of conspiracy to cause explosions as part of the IRA's mainland campaign who was sentenced to 25 years imprisonment at the Old Bailey in 1993

19 Table 3.10, HO Statistical Bulletin, 1995

20 Tables S2.11; S2.6 H.O. Statistics of Drug Seizures and Offenders Dealt With, UK, 1994, Supplementary Tables:July 1996; and unpublished Home Office statistics produced on 8 May 1997

21 *Aramah*, (1982) 4 Cr. App. R. (S.) 407

22 *Hansard* [Lords], Committee Stage, Controlled Drugs (Penalties) Bill, 27 June 1985: 838

23 *Hansard*, ibid. (27 June 1985: 838)

24 ibid.

25 *Bilinski* (1988) 866. App R 146

26 See Kay, L '*Aramah* and the Street Value of Drugs', *Criminal Law Review*, 1987 p. 184 for a discussion of the determination of street value. Estimates are based on information gathered by the National Criminal Intelligence Service (NCIS) which in turn are based on local police intelligence and 'police buys' and on laboratory analyses of the purity of a particular drug consignment

27 *Aranguren, Aroyewumi, Bioshogun, Littlefield and Gould* (1994), 99 Cr. App. R. 347

28 See *Attorney-General's References Nos 3, 4 and 5 of 1992* (1993), 14 Cr. App. R. (S.) 191)

29 Tables S2.6, S2.11, *Statistics of Drug Seizures and Offenders Dealt With, UK 1996*

30 See especially Green, P, 1990 *Drug Couriers*, Howard League:London; Green, Mills and Read, 'The Characteristics and Sentencing of Illegal Drug Importers', *British Journal of Criminology*, Vol. 34, No. 4, Autumn 1994

31 Between 1984 and 1994 the proportion of all drug offenders found guilty, cautioned or dealt with by compounding, sentenced to immediate custody declined from 15% to 8% for males and 13% to 7% for females. Concomitantly the same period saw a dramatic increase in the use of the caution — from 10% in 1994 to 55% in 1994. (HOSB 1995, Supplementary tables S2.4 and S2.5)

32 Home Office, Unpublished statistics 1997; *Prison Statistics England and Wales 1995* Cm 3355, Government Statistical Services (prison receptions for women totalled 2,897 in 1995 while the equivalent figure for men was 49,875; according to Prison Department figures drug related receptions amounted to 7.8% for men and 12.3% for women)

33 Average comparisons cannot be made as the statistical information relating to average sentence length by gender and offence is unavailable. Home Office Supplementary Tables 1995; HO unpublished data 1997

34 See *Gary Royle and Stephen Pollitt* (1997), 1 Cr. App R. (S.) 184. In this case an appeal was lodged against sentence based on the appellants' arguments that their guilty pleas had not been taken into account. The first appellant had been sentenced to seven years and the second to 13 years (one year below the maximum). Lord Bingham in refusing the second appellant's appeal commented on the fact they were caught red-handed and therefore had little choice but to plead guilty and due to his 'key part' and the serious nature of the offence (the importation of £5.5 million of cannabis) the sentence was justified. With regard to the first appellant, the lesser role was accepted (he was merely a hired hand on the yacht purchased by Pollitt). The view of the trial judge, however, that 'the enterprise could not have been conducted without you. You played an essential

part and therefore the sentence that I impose must be a substantial one', was upheld.

35 *Aramah*, ibid
36 Green, P, Mills C and T Read, 'The Characteristics and Sentencing of Illegal Drug Importers', *British Journal of Criminology*, Vol. 34, No. 4 Autumn 1994
37 For further information on foreign national prisoners see Hedges J, and Tarzi, A, *A Study of Foreign Prisoners*, Inner London Probation Service, 1990; Abernethey, R, Hammond, N, *et al*, *Drug Couriers: A Role for the Probation Service*, Middlesex Probation Service, London, 1992
38 The drugs provisions of the Criminal Justice Act 1993, including the power to forfeit drug trafficking money imported into or exported from the UK, were consolidated in the Drug Trafficking Act 1994
39 Controller and Auditor General, *HM Customs and Excise: The Seizure of Drug Trafficker's Assets*, HC 668 Session 1995-96, 23 August 1996, National Audit Office
40 1996: paras 2.16, 2.17
41 According to Directive 63/360/EEC, article 10
42 The Immigration and Nationality Directorate did not begin breaking down the deportation statistics in terms of broad offence categories until 1994
43 Personal communication, Enforcement Policy Group, Immigration Service Enforcement Directorate, 9 April 1997.

CHAPTER EIGHT

The Scapegoat Solution

It is common knowledge that in the late twentieth century illegal drugs are highly priced commodities in Western markets. Less well understood is the fact that the ideologies, politics and policies framing illegal drug control have also become highly priced commodities where the dollar value has been replaced by the currency of electoral populism. Over the past two decades votes have become a central motivating force behind much criminal justice policy. Being 'tough on crime, tough on the causes of crime'; accepting that 'prison works'; endorsing 'fast track punishment for young offenders'; these linguistic 'truths' have become the cues to winning votes in the law and order debate. The image of the drug trafficker provides an impeccable rationale for the validity of these claims.

The demonisation process, so much a part of the criminalisation of drug traffickers, has framed a drug control strategy oriented around those at the bottom of the trade. The major players and the trade itself remain unhindered. As we have seen, Western demand for drugs ensures that it remains in the interests of some countries to maintain a lucrative drugs industry. In terms of international questions of political economy the continuity of the trade may also service certain Western interests. Within the international trade the range of players is vast— governments, individual drug lords, families and cartels, law enforcers, side-lining business entrepreneurs, looser networks of racketeers, dealers at high levels, dealers at low levels and the courier. As in most business enterprise these roles are distinguished by those features first delineated in the *Introduction* to this book—power, control, wealth and cognisance. As the evidence amassed in this book suggests the anti-racketeering rhetoric which accompanies the law enforcement strategy is unable to distinguish between high-level and low-level players. Similarly the law demonstrates the same inability. Through criminalisation, all those involved in the trafficking enterprise are dealt with by the same broad brush. What this means in practice is that those most vulnerable to arrest and prosecution are dealt with, conceptually, as major traffickers.

Drug traffickers and the drug importers that this book has focused on have been central to the continuing discourse on British and European drug enforcement, if, for no other reason than the borderline nature of the crimes committed. Borders have occupied a central pillar of resistance to the political and economic changes which are defining

175

the new Europe. It is therefore around the issue of borders that the consolidation of fear and danger has been orchestrated. The pressure toward increasingly repressive drug and immigration control strategies operates at one important level to allay insecurities over the threatened changes in geo-politics to come. Drug demonisation cements the variously whipped up fears seen to threaten 'national identity' and concentrates public anxieties into a manageable forum.

Foreign drug importers come to embody the weaknesses in the process of unification and measures to address the alien threat—not just foreign, but poisonous as well—are welcomed as central to preserving national security as well as identity.

But even before the threat to the integrity of internal European frontiers became a central issue, drug trafficking occupied an important niche in the list of UK public enemies as outlined in *Chapter 6*. Here the 'conventional wisdom' understands illegal drugs as foreign by source and traffickers as foreign by corollary. What is required in the construction of a public enemy is a bridge between group identity and an experience or perception of social threat. Thus we have illegal immigrants 'threatening jobs and culture'; Jamaican Yardies threatening the community with street violence and 'crack' cocaine; Turkish mafia gangs trading in heroin; Islamic fundamentalism; and Nigerian 'fraudsters and drug lords' undermining the economy. Mediating the relationship between the designated target groups and the bigger threats they signify to the body politic and individual integrity is the symbol and reality of the illegal drug trafficker. The trade, reduced in this instance, to the individual drug courier—the vehicle of cross-border contagion—now has its subject.

The instigation of a second IRA ceasefire in July 1997 and the subsequent Northern Ireland political settlement agreed at Easter 1998 have dramatically diminished the reality and ideological value of the 'terrorist threat'. The peace agreement and its overwhelming support by the people of Northern Ireland now ensure the prominence of the drug trafficker as the enemy to consolidate criminal and political policy into the new millennium.

As *Chapters 4* and *5* demonstrate, the politically constructed archetype of the drug trafficker stands in glaring contrast to the reality of the imprisoned drug importer. But the incongruence of 'drug baron' myth and 'courier' reality is lost in the battle cry of prohibition discourse. Harsh sentences must mean serious high level traffickers; the fact that foreign importers are over represented in British jails is evidence that the drug threat is an imported one; the emphasis on supply and border interdiction is a logical extension of recognising the threat as an alien one; the escalation in drug control repression is a

176

necessity if Britain is not to be 'swamped' with narcotics and so on. All this against a backdrop of escalating drug convictions, increased seizures by customs, racially informed policing and reporting of drug crimes, repressive new measures against low level street dealers and complex international laws and mechanisms to locate the profits of the drug trade. Conventional drug 'wisdom', then, is reinforced by the actuality of drug control policy and judicial practice.

In the new Europe drug control is heavily freighted with bureaucratic over-load—of which there seems an endless expanse of incremental possibilities. As European enforcement measures proliferate, the impact is more symbolic than pragmatic. The *Americanisation* of, not only drug enforcement but crime control more generally, has ensured the politics of punishment a secure status in the new Europe. Developing countries must show a willingness to conform to European (and, by association, American) ideas about the control of illegal drugs. They must introduce approved enforcement strategies and demonstrate that headway is being made in the fight against illegal drugs using the same performance indicators which say so little about the impact of prohibition and its armoury in Britain. Why, we must ask, if the same strategies have been so unsuccessful in reducing the quantity and consumption of drugs here in the UK, would they be any more successful in countries like Nigeria, the Caribbean or Burma? The evidence suggests that drug-specific foreign policy and aid initiatives operate, as in the domestic schema of drug policy, very largely at the level of symbolism. As was documented in *Chapter 3,* the sums donated by the UK to assist drug control programmes abroad have been insignificant on any scale and the system of special trade preferences instituted by Europe for certain drug-producing countries is structurally doomed to failure. Drug-related foreign aid initiatives also act, using the undisputed demonology of illegal drug trafficking, to place certain developing countries under the influence of Western governments who have power and influence over the World Bank, the IMF and other international sources of credit. The symbolic noises and real threats made by the west about drug control in transit and producer countries will, however, continue to fall on deaf ears until the foreign debt crisis crippling these countries is removed.

The case of Nigeria provides a concrete means of understanding the centrality of underdevelopment and economic crisis in perpetuating the cycle of Third World involvement in the drugs trade. Nigeria's role as a transit port for drugs from other parts of the world and in providing a pool for the recruitment of couriers is intelligible only in the context of that country's recent history. Within the fabric of enormous economic, political and social dislocation, widespread corruption and spiralling poverty, the crime of running drugs inevitably loses much of its 'ugliness'. The urgent needs of daily existence take priority over a morality imposed by former colonial masters.

British domestic drugs policy and practice are thus confronted by a set of circumstances which they have been unwilling to accommodate and which render them little more than cosmetic symbols of alternative agendas. In light of the minimal impact that current practices of seizure and interdiction have on the drugs trade such analyses should force a major re-think in British drug control strategy. Since the beginning of the 1980s, in the UK, we have seen a dramatic rise in the costs associated with drug enforcement with well over £520 million now expended on drug control per annum. Yet as shown in *Chapter 7*, by all obvious measures of success, these many millions injected into a war against drugs have resulted not only in a worsening of the problems associated with drug misuse but paradoxically have reinforced the state's commitment to existing strategies. It is, as Christina Johns writes, a case of skewed logic—at least ostensibly so:

> Prisons have been a failure, so more prisons will be a success; punishment has been a failure so more punishment will be a success; criminalisation and enforcement have been a failure, so more criminalisation and enforcement will be a success. (Johns 1992:173)

Of course if we accept the argument that the drugs war has other motives, other agendas, then the 'skewed' logic is misapplied. There is a strong argument to be made that in addition, and related to, the electoral value inherent in the drug war is the medium it lends its masters for the exercise of social control. As Diana Gordon writes in relation to US drug control:

> . . . what is also at stake . . . are fundamental hierarchies of authority — parents over children, the affluent over the poor, lighter races over darker ones, accumulators over dependents . . . (1994:19)

If this is the case then a rational approach to the control of illicit drugs has deeper and more intractable hurdles to negotiate. Like Diana Gordon, I would argue that drug control reform is possible but that it is unlikely to be stimulated by rational arguments which site prohibition at the heart of the drug control malady. Rather it will be the force of political pragmatism, economic rationalism, a prison system bursting at the seams or some other expedient pressure which may motivate reform. And that pressure, as we have seen, will have to be greater than the expression of concern by senior police chiefs over unworkable drug laws. Even then we are unlikely to see the abandonment of a symbolic metaphor so useful in coalescing public opinion and building state resources. Gordon's analysis of drug policy in the USA supports the evidence provided in this book when she writes that it is '. . . a resource for furthering values—of security, order and participation—and staking claims—to material and political success, to public goods . . .' (1994:7) Until a suitable new enemy can be constructed and until the pressures on the system created by the prohibition of drugs reaches explosive dimensions the value inherent in the demonisation of illegal drugs will continue to service the needs of Britain's 'shadow agenda' of social control.[1]

The testimonies of the drug couriers interviewed for this book and the evidence provided on the operation of the British war on drugs, prove that the crude postivistism of current policies obscures a complex international problem which has its roots in political economy. There are no easy answers despite the blinkered vigour with which supply-oriented strategies are currently pursued. The courier narratives highlight the centrality of ordinary people's daily struggles in understanding the foundations and dynamic of the drug trade. These daily struggles, in both the industrialised and the developing worlds, must be understood and integrated into any rational and humane drug control policy. Without them drug policies will remain cruelly misplaced and society's 'victims' will continue to remain the target for the state's political scapegoating. Drug traffickers and specifically those couriers who find themselves arrested and imprisoned in the UK are simply not in the 'demon' mould the image makers would have them in. The stereotype of the ruthless drug lord may fit the likes of Pablo Escobar or David Telliagaoglu[2] but as the interviews reveal it does not fit the reality of the very visible, and therefore vulnerable faces, of drug trafficking. And it is, as we have seen, those visible faces who disproportionately face severe criminal justice sanctions and who provide substance for the perpetuation of the drug threat myth and for the development of anti-trafficking legislation. While drug control strategies remain fixated with producer countries and the individual suppliers of drug—that is while the focus remains on an external enemy—the courier will be the individual embodiment of the enemy. What is also evident from the interview testimony is the diversity of individuals who become involved in smuggling drugs at this low level. While there are certain uniformities of experience shared by couriers, those uniformities relate to contextual issues of political economy, relative poverty and personal need—not to individual character or personality structure. There is no new type-cast to replace the illusory stereotype.

179

This book offers an insight into an offence—the smuggling of drugs across borders—which in many ways exemplifies the more general fears engendered by the drugs trade. By tracing the historical evolution of the drug trafficker as both a central player in the trade and as 'demon' in the popular lexicon we have a context in which to place the drug courier of the late twentieth century. The concern is less about the physiological impact of the drugs in question and much more about social cohesion and ultimately social control. The disturbing consequences of prohibition are instead heaped onto the chemical properties of the drugs themselves—blame is thus transferred. All illegal drugs are reduced into some amorphous poison. How else can we explain why cannabis, a safe and widely popular drug, remains at the centre of drug enforcement operations. Cannabis is the drug most widely seized and it is the drug for which most users, dealers and traffickers are criminalised. Political and media hyperbole centres on the class A drugs, heroin, cocaine and more recently Ecstasy, and the individual tragedy they wreak. These are the demon drugs which service the real campaign against cannabis. In similar vein it is the sensationalism surrounding the existence of drug lords and barons which services the real criminal justice campaign against those in the trade least culpable and most vulnerable to arrest.

The threat to individual security that drugs are claimed to pose, the foreign nature of their origins and the implied alien threat of foreign national traffickers, build upon more basic fears engendered within the body politic. In an economically and socially insecure world scapegoats provide an important safety-valve and provide a source of cohesion for national rulers which might otherwise be lacking. The mechanisms by which this scapegoating takes place have been outlined in previous chapters.

Why is there a dogged insistence on the part of the policy makers to continue with law and order strategies—despite a recognition that, law enforcement is failing; that the importance of addressing demand is undervalued; that the drugs trade is central to many Third World economies; that drug-related foreign aid is but an insignificant drop in the ocean? The foregoing chapters have sought to highlight the geo-political dimension behind British and European resistance to come to grips with the fundamental issues of cause and effect in the dynamic of the international trade.

Listening to and addressing the needs expressed by those involved in carrying drugs is the first stage in moving forward. If those needs are taken seriously we are led back to the complex world of political economy, the capitalist ideals of profit and competition, divisions between the developed and underdeveloped worlds and the basic hardships of those at the bottom struggling to survive in the late twentieth century. Criminal policy offers no solutions. Unless drug control policy is prepared to move beyond criminal policy, to veer away from law enforcement into the arena of development politics, domestic welfare, political economy, international poverty and Third World debt, there will be no question of an end to the human tragedy exemplified by the imprisoned couriers in this study. Their plight, along with the flourishing of the international illicit drugs industry, will remain untouched.

ENDNOTES

[1] Diana Gordon uses the term 'shadow agenda' to explain the continued commitment to a patently impotent and failing drug control strategy. The 'shadow agenda' includes control over minorities; the preservation of 'hierarchies of authority'; reinforcing the legitimacy of the law; furthering a sense of national identity and security as well as securing material resources for state agencies (1994:7)

[2] David Telliagaoglu, from Sussex, was jailed for 25 years in 1996 for masterminding the importation of £10 million worth of heroin. In 1982 he returned to the UK having served five years of a nine year sentence in Germany for drug smuggling (*The Observer*, 27 July 1997).

Bibliography

Abernethy, R, N Hammond, M Frost, P Green, T Read and S Hobson, *Drug Couriers: A Role for the Probation Service*, London, Middlesex Area Probation Service, 1992

Aderinda, Dapo, 'Drug War is No Ploy to Rid UK of Nigerians, Says Envoy', *The Times*, 17 April 1990

—, 'Drug Convicts Abroad may be Retried Here', *The Times*, 31 July 1990

Advisory Council on the Misuse of Drugs (Caymen Islands), Reports 1989, 1990, 1992, 1993

Afolabi, Tayo, 'Drug Trafficking: Nigerian Women Languish in British Jails', *The Times*, 23 July 1990

Africa Economic Digest, *Nigeria: 25 Years of Independence, An AED Special Report*, September 1985

Africa This Week, Nigeria, 'NDLEA Vetting', 17-23 June 1996

—, 'NDLEA Sacking', 3-9 June 1996

—, 'Nigeria Narcotics Controversy', 20-26 May 1996

—, 'Nigeria', 4-10 September 1995

—, 'Drug Offences', 10-16 July 1995

—, 'Drug Raids', 19-25 June 1995

—, 'Double Jeopardy', May 29-June 4 1995

Ahire, Philip, *Imperial Policing*, Milton Keynes: Open University Press, 1991

Albrecht, Hans-Jorg, 'Drug Policies and National Plans to Combat Drug Trafficking and Drug Abuse: A Comparative Analysis of Policies of Co-ordination and Co-operation' in Estievenart, Georges (Ed.), *Policies and Strategies to Combat Drugs in Europe: The Treaty on European Union; Framework for a New European Strategy to Combat Drugs*, Dordrecht:Martinus Nijhoff, 1995, 182-196

— 'Drug Couriers, the Response of the German Criminal Justice System', in Green, P (Ed.), *Drug Couriers: A New Perspective*, London: Quartet Books, 1996

— and A van Kalmthout (Eds.), *Drugs Policies in Western Europe*, Frieburg: Max-Planck Institute for Foreign and International Penal Law, 1989

Aina, W, A, 'Special Report on the Trial of Drug Barons', *The African Guardian*, 23 July 1990

Association of Chief Police Officers, *The Way Forward: National Drugs Conference 1995: Final Report*, London: ACPO, 1995

Austin, Hal, 'Straw Warned of Threat to London from Serbian Gangs', *The Independent*, 1 June 1997

Aziz, Christine, 'Dutch Courage to Close the Joint', *The Guardian*, 31 October 1995

Babarinsa, D, 'Killing by Another Name = Murder', *Newswatch*, 11 December 1989

Bachman, J G, L D, Johnston and P O'Malley, 'Explaining the Recent Decline in Cocaine Use Among Young Adults: Further Evidence That Perceived Risks and Disapproval Lead to Reduced Use', in *Journal of Health and Social Behaviour*, 31 June 1990, 173-184

Banks, T, 'No Smoke Without Fire', *The Guardian*, 31 October 1995

Banner, G and S Sengoz, *Feasibility Research Into the Controlled Availability of Opioids: Working Paper 10*, Canberra: National Centre for Epidemidology and Population Health, 1994

Bassiouri, M C, 'International Aspects of Drug Abuse: Problems and a Proposal', *John Marshall Journal*, 9(1), 1975, 3-45

Bean, P, *Drugs and Social Control*, Oxford: Martin Robertson, 1974

Bennetto, Jason, 'Police "Using Dubious Tactics" with Informers', *The Independent*, 25 September 1995

Berridge, Virginia, 'Drugs and Social Policy: The Establishment of Drug Control in Britain 1900-30', *British Journal of Addiction*, 79, 1984, 17-29

— 'War Conditions and Narcotics Control: The Passing of Defense of the Realm Act Regulation 40B', *Journal of Social Policy*, 7, 1978, 285-304

— and G Edwards, *Opium and the People: Opiate Use in Nineteenth Century England*, Allen Lane, Second edition, New Haven: Yale University Press, 1987

Boseley, S and T Radford, 'Drugs Mule Dies in Tragic Trade with Fatal Pay-off', *The Guardian*, 23 September 1992

Brack, G, 'MEPs Fear Hard Drug Explosion', *The Times*, 15 October 1990

Braid, M, 'Courts to Study Personal Files on Drug Traffickers', *The Independent*, 7 October 1992

Bruggeman, W, 'Europol/ EDU', Paper presented at the Association of Chief Police Officers' National Drug Conference, West Yorkshire Police Training School, 8-10 June 1994

Bucknell, P, 'The Crack Explosion', *Criminal Law Review* , 1992, 359-360

Bunting, M, 'Europe's Broad Band of Penalties', *The Guardian*, 15 February 1994

Bunyan, T, *Statewatching the New Europe: Handbook on the European State*, London: Statewatch, 1993

—, *The Europol Convention*, London: Statewatch, 1995

Burchill, J, 'Victims of Drug Culture', *The Sunday Times*, 19 November 1995

Campbell, Denis,

—, S Wilford and C Pepinster, 'Police Make £5000 Pay Out', *Time Out*, 2 December 1992

—, 'Excessive Force', *Time Out*, 16-23 October 1992

Campbell, Duncan

—, 'Judges Rate Drugs Worse than Murder', *The Guardian*, 20 August 1996

—, 'Drug Sellers Face Longer Jail Terms', *The Guardian*, 1 January 1996

—, 'Police Win Battle for British FBI', *The Guardian*, 6 October 1995

—, 'Police Accused of 80-fold Mark Up on Drug Values', 4 February 1995

—, 'Victims of a Dirty War', *The Guardian*, 2 February 1995

—, 'Cocaine Seizures by Customs up by 224pc', *The Guardian*, 20 January 1995

—, 'Appeal Court Frees Man Due to "Tainted" Evidence from Police', *The Guardian* , 6 July 1994

—, 'Corruption Claims "the Worst for 20 Years"', *The Guardian*, 4 February 1994

—, 'Pressure Builds for New Drugs Deal', *The Guardian*, 16 October 1993

—, 'Police Station Cleared of Organized Drug Dealing', *The Guardian*, 16 September 1993

—, 'Two Freed Over "Rotten" Evidence', *The Guardian*, 16 February 1993

—, 'Drug Arrest Puts Police in Front Line', *The Guardian*, 11 July 1992

—, 'Customs Braced for 1992 Drugs Battle', 16 January 1991

—, and L Donegan, '"Bent Copper" Gets 10 Years', *The Guardian*, 25 February 1997

—, 'Rethink Drugs War: Police Chief', *The Guardian*, 18 August 1997

—, 'Minister Plans Drug Courts', *The Guardian*, 19 August 1997

Campodonico, Humberto, 'Drug Trafficking, Laundering and Neo-Liberal Economics: Perverse Effects for a Developing Country' in Dorn, N, J Jepson and E Savona (Eds.), *European Drug policies and Enforcement*, Basingstoke: Macmillan Press Ltd., 1996, 231-41

Carlen, P, *Women, Crime and Poverty*, Milton Keynes: Open University Press, 1988

Carrell, S, 'Seizures of Illegal Drugs on Increase', *The Scotsman*, 22 March 1994

Carvel, J, 'Drug Seizures Rise to £300m', *The Guardian*, 3 October 1991

—, 'Labour Fights Shy of Going Soft on Drugs', *The Guardian*, 18 June 1991

—, 'Double Jeopardy, Inmates Abscond', *The Guardian*, 19 December 1990

—, 'Cash Seizure Plan to Curb Drug Traffic', *The Guardian*, 28 March 1990

Chambliss, W J, 'The Political Economy of Crime: A Comparative Study of Nigeria and the USA' in Taylor I, P Walton and J Young, *Critical Criminology*, London: Routledge, 1975, 167-179

Cheney, D, *Into the Dark Tunnel: Foreign Prisoners in the British Prison System*, London: Prison Reform Trust, 1993

Chomsky, N, *Deterring Democracy*, London:Vintage, 1993

Christie, N, *Crime Control as Industry: Towards GULAGS, Western Style?*, London: Routledge, 1993

—, '1989 Reflections on Drugs', in Albrecht, Hans-Jorg and A van Kalmthout (Eds.), *Drugs Policies in Western Europe*, Frieburg: Max-Planck Institute for Foreign and International Penal Law, 1989, 41-8

Clark, C A and Sanctuary, C J, 'Anti Drug Smuggling Operational Research in HM Customs and Excise', *Public Administration* , Vol. 70, No. 4, 1992, 577-89

Clutterbuck, Richard, *Crime and Corruption: Thinking the Unthinkable*, Basingstoke: Macmillan Press Ltd., 1995

—, *Drugs, Terrorism Drugs and Crime in Europe: After 1992* , London: Routledge, 1990

Collinson, Mike, 'Punishing Drugs: Criminal Justice and Drug Use', *British Journal of Criminology*, Vol. 33, No 3, 1993, 383-395

Commission of the European Communities, *Strengthening the Mediterranean Policy of the European Union: Establishing a Euro-Mediterranean Partnership*, Brussels: European Commission, 1994, Com (94), 427, Final

Cotic, D, *Drugs and Punishment: An up-to-date Interregional Survey on Drug Related Offenses* Rome: UNSDRI, 1988

Cotts, C, 'Smart Money', *Rolling Stones Magazine*, New York Issue, 681, 5 May 1994

Cowdry, Q, 'MPs Demand Extra Powers to Confiscate Drug Baron's Profits', *The Times*, 8 December 1989

CPSA and NUCPS, *Customs and Excise: Campaign for Public Service*, CPSA and NUCPS, 1993

Crown Prosecution Service, 'Operation Jackpot: Two Officers to be Prosecuted', *Press Release*, 26 July 1994

Curtis, R and P Durrant, 'HMP Highpoint and Drug Couriers', *Prison Service Journal*, 90, 1993, 2-6

Daily Champion, 'Commission to Cater for Abandoned Kids', *Daily Champion*, 22 October 1990

—, 'Our Kids in UK', *Daily Champion*, 23 October 1990

Daily Satellite, 'Help Educate Parents', 17 October 1990

Daily Star, 600 'Nigerians Arrested for Drug Trafficking', 14 May 1990

Daily Telegraph, 'Courts Increasing Drug Cautions', 14 September 1991

—, 'Mrs Babangida Opens Workshop on Monday', 11 October 1990

Darbyshire, N, 'Customs Reward Over Drug Cash', 6 November 1990

Daruvalla, A, 'Liberal Dutch Finally Get Tough on Drugs', *The Independent*, 25 September 1995

Dateline, 'Nigeria, Drug Problem', 13-19 March 1995

Davis, M, *City of Quartz: Excavating the Future in Los Angeles*, London: Vintage, 1992

Dibden, T, 'Dangers Will Not Make Us Change Our Habit', *The Times*, 17 November 1995

Dorn, N, 'Borderline Criminology: External Drug Policies of the EU' in Dorn, N, Jepson J and Savona E (Eds.), *European Drug Policies and Enforcement*, Basingstoke: Macmillan Press Ltd., 1996, 242-265

—, 'Drug Markets and Law Enforcement in Europe' in Green, P (Ed.), *Drug Couriers: A New Perspective*, London: Quartet Books, 1996, 169-182

—, *A European Analysis of Drug enforcement*, Paper to the European Scientific and Technical Seminar on Strategies and Politics to Combat Drugs, European University Institute, Florence Italy, December 1993

—, *Drug Trafficking and Enforcement Countermeasures in Europe: A Comparative Perspective on Public Perceptions and Policy Priorities*, Paper to the Centre for the Study of Public Order, Leicester, September 1993

—, 'Subsidiarity, Police Co-operation and Drug Enforcement: Some Structures of Policy Making in the EC', *European Journal on Criminal Policy and Research*, 1/2, 1993, 30-47

—, 'The Quiet Harmony of the Police: Enforcement, Welfare and Single Market Perspectives on Policing in Europe with Special Reference to Illegal Drugs', in *Narkotikapolitik, I Internationellt Perspektiv*, NAD PUBLIKATION, No. 24, 1993

—, Jepson J and Savona E (Eds.), *European Drug Policies and Enforcement*, Basingstoke: Macmillan Press Ltd., 1996

—, Karim M and N South, 'Drugs, Crime and Law Enforcement: Some Issues for Europe', in Heidensohn, F and M Farrell (Eds.), *Crime in Europe*, London: Routledge, 1991

— and N South (Eds.), *Traffickers: Drug Markets and Law Enforcement*, London: Routledge, 1992

— and —, 'Drug Markets and Law Enforcement', *British Journal of Criminology*, 30, 2, 1990 17-88

— and N South, *A Land Fit for Heroin: Drug policies, Prevention and Practice*, London: Macmillan, 1987

Downes, D, *Contrasts in Tolerance, Post-War Policy in the Netherlands and England and Wales*, Oxford: Oxford University Press, 1988

185

− and P Rock, *Understanding Deviance: A Guide to the Sociology of Crime and Rule Breaking*, Oxford: Oxford University Press, 1988

Driscall, M., 'Child of Our Times', *The Sunday Times*, 19 November 1995

Drug Enforcement Agency, 'Cocaine Trafficking Trends in Europe', *Drug Enforcement*, Fall, 1982, 21-2

Duke, Steven B and Albert Gross, *America's Longest War: Rethinking Our Tragic Crusade Against Drugs*, New York: Tarcher Putnam, 1993

Duncan, Gary, 'Customs Men Claim Cuts Have Damaged Service', *The Scotsman*, 6 March 1992

Dunkel, T, 'Saving Hapless Americans Abroad', *Insight*, 26 March 1990

Eastern Morning News, 'Drugs Menace is Bigger than Ever', 20 January 1994

Economist, The, 'Nigeria Survey: After the Ball', 1986, 3-42

−, 'The Political Economy of Nigeria', 1984, 1-32

Edake, E, 'Nigeria Marks Family Week', *The Republic*, 11 October 1990

Ellison, E, *Police Review*, 15 November 1993

Enright, S, 'Charge or Caution', *New Law Journal*, 143, 1993, 446

Epstein E J, *Agency of Fear: Opiates and Political Power in America*, London: Verso,1977

Estievenart, Georges, 'The European Community and the Global Drug Phenomenon: Current Situation and Outlook', in Estievenart, G, (Ed.), *Policies and Strategies to Combat Drugs in Europe: The Treaty on European Union; Framework for a New European Strategy to Combat Drugs*, Dordrecht: Martinus Nijhoff, 1995, 50-97

Etoh, B, 'Nigerian Women Drug Traffickers in British Prisons', *Evening News*, 13 November 1990

−, 'Nigerian Children Abandoned in Britain', *The Standard*, 25 October 1990

European Commission, *Communication from the Commission to the Council and the European Parliament on a European Union Action Plan to Combat Drugs*, 1995-1999, COM (94) 234 Final, Brussels, 1994a

−, *Strengthening the Mediterranean Policy of the EU: Establishing a Euro-Mediterranean Partnership*, COM (94) 427 Final, Brussels, 1994b

Europol Drugs Unit Working Programme, March, *Report on the Activities of the Europol Drugs Unit in 1996*, 1997

Farrell, A. *Crime, Class and Corruption: the Politics of the Police*, London: Bookmarks, 1992

Feldman, David, 'A Survey of English Forfeiture Law' in Flood, S (Ed.), *Illicit Drugs and Organized Crime: Issues for a Unified Europe*, Chicago: University of Illinois, 1991, 13-24

Ford, R, 'Thousands Take Tablets Every Week', *The Times*, 14 November 1995

Foreign and Commonwealth Office, *Background Brief, Trends in Drug Trafficking*, London:FCO Information Department, 1995

−, *Nigeria: Background Brief* , London: FCO Information Department, 1995

−, *Background Brief, Tackling Drugs Together: Britain's New Strategy Against Drug Misuse*, London: FCO Information Department, 1995

−, *Central America, The Caribbean and Mexico; The Fight Against Drug Trafficking*, London: Chadwyck-Healy Ltd., 1993

−, *Drugs in the Caribbean*, London, Chadwyck-Healy Ltd., 1990

Fortson, R F, 'Sentencing of Drug Couriers' in Green, P (Ed.), *Drug Couriers: A New Perspective*, London: Quartet Books, 1996, 79-111

−, *The Law on the Misuse of Drugs and Drug Trafficking Offenses*, Second edition, London: Sweet and Maxwell, 1992

Fuller, Mark, Cocaine Fear for 1992, *The Times*, 8 May 1991

George, S, *The Debt Boomerang: How the Third World Debt Harms Us All*, London: Pluto Press, 1992

− and F Sabelli, *Faith and Credit: The World Bank's Secular Empire*, London: Penguin Books, 1994

Ghomoral, V, 'Child Abandonment in UK: Shift in Value Placed on Living Abroad, Nigerians Told', *Regional Concord*, 23 October 1990

Gilmore, W C, *Dirty Money: The Evolution of Money Laundering Counter-measures*, Strasbourg: Council of Europe, 1995

Goddey, J, 'Met Chief Praise for KX Swoops', *Camden and St. Pancras Chronicle*, 19 May 1994

186

Gordon, D, R. *The Return of the Dangerous Classes: Drug Prohibition and Policy Politics*, New York: W W Norton and Co, 1994

—, 'Drugspeak and the Clinton Administration: A Lost Opportunity for Drug Policy Reform', *Social Justice*, Vol. 21, No. 3, Issue 57, Fall, 1994

Government of the Federal Republic of Nigeria, *International Co-operation in Crime Prevention and Criminal Justice for the 21st Century, The Nigerian Perspective*, Paper presented to 8th UN Conference on Prevention of Crime and the Treatment of Offenders, Havanna, Cuba, 27 August-9 September 1990

Green, P (Ed.), *Drug Couriers: A New Perspective*, London: Quartet Books, 1996

—, 'Drug Couriers: The Construction of a Public Enemy' in Green, P (Ed.), *Drug Couriers: A New Perspective*, London: Quartet Books, 1996, 3-20

—, *Drug Couriers*, London: Howard League for Penal Reform, 1991

—'A Phoney War: Drug Traffickers in British Prisons', *Criminal Justice Matters*, No. 5, Winter, 1990

—, Chris Mills and Tim Read, 'The Characteristics and Sentencing of Illegal Drug Importers', *British Journal of Criminology*, Vol. 34, No. 4, 1994, 479-86

— and I Purnell, *Measuring the Success of Law Enforcement Agencies in Australia in Targeting Major Drug Offenders Relative to Minor Drug Offenders*, Report Series: 127, National Police Research Unit:Adelaide, 1996

Gridden, R, 'Drug Seizures from EC Highlight Fears Over "Open Frontier"', *Daily Telegraph*, 7 November 1990

Grove, V, 'The Ecstasy and the Agony', *The Times*, 14 November 1995

Guardian, The, 'Short Shrift on Soft Drugs, Ignore Serious Debate and Shoot the Messenger', *The Guardian*, 31 October 1995

—, 'Father Wins Unexpected Support as He Continues Fight to Prove Allegations of Planted Evidence', *The Guardian*, 8 November 1993

—, 'Europe "Faces Havoc" from Cocaine Flood', *The Guardian*, 5 December 1991

—, 'Yard Squad to Combat Drug Gangs', *The Guardian*, 10 August 1991

—, 'Cocaine Threat Worries Patten as Seizures Increase by 50pc', *The Guardian*, 7 September 1990

—, 'Sinister Proof of the Smugglers Pudding', *The Guardian*, 11 January 1990

HM Customs and Excise

—, 'Minister Announces Large Scale Increases in Drug Seizures During 1994: Another Outstanding Year for Customs', News Release, 6/95

—'PM Welcomes Record year for Drug Seizures During 1995; Another Outstanding year for Customs', News Release, undated

—, *Reports of the Commissioner of Customs and Excise 95/96*, London: HMSO, 1996

—, *Annual Report*, London: HMSO, 1995

—, *Reports of the Commissioner of Customs and Excise 94/95*, London: HMSO, 1995

—, *Annual Report*, London: HMSO, 1992

—, *Reports of the Commissioner of Customs and Excise 91/92*, London: HMSO, 1992

—, *Annual Report*, London: HMSO, 1990

—, *Drugs Brief 1992: Frontier Checks and the Free Movement of People*, London: HM Customs and Excise, 1990

—, *Annual Report*, London: HMSO, 1989

—, *Annual Drug Seizures*, London: HMSO, 1983

Hackney Gazette, 'Judge Raps Corruption Probe as More Convictions are Quashed', 17 December 1993

Hammond, N, 'Turning Back the Clock; Implications for Pre-sentencing Reports of the Criminal Justice and Public Order Act 1994', in Green, P (Ed.), *Drug Couriers: A New Perspective*, London: Quartet Books, 1996, 151-9

—, 'Pre-sentencing Reports on Foreign National Drug Traffickers: Present and Future', *Probation Journal*, 42(1), 1995, 17-23

—, *The Value of Pre-sentence Reports on Foreign Nationals*, Middlesex Probation Service, Foreign Nationals Unit,1994

— and John Walters, *Perspectives of Nigeria, Report of a Study Tour of Nigeria, 24 October-7 November 1992*, Middlesex Area Probation Service, 1993

Hansard, 'Drug Imports', Written Answers, 15 April 1996, Col. 368

—, 'Illegal Drugs (Imports)', Written Answers, 13 February, 1992 Col. 586

—, 'Drug Abuse', 9 June 1989, Col. 477

—, 'Drugs', Written Answers, 8 November 1989, Col. 760

— (Lords), Committee Stage, Controlled Drugs Penalties Bill, 27 June 1985

—, Controlled Drugs (Penalties Bill), 19 April 1985, Cols. 563-76

—, 13 February 1992, 1581, col. 586.

Heaven, O, 'Working with Nigerian Women Prisoners', in Green, P (Ed.), *Drug Couriers: A New Perspective*, London, Quartet Books, 1996, 160-6

Hebenton, B and T Thomas, 'Rocky Path to Europol', *Druglink,* November/December 1992, 8-10

Herman, E S, 'Drug Wars: Appearance and Reality', *Social Justice,* Vol.18, No. 4, 1991, 76-84

Hedges, J and A Tarzi, *A Study of Foreign Prisoners*, London: ILPS, 1990

Helm, S, '"Rivalry and Corruption" Hampering Drugs Fight', *The Independent*, 13 May 1988

Hillyard, F, *Suspect Community: People's Experience of the Prevention of Terrorism Acts in Britain*, London: Pluto Press, 1993

Home Office, 'Statistics of Drug Addicts Notified to the Home office, United Kingdom 1995', *Home Office Statistical Bulletin*, 15/96, 26 July 1996

—, *Criminal Statistics England and Wales 1995*, London: HMSO, 1996, Cm 321

—, *Statistics of Drug Seizures and Offenders Dealt With, United Kingdom 1994, Area Tables*, London: HMSO,1996

—, *Statistics of Drug Seizures and Offenders Dealt With, United Kingdom 1995, Supplementary Tables*, London: HMSO, 1996

—, Conference Report, Criminal Justice Conference, 28 February-1 March 1996, Liverpool: Home Office Special Conference Unit, 1996

—, *Tackling Drugs Together: A Strategy for England 1995-98*, White Paper, CM 2846, 1995

—, 'Statistics of Drug Addicts Notified to the Home Office, United Kingdom 1994', *Home Office Statistical Bulletin*, 17/95, 19 July 1995

—, *Statistics of Drug Seizures and Offenders Dealt With, United Kingdom 1993, Area Tables*, London: HMSO, 1995

—, *Statistics of Drug Seizures and Offenders Dealt with, United Kingdom 1993, Supplementary Tables*, London, HMSO, 1995

—, *The Misuse of Drugs (Amendment) (No 20) Regulations 1995*, London: HMSO, 1995

— *Tackling Drugs Together: A Consultation Document on a Strategy for England 1995-98*, Green Paper, October 1994

—, *Crime Statistics England and Wales 1991*, London: HMSO, 1992

—, *Drug Prevention Initiative Progress Report 1990-1991*, London: HMSO, 1992

—, 'The Government Response to the Seventh Report from the Home Affairs Committee 1988-89 and the Sixth (Internal) Report (UC 356), "Crack: The Threat of Hard Drugs in the Next Decade" 1989-90', CM1164, London: HMSO, 1990

—, 'Statistics of the Misuse of Drugs: Seizures and Offenders Dealt with, United Kingdom 1989' (and supplementary tables), in *Statistical Bulletin 1990,* London: HMSO, 1990

—, *Drug Offenders: Nationality of Import/Export Cases*, Unpublished, 1990

—, *UK Action Plan on Drug Misuse, The Government Strategy*, London: HMSO, 1990

—, 'More Help for Drug Addicts Under Criminal Justice Proposals', News Release, 7 February 1990

—, *Crime Statistics, England and Wales 1989*, London: HMSO, 1990

—, *Prison Statistics in England and Wales*, London: HMSO, 1989, Cm 1221

—, *Tackling Drug Misuse:A Summary of the Government's Strategy*, Third edition, 1988

Home Office Research and Statistics Directorate, *Research Finding No. 50, Persistent Drug Misusing Offenders*, London, HMSO, 1997

Hopkinson, N, *Fighting Drug Trafficking in the Americas and Europe*, Wilton Park Papers 43, London, HMSO, 1991

House of Commons Home Affairs Committee, Session 1984-85, *Misuse of Hard drugs, Minutes of Evidence from HM Customs and Excise*, London: HMSO, 1985

House of Commons, Session 1994-95, Home Affairs Committee, Third Report, *Organized Crime*, London: HMSO

House of Lords Select Committee on European Communities, HL 51, 1995

Hudson, C, 'Who Really Killed Leah Betts?', *Daily Mail*, 26 April 1997

Huling, T, 'Women Drug Couriers: Sentencing Reform Needed for Prisoners of War' *Criminal Justice*, Winter 1995, 15-19 and 58-61

— 'Prisoners of War: Women Drug Couriers in the United States' in Green, P (Ed.), *Drug Couriers: A New Perspective*, London: Quartet Books, 1996, 46-60

Ihonvbere, J O, *Nigeria: The Politics of Adjustment and Democracy*, New Brunswick: Transaction Books, 1994

Inciardi, J A (Ed.), *The Drug Legalization Debate*, Newbury Park, Ca: Sage, 1991

—, *The War on Drugs: Heroin, Cocaine, Crime and Public Policy*, Palo Alto, CA: Mayfield, 1986

Inner London Probation Service, *A Prison Within a Prison: A Study of Foreign Prisoners*, London: ILPS, 1990

Institute for the Study of Drug Dependence, *Drug Misuse in Britain*, London: ISDD, 1991

— and M Ashton, *National Audit of Drug Misuse in Britain*, London: ISDD, 1992

— *International Criminal Police Review*, 'A New Relationship Between Customs Departments and Commercial Operators', September-October, 1990, 34-36

—, 'Heroin Trafficking in Africa: Its Impact on Europe', September/October, 1989, 25-28

—, 'The Drug Problem: The Situation In Africa 1982-84', 396, 1986, 65-70

Interpol, 'The Drugs Situation in Europe after 1992', July/August, 1990, 25-32

Ipimesho, T, 'Drug Convicts', *The Times*, 27 July 1990

—, 'Nigeria Now Unsafe for Drug Pushers', *The Times*, 20 April 1990

—, 'Nigerians Languish in Thai Prisons', *The Times*, 19 April 1990

Jenkins, J, 'Foreign Exchange', *New Statesman and Society*, 28 July 1989, 12

Johns, C, 'The War on Drugs: Why the Administration Continues to Pursue a Policy of Criminalization and Enforcement', *Social Justice*, Vol.18, No. 4, 1991, 147-165

— *Power, Ideology and the War on Drugs: Nothing Succeeds Like Failure*, New York: Praeger, 1992

Joshua, L, 'Nigeria, Drug Trafficking and Structural Adjustment: Overcoming the Impediments to Dialogue' in Green, P (Ed.), *Drug Couriers: A New Perspective*, London: Quartet Books, 1996, 21-29

Kay, L, '*Aramah* and the Street Value of Drugs', *Criminal Law Review*, 1992, 814

Kendall, R E, *Drugs and Criminality*, Paper presented at the Association of Chief Police Officers' National Drug Conference, West Yorkshire Police Training School, 8-10 June 1994

Keith, M, *Race, Riots and Policing: Lore and Disorder in a Multi-racist Society*, London: UCL Press, 1993

Kerr, Michael, 'National CID Unit Sought to Crack Organised Crime', *Daily Telegraph*, 7 June 1990

King, L A, 'Estimating the Proportion of UK Drug Consumption which is Imported on the Basis of Customs and Police Seizures for Particular Drugs', *Forensic Sci Int*, 76(3), 1995, 217-25

Kirby, T, 'Police Could Face Criminal Charges After Drugs Inquiry', *The Independent*, 4 February 1994

—, 'Drug Convictions Overturned After "Planting" Claims', *The Independent*, 3 March 1993

—, 'Six Questioned After £160M Cocaine Seizure', *The Independent*, 24 November 1992

Kratz, J, 'Repression Has Been a Stunning Failure', *The Los Angeles Times*, 21 March 1990

Krauss, C, 'US Sugar Quotas Impede US Policies towards Latin America', *Wall Street Journal*, 26 September 1986

Labour Party, The, *Drugs: A Consultation Document*, 1991

—, *Cutting the Lifeline: A Survey of Increases in Drug Use and Cuts in Provision*, 1993

—, *Breaking the Vicious Circle: Labour's Proposals to Tackle Drug Related Crime*, 1996

Land, T, 'New Euro Bid to Fight Drugs', *Lloyds List*, 10 July 1990

Lawrence, J, 'Leah Betts Died of Drinking Water to Counter Drug Effect', *The Times*, 22 November 1995

Lee, R W. and S. MacDonald, 'Drugs in Post-Communist Societies', Perl, R F. (Ed.), *Drugs and Foreign Policy: A Critical Review*, Boulder: Westview Press, 1994

189

Levi, M, 'Pecunia non olet: cleansing the Money Launderers from the Temple'. Crime, Law and Social Change, 16: 217-302, 1991

Levitsky, M, 'US Efforts in the International Drug War' in Krauss, M B and E P Lazear, *Searches for Alternatives: Drug-control Policy in the United States*, Stanford: Hoover Institute Press, 1991, 360-376

Lewis, R, 'European Markets in Cocaine', *Contemporary Crisis*, 13, 1989, 35-52

Lindesmith, A, *The Addict and The Law*, New York: Vintage Books, 1965

Linton, L and A Fresco, 'Drug Anger of Coma Girl's Father', *The Times*, 13 November 1995

Livingstone, R, 'EC is Set to Tackle the Drugs Menace', *Evening Standard*, 18 May 1992

Lyioia, D, 'Horrors of British Prisons', *African Concord*, 7 August 1989

—, 'A Personal Testimony, My Four Week Ordeal in a British Prison', by a South African Penelope Lee Ahem, *African Concord*, 7 August 1989

—, 'And the Kids Plights, Babies Separated from Mothers Serving Jail Terms', *African Concord*, 7 August 1989

Maden, A, M Swinton and J Gunn, 'The Ethnic Origin of Women Serving a Prison Sentence', *British Journal of Criminology*, 32, 1992, 218-21

Maguire, M, R Morgan and R Reiner, *The Oxford Handbook of Criminology*, Oxford: Oxford University Press,1994

Manderson, D, *From Mr. Sin to Mr. Big: A History of Australian Drug Laws*, Melbourne: Oxford University Press, 1995

Marks, H, Short Steps to Sanity, *The Guardian*, 31 October 1995

Matthews, A. 'Britain Fosters International Co-operation', *International Journal on Drug Policy*, Vol. 4, No. 1, 1991/92, 2-3

Mathiesen, Thomas, 'Towards an integrated Surveillance System: The Case of Europe'. Paper prepared for workshop on Criminal Policy in Transition, International Institute for the Sociology of Law, Onati, May 1998.

Mbonye, F, 'Give Children Priority,' *Daily Star*, 17 October 1990

McCarthy, T and T Kirby, 'Nigerian Heroin Link Expands Golden Triangle', *The Independent*, 24 July 1990

McCoy, A W, *The Politics of Heroin in Southeast Asia*, New York: Harper and Row, 1972

—, *Drug Traffic: Narcotics and Organized Crime in Australia*, Artarmon, NSW: Harper and Row, 1980

McGreal, Chris, Nigerians Attack British Hypocrisy, *The Guardian*, 21 July 1995

Mennens, A., 'European Community Drug Control Policy', *CIIR Seminar Papers*, 1993

Michael, A, *Cutting the Lifeline: A Survey of Increases in Drug Use and Cuts in Provisions*, The Labour Party, 1995

Mills, Heather, 'Drug Addicts "Commit Half of all property Crimes"', *The Independent*, 12 February 1994

Millward, D, 'Britain Joins UN Pact to Step Up Drug War', *Daily Telegraph*, 29 June 1991

—, 'Europe Unites to Fight Drug Barons', *Daily Telegraph*, 6 May 1991

Ministry of Health, *Drug Addiction, The Second Report of the Interdepartmental Committee*, London, HMSO, 1965

—, *Drug Addiction, Report of the Interdepartmental Committee*, London, HMSO, 1961

—, *Departmental Committee on Morphine and Heroin Addiction*, London, HMSO, 1926

Monaghan, G, *Trends in UK Drug Enforcement*, Paper presented at the Association of Chief Police Officers' National Drug Conference, West Yorkshire Police Training School, 8-10 June 1994

—, 'Powers of Arrest for Cannabis', *Druglink*, Vol. 6, Issue 1, January/February 1991

Monahan, J, 'West Left Wanting in Drugs War's New European Front', *Financial Times*, 20 March 1990

Moran, T K, 'US Drugs Strategy: Is there a Change of Emphasis', Paper presented at the Association of Chief Police Officers' National Drug Conference, West Yorkshire Police Training School, 8-10 June 1994

Morgan, R, and T Newburn, T, *The Future of Policing*, Oxford: Clarendon Press,1997

Mouat, L, 'Drug Traffickers Link Up in 1990', *The Christian Science Monitor*, 9 January 1991

Mukherjee S K, *Profile of Federal Prisoners*, Canberra: Australian Institute of Criminology, 1981

Nadelman, Ethan, A, 'The Case for Legalisation', *The Public Interest*, 92, 1988, 3-31

—'International Drug Trafficking and U.S. Foreign Policy', *Washington Quarterly*, Fall, 1985, No.4

— *Cops Across Borders: The Internationalization of U.S. Criminal Law Enforcement*, Pennsylvania: Pennsylvania State University Press,1993

National Audit Office, *HM Customs and Excise: Custody and Disposal of Seized and Detained Goods 1991-92*, London: HMSO, 1996

Neil, A, 'Public Agony is a Poor Weapon Against Ecstasy', *The Sunday Times*, 19 November 1995

New Nigerian, 'Embassy to Help Abandoned Nigerian Children', 19 October 1990

—, 'British Social Workers for Lagos', 12 October 1990

Nigerian Tribune, 'Law Against Dumping of Nigerian Children Abroad Soon', *Nigerian Tribune*, 11 October 1990

O'Connor, J, 'The Policing of Drugs in London: A Police Commander's Personal View', in Green, P (Ed.), *Drug Couriers: A New Perspective*, London: Quarter Books, 1996, 191-8

O'Malley, Pat and Stephen Mugford, 'The Demand for Intoxicating Commodities, Implications for the War on Drugs', *Social Justice*, Vol.18, No. 4, 1991, 49-75

Oakley, R, 'Britain Leads Drive for EU Drugs Intelligent Unit', *The Times*, 14 June 1990

Obi, D, 'Law on Child Abuse Soon', *New Nigerian*, 11 October 1990

Obot, I S, 'Ethical and Legal Issues in the Control of Drug Abuse and Drug Trafficking: The Nigerian Case', *Soc. Sci. Med.*, Vol. 35, No. 4, 481-93

Observer, The, 'Turncoat Labour Lords Wreak Criminal Damage', *The Observer*, 23 March 1997

Office of National Drug Control Policy, Office of the President, *National Drug Control Policy*, Washington DC: US Government Printing Office, 1991

Oladepo, W and Mba, J, 'Losing the Drug War', *Newswatch*, 19 February 1990

del Olmo, Rosa, 'Drug Couriers: Discourses, Perceptions and Policies' in Green, P (Ed.), *Drug Couriers: A New Perspective*, London: Quartet Books, 1996

—, 'The Geopolitics of Narcotic Trafficking in Latin America', *Social Justice*, Vol. 20, Issue 53-54, Fall-Winter, 1993, 1-23

—, 'The Hidden Face of Drugs', *Social Justice*,Vol. 18, No. 4, 1991, 10-48

—, 'The Economic Crisis and the Criminlisation of Latin American Women', *Social Justice* Vol. 17, No. 2, 1990, 40-53

Organization for Economic Cooperation and Development, *The Role of Development Assistance in Narcotics Reduction in Developing Countries*, Pari: OECD, 1987

Overseas Development Administration, *Nigeria: Country Aid Programme Statement 1996/97 Update Supplement*, London, ODA, 1996

Pallister, D, 'DPP Considers Charges Against 45 Police Officers', *The Guardian*, 4 February 1993

Palmer, Phil, *In Support of Community Intolerance, Zero Tolerance, Crime Control and the British Police*, University of Southampton, Unpublished

Parker, H, F Measham and J Aldridge, *Drugs, Future Changing Patterns of Drug Use Amongst English Youth*, London, ISDD, 1995

Pearson, G, *The New Heroin Users*, Oxford: Basil Blackwell, 1987

—and Phillips, S, *Drugs, People and Services In Lewisham*, Final Report of the Drug Information Project, the Lewisham Safer Cities Project, Goldsmiths College, Drug Information Project, 1991

Perl, R F (Ed.), *Drugs and Foreign Policy: A Critical Review*, Boulder: Westview Press, 1991

Petre, J, 'Drug Cash to Boost War on Traffickers', *Daily Telegraph*, 9 April 1991

Pilkington, E, 'The Smack Doctor', *The Guardian*, 26 October 1995

Police Review, 'Maastricht Treaty Creates "Europol" Intelligence Unit', *Police Review*, 13 December 1991

Rayner, J and T Kirby, 'Breaking the White Wave of Evil', *The Independent on Sunday*, 5 April 1992

Release, *Release National Drug Survey August 1994*, London: Release,1994

Refugee Council, The, *Beyond Belief: The Home Office and Nigeria*, London, The Refugee Council, 1995

Reuter, P, *Disorganized Crime: Illegal Markets and the Mafia*, Cambridge, Mass: MIT Press, 1984

191

Richards, M, McWilliams, N Batten, C Cameron and J Cutler, 'Foreign Nationals in English Prisons: 1. Family Ties and their Maintenance', *Howard Journal of Criminal Justice,* 34 (2), 1995, 158-75

Roberts, Y, 'To the Slaughter', *New Statesman and Society* 13 October 1989

Robertson, K, 'Crime, Frontier Controls and 1992', in Flood, S, (Ed.), *Illicit Drugs and Organized Crime: Issues for a Unified Europe,* Office of International Criminal Justice, University of Illinois at Chicago, 1991

Rose, D, '£1m Scheme to Pay Drug Informers', *The Guardian,* 15 February 1990

—, Crime Bill Could Fill 60 New Jails, *The Observer,* 23 March 1997

Ruggiero, Vincenzo, 'Brixton, London: A Drug Culture Without a Drug Economy', *International Journal of Drug Policy,* 4, 1993, 83-90

—and N South, *Eurodrugs: Drugs Use, Markets and Trafficking in Europe,* London, UCL Press Ltd., 1995

— and A Vass, 'Heroin Use and the Formal Economy', *British journal of Criminology,* 32, 1992, 273 - 91

Rutherford, Andrew, 'Women, Sentencing and the Prison Service', *New Law Journal,* Vol 147, March 1997, 424-425

—, *Transforming Criminal Policy,* Winchester: Waterside Press, 1996

—, *Criminal justice and the Pursuit of Decency,* Winchester: Waterside Press, 1994

—and P Green, 'Illegal Drugs and British Criminal Justice Policy' in Albrecht, Hans-Jorg and A van Kalmthout (Eds.), *Drugs Policies in Western Europe,* Frieburg, Max Planck Institute for Foreign and International Penal Law, 1989

Sabbag, R, *Snow Blind: A Brief Career in the Cocaine Trade,* London: Picador, 1976

Saltmarsh, G. 'Cleaning Up with Dirty Money', *Police Review,* 97, 1989, 390-91

Savona, E, 'Money Laundering, The Developed Countries and Drug Control: The New Agenda' in N Dorn, J Jepson and E Savona (Eds.), *European Drug Policies and Enforcement,* Basingstoke: Macmillan Press Ltd., 1996, 213 - 30

Sayo, I and T Odediran, 'Law Against Child Abandonment Underway', *The Times,* 11 October 1990

Scloilino, E, 'Lagos Regime is Behind Drugs Flood, US Report Says', *The Guardian,* 6 April 1994

SCODA, *Annual Report 1991/92,* London: SCODA, 1992

Seward, V, *Combating Drugs Trafficking and Abuse: The Challenge to Europe,* Wilton Park Paper 65, London, HMSO, 1993

Shapiro, H, '"Contemporary Cocaine Use" in Britain', in Institute for the Study of Drug Dependence (Ed.), *Drug Misuse in Britain,* London, ISDD, 1991

Sharkey, A, 'Just Get a Whiff of that Dutch Skunk', *The Independent,* 14 November 1992

Sharrock, D, 'Six held After £160 m Cocaine Raid', *The Guardian,* 24 November 1992

Single European Act, Article 8A, Council of the European Communities, Office for Official Publications, Luxembourg, 1986

Smart, C, 'Social Policy and Drug Addiction: A Critical Study of Policy Development', *British Journal of Addiction,* 1984, 31-39

Smit, B, 'Dutch Reap Rewards of Soft Line on Drugs', *Daily Telegraph,* 18 January 1991

Soloman, G B H and R M Jenkins, 'The Impact of EC 1992 on Terrorism and Drug Trafficking in Europe: The US Concerns', *Terrorism,* Vol. 13, 15-22

South, N, 'Drugs: Control, Crime and Criminal Studies', in Maguire, M, R Morgan and R Reiner (Eds.), *The Oxford Handbook of Criminology,* Oxford: Oxford University Press, 1994, 393

Spectator, The, 'Opium and the People', *The Spectator,* 11 June 1990

Standard, The, 'Checking Child Abandonment Abroad', 26 October 1990

—, 'High Commission to Cater for Abandoned Nigerian Children', *The Standard,* 20 October 1990

Stanley, A, 'Deportation and Drug Couriers' in Green, P (Ed.), *Drug Couriers: A New Perspective,* London: Quartet Books, 1996, 112-26

Statewatch, NCIS Annual Report, Vol. 6 No. 4, July-August 1996

—, 'Prison Drugs Policies', Vol. 6 No. 3, May-June 1996

—, 'Europol: Defining "Organised Crime"', Vol. 4 No. 4, July-August 1994, 12

—, 'Europol', Vol. 4 No. 3, May-June 1994, 16-17

—, 'Europol and Immigration', Vol. 3 No. 1, January-February 1993, 10-11

—, 'Which way for MI5?', Vol. 2 No. 2, March-April 1992, 5-6

—, 'Europol Given Go Ahead by Trevi', Vol. 2 No. 1, January-February 1992, 1

Stevenson, R, 'Legalise Them All', *The Guardian*, 31 October 1995

Stimson, G, 'The War on Heroin: British Policy and the International Trade in Illicit Drugs', in Dorn, N and N South (Eds.), *A Land Fit for Heroin: Drug Policies, Prevention and Practice*, London, Macmillan, 1987

Straw, J, *Breaking the Vicious Circle, Labour's Proposals to Tackle Drug Related Crime*, The Labour Party, 1996

Stuttaford, T, 'Every Illegal Maker has a Recipe, There is No Unadulterated Dose', *The Times*, 15 November 1995

Sunday Times, The, 'War on Drugs Yields Results', *The Sunday Times*, 29 July 1990

—, Leah's father in Threat to Dealer, *The Sunday Times*, 19th November 1995

Sutton, M and A Maynard, 'What Is the Size and Nature of the "Drug" Problem in the UK', YARTIC Occasional Paper 3 presented at the Centre for Health Economics, University of York, 1992

—'Trends in the Cost-effectiveness of Enforcement Activity in the Illicit Heroin Market, 1979-1990', YARTIC Occasional Paper 4, Centre for Health Economics, Leeds Addiction Unit, York, 1994

Taylor, I, 'The International Drug Trade and Money laundering: Border Controls and Other Issues', *European Sociological Review*, Vol. 8, No. 2, September 1992, 181-93

Tendler, S, 'Gang Killings Linked to Leah Case', *The Times*, 8 December 1995

—, 'Seizures of Heroin Double', *The Times*, 16 April 1991

Thomas, D A, 'The Criminal Justice Act 1993: (1) Confiscation Orders and Drug Trafficking', *Criminal Law Review*, 1994, 93-100

Thomas, D, 'Judge Jails Five in LSD Gang to a Total of 42 Years', *The Independent*, 29 May 1992

Time Magazine, 'Hitting Back at Heroin Control', 18 April 1994

Time Out, 'Stinging the Blues', 2 February 1994

—, 'Victim of Corrupt Police Goes Free', *Time Out*, 23-30 September 1992

Times, The, Leah Betts Man May face Retrial, *The Times*, 18th December 1996

—, 'Customs Drug Cash Haul "Not Enough"', *The Times*, 23 August 1996

—, 'Leah's Funeral to be Used as a Lesson', *The Times*, 2 December 1995

Tisdall, S, 'America Hit by Heroin-Eaters', *The Guardian*, November 1990

Trebach, A, *The Heroin Solution*, New Haven, Conn: Yale University Press, 1982

Travis, A, 'Customs Cuts "Open Drug Door"', *The Guardian*, 1 December 1994

—, 'Blair Warns of Drug Crime', *The Guardian*, 1 June 1994

Tullis, L, *Unintended Consequences: Illegal Drugs and Drug Policies in Nine Countries,*, London: Lynne Reinner Publishing, 1995

Turner, D, 'Pragmatic Incoherence: The Changing Face of British Drug Policy' in Krauss, M B and E P Lazear, *Searching for Alternatives, Drug-control Policy in the United States*, Stanford: Hoover Institute Press, 1991

US Congress Senate Committee on Foreign Relations, *Treaty Between the US and the Federal Republic of Nigeria on Mutual Legal Assistance in Criminal Matters*, Washington DC: USGPO, 1992)

United States Department of Justice, *An Analysis of Non-Violent Drug Offenders with Minimal Criminal Histories*, Washington DC: DOJ,1994

US State Department, *Agreement Between the United States of America and Nigeria, Narcotic Drugs*, Washington DC: USGPO, 1989

United Nations Commission on Narcotic Drugs, 'Situation and Trends in *Drug Abuse and the Illicit Traffic: Review of the Illicit Traffic in Narcotic Drugs and Psychotropic Substances During 1985*, Vienna: UN, 1987

Varley, N, 'Anger at 11 Years Jail for "Gullible" Drug Courier', *The Guardian*, 22 February 1997

Wagstaff, A and A Maynard, *Economic Aspects of the Illicit Drug Market and Drug Enforcement Policies in the UK*, London, HMSO, 1988

Walton, D A, 'Drug Couriers and the Role of Customs and Excise: A Custom's Senior Manager's Personal View' in Green, P (Ed.), *Drug Couriers: A New Perspective*, London: Quarter Books, 1996, 183-90

Watson, R, 'Drug Supersquad for EC', *The European*, 23 April 1992

Weale, S, 'Legalisation Creates Problems It Does Not Solve Them', *The Guardian*, 31 October 1995

Webb, G, 'Charges Soon in Police Drug, Theft Corruption Scandal', *Evening Standard*, 3 February 1994

West Riding Yorkshire Post, 'Police Charged Over Operation Jackpot Corruption Claims', 27 July 1994

White House, *National Strategy for the Prevention of Drug Abuse and Drug Trafficking*, Washington DC: US Government Printing Office, 1984

—, *National Drugs Control Strategy*, Washington DC: US Government Printing Office, 1988

Wilkinson, P, 'Policewomen Jailed for Supplying Their Friends with Drugs', *The Times*, 11 October 1995

—, 'Police Target Ecstasy', *The Times*, 10 January 1992

Wiltshire Gazette and Herald, 'Steer Clear of "Big E" Warning', 23 January 1992

Wintour, P, '"Political Cowards" Anger MP', *The Guardian*, 31 October 1995

Yorkshire Post, 'Customs Officers Given Powers to Seize Drug Cash', 23 September 1991.

Index

196

197

198

internal concealment 90 *et al*
Interpol 16 19 20 29 137
Iran 32 43 47
Ireland 24
ISDD 133
Islamic countries/aspects 18 71 176
Istanbul 41
Italy 20 23 43 47

Jamaica(n) 17 80 86 96 144 146 160 176

Labour/New Labour 123 *et al*
Laos 47
Latin America 35 37 45 59 62 84 89
legalisation 14 23 121 *et al* 124 129 138 et al
Lome Convention 42
low-level players 9 10 47 80 *et al* 131 171 175
    women as 85

Maastricht Treaty 21 23
Macedonia 43
Mafia 17 176
MAGHREB 18 29
manufacture 135
medical practitioners 108 *et al*
Methadone 133
Mexico 31
Middle East 18 43
miscarriage of justice 141 *et al* 147
Misuse of Drugs Act 1971 113
MI5, MI6 137
money laundering 15 22 38 118
monitoring 20 28 38
morphine 109 111
Mutual Legal Assistance Treaties (MLATS) 39

National Drugs Intelligence Unit 136
National Drug Survey (Release) 133
'narco dollars' 120
Nazi/neo-Nazi 18
NCIS 17 25 119 136
NDLEA (Nigeria) 60
Netherlands, The 20 23 24 47 130
New Labour Because Britain Deserves Better 127
Nigeria(n) 13 18 32 36 43 45 *et al* 80 82 87 90 105 160 164 176 177
normalisation 132
North America 48

199

Russia 43

scapegoating 62 175
Schengen Convention 23 29 130
SCODA 131
Scotland 139
search/seizure 113 148 149 153 177
sentences: see *punishment, harsh punishments*
seriousness (drug offences) 10
shaming 62 67 105
Single European Act 15
smuggling 55 135 148 *et al* 180
social control: see *control etc.*
South Africa 18 47
South America 18 48 80 82
   and see *Columbia* in particular
Spain 47 99 100
stereotypes 17 79 147 179
street values 158
Structural Adjustment Programme (SAP) 56
surveillance 15 24 38
   and see *monitoring*
supply reduction/orientation 20 33 35 37 38 45 116 117 126 130 134 *et al*
   179
symbolism/symbolic gestures 33 40 128 130 177
Syria 32

Tackling Drug Misuse 117 136
Tackling Drugs Together 122 132 151 171
TALIS programme 29
targeting/target groups 18 34 45 48 80 *et al* 135 136 147 149
tariff reduction 36
terrorism 136 155 176
Thailand 36 47
Third World 86 90 120 148 180
trade preferences 40 42 177
traffickers (special emphasis) 79 115 160 162 *et al* 175 *et al*
TREVI 16 21 27 29
Triads 17
Turkey/Turkish 17 29 43 176

UNDCP 30
UK 27 33 80 107 *et al* 130 *et al*
USA 9 18 25 31 37 *et al* 47 57 59 80 83 119 130 134 145
   and see North America
USSR (former) 42

The Sentence of the Court Series

This excellent series created by experts with day-to-day responsibility is essential reading for anyone interested in magistrates' courts:

📖 **The Sentence of the Court** Michael Watkins, Winston Gordon and Anthony Jeffries. **Foreword: Lord Bingham, Lord Chief Justice.**

- Excellent *The Law*
- An extremely clear, well written book *The Magistrate.*

Second edition 1998. 192 pages. ISBN 1 872 870 64 3 *Published May 1998* £12.

📖 **Introduction to the Youth Court** Winston Gordon, Michael Watkins and Philip Cuddy.

- A must for those interested in the work of the youth courts *The Magistrate.*
- Extremely useful and practical *The Law.* (1996)

New second edition scheduled for late 1998. ISBN 1 872 870 36 8. £12

📖 **Introduction to Road Traffic Offences** Winston Gordon, Philip Cuddy. A complete overview of this everyday topic. (1998) ISBN 1 872 870 51 1. £12

Also produced under the auspices of the Justices' Clerks' Society:

Magistrates Bench Handbook
A Manual for Lay Magistrates

A range of key materials for training and day-to-day reference purposes. An invaluable resource for anyone interested in magistrates' courts. Includes *The Sentence of the Court*, Magistrates' Association *Sentencing Guidelines.* Judicial Studies Board Structured Decision-making Charts, a selection of Reference Sheets and Court Pronouncements in Plain English. Loose-leaf. ISBN 1 872 870 62 7. Direct mail price (includes binder, contents and printed section dividers) £28.50 plus £3.50 p&p per copy. UK only.

And *Introduction to the Family Proceedings Court* (see under *Introductory Books*, p. 204).

Series Editor Bryan Gibson

Other introductory books from Waterside Press

📖 **Introduction to the Magistrates' Court** Bryan Gibson (Third edition scheduled for late 1998). A basic outline — plus *Common Practices and Procedures* and an extensive *Glossary of Words, Phrases and Abbreviations*. An ideal introduction *Law Society Gazette*. (1995) ISBN 1 872 870 15 5. £12

📖 **Introduction to the Family Proceedings Court** Elaine Laken, Chris Bazell and Winston Gordon. **Foreword: Sir Stephen Brown**, President of the Family Division of the High Court. Produced under the auspices of the Justices' Clerks' Society. Because of its clarity of information and its lucidity of language and explanation *Introduction to the Family Proceedings Court* is a very accessible handbook *The Magistrate*. (1997) ISBN 1 872 870 46 5. £12

📖 **Introduction to the Probation Service** Anthony Osler. An overview of work with offenders. Also includes the role of the Court Welfare Service in family matters. (1995) ISBN 1 872 870 19 8. £12. A new second edition by Dick Whitfield will be available from Autumn 1998

📖 **Introduction to the Criminal Justice Process** Bryan Gibson and Paul Cavadino. Rarely, if ever, has this complex process been described with such comprehensiveness and clarity *Justice of the Peace* (First reprint, 1997) ISBN 1 872 870 09 0. £12

📖 **Introduction to Prisons** Nick Flynn *et al* **Foreword: Lord Hurd.** In association with the Prison Reform Trust. (Autumn 1998) ISBN 1 872 870 37 6. £12

📖 **Introduction to Criminology** A Basic Guide Russell Pond A lay person's guide written with people working in the criminal justice arena in mind. The basic ideas of criminology and their sources. (Autumn 1998) ISBN 1 872 870 42 2. £12

A selection of other titles from Waterside Press

📖 **Criminal Classes** Offenders at School Angela Devlin
If you are in any doubt about the links between poor education, crime and recidivism, read it: Marcel Berlins *The Guardian*. (First reprint, 1997) ISBN 1 872 870 30. £16

📖 **Children Who Kill** Paul Cavadino (Ed.) With contributions by **Gitta Sereny** and others. From the tragic Mary Bell and Jamie Bulger cases to comparable events world-wide. Highly recommended *The Law*. A rich source of information *BJSW*. (1996) ISBN 1 872 870 29 5. £16

📖 **Tackling the Tag** The Electronic Monitoring of Offenders Dick Whitfield A comprehensive and balanced guide *Prison Report*. Each court library would benefit from a copy *The Justices' Clerk*. (1997) ISBN 1 872 870 53 8. £16

📖 **Interpreters and the Legal Process** Joan Colin and Ruth Morris Weighty and immensely readable *Law Society Gazette*. An extremely practical guide *The Law*. A scholarly work with everyday practical messages for all professionals *Wig and Gavel*. (1996) ISBN 1 872 870 28 7. £12

📖 **Prisons of Promise** Tessa West **Foreword: Sir David Ramsbotham**, Chief Inspector of Prisons. Extremely well-researched . . . Should be seriously considered by the home secretary *Justice of the Peace*. Deserves to be made available to every magistrate *The Justices' Clerk*. (1997) ISBN 1 872 870 50 3. £16

📖 **I'm Still Standing** Bob Turney The autobiography of a dyslexic ex-prisoner, now a probation officer. A truly remarkable book *Prison Writing*. (1997) ISBN 1 872 870 43 0. £12

📖 **Justice for Victims and Offenders** Martin Wright An informative addition to the excellent Waterside Press series *Vista*. ISBN 1 872 870 35 X. £16

📖 **Hanging in the Balance** Brian Block and John Hostettler A history of the abolition of capital punishment in Britain. **Foreword: Lord Callaghan.** A masterwork *Justice of the Peace*. (1997) ISBN 1 872 870 47 3. £18

📖 **Conflict Resolution** A Foundation Guide Susan Stewart Of interest to people who deal with disputes — of whatever kind — including through mediation and alternative dispute resolution procedures. (1998) ISBN 1 872 870 65 1. £12

📖 **Domestic Violence and Occupation of the Family Home** Chris Bazell and Bryan Gibson A key work for family law practitioners. Includes the interface with the Protection from Harassment Act 1997. (Autumn 1998 onwards) ISBN 1 872 870 60 0. £18

📖 **Invisible Women** What's Wrong With Women's Prisons? Angela Devlin As featured in the national press. ISBN 1 872 870 59 7. £18

📖 **Drinking and Driving** A Decade of Development Jonathan Black Strongly recommended *Justice of the Peace* (1993) ISBN 1 872 870 12 0. £14

📖 **Principled Policing** John Alderson From Northern Ireland to Tiananmen Square, Nazi Germany to Edgar Hoover's days at the FBI: a call for decency, fairness and moral values to act as touchstones for police officers everywhere. By the former Chief Constable of Devon and Cornwall. ISBN 1 872 870 71 6. £18

📖 **Until They Are Seven** His Honour John Wroath An absorbing account of the origins of women's legal rights. A true story which reads like a Victorian novel. ISBN 1 872 870 57 0. £16

Forthcoming

📖 **Going Straight** Angela Devlin and Bob Turney Interviews with people who have 'succeeded' after a life inside/criminal career. ISBN 1 872 870 66 X. £18

📖 **Communities Against Crime** Rob Allen A first-hand investigation of promising initiatives in the USA which may be worthy of replication in the UK. Details tba.

📖 **A to Z of Criminal Justice** Paul Cavadino A 'mini-encyclopaedia' of terms and terminology. ISBN 1 872 870 10 4. £18

📖 **Geese Theatre Handbook: Working With Offenders and Youth at Risk** Drama based group work and interactive theatre for offenders including practical exercises and instructions. A practical guide to drama-based learning, with exercises and hundreds of suggestions. (Scheduled for late 1998/early 1999) ISBN 1 872 870 67 8. £20

📖 **Murderers and Life Imprisonment** Eric Cullen and Tim Newell ISBN 1 872 870 56. £20 Details tba

Other Titles in the Waterside Press Criminal Policy Series

A range of publications by leading commentators on criminal justice and criminal policy

Transforming Criminal Policy Andrew Rutherford Excellent and highly readable *Vista*. (1996) ISBN 1 872 870 31 7. £16

Capital Punishment Global Issues and Prospects Peter Hodgkinson and Andrew Rutherford (Eds.) Deserves to be widely read *Law Quarterly Review*. ISBN 1 872 870 32 5. £18

Criminal Justice and the Pursuit of Decency Andrew Rutherford Without people committed to humanising penal practice, criminal justice can so easily sink into apathy and pointless repression *Sunday Telegraph*. (Reprint 1994) ISBN 1 872 870 21 X. £12

Criminal Justice 2000: Strategies for a New Century Michael Cavadino, Iain Crow and James Dignan. Details tba

Golden Threads of Evidence and Procedure Roderick Munday. Details tba

Series Editor Professor Andrew Rutherford

Matthew Tillotson
L6SS
Janette Spurr
L6HB
Richard K Hodgson L6ARB—U6ARB
Michael Woodhead L6 EM
D. A. Leatherdale L6 RJM

Brixdal Glacier, Norway. Note the intensely crevassed surface of the glacier, the cave at the snout, the rocky morainic deposit in the foreground, and the lake at the ice front. (*Bergen Line*.)

MORPHOLOGY

AND

LANDSCAPE

BY

HARRY ROBINSON, Ph.D., M.Ed., B.A.

HEAD OF DEPARTMENT OF GEOGRAPHY AND GEOLOGY,

THE POLYTECHNIC, HUDDERSFIELD.

UNIVERSITY TUTORIAL PRESS LTD

9-10 GREAT SUTTON STREET, LONDON, E.C.1

Published 1969
Reprinted (*with minor alterations*) 1970
Second Edition 1973

ISBN: 0 7231 0615 0

PRINTED IN GREAT BRITAIN BY UNIVERSITY TUTORIAL PRESS LTD, FOXTON
NEAR CAMBRIDGE

PREFACE

THIS book provides the Sixth Form student with an introduction to the branch of physical geography which we call geomorphology. However, I have entitled this book *Morphology and Landscape* since it is concerned primarily with landscape features and I wish to emphasise the skeletal importance of topographic features and to show how they have been developed.

In writing a text for Sixth Formers the twofold problem arises of, first, translating geomorphological jargon into understandable English and, secondly, of deciding the extent to which new concepts should be introduced. I hope the matter is presented in such a way that the student can not only understand it readily but also find the book readable. To assist the verbal comprehension, I have made use of many simple diagrams and included many specially selected photographs. The latter should be carefully studied and referred to when reading the text.

The introduction of new ideas to the Sixth Form student helps him to realise that the textbook is not gospel and that he must beware of accepting without question what may seem to be perfectly obvious and rational statements; moreover, it demonstrates to him that geography is a dynamic discipline and that there are many problems of an interesting nature still teasing and perplexing the geomorphologist. The ultimate purpose, of course, is to get the student to *think* and not merely to ingest yet more geographical information.

The whole approach to geomorphology is changing and many of the former explanations of features and processes are not only being questioned but in some cases have been shown to be inaccurate. There is now a growing awareness that climate, vegetation and soil, and even man himself, have played a much more important role in landscape development than was formerly believed; the Davisian interpretation of landscape evolution has come under heavy fire; the role of mass wasting in landscape formation is now receiving increased attention; and we are beginning to look more closely at arid, semi-humid, and humid tropical environments. I have

iii

attempted to introduce and briefly discuss some of these newer developments without departing too much from the traditional approach to physical studies. There is a formidable gap to be bridged between "O" and "A" Level geography and this bridging has to be done in easy stages. This book will provide a basic introduction so that the student can then go on to more advanced texts and read and understand them with greater facility.

I wish to acknowledge my most grateful thanks to many people who have helped in the writing and production of this book; to those authors, editors, and publishers who granted me permission to use quotations and diagrams (acknowledged in the text); to organisations, agencies, and individuals who helped with the illustrative material; to D. C. Money and my colleague A. Potter who read and criticised the MS. and who made innumerable suggestions; to my students who, in a sense, were my guinea pigs; and to my wife for her support and forbearance. I would emphasise that I alone am responsible for any inaccuracies that may occur in the text.

H. R.

NOTE TO THE SECOND EDITION

In the new edition, changes to take account of more recent research have been made in the diagrams, and recent developments in crustal plate theory have been reviewed.

H. R.

CONTENTS

LIST OF ILLUSTRATIONS

CHAPTER 1

THE EARTH—ITS SHAPE, COMPOSITION, AND STRUCTURE

Early Speculation

According to Archbishop Ussher, an Irish prelate who lived in the middle of the seventeenth century, the earth was created at exactly nine o'clock on the morning of 23 October, 4004 B.C.[1] The biblical interpretation of the origin of the earth and the universe is that of Divine Creation: "In the beginning God created the Heaven and the Earth". This Christian belief dominated European theology and philosophy until modern times. But it is interesting to note that from the very earliest days peoples have speculated upon the origin of the earth and the universe. The study of the evolution of ideas regarding the earth and its relation to the solar system and of the latter to the universe is known as *cosmology*. Such a study really lies outside the scope of geography but it is useful to have some slight background knowledge of the subject.

From the very beginning man was fascinated by the heavens and the earth and pondered upon their origin. Peoples of early civilisations had their versions of creation and of the nature of the universe and some of these early ideas were highly elaborate and not infrequently fantastic. The Greek philosophers were the first to query the mythological fabrications of the earlier civilisations and they tried to find a more satisfactory and more rational explanation for the form of the world.

Who it was who first propounded that the earth was spherical is not known for certain but it is recorded that Thales of Miletus, who flourished during the sixth century B.C., believed the earth to be a sphere. Two centuries later, both Aristotle and Plato argued that the earth must be spherical in shape. Ptolemy, the last of the great Greek astronomer-geographers, held that the earth was a

---

[1] According to the geologists' reckoning the earth is about 4,500 million years old.

sphere but was a stationary body and that all the planets and stars revolved around it. The Ptolemaic system, embracing the idea of the earth as the centre of the universe, persisted throughout medieval times and dominated scientific thought.

In A.D. 1543 a Polish astronomer, Copernicus, published his revolutionary theory which put the earth in its proper place and fixed the sun as the centre of the solar system. According to Copernicus' theory, the earth was merely one of several planets revolving around the sun. This new hypothesis was hotly disputed by the Church and it was many years before this *heliocentric theory,* as opposed to the traditional *geocentric theory,* won complete hearing and support.

The Shape of the Earth

To early man, with his limited powers of perception, the earth was flat. This belief of a flat, disc-like earth was common to all the peoples of antiquity and the concept persisted until the Greek philosophers began to teach otherwise. After the collapse of the Roman Empire, the scientific learning of the Ancient Greeks was, for the most part, lost and during the period known as the Dark Ages, approximately from the fifth to the thirteenth centuries A.D., reason was at a discount. Learning fell into the hands of monks and clerics and knowledge came to be based upon the literal interpretation of the Scriptures. The earth thus came to be regarded, once again, as a plane. Did not the expression "the four corners of the earth", plainly stated in the Book of Revelation, prove beyond any shadow of doubt that the earth was a rectangular plane? The Scriptures were the supreme authority and the churchmen effectually had their way. A Christian merchant, one Cosmas, in his theological zeal, wrote a book entitled *Christian Topography* (circa A.D. 540), to confound what he thought were the erroneous views of "pagan" authorities. He ridiculed their idea of a spherical earth by drawing a picture of a round ball with four men standing upon it on opposite sides, triumphantly asking how could men possibly stand upside down? Not all men, however, not even all churchmen, succumbed to Scriptural persuasion; a few, like Bede, persisted in their belief of a spherical earth. But the majority pinned their faith to biblical teaching and accepted without question the Scriptural interpretations of the form of the earth. Not until the sixteenth century did the flat earth theory become finally superseded by a spinning, spherical earth.

The heliocentric theory of Copernicus together with the discovery of the laws of gravitation by Newton and the investigations into circular motion by Huyghen caused the scientists to think afresh upon the form of the earth. They argued that if the earth was a motionless body, the mutual attraction of its several parts would cause it to have a perfectly spherical shape; but, it was accepted that it was a rotating body and as such, therefore, it was subject to centrifugal forces and would, accordingly, tend to bulge out in those parts furthest removed from the axis of rotation, *i.e.* in its equatorial regions. In this way Newton deduced the earth had a shape something like an orange—that it departed from the perfect spherical form through slight polar flattening.

A pendulum experiment, undertaken by Jean Richer in 1671, confirmed Newton's theory. The French astronomer went to the island of Cayenne, in French Guiana, to make certain observations and here, near the equator, he found that a clock, which kept exact time in Paris, lost nearly two and a half minutes every twenty-four hours. This he correctly attributed to the difference in the force of gravity between Paris and Cayenne. The nearer a pendulum is to the centre of the earth the faster it swings, thus it was deduced that Cayenne must lie slightly more removed from the centre of the earth than Paris or, in other words, there must be a slight bulging of the earth in equatorial latitudes.

At this juncture there was another development: let us quote Dr E. G. Woods: "Simultaneously with the announcement of Newton's discovery, two French astronomers named Cassini had, through errors in their measurements, arrived at the conclusion that the earth was elongated like an egg; hence, in France, Newton's 'orange' became a 'lemon'. Thus arose a furious controversy, most amusingly parodied by Swift in *Gulliver's Travels,* where the Court was torn by factions between the Bigendians and the Littlendians. Finally the French Academy settled the dispute in favour of Newton by sending expeditions both to Lapland and Ecuador. 'Thus,' grimly remarked Voltaire, '(they) flattened both the poles and the Cassinis'." [1]

Later measurements confirmed Newton's definition of the earth's form as a sphere compressed along the polar axis and bulging slightly around the equator, although the flattening is more pronounced than the bulging. Such a form with its two deviations from perfect sphericity is called an *oblate spheroid* or an *ellipsoid of revolution*. The earth's oblateness is attributed to the centrifugal force of the earth's rotation, which produced the oblate spheroidal form when the earth was in its formative stage and in a plastic condition. The oblate spheroidal form has not been accepted without challenge, however, and, in 1903, Jeans calculated that the earth was more pear-shaped than orange-shaped! [2] To surmount the difficulties of describing the exact shape of the earth the term *geoid* was invented, although this does not get us very far since it simply means "earth-shaped"!

The study and determination of the exact form and dimensions of the earth is the science of *geodesy*. Geodetic survey together with satellite observations gives the earth's dimensions as follows: equatorial diameter 7,926·42 miles, polar diameter 7,899·83 miles, giving a difference of 26·59 miles. This departure from the perfect spherical form is only slight and it must not be over-emphasised. Viewed from the moon, the earth would appear as a true sphere. Again, the earth reduced to the size of a 16-inch globe would not depart sensibly from the spherical. Thus for all practical purposes we can assume the earth to be a perfect sphere.

PROOFS OF THE EARTH'S SPHERICITY

A person possessing no previously acquired knowledge of the world in which he lives might be forgiven for assuming the earth was flat. The rotundity of the earth is not easy to perceive from ground level. Acute observation and careful thought, however, will convince one of the earth's spherical form. But this sphericity

[1] *The Principles of Geography, Physical and Human,* Oxford University Press, 1937, p. 24.

[2] The latest measurements reveal that Jeans was correct. British Association, 1965.

was not always believed in, as we have already seen, and a story is told of Paul Kruger, President of the Transvaal towards the end of the nineteenth century, who was affronted when a person in his company referred to the earth as being round! Stranger still, however, are those people, "the flat-earthers", who to this day persist in believing the earth is flat. A flat earth contravenes one or all of the usually accepted proofs of the earth's sphericity.

The following arguments may be adduced in witness of the earth's spherical shape.

(1) Circumnavigation, first accomplished by Magellan's ship, the *Vittoria,* and since repeated innumerable times, provides striking proofs of the earth's roundness. Travel, along the surface on a constant bearing, from any point on the earth's surface, will eventually bring one back to the point of departure.

(2) If the earth was flat, the sun would rise (and set) at precisely the same moment over its entire surface; moreover, the angle at which the sun's rays struck the earth would be uniform over the whole surface, but we know it is not and that it varies from 0 to 90 degrees, thereby proving the curvature of the surface.

(3) The dip of the horizon is everywhere the same. Again, the horizon is always circular to an observer and, with increasing height, the horizon continually expands to give an ever-widening view; this is a feature characteristic of a sphere.

(4) The altitude of the Pole Star increases regularly (1 degree higher for every 69 miles) as an observer travels from the equator to the poles, indicating the earth is curved in a north-south direction. We can prove that all arcs drawn from equator to pole are arcs of circles and, therefore, that the earth is spherical.

(5) In lunar eclipses the earth's shadow on the moon is always seen to be circular and the only geometrical form which at all times and under all circumstances always casts a circular shadow is a sphere. Thus the inference is the earth must be round.

(6) The sun and all the planets of the solar system have been observed to be spherical bodies and, since the earth is merely one of the planets, originating in the same way as all the others, by analogy, it may be assumed to be, like the rest, spherical in shape.

(7) Apart from the very slight differences we have already noted in connection with Richer's experiment, the force of gravity is practically the same the world over. Thus, the force of gravity requires the earth to be spherical in form.

(8) The Bedford Level experiment, first performed in 1870 by A. R. Wallace, gave practical proof of the earth's rotundity. If three poles of equal height are set up at equally spaced intervals on a water surface and the top of the third is sighted from the first, the middle pole will be found to project above the line of sight, thereby proving the curvature of the surface, which is of the order of 6 feet in 3 miles.

(9) Aerial photography offers the latest and most convincing proof. Examination of photographs taken by rockets at very high altitudes—200 miles and more—shows the horizon as a curved line. A series of photographs taken in many widely separated parts of the earth would provide indisputable evidence of a spherical form.

Cumulatively, these various arguments demonstrate beyond any shadow of doubt that the earth is a sphere.

SURFACE IRREGULARITY

Although the earth has a spherical form, it is obvious that the earth's outer surface is by no means smooth. High mountains and ocean deeps produce a notable irregularity of surface relief. The continents exhibit a varied relief of mountains, plateaus, and plains, and continental relief culminates in Mount Everest with an elevation of 29,141 feet above sea level. Similarly, the ocean floors, though generally less diversified than the land masses, possess ridges, rises, depressions, and deeps, with the greatest recorded depth occurring in the Mariana Trench, off the island of Guam in the Pacific, 37,800 feet below sea level. The total vertical range of the surface of the earth is thus 66,941 feet, or just over 12 miles (see Fig. 1).

We should not be unduly impressed by this irregularity of the earth's surface, for 12 miles is only about 0·154 per cent. of the earth's diameter. The amount of irregularity can be illustrated in a number of ways. For example, if the earth is reduced to the size

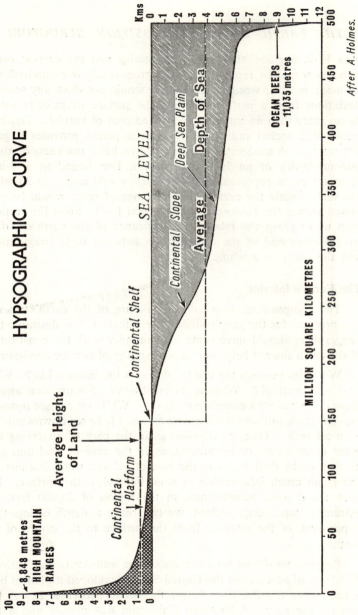

Fig. 1.

The diagram shows the areas of the earth's crust between successive levels from the highest mountain peak, Mount Everest 29,141 feet, to the greatest known ocean deep, Mariana Trench 37,800 feet.

of a 16-inch globe, the highest mountains and the deepest ocean trenches would be represented by approximately one-hundredth of an inch; in other words, such a globe would not show any sensible deviations from a perfect sphere. The surface irregularity would be no more than an imperfectly applied coat of varnish. Again, a circle of 2 inches radius drawn with a pencil provides a good illustration. A moderately thin pencil line has a thickness of about one-hundredth of an inch and such a line bounding a 4-inch diameter circle, representing 8,000 miles, would represent 20 miles. On such a scale the earth's vertical range of relief would be contained within the thickness of the pencil line! Such illustrations help us to grasp the relative insignificance of the earth's surface irregularities and of the true relation between these irregularities and the earth as a whole.

The Earth's Interior

The composition, structure, and nature of the earth's interior is a problem for the geophysicist. Nevertheless, it is desirable that geographers should have some acquaintance with the constitution of the earth since it helps our understanding of surface conditions.

What lies beneath the crust? What is the interior like? What does it consist of? What is its condition? No one can answer these questions with complete certainty. While we can see upwards into space for millions of miles, we are unable to see downwards for even an inch. True, by digging, as in the case of quarrying and other excavations, or by mining, as in the case of coal and gold mining, or by drilling, as in the case of oil and water borings, we can glean much information of what lies below the surface. But even the deepest penetrations, in the region of 20,000 feet, are extremely superficial; indeed, we can reach a depth of less than 1 per cent. of the distance from the surface to the centre of the earth.

Because we know so little about the sub-crust, the National Academy of Sciences in the United States developed a plan to bore a hole some 6 miles deep below the ocean bed (Fig. 2). A site just off the shore of Southern California was chosen and a test drilling has already taken place. The aim was to drill through the overlying crust under the ocean where it is relatively thin

THE MOHOLE PROJECT

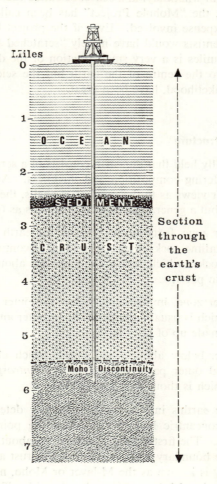

Section through the earth's crust

Fig. 2.

In order to probe the earth's crust, with a view to finding out more about its constitution and character, it was planned to drill a hole to tap the mantle below the Mohorovičić discontinuity but, temporarily it is hoped, the project has been called off.

(about $2\frac{1}{2}$ miles) to probe and secure samples of the sub-crust. Scientists would have been able to study the cores brought up by the drilling.   Such cores would have provided authentic samples of material from what may, in a sense, be called the earth's interior. Unfortunately, the "Mohole Project" has been called off because of the great expense involved.   Even if the project had been completed, the scientists would have merely "scratched the surface" as it were, for 6 miles is a very small fraction of the distance—some 4,000 miles—to the centre of the earth but the scientific rewards would, in all likelihood, have been great.

The Earth's Structure

It is generally held that the earth consists of a series of layers or "shells" of differing composition and thickness.   Authorities vary slightly in their views as to the number of shells, their constitution, and thickness but a generally accepted scheme is as follows:

(i) an outer zone, forming the crust of the earth which is composed of crystalline rocks with a thin and discontinuous layer of sedimentary rocks, which has a thickness of about 25 miles or slightly more in parts;

(ii) an inner zone, immediately below the outer crust, forming the *mantle,* which is usually divided into an outer and inner mantle and which is made up of ultra-basic rocks;

(iii) a core, below about 1,800 miles, which also appears to have inner and outer parts, known as the *centrosphere* or *barysphere* and which is thought to be metallic.

Within the earth's interior are two clearly detectable changes between the concentric layers;   these dividing points are termed discontinuities.   The first occurs at a depth of about 20 to 30 miles and marks the boundary between the earth's crust and the mantle. This boundary is known as the M-layer or Moho, named after the Yugoslav scientist, Mohorovičić, who first identified it from his study of earthquake waves which, he noted, suddenly increased in velocity at a depth of about 20 miles thereby indicating an increase in rock density.

The second major discontinuity, called the Gutenberg discontinuity, after the scientist who discovered it in 1914, occurs at a depth of 1,800 miles. At this depth the mantle of ultra-basic rocks gives way to the core which is thought to be metallic. Some geophysicists believe the Gutenberg discontinuity marks the change from a solid to a liquid state. Whatever the core may be made of

STRUCTURE OF THE EARTH

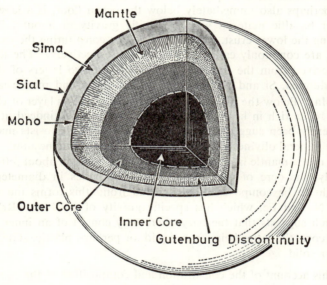

Fig. 3.

A "cutaway" of the earth to illustrate the hypothetical structure of the interior. It is believed that the interior consists of a series of onion-like layers. The different layers are not drawn to scale.

and whatever state it may be in, there is no doubting that at a depth of some 1,800 miles there is change for the core offers resistance to earthquake waves: the so-called S-waves disappear while the P-waves travel on at a reduced speed (see p. 55). Fig. 3 shows a "cutaway" of the earth to give a cross-section of its interior structure.

Composition and Nature

The outermost layer of the earth consists of crystalline rocks with sedimentary rock cappings. The greater part of the land surface is covered with sedimentary rocks, such as limestones, sandstones, shales, and clays, in places several miles thick; but evenly spread over the earth's surface they would form a cover only about half a mile deep. The sedimentary rocks of the continental surfaces lie on granitic crystalline basement rocks. The sedimentary and granitic rocks have a specific gravity of 2·0-2·7. Beneath these, and perhaps also immediately below the ocean floor, is a layer of denser basaltic material with a specific gravity of about 2·7-3·0 forming the lower crust. These two layers, constituting the earth's crust, are commonly called *sial* and *sima* respectively. The terms are derived from the combination of the first two letters of silica and alumina, Si and Al respectively, and silica and magnesia, Si and Ma. Below the Mohorovičić discontinuity lies a layer of ultrabasic rocks rich in heavy iron-magnesium minerals; indeed, it has frequently been suggested that this layer probably consists mainly of the mineral olivine, a heavy silicate of iron and magnesium. The rocks of the mantle have a specific gravity of between about 3·0-5·0. Finally, the core of the earth, some 4,000 miles in diameter, is thought to be composed of nickel and iron; this forms the *nife*, from Ni and Fe, which has specific gravity of 5·0-13·0. Recent research suggests that the barysphere may consist of an inner and outer core, the latter being in a liquid, or perhaps plastic, state, the former solid.

This account of the constitution and composition of the earth is essentially hypothetical. It is based upon reasonable interpretation of geophysical exploration and observation. There are sound and good reasons for believing that the earth's interior resembles the picture outlined above, but these interpretations should not be accepted as ascertained facts.

And what of the nature of the earth? It is established beyond any shadow of doubt that temperature and pressure increase with depth below the earth's surface. Whatever the exact figures may be, we can be assured that at the earth's centre tremendously high temperatures and enormous pressure prevail. Under the great heat, one would expect the material of the core to become liquid, perhaps even gaseous, but, as a result of the terrific pressure, it is in a condition such as we cannot comprehend. Scientists ask us to imagine the earth as a ball as rigid and as strong as steel and yet, at the same time, possessing a certain plasticity!

CHAPTER 2

ROCKS—THEIR CHARACTER, CLASSIFICATION, AND
IMPORTANCE

What is Rock?

In the foregoing section we have already referred to rocks of various kinds—limestone, sandstone, granite, basalt—which constitute much of the earth's crust. Since a great deal of what follows in this book will be concerned with rocks, it is important that we should be clear as to terms and familiarise ourselves with the chief types of rock.

First, what is meant by "rock"? To the geologist, and the geographer too, rocks include not only hard, massive slabs or boulders of stone, but such softer materials as muds, clays, and sands. In the strict geological sense rock is any naturally occurring agglomeration of mineral particles. Thus we can say rocks are composed of *minerals*. But what is a mineral? The term is difficult to define with precision[1] but scientifically a mineral is any natural inorganic homogeneous substance which has a distinct chemical composition. Altogether about 1,500 mineral species are known; to these, and their varieties, many thousands of names have been given. Of these many hundreds of kinds of minerals only relatively few are important "rock-forming" minerals, although these few collectively make up something like 99 per cent. of the rocks of the crust.

Minerals, in turn, are composed of *elements, i.e.* substances which cannot be split up into simpler substances by chemical means. Of the 103 elements known, many are extremely rare and are of little importance in the composition of rocks. It has been estimated

[1] In everyday usage the term mineral is generally used to connote all substances obtained from beneath the surface of the earth such as sand, limestone, coal, salt, metallic ores, etc. Used in this way it is not a scientific term; it is purely a commercial or economic term.

that the crust of the earth is made up, in the main, of the following eight elements:

oxygen	46·71 per cent.	calcium	3·65 per cent.
silicon	27·69 per cent.	sodium	2·75 per cent.
aluminium	8·07 per cent.	potassium	2·58 per cent.
iron	5·05 per cent.	magnesium	2·08 per cent.

Many of the other elements, *e.g.* gold, tin, copper, sulphur, though very rare in ordinary rocks, are locally concentrated in deposits which may be profitably worked.

None of the above eight main elements, with the exception of iron, exists as such in mineral form. Some of the other elements may exist naturally by themselves making minerals, *e.g.* gold, copper, sulphur, carbon (in the form of diamonds and graphite). In most cases, however, two or more elements are chemically combined; for example, oxygen and silicon may be united to form the mineral quartz, a common constituent of many rocks. Minerals are thus *compounds* of their constituent elements while rocks are *mixtures* of their component minerals.

Most ordinary rocks are made up of two or more minerals bound together. The heterogeneous rock can, in fact, be taken to pieces and the different homogeneous minerals that compose it be separated out. Inspection of a piece of granite, for instance, shows that it consists of several distinct minerals which are readily distinguishable: hard, clear, glassy grains of quartz; hard, pinkish grains, often with smooth faces, of felspar; and small silvery white or black soft, scaly flakes of mica. An analysis of a certain sandstone reveals, for example, that it is composed of rounded grains of quartz, felspar, augite or hornblende, with rutile, tourmaline, zircon, and a number of other minerals. Certain rock formations are virtually made up of a single mineral in the form of numerous individual particles as, for example, pure limestone which may consist wholly of calcite (the crystalline form of calcium carbonate) or pure sandstone which may contain only grains of quartz. Finally, it should be noted that, although the vast majority of rocks are made up of minerals, a few substances of organic origin, such as coal, peat, guano, are also classed as rocks.

A knowledge of rocks is important because upon them depends very largely the nature of the surface relief, the formation of soil, the occurrence of mineral wealth, the availability of water resources, etc. Rocks can be classified in three ways: (1) by their origin, (2) by their physical and chemical characteristics, and (3) according to their age.

CLASSIFICATION BY ORIGIN

Adopting a classification based on mode of origin and composition, a threefold division is recognised.

1. IGNEOUS ROCKS

The name derives from the Latin *ignis,* meaning "fire". This group of rocks, as the name implies, constitutes materials that have originated from an initially molten condition. All have solidified from the molten material or magma which occurs beneath the crust and are characteristically either crystalline in structure or glassy in appearance. Igneous rocks can be further subdivided into:

(*a*) *Plutonic rocks* which have cooled very slowly at considerable depths under pressure and which exhibit a coarsely crystalline structure, since the gradual cooling promoted the growth of large crystals. Such rocks are known as *intrusive rocks* for they have been intruded into the surface rocks from the magma reservoirs below; usually, too, they occur in large masses. Examples of plutonic rocks are granite, diorite, syenite, and gabbro.

(*b*) *Hypabyssal rocks* result from magma being intruded into other rocks, often overlying layers of strata, at shallow depths beneath surface level. Since the molten rock undergoes relatively rapid cooling in dykes (vertical fissures) and sills (horizontal sheets), crystallisation is speeded up and the rocks are, therefore, finer in texture than the coarsely crystalline plutonic rocks. Porphyry and dolerite are examples of this fairly well-defined intermediate category of rocks.

(*c*) *Volcanic rocks* are igneous rocks which have been thrown out or poured out on to the surface and have thus been cooled quickly. They are characteristically very finely crystalline and

PLATE I

Above: Folded strata showing anticlines and syncline disposed asymmetrically. (*A. Potter.*)

Below: The Caernarvonshire coast at Vwchymynydd. The bedding planes of the rock strata can be clearly distinguished. Note the fracture in the cliff face on the left which marks a fault. (*Aerofilms.*)

PLATE II

Above: A dyke of igneous rock. *(Crown Copyright Reserved.)*

Below: Fair Head Sill, in the north-eastern corner of County Antrim. This is a Tertiary dolerite sill, 250 ft thick, which has been intruded into Carboniferous strata. Fair Head rises 636 ft above sea level. Note the scree which litters the lower slope and the flat surface of the exposed sill. *(Aerofilms.)*

often glassy in appearance. The molten rock or lava which is poured out forms *extrusive rocks, e.g.* basalt, rhyolite; the ejected material forms *eruptive rocks, e.g.* pumice, tuff. The geologist usually classes the latter, which consist of the accumulated fragments of explosive volcanic activity, as a distinct group known as *pyroclastic rocks.*

The geologist also makes a classification of igneous rocks according to their chemical composition. This classification is given in Table I.

TABLE I

IGNEOUS ROCKS

	VOLCANIC OR EXTRUSIVE	HYPABYSSAL OR INTERMEDIATE	PLUTONIC OR INTRUSIVE
Solidified	on the surface	below the surface	deeply below surface
Cooling rate	rapid	medium	slow
Crystal size	small	medium	large
Forming	lavas	dykes and sills	massive bodies
ACID	RHYOLITE	QUARTZ PORPHYRY	GRANITE
Over 66 per cent. silica	OBSIDIAN		
Under 35 per cent. basic oxides			
Specific gravity 2·4-2·7			
INTERMEDIATE	TRACHYTE	SYENITE PORPHYRY	SYENITE
Between 65-55 per cent. silica	ANDESITE	PORPHYRITE	DIORITE
Between 35-45 per cent. basic oxides			
Specific gravity about 2·8			
BASIC	BASALT	DOLERITE	GABBRO
Between 55-45 per cent. silica			
Between 45-55 per cent. basic oxides			
Specific gravity 2·9			
ULTRABASIC			PERIDOTITE SERPENTINITE
Below 45 per cent. silica			
Over 55 per cent. basic oxides			
Specific gravity 3·0 or above			

TABLE II

SEDIMENTARY ROCKS

	DOMINANT CHARACTER	RAW MATERIAL UNCONSOLIDATED	CONSOLIDATED ROCKS
MECHANICALLY FORMED	Argillaceous (muddy)	Muds, Clay Varve clays Loess	Brickearth, Shale, Mudstone, Fullers earth.
	Arenaceous (sandy)	Sand Silt	Grit, Greywacke, Arkose, Sandstones of various types, Siltstone.
	Rudaceous (pebbly)	Scree (talus) Gravel Boulder clay	Breccia, Conglomerate, Tillite.
ORGANICALLY FORMED	Calcareous	Shell sand Coral reef Algal sand Oozes $\begin{cases} \text{Globigerina} \\ \text{Pteropod} \end{cases}$	Limestones, *e.g.* shelly, coral, crinoidal, foraminiferal (chalk), siliceous, etc.
	Siliceous	Oozes $\begin{cases} \text{Radiolarian} \\ \text{Diatom} \end{cases}$ Diatomaceous earth	Radiolarian Cherts
	Carbonaceous	Peat	Lignite, Cannel coal, Bituminous coal, Anthracite.
	Ferruginous	Bog iron ore	
	Phosphatic	Guano	Phosphorite, Bone breccias.
CHEMICALLY FORMED	Calcareous	$CaCO_3$ precipitated from solution. $CaCO_3$, $MgCO_3$ of precipitation or replacement origin	Limestones, *e.g.* oolitic, dolomitic, travertine. Dolomite, Magnesian limestone.
	Siliceous	Silica gel	Flint, Chert, Jasper, Sinter.
	Ferruginous Saline	Fe_2O_3 hydrosol Salt lake deposits	Clay ironstone Gypsum, Anhydrite, Rock salt, Potash, and Soda salts Nitrates.

2. SEDIMENTARY ROCKS

All sedimentary rocks are of external origin; that is, they have been derived either from the disintegration of pre-existing rocks or from chemical or biological activity on the surface. They have been formed by deposition either upon the land surface or under water. Many occur arranged in layers, or strata, when they are said to be stratified, though not all sedimentary rocks, it should be noted, are stratified. Sedimentaries constitute perhaps some 75 per cent. of the earth's *surface* rocks. This group may be classified in a variety of ways but, since they are formed by the deposition of fragments of other rocks, by organic accumulation and by chemical precipitation, a useful threefold division upon this basis may be adopted.

(*a*) *Mechanically-derived rocks*, sometimes called *clastic* rocks, are formed of small particles or fragments of rock waste carried by water, ice, or wind and re-deposited in layers of varying thickness. Such accumulations of mineral matter become compacted by pressure to form alluvia, clays, sandstones, conglomerates, etc. Sediments which have been deposited upon the land surface, such as aeolian or wind-blown (*e.g* loess), fluviatile (*e.g.* river gravels), lacustrine (*e.g.* lake muds), and glacial (*e.g.* boulder clay) deposits, are often grouped as continental deposits, in contrast to marine deposits which have been laid down under the sea. All clastic sedimentaries, in which transportation and deposition have been effected mainly by mechanical means, are formed of terrigenous debris. The geologist subdivides the mechanically formed rocks into *argillaceous* or clayey rocks (very fine grained), *arenaceous* or sandy rocks (fine or medium grained), and *rudaceous* or rubbly rocks (coarse grained).

(*b*) *Organically-derived rocks* are rocks which consist wholly or largely of the remains of organisms, either plant or animal, deposited in water or on land. Such rocks as coral, shell-limestones, coal, and guano are examples of organic sediments. Organic rocks are commonly divided into two groups according to whether they are derived from the remains of animals or are of vegetable origin. Many *calcareous* rocks, *e.g.* chalk, coral, diatomite, and some limestones, are composed of the skeletal and shelly remains of tiny marine creatures. The *carbonaceous rocks* are of vegetable origin and consist largely of carbon, together with other substances in small amounts. They include such fuels of great economic importance as peat, lignite, coal, petroleum, and bitumen.

(*c*) *Chemically-derived rocks* are those formed as a result of precipitation by various chemical reactions: amongst such rocks are gypsum, flint, rock-salt, and travertine. Some limestones are of chemical origin, the calcium carbonate being precipitated by inorganic processes. Some chemical sediments derive from the evaporation of chemically-charged waters; rock-salt and gypsum originate in this way. Chemically-derived rocks, owing to the processes involved in their origin, are characteristically consolidated rocks, *i.e.* the constituent particles are closely bound together forming a coherent mass. Chemical sediments are not very extensive and constitute only a small class; such rocks are, nevertheless, of importance economically. It is important to note that many sedimentary rocks are mixtures, *i.e.* they may be part mechanical, part chemical in origin, *e.g.* sandy limestones.

3. METAMORPHIC ROCKS

The name derives from the Greek *meta-morphe*, which means "change of form". Metamorphic rocks, which were originally igneous or sedimentary in origin, have been subjected to alteration, becoming changed in both character and appearance. All rocks can be changed, the ease and degree of change depending upon a variety of factors:

(*a*) the resistance of the rocks to crushing;

(*b*) the grain size of the rocks being altered;

(*c*) the porosity of the rocks;

(*d*) the solubility of the constituents of the rocks;

(*e*) the chemical action of the minerals; and

(*f*) the stability of the minerals that are produced.

The metamorphosis, or change from the original state, may have resulted from:

(i) heat which causes the minerals to re-crystallise; such action is called thermal metamorphism;

(ii) stress which causes alteration in the rock structure; known as cataclastic metamorphism;

(iii) the action of heat and stress in combination producing regional metamorphism;

(iv) the action of water, which dissolves some rock material and deposits other mineral matter.

Metamorphism thus may be classed as being of three kinds: (1) *contact metamorphism* caused by the action of heat, gases, or chemical solutions; (2) *dynamic metamorphism* caused by the action of great pressure; (3) *regional metamorphism* involving relatively high stress and temperature. Contact metamorphism takes place, for example, where intrusive or extrusive rocks make contact with other rocks and, as a result of their heat, causes changes to occur or where gases associated with igneous magma effect changes in the surrounding rocks as a result of their combination with the matter already there. Dynamic metamorphism results from purely physical forces. Intense pressure coupled with shearing stresses produces a rearrangement of the molecular structure of the rock. Regional metamorphism, as the name implies, takes place on a wider scale, as for example, in areas where mountain building has occurred.

British metamorphic rocks show a wide range. This is to be expected since both the original rocks from which they are derived and the methods of alteration vary greatly. Most igneous and sedimentary rocks have a "metamorphic equivalent": for example, clay becomes slate, sandstone—quartzite, limestone—marble, and granite —gneiss. Sometimes metamorphism has been so great that it is practically impossible to tell from which rocks metamorphic rocks were originally derived, *e.g.* gneiss. Metamorphic rocks provide us with many rocks and minerals that are highly prized, *e.g.* rocks used in industry, ornamental building stones, and many gemstones.

CLASSIFICATION OF ROCKS BY AGE

An alternative classification of rocks may be made according to their age; indeed, the geologist finds it necessary to know the age of rocks and to use terms to describe their age. Accordingly, he has devised a chronological table which enables him to show the sequence in which the different layers of rock or strata making up the earth's crust were formed. In building up this chronological table he makes use of a basic geological principle which states that a sedimentary stratum occurring at the surface was laid down subsequently to the bed immediately below it, and that beds of rocks become progressively older as a succession of strata go deeper. This principle is known as the *Law of Superposition*. Its application is universal unless earth movements have disturbed and displaced the strata relatively to each other. It should be borne in mind, however, that this law does not normally apply to igneous or metamorphic rocks: it is applicable mainly to sedimentary strata.

The earth has been in existence for some 4-5,000 million years. Just as historians divide historical time into eras and periods to enable them to place events and developments in the correct time sequence and to distinguish major phases of cultural advancement and civilisation, so geologists, for the sake of the same convenience and precision, have adopted a similar division of geological time. This geological time-scale, divided into units, is accepted internationally. It is applicable the world over, although the rock sequences that occur between place and place may differ since the conditions which give rise to successions of beds may have, and usually will have, differed. The datum of this time-scale has been equated with the appearance of distinctly recognisable and fairly abundant life—preserved in fossil form—on the earth. The first rocks containing observable fossils are termed "Cambrian". Some older rocks appear to contain faint traces of life in the form of very primitive, simple organisms, but in most pre-Cambrian rocks there is little fossil evidence of the beginnings of life. This is readily understandable since the earliest forms of life must have been made of jelly-like substances which were not suited to preservation in fossil form. Thus we accept the Cambrian rocks as marking the beginning of the fossiliferous time-scale.

More recent geological time, which accounts for only about one-seventh of the total geological time, is divided into four eras based upon the forms of animal life which are represented by the animal fossils occurring in the rocks. In the "era names", the ending "zoic", which comes from the Greek *zoon* meaning "animal", may be loosely interpreted as "the form of life". The four eras are:

Archaeozoic—before any forms of life;

Palaeozoic —"ancient" (*palaeos*) forms of life;

Mesozoic   —"intermediate" (*mesos*) forms of life;
Cainozoic   —"recent" or "new" (*kainos*) forms of life.
Alternative names for these four eras are: Pre-Cambrian, Primary, Secondary, Tertiary. With characteristic perverseness the British commonly use a scheme which is a combination of both, *viz.* Pre-Cambrian, Palaeozoic, Mesozoic, Tertiary.

The four eras or major divisions in the geological time scale are thus:

(i) the *Pre-Cambrian Era*, in which many series of rocks were formed over a vast length of time—some 3,900 million years—and in which there is little, if any, real fossil evidence of forms of life;

(ii) the *Primary* or *Palaeozoic Era*, extending over a period of perhaps 345 million years, whose rocks contain "ancient" forms of life such as spineless creatures, primitive fishes and the first plants;

(iii) the *Secondary* or *Mesozoic Era*, extending over about 155 million years, a period of "intermediate" forms of life, when reptiles were especially numerous and plant forms were being elaborated;

(iv) the *Tertiary* or *Cainozoic Era*,[1] covering perhaps 65 million years, during which "recent" forms of life, such as mammals and flowering plants, developed.

These great eras are distinguished by the forms of life that were in existence during the geological time span, and they indicate the gradual evolution from the most simple and primitive forms to the most complex and highly developed forms. During each era many kinds of rocks were formed, each containing fossils characteristic of their time; it is, therefore, necessary to have a more detailed system of classification. Each of the above major time divisions is thus subdivided into *periods* or *systems*—themselves major divisions of geological time. Each period is, in turn, subdivided into rock series or sub-systems. These various periods are based upon, and recognised by, distinctive rock types and the animal and plant fossils which characterise the rocks. Thus, during a given period of time within an era, a series of rocks, *e.g.* sandstones, limestones, and shales, were laid down which contain specific kinds of fossils. In this way we are able to distinguish definite systems of rocks.

[1] It is now common practice among geologists to divide the Cainozoic Era into two: the Tertiary and the Quaternary. The Quaternary covers the last two million years or so during which time man evolved.

These systems are named in different ways. They are of a very mixed nature, but illustrate well the gradual growth of the science of geology, both in time and space. Their derivation is:

(*a*) by describing the characteristic rocks, *e.g.* Carboniferous—coal bearing, Cretaceous—chalk;

(*b*) by describing the nature of the fossil contents, *e.g.* oligocene—a few fossils in recent formation, holocene—entirely recent;

(*c*) by using the place-names where the rocks were first recognised and studied, *e.g.* Devonian from Devon, Permian from Perm in the Soviet Union;

(*d*) by using ancient tribal names, *e.g.* Silurian after the ancient Welsh tribe of the Silures, Ordovician after the Ordovices;

(*e*) by indicating the divisions within the system, *e.g.* Triassic implying a threefold division.

The accompanying geological time scale (Table III) is a guide to the geologist's classification of the earth's rocks in terms of eras and periods of time.

Rocks and the Landscape

As a result of their composition, character, and structure, rocks are of great importance to the geographer. They influence the development of landforms, they largely determine the nature of the landscape, they influence the character of soils (and thereby agriculture), they are the source of mineral wealth, and they affect the quantity and quality of surface and sub-surface water supplies. For these very important reasons it is necessary that we should look at the types of rocks a little more closely and note the important varieties.

The nature of the topography or surface relief and the landforms which characterise it are influenced to a very marked degree by the kind of rock or rocks present. One has only to compare a topographical map with a geological map to see that there is frequently a close correspondence between the relief and the underlying rocks. It becomes clear, therefore, that the character and arrangement of rocks are fundamental in landform development. Rock affects the

TABLE III

GEOLOGICAL TIME-SCALE

ERA	PERIOD	YEARS AGO (in millions)	GEOLOGICAL ACTIVITY	CHIEF ROCKS (with examples from British Isles)	FORMS OF LIFE
QUATERNARY	Holocene or Recent	0·01		Alluvium (Fenlands), Sands (culbin).	Homo sapiens emerged about 40,000 years ago. Species of man and present-day animals appear.
	Pleistocene	1·5-2	Period of Great Ice Age.	East Anglian boulder clay.	
CAINOZOIC OR TERTIARY	Pliocene	7		Sands and gravels (East Anglia).	Mammals dominant creatures.
	Miocene	26	Alpine orogeny: Alps, Dinarics, Himalayas, etc.	Clays and sands (Hampshire Basin).	Flowering plants.
	Oligocene	38		Clays, sands, and gravels (London Basin).	Emergence of earliest primates.
	Eocene	54		Thanet sands, Reading beds.	
	Palaeocene	65			
MESOZOIC OR SECONDARY	Cretaceous	136	Development of geosynclinal sea of Tethys.	Chalk of Downs and Wealden clays and sands.	Mammals appear; modern-type plants appear.
	Jurassic	195		Limestone escarpments of eastern England; sandstones and shales.	Great age of reptiles; first primitive birds.
	Triassic	225		New Red Sandstone and marls of Midlands.	Reptiles abundant.
PALAEOZOIC OR PRIMARY	Permian	280	Hercynian orogeny; building of mountains now represented by blocks of central Europe.	Magnesian limestone.	
	Carboniferous	345		Coal Measures, Millstone Grit and Carboniferous Limestone (Pennines and Mendips).	Land plant life develops.
	Devonian	395	Caledonian orogeny; building of ranges now represented by stumps of mountains found in Scotland and Scandinavia.	Old Red Sandstone of Cheviots and Exmoor. Sandstones, shales, and limestones.	Amphibians.
	Silurian	440		Sandstones, shales, and limestones.	First primitive fishes.
	Ordovician	500		Sandstones and slates (central Wales).	Spineless creatures.
	Cambrian	570		Slates and sandstones (North Wales).	Marine life clearly distinguishable; invertebrates.
PROTEROZOIC EOZOIC AZOIC	Pre-Cambrian	4500	Three, and perhaps more, phases of mountain building occurred in this remote period which stretched over some 3,000 million years.	Sandstones in extreme north-west of Scotland.	

N.B. Figures refer to base of each period.

extent to which the land is worn away and shaped by means of:

(i) its structure, *e.g.* whether it is massive, stratified, folded, faulted, etc., and

(ii) its lithological qualities, *e.g.* its permeability, solubility, hardness, jointing, etc.[1]

Broadly, the rock structure influences the general pattern of the relief, while the lithological character of the individual rocks is largely responsible for the topographical details. While in general terms what we have just said is true, it should be noted that there are areas where the relief does not appear to be a reflection of the rocks.

In the first place, it is clear that soft rocks will wear away more

LANDFORMS AND ROCK STRUCTURE

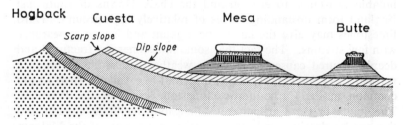

Fig. 4.

Diagram illustrating the relationship of certain erosional and residual landforms to the structure and disposition of the strata from which they have been formed.

readily than hard rocks, although the speed at which the soft rocks (and the hard ones too) will be worn away depends upon many factors. Clays, which are soft and easily eroded by water action, usually form lowlands, especially if they occur in juxtaposition with other rocks as in the case of the English Plain where the clay vales are separated by upstanding ridges of harder rocks. Other soft rocks of moderate resistance, such as chalk, produce a rolling topography of low, gently-rounded hills, although the lack of surface drainage on much of this porous rock helps to maintain it as a prominent landscape feature, despite its relative softness. On the

[1] Lithology is the study of rocks in connection with their physical, chemical, and textural character.

other hand, hard rocks which are resistant to erosive forces tend to give rise to bold, upstanding relief; for example, the hard, tough Pre-Cambrian rocks of Charnwood Forest project through the Triassic sedimentaries of the Midlands while the line of volcanic hills extending between the Firths of Clyde and Tay in the Midland Valley of Scotland rise up as prominent hill masses from the floor of Carboniferous rocks. Providing all other things are equal, the harder rocks form the higher ground; but even these may be reduced in time, as in the so-called "shield areas" of the world where prolonged erosion of very hard rocks has succeeded in wearing them down to relatively flat, low-lying areas.

Permeable and soluble rocks, such as chalk and limestone, have little surface drainage though they possess subterranean watercourses. Rocks such as chalk which permit ready percolation of water (and consequently suffer reduced run-off) may exhibit a notable resistance to erosion and the chalk Downs of south-east England form upstanding ridges of relatively high ground. Hard limestones may give the landscape a gaunt and barren appearance with few streams. The fact that some limestones are fractured and deeply fissured causes the rock to weather and erode to produce vertical faces, precipices, crags, and wall-like valleys, such as are common in the Carboniferous limestone areas of the Pennines. The joints in the Carboniferous limestone facilitate erosion and this can be clearly seen in the limestone pavements of the Malham area in Yorkshire where the joints have been opened up to produce a "pavement" of limestone blocks separated by often wide and deep crevices. On the other hand, the presence of fissures in the limestone clearly increases the permeability of the rock and this tends to increase its resistance to surface erosion.

Hard sandstones, which are stratified, wear away to give a tabular topography if the dip is slight, as is exemplified in the *tableiros* of the Brazilian Plateau, while, if the sandstones alternate with less resistant rocks, such as shales, as in the upper valleys of the Colne and Calder Rivers of the West Riding of Yorkshire, they produce a step-like landscape—a scarp and bench topography. Hard, impermeable, and insoluble rocks frequently give rise (as a result of the effects of climatic and other weathering) to rounded, boulder-strewn landscapes. In our cool temperate moist regions granite, for instance, produces rounded hill ridges (as in Brittany) with, sometimes, distinctive block-like outcrops (as on Dartmoor—the tors); while the wearing away of gneiss under moist tropical conditions in the vicinity of Rio de Janeiro has produced the "sugarloaf" hills. Quartzites, which are metamorphosed sandstones, are highly resistant to water erosion and often weather to give sharply defined serrated crests, tooth-like peaks, and a general ruggedness of outline.

SECTION FROM MALVERN TO CHILTERN HILLS
SHOWING HILL RIDGES AND VALES

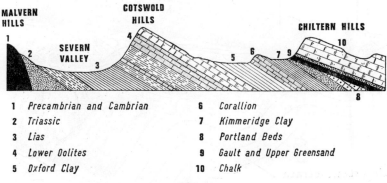

1	Precambrian and Cambrian	6	Corallion
2	Triassic	7	Kimmeridge Clay
3	Lias	8	Portland Beds
4	Lower Oolites	9	Gault and Upper Greensand
5	Oxford Clay	10	Chalk

Fig. 5.

Where rocks of differing hardness and resistance outcrop at the surface they will undergo differential erosion. In this case the tilted strata have given rise to bold escarpments and hill ridges with intervening vales. The vertical scale is exaggerated.

Perhaps enough has been said to indicate how the lithological qualities of rocks may, and usually do, affect the landscape and we can now turn to the effects of structure. Alternating bands of resistant and less resistant rocks, outcropping at the surface, result in asymmetrical hill ridges with scarp (steep) and dip (gentle) slopes, a landscape feature well illustrated in the scarplands of southeastern England, where limestone and chalk beds are separated by softer clays and sands (Fig. 5). If the outcropping beds have no significant lithological differences, then the structure may not affect the relief to any appreciable extent; for example, the Upper Jurassic series in the East Midlands comprise three clay formations, the Oxford, Ampthill, and Kimmeridge Clays, all of roughly uniform resistance with the result that there are no appreciable relief differences between each and the three together form a wide belt of generally level, low-lying land. In like manner, the Silurian and Ordovician rocks of the Southern Uplands of Scotland have a

JURAS: PARALLEL RIDGES AND VALLEYS

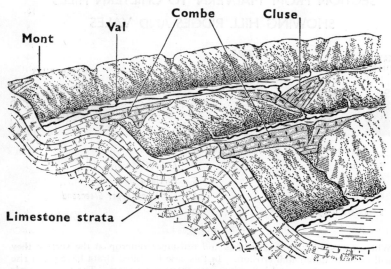

Fig. 6.

The Jura Mountains result from a simple fold structure, the anticlines forming the ridges and the synclines the longitudinal valleys. Streams, such as the Doubs, pass from one *val* to another through *cluses* (transverse valleys) and the entire drainage system, as well as being antecedent, forms a trellis pattern. In the crests of the ridges are stream-eroded hollows known as *combes*.

measure of lithological uniformity with the result that even the complicated fold structure of the Uplands is not always clearly reflected in the relief.

Symmetrically folded beds may produce a pattern of long parallel ridges and valleys. This is well exemplified in the case of the Jura Mountains (Fig. 6). Here the rocks, mainly oolitic and marly limestones of Jurassic age, are folded into parallel ranges on the inner or eastern side of the Juras. The anticlines of the Jura folds form the ridges and the synclines the longitudinal valleys. Where a structural dome occurs, *i.e.* where the rock strata are gently flexed upwards to form a dome shape, a distinctive relief pattern may result from its denudation. Study of a geological map of the Lake District (see Fig. 71, p. 196) shows that in the central area old Palaeozoic rocks, Ordovician and Silurian, occur coinciding with the highest relief; around this core, and more particularly on the northern side, younger rocks are arranged roughly concentrically in order of age. The whole clearly marks an eroded dome.[1] The Weald is also a dome structure but it does not form a physiographic dome. The Black Hills of South Dakota in the United States form both a dome-shaped landform and a structural dome; here the old crystalline basement rocks of the continent break through the overlying sedimentaries in a dome-like swelling, forming a welcome change to the general monotony of the plains.

Domed landforms may result in another way. Many igneous intrusions into sedimentary rocks are roughly circular or oval in plan and are dome-shaped bodies, *e.g.* batholiths, bosses, laccoliths. The domed form of such intrusions may be reflected in swellings of the land surface. When such intrusions are exposed by denudation, the resistant igneous rocks may continue to show their domed form; for example, the Henry Mountains of Utah, in the United States, are laccoliths in origin and exhibit dome-like features. The domed form of exposed intrusions seldom survives over large areas for the jointing, which is characteristic of many igneous rocks, leads to the etching and modification of the surface. The section across the Wicklow Mountains largely formed from a great granitic boss, shows how the original exhumed dome has been modified (Fig. 7).

Other forms of intrusion, such as dykes and sills (see pp. 82-3), often show special resistance to erosion and, accordingly, after exposure, often stand out dramatically as ridges or form impressive escarpments. For example, the Whin Sill in the north of England is a bluish-grey dolerite intrusion 60-100 feet thick and, being more

[1] See page 195.

resistant than the limestone into which it was injected, it now out-crops as a marked ridge causing spectacular waterfalls, as at High Force in Teesdale (70 feet high), the lofty crags of High Cup Nick, the blunt, cliffed promontory on which Bamburgh Castle is sited, and the sea shattered fragments which form the Farne Islands. Clearly such outcrops can have striking scenic effects.

SECTION ACROSS WICKLOW MOUNTAINS

(After Charlesworth)

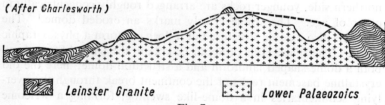

▨ *Leinster Granite*   ⁺⁺⁺ *Lower Palaeozoics*

Fig. 7.

The diagram shows how the exhumed granitic boss, which forms the Wicklow Mountains, has been eroded so that the domed form of the original surface of the intrusion no longer survives.

The effects which rocks, through their characteristics and structures, have upon relief in general and landforms in particular will become more clearly apparent as we proceed; here we have been concerned in drawing attention to the important role which rocks play in influencing landscape and landscape features. The student is advised to follow up this chapter by reading Chapter 7 in Sparks's *Geomorphology.*

CHAPTER 3

THE ORIGIN OF CONTINENTS AND OCEANS

Although the poets have written of the "everlasting hills" and although the earth appears stable enough and the features of the landscape seem fixed and changeless, yet the earth is by no means a stable, quiescent body, neither are the surface relief features permanent. Changes are taking place continuously both beneath and on the surface of the earth. Apart from such readily recognisable active phenomena as earthquakes and volcanoes, sudden subsidences and landslides, most changes in the terrestrial landscape are so slow as to be imperceptible. Since visible changes usually take so long to effect, the land surface appears not to alter.

A succession of slow, remorseless changes does occur however and the landscape passes through a life-cycle of stages: from youth, through maturity, to old age. In this and the succeeding chapters we shall trace the various earth movements and note the terrestrial agents which have blocked out the major lineaments of the relief and have shaped and fashioned the topographical details of the land surface.

Relief, whether large- or small-scale, results from the action of two forces:

(i) *tectonic forces, i.e.* those giving rise to upheaval, subsidence, folding, fracturing, and eruption; they produce, generally speaking, the major structural units of the earth and the major or second order relief forms[1] such as the mountain ranges and many of the great plateaus and plains; in a word, they rough-hew the topography;

(ii) *denudative forces, i.e.* those giving rise to the etching, smoothing, and polishing of the land surface; they destroy, carve, and mould the major relief features into an infinite variety of detail producing such topographic features as hills and valleys, spurs and scarps, caves and cliffs.

---

[1] First order relief features are the continental areas and the ocean basins.

Diastrophism

The major relief features have mostly been brought about through the action of internal forces, *i.e.* those beneath the earth's crust. To such forces disturbing and dislocating the crust the general term *diastrophism* is applied. Diastrophism embraces all movements of deformation, but is the outcome of two main types of movement:

(i) vertical movements tending either to lift or depress segments of the crust bodily, which are commonly termed *epeirogenic,* or continent-building, movements; for example, the Russian Platform, the African Plateau, and the High Plains of North America have resulted from such movements while some oceanic areas would appear to owe their origin to large-scale down-warping or subsidence;

(ii) tangential forces, which are horizontal movements tending either to compress or extend the crust, compression involving the folding and faulting of the earth's rocks, tension involving fracturing and faulting; these, known as *orogenic* or mountain-building movements, have been responsible for the great young folded mountains of the Alps, Himalayas, Andes, etc., the old complex folded mountains of the Appalachians, and the massive block faulting of the Eastern Highlands of Australia.

FOLDS

That layers of rock are capable of being crumpled or buckled into folds is a matter of simple observation: the folds can often be seen in the faces of cliffs or railway cuttings. The folding of rock strata is due to compressive forces in the earth's crust. There are three simple geometrical forms of folding: (i) where the strata are bent upwards into a symmetrical upfold, called an *anticline*; (ii) where the strata are bent downwards in a symmetrical manner to form a *syncline*; and (iii) where horizontal beds dip and then flatten out again, forming a simple flexure known as a *monocline*.[1] The centre line of the upfold or downfold is called the axis while the two sides of the folds are termed the limbs. Folds may not be, in fact

---

[1] N.B. Monoclines are also often associated with vertical movements (faulting).

PLATE III

Above: Giant's Causeway, County Antrim, Northern Ireland. The "honeycomb" structure resulted from the cooling of the igneous rock which forms the Antrim Plateau. Each block is hexagonal in shape. (*Aerofilms.*)

Below: Pahoehoe lava flow on the Kau desert south of Kilauea in the Hawaii National Park, Territory of Hawaii. Cinder cones can be seen in the background. (*USIS.*)

PLATE IV

Above: Stac Polly, Wester Ross, in extreme north-west of Scotland showing aiguille, *i.e.* a needle-shaped rock peak, due to frost-wedging. (*Eric Kay.*)

Below: Details of the cap stones forming earth pillars in boulder clay, Val d'herens, Switzerland. (*Eric Kay.*)

seldom are, perfectly symmetrical and where in such a fold structure one limb is steeper than the other it is said to be asymmetrical
(see Fig. 8 and Plate 1).

The character of any fold structure depends upon the intensity
of the compressive forces creating it together with the nature of

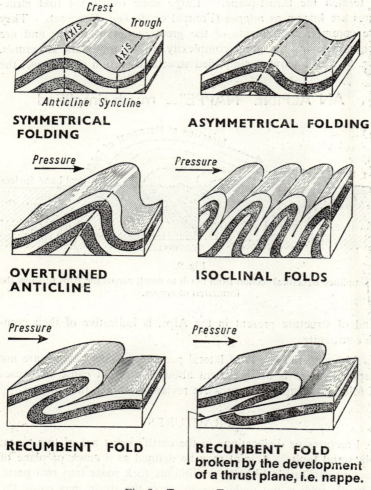

Fig. 8. TYPES OF FOLD.

the rock. An asymmetrical or inclined upfold may be pushed right over to form an *overfold*, or overturned fold. If a fold is overturned to such an extent that the axial plane lies horizontally it is said to be *recumbent*. Sometimes the pressure exerted upon a recumbent fold is sufficiently great to cause it to be torn from its roots and to be thrust forward. The tear, or plane of fracture, is termed the thrust-plane. Large scale overthrust fold structures are known as *nappes* (French) or *decken* (German). They are common components of the great mountain ranges and are responsible for the great complexity of the mountain structures. Fig. 9. which shows a simplified structural section of a *nappe*, the

AN ALPINE "NAPPE" — much simplified

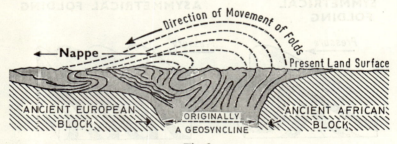

Fig. 9.

A simplified structural section from north to south across the Alps to show the formation of *nappes*.

kind of structure present in the Alps, is indicative of their complex structure.

Although the effects of lateral pressure or compression are not disputed, there is disagreement about the actual cause or causes of folding. Suggested causes are reviewed later in this chapter.

FRACTURES

Fractures or dislocations in the earth's crust are of two types: joints and faults. A joint may be defined as a crack or plane of fracture dividing a hitherto continuous rock mass into two parts. If brittle rock is put under severe stress the strain may cause the rock to break or fracture. Joints differ from faults in that little or no actual displacement has taken place along them. Many rocks, such as limestone, sandstone, and granite, have joints in them but these are not always due to tectonic strains and stresses; in some sedimentary rocks, they may be due to shrinkage resulting from slow drying out; and in the case of igneous rocks they are caused by contraction on cooling.

A fault is a fracture involving the displacement of the rocks on either side of it relative to one another; in other words, there has been an actual dislocation or movement along the plane of fracture. The movement of the rocks may be vertical or horizontal or a combination of both. The vertical displacement of the strata, which may vary from a fraction of an inch to hundreds of feet, is termed the *throw*. Where the fault is inclined, lateral displacement occurs which is called the *heave*. The inclination or angle between the fault-plane and the horizontal is known as the *dip*, while the angle between the fault-plane and the vertical is described as the *hade* (Fig. 10).

Faults may be classified by the movements which have taken place along them. A normal fault is one which has both the hading and the down-throw in the same direction. In this case a rock mass moves down the dip of the fault-plane. *Normal faults* are the product of tension. Compression, on the other hand, results in the beds on one side of the fault-plane being thrust over those on the other side; in other words, there is over-thrusting up the dip, and the fault hades to the up-throw side. These are known as *thrust faults* or *reverse faults*. *Tear-faults* or *wrench-faults* are formed where the movement is in a horizontal direction although the fracture is vertical; these are sometimes called transcurrent faults. The Great Glen fault, separating the North-western Highlands from the Grampians, in Scotland, is a wrench-fault; the horizontal displacement is of the order of 65 miles.

The presence of faults, whether singly, in parallel, or *en echelon*, indicate that forces have been acting on the crust, and that the stresses and strains exerted by these forces have been stronger than the strengths of the rocks which have yielded to them.

Folding and Landforms

Many of the most recently formed mountains are called fold mountains because they are built up of strata which have

FAULTING

1 — NORMAL FAULT

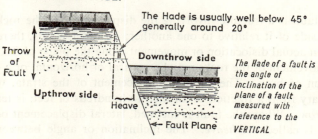

The Hade is usually well below 45°
generally around 20°

Throw of Fault

Downthrow side

Upthrow side

Heave

Fault Plane

The Hade of a fault is the angle of inclination of the plane of a fault measured with reference to the VERTICAL

Normal Faults are produced by tension and indicate a pulling apart of the strata. NOTE :- If a bore-hole was put down along the fault, no duplication of beds would occur — beds would be missing.

2 — REVERSE FAULT

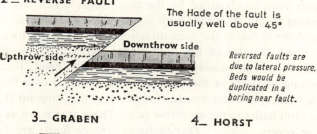

The Hade of the fault is usually well above 45°

Downthrow side

Upthrow side

Reversed faults are due to lateral pressure. Beds would be duplicated in a boring near fault.

3 — GRABEN

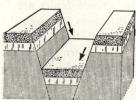

4 — HORST

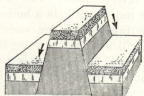

Two normal faults due to tension with a depressed, or rift block, or graben, between them.

Two normal faults with an elevated block, or horst, between them.

Fig. 10.

suffered folding of one kind or another. Their building presupposes two conditions: (i) vast accumulations of sedimentary deposits, and (ii) a mechanism to produce folding and uplift. Let us turn our attention to these two problems.

Geosynclines. Geologists have shown that immense thicknesses of sedimentary rocks are involved in mountain building; for instance, something of the order of 25,000 feet of sedimentary strata went into the building of the Appalachian Mountains. Many centuries ago, long before geology developed as a scientific study, that Renaissance genius, Leonardo da Vinci, observed that marine fossils were to be dug out of Alpine peaks and concluded, rightly, that the rocks making up those mountains must at one time have lain beneath the sea. Thus the strata making up fold mountains are marine sediments occurring in vast thicknesses. How these accumulations came into being raises the first problem in mountain building. It is postulated that rock waste, brought down from neighbouring land masses, was deposited in long and relatively narrow depressions in the floor of adjacent seas. These elongated belts of accumulating sediments are called *geosynclines* or geosynclinal troughs. It is thought that these troughs sag or sink either through downward drag by convection currents in the mantle or under the weight of their accumulated deposits but that deposition keeps pace with the rate of subsidence. Only in such subsiding trenches, it is thought, could sufficient sediments accumulate to explain the vast thicknesses of rock strata involved in young fold mountain building.

It is generally held that a great linear depression extended across the mid-Old World land mass in early Tertiary times. This depression formed the Sea of Tethys, as the geologists call it, and formed a great geosynclinal trough in which were deposited the sediments which later were squeezed, crumpled, folded, and uplifted to form the mountain systems of the Alps and Himalayas. This idea seems reasonable enough but, if we are to accept geosynclines as a pre-requisite for mountain building, the question naturally arises: can we distinguish any comparable zones of accumulation at the present time? It is suggested that the Mediterranean Sea, the Indo-Gangetic Plain (in which there are alluvial deposits *at least*

4,000 feet thick and probably considerably thicker), and the marginal seas of eastern Asia may well be embryonic geosynclines.

Orogenesis. The second main problem in mountain building relates to the folding and uplift of the geosynclinal deposits: how was the folding and uplift achieved? There is no sure answer to this problem. Most modern theories involve the idea of one or two "forelands" (the leading edges of continental blocks) moving and squeezing the geosynclinal strata so that they become compressed and folded and are then uplifted and overthrust.

HOLMES' CONVECTION CURRENT THEORY

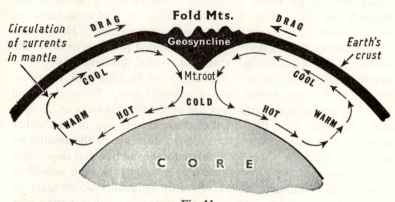

Fig. 11.

The diagram illustrates Holmes' idea of currents in the plastic sub-crustal zone which could lead to down-warping of the outer crust and associated crumpling of geosynclinal sediments to cause mountain folds.

Various theories of causation of mountain building have been put forward; here a brief reference will be made to two; but students who are interested in this rather complex problem of orogenesis should read Chapter 4 of Professor Steer's book *The Unstable Earth* in which he summarises the principal ideas.

Holmes has suggested that not only the process of building but the creation of geosynclines may be due to convection currents in the sub-crustal zone arising possibly from unequal cooling or from unequal heating due to radioactivity in segments of the earth (Fig. 11). The idea postulates ascending currents in the sub-crustal zone beneath the continental land masses. These currents then flow horizontally beneath the continental blocks and cooling takes place. This cooling causes a downward flow of sub-crustal material and the drag created by this down flow results in a down-warp or geosyncline. Continued down-warping leads to the compression and buckling of the geosynclinal sediments to form fold belts. It would also account for the low densities of the deep mountain roots which would be developed. It is a fact that all mountain areas have a relatively low gravitational pull and this theory helps to explain it.

Another theory, first seriously suggested by Wegener, attempts to explain mountain building in terms of moving or drifting continents. The hypothesis argues that the continental blocks, being composed of relatively light sial material, float in the denser sima or sub-crustal material and are free to drift, just as ice-floes move in the sea. The movement laterally of such continental blocks, it is maintained, could lead to the compression of sediments lying on the continental margins, or even of the continental margins themselves, or alternatively to the compression of geosynclinal deposits that might lie between two wandering blocks. This, like all other theories, has its snags; we shall return shortly to a fuller discussion of this interesting hypothesis of continental wandering.

ISOSTASY

It seems very likely that fold mountains undergo two phases of uplift: first as a result of compression, and second as a result of what is known as isostatic readjustment. The theory of isostasy is, simply put, the concept of a state of equilibrium or balance existing in the earth's crust. It implies the idea of continental land masses, *i.e.* sial, composed of materials of lighter density, "floating" in a substratum of denser material, *i.e.* sima (Fig. 12). Just as only about one-seventh of an iceberg shows itself above the sea surface, so it is estimated only about one-ninth of the continental blocks appear at the surface, the remainder being "buried" in the simatic substratum.

The idea of isostasy can perhaps best be grasped by thinking of several blocks of wood of the same cross-section but of differing heights floating in a tank of water. The individual blocks raise

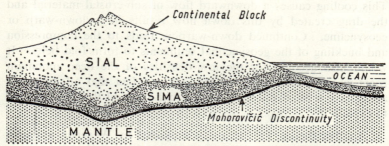

DIAGRAMMATIC CROSS-SECTION
OF THE EARTH'S CRUST

Fig. 12.

The continents form sial blocks which, because they are formed of materials of lighter density, are envisaged as "floating" in the sima or denser material of the sub-crust.

PRINCIPLE OF ISOSTASY

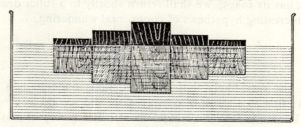

Fig. 13.

A series of wooden blocks of different heights floating in a tank of water to illustrate the concept of isostatic balance between adjacent "columns" in the earth's crust.

themselves above the water level by amounts which are proportional to their respective lengths. Such a series of blocks are said to be in a condition of hydrostatic balance. It is possible to conceive of blocks of the outer crust, floating in the sima, being in a comparable state of balance—isostatic balance. Now if an inch was sawn off one of the wooden blocks that particular block would adjust itself in the water: a portion of the block previously submerged would lift itself above the water level and the submerged portion would not sink as deeply into the water as in its original position (see Fig. 13). In like manner, the denudation of a land mass, whether it be a mountain range, a plateau, or a plain, and the removal of the rock waste will upset the isostatic equilibrium of the mass of land and it will rise until the correct adjustment has been made.

Supposing, to come back to our wooden blocks again, the inch sawn off one block was placed on top of an adjacent block, this would have the effect of depressing the latter and causing the underwater portion of the block to sink deeper. Similarly, if the load of rock waste from, say, a mountain is deposited upon an adjacent plain this will lead to the sialic "column" beneath the plain becoming depressed; in other words, the plain, because of its increased load, will have to make an appropriate readjustment to achieve isostatic balance. Fig. 14 will help to make this clear.

The whole idea and process of isostatic readjustment can be illustrated by the effects produced by the great glaciation of Pleistocene times. The formation of the ice-sheet over Scandinavia resulted in the land becoming depressed by the enormous weight of the accumulated ice. But when the ice cap melted away the land began to rise with the gradual easing of the load. The melting of the Scandinavian ice has led to a compensation of several hundreds of feet—even up to 900 feet in places. This uplift is indicated by the presence of raised beaches. Uplift is still going on and is illustrated by changes along the Bothnian coast of the Baltic; Fig. 15 shows the rise or fall of harbours in millimetres per year in Europe. The Finnish port of Vaasa is several hundred years old but its modern port is situated about six miles west of the original harbour site—a fact which shows how the continuing uplift along this coast (as along the Swedish coast opposite) has rendered some of the original harbours quite useless.

Finally, we should note that this vertical readjustment which goes on probably induces movements in the material in the substratum. Increases or releases in the pressure exerted upon the substratum material lead to a slow flowage in the sima. Clearly, unless there is a transfer of material in depth the sial blocks could not remain in isostatic equilibrium.

Faulting and Landforms

The stresses and strains imposed on the crust by the forces of compression and by changes in level frequently cause severe fracturing and faulting. Areas of old, hard rocks seldom yield to

ISOSTATIC EQUILIBRIUM IN THE CRUST

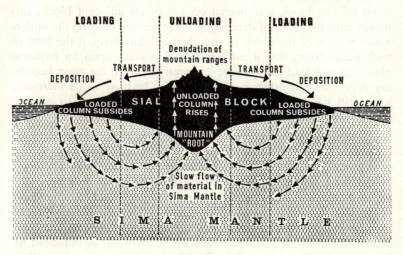

Fig. 14.

Denudation and deposition on the land surface give rise to compensations at depth: in other words, loading in one area causes subsidence resulting, in turn, in a slow flowage at depth; on the other hand, unloading allows the land to rise and this uplift is augmented by sub-crustal flowage.

folding; the brittle rocks tend rather to fracture and fault. In regions of old mountains, where a measure of stability has been achieved, renewed pressures will lead to large-scale faulting which may come to dominate the landscape. For example, the Rhine Uplands and the Eastern Highlands of Australia consist of a series of faulted blocks which have produced distinctive landform features.

Faulting gives rise to two main topographical forms. Faulting and subsidence on an appreciable scale produces *rift valleys* or *graben* such as the Central Lowlands of Scotland and the Rhine Rift

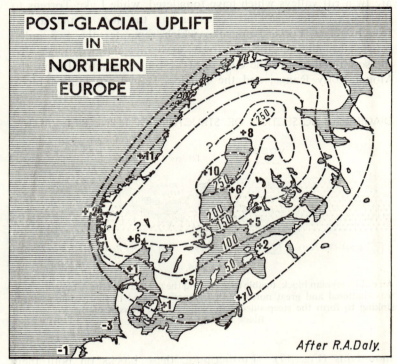

Fig. 15.

The melting of the Pleistocene ice cap, which had depressed the area, allowed the Fennoscandian region to adjust itself isostatically. The pecked lines show the amount of uplift in feet in different parts of the area. The figures having positive and negative values show the rise and fall in sea level in millimetres per year along different parts of the coast. Note the general correlation of the latter with Daly's estimate of the amount of land uplift.

Valley (Fig. 16). Faulted blocks which have been uplifted are known as *horsts,* and characteristically they are bounded by steep, often cliff-like slopes, termed *fault-scarps.* Typical examples of horst blocks are the Vosges and Black Forest which margin the

Rhine Rift Valley, the Ruwenzori massif in East Africa, and the Mount Lofty and Flinders Ranges in South Australia. The State of South Australia, in fact, provides us with a good example of a sequence of rifts and horsts. The gulfs of Spencer and St Vincent are twin rift valleys which have foundered, while Lake Torrens to the north of Spencer Gulf forms part of the floor of the faulted trough. The Yorke Peninsula, which separates the two gulfs, resisted foundering and now forms a slightly elevated horst. To the south and east of the Gulf of St Vincent, Kangaroo Island, the Mount Lofty Range, and the Flinders Range are faulted block

DIAGRAMMATIC SECTION OF STRUCTURE OF RHINE RIFT VALLEY

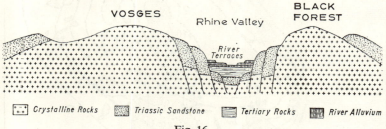

Fig. 16.

An old Hercynian block, unable to withstand the pressures of the Alpine orogeny, was shattered and great north-south fractures resulted in the middle segment sinking to form the steep-sided Rift Valley. The massifs of the Vosges and Black Forest form horsts.

mountains (Fig. 17). Furthermore, these blocks on both their eastern and western faces exhibit step faulting, that is parallel faults throwing in the same direction, and three levels are discernible at about 400, 1,000, and 1,500 feet.

Another interesting example of the effects of faulting is provided by the so-called Basin and Range Province within the cordilleran system of the United States (Fig. 18). Here a series of tilted fault-blocks uplifted in comparatively recent times have produced a number of north-south trending mountain ridges separated by depressions. Lines of volcanic cones appear along some of the fracture lines.

FAULTS AND BLOCKS OF
SOUTH AUSTRALIA

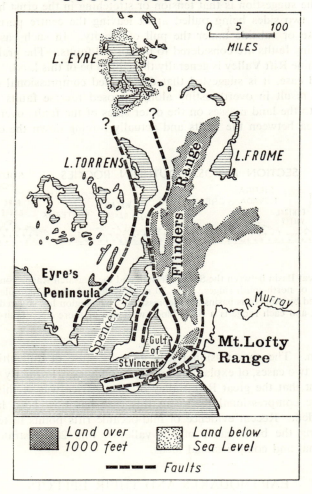

0   5   100
MILES

L. EYRE

?   ?

L. TORRENS

Flinders Range

L. FROME

Eyre's
Peninsula

Spencer Gulf

R. Murray

Gulf
of
St Vincent

**Mt. Lofty
Range**

Land over
1000 feet

Land below
Sea Level

Faults

Fig. 17.

In South Australia extensive faulting has produced a series of graben and horsts.
Spencer Gulf and Lake Torrens occupy a down-faulted depression which
probably continues northwards to bound Lake Eyre.

The mechanics of the formation of rift valleys is not fully under-stood. There are several hypotheses but the two principal explana-tions relate to the ideas of tension and compression. In the first case the suggestion is that tension or stretching in the crust has led to the two sides being pulled apart leaving the centre portion to collapse or subside under the pull of gravity. In such cases the bounding faults are considered to be normal faults. The graben of the Rhine Rift Valley is generally thought to be of this kind. In the second case, it is suggested that deep-seated compressional move-ments result in overthrusting along opposed reverse faults which leads to the land masses on the outer sides of the faults overriding the area between the faults and actually forcing down the central

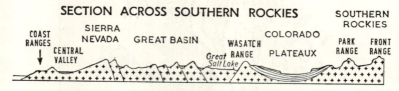

Fig. 18.

The Great Basin between the Sierra Nevada and the Wasatch Range consists of a series of north-south ridges, 10 to 20 miles wide and up to 100 miles long, separated by numerous basins and depressions. The region has suffered severe faulting and each range is a tilted block with one or more steep fault-scarps.

portion. The compressional idea arose because of difficulties, in one or two cases, of explaining gravity anomalies. Formerly it was thought that the great Rift Valley of East Africa was of this type but the compressional theory in this case has now been largely discarded. Recent evidence of mid-oceanic rifts points to tension as being the basic cause of rift valleys. Fig. 20 illustrates the tensional and compressional ideas.

EARTHQUAKES AND THEIR EFFECTS

An earthquake or earth tremor, simply stated, is the shaking or vibrating of the earth's crust. Such tremblings vary greatly in their intensity: some are so slight as not to be generally noticeable

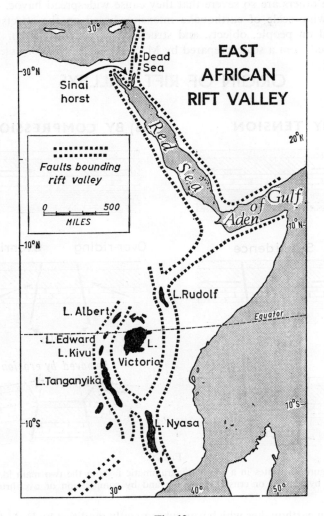

Fig. 19.

The Great Rift Valley of East Africa is the greatest fault structure on the face of the earth. As the map shows it has great ramifications. Various theories have been put forward to explain the origin of the Great Rift but both Gregory's early tensional theory and Wayland's compressional theory have been challenged.

while others are so severe that they cause widespread havoc. The following scale of earthquake intensity, based on the effects produced on people, objects, and structures, is generally used. It is derived from a scale prepared by M. S. Rossi in 1873 for assessing

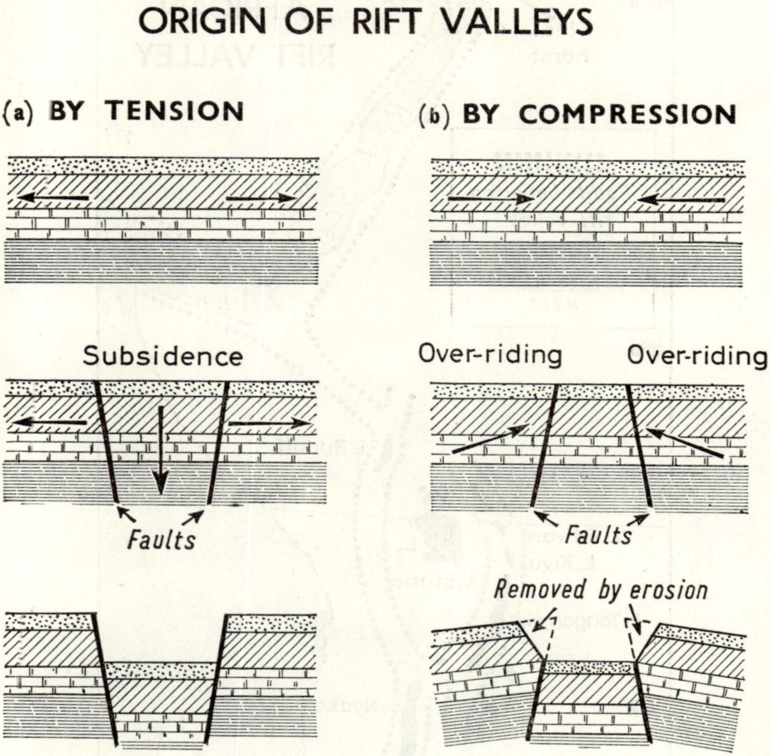

ORIGIN OF RIFT VALLEYS

(a) BY TENSION   (b) BY COMPRESSION

Fig. 20.

The figure illustrates in a simple diagrammatic fashion the two main ideas of origin by tension or crustal stretching and by compression or overthrusting.

Italian earthquakes which was subsequently modified by F. A. Forel for use in Switzerland.

ROSSI-FOREL SCALE OF SEISMIC INTENSITY

1. Noticed only by an experienced observer.

2. Noticed by a few people at rest.
3. Generally felt by people at rest.
4. Felt by people in motion; doors and windows rattle.
5. Felt generally; disturbance of furniture.
6. Sleepers awakened; hanging objects such as chandeliers set in motion.
7. Causes panic; moveable objects overthrown; church bells ring.
8. Damage to buildings; chimneys fall and walls are cracked.
9. Some buildings destroyed.
10. Widespread destruction.

In the world at large an average of about four shocks are registered every day; these are only minor tremors but approximately once every three weeks shocks of considerable intensity occur and some three or four earthquakes, usually involving death, happen on the average every year. A year chosen at random, say 1955, will illustrate this.

STATISTICS OF EARTHQUAKES, 1955

Date 1955	Location	Killed	Injured	Homeless
April 1	South Philippines ...	432	2,000	12,000
April 14	Kangting, China ...	39	113	?
April 19-20	Volos, Greece ...	6	60	3,000
July 20	Ecuador			6,000

During the present century catastrophic earthquakes have occurred in different parts of the earth—at San Francisco, at Latakia in the Lebanon, in Turkey, in Tokyo, in Cyprus, at Orleansville in Algeria, in Greece, in the Philippines, in El Salvador, at Skopje in Yugoslavia, at Agadir in Morocco, and in central Chile.

The phenomena associated with earthquakes may be grouped for purposes of convenience into three classes: the sounds accompanying seismic disturbances, the peculiar atmospheric conditions which are often associated with earthquakes, and the various physical happenings resulting from the shock. The amount of noise accompanying earthquakes is broadly linked with their severity; in severe tremors there is often a dull rumbling sound which is faint at first, increases in intensity, and finally dies away gradually; in nearly every case the duration of the noise is greater than that of the state of tremor. Strange atmospheric phenomena often accompany earthquakes, *e.g.* sudden winds, torrential rains, the reddening of the sun, and luminous phenomena, such as the "blood-red glow" which accompanied the Valparaiso earthquake of 1932. Some of these atmospheric disturbances, and especially the manifestation of luminosity, cannot adequately be accounted for and remain something of a puzzle. The third class of phenomena includes the uplift and depression of the land surface locally, the cracking and fissuring of the land surface, and flooding resulting from water disturbances. There are many attested cases of uplift and subsidence but one of the most spectacular examples is that provided by the Alaskan earthquake of 1899 where a section of the coast was lifted up 47 feet! Gaping cracks or fissures, some up to several feet in width, are a not uncommon occurrence. Sometimes these fissures remain open; sometimes they close up again. Where an earthquake affects the sea bed, great waves may be propagated which may travel long distances and flood coasts thousands of miles away. The central Chilean earthquake of 1960 resulted in great waves which travelled across the whole breadth of the Pacific and produced coastal flooding in Japan. Such waves are called *tsunamis,* a Japanese term.

Distribution of Earthquakes

Earthquakes do not occur equally or everywhere on the earth's surface. A map showing their distribution (Fig. 21) indicates that they tend to occur in certain zones or belts and these, as will be seen later, correspond fairly closely with the great zones of crustal weakness, *i.e.* the belts of young fold mountains and along major lines of faulting such as that of the great Rift Valley of East Africa.

There are two main zones of earthquake activity: (i) the mid-Old World belt which runs from Iberia and Morocco through the Mediterranean, Turkey, Iran, the Himalayan region to China; and (ii) the circum-Pacific belt which follows the western coastal zone of the Americas, the Aleutian Islands, the Japanese and Philippine

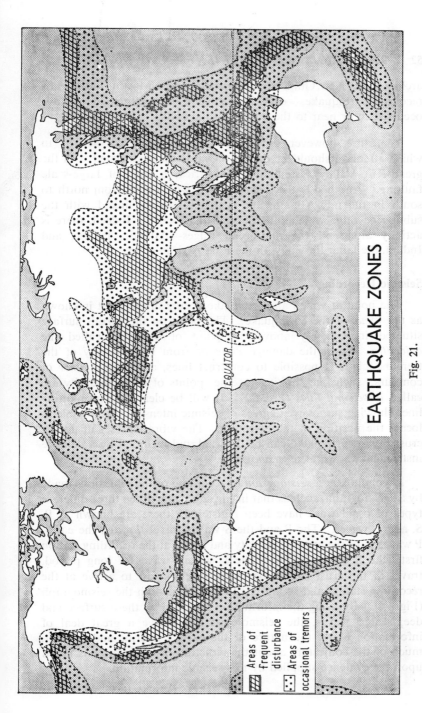

EARTHQUAKE ZONES

Fig. 21.

The earth's susceptibility to tremors may be correlated with the great zones of crustal weakness, *e.g.* the belts of young fold mountains, the zones of major fracturing, and the mid-ocean rises.

archipelagos, New Guinea, and New Zealand. Most of the world's recorded earthquakes—over 75 per cent.—are estimated to have occurred in or near to these two seismic belts.

There are, however, other distinguishable zones of activity to which attention should be drawn. One is that associated with the great Rift Valley system of East Africa, a zone of large-scale faulting. Another is the S-shaped belt which runs from north to south in the mid-Atlantic and which is closely linked with the submarine ridge which runs through that ocean. Indeed, there is activity along all the mid-ocean ridges—Atlantic, Pacific, and Indian, the latter linking with the East African zone.

Seismic Recording

The point at which an earthquake occurs in the crust is known as the *focus* of the earthquake. The point on the earth's surface situated immediately above the point of origin is called the *epicentre*. From the damage done or from the intensity of the tremors felt it is possible to construct lines, after the manner of contours; such lines linking together points of equal intensity are called *isoseismal lines* (Fig. 22). It will be clear that by plotting lines showing successive degrees of seismic intensity it is possible to locate the position of the epicentre. The vibrations set up in the crust by an earthquake can be detected and recorded by a delicate instrument known as a *seismograph*.

If you look at a *seismogram* or recording of the vibrations made by a seismograph, such as that in Fig. 23, you will see three different types of oscillations have been registered; these are known as P, S, and L waves. The P and the S waves travel *through* the earth. P waves have the greatest velocity and arrive at the recording station first; the S waves follow. The L waves, waves of long period, travel in the crust *round* the earth, take longest to arrive at the recording station and so are last to be recorded on the seismograph (Fig. 24). By using the information provided by these surface and deep-seated waves, the seismologist can derive a great deal of information about the nature of the earth's interior and, in fact, much of the conjecture about the structure of the interior is based upon the evidence supplied by this seismic information.

Causes of Earthquakes

Finally we come to the problem of what causes earthquakes. While some earthquakes are associated with vulcanism (though the two are not necessarily or inevitably related), most of them are

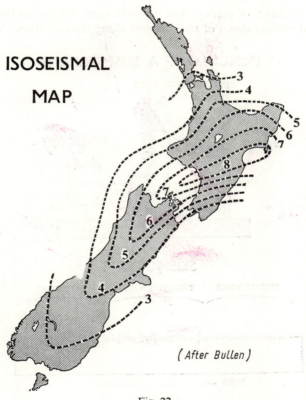

ISOSEISMAL

MAP

(After Bullen)

Fig. 22.

The pecked lines link together, after the fashion of a contour map, the points of equal intensity of earth tremors. Thus, in New Zealand, the area between Wanganui and Gisborne in North Island suffers the greatest degree of seismic intensity.

tectonic, that is they are due to sudden movements within the rock crust particularly where there are fractures. For various reasons stresses build up within the crust and when a certain point of intensity is reached breaks or slips occur.   These produce locally a jolt or shock, the effects of which are to send out vibrations.   The intensity of the earthquake depends upon two factors, (*a*) the amount of slip or movement along a fault, and (*b*) the size of the rock mass involved in the movement.

The majority of earthquakes it would seem are due to the slipping and settling down of rock masses along fracture lines.   Areas

PRINCIPLE OF A SEISMOGRAPH

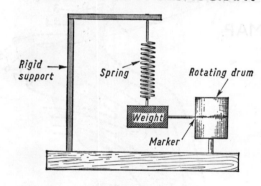

SEISMOGRAM

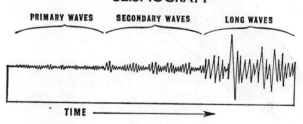

Fig. 23.

A variety of instruments have been devised to record earth tremors.   A seismograph is simply an instrument designed to measure the displacement of the ground with respect to a mass.   In the type of seismograph shown here a mass is suspended by a spring; a tremor will agitate the spring causing the weight to move up and down; as it does so the attached pointer will register its vertical movements upon the rotating drum.   Another type of seismograph measures horizontal movements.   The lower diagram, a seismogram, records the different types of waves generated by an earthquake and indicates the time of their arrival at a station.

of young fold mountain building have also suffered fracturing and this explains why the great seismic belts are to be correlated with the zones of recent mountain building. While such mountains were being built, earthquakes must have been common phenomena and

THE EARTH
AND EARTHQUAKE WAVES

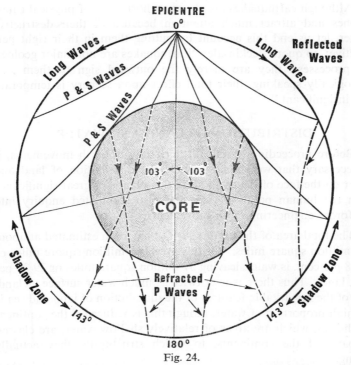

Fig. 24.

The paths of earthquake waves through the earth. The P waves (primary or longitudinal waves) and the S waves (secondary or transverse waves) travel through the earth while the L waves (surface waves) travel round the earth. Note that the S waves do not penetrate the core; also, that the P waves have their speed of movement reduced as they travel through the core while the waves are refracted or bent. Note, too, the shadow zones between 103° and 143° distant from the epicentre where no P or S waves are received.

as Sir Dudley Stamp has said: "The earthquakes of to-day are like the final murmurs of a great storm which has passed."

R. P. Beckinsale has drawn attention to another possible cause.[1] Local intense surface loading may dispose towards earthquakes and he cites the area around the Mississippi delta where there has been excessive surface loading due to the deposition of vast quantities of alluvium and the loess region of North China which has accumulated a great spread of desert derived dust; both these areas are regions suffering seismic tremors.

Although earthquakes are the most horrifying of physical catastrophes and attract much attention because of their destructive power, let us end this account by putting them in their right perspective; to quote Beckinsale: "Earthquakes are not major geological processes; they are merely the outward sign of them . . . geologically speaking, their total effect upon scenery is temporary and insignificant." [2]

DISTRIBUTION OF LAND AND WATER

Before proceeding to any further study of earth movements, it is necessary that we should look at the distribution of land and water on the face of the earth since this plan is of great significance from the human point of view and also stimulated enquiry into the forces engineering earth movements.

The total area of the earth's surface has been estimated at about 197 million square miles. Of this area 140 million square miles or 70·78 per cent. is water, leaving 57 million square miles or 29·22 per cent. land. Thus there is over twice as much water surface as land. One of the remarkable features of the distribution of land and sea is the high proportion of water, though this is reduced if the continental shelves, which are areas of relatively shallow water, are classed as parts of the continents, to which structurally they actually belong.

A second interesting feature is the disposition of the land areas. A glance at a globe shows that the land is very unevenly distributed. The greater part of the land area lies north of the equator. The

---

[1] *Land, Air and Ocean*, Duckworth, 2nd edit., 1965, p. 186.
[2] *Idem.*

southern hemisphere, on the other hand, is predominantly sea; 81 per cent. of the total surface area is water. In the northern hemisphere the proportions of land and water are more nearly equal, though even here there is an excess of water area over land area (40 per cent. land, 60 per cent. sea). The globe is most nearly encircled by land in latitudes 60 to 70 North, and almost completely encircled by sea in latitudes 40 to 70 South.

A useful division of the earth is into land and water hemispheres. The *Land Hemisphere* is that half of the globe which contains the maximum possible amount of land area. An American, Parker van Zandt, calculated that by constructing a hemisphere with its centre at Nantes, in France, the highest possible proportion of land surface could be enclosed (about 85 per cent. of the land). Even in the land hemisphere, however, water covers rather more than half of the total area. Similarly, a *Water Hemisphere* can be delineated by centring a hemisphere upon New Zealand. In the water hemisphere only a small fraction of the earth's land surface is to be found. In it are contained Australia, New Zealand, the southern part of South America, Antarctica, and many small islands.

The antipodal arrangement of land and water together with the other peculiarities of land distribution and the roughly triangular shapes of several of the land masses led, in the past, to some theorising about the earth's form; for example, Lowthian Green formulated his Tetrahedral Theory in which he compared the earth to a tetrahedron—a three-sided pyramid with a flat base. But the curious features of land shape and distribution are, in all probability, completely accidental.

THE THEORY OF DRIFTING CONTINENTS

A problem which has taxed and teased geologists and geophysicists for some time is to what extent the continents and their geographical positions have remained stable and constant during geological time. This basic problem of earth science has been, and continues to be, debated at length. There are two main schools of thought: the first believes that the general framework of the earth has remained essentially stable throughout the greater part of earth history; and the second believes that continental changes and movements have happened on a large scale so that the earth-plan has been continually modified.

The suggestion that lateral movement of the continental land masses might have occurred was first mooted just over a century ago (1858) by Antonio Snider. The scientific climate of opinion at that time prevented any serious consideration of Snider's suggestion; it was dismissed as fantastic and became forgotten. At the beginning of the present century an American, F. B. Taylor, and an Austrian, Alfred Wegener, postulated continental displacement on a gigantic scale. Both, incidentally, developed their unorthodox ideas quite independently. It was not until Wegener published his now famous book on the subject, *The Origin of Continents and Oceans,* in 1915, that the idea of continental drifting attracted world attention and began to receive serious consideration.

Wegener was a biologist and came to devote attention to the possiblity of continental movement as a result of the difficulties he encountered in trying to explain the distribution of flora throughout the world. Certain distributions were only explicable if land bridges existed linking one land mass to another. He found that there was no evidence for such land bridges and therefore concluded that the land masses themselves must formerly have been close together. He was struck, as others before his time had been, by the parallel coasts of the Atlantic and their jig-saw fit. Thus he was led to develop his theory.

Wegener's Theory

Briefly, according to Wegener, the present day distribution of the continents is due to the breaking up by rifting of an original single major land mass or proto-continent which he called *Pangea* (Fig. 25). As a result of its initial breaking two continental land masses developed, a northern continental block, known as *Laurasia,* which comprised most of present day North America, Europe, and Asia, and a southern block, styled *Gondwanaland,* which included most of South America, Africa, Arabia, the Indian Deccan, and Australia. The two great continental land masses came to be separated by a great midland, east-west stretching sea, the *Sea of Tethys.* Subsequently, these two continental blocks of Laurasia

THE EVOLUTION OF THE CONTINENTS
ACCORDING TO WEGENER

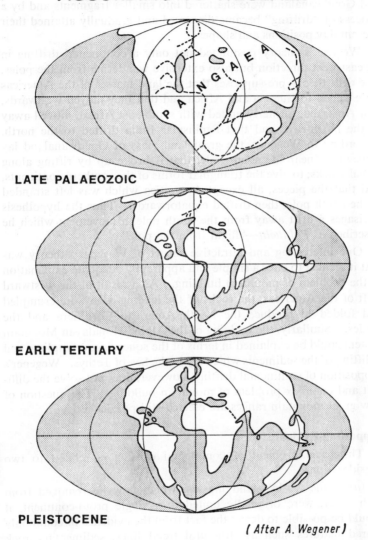

LATE PALAEOZOIC

EARLY TERTIARY

PLEISTOCENE

(After A. Wegener)

Fig. 25.

The diagram shows the evolution of the continents according to Wegener. In late Palaeozoic times the continents formed a single land mass, *Pangea*. By early Tertiary times the rifting and displacement of this proto-continent had begun. By Pleistocene times the continents had assumed their present locations and their present-day shapes had been more or less lined out.

and Gondwanaland were shattered into smaller fragments and by a process of "drifting" became dispersed and gradually attained their present day positions and shapes.

Wegener's theory postulated not only a continental drifting in an east-west direction but also extensive wandering from the poles. The drift theory pre-supposes that the land masses of the Americas were joined to Eurasia and Africa and that they moved westwards, that Australia, formerly united with south-east Africa, moved away to the north-east, and that Peninsular India drifted to the north. According to Wegener, the great land mass of Gondwanaland lay somewhere near the south pole, that it broke up by rifting along radial cracks, to give the triangular forms of the southern continents, and that the pieces, all except Antarctica which was left stranded at the south pole, then drifted equatorwards. Thus the hypothesis envisages a drift away from the south pole, a movement which he described as *Polflucht*—"flight from the pole".

One interesting and attractive aspect of Wegener's theory was that it seemed to offer a simple and apparently adequate explanation of the problem of mountain building. As a result of the westward drift of the Americas, the rocks of the leading edge were crumpled and folded to produce the North American Cordillera and the Andes. Similarly, the building of the Alpine-Himalayan Mountain System could be explained in terms of the squeezing, crumpling, and uplifting of the sediments which lay in the Sea of Tethys. Wegener's proposition of continental drifting, however, does not solve the difficult and complex problem of mountain building. The question of how great mountain ranges are erected still puzzles us.

Supporting Evidence

The basic problem of continental drifting is related to two considerations:

(*a*) If the world's land masses, which now lie removed from each other, were originally united in a single proto-continent, it should be possible to detect the fact from the evidence of commonly shared features such as structural trend lines, sedimentary rock sequences, and fossil remains.

(*b*) If the present day continents formerly had widely different geographical positions, then climatic differences, too, should have characterised the land masses; such past climates, which can be inferred from geological evidence, should be apparent.

Wegener and, later, his disciple Du Toit, the South African geologist, assembled an impressive array of evidence to support the theory. Here it is impossible to do more than indicate some of the main points which tend to support drifting. Evidence in favour of the theory is provided by the following:

(i) The parallelism of the opposing coasts of the Atlantic is a striking feature and if the two coasts were drawn together they would make a rough jig-saw fit. Wegener also drew attention to similar parallelism elsewhere, noting especially the relation of Greenland to Ellesmere Land, Baffin Land, and Labrador.

(ii) There is a close resemblance in many structural features of the American and African coasts; for example, the transverse orogenic zones match up surprisingly well and the same types of rock occur in Africa and South America. Geological similarities on the two coasts of the Atlantic thus provide strong evidence which ties up with the parallelism (see Fig. 26).

(iii) There is evidence from the distribution of certain past plant and animal species whose occurrence is inexplicable unless continental drifting is invoked. Striking correspondences are to be found in the fossil remains of the rocks of Permo-Carboniferous age found in South America, Africa, and India. The distribution of the Glossopteris flora, of marsupials, of the fresh-water worm Phreodrilus, etc., all seem to point to former land connections.

(iv) Traces of glaciation dating from the Carboniferous period are to be found in the far-separated land masses of South America, Africa, India, and Australia but with these different continental areas in their present position the distribution of the Carboniferous glaciation, which apparently affected all of them, is inexplicable.

(v) If the great Tertiary fold mountain systems were formed by geosynclinal sediments being squeezed, folded, and uplifted by advancing shield forelands, then Wegener's postulated equatorward drift might explain the great young fold mountain ranges of Europe, North Africa, and Asia and his postulated westward drift the creation of the American cordilleran systems.

Difficulties

The cumulative evidence in support of continental drifting is massive and when one reviews *all* the evidence it is difficult not to be carried away by Wegener's theory. But even weighty circumstantial evidence and the fact that the theory appears adequately to account for a number of puzzling phenomena does not necessarily

GEOLOGICAL SIMILARITY ON
THE TWO SIDES OF THE ATLANTIC

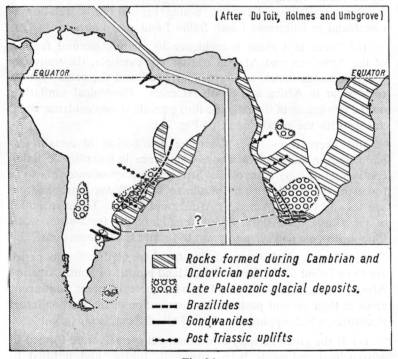

Fig. 26.

The rock structures of the African and South American coasts as worked out by the South African geologist A. L. Du Toit and others. Affinities of rocks and structures provide strong evidence supporting Wegener's theory. Imagine South America twisted round so that the shoulder of Brazil fits into the Gulf of Guinea and these similarities match up surprisingly well.

prove that the hypothesis is true. Perhaps the greatest weakness in the theory, and a stumbling block which has yet to be surmounted, is to find a means of "engineering" continental drift. The forces suggested by Wegener (*a*) to cause the disruption of Pangea and, later, Laurasia and Gondwanaland, into gigantic fragments, and (*b*) to cause lateral displacement of those fragments over distances of thousands of miles, are utterly inadequate. Upon this key problem the theory has largely foundered.

There is another important weakness which relates to the time of drifting. According to Wegener the breaking up of the protocontinent mainly occurred in early Tertiary times. Thus, even if we accepted continental drifting as causing mountain building and being responsible for the Tertiary mountain ranges, we are still left with the problem of accounting for the formation of mountain systems, of which there are many, *before* the Tertiary period.

If all the points in the theory could be established and an adequate motive force discovered then, as Shand has said, "we should have to credit Professor Wegener with the greatest piece of geological synthesis that has ever been accomplished".[1] Whether or not continental drift is the answer to the problem of the origin of continents and oceans, there is no denying its impact on modern thought. Many geologists, even if they do not go all the way with Wegener, still adhere to the principle of continental wandering.

PALAEOMAGNETISM

Wegener's theory, which had long been discredited by many scientists, has been resurrected and found a new respectability during recent years as a result of palaeomagnetic studies, *i.e.* the study of the earth's magnetism during the geological past. Palaeomagnetic investigation discloses the orientation of the magnetic field of the rocks when they were originally laid down. This orientation arises in the following way: when igneous rocks are initially laid down or extruded, the magnetic particles within them take on the same direction and the same dip as the local geomagnetic field at the time of their consolidation.

---

[1] *Earth Lore*, Thomas Murby and Co., 1933, p. 131.

Recent research into the magnetic structure of rocks shows that the magnetic orientation of the fields of the rocks of the continents varies between one geological period and another. Expressing this in a different way, "fossil" magnetism offers a means whereby the positions of the continents may be located at various times during

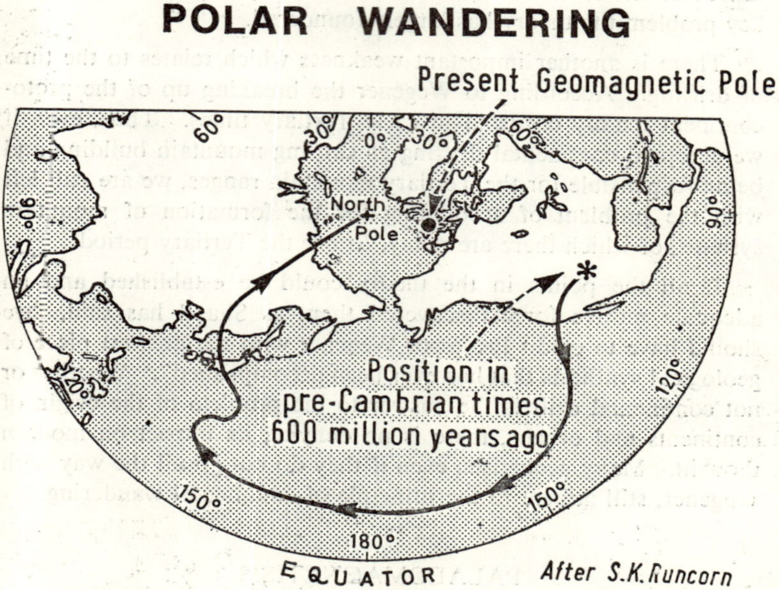

POLAR WANDERING

Present Geomagnetic Pole

Fig. 27.

The map shows the curve of polar wandering as worked out by S. K. Runcorn. This curve traces the route by which a continental block has moved since Pre-Cambrian times, *i.e.* during the past 600 million years.

past geological ages (see Fig. 27). The use of the term "polar wandering" is rather unfortunate as it suggests that the poles have moved; this is not so: it is the continents which have changed their positions.

By using the evidence from the rocks it has become possible to track the past movements of a continental area relative to its nearest magnetic pole. A "polar wandering curve", as Professor Runcorn

PLATE V

Above: Alluvial fan built up by a mountain stream at Jotunheimen, Norway. (*Eric Kay.*)

Below: Thornton Force, Ingleton. This waterfall exposes an unconformity, the limestone having been deposited horizontally upon the Ingletonian beds. Note the lip of the fall, the overhang, and the plunge pool.

PLATE VI

Above: Meanders of the River Cuckmere in Sussex. (*Eric Kay.*)
Below: Incised meander of the Afon Rheidol, Cardiganshire, Wales. (*Eric Kay.*)

termed it, is a reflection of the past movements of a continent. Although the poles, it would seem, have been reversed, it should be emphasised that the poles themselves have not wandered widely— Runcorn's term "pole wandering curve" is confusing in that it implies a large-scale movement of the poles which, in fact, has not taken place. It has been shown that each continent has its own wandering curve.

Thus, because the magnetic poles have been more or less stationary throughout geological time and because each continent possesses rocks showing different magnetic orientations, the following conclusions may be made: (i) since each continent has a polar wandering curve it must have moved about the surface of the earth; and (ii) since these curves are different for each continent then the continents must have moved relative to each other. Palaeomagnetic studies have, therefore, greatly strengthened the idea that continental drifting has taken place. While the evidence of palaeomagnetic studies supports the thesis of former world-wide movements on an appreciable scale, palaeomagnetism also lends support to another new theory, that of an expanding earth.

THE EXPANDING EARTH

Until fairly recently, the orthodox belief was that the earth was contracting. Originally an intensely hot body, it was assumed to be gradually cooling. This cooling caused contraction which, in turn, produced stresses in the crust as it accommodated to the shrinking interior. Gravity tended to pull the crustal layers towards the centre of the earth. As the crustal layers were rigid, buckling and crumpling ensued. The earth was thought to resemble an apple, the skin of which, as it dries, becomes puckered and wrinkled all over. Mountain building was, formerly, thus explained. But if mountains were due to contraction, then they should cover all the earth's surface like the uniform wrinkles of a withered apple. But mountains occur in lines or zones; they do not form a regular all-over pattern. The contraction theory is also unsatisfactory quantitatively; it is doubtful if the degree of contraction by cooling would be sufficient to produce the amount of wrinkle required to build mountain ranges. It is also difficult to explain tensional zones on the earth's surface under the contraction theory. Hence, as a complete explanation orogeny by contraction has been discounted.

The idea that the earth is expanding was first advanced in 1935 by J. K. E. Halm, who suggested that expansion would cause the splitting and gradual separation of continental land masses as they

THE EXPANDING EARTH

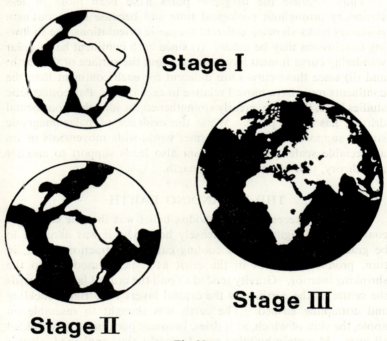

Stage I

Stage II

Stage III

Fig. 28.

Stage I shows the sialic layer, which originally covered the entire surface of the earth, just beginning to break up. Stage II shows an expanded earth with the continental segments now separated by embryonic ocean basins. Stage III depicts the earth as it is at the present time.

moved radially outwards. The ocean basins are explained as resulting from this separation.

The gist of the theory is as follows. The continents consist of light rock which, early in the earth's development, rose to the surface as a thin scum of granitic material originally covering the entire surface of the earth, then much smaller than it is now. Expansion caused the outer shell to crack into pieces, forming "continental rafts", the ancestors of the present continents. Now, assuming that the earth is expanding and that the "continental rafts" have remained roughly the same size, additional crust would have to be formed. This new crust is alleged to have been formed in the oceans by basaltic rock being forced through from below and spreading out to form the ocean bed. Thus, as the ocean bed grew, so would the continental masses become further and further separated (Fig. 28).

This offers an explanation which overcomes some of the difficulties of Wegener's drift theory: (1) The origin of the ocean basins, which have long puzzled scientists; (2) the differences in the rocks forming the continents (sial) and the ocean floor (sima); (3) the absence of deformations in the ocean floor which should have occurred through the drifting of the continents across it; (4) the earth's expansion would produce a change in the relative positions of the continents and this would explain the land mass movements indicated by palaeomagnetic studies; (5) at the same time it allows the evidence of former land mass connections, such as structural links, glaciation, etc., to stand unchanged; (6) it ties up with the great mid-ocean ridges and their associated fissures which mark belts of intense seismic activity and crustal weakness; (7) and finally how, in spite of denudation over several billion years, the land continues to lift its head above the water. The sea level over the entire geological time span may in fact be falling. In an expanding earth the continental areas will remain virtually unchanged in size whereas the ocean areas will increase and sea level fall.

THE THEORY OF PLATE TECTONICS

A completely new theory of the origin of continents and oceans has now superseded—though not necessarily exploded—all the other theories outlined in this chapter. The theory of plate tectonics links together the ideas of sea-floor spreading with the older hypothesis of continental drifting. There are two parts to the theory: (a) a geometrical part which conceives of the lithosphere, or outermost shell of the earth as a mosaic of "plates" or stable, rigid segments of crust and upper mantle, which may be part continent and part ocean; and (b) a kinetic part, suggesting that the various plates are in constant relative motion. The earth's outer crust is made up of a number of rigid, shifting plates of greatly varying size, which slide past one another, converge or move apart; continents

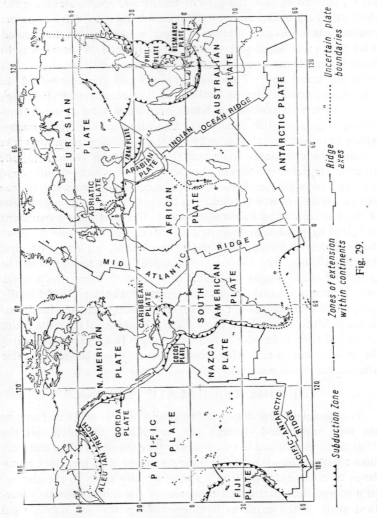

Fig. 29.

drift, mountains are formed, and new crust comes into being. Fig. 29 shows the various plates that are recognised, and zones of new crustal formation.

Mountain formation has long been a puzzle. Geologists have long known that vast accumulations of sedimentary deposits have been squeezed, folded and uplifted but the precise mechanism is not clear. Many suggestions have been put forward, *e.g.* the cooling and shrinkage of the earth, the advance of continental forelands, etc. Plate tectonics offers a satisfying explanation. When two plates

STAGE 1

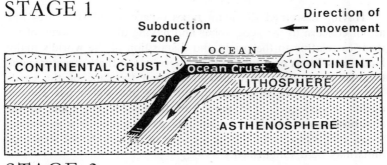

STAGE 2

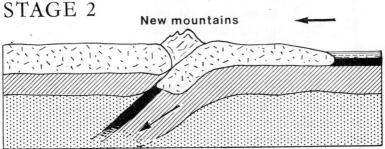

COLLISION OF TWO CONTINENTS Fig. 29a.

collide, the leading edge of one is subducted or forced under the edge of the other plate and plunges down into the mantle where it is destroyed and absorbed into the mantle. However, since the continental crust of the other plate is too buoyant to be forced down into the mantle—the continental crust has a lower density and so is buoyant —mountains are formed along its edge by the crumpling of the marginal rocks and their upthrusting by the subsiding plate. Fig. 29(a) will help to make this clear. It is believed that the Himalayas were formed when the plate of the Indian Deccan, an ancient, rigid plateau block, collided with the old Asian plate in mid-Tertiary times.

CHAPTER 4

THE EARTH'S STRUCTURAL AND RELIEF PATTERN

Having described the main types of geological structures that are of concern to the geographer and having discussed some of the theories relating to the origin and disposition of the world's major land areas, let us now turn to the pattern which these structures and tectonic movements have produced upon the face of the earth. The pattern which now presents itself is one which has evolved during a very prolonged period of time, although some of the structural units which make up this pattern are, in a geological sense, relatively recent. In a broad way, five principal structural units may be distinguished:

        (i) ancient shield areas;
       (ii) old plateau blocks;
      (iii) old fold mountains;
      (iv) young fold mountains;
       (v) recent sedimentary plains.

Representatives of these basic structural components are to be found in almost every continent, although the continents do show considerable variations in their structural make-up and their structural complexity.

Relief is to a great extent the outward expression of the internal structure. Topographically it is usual to recognise four kinds of relief: mountains, hills, plateaus, and plains; but it is not always easy to be precise about the connotations of these terms. For example, the Siwalik Hills, which flank the Lesser Himalayas on their southern side and which rise up to several thousand feet, appear as mere hills beside the towering Himalayas but in another regional context they might well be termed mountains. It is like the man from the Fenlands who comes to visit the West Riding of Yorkshire and is appalled by the "mountainous" terrain, whereas the Yorkshireman takes the hills in his stride and is hardly aware of their existence.   Generally, however, the qualities of elevation and ruggedness help us to categorise the surface relief.

Fig. 30 attempts to illustrate the main structural features of the earth's land surface.   The structural components we will describe in turn indicating at the same time their characteristic relief features.

The Earth's Structural Units

(i) *The ancient shields*

Disposed over the earth's surface are a number of old blocks which have formed rigid masses for long periods of geological time.   These have been termed "shields" (because they are shaped roughly like a shield) and it has been customary to distinguish four, *viz.* the Laurentian or Canadian Shield, the Baltic or Fenno-scandian Shield, the Siberian Shield or Angaraland, and Antarctica. (The old plateau blocks are also in a sense "shields" but here it is proposed to look upon them as a distinct type of structural unit.) The shields, as resistant masses, have served as nuclei around which the continents in the northern hemisphere have grown.   They consist primarily of very old igneous and metamorphic rocks dating from Pre-Cambrian times, and these ancient materials are commonly referred to as "the basement complex".   The shields were once mountainous areas, which had been built up by very early orogenies, the details of which we know very little.   But, as a result of aeons of weathering and erosion and uplift and denudation, they have been peneplained down so that now, for the most part, they lie only a little above sea level.   Because of their general situations in high latitudes, they became seats of ice accumulation during the Pleistocene Ice Age.   As a result they exhibit extensive areas of ice-scoured bare rock, in some parts bereft of soil, with on their peripheries accumulations of glacial debris.   So tough and resistant were these old stable masses that they largely withstood the pressures of the several episodes of orogenesis which have occurred since the end of Pre-Cambrian times.   The shields did not go completely unscathed, however, for they show injections of igneous rocks, are faulted, and locally heavily mineralised.   Topographically the shields are typically low-lying, smooth, and monotonous.

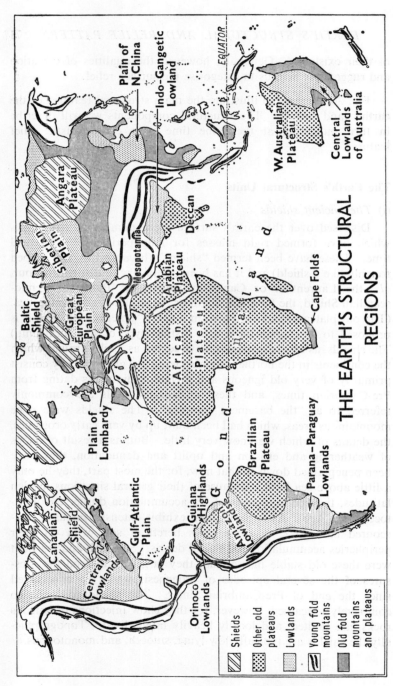

THE EARTH'S STRUCTURAL REGIONS

Fig. 30.

Shields
Other old plateaus
Lowlands
Young fold mountains
Old fold mountains and plateaus

Baltic Shield
Canadian Shield
Great European Plain
Siberian Plain
Angara Plateau
Plain of N.China
Indo-Gangetic Lowland
Mesopotamia
Arabian Plateau
Deccan
African Plateau
Cape Folds
Central Lowlands
Gulf-Atlantic Plain
Plain of Lombardy
Orinoco Lowlands
Guiana Highlands
Amazon Lowlands
Brazilian Plateau
Parana–Paraguay Lowlands
Gondwanaland
W. Australian Plateau
Central Lowlands of Australia
EQUATOR

(ii) *The plateau blocks*

The old plateau blocks of Brazil-Guiana, Africa, Arabia, India, Australia, and China differ from the shields in their greater elevation though they are nowhere of very great height; generally they are two or three thousand feet high, occasionally rising up to 5,000 feet or slightly more. The African Plateau, which is the largest of these plateau blocks, is composed, like the shields, of very old crystalline rocks, but is covered in many areas with sedimentary layers. Its surface is surprisingly uniform over extensive areas, however, and the general effect is one of great monotony. While wide expanses are completely level or only gently undulating, in many areas inselberge or steep-sided residual hills rise up sharply. The plateau surface, or rather surfaces, for there are several lying at varying elevations, are bounded by steep scarp-slopes. The African plateau, though stable and resistant, has obviously yielded to certain pressures for lava outflows, volcanic eruptions, and large-scale faulting have occurred. Some of the plateau blocks, *e.g.* the Brazilian Plateau and the Deccan, have been uplifted and tilted, suffering faulting, igneous intrusion, and volcanic outpourings in the process. The scattered plateau blocks of the southern continents and southern Asia share many geological and topographical features and they are generally regarded as parts of a former, very extensive land mass, called, as we have already noted, Gondwanaland, which was fractured and whose portions became dispersed through the operation of continental drifting.

(iii) *The old fold mountains*

A number of orogenies have occurred since the end of Pre-Cambrian times and the mountain zones which diversify the earth's surface are the outcome of these earth-storms. The earlier orogenies—the so-called Caledonian and Hercynian orogenies—have given rise to what are now termed "old fold mountains" in contrast to the "young fold mountains" which resulted from the most recent of the mountain-building epochs, the Alpine. The old fold mountains belong to two phases of mountain building, the Caledonian, which occurred about 400 million years ago in the Siluro-Devonian periods, and the Hercynian, which happened some 270 million years ago in the Carbo-Permian periods. The Caledonian take their name from Caledonia, the Celtic name for Scotland, where they are well represented; the Hercynian (alternatively called the Armorican or Variscan Mountains) derive from the Harz Mountains of central Germany. All the continents show some evidence of these orogenies and the tattered, worn-down remains of them tend to flank and encircle the old shield areas which played an important part in their formation. The mountain systems consist mainly of the stumps or residual relics of the former mountainous masses and, due to the subsequent pressures which were exerted upon them, they were fractured and shattered to produce tilted blocks or horsts. Topographically, they tend to form "big hills" rather than mountains and, as a result of erosion and peneplanation, they tend to exhibit blunt outlines and to display accordant summit levels. Except where faulting has taken place or where there has been renewed down-cutting by streams as a result of rejuvenation, steep slopes are relatively rare. The Caledonian and Hercynian Mountains owe their elevation to re-uplift rather than to the initial earth movements which were responsible for their origin. The Appalachian Mountains (which show evidence of both the Caledonian and the Hercynian orogenies) and the Eastern Highlands of Australia are examples of old fold mountains. Other old fold mountains are shown in Fig. 30.

(iv) *The young fold mountains*

The most impressive relief features on the world map are the young fold mountains represented by the Alps and their associated ranges, the Himalayan system, the Andes, and the North American Cordillera. These mountains are characteristically high, rugged, and peaked. The young fold mountains are collectively known as Alpine mountains after the Alps which typify their structure and relief features. They were built during the last great orogeny, the Alpine, in mid-Tertiary times approximately 35 million years ago. However, it is wise to think of the Alpine movement as extending over a wide period, perhaps as far back as Jurassic times when some embryonic activity took place and even continuing, in a dying form, to the present for it may well be that the mountains of the West Indian Antilles and those of the East Indian region are ranges in process of elevation. The principal uplifts, however, seem to have occurred in Oligocene-Miocene times. One of the striking features of the new fold mountains is their occurrence in long and relatively narrow belts and two main zones can be readily perceived: the mid-Old World belt, consisting of the Alps and their extensions and the Himalayan system and the circum-Pacific girdle which stretches along the entire length of the western side of the Americas and is continued in the island arcs which swing off eastern Asia. The young fold mountains have a number of distinctive and distinguishing features: they are spectacularly massive and attain great heights; they are rugged and jagged in outline (the term sierra = "saw-toothed" is often applied to them), largely because they are high enough to have suffered glacier attack and especially frost shattering; they tend to consist of ranges which have an arcuate form; and the ranges frequently splay out and then converge to enclose high intermontane plateaus. Although these young fold mountains are of recent build, it is likely that many ranges have already undergone drastic reduction and suffered renewed uplift. It seems very probable, however, that these young fold mountains were never much higher than they are now, in spite of denudation, but that isostatic readjustment has maintained their general high elevation.

(v) *Recent sedimentary plains*

The fifth component in the general structure of the earth's surface comprises the generally low-lying and generally level areas, constituting the lowlands and plains, which are built up of sedimentary deposits. The two main types of plains can be recognised: the sedimentary platforms and the alluvial lowlands: but it is not always possible to be quite clear-cut about this division. In many areas, usually between the shields and the resistant blocks of Caledonian and Hercynian origin, marine inundations have often taken place and in these epicontinental seas relatively thin sediments were laid down upon the land surfaces thus submerged. Subsequently, these depressed or down-warped surfaces were lifted up to form dry land; the Great Plains of North America are a case in point.

Most of the great lowland areas were formed in large part from areas transgressed by fluctuating epicontinental seas. Since the newer beds of sedimentary rocks were deposited upon old, hard, peneplains the new layers have suffered no disturbance, except perhaps a gentle warping as happened in the case of the Russian Platform, by subsequent earth movements and hence display a fairly level or gently undulating surface relief. In some places the infilling of depressions or arms of the sea by alluvium has occurred, *e.g.* the Indo-Gangetic Lowland and the Great Plain of North China; but in many areas, as in the Amazon lowlands or in the smaller plains of South-east Asia alluvial top-dressings cover marine laid sediments. Topographically these plains are level or undulating, often, though not inevitably, low-lying (cf. the Great Plains of North America) and provide the more important arenas for human settlement. Some have been improved for occupancy by man through the legacy of the Ice Age (*i.e.* by deposits of loess and boulder clay) but sometimes the reverse has occurred.

Vulcanicity and Faulting

To conclude this very brief survey of the earth's surface structure let us note that geological and topographical units of the present continents are not the result purely of the effects of orogenic folding, vertical uplift, and subsequent denudation. Locally, vulcanicity, frequently related to the young fold mountain zones, is of considerable significance, giving rise either to volcanoes, as occur in the Andes and in the mountain arcs of eastern Asia, or to fissure eruptions which have produced extensive lava spreads as in the case of the Deccan and the Columbia Plateau. Elsewhere, faulting has been a major factor. Major fault lines can sometimes be related to areas of recent mountain building as in the case of the San Andreas Fault in California. But large scale faulting is a feature of many areas with the Great Rift of Africa providing one of the major lineaments of the earth's surface (see Fig. 19, p. 47).

The Structural Evolution of Europe

Let us now turn to a specific continent, Europe, and trace its structural evolution.

The geological history of Europe is largely the history of the formation, erection, and destruction of a series of mountain chains which have been built up around a shield that formed the nucleus.

Since the beginning of Palaeozoic times Europe has witnessed the completion of three great geological cycles, the orogenic movements of the Caledonian, Hercynian, and Alpine. Briefly, then, we can visualise the growth of Europe as being due to a series of orogenies which grafted successive mountain systems on to an ancient stable core. (In general terms, all the continents have been built up in a similar manner.)

(a) The Fennoscandian Shield

The core of Europe is the Baltic or Fennoscandian Shield. This primitive mass of old, hard, highly metamorphosed rocks, probably underlying much of northern, central, and eastern Europe but out-cropping only in Finland and parts of Sweden, has remained rigid and stable since at least the Cambrian period. In its original state it must have formed an area of high mountains which was denuded and subsequently re-elevated and reduced—perhaps several times—so that now only the mountain roots remain, planed down practically to sea level and presenting a low, undulating surface.

(b) The Caledonian System

In the marginal seas to the north and west of the shield, debris from the mountains slowly collected to form Cambrian, Ordovician, and Silurian sediments. Then, somewhere about 440 million years ago, at the end of Silurian times, the first of the earth storms after Pre-Cambrian times took place. As a result the long accumulated sediments were raised up into a huge range of fold mountains producing the Caledonian system which probably presented during the Palaeozoic Era a gigantic and continuous mountain range swinging in a great arc from Ireland, through Scotland and Norway, to Spitzbergen.

(c) The Hercynian System

After the formation of the Caledonian Mountains a period of quiescence followed. A continental period followed in northern Europe, while to the east and south new geosynclines began to develop and fill with sediments, one along the site of the present-day Ural Mountains, the other across central and southern Europe stretching from Ireland to southern Russia. On the existing land, rocks of the Old Red Sandstone were laid down by aerial deposition. During early Carboniferous times the sea spread over the southern margins of the land and great beds of Carboniferous limestone were deposited over the central areas of Europe. Later the waters receded and in the swamps, shallow lagoons, and great river deltas which now covered much of the area a thick, tropical vegetation, similar to that found in the Everglades of Florida at the present day, grew and gave rise to the coal seams of the late Carboniferous rocks. As a result, a great "coal trough" runs across central Europe from Britain, through France and Belgium, Germany and Poland, to the Donetz basin of southern Russia.

The great Carboniferous geosynclines became transformed into orogenic belts during late Carboniferous and early Permian times. The mountain-building movement which occurred resulted in the Hercynian mountain system. Originally the system formed an enormous range, comparable to the present day Alps, which stretched across central Europe. Following upon later earth movements, the Hercynian mountain belt was broken up into a series of isolated blocks forming the present massifs of southern Ireland, South Wales, Cornwall, Brittany, the Central Plateau of France, the Ardennes, Vosges, Black Forest, and Bohemia. The general direction of the Hercynian fold mountains is roughly west to east, but actually the system consists of two arcs, the Armorican arc in the west and the Variscan arc in the east. Roughly contemporaneously in eastern Europe the Ural Mountains were erected.

(d) The Alpine System

Apart from minor oscillations, a long quiet continental period followed the Hercynian orogeny. As a result, denudation worked uninterruptedly and reduced the Hercynian Mountains down to their stumps and deposition took place upon the land, in inland seas, and in the open sea to the south. In the latter, which the geologists have called the Sea of Tethys, continuous deposition took place from early Mesozoic times and vast thicknesses of marine sediments steadily accumulated. Towards the end of Triassic times the sea in the south began to invade the southern margins of the continent and during the succeeding Jurassic and Cretaceous periods it

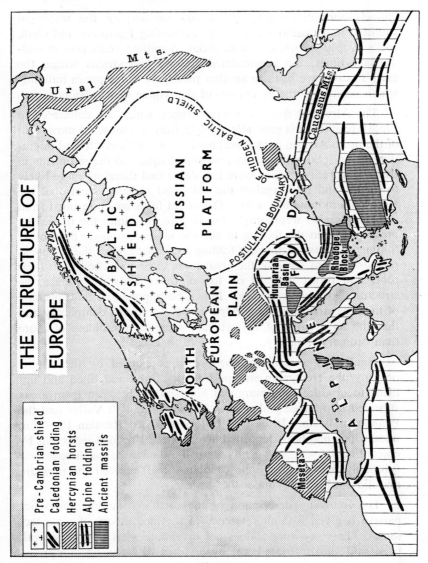

Fig. 31.

The structural pattern of Europe may be thought of as an ancient stable core, the Fennoscandian Shield, around which three great mountain systems, the Caledonian, Hercynian, and Alpine, were successively grafted.

spread more extensively, practically submerging the whole of southern and central Europe and depositing limestone and chalk rocks over great areas.   Then, about 35 million years ago, in mid-Tertiary times, the accumulated stresses and strains within the earth's crust gave birth to another paroxysm of mountain building, which resulted in the mountains of the Alpine system being raised.

The Alps and their associated ranges, which are delineated in Fig. 31, resulted, it is generally thought, from a northward movement of the proto-African continental land mass.   This northward migration of the solid resistant African shield squeezed the sediments in the Sea of Tethys, which were less dense and therefore more likely to buckle and fold, against the old, hard resistant stumps of the Hercynian mountain system.   The initial folds which resulted from the compression were simple but in Miocene times the increasing pressure caused the folding to become more complex.   First over-folding and next recumbent folding took place, then the relentless pressure caused some of the great folds to be wrenched from their roots and thrust forward on top of other folds to produce the structures known as *nappes*.   It will be appreciated that, because of this, the structure of the Alps is one of extreme complexity and that the unravelling of its structure presents a problem of more than ordinary difficulty.

Finally, as a result of the pressures exerted by the Alpine orogeny, the Hercynian stumps were fractured and tilted and up-lifted to produce fault-margined horsts while between them areas subsided to produce graben such as the Rhine Rift Valley and the Pannonian Basin.   In eastern Europe the vast Russian Platform, upon which had been deposited layers of level-bedded sediments by epicontinental seas, was gently warped although its tough basement (probably part of the Fennoscandian shield) resisted the pressure and did not break up under the strain.

The foregoing description of the earth's structural and relief pattern is given without reference to the new theory of plate tectonics.   This new theory does not invalidate what has, in general, been said above; indeed, the events described can be interpreted in terms of plate tectonics.

PLATE VII

Above: The Grand Canyon of the Colorado River, Arizona, U.S.A. This mighty canyon, incised deeply (4,000 ft) into the plateau surface, cuts through a series of level-bedded strata containing limestones and sandstones. These rocks of variegated colours add to the visual impact of this impressive natural feature. (*Aerofilms.*)

Below: The River Avon at Clifton, Bristol, England. At this point the river has carved a deep gorge through the limestone. (*Eric Kay.*)

PLATE VIII

Above: The Mississippi Delta looking south from the Head of Passes. Note the distributaries, lakes and birds' foot formations. (*U.S. Army Corps of Engineers.*)

Below: The Rakaia River flowing from the Southern Alps in South Island, New Zealand, in an entrenched course through broad terraces. Notice the braiding, the great quantity of alluvium, and the different heights of the terraces. Wind-breaks line the flat fields. (*Aerofilms.*)

CHAPTER 5

VULCANICITY AND VOLCANIC LANDFORMS

The term vulcanicity may be said, broadly, to include all those processes by which gaseous, liquid, and solid substances are injected into the earth's crust or ejected on to the surface. More narrowly, vulcanicity is sometimes used to describe volcanoes and volcanic activity. But much unseen and less spectacular activity occurring beneath the earth's surface should also be taken into account for it is not less important. Vulcanicity is closely related to the orogenic cycle and usually occurs when mountain building is in progress or severe crustal dislocation takes place.

Periodically throughout geological time, masses of magma (a general term for molten rock material) have forced their way into the earth's crust where they have cooled and solidified to form bodies of igneous rocks of varying shapes and sizes. It has already been noted that rocks injected into the crust are called *intrusive rocks*. Occasionally, some of the molten rock material finds its way through the crust, pouring out on to the surface or being forcibly ejected; such material solidifies to form *extrusive rocks*.

This igneous activity may, in either case, exert an important influence upon surface features, *e.g.* intrusive rocks ultimately may be exposed by the removal of covering strata; ejected material may accumulate to build up volcanic cones. The various landforms which result in this way form, in the terminology of the geomorphologists, localised landscape accidents.

Intrusive Bodies

The intrusive forms resulting from the cooling and solidifying of the molten magma depend, to a very large extent, upon two factors: (i) the degree of fluidity of the magmatic material, and (ii) the character of the rock strata in the upper crust. For instance, the greater the mobility of the magma, the further and the easier will it flow and penetrate rock strata; the weaker the bedding planes of strata and the more joints and faults there are in them, the greater will be the facility for magma to intrude itself. Geologists distinguish numerous intrusive forms but the more important are as follows.

Extensive deep-seated intrusions of plutonic rock are known as *batholiths*. Since the masses of magma cooled slowly, they form coarsely crystalline rocks such as granite. In due course, as a result of denudation, these masses may become exposed at the surface and the granite mass of Dartmoor is often cited as an example of

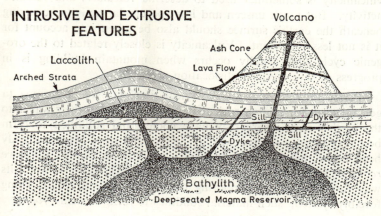

Fig. 32.

Intrusive and extrusive features result from magma in the sub-crust finding its way into the upper crust or out on to the surface through lines of weakness, *i.e.* along bedding planes or along faults and joints.

an exposed batholith. Similar, but smaller, intrusions are termed *bosses* or *stocks*. Where magma has forced its way into the overlying strata causing doming to take place a *laccolith* is formed. The Henry Mountains of Utah, in the United States, provide the classic example of laccoliths. Similar lenticular intrusions forming saucer-shaped bodies, *i.e.* having sagging floors, are called *lopoliths*. Where magma has been injected between bedding planes to form more or less horizontal sheets sills are created and the Great Whin Sill of north-eastern England provides a good example of this type of intrusion. Vertical intrusions cutting across the bedding planes (and probably taking advantage of the presence of a fault or joint) and forming "walls" of igneous rock are termed *dykes*. More properly, a sill may be defined as being concordant with the strata; a dyke discordant with it. These various features are illustrated in Fig. 32 and in Plate 11.

Types of Volcanic Eruption

The magmatic material which is forced to the surface gives rise to some highly distinctive landforms. The type of volcanic eruption depends upon two principal factors: (i) the nature of the exit channel, and (ii) the composition of the magma.

The crustal aperture is, broadly, one of two types: it may be a great crack or fissure in the crust through which the magma wells up and pours out on to the surface or it may be a localised vent hole through which the magma is forcibly ejected. Such eruptive forms are sometimes called, respectively, the *linear* or *fissure* type and the *central* or *vent* type.

It is around the latter that ejected materials accumulate to build up the distinctive landforms known as volcanoes. The shape and form of volcanoes depend very much upon the composition of the magma. If the lava is acid it is viscous and so will solidify quickly and not flow very far, thus tending to build up high, steep-sided cones; on the other hand, if the lava is basic it is fluid, flowing easily and extensively and solidifying slowly and so tending to produce flatter cones of greater diameter. Hence, the nature of the relief reflects to a considerable extent the character of the magma.

Fissure Eruptions.—These form the simplest type of eruption. Usually there is little or no explosive activity associated with fissure eruptions (though there are instances of minor explosions and the ejection of ash taking place, *e.g.* the Laki eruption, in Iceland, in 1783 and the Tarawera eruption, in New Zealand, in 1866) and normally the lava wells up and pours out quietly, flowing easily, and gradually smothering the existing land surface under a blanket of basalt. The molten material finds its way to the surface through lines of weakness in the crust, such as a fracture or series of fractures. The lava may be extruded from the entire length of the fracture or, more erratically, at a series of points. Such eruptions, moreover, usually occur in successive flows which, taken as a whole, exterd over a long time. Each outpouring is not normally very thick: the individual flows average a thickness of about 20 feet; seldom do flows exceed 100 feet. However, the total accumulated thickness of successive outpourings may amount to several thousands of feet.

Except along the mid-oceanic fissures where eruptions are occurring on a large scale few eruptions of this kind are happening in the world at the present day. During past geological ages, however, fissure eruptions on an extensive scale took place. One of the largest outpourings occurred on the Deccan Plateau of India where nearly 400,000 square miles are covered with basalt which attains a general thickness of some 4-6,000 feet but which is nearly 10,000 feet thick on the west coast near Bombay. It is interesting to note that a sample boring revealed twenty-nine distinct flows which averaged 40 feet in thickness. Another major basalt sheet is that of the Columbia Plateau in the United States which covers approximately 250,000 square miles and has a maximum thickness of about 5,000 feet. The Stormberg lavas of South Africa and the basalt plateau of Parana in southern Brazil are further examples of extensive fissure eruptions. It is thought that the basalt plateau of Antrim, in Northern Ireland, together with portions of the Hebrides, Faroes, Iceland, Jan Mayen, and Greenland, may represent the remains of a former vast sheet of basalt which, for the most part, has now foundered (Fig. 33).

Central Eruptions.—In the majority of cases where the eruption is of the central type, the focus of activity is localised; in other words, the outpouring of material is concentrated at a point instead of along a fracture or a series of fissures. At such a point, where there is an orifice or opening, material is forced out on to the earth's surface and this builds up to form some kind of cone. Such a conical accumulation gives rise to a volcano in the narrowly accepted meaning of the term (Fig. 34).

The ejected material from a central eruption may be gaseous, liquid, or solid in form. Gaseous substances play no constructive role in fashioning the volcano; they do provide, however, much of the motive power through their explosive capacity. The cone itself is constructed of ash, cinder, and lava together with a variety of

BASALT PLATEAUS

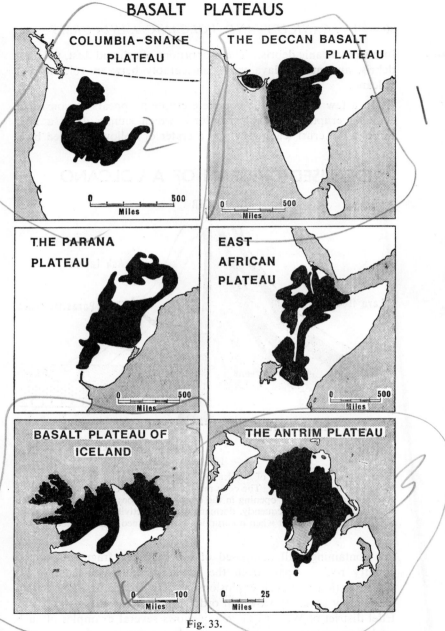

Fig. 33.

In various parts of the world fissure eruptions have resulted in extensive accumulations of basalt which have smothered the pre-existing topography and given rise to basalt plateaus.

forms of volcanic debris. The proportions of ash and dust, volcanic debris, and molten lava vary considerably between volcano and volcano.

In a few instances the complete eruption appears to consist of a single eruption of explosive force which simply drills a hole through the crust leaving behind a crater or hollow encircled by a

IDEALISED DIAGRAM OF A VOLCANO

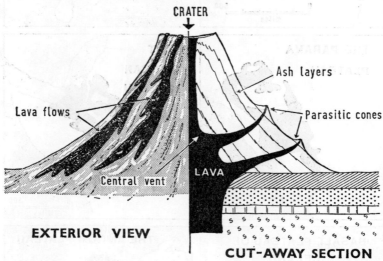

Fig. 34.

External and interior view of a volcano. Volcanoes may be likened to safety-valves in the earth's crust. The cone may be built up of ejected ash or lava or both around the vent or opening in the crust. Volcanoes are said to be active when eruptions occur frequently, dormant when no activity has taken place for a long time, and extinct when no eruption has happened within historic times.

low containing wall composed of the shattered fragments of the country rock. Apart from the initial punctuation, there is no further action and such explosions would seem to function purely and simply as safety-valves in order to relieve local stresses. The Eifel district of Western Germany shows several examples of such explosion-craters.

Occasionally volcanoes are built through a single phase of vigorous activity. Monte Nuovo, near Naples, which erupted in 1538, formed a cone 440 feet high within three days. Less spectacular in its growth was Parícutin, in Mexico, whose complete life-cycle extended over nine years, although most of the cone, which reached a height of over 1,400 feet, was constructed during the first two years of activity. Long-continued activity, perhaps extending over many centuries, will eventually give rise to very large cones several thousands of feet in elevation and with diameters many miles in extent, such as the volcanoes of Hawaii, Indonesia, and the Andes.

The ejected material does not always accumulate in cone-shaped mounds and it should be emphasised that there are widespread areas of accumulated ash which have covered the original land surface and which have become consolidated to form volcanic tuff; for example, there are large areas in southern Etruria in Italy which have been blanketed in this way.

Extrusive Materials

The materials that are extruded on to the surface are in three physical states—in gaseous, liquid, and solid forms.

Gases.—A variety of gases are given off as a result of volcanic activity but those emitted by volcanoes contain 60-95 per cent. super-heated steam. Most of this water has been formed by distillation from the deeply-seated magma chamber. Carbon dioxide is given off in large quantities and gaseous compounds of sulphur, particularly sulphur dioxide and sulphuretted hydrogen, are also common. The sulphur dioxide becomes dissolved in the steam to produce a weak solution of sulphuric acid and it is largely this which is responsible for the killing off of vegetation in areas of vulcanicity. Chlorine and fluorine are also given off by some volcanoes while a few emit boron. The eruptions of the West Indian volcanoes, Mont Pelée and Soufrière, in 1902, were accompanied by unusual outpourings of gases which rolled down the mountain slopes and caused the loss of many lives. Without doubt these various gases, in conjunction with steam, contribute much to the mechanism of volcanoes, especially those of an explosive disposition.

Water.—During eruptions some steam is usually produced and given off. In eruptive phases, temperatures are usually so high that any water present is inevitably converted into steam whose expansive force has explosive tendencies. When the emitted steam comes into contact with the cooler air condensation occurs, cloud is formed, and rain falls. Torrential rains are, in fact, a frequent accompaniment of volcanic eruptions. Such heavy downpours sometimes mix with the fine dust which is ejected to produce mud flows such as those which overwhelmed the Roman town of Herculaneum at the foot of Monte Somma; as a result of this "cast" of solidified mud Herculaneum was perfectly preserved for posterity. Sometimes destructive floods occur as a result of the sudden melting of snow and ice which may cover the upper slopes of high volcanoes. An instance of this occurred in 1877 when molten lava oozing out of the Ecuadorian volcano of Cotopaxi melted the snows of its summit to produce a flood which poured down the mountain slopes. In such phenomena as geysers, hot springs, and mud volcanoes, water is the only, or most important, product of volcanic activity.

Lava.—The other liquid product of vulcanicity is lava, the name given to molten rock. Rock is "liquefied" within the crust through the combined action of temperature and pressure. It would appear that lavas start moving in the mantle from a depth of 200-300 km. The degree of fluidity of lava depends very largely on its composition: an acid lava remains very viscous while a basic lava is highly mobile. The degree of the lava's fluidity will therefore have a very important bearing upon the forms of cones built up of lava-flows, *i.e.* whether they will have steep or gentle slopes.

Solid Debris.—Most volcanoes eject a certain amount of material in solid form. The nature of this ejected matter varies considerably but a grouping of the chief kinds of solid debris may be made as follows. (*a*) Most important is the solidified *lava* which has formed in the crater or chokes the pipe and is shattered with the onset of volcanic activity: such material is usually ejected as angular fragments of different size which form the rock known as *volcanic breccia.* (*b*) *Pumice,* the solidified froth and scum from the surface of the lava, has a sponge-like, cellular nature and its low specific gravity is due to the presence of much gas and steam in the lava when the pumice was formed. (*c*) Material which is of a more cindery character is known as *scoria*. Its origin is essentially the same as that of pumice although it is usually of more basic composition. It has the same coarsely cellular appearance caused by escaping gases. (*d*) *Lapilli* is a term applied to small, usually round but sometimes angular, stony fragments, ranging up to the size of a walnut, which are thrown out during eruptive phases. (*e*) *Volcanic bombs* are masses or clots of lava, usually of approximately rounded form and often of considerable size, which are ejected from the crater. They are usually in a more or less viscous condition becoming shaped as a result of their passage through the air. (*f*) *Tuff* is the name applied to finely divided material or volcanic dust which piles up to form partially or completely consolidated masses of rock.

Birth of a Volcano—Parícutin

Occasionally man is able to witness the birth and growth of a volcano; such happenings are relatively few, however, and no more than about a dozen have come into existence during historic times. One, Parícutin, of which we have a complete life history, was born on February 20th, 1943. Less than a decade later, it had become quite inactive but during its nine-year growth it was studied very closely in all details and vulcanologists were able to secure important statistics of great value in the study of volcanic activity.

The record of Parícutin's birth runs as follows. Early after noon on that February day, a Mexican peasant, Dionisio Pulido, was ploughing a cornfield when he felt the earth shake and noticed a wisp of smoke issuing from a crack in the ground. During the course of the afternoon more smoke began to escape, the ground began to get warm, and faint deep-seated rumbling noises were heard. Just before 4 o'clock the earth shuddered and the ground was ripped open by an earthquake. Explosions began to occur every few seconds, dense clouds of smoke and steam were emitted, and ash and dust were hurled into the air.

The explosive activity gradually increased in violence and red-hot rocks were thrown out to a height of 2,000 feet. Severe explosions every few seconds continued day and night for several weeks. The ejected debris began to pile up to form a cone: within five days it had reached a height of 300 feet, at the end of the second week it was 550 feet, within ten weeks 1,000 feet, at the end of the first year 1,400 feet, and at the end of the second year 1,500 feet.

At first, the eruption was of the dry type, that is it ejected ash and cinders only, although some lava did well up from a fissure about 1,000 feet away two days after the eruption started. But it was four months before molten lava began to bubble out of Parícutin's vent and flow down the sides of the cinder cone. By this time, not only had Pulido's farmstead been destroyed and engulfed but the villagers had had to evacuate their homes which gradually were burnt out and smothered with volcanic debris. Fortunately, no one was killed by the eruption but all the trees and vegetation for miles around were destroyed. Finally, after nine years of activity, the eruptions stopped and Parícutin's destructive power came to an abrupt end. Thenceforth, it settled into quiescence and has now become just another of several small dead cones in the locality, all of them perhaps satellites of Toncitaro.

According to the records which were made from survey and calculation, Parícutin threw out, between 1943 and 1952, 2,500,000,000 tons of cinders and rocks and spewed up 1,500,000,000 tons of lava. Peak activity was reached in May, 1945 and, from tests of the clouds emitted at that time, it was estimated that 16,000 tons of water vapour were given off each day and 100,000 tons of lava squeezed out.

Phases of Volcanic Eruption

The foregoing brief account of Parícutin's career helps us to appreciate the various phases in a volcanic eruption. Geologists usually distinguish six main phases in the life history of a volcano.

(i) Action is initiated by an intrusion of magmatic material into the upper crust from a local reservoir of magma. The pressure of the volatile substances gradually increases and premonitory signs, *e.g.* rumbles, thunder, earth tremors, etc., are heard and felt.

(ii) The build-up of pressure ultimately results in eruption which may be fluid or explosive. Material is ejected until the pressure in the magma reservoir has been fully relieved; the time taken to relieve such stresses varies.

(iii) Relief in pressure results in the phase of dormancy setting in. The volcano becomes quiet or sleeps and the vent hole or fissure becomes plugged up. The closing of the orifice, however, enables the pressure to build up once again.

(iv) While some volcanoes may close their life-cycle after a single eruption, as Parícutin appears to have done, most go through a succession of eruptions, frequently at regular intervals, as in the case of Vesuvius. Ultimately, however, these eruptions cease and the volcano becomes dead.

(v) After the last eruption there follows a period of decadence and extinction. This is a sign that the crustal stresses have become adjusted. Extinct volcanoes are associated with a stable adjustment of the earth's crust.

(vi) Finally, the denudation of the volcanic cone and the extruded material takes place. The whole of the accumulated volcanic matter eventually may be eroded away and only the presence of a protruberant plug-remnant is left as a reminder of a former volcano, *e.g.* the rock upon which Edinburgh castle now stands. See Plate XXIV which shows a volcanic plug.

The Distribution of Volcanoes

Evidence of volcanic activity is to be found in rocks of all ages the world over. Thus it is apparent that volcanoes have been a feature of the terrestrial landscape throughout geological history. A further fact which emerges from a study of volcanoes is that geographically they show no predilection for any particular environment being found in mountains, on plains and plateaus, and in the oceans. However, when we come to study the distribution of the eight hundred or so volcanoes which are active or are known to have been active within the historical period it is found that they occur mostly in distinctive belts or zones. They tend to occur:

(i) in association with continental coastlines;
(ii) along mid-ocean submarine ridges;
(iii) in regions of earthquake occurrence;
(iv) in zones of recent mountain building.

Quite clearly, therefore, volcanoes appear to be linked with crustal movements and lines of weakness in the lithosphere.

The map (Fig. 35) indicates that there are two main belts of volcanoes:

(i) the Circum-Pacific Girdle;

(ii) the Alpine-Himalayan Belt.

Some two-thirds of the world's active volcanoes and a large number of those not long extinct occur around the rim of the Pacific Ocean where they form what has been called "a girdle of fire". This volcanic girdle runs through South and Central America in association with the great belt of young fold mountains and in the northern and western Pacific takes the form of linear or arcuate belts. Offshoots from the main girdle are the volcanic loops of the West Indies and the Southern Antilles, which links Patagonia with Grahamland. Within the main basin of the Pacific are several volcanic groups usually arranged along lines having a north-west to south-east trend.

The second major belt of volcanoes is associated with the Alpine-Himalayan mountain system. Except for those in Indonesia, which follow the arc-like pattern of the Pacific volcanoes, the volcanoes exhibit a more sporadic distribution. The volcanic zone can be traced from the Canary Islands, through the Mediterranean and Middle East to South-eastern Asia. Noteworthy is the fact that the Alps and the Himalayas are completely devoid of volcanoes —regions where, in fact, one would expect them to occur. The reason for this is obscure but it may be due to the intense folding and overthrusting which have blocked the passageways along which magma might have forced its way to the surface. A major offshoot from this mid-Old World belt is the volcanic zone associated with the Great Rift Valley of Africa. In the Atlantic, volcanoes occur in Iceland, Jan Mayen Island, the Canary Islands, the Azores, Cape Verde Islands, St Helena Island, and Ascension Island. Volcanoes in the Indian Ocean are found on Madagascar, Mauritius, Reunion, Rodriguez, and Kerguelen.

This brief account of the distribution pattern of volcanoes serves to corroborate the points made at the beginning of this section, namely, that volcanic activity is related to continental margins and to zones of crustal deformation.

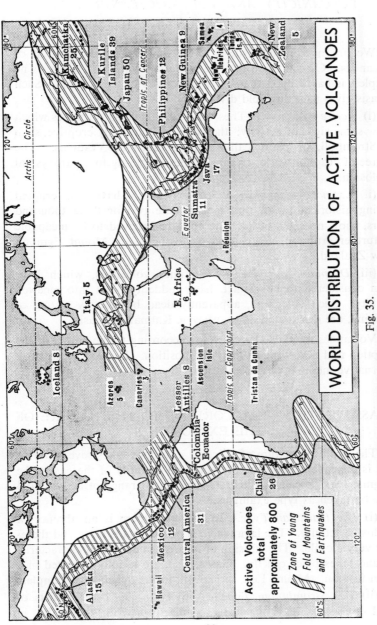

Fig. 35. WORLD DISTRIBUTION OF ACTIVE VOLCANOES. In some areas, as in Japan and Java, they lie too thick upon the ground for every volcano to be shown. Note the correlation of most volcanoes to the zone of young fold mountains and earthquake occurrence.

The map attempts to show the world distribution of active volcanoes. In some areas, as in Japan and Java, they lie too thick upon the ground for every volcano to be shown. Note the correlation of most volcanoes to the zone of young fold mountains and earthquake occurrence.

93

TYPES OF VOLCANOES

We are now in a position to attempt some classification of volcanoes. Classification may be made in a variety of ways. The simplest is based upon the *degree of activity* of the volcano. Such a basis gives us a threefold division.

(i) *Active volcanoes.*—These may be defined as volcanoes which show some signs of activity: they may be constantly eruptive, such as Stromboli, or periodically eruptive, such as Vesuvius. The degree of eruption varies from a gentle simmering to a paroxysmal explosion.

(ii) *Extinct volcanoes.*—Volcanoes which have not erupted during historical times, that is for some two or three thousand years, show no signs of activity, and are believed to be incapable of further eruption, are classed as extinct; *e.g.* Mount Egmont, New Zealand.

(iii) *Dormant volcanoes.*—Sometimes volcanoes, which have been considered to be extinct, have suddenly burst into renewed activity. Such volcanoes, apparently dead but merely resting or sleeping, are designated dormant; *e.g.* Katmai in Alaska.

Volcanoes may also be classified according to the nature of the eruption and according to their composition. Let us look at these alternative methods of classification.

CLASSIFICATION—1. ACCORDING TO THE NATURE OF THE EXPLOSION

The explosive nature of volcanic eruptions takes several forms and is dependent upon the pressure and quantity of the gas in the magma. Six volcanoes illustrate the general range of activity and may be taken as type examples.

(i) *The Hawaiian Type.*—In this type there is an absence of explosive activity. The lava which is poured out is basic and therefore very mobile. The effusion of lava is the dominant characteristic and takes place quietly. Gases, also, are usually liberated in a quiet fashion. Mauna Loa, in Hawaii, forms the classic example.

(ii) *The Strombolian Type.*—Activity in this case consists of mild explosions recurring, often regularly, at short intervals; in the case of Stromboli minor explosions occur every few minutes. With every explosion red-hot clots of lava are thrown out which form "bombs" of scoria. Luminous clouds accompany phases of more intense activity.

(iii) *The Vulcanian Type.*—This type, named after Vulcano in the Lipari Islands, has more violent and more irregularly spaced explosions. The lava, being more viscous, crusts over and the pent up gases accumulate until they explode with considerable violence. Dark clouds and much steam accompany the explosion.

(iv) *The Vesuvian Type.*—Vesuvius provides the type example. In this instance, violent explosion follows a long period of mild activity or apparent quiescence. Gases gradually accumulate and the magma becomes highly charged with them. The condition becomes highly explosive and when the critical point is reached the rock plugging the vent is shattered and the magma is expelled with explosive force.

(v) *The Krakatoan Type.*—Extreme explosive violence was reached in the eruption of Krakatoa. In this case no lava was emitted but enormous quantities of volcanic dust were ejected. The explosion was so tremendous that not only was the volcano demolished but a hole was blasted beneath the sea surface.

(vi) *The Peléan Type.*—This type of explosive eruption is characterised by blasts of dark or incandescent ash and gas which issue through lateral cracks since the material cannot escape upwards due to the vent being sealed. These blasts, known as *nuees ardentes,* roll downslope and may, as in the case of the explosion of Mount Pelée in Martinique, cause great loss of life.

CLASSIFICATION—2. ACCORDING TO COMPOSITION

Classifying volcanoes according to the type of material which has accumulated around the vents, we have a fourfold division.

(i) *Shield Volcanoes.*—When there is an absence of explosive activity and, therefore, an absence of ejected fragmentary material also, the volcanic material consists almost solely of lava which is poured out quietly. If the lava is basic, it is, as we have already noted, very mobile and can flow for considerable distances before it cools and congeals. The very fluid lava erupted from Mauna Loa in Hawaii travels at the rate of about 3 feet per minute and flows for distances of 20 to 30 miles. The result is the building up, by successive outpourings, of cones which are much broader than they are high with small angles of slope, rarely steeper than 10 degrees near the summit and 2 degrees near the base. The five great volcanoes of Hawaii are of this kind; Mauna Loa, the largest, for instance, reaches up to 13,675 feet at its summit but since Hawaii has a diameter of 70 miles at sea level its slopes are only gentle. Such great basaltic lava cones are known as shield volcanoes.

(ii) *Dome Volcanoes*.—The second type of effusive or lava volcano is called the dome volcano. In the case of viscous lava, the cooling and congealing is rapid, hence the lava does not flow very far. The result is the formation of a dome-shaped cone with steep, convex sides and frequently without a visible crater. Such acid lava volcanoes have an elevation which is great in proportion to the basal diameter. Typical domes of this type are found in the region of Auvergne, in the Central Massif of France. These extinct volcanoes—the *puys d'Auvergne*—with their rounded shapes give rise to the very characteristic landscape of the area. The highest of the puys is the Puy de Dôme, 4,806 feet. It seems likely that some of these dome volcanoes had their distinctive shapes accentuated by internal pressure and expansion. Later uprisings of lava were contained by the hardened surface layers and, unable to find an exit, swelled these layers outwards.

(iii) *Cinder Cones*.—Explosive activity gives rise to showers of fragmental material—dust, ash, cinders, lapilli, bombs, etc.—and this volcanic debris, as it falls back to earth around the vent, gradually accumulates to form a cone which is normally slightly concave in shape as a result of the spreading outwards of material near the base. The larger fragments usually fall near the vent, helping to build the cone upwards, while the finer material is ejected further to fall on the sides of the cone. Small cinder cones sometimes sprout up on the flanks of larger volcanoes. Cinder cones are steep-sided with slopes of 30 to 40 degrees; seldom, however, do they attain any great height. While Volcano de Fuego, in Guatemala, is an ash-cone reaching an elevation of 11,000 feet, the majority rarely rise above one or two thousand feet. Examples of

PLATE IX

Above: Eglwyseg Mountain, north of Llangollen, Denbighshire. Below the free face of the limestone beds lies the constant slope determined by the angle of rest of the scree; the latter passes into the concave slope that leads down to the river. (*H.M. Geological Survey.*)

Below: Cliff slumping and flow in Barton Beds at Barton-on-Sea, Hampshire, England. (*Eric Kay.*)

PLATE X

Above: Flimerstein, Bergsturz, Switzerland. This mountain block clearly shows the vertical cliffed free face and a series of fans, now largely forest-covered, along its base. Note the rock and earth flow to the right which can be clearly picked out by the shrub and tree growth which has developed on the tongue of the flow. (*Aerofilms.*)

Below: Water sinks or swallow hole forming an incipient pot-hole near North Craven Fault, North Pennines. (*Eric Kay.*)

cinder cones are Parícutin in Mexico, Monte Nuovo near Naples, and the numerous cones at Rauoholar, in Iceland.

(iv) *Composite Cones.*—The alternate eruption of fragmental material and effusion of lava builds up cones which are commonly called composite volcanoes. Composite cones are the most com-

TYPES OF VOLCANOES

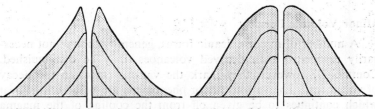

Ash and cinder cone giving steep concave slopes, e.g., Vulcano de Fuego, Guatemala.

Viscous lava gives rise to steep convex slopes, e.g., the volcanoes of Auvergne, France.

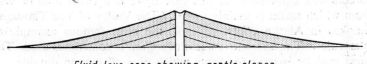

Fluid lava cone showing gentle slopes, e.g. Mauna Loa, Hawaii.

Fig. 36.

The shapes assumed by volcanoes depend very largely upon the materials from which they are built. If the lava is basic or mobile the cones will have low angles of slope; if viscous or slow-flowing dome-shaped cones with steep sides usually result. Composite cones are typically cone-shaped and usually give high, steep-sloped imposing volcanoes.

mon type of volcano and it may perhaps be said that the composite cones provide the "typical" volcano. They are characterised by slopes of about 30 degrees at the summit, tapering off to about 5 degrees near the base. Composite cones, almost without exception, provide us with the highest and most imposing volcanoes and such well-known cones as Mount Etna and Vesuvius in Italy, and Chimborazo and Popocatopetl in South America, belong to this type. Such cones are composed of ejected pyroclastic material and lava which originate from the same vent, though commonly there is much more fragmental matter than lava. Composite cones usually possess a well-developed crater and may exhibit "nested" (*i.e.* one inside the other) craters, resulting from violent eruptions following upon long periods of quiescence. Some composite volcanoes, *e.g.* Mount Etna, develop secondary cones upon their slopes.

Minor Volcanic Forms

A number of minor volcanic forms, generally though not necessarily associated with decayed volcanoes, may be distinguished. Commonly, however, they mark the various stages in the decay of volcanoes. The various minor phenomena are based on the heat which continues to be given off from the cooling of the magma which goes on for a long time after active vulcanism has ceased. A variety of names are given to vents emitting volatile gases and steam. The term *solfatara* is given to a vent which emits sulphurous gases: typically these indicate the approaching extinction of volcanic activity. A *fumarole* marks a further step along the road to complete extinction: in this case there is a small hole or vent from which steam is mainly issued. The Valley of Ten Thousand Smokes in Alaska offers, perhaps, the most famous example of fumaroles. The alternative name of *soffoni* is sometimes used. The term *mofette* is used for vents which give off carbon dioxide. It will be noted that these various names are Italian since the phenomena were first observed and described in the volcanic area of the Phlegraean Fields, near Naples.

In some areas of present or past volcanic activity ground water comes into contact with the heated rocks below: this gives rise to *hot springs* and *geysers*. The latter comprise jets of hot water with some steam which, either at regular or irregular intervals, are thrown up into the air. Geysers are caused by the accumulation of superheated steam in deep cavities; when a critical pressure is reached, the steam forces the water in the upper part of the geyser pipe to the surface in the form of a fountain. When the pressure has been released the fountain subsides and its next emission has to await the build up of the appropriate pressure. "Old Faithful" in Yellowstone National Park, U.S.A., has a fairly regular eruption interval, roughly once every hour on an average, throwing 10-20,000 gallons of water into the air to a height of more than 120 feet. Iceland and North Island, New Zealand, have numerous geysers. Geysers may be looked upon as the next stage, after the fumarole, in the decay of volcanoes.

Finally, there are hot or thermal springs which may be said to mark the virtual end of volcanic activity in an area. Iceland possesses many thousands of hot springs and they are a feature of the volcanic district of New Zealand. Hot springs are known to occur in non-volcanic areas and those of Bath in England are per-haps the best known. The so-called *mud volcano* occurs where the spring water becomes mixed with mud and wells up as hot liquid mud, sometimes building up small short-lived conelets.

A feature of some volcanic areas are terraces built up around geysers or thermal springs. The hot water contains mineral matter in solution, particularly dissolved silica, and this may be deposited in the form of travertine or siliceous sinter to build up terraces.

VOLCANIC LANDSCAPES

Volcanic landscapes, though of limited occurrence, show an astonishing variety of landforms. In some areas, notably the Andes, the Central American Cordillera, Japan, and Indonesia, volcanoes are important elements in the structure and imposing features of the relief. Isolated cones, such at Etna in Sicily and Egmont in New Zealand, form dominant elements in the landscape. Few relief features are so imposing and impressive or so beautiful and majestic as high-peaked volcanic cones. Some active volcanoes, such as Izalco, in El Salvador, which is almost continuously aflame —hence its name "the lighthouse of the Pacific"—bring a dramatic element into the landscape. Not all volcanoes tower up to form great cones. Topographically, there is little in common between such graceful steep-sided cones such as those of Cotopaxi and Fujiyama and the low, flat-topped shield volcanoes such as Mauna Loa. Distinctive, too, are the round-topped, dome-shaped, crater-less volcanoes of Auvergne.

A spectacular landscape feature associated with volcanoes is the *caldera*. The term, which means a basal wreck, is applied to the large, shallow cavities or depressions which are much larger than volcanic craters and may be up to about 10 miles in diameter. The origin of these more or less circular depressions is disputed: while some are thought to be pits left behind after

DEVELOPMENT OF A CALDERA

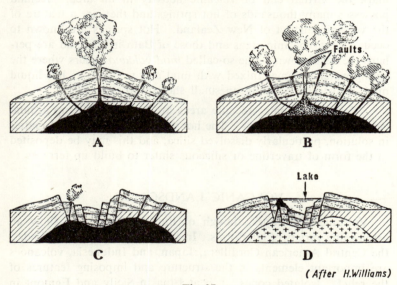

(After H.Williams)

Fig. 37.

The diagram shows the stages by which a caldera is formed. According to one view they are thought to be due to the collapse of former volcanic cones which have been weakened and in which perhaps faulting has developed.

paroxysmal explosions have removed the summits of former cones, others appear to have been created through the subsidence of the upper parts of cones weakened by explosions and the occurrence, in some cases, of roughly circular faults bounding the areas of subsidence supports this view (see Fig. 37).

There is also considerable evidence to suggest that the sheer weight of cones causes downward sagging and the formation of circular faults giving rise to ring dykes and cone sheets (funnel-shaped zones of dykes). Perhaps the most famous caldera is occupied by Crater Lake, in Oregon, U.S.A.; it is nearly six miles across. Another fine example is Askja caldera in central Iceland, almost five miles in diameter, which also contains a lake, Oskjuvatn, occupying a crater pit in its south-eastern corner (Fig. 38). The

ASKJA CALDERA, ICELAND

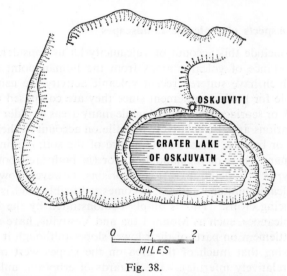

Fig. 38.

Askja caldera, in central Iceland, which is roughly five to six miles in diameter, is a fine example of a caldera. In the south-eastern part of the caldera is the crater lake of Oskjuvatn which is over 500 feet deep. Oskjuviti is a crater pit within the caldera which last erupted in 1875.

cone of the present volcano Vesuvius lies within the caldera walls of old Monte Somma (Fig. 39). At Slieve Gullion, in northern Ireland, a huge ring dyke encircles a collapsed area, some seven miles in diameter, which forms the floor of an old caldera.

In the case of extinct volcanoes, erosion has much modified their original shapes. Where the original conical shape has suffered advanced stream erosion *planèzes* are formed. These are isolated triangular plateaus fashioned by radial drainage deeply dissecting the volcano. They are well-developed in the region of the Cantal, a much dissected volcano, in the Central Massif of France. Where erosion has reached an advanced state, the cone may be largely destroyed. The lava plug in the vent of the volcano, being tougher than the accumulated material, is much more resistant to erosion and remains. Plate XXIV shows Wase Rock, 100 miles southeast of Jos, in Nigeria, a great volcanic plug, the final residual remnant of what must once have been a great volcano.

Human Aspects of Volcanic Landscapes

To conclude this account of vulcanicity let us consider, briefly, the importance of volcanic areas from the human point of view. Areas which have suffered recent volcanic activity are usually unfavourable for human settlement since they are composed of either bare rock or scoriaceous material while many areas of older volcanic accumulations are also relatively infertile on account of their undue porosity or because of the acidic nature of the soil, *e.g.* in Etruria and in many parts of highland Ecuador (in both are poor heath/ broom types of vegetation). It is surprising, however, how quickly some volcanic matter weathers, becomes cultivable, and is capable of producing crops. This is amply demonstrated by the fact that active volcanoes, such as Mount Etna and Vesuvius, have attracted dense settlement on parts of their lower slopes (although it is worth emphasising that much of the area on the slopes west of Mount Etna is relatively infertile). The hazards of eruption, unless it be violent, seem to trouble the peasants not at all. Basaltic outpourings, generally speaking, in time weather to give rich soils. The deep, black, moisture-retentive cotton soils, known as *regur,* of the north-western part of the Indian Deccan are frequently quoted as an example of rich and fertile soils derived from basalt; by and large, this is so, for true *regur* is a fine-textured, heavy clay loam with a well-knit structure, is fairly rich in iron, possesses adequate lime, and contains some humus, but it is its water-holding capacity, due to its high clay content, which makes it especially important to the peasant. Most of the *regur* overlying the Deccan trap formations has a fairly high degree of fertility, but there are areas of *regur* soil which are not particularly rich. The *terra roxa* or reddish earths of southern Brazil, largely localised upon the *terra roxa* formations which are interbedded with sandstones, are derived from weathered basalt and have proved to be rich and fertile and ideal for coffee planting.

The dangers from vulcanism, in spite of what has been said above, should not be underrated. Fortunately, warnings of incipient eruption are usually given and, if these be heeded, loss of life need not be great. Calamities such as those of Herculaneum-Pompeii

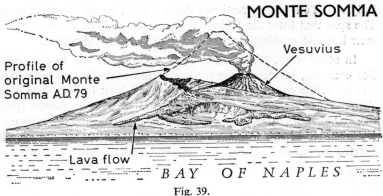

VESUVIUS HALF ENCIRCLED BY THE CALDERA
OF
MONTE SOMMA

Vesuvius

Profile of original Monte Somma A.D. 79

Lava flow

BAY OF NAPLES

Fig. 39.

This sketch shows the caldera of Monte Somma and the profile of the great volcano before its collapse. The cone of present-day Vesuvius lies within the encircling walls of the caldera.

and Mont Pelée are, thankfully, rare; occasionally, however, disasters do occur as in 1963 when Mount Agung on the island of Bali erupted killing 1,460 people and devastating 53,700 hectares of paddy fields. Death and destruction from earthquakes are usually much greater than from volcanoes, though the two may be intimately related as in the case of the disaster which overwhelmed south central Chile in 1960.

One very important effect of vulcanism is related to the occurrence of minerals. Many metallic minerals and the precious stones are associated with igneous rocks which are the product of vulcanism. Examples of this association are: the diamond deposits of

South Africa which have been formed by direct magmatic crystallisation in volcanic pipes; the copper-nickel deposits of the Sudbury district of Canada which occur in a volcanic intrusion; the magnetite iron ores of Sweden which were formed by the injection of the dense metalliferous parts of the magma into faults and fissures; and the copper deposits of Butte, Montana, U.S.A., which are found in a large batholith.

Volcanic areas with their strange landscapes, geysers, hot springs, mineralised waters, and the like have attracted tourists and many countries have capitalised their volcanic phenomena to this end.   Iceland, North Island, New Zealand, the Naples region of Italy, and Yellowstone National Park, U.S.A., are all tourist centres. The spas that litter the Rhine Gorge region of West Germany owe their hot and medicated waters to the effects of vulcanism.

In other ways, too, man has put volcanic activity to good use. For example, in Iceland he has piped the naturally hot waters to Rekjavik, the capital, where it is on tap; whilst in Italy and New Zealand natural steam is used to generate electric power (geothermal energy).   Lastly, and not to be neglected though we cannot elaborate the theme here, is the influence which vulcanism has exerted on man's aesthetic and religious experiences.

CHAPTER 6

THE CYCLE OF EROSION

The surface relief of the earth has resulted from natural forces working slowly but persistently through the countless years of geological time. These same forces are still at work to-day. Because these forces work slowly, almost imperceptibly, it is not easy to realise that they are capable of radically changing the face of the earth. Given time, however, they can accomplish vast and unbelievable changes.

Broadly speaking, the earth's relief features result, as we have already noted, from the constant conflict between two quite distinct sets of forces: those that tend to elevate and build up the land surface and those that continually strive to destroy and reduce it, forces known, respectively, as tectonic and denudative forces. In Chapters 3 and 4 we saw that the tectonic forces originated within the earth and caused structural changes. Such deformation embraces the forces of diastrophism which fold and fracture the earth's crust and vulcanism which builds up the surface. By and large, the tectonic forces are responsible for the major structural units and major topographic inequalities of the earth's surface. No sooner do the tectonic forces begin to raise up and build up the surface than the denudative forces commence their processes of destruction. These destructive processes, which oppose the constructive processes, have the effect of reducing the elevations and filling in the hollows; in other words, they tend to level off the inequalities of the land surface.

THE PROCESSES OF DENUDATION

The earth's surface has been carved, chiselled, and modelled by a number of natural agents. These agents are:

(i) the atmosphere;

(ii) running water;

> (iii) gravity;
>
> (iv) ground water;
>
> (v) moving ice;
>
> (vi) wind action;
>
> (vii) waves and currents.

These agents undertake different types of work. The particular destructive processes in a given area are largely controlled by the climatic conditions. The kind of scenery that is produced in any region very largely depends upon the agent or agents modifying it; the other main factor affecting the nature of the scenery is the rock, its structure, hardness, etc. These destructive agencies operating upon the land surface are sometimes called *destructional forces*.

Denudation

Before proceeding further, it will be useful to be clear as to terms; let us, therefore, define the chief terms involved in the process of erosion. The various processes involved in the sculpturing of the land surface are commonly grouped together under the term *denudation* which comes from the Latin, *denudare*, meaning "to lay bare". The term really embraces three processes: (1) the disintegration or breaking up, into particles or fragments, of the original rock mass; (2) the wearing away of the land surface by scraping, scratching, carving, chiselling, etc.; and (3) the removal of the loose material from its site of origin to elsewhere. The first of these processes, concerned with the rotting and breaking up of the rock material by the action of the weather, is known as *weathering*. The second process, concerned with the actual gradation of the surface by such means as corrasion (cutting and scraping action) and solution (dissolving action), is known as *erosion*. The third process, involving the removal and carriage of rock debris, forms *transportation*.

Deposition

In addition to the actual processes of denudation, the geographer must note the process of *deposition* for both are very closely related. Whenever and wherever denudation occurs there is also deposition for the disintegrated loose materials of the land surface, resulting from weathering and erosion, though removed from their original position, must find another resting place, even though it may be merely temporary, whether nearby or far away. The deposition of transported debris cannot very well be divorced from the denudative processes since one is the logical outcome of the other and it is, therefore, customary to deal with the process of deposition in conjunction with denudation.

Landforms

The details of the scenery resulting from weathering, denudation, and deposition are multitudinous, but the landforms produced all fall into three groups:

(*a*) *erosional forms,* that is landforms that result from the erosion of the surface by corrosion and solution, *e.g.* valleys, cirques, pot-holes, caves, bolsons, etc.

(*b*) *residual forms,* that is landforms resulting from, and left behind by, wear and tear, *e.g.* hills, earth-pillars, arêtes, sea-stacks, mesas, etc.

(*c*) *depositional forms,* that is landforms due to the deposition of weathered and eroded material, *e.g.* glacial erratics, drumlins, sand dunes, stalagmites, alluvial fans, etc.

The Cycle of Erosion

To the sequence of events, consequent upon the process of weathering, erosion, and deposition, which lead to the complete process of land change, from initial uplift of the land to its final destruction, geographers and geologists have applied the term *cycle of erosion* or *geomorphic cycle.* These terms are useful, all-embracing terms which cover all the varied activities and transformations occurring upon the earth's surface as a result of modifying agents other than tectonic.

The term geomorphic cycle is less commonly used than the cycle of erosion, although it has an advantage over the latter. One is apt to confuse the terms "erosion" and "cycle of erosion" if due care is not exercised. It should be remembered that the process of erosion is merely one part of the cycle of erosion. Use of the alternative geomorphic cycle would get over this difficulty but, unaccountably, perhaps because it smacks too much of jargon, it is seldom employed.

THE DAVISIAN CONCEPT

The great American geomorphologist, W. M. Davis, enunciated the principle: "Landscape is a function of structure, process, and stage." By this he meant that the landforms which make up the landscape are the resultant of the interaction of the structure and character of the rocks, of the various denudative processes which modify these, and of the degree of transformation to which they have been subjected. Let us consider, briefly, these factors in landscape development.

Structure

Structure involves two distinct aspects: firstly, the actual build of a given area of the earth's surface and, secondly, the nature of the rocks, *i.e.* their hardness, resistance, solubility, etc. We have already noted the main types of structure, and there is no need to elaborate further upon them. Suffice it to say that the build of an area is the result of its geological history and that four primary types of build may be recognised, *viz.* layered, massive, volcanic, and combined builds. Von Engeln has gone a stage further than this and recognised nineteen different geomorphic units and the student who wishes to delve further into this aspect of structure should consult his *Geomorphology*.[1]

The characteristics or qualities of rock, such as hardness, resistance, permeability, solubility, etc., will influence the way in which the land is shaped. Hard, resistant rocks, if old, become worn down to produce level or nearly level plains but if such rocks are recent or have been re-elevated they give rise to rugged, upstanding scenery. Young soft rocks, which are easily worn away, produce gentle topography. The influence which rock type exerts on topography may be illustrated by the following examples from humid temperature regions: hard, resistant igneous rocks give rise to upstanding ridges (the Great Whin Sill) and volcanic plugs (Arthur's Seat); granite weathers to produce block-like outcrops or tors; Millstone Grit, coarse, hard, and resistant, gives rise to a

---

[1] Especially Chapter IV.

distinctive tabular and step topography; limestone, which is permeable and usually fissured, produces deep, steep-sided gorges
(Cheddar Gorge); Chalk, which is soft and porous, gives rise to
gentle, undulating surfaces (the Downs); while alternating tilted
hard and soft rocks produce scarplands (south-eastern England).

Process

Process refers to the collective work of the various agencies of
earth sculpture, *i.e.* weathering and the action of water, wind, ice,
and gravity. When dealing with the various processes of denudation it is usual to speak of "normal" processes when the activity is
performed by atmospheric weathering and running water. These
two factors in temperate and humid areas are the dominant agents
effecting wear and tear. Those processes which are active under
arid conditions and glacial conditions are treated separately. Davis
termed them *climatic accidents*. In both cases the specialised work
of wind and ice is characteristic of relatively restricted areas. So,
too, is the work of the sea which is confined to the margins of the
land, hence marine erosion is also treated separately. In referring
to the work of atmospheric weathering and running water as
"normal" the implication is that the other processes are "abnormal".
But this is not so, for one process of land sculpture is just as normal
as any other. It is, therefore, arguable that the term "normal" is
an unfortunate and unsuitable designation, but, as so often happens,
common usage of the term for several decades has led to its acceptance and now it is customary to distinguish the operational activities
of the different sculpturing agents into normal and other processes.

Landscapes which owe their topographic features to the normal
processes of atmospheric weathering and running water are termed
"normal landscapes". Such landscapes, carved and shaped by the
rills, streams, and rivers and etched and fretted by the air, are
not dominant over the face of the earth and it has been estimated
that less than 25 per cent. of the total land surface has been
fashioned by normal processes. Over the remainder of the earth's
surface denudation has been carried out by more specialised means:
either by the "climate-controlled agencies" of wind and ice under
arid and glacial conditions or by the sea whose erosive activity is
narrowly delimited to the continental margins.

Stage

The surface relief undergoes constant modification at the hands of the different agents of denudation. Slowly but surely the landscape suffers a series of changes. These changes occur in an ordered sequence. Let us assume a land area emerges from the sea; it presents an entirely new land surface which has not been affected by any agents of denudation. However, immediately the land breaks the sea surface, it becomes subjected to atmospheric weathering and, in due course, when streams have developed, it is eroded by running water. The initial land surface will be eroded and lowered; as time goes on further denudation will take place; and, ultimately, the entire land area will be worn away so that it is reduced to sea level. The reduction of the land surface by running water to its lowest level will produce a peneplain (pene = almost); this, alternatively called base-levelling, is the theoretical termination of the cycle of erosion.

This is the *theoretical* cycle which applies to all land areas. Whether, in practice, this theoretical cycle is ever achieved is doubtful; usually something occurs to interrupt it. "Stage" may be defined as the degree to which the relief has been altered by the denuding agents, whether it has been little changed, much changed, or radically changed. "When a geomorphic feature," writes the geomorphologist von Engeln, "is said to be in a certain stage, it is meant to indicate that its development by process has proceeded to a given one of the characteristic points in a series of changes that must ensue between a beginning and an end condition." [1]

The concept of a cycle of development in relation to land surfaces is a useful and well-established idea. And to help us understand this cycle more clearly Davis, borrowing from the human life-cycle, chose the terms "youth", "maturity", and "old age" to illustrate the different stages in the cycle. These terms imply a succession of phases, much as cycle is an implication of gradual change. It is worth emphasising that "stage" is not a measurement of time although obviously time is involved in the cycle of development; let us look upon stage as one of the phases in the successive changes that occur rather than as a length of time.

[1] *Geomorphology,* Macmillan, 1942, p. 76.

Criticism of the Davisian Concept

We headed this section the Davisian Concept. This, rather than the concept of the cycle of landform development, was deliberately chosen. Now we must note that although Davis's ideas were widely and commonly accepted in the United States and Britain, and elsewhere too, they were not wholly accepted by some geomorphologists. Davis's scheme of things came under fire, chiefly on two counts, from two German geomorphologists, Albrecht and Walther Penck, father and son. Davis postulated, first, a smooth surface for the commencement of the cycle and, second, a relatively rapid uplift of land surfaces. The Germans emphasised the unreality of the first condition since a perfectly smooth initial surface is an impossibility and looked upon slow, and not rapid, uplift of land as being the usual second condition. For these and other reasons there is, therefore, an opposing school of thought. To follow out these differing ideas would lead us into difficulties and we must be content with remembering that the Davisian concept has been challenged.

The concept of the cycle of erosion, developed and formalised by Davis at the beginning of the present century, involved the modification of the physical landscape through the natural agencies of weathering and of erosion in an orderly progressive sequence of changes. For the purpose of demonstrating this cycle Davis introduced two assumptions: (i) that the cycle worked itself out on a newly uplifted land surface which ultimately ended up as a low and almost featureless plain, and (ii) that the successive stages in this cycle progressed through the three phases of youth, maturity, and old age.

The whole Davisian concept has come under heavy criticism in more recent times but in all fairness to the great geomorphologist it should be emphasised that he was propounding a largely hypothetical concept. Davis made certain assumptions in order to simplify his ideas but he was well aware that they could not be justified in nature. He was well aware of the artificiality of a newly uplifted land surface and of the life sequence but these were introduced as an aid to understanding. Davis's ideas have been attacked upon other grounds as well. For example, it is averred that no cycle can ever be completed: that interruptions, such as those due to climatic changes or alterations in the level of base level, are bound to interfere with the orderly progress of the cycle. Furthermore, it is doubtful whether there can ever be any simple cycles since climate is unlikely to be sufficiently stable over periods long enough for a cycle to be completed; "regional studies . . . have shown that relief usually has been formed under the influence of a series of partial cycles. often with the intervention of changes of climate."[1] Landscapes are therefore polycyclic rather than monocyclic and polygenetic; that is, features are the result of several erosion processes.

In addition to the climatic instability, which played no part in the Davisian scheme of things, no consideration was given to biogeographical influences. It is now becoming increasingly recognised that the evolution of landscapes also owes much to the soil cover and the characteristics of the soil, to the vegetation cover, and to human activities. To quote Professor Kenneth Walton: "In addition to the under-estimation of the role of vegetation, the Davisian system pays no attention to the most important process in the evolution of the physical landscape during the last million years. This, surely, is the introduction of human activities which have consciously been directed towards transformation of the physical environment to man's own ends and, often without pre-vision, have changed the type and intensity of process out of all proportion to the numbers of people or their level of technological achievement."[2]

The Use of the Cycle

Though there are many objections to Davis's concept of a geo-morphic cycle, it cannot be denied that it has a useful purpose to serve in geography. As Sparks says: "It provides a comprehensive geomorphological scheme which can be dissected and discussed in its more important parts: it provides a framework in which the significance of the processes . . . may be seen. Finally, it repre-sents the most sensible general view of the course of sub-aerial erosion, and, for want of anything better, its study is still of use to the geomorphologist."[3]

[1] B. W. Sparks, *Geomorphology,* Longmans, 1960, p. 20.
[2] *Scottish Geographical Magazine,* Vol. 84, No. 1, 1968.
[3] ibid.

PLATE XI

Above: Malham Cove, Malham, Yorkshire. This spectacular semi-circular scar, nearly 300 ft high, composed of Carboniferous limestone, owes its origin largely to the Mid-Craven Fault. The actual fault line lies just south of the Cove: erosion has caused the Cove to retreat north of the fault. The stream in the foreground has its origin in the Vauclusian spring which issues strongly from the base of the Cove. (*Aerofilms.*)

Below: Gordale Scar, Malham. The deeply penetrating cleft in the Scar is thought by many to represent a collapsed pot-hole. In the foreground are many springs and after heavy rains water can be seen bubbling up from the many underground watercourses which riddle the area. (*A. Potter.*)

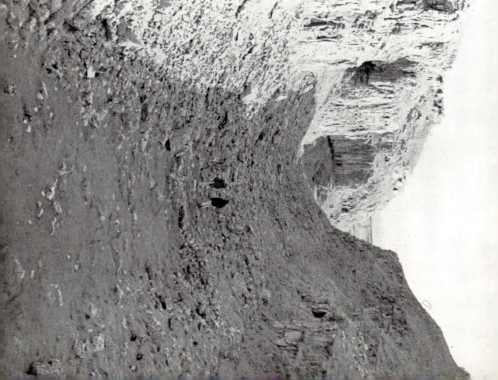

CHAPTER 7

THE WEATHERING PROCESS

Factors Affecting Weathering

The surface of the earth everywhere is gradually but persistently breaking up and crumbling to pieces as a result of the disintegration and decay of the rocks. To all the processes whereby rocks are loosened, broken up, and decomposed because of exposure at or near the earth's surface we apply the term *weathering*. The action of weathering prepares the rocks for removal by other agents of erosion. While the effects of such agents as streams, glaciers, etc., is localised, weathering is all pervasive and operates over the entire surface of the earth.

The degree and nature of the weathering depends upon several factors, chief of which, according to Lobeck, are:

(i) the kind of rock, *i.e.* its mineral composition, structure, hardness, or softness;

(ii) the climatic conditions, *i.e.* whether conditions are hot or cold, dry or humid, uniform or changing;

(iii) the presence or absence of a vegetative cover and the character of this cover;

(iv) fortuitous conditions, *e.g.* the slope of the land surface, the degree of exposure to sun, wind, and rain, etc.

A wide variety of destructive processes are embraced by weathering; they include: heating, cooling, freezing, thawing; mechanical hammering and attrition, or the wear and tear involved in the disturbance of material; the prying and prizing action of

---

PLATE XII

Above: Limestone pavement, showing clints and grikes, above Malham Cove. Note the terrace features in the valley. (*A. Potter.*)

Below: The Dry Valley above Malham Cove. Water once flowed down this valley and cascaded over the top of Malham Cove to give what must have been a spectacular waterfall. (*A. Potter.*)

ice, plants, and animals; solution and leaching; and such chemical changes as oxidation, hydration, carbonation, and desilication.

It is customary to think of, and to consider, the processes of weathering as operating in three ways, *viz.* mechanically, chemically, and biologically, and it will be convenient to discuss them under these three heads.

MECHANICAL WEATHERING

Mechanical, or physical, weathering results very largely from the activities of the climatic elements (sun, rain, frost, etc.), although biological activity contributes to the process. Mechanical weathering is most emphatic in arid areas and on exposed mountain summits. In such areas vegetative cover is largely or entirely absent and vegetation, in the main, helps to resist disintegration by protecting the rocks.

Temperature variations.—It is common knowledge that most substances expand when heated and this is equally true of the rocks of the earth's crust and of the mineral particles which make up those rocks. Thus when bare rock surfaces are exposed to the direct rays of the sun they become greatly heated. This heating is confined to the surface of the rock, however, since rock is a poor conductor of heat; the underlying layers are scarcely affected. This means that the heated surface layers of rock are expanding away from the underlying rock that has not been heated. The constant alternate heating and cooling of the rock surfaces causes mineral expansion and contraction, with the various mineral constituents expanding at different rates. This repeated action may lead to the breaking off of individual mineral grains, the splitting off of thin layers of rock, and the shattering of the bedrock into blocks. The grain-by-grain break-up of rocks is called *granular disintegration;* the peeling- or shelling-off in onion-like layers is called *exfoliation,* or *spalling;* while the breaking up of bedrock into blocks is termed *block disintegration.* The small fragments that break off are angular and ragged and the resultant sand which derives from the rock is rough and angular. The rock mass from which the fragments originate may, however, be smooth and take on rounded forms; bed rock or boulders may show rounded surfaces and when such rocks are gradually reduced in size by exfoliation the process is sometimes called *spheroidal weathering.*

Insolation is strongest in lower latitudes where the noonday sun is more nearly vertical; especially in summer in the cloudless regions of the sub-tropical and tropical deserts, and at high altitudes, such as on mountain summits and high plateaus, like the Andean and Tibetan Plateaus, where the air is rarefied. Re-radiation is most rapid in regions that have greatest surface temperatures and great contrasts between day and night temperatures, *e.g.* desert areas. This rapidity of heating and cooling, and so of the forces of expansion and contraction, hastens the break-up of the rocks although laboratory experiments have shown that this kind of weathering must have *some* moisture present. Hence, as one might expect, purely mechanical disintegration induced by temperature changes, reaches its maximum in the hot and warm arid and semi-arid areas. It is also considerable in high exposed areas where the sun's rays are powerful.

Action of Frost.—Frost action depends upon the fact that when water changes to ice by freezing expansion takes place. Conversely, when ice melts contraction occurs. Rain water percolates into the pores, cracks, and crevices of rock and, when this moisture freezes, the consequent expansion causes stresses to occur in the openings, widening them or loosening individual mineral grains. Such continued stresses ultimately result in the breakage of the rock. Slowly but surely angular fragments of rock are split off from the bedrock while even great blocks may be disrupted and dislodged. The mechanical action is thus one of repeated freeze-thaw process than of frost action in itself.

Frost action, naturally, is most common in cold lands and at high altitudes where low temperatures are experienced. In such areas the process is usually extremely active. Exposed summit areas suffer frost-wedging and eventually show shattered needle-shaped peaks, called *aiguilles,* as illustrated in Plate IV. The piles of sharp, angular rock fragments that lie at the foot of, or on the slopes of, mountains, known as *scree* or *talus,* originate from frost action, the various pieces having been split off from the exposed bedrock and piled up due to the pull of gravity.

Frost action is not restricted to cold environments or high mountain areas; whenever and wherever it occurs its action produces the same results, though obviously such results will take longer to show themselves. Even in Britain porous rocks which become impregnated with water will be gradually affected by frost action and suffer frost-wedging, while the occasional frosts of winter will "lift" lawns necessitating rolling in spring and the clods of autumn-ploughed fields will break down by spring ready for sowing.

Action of Rain.—The mechanical weathering action of rain (which also has a chemical action) occurs wherever rain falls, but is especially pronounced when the rain is torrential in its character. Heavy rain of this kind, which comes in periodic downpours, will rapidly wash away loose sands. Where boulders or hard layers occur in such loose deposits, they serve as protective "caps" and result in *earth pillars* being formed. See Plate IV.

The impact of raindrops may help to loosen particles, but in many areas the action of rain is probably more effective chemically than physically. It is worth noting that rain water fulfils a useful function as a lubricant; mantle material may become unstable through the lubricating action of the percolating water and yield to the force of gravity.

CHEMICAL WEATHERING

Weathering includes many chemical processes. Chemical changes involve actual chemical reactions; such substances as oxygen or carbon dioxide are added to the elements comprising the mineral matter of rocks. Much chemical weathering results from various acids in weak solutions in water penetrating and attacking the mantle and bedrock. Some mineral particles may be completely dissolved away and removed in solution: there are others, of course, which are little affected.

The effects of chemical weathering are: (*a*) to make chemical products that are softer or more mobile than the original minerals and which can the more easily be removed mechanically; (*b*) to produce secondary minerals from the original minerals that are soluble in water and which can therefore be readily removed by running water; and (*c*) to produce chemical compounds that take up greater volume than the original minerals with the result that the weathered rock swells, is weakened, and breaks up more easily.

The chemical changes that occur in weathering involve chiefly solution, oxidation, reduction, hydration, and carbonation. Oxidation affects metals and various metallic compounds to produce oxides; this is most readily seen in rocks containing iron. Iron is a common element but usually occurs in the ferrous state; this may become oxidised to the ferric condition forming a brown or yellow crust which crumbles easily. The reverse process, or loss of oxygen, is known as reduction; this is a less common occurrence. It happens when percolating water becomes charged with humic acid, a complex organic acid formed by the partial decay of vegetable matter. This helps in the chemical weathering of rocks; for example, ferric compounds are affected by the solution and undergo reduction to the ferrous state. Hydration means the taking up of water as a chemical constituent. The hydration of felspar, for instance, results in the formation of clay. The China clay, found on Dartmoor, for example, results from the rotting of granite which is composed mainly of the minerals, quartz, mica, and felspar; whilst the former minerals are almost insoluble, felspar becomes changed to soft kaolinite. Carbonation involves the conversion of carbonates into the much more soluble bicarbonates. Rain water which has absorbed carbon dioxide gas from the air is turned into a very weak carbonic acid; this diluted acid reacts upon such calcareous rocks as chalk and limestone, converting the calcium carbonate of which they are composed into the much more soluble form calcium bicarbonate. Finally, desilication is the process of removing the silica from rocks. Many rocks contain much silica, and igneous and metamorphic rocks contain silicate minerals. Chemical action readily breaks up the complex molecules of silicate minerals. The hydration of felspars, which are mainly silicates of aluminium, could be called desilication.

The rate of chemical weathering varies considerably in different parts of the world. It is at its maximum in the hot, humid regions of low latitudes, where both the high temperatures and abundant moisture accelerate the speed at which chemical reactions take place. On the other hand, in high latitudes and high altitudes the cold may virtually halt chemical processes; in addition, there is often little water in the liquid state; hence, in such areas chemical weathering tends to be at its minimum. Nevertheless, it is worth noting that research tends to indicate a surprising amount of chemical change even in cold latitudes. In hot, arid desert regions, where there is a dearth of moisture, chemical decay goes on at a reduced rate, but often plays an important part in the disintegration of rocks.

BIOLOGICAL WEATHERING

Biological or organic weathering refers to the weathering activities wrought by animal and plant action. Biological weathering is at once mechanical and chemical. While the activities of organisms are especially significant for, and, indeed, are chiefly concentrated on, the formation of soil, locally they do assist the decomposition and disintegration of solid rock.

The mechanical disintegrating effect is due primarily to the prying action of roots and the burrowing of animals. Tree roots penetrate cracks, and as the roots grow they exert a powerful force widening the cracks and sometimes dislodging rocks. The prying action of roots also allows water and air to penetrate more deeply into the rocks thus allowing them to carry their work of weathering to greater depths. Animals, such as moles, rabbits and other burrowing creatures, and earthworms help to loosen and weaken the soil and rock and make it more easily movable by other agents. Certain marine organisms are capable of boring into rock and in this way they may weaken the rock structure.

The organic acids produced by animals and plants and secreted by them also aid the process of weathering by promoting decay. Plants produce humic acid which, as we have already noted, helps in the reduction of ferric compounds and affects the processes of soil formation by encouraging the removal of strong bases from the upper layers. Marine organisms secrete chemicals which attack calcareous rocks. The urination of animals is yet another contributory factor. The bacteria in the decaying vegetable matter of soils play a very important role in the formation of soils. In these and various other ways organisms undertake useful work in the disintegration and decomposition of the land surface.

Summing up, we can say that the weathering process is the outcome of physical, chemical, and biological actions but, whilst we have considered these three activities separately, *in any given situation all are usually at work* even if one is of dominant importance.

Table IV summarises the various factors which are responsible for weathering and which affect the thickness of the weathered mantle of unconsolidated material.

TABLE IV

FACTORS AFFECTING WEATHERING

1. Geological Factors

Factor	
(i) Parent rock.	Rocks offer a wide range of resistance to weathering, owing to both mechanical and chemical factors. Rocks composed of cemented particles are more likely to yield to weathering than those composed of tightly interlocking crystals. Much, too, will depend upon the mineral composition of the rock; for example, rocks high in carbonates are very amenable to solution.
(ii) Structure.	Rocks of massive structure are more likely to show a greater resistance to weathering than those that are bedded. Rocks broken by cracks and fissures provide conduits for percolating water and so assist solution.

2. Topographic Factors

(i) Elevation.	The higher the elevation the better chance is there for active water movement through the rock. In low-lying areas the drainage may be poor; moreover, the water tends to become saturated with dissolved material and, as a result, becomes incapable of undertaking further solution.
(ii) Slope.	High, and especially steep, slopes lead to the down-slope washing and creep of weathered material. There is a tendency for rain water to flow off the surface rather than to percolate downwards and so undertake some solution.
(iii) Aspect.	Slopes exposed to wind and rain will be more prone to weathering than sheltered slopes. Again, slopes facing the sun in high altitudes will be more subject to freeze-thaw action than those which are always cold and sunless.

3. Mechanical Factors

(i) Frost action.	Water penetrates into cracks and crevices and then freezes. Continual freeze-thaw action acts like a wedge forcing the rock apart. Freezing and thawing action also keeps the weathered blanket or loose mantle material porous and promotes the movement of water which, in turn, assists creep, sliding, and slumping of the unconsolidated material.

(ii) Temperature fluctuations.	Rapid temperature fluctuations may cause expansion and shrinkage of the mineral particles or the surface face and promote granular disintegration or exfoliation.
(iii) Organisms.	Plant roots may exert a wedging effect where they penetrate cracks in the rock. Burrowing animals may undermine and loosen the soil and so make it easier for the other factors to do their work.

4. Chemical Factors

(i) Temperature.	High temperatures, especially if they are associated with moisture, promote chemical reactions and speed up rock decay. As a general statement it may be said that an increase in the temperature of 10° C. (*18° F.*) roughly doubles the chemical reaction rate.
(ii) Rainfall.	The higher the rainfall the more water will there be available to promote dissolving action and to react with the rock.
(iii) Organisms.	Plants may act as a protective cover and so prevent the wasting of soil: on the other hand, their roots may assist the penetration of water and so help solution. Plants may also extract certain constituents from the soil and mantle and so help to break them down. The secretions of animals, too, may assist in a small way.

5. Time Factor

Interval of exposure.	The length of time a rock surface has been exposed to the weathering process will affect the degree to which a particular type of rock is weathered and the thickness of the weathered mantle.

CHAPTER 8

GROUND WATER AND SPRINGS

Ground water and gravity are two quite distinct agents operating on the earth's surface, or near to the surface, and undertaking destructive work, but their respective activities are closely linked and it is convenient to treat them together. The term ground water simply means water that is underground or beneath the surface in contrast to the water that occurs on the earth's surface. In the main, it brings about a different kind of work to that which flows over ground as streams and rivers. Gravity, of course, is merely the "pull" which the mass of the earth exerts, but this force, by displacing loose surface materials, helps considerably—often to a much greater extent than is generally realised—in the shaping of the topography and in the fashioning of relief features.

GROUND WATER

Origin of Ground Water.—Water, in lesser or greater quantities, is almost everywhere present in the soil, subsoil, and bedrock: it is this water, beneath ground level, that we call *ground water*. It is of either *external origin, i.e.* derived from the atmosphere or surface waters, or *internal origin, i.e.* derived from the rocks forming the crust. The bulk of ground water, perhaps 95 per cent., or even more of it, comes from atmospheric precipitations; such water is known as *meteoric water.* A certain amount of moisture seeps downwards from streams, rivers, springs, lakes, etc., but this water derives from atmospheric precipitation and so is also meteoric water. A small proportion of ground water, however, is of internal origin. It is of two kinds: some is retained in sedimentary rocks from the time when they were laid down and such water is called *connate water;* and some is liberated as a result of igneous activity, *e.g.* during the crystallisation of magma, and is known as *magmatic* or *juvenile water.*

Percolation of Water.—Three things happen to the rain or other forms of atmospheric precipitation which falls on to the land surface: (i) it may evaporate directly back into the the air or be returned to the atmosphere through transpiration by plants; (ii) it may flow over the land surface and be collected by streams and rivers and carried to the sea; and (iii) it may sink into the ground and percolate through the soil and rocks to form ground water where it remains unless it reaches the surface again as spring water. The proportionate amounts evaporating, running off, and sinking into the ground vary widely between place and place and region and region according to the influence of several factors.

The factors which determine the amount of surface moisture entering the ground may be enumerated as follows:

(i) the abundance and nature of the rainfall: gentle or drizzly rains will allow the moisture to sink in gradually, whereas heavy, torrential rains produce much run-off;

(ii) the slope of the land surface: steep slopes induce rapid run-off whereas fairly level land prevents run-off and assists percolation;

(iii) the porosity and permeability of the surface layers: if the soils and rocks have few openings in them the water will not be able to seep downwards;

(iv) the rate of evaporation: if the air is dry and warm and there is much wind, surface moisture will be readily evaporated and hence less will be able to sink in;

(v) the nature and extent of the vegetative cover: a thick mat of vegetation will help to protect the soil surface from evaporation whilst roots and stems will assist percolation; on the other hand, plants draw water up from the soil and readily evaporate it from their leaf surfaces;

(vi) the amount of moisture already in the soil: if the soil is dry it will absorb moisture readily, but if it is already saturated it will be unable to take in further water.

Porosity and Permeability.—The qualities of porosity and permeability are important characteristics of rock since they determine the capacity of a rock to hold and transmit water. The characteristics of porosity and permeability are intimately linked with rock structure and texture. Moisture percolating through the surface soil into the underlying layers moves through, and is stored in, the spaces between the constituent parts of the rock. The size and arrangement of these spaces are classified either as pores or fissures. These voids in the rock material are of great importance since they control (a) the rate of flow of water through the rocks, and (b) the amount of water that can be held in the rocks.

Rocks which possess tiny inter-connected air-spaces, termed pores, and can absorb and hold variable quantities of water are said to be *porous* and the porosity of a rock may be defined as the proportion of pore-space in a rock compared with its total volume. The capacity of a rock for containing water depends therefore upon the volume of the inter-communicating or interstitial spaces and this volume, in turn, is determined by the size of the individual rock particles, their shape, their arrangement, and the extent to which the pore spaces between the constituent parts of the solid material is filled with bonding cement (Fig. 40). Greater pore-space occurs in rocks made up of rounded grains than in those angular grains which pack more closely together. Large, well-sorted grains of rock give large pore-spaces while ill-sorted material has much of its pore-space filled with tiny particles. Well-cemented rocks have their pore-spaces largely filled in with cement. Thus a coarse-grained, well-sorted rock with little cement such as a well-screened gravel, will hold much water, whereas an ill-sorted, well-cemented rock, such as Millstone Grit, will have a poor water holding capacity. Well-sorted deposits of uncemented gravel, sand, or silt, possess a high degree of porosity, irrespective of whether they consist of large or small grains.

Permeability, or the perviousness of a rock, may be defined as the capacity of a rock to transmit water. Rocks which permit the passage of water are termed *permeable*; those which prevent the passage of water *impermeable*. Perviousness as a rock characteristic must be clearly distinguished from porosity. A rock may be highly porous in the sense that it will absorb much water, yet it may prevent the free passage of water through it and only yield up its water reluctantly. Argillaceous rocks, while distinctly porous, are nevertheless essentially *impervious*. Grain size is the critical factor in such rocks. Clays are very porous, some holding up to 50 per cent. of their volume of water, but the pore-spaces are so minute that the water clings by molecular attraction to the fine grains, with the result that the rock yields up little water and may even prevent the passage of water through it. Crystalline rocks, such as granite

POROSITY IN ROCKS

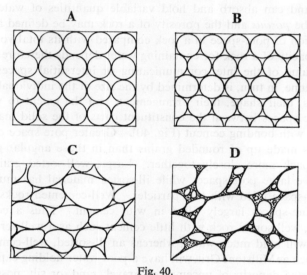

Fig. 40.

A and B show the effect of the packing of grains upon pore-space; the interstices between the grains in B are much smaller than in A. C shows a natural sand with a good sorting of grains, thereby giving a high degree of porosity. D shows a poorly sorted sand with a matrix of clay giving a low degree of porosity. The porosity of a rock is determined by the size, shape, and arrangement of the particles making up the rock and the extent to which the voids between the individual particles are filled with a bonding cement.

which is made up of interlocking crystals, are compact and solid and show but the slightest porosity yet, at the same time, they are generally fractured and fissured thereby allowing water to pass freely through them. Hence, intrinsically non-porous rocks may be *pervious*.

Most rock strata possess some degree of permeability, though there is a wide variation and gradation between those of high permeability and those of very low permeability. Well-jointed compact limestones are highly permeable. High permeability is characteristic of loose, unconsolidated agglomerates like river gravels. Chalk absorbs up to 50 per cent. of its volume of water and where it is fissured possesses a high degree of permeability. Sandstones vary widely from the very permeable greensand to the much less permeable Millstone Grit. Clays, once wet, are impermeable to the passage of water.

THE WATER-TABLE

The bulk of ground water is limited to the upper half mile of the earth's crust. The downward percolation of water is halted by impervious rock. Note that at great depths imperviousness may be due to the pressure in the crust closing the interstices in the rocks. Let us look at a cross-section of the upper crust where layers of permeable rock overlie layers of impermeable rock strata.

Rain water seeps slowly downwards through the pores in the rocks and through fissures until it is halted by a layer of impervious rock. Since the water cannot drain downwards any further, it will begin to accumulate above the impermeable layer. To beds of rock that are capable of holding water we apply the term *aquifer*. Above an impermeable layer three zones are usually distinguished:

(i) The upper zone through which the water descends and in which air as well as percolating water is found; this is known as the *zone of aeration* or the *vadose-water* (*i.e.* wandering water) *zone*.

(ii) The lower zone immediately above the impermeable rock where the water accumulates and from which the air has been completely dispelled; this is termed the *zone of saturation*.

(iii) The intermediate zone, which holds water after long-continued rain but dries out during periods of drought; this in-between zone is called the *zone of intermittent saturation*.

The upper surface of the zone of saturation forms the *level of saturation* or, as it is more commonly called, the *water-table*. The height of the water-table varies from place to place and from season to season, but it is normally within a few hundred feet of the surface. Generally speaking, the water-table reflects, in a subdued way, the profile of the land surface: in other words, the water-table tends to rise under the hills and fall under the valleys (see Fig. 41).

Ground water, besides moving vertically, also moves horizontally. Locally, the water-table will rise after heavy or continuous rainfall and create a sufficient head of water to cause a gradual seepage laterally. This horizontal seeping is a gradual and slow

MOVEMENT OF GROUND WATER

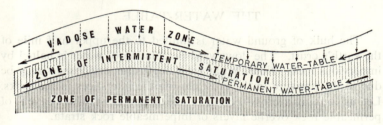

- - - - - - → *Downward percolation of water*
————————→ *Horizontal movement of water*

Fig. 41.

The diagram shows the two principal movements of water in the soil: the downward percolation and the horizontal movement. Water moves downwards until it reaches the level of permanent saturation and will continue to "pond up" above that level until it drains off horizontally. Hence, in times of abundant rainfall a zone of intermittent saturation will build up. Conversely, in times of drought the temporary water-table will drop until it reaches the zone of permanent saturation. Note how the water-table reflects, in a subdued way, the profile of the land surface.

process seldom exceeding more than a few hundred yards per year. The rate of movement depends very much upon the size of the pore-spaces in the rock. The horizontal movement of water is exemplified in areas with artesian wells, as we shall see in a moment.

Finally, we should note that the water-table is a sub-surface feature of considerable complexity. We must guard against thinking (*a*) there is *always* a water-table; (*b*) the level of saturation is always *level*; and (*c*) there is only *one* water-table in an area. Whether ground water is present depends, as we have seen, upon the type of rock beneath the land surface, though commonly water is present. There is an approximation to a level water-table only in areas of homogeneous rock structure and even then the water-table, as noted above, is sympathetic to the surface relief, tending to be higher beneath the watersheds and lower beneath the valleys. In localities where alternating pervious and impervious rock layers occur there is a tendency for the impervious beds to form their own water-tables. Such water-tables may lie high above the main water-table of a region, when they are known as *perched water-tables* (Fig. 42). An example of a perched water-table occurs in the

PERCHED WATER - TABLE

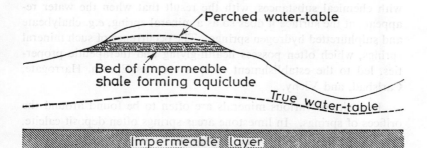

Fig. 42.

Sometimes a band of impermeable rock within the vadoze zone produces a localised, isolated area of ground water which lies above the water-table proper; this forms a "perched" water-table.

Cotswolds; here in the limestone is a thin layer of Fuller's Earth, which is impermeable, and this has produced a perched water-table in the uplands. Perched water-tables are of common occurrence and of immense human importance in many parts of the world, *e.g.* in Italian and Spanish hill settlements.

DEFINITION AND NATURE OF SPRINGS

A spring may be defined as a natural outflow of water from the ground, the point of emergence of ground water. The rate of flow is variable: it may gush out forcibly, flow strongly, or seep out gently. The flow, moreover, is likely to vary seasonally. Springs are often classed as permanent, if they have a continuous flow, or intermittent, if they dry up temporarily. Spring water may vary in its physical and chemical character: it may be cold or warm, soft or hard, mineralised or non-mineralised. If spring water is warm and mineralised it is likely to be of internal origin and is often, indeed most usually, associated with volcanic activity, *e.g.* the numerous thermal springs of Iceland or North Island, New Zealand. Hot springs do occur, however, in non-volcanic areas, witness the well-known warm waters of Bath.

Mineralisation is not necessarily linked with either water of internal origin or with volcanic activity. Meteoric water, or rain water, percolating underground may dissolve and become charged with chemical substances, with the result that when the water reappears at the surface it does so as a mineral spring, *e.g.* chalybeate and sulphuretted hydrogen springs. The occurrence of such mineral springs, which often possess health-giving and therapeutic properties, led to the establishment of spas such as Epsom, Harrogate, Carlsbad, and Vichy.

Deposits of various minerals are often to be found around the orifices of springs. In limestone areas springs often deposit calcite, *e.g.* the famous "petrifying" springs at Knaresborough, in Yorkshire, where objects placed in the spring water become encrusted with calcite. Calcareous springs often deposit thick layers of calcite, commonly known as tufa or travertine. Similarly, crusts of siliceous sinter are frequently built up around geysers and hot springs.

A brief reference may be made to ebbing-and-flowing wells; these are rather different from the intermittent springs mentioned above, since their flowing is usually of a short-term cycle, sometimes only a matter of hours. Hence the mechanism that works them is different from the seasonal drying up which lowers the water-table which, in turn, produces the intermittent flow. In honeycombed limestone areas, additional supplies of water (after rains) may result in the local raising of the water-table, which may produce an ebb and flow at a spring point. Again, in coastal areas made up of pervious rocks fresh ground water may lie on top of denser sea water and the pulsations of the tides may produce a rise and fall in the water-table, which causes the ebb and flow of a well.

The Origin of Springs

Springs result from variations in the rocks and structures of the crust. Neither the land surface nor the geology of the crust is uniform. Topographic variations, differences in rock type, and geological accidents produce conditions conducive to spring formation. Broadly, however, the occurrence of springs depends upon three factors or conditions: (i) the shape of the land surface, (ii) the position of the water-table, and (iii) the character and relationship of the rocks.

Springs are of numerous and varying origins, but mostly they are related to the arrangement of pervious and impervious strata and to geological structures such as folding, faulting, jointing, etc. The more common types (see Fig. 43) may be classified as follows:

(i) *Water-table springs.* These are found where the water-table is cut by a valley or depression. Springs of this type are common in glacial drift. Oases in desert regions are due to the water-table being cut locally by the ground surface. Another type of water-table spring, usually termed an overflow spring, occurs where the water-table of a water-bearing bed impinges upon an overlying impervious stratum. A perched spring may result from the occurrence of a minor local impervious rock layer which has given rise to a perched water-table.

(ii) *Scarp-foot and dip-slope springs.* Scarp-foot springs occur at the foot of scarp-slopes and owe their origin to an impervious bed underlying pervious rocks. For example, water will percolate through a layer of chalk which is a pervious rock but eventually its downward progress will be checked when it reaches an impermeable layer, such as a band of clay which may underlie the chalk; then the water will flow along the surface of the clay until it breaks the land surface at the point of junction of the chalk and clay. Scarp-foot springs of this type are commonly associated with escarpments in chalk or limestone country, *e.g.* around the bases of the Lincolnshire Wolds, the Lincoln Heights, and the Cotswolds, where strings of wet-point, scarp-foot villages may be seen.

TYPES OF SPRINGS

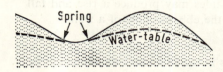

DIMPLE SPRING

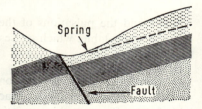

FAULT SPRING

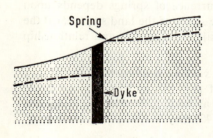

DYKE SPRING

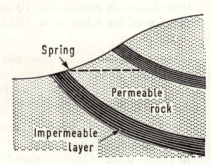

SYNCLINAL SPRING

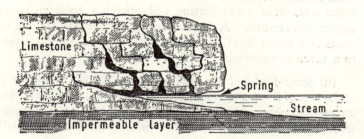

VAUCLUSIAN SPRING

Fig. 43.

The occurrence of springs is related to the character and relationship of rocks, particularly of permeable and impermeable beds. A dimple or depression spring is one that exists simply because the land surface extends down to or cuts the water-table. Many desert oases originate in this way. Fault, dyke, and synclinal springs are sometimes termed contact springs since they are caused by water flowing to the surface from a permeable bed where the latter comes up against an impermeable bed or an obstacle such as a dyke. A Vauclusian spring or resurgence results from water percolating through fissured rock and issuing from that rock where it meets an impermeable stratum.

Springs may occur on the dip-slopes of escarpments. Such springs are due to the level of the water-table in the permeable rock breaking or intersecting the surface. They are likely to occur on

SCARP AND DIP-SLOPE SPRINGS

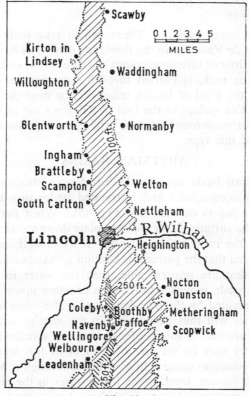

Fig. 44.

To the left are the scarp-foot springline settlements; to the right the dip-slope springline settlements.

the edge of an impervious covering rock, for the water descending the dip is unable to find room for itself in the already saturated aquifer and so seeks an outlet at the surface (see Fig. 44).

(iii) *Fault and joint springs.* Springs which are directly related to structures in the rocks such as faults, joints, or intrusions fall into this category. Faulting resulting in an arrangement of pervious and impervious strata which causes water to accumulate, as in the diagram (Fig. 43) for instance, will lead to the occurrence of springs along the fault. An igneous dyke, cutting the land surface, will produce the same result. Joint springs occur where water contained in a system of jointing issues at the surface, *e.g.* in the Black Cuillins in Skye.

(iv) *Vauclusian springs.* These, which take their name after the Fontaine de Vaucluse in the limestone district of Savoy, France, are characteristic of limestone country, where water, sinking through fissures in the rock, is carried through subterranean channels to issue below the level of intake, usually at or near the base of the limestone. The springs at the foot of Kilnsey Crag in Wharfedale, where the Carboniferous limestone rests upon impermeable Silurian slates, are of this type.

ARTESIAN BASINS

An artesian basin may be described as a structural basin in which water accumulates and is trapped under pressure between impermeable layers of rock (see Fig. 45). When pervious rocks outcrop at the surface, water will percolate downwards and become absorbed in the rock strata at depth. If the underlying rock beds are so arranged that the permeable stratum is "sandwiched" between two layers that are impermeable, then the water in the aquifer becomes trapped; movement of the water either upwards or downwards is prevented by the over-lying and under-lying impermeable strata. Water will thus accumulate in the aquifer until the latter becomes saturated. If the aquifer occurs in a synclinal structure a head of water may be set up; the weight of this water provides sufficient pressure to cause a flow of water through a bore. Water tends to find its own level, hence if the water in the aquifer, in its higher part, reaches a higher level than that in the trough of the syncline, then the hydrostatic pressure induces an upsurge of water immediately the impermeable capping rock is pierced by a bore. The flow of water from an artesian bore is not usually very spectacular since the hydrostatic pressure becomes lessened due to the effects of friction within the rock. In an artesian well the water flows freely without the use of pumps. If the water has to be pumped up, then the well is termed sub-artesian.

The term artesian derives from Artois in northern France where such wells were first sunk. Artesian wells occur widely throughout

ARTESIAN BASINS

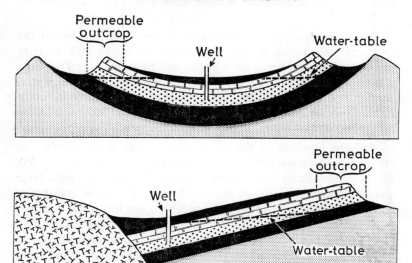

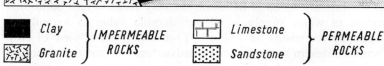

Fig. 45.

The diagrams show the structural nature of artesian basins. The upper diagram shows a synclinal basin as in the London Basin. The lower diagram shows how inclined strata coming up against impermeable may produce the same artesian condition. In an artesian structure aquifers, or water-holding beds, are enclosed above and below by impermeable strata.

the world. In some cases the water lies fairly near the surface, but very often it lies at great depths and requires deep borings to tap it. The London Basin provides us with a home example of an artesian basin: here rain, falling on the chalk hills of the Chilterns to the north and North Downs to the south, percolates downwards through the porous chalk until it is halted by the impermeable layer of Gault Clay that lies beneath. The Chilterns and the North Downs are merely the upstanding outcrops of a great sheet of chalk that is gently downfolded. While older impermeable clay underlies the chalk, younger clay lies on top; hence the "sandwich" conditions necessary for artesian water are present. London, in fact, secures about one-fifth of its water requirements from wells sunk into the chalk.

Oil prospecting in the Sahara in recent years has led to the discovery of artesian water. The large Secondary and Tertiary basins have been shown to contain prolific aquifers. The most famous of these aquifers is the *nappe albienne,* a thick water-bearing bed of Jurassic to Cretaceous age, which extends south-wards from the Atlas Mountains. Hence, since 1950, several deep boreholes have been sunk in the Algerian Sahara.

Perhaps nowhere in the world are artesian water supplies so important as in Australia. Here occur several great basins (Fig. 46). The most important is the Great Artesian Basin which yields large quantities of water from some 6,000 bores. The cattle industry of northern Australia is largely dependent upon the water supplies from the basin. The other basins are of less importance. But, taking them as a whole, it may be said that Australia makes great use of their water resources; they provide a valuable supplement to the rainfall which is deficient in many areas. This additional source of water supply is of considerable value to agriculture, especially for pastoral activities. From the point of view of crop farming artesian water has one disadvantage: it contains dissolved mineral matter and this sometimes is present in such quantities as to render it quite useless for irrigation purposes. Again, artesian water is of value to towns, for which it sometimes acts as the sole source of supply.

THE WORK OF GROUND WATER

The work of ground water is dual in its nature: it is mechanical and chemical in its action. The mechanical action is closely connected with the action of gravity. Ground water acts as a lubricant and its mechanical action depends almost entirely on its lubricating action. Lubrication has a twofold aspect: first, the presence of water in the soil or mantle reduces internal friction within the mass of material and, secondly, it reduces the friction between the unconsolidated material and the bedrock. Hence the presence of

ARTESIAN BASINS OF AUSTRALIA

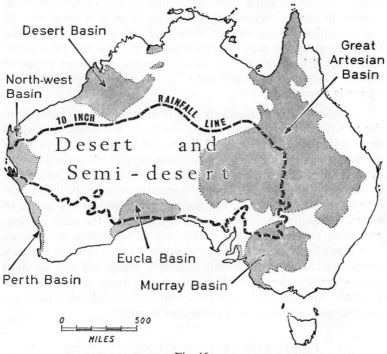

Desert Basin

North-west Basin

Great Artesian Basin

Desert and Semi-desert

Perth Basin

Eucla Basin

Murray Basin

0   500
MILES

Fig. 46.

Some of the greatest artesian basins occur in Australia. The Great Artesian Basin results from Jurassic sandstone aquifers which dip gently towards the interior of the continent. Outcropping in the Eastern Highlands, they derive their intake of water from the rains falling upon those highlands. There are about 5,000 artesian bores in Queensland alone.

water in the soil and mantle allows it to creep or slide downslope as a moistened mass. By facilitating movement, ground water is partly responsible for such phenomena as soil creep and landslides.

Ground water, too, by moistening layers of rock, such as clay, and making them greasy, enables masses of bedrock to slide or slump.

Ground water does a certain amount of mechanical erosion on its own account. In underground tunnels and caverns rushing waters carry boulders along, as well as finer debris, and a certain amount of scouring action takes places. The force of these underground streams is often tremendous and in one of the limestone caverns in the Derbyshire Peak District there is a great slab of rock, weighing 20 tons, wedged in the roof; it was swirled and lifted and wedged by the water which once surged through the cavern. Thus, it will be clear, that in addition to the dissolving action of ground water, a certain amount of wear and tear by mechanical means is also effected.

Ground water in finding its way underground sometimes gives rise to such surface features as swallow-holes, pot-holes, etc., which are especially characteristic of limestone areas since these rocks are highly susceptible to solution. Solution of rock material forms the chief chemical work of ground water. Rocks differ, of course, in their solubility: some, like sandstones, dissolve but little, whereas others, such as limestone, are particularly prone to the action of water. Areas of Carboniferous limestone show the most obvious and most wonderful results of the action of underground water. The erosive activity of water as it works its way through the rock strata produces "underground scenery", which reaches its most spectacular development in the limestone areas where the rock becomes honeycombed with subterranean channels and passages, caverns and chambers with pools and waterfalls.

FEATURES OF LIMESTONE REGIONS

Of the permeable rocks, limestone is the most important and is widely distributed throughout the world. Since it is partially soluble, as well as permeable, it gives rise to a distinctive type of landscape with unique features.

Limestone occurs in a variety of forms: as Mountain limestone of Carboniferous age, which is common in the Pennines; as Oolitic limestone, such as that in the Cotswold Hills and the Jura Mountains (from whence it derives its name); as Magnesian limestone, a dolomitic limestone, a narrow band of which runs from Nottingham to Newcastle, and which also occurs in the Alps; and as Chalk which is widely spread in south-eastern England and forms the hill ridges of the Chilterns and North and South Downs. Chalk frequently is too soft and porous, and contains too great an admixture of clay, to develop the complete range of features associated with the harder limestones though locally it may exhibit some of the features.

The Illyrian Alps in Yugoslavia, which extend south-eastwards from the Istrian Peninsula into the old kingdom of Montenegro, are composed of a belt of limestone more than a hundred miles wide. Here is found limestone scenery in its most highly developed form, especially in the region known as the Karst where all the various landforms associated with limestone areas are uniquely developed. So distinctive is this limestone topography that the term *karst* has come to be commonly applied to similar limestone areas elsewhere, even though the distinguishing features may not be so extravagantly developed nor so well defined elsewhere.

The Causses regions of the Central Massif of France exhibit the same highly developed limestone scenery as is found in Yugoslavia. On a smaller scale, it occurs in the Pennines, being notably well-developed in the Ingleton-Malham area, and in the Mendip Hills.

Surface Features.—Let us look at the surface features that are developed on limestone. Rain water, which takes up quantities of carbon dioxide as it falls through the air, is turned into a very weak acid which acts upon the limestone to form the very soluble salt, calcium bicarbonate. This acidic ground water percolating through the limestone causes solution which proceeds most rapidly along the various lines of weakness—the fissures, the joints, the bedding planes—occurring in the rock. In Britain there are several kinds of limestone, but the Carboniferous limestone, which is especially massive, possesses distinct bedding planes and is highly fissured, and which occurs predominantly in the north of England, shows karst features best. Deep, narrow gorge-like valleys are cut into the hills and because of fissuring the valley sides frequently stand up in steep cliffs or precipices. Massive escarpments, towering up, are characteristic features of the limestone relief. The Jurassic limestone, though exhibiting some of the typical features of karst country, is less impressive and "caving", for example, is much less extensive than in the Carboniferous limestone.

Since limestone is permeable, surface streams are usually lacking. If streams do occur, they seldom flow for long distances and normally plunge into holes or sinks to reappear later, sometimes several miles distant, at lower levels. Occasionally, after heavy rains, streams may run on the surface; this is unusual and is due to the fact that the sub-surface channels are unable to drain away the excess water quickly enough. The plateau surfaces are often cut and trenched into irregular blocks if the bare bedrock is exposed; the blocks of the dissected surface are known as *clints,* the solution furrows, often a foot or two wide and several feet deep, are called *grikes.* Walking across such a network of fissures and, occasionally wobbly, blocks is strenuous and dangerous work. See Plate XII.

Various other surface features are found in karst areas. Broad, funnel-shaped hollows or water-sinks are known as *dolines*; enlarged swallow-holes, resulting from the coalescence of several sinks, are called *uvalas*; shallow, steep-sided depressions with flat, and sometimes marshy, floors are known as *poljes.* Poljes, like the other features, are formed by solution but they may be several miles in diameter. They are of especial importance in bare, barren mountainous areas since the thin residual soil that accumulates on their floors provides the only possible cultivable land and in Yugoslavia villages often cling to the rims of these depressions.

Two limestone areas with somewhat specialised and distinctive features deserve a mention. The first area is the Dolomites in northern Italy. Here, in the Alps, the dolomitic limestone, creamy pink in colour, has suffered frost shattering and given rise to magnificent scenery; fantastic formations with precipices, arches, pillars, and pinnacles produce a picturesqueness and grandeur that must be seen to be believed. The other area is central Ireland where conditions are to be found that are rather out of character in limestone areas. Here, along the middle course of the Shannon, solution has occurred which causes the river to widen out and form a series of loughs or lakes. The explanation of this unusual feature lies in the fact that the water-table is near the surface; the rocks are saturated almost to surface level; hence surface streams do not, cannot, go underground. Somewhat similar conditions occur in the low limestone plateau of Yucatan, in Mexico, and in Florida where during the rainy season the land becomes completely saturated and sheets of water lie upon the limestone.

Karst features tend to show themselves wherever limestone outcrops, but the extent and degree to which such features develop is

FORMATION OF A GORGE
IN A LIMESTONE
ESCARPMENT

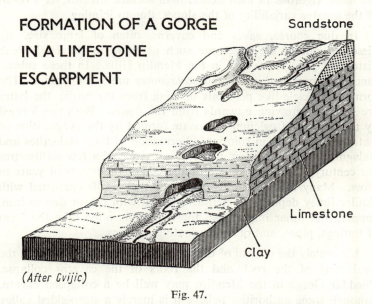

Sandstone

Limestone

Clay

(After Cvijic)

Fig. 47.

Streams, running off the sandstone, disappear into and percolate through the limestone. The percolating water dissolves out subterranean channels and caverns. In due time the roofs of such underground caverns may collapse and a steep-sided gorge will result. Sometimes, as at Gordale Scar, Malham, parts of the former roof survives to form an arch.

related to the nature of the limestone, its structural characters, and to the amount of rainfall.

Underground Features.—The relative absence of surface waters stands in marked contrast to the usually abundant sub-surface waters. Surface moisture rapidly moves underground through cracks and crevices, joints and fissures to form streams which travel underground. Subterranean channels and passages thread the limestone after the fashion of a rabbit warren. Water seeping along cracks and through joints attacks the limestone and widens the openings to allow rushing waters to make their way through the rock. The turbulence and splashing which results assists further the chemical decomposition. Mechanical erosion is also aided by the swiftness of flow; it is more than likely that sub-surface streams are more vigorous in their action than surface streams, as a result of the greater variability of the slopes, due to jointing.

In due course, caves and caverns, often of large size, are dissolved out of the limestone such as those in the High Peak district of Derbyshire and in the Mendip Hills. In these subterranean caverns *stalactites* and *stalagmites* are often found. The former are icicle-like pendants hanging from the roofs; the latter are columns growing upwards from the floors. Both are formed by the deposit of calcium carbonate formed by the evaporation of water containing it in solution. Formation of both stalactites and stalagmites is a very slow process—a matter of a few millimetres per century. Some have taken hundreds of thousands of years to grow. Many of the caverns also have their walls encrusted with similar limey deposits, sometimes stained with colour due to iron, copper, and other impurities; these deposits often take the form of flutings, pipes, and other fascinating patterns.

Ultimately the growth of the underground caverns results in the weakening of the rock and the roofs of the caverns collapse. Cheddar Gorge in the Mendips may well be a collapsed cavern, although some authorities believe it is merely a steep-sided valley which has been cut in the limestone by a now vanished river.

Malham: An Example of English Karst Country

The Malham area in the West Riding of Yorkshire provides a now famous and excellent example of karst country; it is, as it were, a Dalmatia in miniature. About half a mile north of Malham village the Craven Highlands of Carboniferous limestone, frequently referred to as the Great Scar Limestone, rise up and the rise is clearly marked by the great scarp, hundreds of feet in height. This great scar marks the line of the Middle Craven Fault. To the south of the fault, which runs roughly east-west, the landscape, exhibiting a fairly advanced state of erosion, shows a rolling, culti-vated countryside developed on shales and sandstones and some limestones. North of the fault lies the bare, rough grazing land of the limestone plateau on which streams are conspicuously infre-quent. Two or three miles north of the Tarn the limestone plateau is capped by residual hills, such as Fountains Fell, composed of younger rocks, the Yoredale Series with their rhythmical succession of beds, and Millstone Grit which crowns the summits.

The Carboniferous limestone, a remarkably pure limestone, is a massive, hard, and resistant rock not easily weathered; on the other hand, in common with all limestones, it is prone to solution by water that is charged with carbon dioxide. Thus surface moisture, instead of flowing away in streams, sinks into the lime-stone through solution joints. These crevices in the limestone run roughly parallel with the Middle Craven Fault, i.e. N.E. to S.W.; secondary joints cut across at right angles, i.e. N.W. to S.E. Thus the limestone is cut up into roughly rectangular blocks (clints), though these are sometimes weirdly shaped, separated by solution-widened joints (grikes), which often penetrate deeply. A limestone "pavement" of clints is particularly well-developed above Malham Cove.

In parenthesis, we may note that there is some dispute as to the exact mode of formation of grikes. The traditional interpre-tation was that the joints had been opened out by solution, as a result of rain water acting upon the bare limestone; but this old view has been challenged and it has been suggested that most of the solution occurred when the limestone was covered by soil. The idea is that after the Ice Age the area was covered by glacial drift and that the drift cover has gradually been removed by percola-tion; in other words, the grikes were formed under the drift. There is some evidence to support this contention; on the other hand, it has been shown that in some areas pavements have been formed from smooth, bare limestone surfaces subsequent to the removal of a drift cover. Clearly, no definite conclusion can be reached about the origin of grikes; it is possible they could have been formed in different ways.

On the plateau there is an assortment of karst features including numerous scars, cliffed exposures of limestone beds, caves, swallow

SKETCH MAP OF THE GEOLOGY OF THE MALHAM DISTRICT

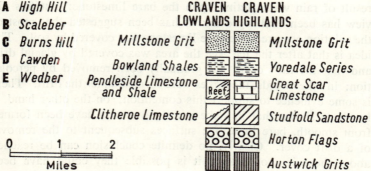

	CRAVEN LOWLANDS	CRAVEN HIGHLANDS
A High Hill		
B Scaleber		
C Burns Hill	Millstone Grit	Millstone Grit
D Cawden	Bowland Shales	Yoredale Series
E Wedber	Pendleside Limestone and Shale	Great Scar Limestone
	Clitheroe Limestone	Studfold Sandstone
		Horton Flags
		Austwick Grits

0   1   2
Miles

Fig. 48.

holes, pot-holes, and dry gorges. Two very spectacular natural features have been formed along the great fault line: Malham Cove and Gordale Scar. The Cove is a great semi-circular cliff or precipice which at its mid-point towers up vertically 285 feet. Seen from a distance or viewed from below the Cove forms a magnificent scenic feature. The water from the Tarn up on the plateau once flowed over the Cove; indeed, on rare occasions, when heavy rain and melting snow provide a larger flow than the subterranean drainage channels can accommodate, some water has come over the precipice. When the Ice Age passed away huge volumes of melt-water eroded the, now dry, valley immediately above the Cove and pitched over the precipice in a mighty waterfall. One can still see the effect of the waterfall action; in the first place, it eroded the straight fault line scarp backwards to form the present curve of the Cove—the present Cove has been cut back several hundred feet from the Mid-Craven Fault line; and, in the second place, the waterfall has cut deepest into the edge of the limestone where the greatest volume of water would be flowing. Plate XI shows a view of the Cove.

The other impressive feature, Gordale Scar, is a great gorge which gashes the scarp face. Opinion varies concerning its origin. Some believe it is essentially a river cut gorge but others think it was produced by the weakening and collapse of the roof of a former vast pot-hole. The huge boulders that litter the base of the Scar lend support to the latter theory. Large quantities of tufa are to be found where Gordale Beck tumbles down the Scar. There is also a fine tufa screen at Jannet's Foss, a waterfall several hundred yards further downstream. From the limestone floor at the base of the Scar numerous springs bubble up: this is due to the base of the limestone resting on impervious Silurian slates. Heavy rain sometimes chokes the subterranean watercourses and the excess water rises up in quantity to flood the valley floor. See Plate XI.

Since the joints in the limestone allow rain to percolate downwards there are few streams on the plateau surface. Between Malham Cove and Gordale Scar is a deep ravine in the limestone known as Gray Gill, and though it has no stream flowing along it, a cave in the gill has water flowing below—the cave floor consists

only of boulders jammed together over an opening of unknown
depth. Also, as we have already noted, immediately north of the
Cove is an old deserted dry river valley (Plate XII). This lack of
surface drainage is what we expect in limestone country but to a
visitor who is unfamiliar with the geology of the area the presence of
a large lake, Malham Tarn, on this limestone plateau comes as a
great surprise. The explanation of this apparent incongruity is the
presence of a plaster sheet of gravelly moraine, formed when a

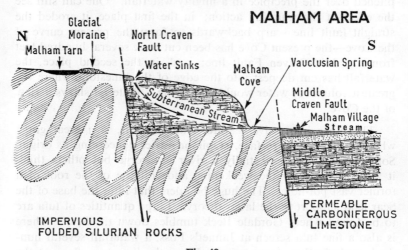

Fig. 49.

former ice-sheet rested here for a while during its retreat northwards. The bed of the Tarn is plastered with impervious boulder
clay while the Tarn itself is impounded by hummocky moraine. The
lake water escapes by means of a small stream which flows for
about 500 yards and then suddenly disappears down a swallow-hole,
known as the Water Sinks. Gordale Beck, which flows for a couple
of miles across the limestone plateau before it descends Gordale
Scar, is also explained by the fact that it flows for some of its length
over the thick glacial drift layer.

The area provides us with an interesting example of the complicated underground drainage characteristic of limestone areas. The map shows two water sinks on the plateau, one south-west, the other due south of Malham Tarn. The latter, which we have already referred to as the Tarn overflow, looks as though it would emerge at the foot of Malham Cove, where there is a Vauclusian spring, since the sink and the spring lie in a direct line and a magnificent dry valley connects them. But, in fact, this is not the case; the water which disappears down the Water Sinks comes to the surface at Airehead Springs south of Malham village while the stream that disappears at the Smelt Mill sink, west of the dry valley, is the one that reappears at the foot of the Cove. This means that these two subterranean streams may possibly cross somewhere beneath the Dry Valley, although they maintain their separate identities. All the evidence goes to show that the limestone is honeycombed with underground streams.

On the high limestone plateau some two to three miles northeast of the Tarn are many enclosed hollows. These vary in their character: some form slight depressions, others are deeply-excavated, while in some cases the depressions break into one another. Douky Bottom forms a spectacular depression further over to the east. In the bottoms of some of these hollows there is a pavement and sometimes an accumulation of limestone boulders. These hollows are doubtless solution hollows and may be equated with similar solution features, such as dolines, uvalas, and the like which are found in the karst region of Yugoslavia.

Chalk Landscapes

Chalk is a variety of limestone, a remarkably pure form, which is composed almost entirely of calcium carbonate. In contrast to most limestones, and certainly with the massive Carboniferous limestone, chalk is soft. Because of its relative softness and porosity, chalk does not develop the spectacular landscape features developed in other limestones and more especially in the Carboniferous limestone. Chalk gives rise to gently swelling scenery with nicely rounded forms: there are few steep faces, few deeply cut valleys, few large caves, few impressive features. Typical karst features are, in fact, largely absent. But chalk, in common with the other limestones, is permeable. It is a well-jointed rock, displaying fissures which are capable of being widened by solution. Thus, because it is porous and fissured, water can readily percolate into it and through it; hence much of the chalk country lacks surface water. The chalk downlands of southern England, the chalk plateaus of Normandy, and the chalk hills of Picardy and Artois are representative of chalk country: they are relatively streamless— surface streams if they exist often have only a periodic regime— exhibit a subdued topography of gentle and smoothly rounded forms, and have valleys which are characteristically wide and flattish bottomed, for any projections are soon smoothed away due to the friable nature of the chalk which weathers fairly rapidly. Although there is much subterranean circulation of water (which makes chalk a valuable storage reservoir and source of water supply) chalk has few large natural underground cavities such as those which are typical of the Carboniferous limestone. The reason for this would seem to lie in the structural weakness of chalk which is incapable of supporting the roofs of large underground caverns and in its porosity and the absence of joint planes.

One of the interesting features of chalk country, notwithstanding its lack of surface water, is its dissection by numerous large dry valleys. It is difficult to interpret these as being formed in any way other than by running water. This implies that once upon a time the surface supported, and was cut by, streams. And the problem naturally arises: where have these streams gone? A number of explanations have been put forward to explain the formation of these dry valleys. One idea is based upon escarpment recession. For instance, as depicted in Fig. 50, the escarpment was located at AB originally so that the surface of the water-table was VB and the water-table controlled the position of the spring line WV. A spring issuing at point O would cause sapping and, together with the stream caused by the running spring water, would lead to the excavation of a valley on the dip-slope. Later, as a result of erosion, the scarp face would retreat to the position CD. Such recession would result in the lowering of the water-table to the position YD; in turn, the new spring line would be positioned lower down the dip-slope at XY. At this stage the spring would emerge from the ground at P, thus leaving the valley above this point dry.

In this view, then, the dry valleys result from the lowering of the level of saturation within the chalk which affects the springs and so the flow of water; in other words, an explanation of these dry valleys is sought in a falling water-table.

A second view is that these dry valleys are a legacy of the Pleistocene. It is supposed that under the extremely cold conditions of that time the chalk would be rendered impermeable by being frozen at depth. This would have sealed up the fissures and

DRY VALLEYS IN CHALK COUNTRY

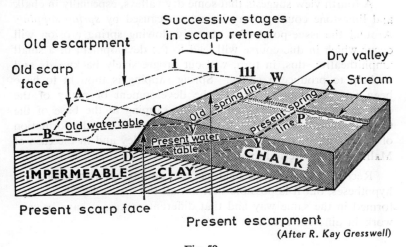

Fig. 50.
Scarp recession, a falling water-table, and the formation of dry valleys. For explanation see text.

effectively prevented percolation underground. During periods of thaw very rapid run-off, confined to the surface, would erode valleys in the land surface. Although it is known that the ground must have been frozen at depth during the Ice Age, the explanation given above has lost favour largely due to the fact that many of the valleys show adaptation to certain structural and topographic controls, whereas if they had been excavated purely by melt-water one would have expected them to be "largely independent of structural guidance".

A third view attempts to explain the origin of dry valleys in terms of climatic changes. It is well known that occasionally, especially after unusually heavy rains, streams sometimes flow in many of the dry valleys of the chalk country and it is thought that perhaps these valleys may relate to phases in the past when more humid conditions prevailed in this country. It is now known quite definitely that there have been wetter phases in the past, as indicated by peat accumulations, certain misfit rivers, etc., and it may well be that some, if not all, of these dry valleys owe their origin to climatic fluctuations.

A fourth view suggests that some dry valleys, especially in chalk and limestone country, may have been caused by *spring sapping*. Around the issue-point of a strongly flowing spring erosion will occur which in due course will lead to the development of a small amphitheatre; this, in turn, will cut progressively backwards and so help to produce a valley. Spring sapping is thought to have been an important agency in the development of many of the combes in southern England. Spring sapping at the base of the Carboniferous limestone is also an active process in the formation of some Yorkshire valleys, *e.g.* the Greta valley and in the case of Malham Cove referred to above.

Recent research in the field has cast doubts upon some of these hypotheses, but it is possible that not all the dry valleys have been formed in the same way and that different processes have been at work in different areas.

CHAPTER 9

SLOPES AND THEIR SIGNIFICANCE

Except in very flat areas, such as some alluvial lowlands, and certain plains that have been eroded to a near level condition, slopes, whether they be steep or gentle, convex or concave, are a feature of the landscape. People dwelling in hilly country are, of course, well aware of the presence of slopes: in the Pennine foothill area of the West Riding, for example, cyclists constantly have to dismount and push their bicycles up the ever present inclines while the motorist is in a perpetual state of gear-changing. Slopes are the upward or downward inclinations resulting from the form of the natural landscape—from the hills and the valleys.

Slopes are an ingredient of the visible landscape and give variety and interest to that landscape, but to the geomorphologist they have come to an inner meaning. They are not merely surface features providing topographic variety: they offer a clue to the interpretation of landscape. As we shall see shortly, the different interpretations of landscape evolution and formation that have been put forward are closely linked with the occurrence and shapes of slopes. For this reason the observation, description, classification, and measurement of slopes have become of great significance to the geomorphologist within recent years; he sees in them the key to the understanding of landscape development. Thus there is a growing emphasis these days on the mathematical measurement and scientific classification of slopes, as against their largely desscriptive and subjective interpretation in the past.

The study of slopes can be divided into two fairly distinct aspects: (i) the study of the way in which mass movements, that is the downward movement of material under the influence of gravity, affect slopes, and (ii) the study of the characteristics and development of slope profiles. The processes of mass movement, or mass wasting as it is sometimes called, are reasonably well understood and fairly comprehensive studies have been made of them. This aspect will be dealt with in Chapter 10. The second aspect presents formidable problems: the study of slope profiles is still very much in its infancy and the interpretations which can be placed upon their study continue to be inconclusive. The study of the evolution of slope profiles poses two complex problems for the geomorphologist to tackle and elucidate: first, there is the question of the development of the so-called convexo-concave slope profile, the kind of profile with which we in cool temperate moist regions are familiar—the broad, gentle convex forms of hills which merge into the equally gentle concave forms of the adjoining valleys; and, secondly, there is the problem of the way in which slopes retreat, whether their recession is due to the progressive lowering and flattening of the landscape or to horizontal, *i.e.* sideways, wasting. Later in this chapter we shall attempt to outline briefly the salient points in this intricate problem of the development of slope profiles but before proceeding to any discussion of this it will be helpful to look at the different types of slope that are recognised and the elements of slopes.

The Origin and Different Types of Slopes

Slopes may be said to fall into three main categories: (i) those due to tectonic action, (ii) those resulting from erosive activity, and (iii) those arising out of the accumulation of material. Those of tectonic origin include scarp-slopes produced by faulting and tilted surfaces arising from earth movements. The second category of slopes originate from the erosive action of such agents as rivers, glaciers, and waves, *e.g.* valley walls, cliff faces. The third category result from the deposition and accumulation of material, *e.g.* alluvial fans, sand dunes.

The geomorphologist, however, has adopted a two-fold basic division of slopes, classifying them as primary and secondary erosional slopes. This division of erosional slopes arises out of their differing modes of origin.

(i) *Primary erosional slopes* are those that have been carved by the different agents of erosion such as rivers, glaciers, wind, or marine action. Examples of primary erosional slopes are vertically excavated river gorges, ice corraded valley sides, wave-cut cliff faces.

(ii) *Secondary erosional slopes* are those that have been developed through the action of weathering and the surface erosion of primary slopes. Note that primary slopes here are meant to include (*a*) the primary erosional slopes we have just referred to, and (*b*) those of tectonic origin which we have noted above.

An illustration will help to make this clear. Under certain conditions, as for instance in an arid region composed of mechanically strong and chemically resistant rocks, a river, through the vertical erosion of its bed, would be likely to carve a deep, slit-like gorge. The vertical, wall-like slopes of such a gorge would form primary erosional slopes since they would result almost purely from the down-cutting action of the river. Under moist temperate conditions, a stream may, in its youthful or torrent stage, initially cut a deep valley with almost vertical sides but almost at once other agencies begin to help the stream in its erosive work; for example, weathering, rain wash, the action of gravity, etc., augment the erosive work of the stream. The result is that not only is there vertical and lateral cutting by the stream but the valley sides are also widened by the wasting back of its slopes. The V-shaped cross-section that eventually emerges is bounded by secondary erosional slopes since these have been produced by weathering action and surface erosion of the primary erosional slopes.

The Elements of Slope

The growing interest in, and analysis of, slopes has led to the recognition of four possible elements in a hillside slope profile. Fig. 51 shows these elements in an idealised form and from top to bottom they are:

(i) The *waxing slope* or, more commonly, the *convex slope* which occurs at the top of a hill where its slope curves over to meet the vertical face next below. It is a soil-covered rock slope and is sometimes referred to as the *upper wash slope*.

(ii) The *free face* which refers to the vertical, wall-like exposure of bare rock. This face is too steep to permit any accumulation of weathered material such as scree. Since any rock waste derived from this face falls or rolls downslope, the free face has also been termed the *derivation slope*.

(iii) The *constant slope* is the straight slope of the lower hill-side which lies at the angle of rest of weathered material. It is the part of the slope profile where scree and other debris tend to accumulate and so is sometimes called the *debris slope.*

(iv) The *waning slope* is the low-angled slope, more or less concave upwards, that lies at the base of the hill and merges into the valley floor. It is called the waning slope because it becomes

ELEMENTS OF SLOPE

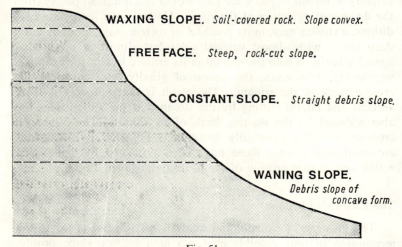

WAXING SLOPE. *Soil-covered rock. Slope convex.*

FREE FACE. *Steep, rock-cut slope.*

CONSTANT SLOPE. *Straight debris slope.*

WANING SLOPE. *Debris slope of concave form.*

Fig. 51.
The figure shows, diagrammatically, the elements of slope. The slope profile has four facets: the waxing slope, the free face, the constant slope, and the waning slope.

less steep as it develops. Alternatively, it is referred to as the *valley-floor basement* or the *lower wash slope.*

Look at Plate IX: the upper photograph shows Mt Eglwyseg, near Llangollen, in North Wales; here can be seen three of the elements in a hillside slope.

This fourfold sequence is, let it be emphasised, an idealised framework of a hillside slope profile, although many hillside slopes do show, quite clearly, these four components or elements. Attention, however, should be drawn to two points. First, some of these slope elements, depending upon local conditions, may not be developed, as for example in areas of low and gentle relief where the free face may be missing and even the constant slope may be barely discernible; on the other hand, some of these elements may be repeated as, for instance, where layers of sandstone and shale are inter-bedded and so cause a repetition of the free and constant slopes. Secondly, these slope elements vary in their importance as the erosion cycle proceeds. In the early phase, when relatively little progress has been made in valley formation, the waxing slopes exhibit increasing prominence; in the middle phase, when down-cutting balances lateral-cutting, the landscape tends to be dominated by constant slopes; while in the late phase, when valley deepening is no longer very active but the sides continue to undergo rapid retreat, the waning slopes become progressively extensive.

One final point may be mentioned. If, as is generally agreed, slopes consist of an upper part which is convex and a lower part which is concave with, very often, a straight slope between them, how do we explain some slopes which *appear to be abnormal, e.g.* a slope which has convexity above but no concavity of slope below? There are slopes bordering river valleys, for instance, which show no waning slopes, no concave profile. Where concavity is absent the reason would seem to be that the concave slope is buried beneath accumulations of alluvium—in other words, it *does* exist but is masked by the heavily aggraded river bed.

The Slope Problem

The foregoing account dealing with types of slope and the elements of slope leads on to the crucial problem of whether slopes are, essentially, *worn down* or *worn back*. In Chapter 6 we referred to the criticism of the Davisian concept made by the German geomorphologists, the Pencks, father and son. The slope problem revolves around Davis's ideas of landscape development and those of Walther Penck.

Davis's ideas of the "normal" cycle of erosion, that is erosion by running water, were based upon his observations of relief features in a humid temperate region; as Holmes puts it the term "normal" "implied a standard of reference based on the landscapes now developing in the humid conditions of a temperate climate".[1] Davis considered that as valleys became widened, their bordering slopes tended to become less and less steep as they retreated sideways. By the time the mature stage had been reached the initial upland surface had practically vanished with only the divides between adjoining valleys indicating the existence of the original surface. The landscape during the stage of maturity was, the valley floors excepted, one of slopes. As time went on these divides were lowered and rounded. Ultimately, as a result of prolonged erosion during the phase of old age, the whole landscape was reduced and subdued to the condition of an undulating plain; this low-lying, levelled erosion surface, the ultimate product of old age, was termed by Davis a peneplain. Peneplanation, or long-sustained denudation leading to the production of a low-lying, gently undulating surface, has come to be intimately linked with two ideas: first, the reduction, smoothing, and flattening of hill slopes as they recede, and, secondly, the accompanying reduction of the divides to produce broad, gently convex forms which merge into the gently concave slopes of the adjacent plains.

It was this interpretation of landscape development that was challenged by Penck. Penck, who had studied the landscapes of tropical Africa and South America, observed that the landscape combined broad gentle slopes with abrupt hillsides. Features such as the kopjes (isolated, steep-sided hills) of Africa, for example, rise up from the broad gently sloping surfaces of the tablelands. Penck and other geomorphologists who have elaborated his ideas see these abrupt slopes as the outcome of the parallel retreat of the hillsides; in other words, the constant slopes (straight slopes) are held to have retreated without their angles of slopes being affected or altered (Fig. 52). As the hill slopes recede, they produce at their bases an ever-widening gently inclined surface, called a pediment. This interpretation sees the landscape as being developed from slope retreat rather than by progressive flattening as Davis argued. Furthermore, if hillsides do suffer parallel recession, and if the slopes remain constant, then the landscape in its mature stage, should present a combination of gentle slopes with steep-sided upstanding

---

[1] *Principles of Physical Geology*, Nelson, 1965 edition, p. 474.

residual hills and not, as Davis would have it, a smoothly undulating landscape where gently convex hills merge into equally gentle concave valley basins.

The crux of the argument, then, resolves itself into the manner by which slopes have retreated, whether, according to Davis, by a process of essentially progressive flattening or, according to Penck, by essentially parallel planing.

The Slope Problem in Humid Temperate Regions

Davis recognised, as we noted in a previous chapter, that

WORN-DOWN AND WORN-BACK SLOPES

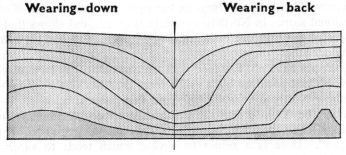

Fig. 52.

The diagram shows contrasting sections of valley profiles from youth to old age: on the left according to the process of wearing-down and on the right according to the process of wearing-back.

erosion was undertaken by agencies other than running water and in addition to the normal cycle he acknowledged that there were other cycles such as those produced under semi-arid and glacial conditions, *i.e.* the "climatic accidents". At this point we may note that Davis was willing to concede that the slopes in arid and semi-arid regions might well be developed in the manner held by Penck, that is by parallel retreat and recession at a constant angle. But he refused to admit that this manner of slope development could be applied to the forested, soil-covered slopes of cool, moist regions.

Another problem poses itself: is Davis's interpretation of landscape development in humid temperate regions correct or is it possible that Penck's idea of landscape development in tropical regions could be applied to moist temperate regions? At the outset, let us emphasise that there has been insufficient exploration, enquiry, and measurement of slopes in humid temperate regions to justify any acceptance of a Penckian interpretation. On the other hand, there are a number of suggestive ideas that are worthy of consideration and which we should note.

(*a*) Broad gentle slopes with abruptly rising hill masses occur in many parts of the world outside the tropics and many claim that they can be distinguished in western Europe and north-eastern North America, that is in those very areas where convex and concave slopes are asserted to be the critical and intrinsic features of the normal landscape. Dury, for example, gives an account of some erosional slopes in Northamptonshire (Fig. 53) and shows that the slopes of the hills are constant, having a gradient of 11°, and he concludes that "there must be at least a suspicion that the erosional side-slopes have not flattened with age, and that they have reached their present positions by lateral retreat".[1] After further discussion of these Northamptonshire hills and their slopes, he says, "it can scarcely be doubted that the features described are fundamentally similar to the pediments and inselbergs acknowledged to exist in Africa". Here is a *prima facie* case which tends to support a Penckian interpretation.

(*b*) Some geomorphologists strongly assert that it is impossible for hillside slopes to maintain a constant gradient and a straight profile under temperate humid climatic conditions and that convexo-concave slopes are, therefore, what one would expect. Their opponents aver that if the convexo-concave profiles of gently undulating landscapes can be substantiated they are most probably the outcome of the flow of sheets of thawed surface mud and rock waste over the frozen subsoil (a process technically called *solifluction* or, in America, *sludging*) during the period of the great glaciations of Pleistocene times. As we shall see in Chapter 13, this process of sludging, which is common in high latitudes, in conjunction with frost-shattering, has the effect of masking breaks of slope and of

[1] *The Face of the Earth*, 1959, pp. 68, 69.

subduing the terrain, and seems to be responsible for the rather featureless character of the landscape over large areas in Arctic regions.

(c) There is a growing body of opinion that denies the applicability of the term "normal" to the landscapes of western Europe and

SOME EROSIONAL SLOPES IN NORTHAMPTONSHIRE

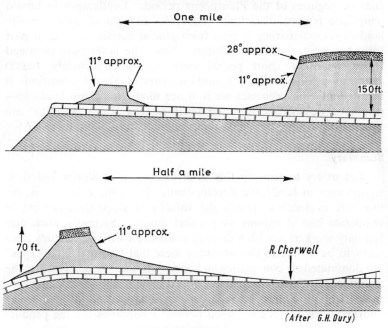

(After G.H. Dury)

Fig. 53.

Erosional slopes in Northamptonshire showing identical slope gradients. Such constant slopes are suggestive of an origin by lateral retreat.

north-eastern North America. The term "normal" in the Davisian scheme of things applied to landscapes developed under humid temperate conditions in which river action was the predominating agency. However, most of the landscapes of these regions, as many geomorphologists emphasise, are not purely nor simply the product of humid temperate conditions, for such conditions have existed for only a relatively short period—far too short a period, in fact, for landscape development.   They emphasise that not so very long ago, geologically speaking, these regions were subjected, for a prolonged period, to glacial conditions when frost action and ice action were prevalent.   Hence it is maintained that the landscapes of western Europe and north-eastern North America must be looked upon as "hybrid landscapes", *i.e.* the landscapes are the product of varying physical conditions which prevailed during the fluctuating climatic regimes of the Pleistocene period.   Landscapes in humid temperate regions, therefore, should be thought of as composite landscapes originating in part from glacial conditions and in part from temperate humid conditions.   Since the latter have obtained for a relatively short period only, say approximately 10,000 years, as against at least 1 million years of glacial conditions it means that "the processes we now see modifying these landscapes (those of western Europe and north-eastern North America) are generally *not* those by which their major features were formed".[1]

Summary

Let us try to sum up this brief discussion of slopes and their significance in landscape development.   First, there is, as yet, far too little evidence to justify the validity of slope development in temperate humid regions by parallel retreat.   Secondly, such preliminary work as has been done in connection with slope study does seem to be averse to the orthodox view that "normal landscapes" are dominated by convexities and concavities of slope.   Thirdly, the traditional or Davisian cycle developed in humid temperate environments can no longer be regarded, in a strict and proper sense, "normal", for Davis's so-called normal landscapes are the product of a succession of varying climatic and eustatic conditions.

---

[1] A. Holmes, *Principles of Physical Geology,* revised edition 1965, p. 477.

CHAPTER 10

GRAVITY AND MASS MOVEMENT

THE DISASTER AT MOULIN-SOUS-FLERON

In the late afternoon of February 3rd, 1961, a 300-ft high slag-heap, built up of waste material discarded by a nearby electric power station, collapsed and smashed down on the small Belgian mining village of Moulin-sous-Fleron, near Liege, burying houses, shops, and motor cars under a 20-ft high mound of rubble and dust and killing some two dozen people. The slagheap, towering above the village and the power station, collapsed suddenly and roared down like an avalanche. Clouds of dust were thrown into the air while slack and mud rolled downslope, surging like lava over everything in its path, engulfing buildings and wrecking power lines, and spreading over a quarter of a mile of country.

This disaster was due to a landslide, the movement in mass of three million cubic feet of slag. The landslide followed heavy rain and flooding in the Meuse valley. The summer, autumn, and winter of 1960 were inordinately wet and the saturated condition of the soil and rock in many areas, not only on the continent but in Britain too, resulted in numerous landslips. In England, for example, a severe landslide blocked the railway line near Basingstoke for several days. In 1966 at Aberfan, in South Wales, a hill composed of coalpit waste, which had been built over springs, slumped and moved downslope to engulf a school and houses and caused the death of 140 children and adults.

Landslides of this kind are one of a number of associated movements involving the displacement of soil and other mantle material and sometimes even of the bedrock. Such movements can be troublesome, and occasionally disastrous, but they are all part and parcel of the continuous process of land change. All the movements help to remove weathered rock and contribute to the denudation of the land surface. Let us first enquire into the conditions which

159

promote these movements of soil and rock; then we will attempt to classify the different kinds of movement that are involved.

TABLE V

CLASSIFICATION OF MASS WASTING
(After C. F. S. Sharpe)

MOVEMENT		TYPE OF MATERIAL		
Kind	Rate	Earth or rock with ice	Earth or rock, dry or with small quantities of ice or water	Earth or rock with water
SLOW FLOW OR CREEP	Imperceptible	Rock glacier creep	Rock creep, talus creep, soil creep	Solifluction
RAPID FLOW	Relatively rapid		Earth flow	Mud flow, debris avalanche
SLIP	Rapid		Landslide, rock-slide, debris-slide, slump	
FALL			Rock-fall, debris-fall	

GRAVITY

Everywhere on the earth's surface the force of gravity exerts a downward pull on all materials. Unconsolidated materials, such as soil and loose mantle rock, are most easily affected, but sometimes even the solid bedrock is disturbed. The term *mass movement* or *mass wasting* is often used to embrace all the different kinds of downslope movement that are due to the pull of gravity.

Mass wasting is closely related to a number of conditions:

   (i) the amount of moisture present, for water acts as a lubricant: movement is greatest during or immediately following very wet weather, especially if rain comes after long, dry periods;

  (ii) when the soil and the mantle rock are loose, or poorly consolidated, and deeply weathered, since such conditions facilitate their disturbance;

 (iii) the angle of rest of the soil and waste mantle material and the degree of inclination of rock strata will influence downslope movement and the rate of movement;

(iv) when hard and soft rocks are interbanded, and especially if the sequence includes clay which takes up water, there is a greater tendency to movement;

(v) the occurrence of thin beds also increases the tendency to movement since there are more bedding planes along which slipping can take place;

(vi) the absence of a substantial cover of vegetation: a grassy sod surface and the binding and holding function of deeply penetrating tree roots help to hold soil and mantle in place.

In addition to these six main factors affecting mass wasting, there are various other influences at work which assist downslope movement, including the alternate heating and cooling of the soil, the freezing of the soil and subsoil, frost heaving which lifts and loosens the soil, the tramping and burrowing of animals, the vibrations from thunder-claps, and the shaking produced by earth tremors.

KINDS OF MOVEMENT

Mass movement varies widely in its nature: at one extreme the movement of material is so slow as to go unnoticed, while at the other extreme it moves with instantaneous and catastrophic suddenness. C. F. Stewart Sharpe, in an exhaustive study of mass movement in soil and rock, has recognised four main kinds of movement: these are (i) slow flowage and creep; (ii) rapid flowage; (iii) sliding and slumping; and (iv) subsidence. His classification is based upon the influence and effects of a variety of factors, chief of which are:

(a) the relative rate of movement, which is regarded as basic;

(b) the water or ice content of the moving mass;

(c) the type of material involved in the movement;

(d) the internal friction and arrangement of the material within the moving mass; and

(e) the relation of the moving material to the land surface and the bedrock.

Fundamentally, a distinction can be drawn between two principal types of mass movement—flows, which are of a relatively slow nature, and slips, which move quickly and usually suddenly. The distinction between the two types of movement depends upon the presence or absence of a slip plane (*i.e.* a surface along which definite shearing action can take place) separating the mass of moving material from the stable ground. Flowage of any kind is a quiet, gradual, and unspectacular but continuous movement and there is no slip plane present; on the other hand, true sliding movements involve definite shearing action on a slip surface and occur with rapid motion. It should be emphasised, however, that there are no hard and fast divisions between the four kinds of movement distinguished above or even between flowage and sliding, for mass movements of a compound character are common. Sometimes initial slipping movements may develop into flows, etc., but typical kinds of mass movement are readily distinguishable in nature and we can accept four major groupings.

(i) *Slow Flowage.* This term embraces the slow movement of surface soil and rock fragments; it includes soil creep, talus creep, rock creep, and solifluction. Movement is so gradual as to be imperceptible, but observations over a prolonged period of time leave us in no doubt as to its occurrence. All manner of materials, from fine particles to big blocks of rock, are affected. The earth or rock may be dry or it may be saturated; and the water may be in the form of interstitial ice. The superficial surface layers alone are, in general, affected. Vegetation and man-made structures are usually carried along with the moving mass (Fig. 54).

The slow downhill movement of soil and weathered mantle rock takes place on any moderately steep slope and is evident in many ways—by bended tree-trunks, by tilted fence-posts, by broken retaining walls, by displaced joint blocks, etc. This imperceptible but continuous downslope movement of the soil is usually referred to as *soil creep.* Terracettes, miniature terraces or steps, a foot or two high, and running horizontally across steep grassy slopes, are formed by creep. These terracettes are common in the Yorkshire Dales and on the Chalk Downs of Southern England where they are frequently, but erroneously, called sheep-tracks. Sheep do make use of these terracettes it is true but they are not made by sheep. Terracettes should not be confused with the Anglo-Saxon lynchets, or cultivation terraces; these are also a common feature of the Yorkshire Dales and the chalk Downlands.

Accumulations of coarse rock waste at the bases of steep slopes produce *talus* or *scree*. Talus creep is most pronounced in cold regions where the alternating expansion and contraction consequent upon freezing and thawing causes lumps of rock to break off from the bedrock. Most mountain slopes in Britain, *e.g.* Ben Nevis, Ingleboro', are littered with shattered rock. This slowly (and sometimes suddenly) rides downslope. This kind of movement

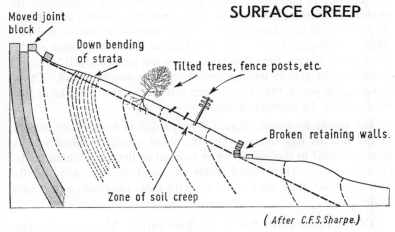

SURFACE CREEP

Moved joint block

Down bending of strata

Tilted trees, fence posts, etc.

Broken retaining walls.

Zone of soil creep

(After C.F.S.Sharpe.)

Fig. 54.

Diagram to illustrate downslope creep. The imperceptible downhill movement of soil results in surface objects becoming tilted, in blocks of rock being displaced, and even outcropping strata being slightly bent.

grades into the related phenomenon of *rock glacier creep*. Rock glaciers may be described as tongues of angular rock waste that form in the high valleys and steep-walled basins of mountainous areas.

Sometimes vertical rock strata, especially laminated rocks, such as shale, or thinly-bedded rocks, exhibit a downhill bending or sagging; this outcrop curvature is styled *rock creep*.

The last type of slow flowage is *solifluction,* which refers to the slow downslope movement of masses of debris saturated with water.

It is a feature especially of arctic and sub-arctic regions and is extremely common on slopes in high latitudes, although it is not confined solely to cold climates. When the upper layers thaw out in spring, the surface soil becomes sodden and saturated since the moisture is unable to percolate into the still-frozen subsoil. As a result, the saturated mass begins to flow, even on the gentlest slopes, producing lobes or terrace effects on hillsides.

The mechanism of these different types of creep is not fully understood; without doubt it is complex. They are probably due to a number of conditions, more especially the type of material, its physical condition, the angle of slope, and the climatic conditions. Any change in the physical condition of the soil or mantle and any slight disturbance that occurs will lead to a rearrangement of the particles and every time this takes place the particles will be urged downslope by gravity which exerts a constant downhill pull. Other things being equal, the rate of creep is directly related to the degree of slope and the amount of water present.

(i) *Rapid Flowage.* Rapid flowage differs from creep mainly in the rate of movement. The increased speed of movement is largely related to the higher water content in the mass which facilitates flowage. Three chief kinds of rapid flowage are usually distinguished: they are known as earth flow, mudflow, and debris avalanche.

Of the three, *earth flow* is the least rapid. Movement is slow but perceptible. Water-saturated masses of earth, varying in volume from a few to several million cubic feet, may shift downslope for distances of up to a mile or more in a matter of a few hours. Earth flows are characteristic of humid areas and are especially common in the humid tropics where the abundant rainfall turns porous weathered material into a plastic-like substance which flows down slopes with gradients as low as three degrees.

Field studies have shown how earth flow is associated with other mass movements. For example, when material on the upper hill slope slumps or falls suddenly away, producing a series of steps or terraces, this results in increased pressure being exerted lower down the slope; this pressure, in turn, causes the soil on the lower slopes to flow like a very viscous liquid and to form lobes. Fig. 55

will help to make this clear.   There is a large solifluction lobe near Sevenoaks, in Kent.

A great earth flow in Slumgullion Gulch, in the San Juan Mountains of Colorado, U.S.A., took the form of a vast tongue of weathered volcanic material, with a consistency like stiff porridge, which flowed down a valley for a distance of six miles before coming to rest, damming a river in the process to create Lake San Cristobal.[1]

Mudflows are amongst the most spectacular forms of mass wasting.   They may be described as streams of semi-liquid mud which flow down valleys in mountain areas.   They differ from earth

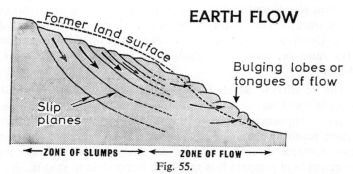

EARTH FLOW

Bulging lobes or tongues of flow

Slip planes

←— ZONE OF SLUMPS —→ ←— ZONE OF FLOW —→

Fig. 55.

The slumping of material on upper hill slopes results in pressure being exerted upon the lower slopes causing earth to "flow".   This flowage takes the form of bulging lobes or tongues of earth which move gradually downslope.

flows in three main ways: first, because of their higher water content, they are much less viscous in their consistency and so flow more easily and more rapidly; secondly, and in contrast to earth flows, they show a common tendency to recur in the same channels; and, thirdly, they are seldom accompanied by slumping and sliding movements being more strictly flow phenomena.   Mudflows frequently arise following sudden rain storms which flush the loose material from slopes and carry it down into the valley where the debris becomes mixed with the water into a thick mud which is capable of carrying great boulders along.   When the mudflow spills out of its confining channel on to flatter, more open country, it

[1] A. N. Strahler, *Physical Geography*, 2nd edition, 1960, John Wiley, pp. 319, 320.

splays out fanwise, spreading a layer of mud and boulders over the land which may vary in thickness from a few inches to many feet. The Roman town of Herculaneum was destroyed by a mudflow in A.D. 79 when dust from the erupting Mount Vesuvius was converted into mud by the torrential rains which accompanied the explosion. Three sub-types of mudflow are sometimes recognised: desert mudflows which occur in arid or semi-arid areas after heavy local rain storms; alpine or arctic mudflows which result from melting snows; and volcanic mudflows known as *lahars,* again due to torrential rains mixing with volcanic dust.

Debris avalanches consist of the flowage of rock fragments from mountain slopes and cliff faces which occur in long and relatively narrow tracks. They build up heaps of rock rubble known as *talus cones.* Debris avalanches are most common in humid regions where heavy rains or, sometimes, earthquake tremors start the talus in motion.

The conditions which favour rapid flowage are very similar, generally speaking, to those promoting slow flowage though one of the more important causes of rapid flowage is reduced internal friction resulting from the abundance of moisture present in the mass. Control of rapid flowage is extremely difficult and once mass movement is in progress it is well-nigh impossible to stop it.

(iii) *Landslides.* Landslides and related phenomena comprise the usually rapid sliding of large masses of earth, mantle material, or rock. They are essentially movements of a catastrophic and destructive nature and on this account they form the most spectacular and most readily recognisable examples of mass movement. Landslides embrace a wide range of movements from small slides along stream banks or railway embankments to sudden devastating collapses of whole cliff faces or entire mountain sides. Geologists divide these different slides into several classes but here we need only make a broad division into two types: landslips and slumps.

Landslips, or landslides, which involve the rapid movement of unconsolidated or poorly consolidated debris or even masses of bedrock, are characteristic of steep slopes. Landslips are more common in Britain than is generally thought. Scarcely a year passes without news of an embankment slipping and blocking a railway line but landslides often occur in the more mountainous areas (and hence tend to go unnoticed) and along cliffed coasts. Landslips are more especially common along escarpments where relatively hard or resistant rocks overlie a softer or less resistant rock as, for instance, where limestone overlies clay. This happens to be the case in the Jurassic scarp, and along the steep faces near Gloucester and Cheltenham there occur repeated slips due to masses of limestone sliding over the greasy basal bands of clay. Slipping is related either to the lubricating action of clay which becomes moistened and greasy after heavy rain or to the sapping action of springs, issuing from the top of the clay, which undermine the superimposed layers. Two well-known landslips in clay occur at Walton's Wood, in Staffordshire, and at Guildford. Similar happenings are of common occurrence in the Central Apennines of Italy; here masses of limestone slide over the underlying clays, sometimes engulfing villages. These landslides are called *frane*. Landslips happen regularly around Britain's coasts. For example, during the first week of May, 1961, thirty families at Cowdrait and Ross, in the fishing village of Burnmouth, near Berwick, were cut off by a landslide. About 500 tons of soil, loosened by heavy rain, fell and blocked the road which runs along the side of the rocky beach, and supplies to the families had to be carried along a quarter of a mile stretch of rocks at low tide.

Sometimes masses of bedrock slide along planes of weakness, *e.g.* bedding planes or faults. Such bedrock mass slips are known as *rock-slides*. Wherever steep mountain slopes are found, there is always the possibility that rock-slides may occur. The Gros Ventre rock-slide, in north-western Wyoming, United States, which happened in 1925, provides an excellent example of a rock-slide. An estimated 50 million cubic yards of rock plunged down the flanks of Sheep Mountain to build up a 250-ft high natural dam across the valley which, in turn, ponded up the river to produce a lake nearly five miles long. Landslides of this order result purely from natural causes.

Slumping (alternatively called shear sliding or slope failure), is akin to landslipping. The term is applied to the movement in mass of unconsolidated material and/or bedrock which slides and falls along a definite shearing surface which is curved (Fig. 56). Slump blocks are massive lumps of bedrock which break off from cliff faces and slither downwards, rotating or tilting backwards along a plane of slip as they slide down. After displacement has occurred, the slump block comes to rest with its upper surface inclined inwards towards the curved shearing surface, the upper part of which now forms a scar where the mass was torn away. Slump blocks may occur as a series of small blocks or as a single major unit (Fig. 56). The latter may be of truly gigantic proportions, as much as a mile or two in length and several hundred feet thick. Displacement, it is worth noting, is usually small in relation

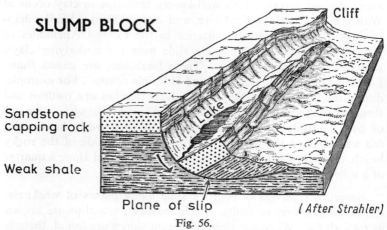

SLUMP BLOCK

Cliff

Sandstone capping rock

Weak shale

Lake

Plane of slip

(After Strahler)

Fig. 56.

Slump blocks shear along a plane of slip and as they fall they rotate backwards with the result that the strata, which originally was horizontally disposed, comes to rest in a tilted position. Here, in the depression between the slumped block and the cliff face, a lake has formed, cf. Lake Gormire in Yorkshire.

to the size of the block. Mam Tor, in the Peak District of Derbyshire, provides good examples of slumping; in fact Mam Tor is locally known as "the shivering mountain".

Slumping on a smaller scale is quite common wherever materials have been cut away and the original slope has been sharply steepened; thus slumping is a common feature along sea cliffs, caving river banks, highway cuts, and railway cuttings. A series of slumps is to be seen on the coast of Kent just to the east of Herne Bay; here London Clay caps the sandy Oldhaven Beds and as the clay becomes wet it weakens and shears away, slumping downwards on to the beach where it spreads outwards in muddy lobes (Fig. 57). See also Plate IX.

The causes of landslides and slumping are many and complex but, briefly, the chief causes are lubrication, the over-steepening of slopes, and over-loading. The effect of lubrication we have already alluded to (p. 160). Over-steepening of the slope may result from erosion or undercutting of the slope at its base and over-loading from the addition of material to the slope or from the additional

SLUMPS NEAR HERNE BAY, KENT

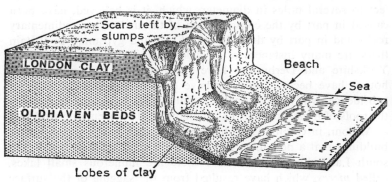

Fig. 57.

The sketch shows some of the slumps near Herne Bay on the Kentish coast. Moistened clay has slumped on to the beach and flowed outwards in muddy lobes.

weight of water in the saturated material. Generally speaking, an individual slip or slump results from the combined action of all three factors. However, it should be understood that the conditions favouring landslip and slump phenomena may exist for some time before any motion occurs but, given the required impetus to "trigger off" the movement, sliding and slumping may take place instantaneously. Where movement is suspected, certain measures can be taken, *e.g.* drainage, to help prevent movement and maintain stability.

(iv) *Subsidence.* Subsidence may be defined as the vertical displacement of earth or rock with little or no horizontal movement.

In this respect, subsidence differs from all the foregoing mass movements. It is characteristically a slow, settling movement resulting from the removal or contraction of underlying material, as happens in mining or draining, or from the down-warping or down-bending of the earth's crust. On the other hand, subsidence occasionally may be rapid, as in the case of the collapse of underground caverns.

Kettleholes in glacial drift have originated, it is generally thought, from the subsidence consequent upon the melting of the underlying frozen mass. But there are other theories; for example, in East Anglia many depressions are considered to be due to chalk solution under drift. On the High Plains of the United States are to be found shallow, saucer-shaped depressions, one hundred feet to several miles in diameter, which, it is believed, have been caused in part by the consolidation of the underlying sedimentary rocks and in part by the solution of salt and gypsum. In Britain there are many instances of subsidence due to mining. Areas in Yorkshire and Derbyshire have suffered from coal mining, *e.g.* houses have become tilted or have even collapsed as a result of subsidence, whilst occasionally yawning gaps have appeared where the roofs of mine workings have collapsed. The haematite workings at Millom, in Cumberland, have created such havoc in the town's buildings that a new town has been built some distance away. In south Lancashire and Cheshire there are numerous small lakes, called *meres,* which have resulted from the sagging of the surface layers consequent upon the extraction of salt. And in the Fenlands the draining of the peaty soils has led to shrinkage of the peat and the general lowering of wide areas. If settling is gradual and uniform over a large area the consequences are not normally very serious but if it is irregular and patchy the outcome may be very serious with extensive damage being done to houses, buildings, drains, roads, railways, pipe-lines, etc.

Sudden collapses may occur sometimes. For example, an earthquake, in 1811, led to a spectacular local collapse which formed Reelfoot Lake, Tennessee, United States. Another instance is provided by the overnight disappearance of about an acre of land with its buildings at Rosel, Kansas, in 1898, leaving behind a pond some 70 feet deep. In limestone regions, underground caverns, dissolved out by water, may collapse, the roof falling in to produce a hollow on the surface. Many authorities believe the deep cleft in the limestone, known as Gordale Scar, at Malham, in Yorkshire, represents a former pot-hole whose roof caved in.

Summing up, we can say mass movement takes a considerable variety of forms, and varies from slow, superficial movements to sudden, spectacular movements which may involve the bedrock in depth; the causes are complex, but moisture plays a leading role in "engineering" the movement; and mass movement phenomena play a more significant part in fashioning the landscape than is commonly supposed. In Britain, for example, mass movements of the rapid kind have been more important than was formerly suspected and were probably connected with former wetter climates. Finally, we might note that from the farmer's point of view soil creep and slumping are the most important movements.

CHAPTER 11

THE DEVELOPMENT OF DRAINAGE SYSTEMS

Flowing surface water is the chief and most effective agent fashioning the landscape. The greater part—at least three-quarters —of the earth's surface has been sculptured by flowing water. In humid areas the land is under constant attack by flowing water in all its forms—rills, streams, and rivers. After storm and flood one can see obvious signs, in the shape of masses of stones, deposits of mud, broken banks, gullied land, changed stream courses, etc., of the work of flowing water, but streams and rivers in their quieter moods are, unobtrusively but insidiously, gradually remodelling the land surface.

The work of running water is quite obviously most effective in humid areas where there is plentiful rainfall, but it is interesting to find that even in the arid lands of the world the effects of intermittent torrents, produced by occasional downpours, are pronounced and many desert areas are scarred by *wadis,* valleys marking former water channels.

River Systems

A river may be defined as water moving under gravity downwards[1] in a natural linear channel of its own making. All streams obtain their water, directly or indirectly, from rainfall or other forms of precipitation. They are fed by immediate run-off consequent upon rainfall, by sub-surface water issuing from springs fed through seepages, and by the release of water which has been held temporarily in swamps, lakes, snowfields, and glaciers. Except in arid regions, the volume of most rivers increases as they flow seawards since they are fed by tributaries.

A strongly flowing spring may form the actual source of a stream, but most rills and streams originate from the sheet run-off

---

[1] This is usually towards sea level, although in some cases, as in certain interior drainage basins, it may be below sea level.

172

in upland areas. The higher areas normally receive the greater rainfall and during heavy, long-continued rains a thinly spread layer of water runs down the hill slopes. This sheet of rain water becomes guided and diverted into small undulations and depressions and soon well-marked lines of water-flow are etched out on the surface: these form rills. Water, trickling down these rills, is concentrated into master rills which feed the headstreams. As the streams flow downslope, they are joined by other streams or tributaries and the river's water supply becomes progressively augmented. In this way a drainage system is established.

The river system occupies a basin or catchment area which may be defined as the entire area of slopes leading into, and drained by, the river and its feeders. Every stream and every river system is separated from its neighbour by a watershed, water-parting, or divide which is the elevated land separating the headwaters tributary to one stream or system from those tributary to another stream or system. The water-parting often has a highly irregular course and, though commonly following the highest land, it does not necessarily follow the highest ridge of a range of hills. Fig. 58 shows, for example, the various main drainage basins and their river systems in North America.

The Description of River Systems

If one looks at the patterns formed by the water channels in a river basin situated in a region of heavy rainfall it will be seen that there is an abundance of surface streams which are fairly evenly spaced at short intervals. If this stream mesh is compared with that developed in an arid area, which has very few streams, it will be obvious that there is a great difference between them. The density of this drainage-net was previously described in *qualitative* terms; for example, one spoke of open-textured or fine-textured nets or widely-spaced or close-spaced nets. Any assessment on these lines however was very largely subjective and of very limited use in comparing one drainage system with another.

A recent development has been that of *quantitative* measure· ment. It is now possible to measure and to express in numerical terms the characteristics of a drainage system. This has brought a great advantage to river study for it enables workers in different regions to make quantitative or mathematical comparisons. This is but another instance of the statistical approach to modern geography and while statistics for the sake of statistics are undesirable any statistical method which enables us to describe and evaluate things

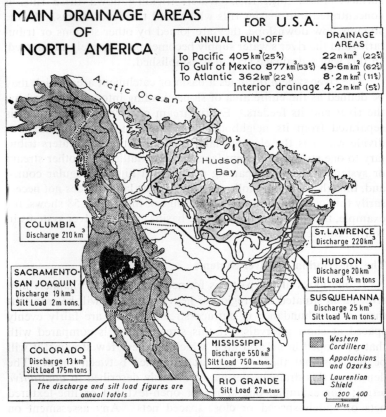

Fig. 58.

more accurately is to be welcomed. This new technique owes much to R. E. Horton who applied statistical treatment to drainage-nets. He concerned himself with enumerating the numbers and lengths of streams, in investigating the relationship between the numbers and lengths of streams to the actual drainage area, and with the density of the drainage-net.

Horton introduced the idea of *orders of streams* as a means of describing river systems. *First-order streams*, or tributaries of the

STREAM ORDERS

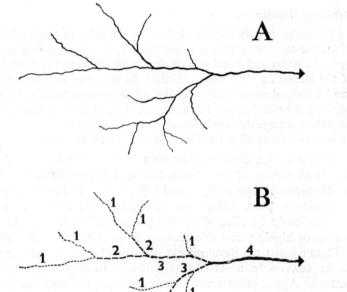

Fig. 59.

A shows a stream with its tributaries. *B* shows the same stream broken down into orders. First-order streams are those with no feeders; second-order streams receive only first-order tributaries; third-order streams result from the union of second-order streams; and so on.

lowliest category, are those which have no branches or feeders; *second-order streams* are those which receive only first-order tributaries; *third-order streams* result from the union of streams belonging to the second order; and so on. Note that it is possible for a second-order stream (made by the union of two first-order streams) to receive another first-order tributary without being raised to the next higher rank (*i.e.* third order). Fig. 59 illustrates this. The application of this stream order concept along with the statistical analysis of drainage-nets is proving very fruitful in the study of rivers, their behaviour, their work, and the landscape patterns which emerge.

Drainage Density

Drainage density may be defined as the ratio of the total length of all the streams within a single river system to the area drained by that system and is calculated simply by dividing the total length of the streams by the area drained. In this way drainage density can be defined numerically and this allows comparisons to be made between area and area; for example, it becomes possible to compare the drainage density between a very rainy and a very dry region or between areas of permeable and impermeable rocks.

The drainage density of an area is of course influenced by a variety of factors or conditions, the most important of which are rock type, soil, slope, climate, and vegetation. The relative spacing of drainage lines, sometimes referred to as drainage texture will obviously be affected by the permeability of the rock: very porous or highly permeable rocks, such as chalk or limestone, will militate against the development of a closely-spaced drainage network; conversely, areas of clay will tend to show a fine-textured pattern. Again, climate will clearly influence the drainage density: in arid regions there will be insufficient moisture to sustain permanent streams while areas of very heavy rainfall are likely to result in an abundance of surface drainage lines.

At this point we may note that youthful landscapes in humid areas will tend to show a greater drainage density than more mature landscapes. There is a distinct tendency for drainage systems to become integrated and to simplify themselves as time goes on; the myriads of streams gradually become superseded by a few main drainage lines, *e.g.* the drainage system of the Brazilian Plateau, which has remained relatively stable for a prolonged period and undergone peneplanation, has become concentrated into a relatively small number of powerful rivers.

Development of a Drainage System

The pattern of streams and rivers in most areas is one of considerable complexity; in its origin it may well be of much greater

STREAM DENSITIES

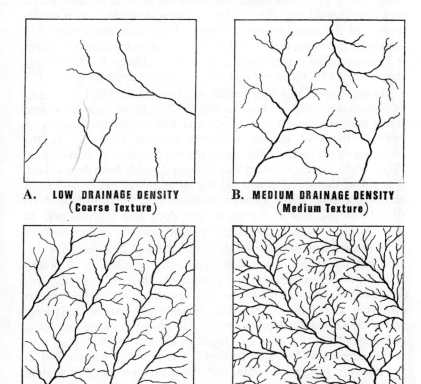

A.   **LOW DRAINAGE DENSITY**
     (Coarse Texture)

B.   **MEDIUM DRAINAGE DENSITY**
     (Medium Texture)

C.   **HIGH DRAINAGE DENSITY**
     (Fine Texture)

D.   **EXTREMELY HIGH DENSITY**
     (Superfine Texture)

Each map represents one square mile of territory.
Fig. 60.

complexity than it appears on the map. In order to understand the complex realities of the present, it may be helpful to study first an idealised case.

Let us imagine that a series of sedimentary level-bedded rocks are raised up above the sea surface to form new land and that in the process of uplift they are slightly tilted so that the uppermost bed presents a gently sloping surface. Immediately this land has emerged it becomes subject to subaerial weathering and erosion. Rain falling upon this surface will run off to form streams which will flow downslope. The water will flow downslope as a consequence of the initial structural slope. Since this initial slope will consist of homogeneous rock there will be no complications, unless it happens to be a very porous or impermeable rock. It is likely that a series of roughly parallel streams will be developed.

In due course, this land surface will become modified as a result of subaerial activity. No longer will the land slope smoothly down; it becomes diversified into ridges and hollows as the underlying beds of rocks of varying resistance become exposed. In the sequence of formations the more resistant beds will stand up as ridges while the less resistant will be worn down to form depressions. The ridges that develop will exhibit an asymmetrical cross-section showing a long, gentle slope, coincident with the dip of the beds (the dip-slope), and a shorter, steeper slope (the scarp-slope); in other words, the upstanding ridges will form *cuestas* or *escarpments*.

The streams which flowed down the original homogeneous surface will, under this new ridged topography, continue in all probability to maintain their original courses but their valleys will show variations or adjustments to the rock structure: where the streams cross the ridges the valleys will be relatively narrow and deep, where they cross the depressions the valleys will be wide and open. Subsequently in the vales developed in the less resistant rock outcrops, streams will also be formed. These, which run parallel to the outcrops of banded strata, join the main river roughly at right angles. Eventually other small tributary streams will develop, some flowing down the dip-slope, some down the scarp-slope of each ridge; the former flow *in the same direction* as the original downslope stream, the latter *in the opposite direction*. Fig. 61 shows the sequence of development.

Stream Nomenclature

Before proceeding any further it will be advisable to note the terms used for streams within the drainage network; these may

DRAINAGE DEVELOPMENT
IN SCARPLANDS

(After J.F.Kircaldy)

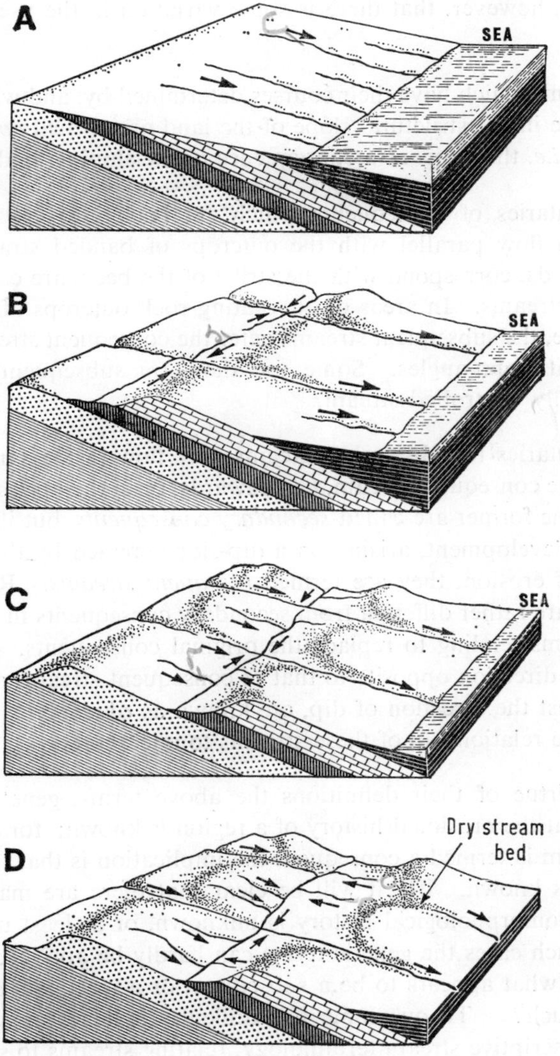

Fig. 61.

A. Initial consequents flowing down original slope.   *B*. Development of strike vales by subsequents.   *C*. A subsequent of the first consequent has captured the headwaters of the second consequent.   *D*. Developed drainage pattern in scarpland topography with wind gap and misfit stream marking the line of the captured consequent.

specify relationships between streams and structures. It should be noted, however, that there is some variation in the use of these terms.

Streams which have their courses determined by, and which flow down, the initial structural slope of the land are termed *consequent* streams, *i.e.* they flow as a consequence of the sloping land.

Tributaries of consequents which cut back into less resistant rock and flow parallel with the outcrops of banded strata or, in other words, correspond with the strike of the beds, are called *subsequent* streams. In areas of alternating rock outcrops of differing resistance, the subsequent streams enter the consequent stream more or less at right angles. Some use the term subsequent for *any* structurally controlled stream.

Tributaries to subsequent streams may flow in the same direction as the consequent stream, *i.e.* seawards, or in the opposite direction. The former are called *secondary consequents,* but if they are of later development, arising on a dip-slope created by the general course of erosion, they are termed *resequent streams.* Resequent streams are rather different from secondary consequents in that they are streams tending to replace the original consequents. Streams having a direction opposite to that of consequent streams and flowing against the direction of dip, are known as *obsequents.* Fig. 61 shows the relationship of these streams to one another.

By virtue of their definitions the above terms, genetic terms, imply that the erosional history of a region is known; for example, if a stream is termed a consequent the implication is that the initial surface is known. But it will be clear that there are many areas whose geomorphological history is unknown, or at least uncertain, and in such cases the genetic terms can hardly be applied, for who is to say what appears to be a subsequent or a resequent stream *is* in fact such? To overcome this difficulty it has been suggested that a descriptive stream terminology, relating streams to structural features, should be used, *e.g.* dip streams, anti-dip streams, strike streams; the use of adjectives in this way makes the position of stream with respect to the structure clearly apparent.

Inverted Drainage

Above we traced the development of the drainage upon a tilted surface which ultimately was fashioned into scarpland topography through the erosive activity of the rivers. Let us now turn to the drainage development on folded rocks. Where there is a series of parallel folds two types of consequent streams will be developed: those flowing along the troughs or along the strike, *i.e.* longitudinal consequents, and those flowing down the limbs of the upfolds which are transverse to the strike, *i.e.* transverse consequents. The former, flowing in the direction of the pitch of the folds, will tend to be less active than the transverse consequents. The latter, being more active, will be responsible for the opening up of strike valleys along the crests of the anticlines. This can be seen in Fig. 6 (p. 28) where *combes,* or stream eroded hollows, occur in the crests of the ridges. These anticlinal boat-shaped hollows have scarped rims which are breached only where the transverse consequent collects the strike subsequents which are eroding the anticlinal vale. Since the anticlinal streams will be more active than the synclinal rivers (due to the greater height of the upfolds above the local base-level of erosion, and also because the arching up of the strata may well have induced a structural weakness compared with the downfolds), the anticlinal vales will be rapidly enlarged and the ridges reduced. Eventually, longitudinal subsequents will develop along the anticlinal axes and these streams if they erode downwards into softer underlying beds may be able to lower their valleys to below the level of the neighbouring longitudinal consequents. If this happens the original anticlines will become the valleys and the synclines the ridges; in other words, the relief will be inverted for the topography will be the inverse of the geological structure. See Fig. 62 which illustrates this development of drainage on folded rocks.

Drainage Patterns

Distinctive patterns are often readily discernible in the drainage features of an area; for example, in northern Sweden there is a striking development of rivers flowing in parallel sequence; while down the steep slopes of symmetrical volcanoes there is usually an emphatic radial pattern. Many different patterns, it is true, may

DEVELOPMENT OF DRAINAGE
ON FOLDED ROCKS

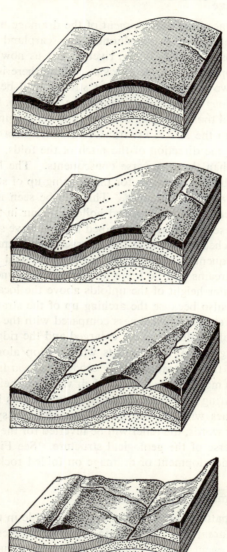

Fig. 62.

1. Initial consequent on folded rocks. 2. First stage in the development of anticlinal vales. 3. Subsequent drainage along anticlinal vales. 4. Inverted relief with capture of initial consequent by subsequent stream.

be seen, but mostly they resolve themselves into three basic types (Fig. 63).

(i) *Dendritic*. Derived from the Greek *dendron*, a tree, this pattern shows a tree-like form which branches at random. Such a pattern

STREAM PATTERNS

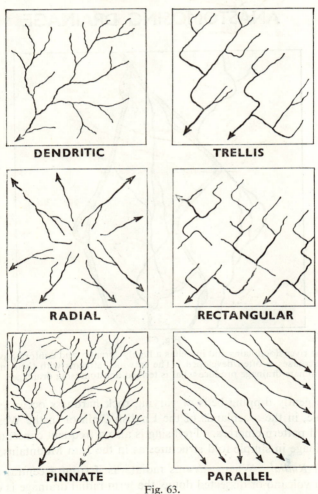

DENDRITIC TRELLIS

RADIAL RECTANGULAR

PINNATE PARALLEL

Fig. 63.

is commonly to be found on homogeneous rock surfaces of uniform resistance, *e.g.* the Shannon, the Amazon.   Incidentally, the ramifying tributaries in the dendritic pattern whose position and direction are entirely fortuitous are often described as *insequent* streams.

(ii) *Trellis.*   A rectilinear pattern, which arises out of the internal geological structure of an area, is developed in many regions.

ANASTOMOSING DRAINAGE

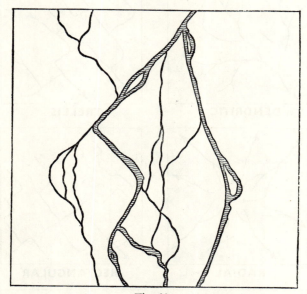

Fig. 64.

On some river floodplains and in deltas a highly complex and contorted pattern of watercourses is often developed.   The entwined streams with their indeterminate drainage produce what is termed anastomosing drainage.

Where gently dipping beds of varying rock hardness occur as, for example, in the scarplands of the English Plain or in the Weald a trellised pattern emerges.   Trellising is also a frequent consequence of drainage in simple fold structures as in the Jura Mountains.

(iii) *Radial.*   Where streams radiate as if from a central area, as on a volcano or dissected dome, the term radial drainage is often applied, but it should be noted that radial drainage may exhibit both dendritic and trellised elements. The rivers of the English Lake District, developed on a dissected dome, show a radial and concentric pattern (see Fig. 71).

While the terms dendritic, trellis, and radial are descriptively useful and while one or the other of the basic patterns tends to be dominant, there are as many variations as there are variations of structure.

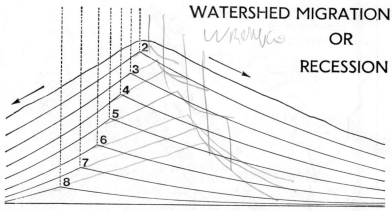

Fig. 65.

In this case streams flowing down the gentle slope are more active than those flowing down the steeper slope. Not only do the headstreams erode headwards and so cause the watershed to retreat but the divide becomes progressively lowered.

A highly complicated intercommunicating pattern of meandering and braided streams is often to be observed on flat plains and in deltas. Such indeterminate drainage is described as *anastomosing*, but it can hardly be classed as a basic drainage pattern. The Mississippi floodplain and the Ganges-Brahmaputra delta provide excellent examples of an anastomosing pattern (Fig. 64).

Watershed Recession

Let us for a moment revert back to our idealised case study of stream development. We noted that at a certain stage in the development of the drainage pattern tributary streams flowing down the dip- and scarp-slopes of the upstanding ridges came into being: these we termed secondary consequents and obsequents. The obsequent streams, since they are flowing down slopes which are

RETREAT of an ESCARPMENT

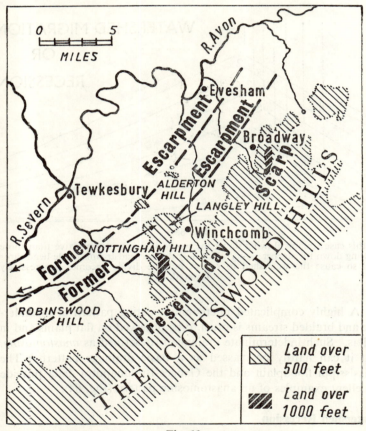

Fig. 66.

The pecked line shows the positions of the Cotswold escarpment in former times. The positions of the former scarp fronts are indicated by remnant hill masses.

steeper (scarp) than those of the secondary consequents (dip), will erode backwards or headwards into the ridge much more vigorously. The ridge which forms a divide between the tributaries of one subsequent and another will gradually undergo modification. The headstreams of the more vigorous obsequents will bite more deeply into the ridge so that in time the ridge divide will take on an irregular form. Interlocking headstreams will produce a definite zigzag pattern (see Fig. 68).

RIVER CAPTURE

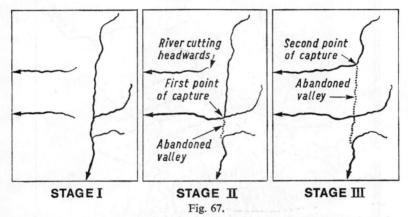

STAGE I   **STAGE II**   **STAGE III**

Fig. 67.

Here two vigorous westward flowing streams are cutting headwards into the divide which separates them from the southward flowing river. In Stage II, one of the westward flowing streams has pierced the divide and beheaded the southward flowing river leaving an abandoned valley below the point of capture. Stage III shows how the second westward flowing stream has captured the headwaters of its neighbour producing a second abandoned valley below the elbow of capture.

Since the headstreams of rivers are constantly eating backwards, the water-parting will undergo constant modification. This backwards movement of the watershed is termed watershed migration or watershed recession. Water divides are, therefore, purely temporary features. Continued headward erosion will also lead to the recession of the whole scarp. An example of the retreat of an escarpment is to be seen in the Cotswold Hills between Cheltenham and Broadway; here are to be found isolated remnants of the previous scarp front and Fig. 66 shows the positions, marked by residual remnants, of the scarp in former times. The streams which eat back the scarp slope not only produce scarp recession but lead gradually to the reduction or lowering of the whole ridge.

WATERSHED RECESSION AND RIVER CAPTURE IN THE LOWTHER HILLS.

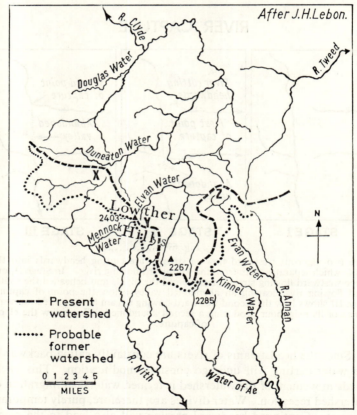

Fig. 68.

This diagram not only shows the headward erosion of contending streams resulting in a zigzagging of the watershed but also provides an illustration of watershed recession and the capturing of river headstreams which has resulted in the migration of the divide.

River Capture

Watershed recession may, and frequently does, give rise to river capture. This is well illustrated in Fig 68. Here in the Lowther Hills in southern Scotland the headstreams of the Clyde and Tweed drain the northern slopes, the headstreams of the Annan and Nith the southern slopes. The latter are swift, vigorous, youthful streams and are actively encroaching upon the more mature Clyde and Tweed; the result is that some of the tributaries of the Clyde and Tweed have been captured by the headstreams of the Annan and Nith. For example, the Evan Water has captured the tributaries of the Clydesburn thereby curtailing the source of the Clydesburn by some four miles.

When a river acquires the headstreams of a contiguous river, enlarging thereby its own drainage area at its neighbour's expense, the process is termed river capture, piracy, or beheading. In the development of the drainage system of any area one river, for a variety of possible reasons, usually becomes more powerful than the others and gradually becomes the "master stream". While a river may enlarge its basin by watershed regression or headward erosion, it may also enlarge its basin by capturing and diverting the tributaries of a neighbouring river system into its own.

As a result perhaps of differences in the amount of rainfall, or the activity of springs in the headwater areas, or of slight variations in rock hardness, one stream may erode more rapidly and downcut more rapidly than its neighbours. This stream will cut back through its divide into the valley of a neighbouring stream and, because it is more vigorous and is at a lower level, it will tap and divert the headwaters of its neighbour into its own. The process is illustrated in Figs. 67 and 69. The Northumbrian and Wealden rivers provide good examples of river capture and it will be helpful to explain how this has come about.

The Rivers of Northumberland

In Northumberland the land slopes eastwards from the Pennine watershed to the North Sea. Originally a series of consequents developed upon the flanks of the Pennines. To-day the Coquet and South Tyne take their rise near the main watershed and flow more or less directly eastwards, but the Blyth and the Wansbeck, which formerly no doubt also arose near the Pennine watershed, now rise mid-way down the Pennine slope. It would seem reasonable to suppose from the map that the Rede, the North Tyne, and the Warks Burn were once the headstreams of the Wansbeck, a tributary of the Wansbeck, and the Blyth respectively. And this is, probably, what they were. The sequence of events which gave rise

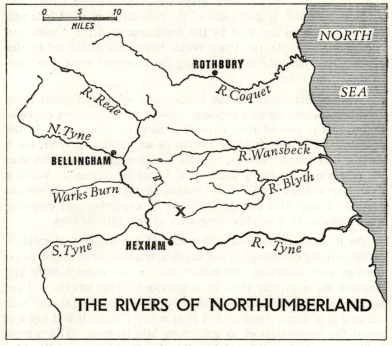

THE RIVERS OF NORTHUMBERLAND

Fig. 69.

X marks the wind gap between the Blyth and the North Tyne and marks out the valley along which the original Blyth flowed. Note how continued headward erosion of the subsequent may, eventually, tap the upper course of the Coquet.

to the present pattern was, in all likelihood, as follows. The North Tyne developed as a subsequent of the South Tyne, and eroding progressively northwards along the soft beds of the Scremerston Coal series it tapped the headwaters of the Blyth and captured and diverted them. Between the headstream (the River Pont) of the present Blyth and the North Tyne there is a well-marked wind gap showing the former valley along which the original River Blyth flowed. The next stage in the development saw the North Tyne continuing its northward erosion and beheading the upper Wansbeck. The point of capture is marked by a sharp bend or "elbow of capture", which is a characteristic feature of river piracy. Moreover, the North Tyne, above the elbow bend near Bellingham, occupies a wide, well-graded valley, which contrasts with the broken, irregular gradient and narrow, deep valley south of the elbow. In other words, the latter is the bed of the younger, vigorous subsequent, the former that of the older consequent river. The third stage is represented by the capture of the Rede and a possible fourth stage can be envisaged, the capturing of the upper Coquet (see Fig. 69).

The Wealden Rivers

Scarpland areas facilitate river capture, and numerous cases may be studied in the scarplands of the English Plain. Few, however, are as interesting as the Wealden rivers, and the Wey-Blackwater river capture is a classic example. Formerly the Wealden area was considered to offer an ideal example of drainage development from a dome but more recent study has shown that this is only partly true. The Weald, as we have already said, is structurally, though not physiographically, a dome: but the area is too complicated to be generally described as a dome, especially in view of the many minor east-west folds on the southern side, and to have a simple consequent drainage pattern. The initial uplift of the Weald, in all probability, did give rise to consequent streams on both sides of the crest but by mid-Tertiary times the region had been reduced to a peneplain, as is indicated by the accordant summit levels generally found throughout the Weald. Subsequent uplift has produced a superimposed drainage system (see p. 194) in the marginal areas with the rivers flowing in both widened and deepened valleys. Several valleys have been eroded along the strike by what are apparently subsequent streams, *e.g.* the Sussex Rother; the rivers then follow the gaps which mark the lines of the old consequent drainage. Most of the dominant rivers exhibit extensive systems of subsequents and numerous wind gaps indicate the former valleys of rivers which have suffered piracy.

Let us look at one of the latest examples of river capture. A subsequent tributary of the River Wey has captured and diverted, near Farnham, a stream which rises near Alton and which once was

RIVERS OF THE WESTERN WEALD

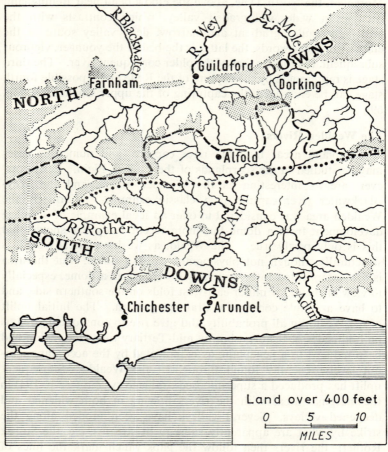

Fig. 70.

The dotted line marks the probable position of the former watershed, the pecked line the position of the present watershed. Note the sharp elbow bends at Farnham and Alfold.

a headstream of the Blackwater. The presence of a wind gap, a sharp elbow of capture, and the misfit stream of the Blackwater testify to the occurrence of river capture in the vicinity of Farnham. It is interesting to note that the Wey, in its turn, has been subjected to piracy in the southern part of its basin. The Arun, which has a shorter course and steeper gradient than the Wey and is, therefore, a more vigorous stream, has succeeded in capturing the former tributaries of the Bramley Wey, which arose in the highland of Hindhead, and diverting them southwards. The valley shapes of the tributaries of the Arun and Wey in the Alfold district exhibit notable differences; the former are deep and steep-sided, indicative of young and vigorous streams, the latter smooth and gentle with wide flat floors, indicating older streams. The Arun's headstreams are, in fact, vigorously eating their way backwards and causing the Arun-Wey watershed to retreat steadily northwards. It is inevitable that further river capture will take place in the future, for the water divides are gradually moving down the side of the gentler gradient, obeying what is termed the *law of unequal slopes*.

The Río Casiquiare

As a third example of river capture, let us briefly note the case of the Río Casiquiare in South America, which provides us with an instance of river piracy in process. The interfluves between the Amazon and Orinoco are so inconspicuous that interpenetration of their headstreams occurs, and in the case of the Casiquiare the river actually links the Amazon with the Orinoco, and water from the upper Orinoco is carried into the Río Negro, one of the Amazon's left-bank tributaries. It would appear that in due course the upper Orinoco, already tapped, will have its waters diverted into the Negro, and a break will occur at the Casiquiare junction.

River capture is a normal incident in the development of river systems and is part and parcel of the unceasing struggle for existence of rivers. Summing up, it may be said that evidence for river capture is provided by:

(i) a sudden change in direction or right-angled bend, known as an elbow of capture;

(ii) marked differences in the valley shapes (cross-sections) above and below the point of capture;

(iii) dry valleys, or dry gaps, linking the valley of one stream to that of another; which indicate the old courses of captured streams;

(iv) river misfits, *i.e.* rivers too small for their existing valleys;

(v) short reversed streams leading from the wind gap to the point of capture may occur if the capture has been long established.

All these signs of capture are not always to be found. The elbow bend is the feature most commonly present, but one must be wary of accepting a sharp bend alone as evidence of capture, for many streams show sharp bends which have nothing to do with river capture. In making any decision upon possible cases of capture, it is advisable to look for at least two, and preferably three, signs of capture.

Finally, let us note that as a result of river capture there is a definite tendency for several small river basins to be replaced by a few large ones, and for the drainage pattern to become simplified. This is well illustrated in the case of the Brazilian Plateau where the drainage system has become reduced to a few master streams.

Superimposed Drainage

A river system normally adjusts itself to the surface structure of the land it drains. For example, in south-eastern England one can clearly discern a rectangular drainage pattern which reflects and is adjusted to the alternating bands of hard and soft rocks; for valleys have been developed along the outcrops of the softer beds, and streams usually cut more or less straight through the cuestas formed by the more resistant chalk and limestone. Sometimes, however, the arrangement of the drainage system appears to show no respect for the surface structure and follows a pattern which is quite unrelated to the nature of the strata being traversed; for example, a river may traverse a band of particularly hard rock several times, or carve out a valley for no apparent structural reason. When a river behaves in such a way, ignoring the structural surface across which it flows, it suggests that the river must, originally, have been developed upon an overlying rock surface which no longer exists. In the first place the river would adapt itself to the original cover of younger rocks, but when these were removed by denudation the river would come to rest upon the underlying rocks of different structure. When, however, the influence of the original structure continues to predominate over that of the newly exposed strata the drainage is said to be *superimposed.*

Superimposed drainage is by no means an uncommon occurrence, and numerous examples are to be found in the upland areas of Britain. One of the classic cases of superimposition is to be found in the Lake District (Fig. 71). Structurally the Lake District is a dissected dome which displays a radial drainage pattern. To-day a ring of limestone surrounds the older, harder rocks of the core. Originally the radial drainage was developed upon the limestone when it completely covered the older rocks beneath. Prolonged erosion led to the limestone layer being progressively removed from the centre of the dome so that now it exists only as a collar around the outer flanks of the dome. The rivers continued, with very little change of course, to cut themselves deeply into the older strata beneath, to whose structure they are now beginning to adapt themselves, although the main rivers continue still to show quite clearly their original radiating pattern. The River Wye, in Monmouthshire, provides another interesting case of superimposed drainage.

Antecedent Drainage

Sometimes rivers show an astonishing independence of relief features, and it is difficult, if not impossible, to explain their present relationships with the geological structure except in terms of antecedent drainage. Antecedent drainage has been defined as: "a drainage system maintaining its original direction across a line of localised uplift".[1] Let us elaborate upon this definition. After a river has fully established itself, it may happen that uplift of the land occurs across its course; but such uplift does not prevent the river from maintaining its original direction, providing that the uplift proceeds sufficiently gradually to enable the river's erosive power to keep pace with it; in other words, the down cutting action of the river proceeds as fast as, or faster than, the uplift. Hence a river's course may bear no relation to the structure of the area; for example, a river may head for and run directly across a mountain

[1] R.G.S. list.

SUPERIMPOSED DRAINAGE: THE LAKE DISTRICT.

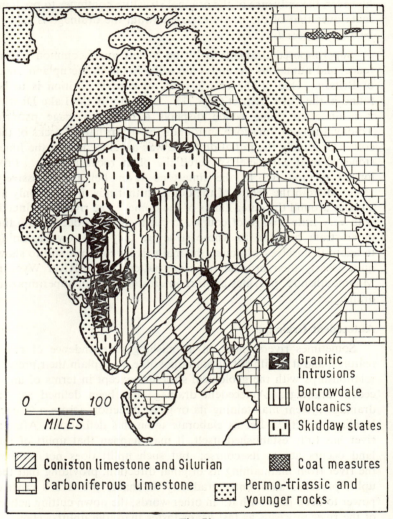

Fig. 71.

The Lake District is an eroded dome. The present radial drainage system originated on the Carboniferous limestone strata which covered the older, harder rocks beneath. The streams in due course cut through the limestone and then continued to incise themselves into the older rocks of the core. Thus, to-day, although the younger rocks have been stripped off except around the periphery of the dome, the rivers retain their radial pattern.

range. Such discordant rivers are termed *antecedent,* because they were established *before* the relief features were developed.

That antecedence has occurred is very difficult to demonstrate, and as Beckinsale has said, "nearly all known postulated cases are necessarily based on obscure and insufficient evidence",[1] and Sparks avers that "antecedence, as a hypothesis, should be the last resort of a geomorphologist seeking to explain an inconsequent pattern of drainage".[2] Both the Indus and the Brahmaputra, piercing the Himalayas, and the Columbia, cutting through the Cascades, are probable examples of antecedent drainage. It is difficult to explain the courses of these rivers unless they are older than the mountains they cross. Although there is nothing inherently impossible in a river's ability to cut downwards at a rate comparable with upwarping or uplift, it should be emphasised that many apparent cases of antecedence might be more satisfactorily explained in terms of river capture. Finally it should be noted that the idea of antecedence is related to *localised* uplift and not to regional land uplift, which would, of course, produce rejuvenation.

[1] *Land, Air, and Ocean,* p. 272.
[2] *Geomorphology,* p. 121.

CHAPTER 12

RIVERS AND VALLEY FEATURES

Rivers may be thought of as instruments, or machines as Strahler has called them, that perform two very important physical functions: they dispose of the superfluous water from the land surface and they work powerfully towards the denudation of the land. In its latter function flowing water accomplishes three main types of work:

(i) it dissolves and erodes the land surface over which it runs;

(ii) it transports the matter it has dissolved and eroded away; and

(iii) it deposits the material which it has carried in suspension or rolled along.

Let us now look more closely at these three aspects of the work of running water.

RIVER EROSION

In discussing the erosive work of a river, three things appertaining to it must be noted: its volume, its velocity, and its load.

Volume of Water

Streams obtain their water, directly or indirectly, from rainfall and other forms of precipitation. Three things may happen to the precipitation: (a) it may evaporate almost immediately; (b) it may soak into the ground; and (c) it may drain off the land surface into streams. The run-off gives rise to the streams, but their supply may be augmented by water which, having percolated underground, subsequently appears at the surface again, at a lower elevation, in the form of a spring. Streams and rivers flow from higher to lower regions, eventually (except in arid regions) emptying themselves into the sea. In humid environments streams normally increase their volume of water as they proceed to the sea, since their drainage basin becomes extended and the stream is fed by tributaries. It is common knowledge, not only that stream volume, in general, increases from source to mouth, but that the volume usually varies seasonally. In areas with marked seasonal rainfall regimes, as in the monsoon lands for example, rivers may alternate between swollen conditions during the period of the rains to little more than trickles in the dry season. On the other hand, a well-distributed annual rainfall will obviously predispose towards a fairly even flow. Irregularities of flow may, of course, in some cases be evened out by snow melt or spring water. The exceptional condition is the stream in arid environments. Here, very often, streams descending from marginal highlands or entering the arid zone may peter out since rapid evaporation quickly reduces their volume and there is no inflow to counterbalance the evaporation.

STAGES OF STREAM DISCHARGE

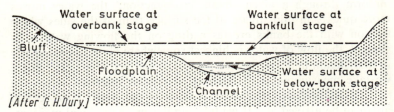

Fig. 72.
Stages of discharge: overbank, bankfull, and below-bank discharge. These may be equated with the states of flooding, when the river channel is full to its brim, and when the river is at low water.

Broadly speaking, a river may be said to have three states of discharge: (i) the bankfull stage, that is when the water-surface in the stream channel reaches to the level of the adjacent floodplain; (ii) the below-bank stage, when the water-surface lies below the tops of the enclosing channel banks, *i.e.* when the river discharge is in a low state of flow; and (iii) the overbank stage, when the water-surface spills over the river banks or, in the colloquial sense, when the river floods (Fig. 72). These concepts relating to the states of discharge of streams, and especially the bankfull stage, are of great importance and significance as will be seen in the following paragraphs.

Stream Velocity

It has long been thought, and commonly stated, that the velocity, or speed of flow, of a river is greatest in the upper courses of streams where the gradients are steepest, and least in the lower courses where the gradients are very gentle. To the observer watching the water tumble down a steep valley or the apparently turgid flow of a wide river in its plains course, such varying velocities seem to be entirely reasonable. Recent research, especially by American hydrologists, on stream flow have shown that these assumptions are erroneous. Careful observations and measurements of water-flow have shown that the mean velocity through the cross-section of a stream, at the bankfull stage, is practically constant throughout the entire length of the stream.

Let us examine this statement a little more carefully. It will probably already be apparent that the velocity of a stream is not uniform through a given stream cross-section; the water moves more quickly in mid-stream at the surface than at the sides where friction with the banks creates a drag on the flowing water. In general, the flow of water is highest somewhere close to the surface in mid-stream and lowest near the banks and bed (Fig. 73). But if we take measurements of the flow at regular intervals across the stream and at depth, the mean velocity of the whole cross-section area can be arrived at. If we take similar cross-sectional measurements at a number of points along the length of the river, whether in its upper, middle, or lower course, we find that the mean velocity through each cross-section is the same providing the river is at the bankfull stage. Clearly, comparisons between one section of a river and another, or between one river and another, cannot very well be made and possess any validity unless they relate to similar conditions, that is to the river's discharge at the bankfull stage. A little thought will show the necessity for this condition. Just as the speed of flow varies from point to point in the cross-section of a river, so the mean velocity through the cross-section does not remain constant at a given place since it is less when the stream is at low water than when it is in spate. Hence for any valid comparisons to be made, corresponding sets of conditions must exist. When these do exist, *i.e.* at the bankfull stage, velocity is constant along the length of the river.

The question arises: why is the velocity constant? Steep slopes, it is true, permit and promote higher velocities than gentler gradients but against this must be set the fact that larger channels exert less friction on the flowing water than do small channels. In other words, the decrease in the gradient, which will tend to slow down the flow, is compensated by the decrease of friction on the moving water. "Velocity can be maintained on a progressively decreasing downstream slope, because the channel becomes progressively more efficient in the downstream direction."[1]

VELOCITY DISTRIBUTION IN AN
OPEN STREAM CHANNEL

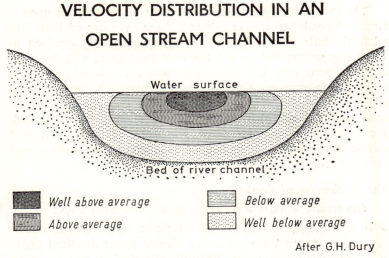

Water surface

Bed of river channel

| Well above average | Below average |
| Above average | Well below average |

After G.H. Dury

Fig. 73.

Velocity distribution in an open channel shown diagrammatically. In general, the flow of water is greatest in mid-stream near the surface where there is a minimum of friction and least near the bed and banks where the flow is retarded by friction.

Stream Load

The volume of water carried and the speed of movement determine the energy of the river and upon the energy of the river depends its carrying capacity and the nature of its load. The carrying capacity of the river is related not only to its volume and

[1] G. H. Dury, "Rivers in Geographical Teaching", *Geography*, Vol. XLVIII, 1963, pp. 23-24.

velocity but also to the character of its *load,* a term used to denote all the materials, solid or in solution, which are moved by water downstream. It will be clear that a stream can carry a much greater quantity by weight of fine material than of coarse. It will also be clear that the more powerful the river (*i.e.* the greater its energy) the greater will be its capacity to move coarse material; for example, during times of flood the swirling waters often carry downstream large boulders which under normal conditions would not be moved. The bed of the River Lyn in North Devon is littered with many large boulders after the disastrous flood of 1952.

The load carried by a river is of great importance for upon it largely depends its erosive power. Running water of itself has relatively little erosive action: its action is mainly confined to dissolving matter; but once it has become charged with debris, it begins to wear away the surface over which it is flowing and with which it is in contact. Thus, generally speaking, the erosive power of a river increases in proportion to (*a*) its velocity, *i.e.* its rate or speed of flow, and (*b*) its load, *i.e.* the amount of matter carried. We must be wary, however, of accepting (*b*) as it stands, for a river carrying too great a load leads to aggradation and the protection of the river bed.

The Mechanism of Erosion

The erosive work of a river acts in six interacting ways:

(i) by *solution* or *corrosion,* the solvent action of water as it flows over the rock; the amount of mineral matter dissolved varies appreciably depending upon the purity of the water and the solubility of the rock, some rocks, such as chalk and limestone, being highly susceptible to solution by water containing dissolved carbon dioxide, others, like gabbro and slate, being little affected;

(ii) by *hydraulic action* or quarrying, due to the prising and lifting effect of rushing water; as the moving water thrusts itself into cracks and crevices, the sheer force may dislodge lumps of rock or even quarry into the bed of the river and lift up slabs of the bedrock;

(iii) by *cavitation* or the collapse of bubbles of water vapour (which form the "foam" which is created when the water is very turbulent); the sudden and violent collapse of such bubbles propagates shock waves which strike adjacent surfaces with hammer-like blows which assist in shattering and disintegrating the rock. Cavitation is really an aspect of hydraulic action;

(iv) by *corrasion* or the scratching and scraping of the river bed and banks by the matter which is carried in suspension, moved by saltation (*i.e.* in jerks and jumps), or moved by traction (*i.e.* rolled along the bed); in other words the river uses its load as a grinding tool which constantly scours and excavates the river channel producing such features as pot-holes, undercut banks, smoothed and rounded boulders, etc.;

(v) by *impaction* or the effect of blows on the stream-bed produced by the lifting of large boulders; during floodtime the surging waters may actually lift boulders bodily to throw them with a crash on to the river bed; the impact of such body blows is sufficient to weaken and sometimes to break the bedrock;

(vi) by *attrition* or the break-up of the load itself into smaller and smaller pieces as a result of the collision and mutual scraping action of the load matter; as a result there is a constant diminution in the size of the fragments being moved and, accordingly, they become easier to transport.

RIVER TRANSPORT

Although the load carried by rivers varies (*a*) between different sections of their courses, and (*b*) between river and river, by and large they carry great quantities of material from one place to another. The load carried by a stream is derived in part from the action of weathering and rain wash on the slopes of the river basin and in part from the solution and erosion of its own bed.

First we might note the different ways in which running water transports its load. Movement is effected by (i) carrying matter in solution; (ii) carrying it in suspension; (iii) rolling it along the bed, *i.e.* bottom traction; and (iv) moving it by a series of jerks and jumps, a process known as saltation. By these four methods matter is carried downstream but, again, the effectiveness of each method varies between section and section of the river's course and also between river and river. An illustration of the kind of load carried and of the methods of transport employed by a river is given by the following figures for the Mississippi. It has been estimated that each year the river carries into the Gulf of Mexico:

340 million tons of matter in suspension,
156 million tons of matter in solution,
40 million tons of matter by traction and saltation.

Although these figures must not be accepted as typical of the quantities of material disgorged by great rivers, the proportions may perhaps be accepted as being reasonably representative.

The amount of material transported by any river depends, as we have already seen, upon the volume and velocity of the river and the size of the load matter. When the turbulence of the flowing water is great and the load consists of fine particles, then not only will a much greater quantity of material be carried but it will be transported much further. A great deal depends also upon the nature of the rocks across which the river flows: swiftly-flowing streams crossing hard gritstones are quite clear because of the relative absence of transportable material; but, on the other hand, even sluggish streams if they happen to cross soft clays will become ladened and darkly discoloured with solid matter in suspension. The Hwang-ho of northern China, which flows across wide areas of a soft, loamy rock called loess, brings down enormous quantities of the buff-coloured material; its waters are stained yellow by it thus giving the river its common name, the Yellow River.

The quantity of matter carried in solution depends upon the solubility of the mineral constituents in rock. Some rocks are more easily dissolved than others. Calcareous rocks are very susceptible to solution. Chalk and limestone are relatively easily dissolved by water, hence streams flowing across such areas carry considerable quantities of lime in solution. A river such as the Shannon, which flows for most of its course across limestone rock, carries an abnormal amount of matter in solution. The various lakes which in fact thread its course are merely solution hollows— depressions dissolved by water out of the limestone floor.

The amount of material that is transported by traction, that is the sliding, pushing and rolling of fragments, pebbles, and boulders along the river bed, and by saltation or the downstream movement of bottom load by skips and jumps, is normally smaller than that moved in solution and very much smaller than that carried in suspension. The transport of bottom load depends upon the force of the running water and the slope of the bed.

RIVER DEPOSITION

When a river current slackens in speed, either as a result of a decrease in volume or a lessening of the slope, some of the materials being transported are deposited. The order in which the materials are deposited is: boulders, pebbles, gravels, sands, silts, and muds, although the change from coarse to fine material is normally imperceptible. Exceptions to this grading occur where local influences as, for example, a break in slope or damming, interrupt the river's course. But the occurrence of a lake in a river's course gives us a clear illustration of the depositional process. Whenever a river enters a lake, the current is slackened with the result that deposition takes place at the point of entry and in due course a fan-shaped delta is built up composed of coarser sands in-shore and finer muds off-shore. The River Rhine, for example, entering Lake Constance as a muddy, glacier-fed stream, has built up an alluvial flat, and then, having been filtered, emerges from the lake as a clear river.

Deposition is not confined to the lower courses of rivers. Much deposition, granted, does occur there but some may occur at almost any point along the river's course. Erosion and deposition often proceed simultaneously; for instance, a river may often erode a concave bank while a sandbank and shingle are formed on the opposite convex bank (Fig. 74). Such deposition is normally of a temporary nature, and a sandbank formed during a phase of reduced velocity is likely to be swept away at a later time.

In the case of many of the larger rivers, such as the Mississippi and the Hwang-ho, the current becomes so slow as the rivers traverse long almost level stretches that it is no longer able to carry its great burden of suspended mud and vast quantities are deposited on the river beds. Through dropping their load, the rivers eventually choke their own beds and, through constant overflowing build up natural embankments or levees composed of mud and silt. The rivers thus confine themselves between such embankments but this merely serves to accelerate the building up, or aggradation, of their beds (Fig. 75). The rivers, especially in floodtime, frequently seek a course elsewhere since the old channel cannot take the excess water, and the levees are breached. ✦ *Diagram opposite.*

STREAM EROSION AND DEPOSITION

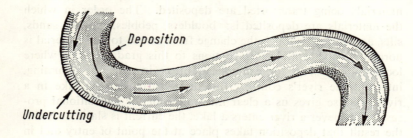

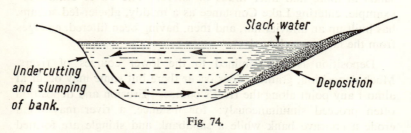

Fig. 74.

Whenever and wherever the velocity of flow is reduced a stream must jettison part of its load. Check in flow occurs at the following points in a river's course: (i) at a break in slope as, for example, where a stream leaves the hills and enters a plain; at such a point an alluvial fan will develop; (ii) where the valley floor widens appreciably thereby allowing the level land on either side of the river to suffer flooding and to receive alluvial deposits; (iii) where a swift river enters suddenly the comparatively tranquil waters of a

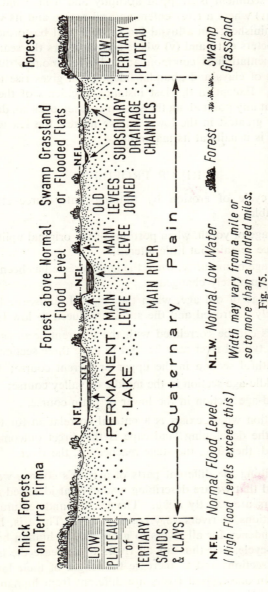

AMAZON BASIN – TYPICAL FEATURES OF THE FLOODPLAINS

Thick Forests on Terra Firma

Forest above Normal Flood Level

Swamp Grassland or Flooded Flats

Forest

LOW PLATEAU of TERTIARY SANDS & CLAYS

LOW TERTIARY PLATEAU

PERMANENT MAIN LEVEE

MAIN RIVER

OLD LEVEES JOINED

MAIN LEVEE

SUBSIDIARY DRAINAGE CHANNELS

Swamp Grassland

Forest

Quaternary Plain

N.F.L. *Normal Flood Level*
(*High Flood Levels exceed this*)

N.L.W. *Normal Low Water*

Width may vary from a mile or so to more than a hundred miles.

Fig. 75.

The diagram shows typical features of the floodplains of rivers within the Amazon lowlands. Levees border the main streams. Temporary drainage channels meander over flats covered with swamp vegetation. Depressions in the alluvial plain are occupied by lakes. Over the plains the rivers shift their braided courses and produce an anastomosing pattern.

lake; here sediment is dropped abruptly and a lake flat or delta built up; (iv) where a river enters an arid region and its volume is rapidly diminished; an alluvial fan or cone will be formed where the water peters out; and (v) where a river enters the sea; in such cases sedimentation is common around river mouths due to the flocculation of clays and abundant deposition gives rise to deltaic formations. Except in the last instance, accidents of these kinds may occur at any point along the stream course; even so, deposition is normally greatest in the lower course nearest the sea where the river's load is usually at its maximum.

RIVER PROFILES

In the cycle of erosion by running water three stages are distinguishable:

(i) the stage of youth, when portions of the original uplifted land surface remain but little altered;

(ii) the stage of maturity, when the land surface has been lowered and completely changed;

(iii) the stage of old age, when the original landscape has been entirely destroyed and the surface reduced to low levels.

These stages can be correlated with the different sections in river courses. A typical river may be said to have three sections:

(i) a youthful section in the upper or torrent course;

(ii) a middle-age section in the middle or valley course;

(iii) an old-age section in the lower or plain course.

The correlation which exists is a natural correlation for the stage reached in the developing landscape is the direct outcome of the work of, and, therefore, the stage reached by, the river.

In describing the different parts of a river's course, we should bear in mind that we are describing a somewhat idealised river for no two rivers are exactly alike. The lengths and features of the different sections of rivers vary considerably. There is, however, a general tendency for all rivers to grow old, as human beings do in their life-cycle, and thus for all rivers to decrease the length of their upper sections and to increase the length of their lower sections. But in one respect rivers are different from human beings;

they can, as we shall see later, become rejuvenated and revert from, say, the mature stage to the youthful stage.

(i) *The Upper Course.* This section of a river, which is the stage of youth, is sometimes called the torrent or mountain course.

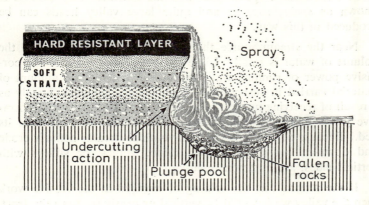

WATERFALLS

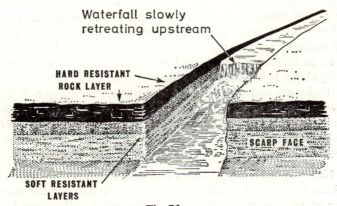

Fig. 76.

The upper figure shows a side view of a waterfall. Here the fall is due to a hard resistant layer of rock overlying softer strata. Waterfalls, however, may result from a variety of causes: by the formation of fault-scarps, by hanging valleys tributary to glacial troughs, and by river capture. But most falls are due to differences in hardness of the rocks forming the river bed. The lower diagram shows the upstream recession of a waterfall.

It is the part of the river that is furthest from its mouth. The river may originate as run-off or as seepage from the spongey, water-holding beds of peat or as a spring. Water flowing out of the ground as a seepage or a spring will gradually remove material and erode backwards or headwards into the hillside. This process is known as *spring sapping* and quite large valley heads can be produced in this way.

Near the stream source the gradient is usually steep but the volume of water is small. Little erosion takes place, for the corrasive power of running water is dependent upon the amount of material carried in suspension. Very shortly, however, largely as a result of receiving matter from rain wash, the stream gains corrasive power and so is able to start work on the excavation of its bed. Because of their energy, such youthful streams actively erode and down-cutting is prominent; hence gorges, or valleys with vertical sides, are common features.

If the stream was the sole agent engaged in the erosive work then the valley walls would be vertical or nearly so, but rain, frost, and other weathering agents attack the sides and the valley becomes V-shaped. The steepness of the valley slopes depends very largely upon the degree of lateral, or sideways, erosion as compared with the rate of downward erosion, and this is related to the resistance of the rock. Thus, if the rocks in which the valley is cut are hard and resistant, such as gritstone, or pervious, so that the water sinks in, as in limestone, relatively little weathering will occur and the valley slopes will be steep and the V narrow. If, on the other hand, the rocks are soft and readily worn away, the valley will tend to be wide with a more open V shape. Typically, however, the torrent course shows a fairly narrow, steep-sided V cross-section. Most of the mountain streams in the Scottish Highlands, in the Lake District, and in North Wales have valleys of this kind.

Not only are young valleys characteristically narrow but there is little room in the valley bottoms for anything other than the stream; the stream usually occupies the entire valley floor because there has not yet been sufficient time for wide floors to develop. A youthful stream tends to follow a winding course since it is easily deflected by obstacles. The bends become emphasised because the current is normally strongest on the outside of a bend. As a result of this swinging of the stream interlocking spurs are developed: these are tongues of land which project alternately into each other. The river bed, moreover, is usually rocky and littered with boulders and typical of the torrent course are such features as pot-holes (circular depressions cut into the bed by swirling pebbles), rapids, cascades, and waterfalls. Thus the longitudinal profile of the upper course of a river is highly irregular, although the stream itself, if we ignore its sinuosity between the interlocking spurs, normally follows a fairly straight, direct course.

RIVER VALLEY: CROSS-SECTION

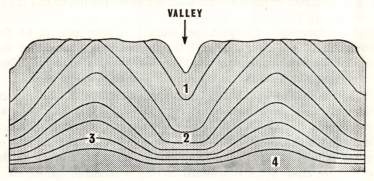

1. Youthful stage   **2.** Mature stage
3. Late maturity   **4.** Old age stage

Fig. 77.

Cross-section to show stages in the development of a valley. As the valley deepens and widens so the interfluves are correspondingly reduced.

The landscape in this youthful stage is characteristically one of deep, narrow, and often straight valleys, separated by broad and often flat-topped summit areas, for the interfluves or divides between the valleys have not yet been destroyed. Youthful landscapes are of restricted usefulness to man: there is little level land for cultivation and the interfluves are often too high and exposed for crop growing; the land suitable for settlement is scarce and aggregations of settlements almost precluded; the streams by their shallowness and rocky beds are useless for navigation; while the narrow, deeply-cut valleys with their steep slopes make land communications not only difficult but very expensive. On the other hand, it is true that the valleys of some young streams provide the only feasible routeways into areas which are difficult of access such as the Swiss Alps and the Colombian Andes. In such areas roads and railways thread their way along the narrow valley-ways. Mountain streams sometimes offer some compensation for they may provide possibilities for the generation of hydro-electric power, while the narrow valleys may offer suitable sites for the impounding of water and the construction of reservoirs.

(ii) *The Middle Course.* The middle or valley course of a river is a transitional or intermediate section linking the upper and lower courses. In this section the work of the river is at once destructive and constructive. The principal work here continues to be the corrasion of the river bed and the downstream removal of the eroded material, although as the plain section is approached increasing attack on the valley sides begins to manifest itself.

In the middle course the volume of water in the river is considerably increased because the effective catchment area (*i.e.* the entire area draining to the river) is increased through tributary streams which augment the water supply. While the volume of water is much greater in the mid-course, the gradients along the valley are less; hence downward cutting is reduced. More effective lateral erosion now begins to show itself.

No stream ever follows a perfectly straight course, at least for any distance, because of the topographical irregularities and structural hazards that it meets. Stream flow is thus affected and the streams begin to swing from side to side. This swinging, already apparent in the torrent track but not pronounced there, becomes more emphatic in the valley course. This swinging of the stream produces, as we have already noted, interlocking spurs. In the upstream portion of the middle course these spurs may continue to interlock but further downstream the spurs suffer river attack and the ends are eroded away, thus producing what are known as truncated spurs; as a result, the spurs slowly recede and what is known as a bluff line is developed.

In the valley section the slopes are not nearly so steep as in the upper course and a "flat" of varying width is developed between the stream bank and the bluff line (Fig. 78). These flats result from the lateral erosion of the river which is now becoming more potent. As the river current swings around each bend it impinges upon the concave side, gradually undercutting the bank and producing a river cliff. On the opposite, or convex side, there is slack water and instead of erosion there is usually some deposition taking

VALLEY FLAT, TERRACES AND BLUFF LINES

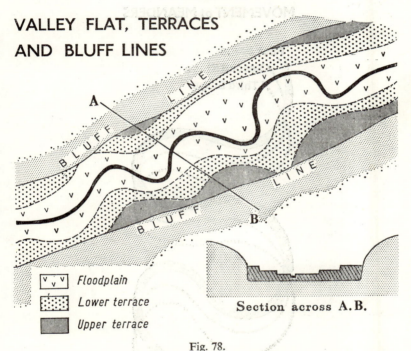

v v v	Floodplain
::::::	Lower terrace
▓▓	Upper terrace

Section across A.B.

Fig. 78.

As meanders migrate downstream they leave behind remnants of the former floodplains as marginal terraces.

place. The slightly sloping spur that is formed is termed the slip-off slope. As each river bend is enlarged, both sideways and downstream, so the bends or meanders move downstream and in so doing they plane off all the spurs and cut a swath along the valley floor which forms the floodplain of the river (Fig. 79). The strips of flat land in the valley bottoms are periodically inundated, for in times of flood the river may spill over its banks; when this happens the river deposits some of its load of silt on the floodplain.

In the middle course all the obstacles, such as rapids and waterfalls, which punctuated the torrent course, forming temporary base

DOWNSTREAM
MOVEMENT of MEANDERS

First Stage
Second Stage
Third Stage

See 220-22
for meanders

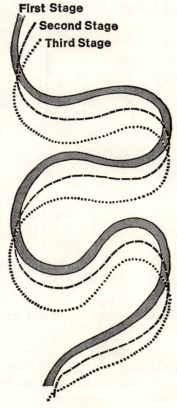

Fig. 79.

The diagram illustrates the downstream movement of meanders. As the meanders move downstream there is a general tendency for them to grow in size, *i.e.* to grow laterally. As they move downstream they widen the valley floor.

levels, have been eliminated. The erasing of such irregularities in the stream course makes the gradient less steep and this action is termed *degrading*. While erosion is dominant in the valley section, the river from time to time and from place to place, wherever conditions are suitable (as, for example, in stretches where the current's speed slackens) causes some deposition to take place. Pebbles and sand will be laid down on the river bed and in places the bed is likely to be built up; this process is known as aggradation, for the river is *aggrading* or raising its surface by the deposition of rock waste.

The stage of maturity brings notable changes in the landscape. The original land surface has been almost completely destroyed. In place of the broad, flat-topped uplands dissected by deep, narrow valleys which were characteristic of the youthful landscape, the relief is now one of wide, deep open valleys, with wide, flat valley floors, separated by fairly sharp divides, all that remain of the original upland surface. Maturity leads to the condition of maximum relief. The ridge-tops of the divides, which lie at the same general level, mark the plane of surface at which the land stood before the mature valleys were cut into it. Thus practically the whole of the former land surface has been eroded away in a mature landscape.

The spacious flat-bottomed valleys of mature rivers with their coating of fertile alluvium offer many advantages to man: they afford sufficient space for agriculture, for aggregated settlement, and for transport. Susceptibility to flooding in some cases is a drawback, and man-made levees have sometimes to be made to protect villages and towns. But the floodplains can be drained and the rich soils usually attract population. The level land also facilitates the construction of highways, whether road or rail, while the rivers themselves because of their depth and unimpeded courses often offer favourable facilities for water transport.

(iii) *The Lower Course*. The lower portion of the river, where it flows across an almost level plain to its mouth, is known as the plain track or course. In this section the river is wide and a greatly increased volume of water is carried over a scarcely perceptible gradient. The main stream of the Amazon, for instance, falls a mere 600 feet in a distance of 2,000 miles; this gives an average gradient of about 3½ inches per mile but in its lowest reaches gradients of 1 inch per mile occur. This very gentle fall in the lower course may be compared with the average gradient of 50 feet per mile in many of the Amazon's headwater streams.

Corrasion of the river bed has, at this stage, virtually ceased and deposition replaces erosion as the main work of the river. The fine mud which is carried in suspension now begins to be dropped on the river bed; the result of this load-shedding is to raise the level of the bed, a process we have already referred to as *aggradation*. There is a distinct tendency for all rivers in their senile state to aggrade their beds, hence the necessity for dredging the mouths of rivers to maintain deep channels if the rivers are used for shipping. The raising of the river bed also implies the raising of the river banks and this occurs during floodtime when the river flowing in spate is obliged to spill some of its water over the banks on to the floodplain. Constant repetition of this and the consequent deposition of sediment leads, as we have already seen, to the building up of levees.

In the lower section of the river there can be no deepening of the valley since there is no longer any vertical corrasion but the river can still continue to wear away its banks and a measure of lateral erosion goes on. Great meanders crawl over the nearly level land, wandering freely and redistributing the alluvium. Any corrasion that may take place is more than balanced, however, by deposition. In the lowermost section of the plain course a river uses practically the whole of its energy in transporting its burden of silt.

In the stage of old age the rivers, full and overflowing and moving downstream in extravagant sinuosities (such as the Tees or the Seine, the Mississippi or the Indus), occupy wide, shallow valleys, only slightly above sea level, which are separated by only very low divides.

The deep alluvial soils of the extensive floodplains of aged streams are rich and fertile and wonderfully productive when cultivated. Their liability to flooding, often on an extensive scale, is a handicap to the farmer (though in certain dry climates it may be turned to an advantage); usually these alluvial plains have to be drained (and dyked) if they are to be effectively used. Settlements, too, are threatened by floods and must perforce seek higher, drier sites, such as the villages in the Nile delta which occupy slight mounds. Though the rivers by their volume and velocity are useful for navigation, they are, at the same time, handicapped by their tortuous channels and estuarine sandbanks; hence, if full use is to be made of the lower courses, the former must be canalised and the estuaries dredged.

The Theoretical Profile of Equilibrium

Having described the various activities of a river from its source to its mouth, we are now in a position to sum up and to draw certain conclusions. We have seen that it is possible to subdivide a river's course into sections, each of which possesses certain fairly well-defined features and characteristics; to these sections we applied the terms torrent, valley, and plain stages which roughly corresponded with the phases of youth, maturity, and old age. Such sections or sub-divisions may be discerned by changes in the gradient of a river bed, and a profile section drawn along the length of a river (known as a long-profile or *thalweg*) will show such changes.

The uppermost section of the river has the steepest gradient but here, because of the small volume of water and because the stream is not heavily charged with debris (this is why mountain streams are normally clear), fairly slow erosion occurs. In the middle section there is usually an abundant supply of water, because the river is being fed by tributaries, and sufficient erosive material in the form of pebbles, grit, and suspended silt to enable abrasion and attrition to be active. But in this section the river is not so heavily laden as to prevent it moving the material it erodes. Sooner or later, however, erosion begins to decrease with the increase in the load that the river is carrying; ultimately, a point will be reached where the amount of erosion just balances the amount of deposition. At such a point where the river has just sufficient velocity to move its load, the profile is said to be graded or in equilibrium.

If we assume for a moment that we have a slope of constant gradient consisting of rocks of uniform resistance to erosion, a river would erode a profile which would show a parabolic curve. It would produce such a curve because of what we have just said:

near the source the erosive activity of the stream is less than average, in the mid-section there is much erosion, while near the mouth there is, again, little erosion because the river is almost fully laden. In reality ideal conditions of this kind seldom, if ever, occur: in the first place, there are usually irregularities in the long profile due to geological or structural accidents such as bands of more resistant rock which may give rise to waterfalls, lakes, etc., and, in the second place, the volume and velocity of the water is not constant.

The outcropping of a band of resistant rock across a stream will cause a temporary obstruction, for the rock will prove to be much more resistant to erosion than the rocks immediately upstream and downstream from it. The river will grade itself in the reach immediately above the obstruction, which will form a temporary base level of erosion. Once the river has graded itself in the reach above the obstruction, then it will begin to concentrate its attack upon the obstruction itself which in due course will be eliminated and the irregularity smoothed out (Fig. 80). In this way irregularities along the whole profile are gradually eliminated: erosion takes place on the steeper sections and deposition on the gentler sections of the profile so that differences in gradient are constantly being reduced and a smooth, curving profile formed.

The volume of water in a river changes constantly as a result of the vagaries in rainfall. Since the volume of water changes over short term periods, so the steepness of all sections of the river should change in agreement with the differing volumes of water. It will be appreciated that after heavy rains, when the river is running in spate, it is deepening its bed; conversely, during dry spells when there is little water, much of the river's load will be dropped and the river will be aggrading its bed. Clearly under short term changes of this kind the river will be unable to adjust itself and in actual fact the long profile of a river must be thought of as the average condition of the various profiles that the river would be likely to assume under differing conditions at different times.

Thus it may be said that a river is constantly striving to attain a perfect profile of equilibrium. The ultimate achievement of a graded course is theoretically possible and many streams have virtually reached this condition; for example, some of the rivers of the English Midlands are quoted by Monkhouse as having attained graded profiles. But it is extremely doubtful whether many rivers have achieved a perfectly graded course, for changes in the level of the land or the sea and climatic changes will destroy its grade.

LONG PROFILE OF A RIVER

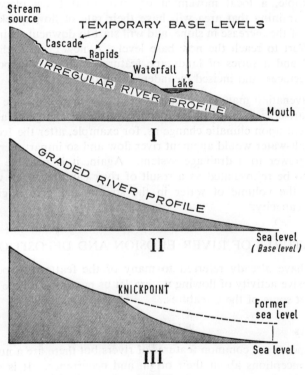

Fig. 80.

I. shows the irregular long profile of a river broken by rapids, waterfalls, lakes, etc., which form temporary base levels. Streams in their upper or torrent courses are characterised by such features. II. shows the graded profile: all the obstructions and irregularities along the river's course have been eliminated and a smooth, curving profile, or profile of equilibrium, has been achieved. III. shows how rejuvenation has led to a new base level being formed; this, in turn, starts a new cycle of erosion and the river recommences down-cutting. The break along the river profile, where the new curve of erosion intersects the former curve of erosion is termed a knickpoint.

Rejuvenation

The revival of erosive activity on the part of a river is termed rejuvenation; it results in an interruption in the cycle outlined above. Rejuvenation may occur for a variety of reasons. It may be caused by (*a*) a fall in sea level or eustatic change, or (*b*) land uplift, which is usually of a local character. In both cases the movements result in a change in base level. It will be clear that if, for example, a local movement of land uplift takes place, the streams draining that area will have their rate of flow quickened, because of the increase in slope, and will start to downcut their beds in an effort to reach the new base level. A new cycle is thereby initiated and a series of landscape features such as knickpoints,[1] paired terraces, and incised meanders result (see pp. 224-8).

Rejuvenation may also occur without any change in base level. It may arise as a result of an increase in the discharge of a river consequent upon climatic change as, for example, after the Ice Age when melt-water would augment river flow and so impart increased erosive power to a drainage system. Again, it is possible for a stream to be rejuvenated as a result of river capture which would increase the volume of water in the stream and give it greater eroding capacity.

FEATURES OF RIVER EROSION AND DEPOSITION

We have already referred to many of the features associated with erosive activity of flowing water: let us now look a little more closely at some of these features.

Meanders

Meanders are common features of rivers but there are a number of misconceptions about their origin and occurrence. It is sometimes said that a stream begins to meander because of some obstruction in the river; it is also often maintained that meanders

---

[1] A term derived from the German *knickpunkt* which is commonly used to refer to any break of slope in the long-profile of a river, *e.g.* a rejuvenation head or an outcrop of resistant rock. In the strict German meaning it refers to a break of slope in the river profile resulting from a change in base level which causes the river to regrade its course. The knickpoint occurs where the new curve of erosion intersects the former curve of erosion.

are associated with the sluggish flow of rivers on floodplains of gentle gradient. Both these ideas are in need of revision. Experiments in the laboratory and field investigations have demonstrated conclusively that obstructions in a river channel tend "to distort meanders, or to suppress them altogether".[1] But even if we relinquish the long-held idea of an obstacle initiating meandering, we must admit that we do not yet know the cause of river meandering. It would seem that meandering begins as a result of the formation of a series of shallows and deeps, technically known as *riffles* and *pools,* on the bed of the river. But why the channel bed should be deformed into a sequence of pools and riffles, and why and how they cause a stream to swing from side to side is not understood (Fig. 81).

Although meanders are associated with level floodplains, it should be emphasised that meanders are not the result of the slowing down of rivers on the gradually decreasing downstream gradient. We must dispense with the idea that meanders are necessarily related to, or are a response to, level floodplains of imperceptible gradient and to low velocities of flow.

The meander-wavelength, that is the distance between the crests of two adjacent loops, is approximately ten times the width of river bed. Meanders, once initiated, tend to enlarge themselves by eroding their outer banks; but there appears to be a limit to this process of enlargement for many meanders exhibit stability or, in other words, they seem to reach a stage where the loops practically cease to grow any larger. Alternatively, the process of growth is brought to an end by the loops being cut off. The neck between two particular loops becomes progressively narrowed until, in time of spate, the river breaches the neck, erodes itself a new channel, and so leads to the loop being cut off. The short-circuiting of loops in this fashion causes most of the water to flow by the new direct route with very little of the water passing round the old meander loop. A cut-off meander quickly loses contact with the new channel, for its ends soon become blocked up by deposits of sand and shingle. The horseshoe-shaped remnant, sealed off from the main stream, forms an *oxbow lake* or *mortlake* ("dead" lake). Slowly, due to the growth of reeds and other plants, the slumping

---

[1] Dury, *op. cit.,* p. 27.

of the banks, and evaporation, the lake becomes filled in and disappears although a scar may be left on the landscape indicating its former presence (Fig. 82).

(A) POOL-AND-RIFFLE SEQUENCE IN A STRAIGHT CHANNEL

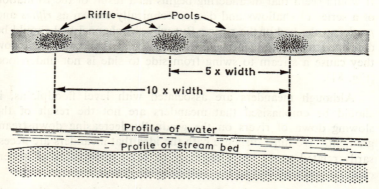

(B) POOL-AND-RIFFLE SEQUENCE IN A MEANDERING CHANNEL

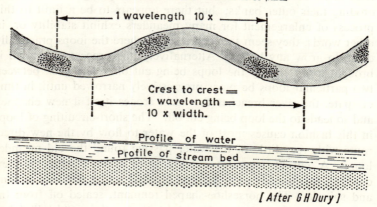

[After G H Dury]

Fig. 81.

A shows the occurrence of pools and riffles and the deformation of the stream bed in a straight channel; B shows the pool-and-riffle sequence in a sinuous channel.

River Terraces

Floodplains may be defined as the flat, or evenly and gently sloping, floors of valleys cut by the lateral erosion of meander-trains as they migrate downstream. The floor is covered by a thin veneer of alluvium deposited when the stream overflows its banks while the floodplain itself is bounded on either side by bluffs. When uplift takes place, the activity of the river will be changed; the river will begin downward cutting again in an attempt to reach its base level. This process of rejuvenation will lead to the river

FORMATION OF A CUT-OFF

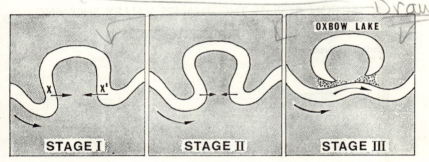

Fig. 82.

The diagram shows the three stages in the formation of a cut-off or oxbow. As the current is attacking the steep concave banks at X and X', the bends gradually approach each other until only narrow "swan's necks" divide them. In floodtime the streams cut across these necks carving out new channels and so shortening the stream's course. The former bends are now abandoned and the deposition of alluvium leads to them being cut off completely.

carving out a new floodplain within its already existing floodplain thereby producing a step-like effect or terrace on either side of the river. The steps on either side now form the bluff lines of the new floodplain. Gradually this new floodplain will be widened by the lateral erosion of the meandering river resulting in the cutting back of the terrace. Along some stretches the terrace may be completely eroded away, so that the terrace no longer forms a continuous shelf but consists instead of a series of apron-like extensions projecting from the original bluff line along the length of the river (see Fig. 78, p. 213).

Paired Terraces

Should further rejuvenation occur, the process will be repeated and a further pair of terraces (lying at a lower level than the first pair) will be produced. A whole series of "paired" terraces may be produced within a river valley. Note that the highest terrace is always the oldest; furthermore, the bluff lines of the uppermost terraces will be much less distinct and cliff-like than the lower ones since they are older and have been subjected to weathering and consequent degrading for a longer period. The height of one terrace above another varies: frequently the difference is only a

SECTION ACROSS THE THAMES VALLEY SHOWING RIVER TERRACES

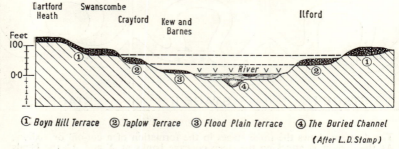

① *Boyn Hill Terrace*   ② *Taplow Terrace*   ③ *Flood Plain Terrace*   ④ *The Buried Channel*

(*After L. D. Stamp*)

Fig. 83.
Compare this with Fig. 78 on p. 213.

matter of a few feet but some terraces may lie 50 or even more feet above their neighbours. Also, it is often possible to correlate the terraces along a valley side with the corresponding knickpoints in the long profile of the river.

Terraces are common features of river valleys. They are particularly well-developed along the Rhine in its rift-valley section and are readily distinguishable along the Wye, the Severn, and the Thames. In the lower Thames valley around London the floodplain reaches a width of about 3 miles; this is bounded by the lower or Taplow terrace which lies some 50 feet above the present floodplain. The upper or Boyn Hill terrace lying at about 100 feet above the present floodplain, or 50 feet higher than the Taplow

UNPAIRED   TERRACES

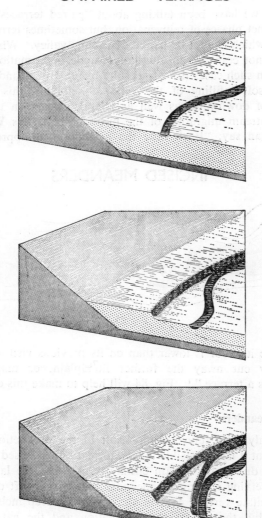

(After Cotton)

Fig. 84.

terrace, is distinguishable at Clapham Common where patches of the terrace gravels are found.

So far we have been talking about "paired terraces" resulting from distinct phases of rejuvenation, but sometimes terraces are to be found which cannot be paired across the valley. Where terrace levels do not coincide an alternative mode of formation must be sought. In such cases the terraces are formed by meanders cutting into the soft infilling of the valley floodplain; this implies a measure of downward, as well as lateral, cutting on the part of the downstream migration of the meander belt. As Wooldridge and Morgan say: "Each time the meander belt approaches the

INCISED MEANDERS

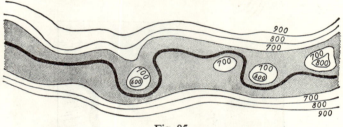

Fig. 85.

valley side its floor is lower than on its previous visit and it may completely cut away the former floodplain, or may leave a remnant as a terrace."[1]   Fig. 84 will help to make this clear.

Incised Meanders

Not only does rejuvenation result in the production of river terraces, but it is responsible for the formation of incised meanders. These are due to the stream cutting deeply into the land surface while preserving its original meander pattern. Uplift of the land will resuscitate vertical erosion and cause the deep incising of the channel; but the degree of rejuvenation and the nature of the valley floor lead to two recognisably different types of incision.

[1] *Geomorphology*, p. 226.

Where relatively quick uplift takes place, and where the rocks are relatively soft, vertical erosion will proceed at a rapid pace and the meanders will become entrenched between steep-sided, symmetrical slopes to produce *entrenched meanders*. If, on the other hand, uplift is only slight and gradual, and the rocks of the valley floor are resistant, the down-cutting takes places more slowly and there is time for the shifting meanders to undertake a certain

INGROWN AND ENTRENCHED MEANDERS

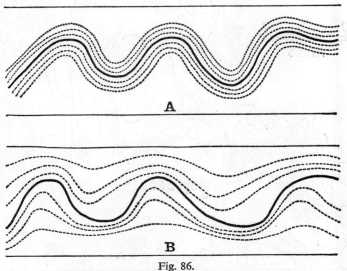

Fig. 86.
A shows entrenched meanders; *B* ingrown meanders.

amount of lateral erosion. In this case the meanders are said to be *ingrown* and their enclosing slopes show pronounced asymmetry of cross profile. Ingrown meanders produce wider and more open valleys with spurs or slip-off slopes projecting into the river loops (Fig. 86).

Excellent examples of incised meanders are to be found along the River Dee in the vicinity of Llangollen, along the River Wye, and on the Wear at Durham. Fig. 87 illustrates the incised meanders of the River Dordogne. It also shows some abandoned meanders, now lying high and dry above the present river bed. Some very fine incised meanders are also to be found along the Meuse as it flows through the Ardennes and in the valleys of other rivers of the Central Massif in France.

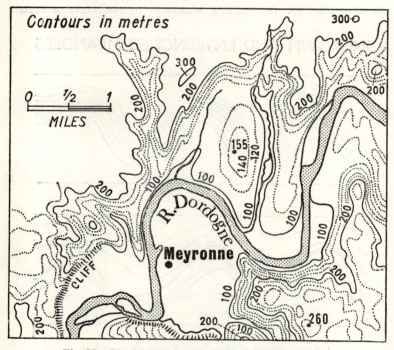

Fig. 87. Incised Meanders on the River Dordogne.

Note the incised meanders of the Dordogne; also the abandoned hanging meander with its two remnant streams. Similar features are to be found on the Wye in Herefordshire and on the Dee near Llangollen.

Braiding

Braiding is the term used to describe the sub-division of a stream channel through the building up of islands. The plaiting effect produced by well-developed branching is sometimes called *anastomosing drainage*. Braiding is initiated by the creation within the river channel of a bank composed of sand and gravel which grows, partly through increasing deposition and partly through the deepening of the channel on either side of it, into an island known as an *ait, ayot,* or *eyot.*

It would seem that braided channels are associated with heavy loads of sediment and with river banks that are extremely easily eroded. If the banks are weak and readily erodible the river is enabled to widen its channel; this, in turn, leads to the shallowing

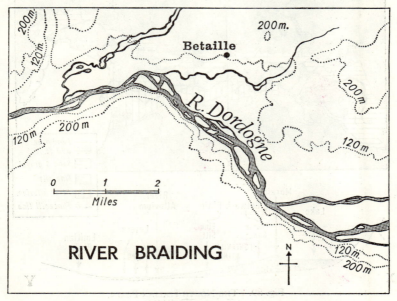

Fig. 88.

of the stream. And with the widening and shallowing of the channel the material on the stream bed becomes more susceptible to disturbance and is shaped into banks of sand and gravel.

Many rivers in their lower courses, especially if they are carrying heavy loads of sediment, show a tendency to braid. The Amazon, Mississippi, and Brahmaputra provide particularly fine examples of braiding on a very large scale. Fig. 88 shows braiding on the River Dordogne, Plate VIII braiding on the River Rakaia in S.I., New Zealand.

Alluvial Fans and Cones

At the break of slope where streams from hill country enter a main valley or plain, the change in gradient—from steep to gentle—causes the streams to jettison some of their load and aprons of gravel, sand, and alluvium are built up. Such fan-shaped masses of accumulated material form *alluvial fans*. Frequently they

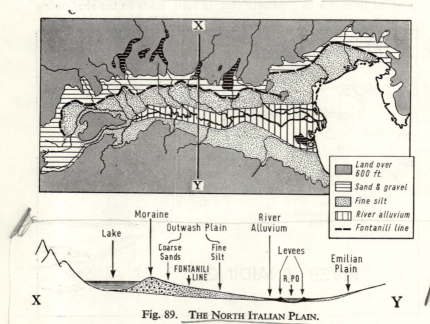

Fig. 89.   THE NORTH ITALIAN PLAIN.

Note: (i) the dry zone of sands and gravels bordering the Alpine foothills; (ii) the line of springs (*fontanili*) at the juncture of the sands and gravels with the fine silt zone; and (iii) the moist alluvial belt immediately adjacent to the River Po.

form the sites of villages as in the case of some of the settlements in Swaledale and Wharfedale in Yorkshire, or in the Rhône valley. An interesting case is provided by the English Lake District where mountain streams falling steeply into the valley containing Lakes Bassenthwaite and Derwentwater built up a series of alluvial fans which eventually coalesced to form a lake delta-flat; this divided the original lake which occupied the valley into two giving the present-day Lakes of Bassenthwaite and Derwentwater. An interesting result of the creation of a series of fans is to be found in the Plain of Lombardy. The rivers issuing from the Alpine valleys have built up a series of broad fans which have had the effect of pushing the main drainage line of the Po southwards. On the southern flanks of the Plain, the streams flowing from the Apennines are smaller and their fans are narrower; hence the Po lies south of the median line of the Plain (Fig. 89).

In some cases as, for example, where a stream occupies a hanging valley and falls abruptly to the flat trough-floor of a glaciated valley, or where, as in semi-arid areas, ephemeral torrents flow in wadis, the deposits of detritus may adopt a cone-like form with slopes as steep as 30 degrees. To these deposits which have a high angle of slope the term *alluvial cone* is preferred. Sometimes the terms fan and cone are used interchangeably, but it is desirable to draw a distinction between the two and to reserve fan for a low-angled deposit and cone for a high-angled deposit. Characteristically, both fans and cones are composed of coarse materials, but there is a graduation in the arrangement of the material, the coarser matter lying at the apex of the deposit, the finer at the edge. An alluvial fan which will ultimately build up into an alluvial cone is illustrated in Plate V.

Deltas

The mechanical load of a river is deposited (*a*) temporarily, either on floodplains or in lakes, to be subsequently removed, and (*b*) finally at the river mouth producing estuarine banks or deltas. Estuarine banks are merely the prelude to the formation of deltas. G. H. Dury has said: "The usual contrast of deltas with estuaries should be discarded . . . the essential difference between an estuary and a delta is that an estuary has not yet been filled in by sediment, and that sedimentary deposits have not yet begun to project seaward on the coast." [1]

A number of conditions or factors predispose towards the deposition of deltaic sediments: (i) the amount and rate of supply of sediment; (ii) the depth of the water at the mouth of the river

[1] *Op. cit.*, p. 20.

(or of the lake in the case of lake deltas); (iii) the rate of sub-sidence of the sea floor (or, on the other hand, the rise in sea level); (iv) the strength and velocity of waves and currents; and (v) tidal range and influence. These factors help to control the shape, areal extent, and volume of deltaic deposits.

A number of misconceptions with respect to the formation of deltas need to be disposed of. First, the idea that lakes or dams along a river's course will check delta formation cannot be sub-stantiated. Second, long plain courses and sluggish flow are not necessary conditions for deltaic formation—think of the short, torrential streams which descend from the Western Ghats in India but which have built up deltas. Third, and perhaps most wide-spread, is the erroneous idea that for successful delta formation the river must debouch into a sea which has little or no tide. While it is true that the absence of tides facilitates deltaic formation, it is not true to say that deltas will not form where tidal ranges are great. Tidal ranges of 25-30 feet occur at the head of the Gulf of California but these have not prevented the formation of the Colorado delta. Again, spring tides in the delta of the Irrawaddy range up to 18 feet. Obviously, then, it is possible for deltas to form in seas which have high tidal ranges. All that appears to be necessary for delta-building is an excess of deposition over removal.[1]

As a river enters the sea its velocity is checked and its load of sediment is released: first, its traction load of sand, gravel, and pebbles is tipped and then its suspended load of fine silt is deposited. Deposition of the suspended matter is assisted by the flocculation or coagulation of the fine particles of clay when they come into contact with salt water. The subaqueous portion of the delta, which slopes gently downwards in a concave slope, con-tains marine deposits as well as fluviatile deposits. The subaerial surface which is level is essentially a continuation of the alluvial deposits of the river floodplain. The upper surface of the delta is extended both seawards and laterally by the continuing bifurca-tion of the distributaries caused by developing mud-banks and the slowly rising surface of the delta.

[1] *The Face of the Earth*, Pelican Book, 1959, p. 106.

Here we cannot go into much detail of the structure of deltas, but a brief mention may be made. Delta structure refers to the sets of beds which are distinguishable within the delta formation; these are threefold:

(i) the *bottomset beds* which lie furthest seaward are roughly horizontal and are composed of the finer detrital matter which has been carried in suspension beyond the delta slope before beginning to sink to the sea bed;

(ii) the *foreset beds* composed of the coarser material moved by traction along the stream bed and successively tipped seawards to produce the progressively advancing front or face of the delta; and

TOPSET, FORESET AND BOTTOMSET BEDS

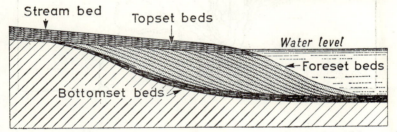

Fig. 90.

(iii) the *topset beds* which lie gently inclined upon the foreset beds and which are to be thought of as a continuation of the alluvial deposits of the river plain (Fig. 90).

This tripartite structure is clearly discernible in lake deltas, but in sea deltas there is often a departure from this "ideal" structure due to the variable conditions of water depth, waves, and currents.

It is possible to distinguish several varieties of delta shape, but broadly there are four main types:

(i) the *estuarine* type, *e.g.* the Rhine, the Susquehanna, where infilling of an estuary occurs but where the delta front does not extend beyond the general line of the coast; this type may be thought of as the delta in embryo;

(ii) the *arcuate* or *fan-shaped* type, *e.g.* the Nile, Rhône, and

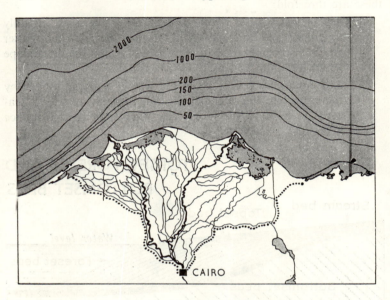

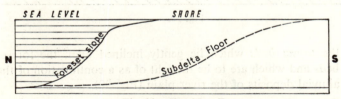

Fig. 91.　The Nile Delta.

The Nile empties itself into the Mediterranean by means of two main distributaries but the entire area of the delta is seamed with watercourses which serve as irrigation channels.　Note how the alluvial deposits are continued off-shore and how they have built up a great submarine platform.

Indus, which with its triangular shape and bow front is usually taken to express the true delta form;

(iii) the *cuspate* type which is shaped or pointed like a tooth, *e.g.* the Tiber and the Ebro;

(iv) the *bird's-foot type* which has a digital or pronged form; this type which is rather unusual and best exemplified by

TYPES OF DELTA

ESTUARINE : Rhine

ARCUATE: Niger

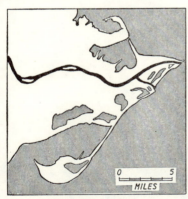

CUSPATE: Ebro

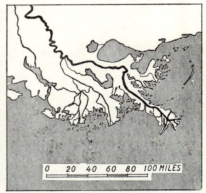

BIRD'S FOOT: Mississippi

Fig. 92.

the Mississippi seems to owe its origin to excessive amounts of silt being brought down and building natural levees along the bifurcating channel edges.

The vast accumulations of deltaic material are apt to cause the underlying sea floor to sag or become depressed with the result that areas marginal to large deltas also tend to suffer sagging and give rise to embayments and lagoons, *e.g.* Atchafayala Bay and Lake Pontchartrain adjacent to the Mississippi, and the Zuider Zee adjacent to the Rhine.

CHAPTER 13

FROST, GLACIERS, AND ICE ACTION

Frost Action

We have already referred in Chapter 7 to the action of frost in the weathering process. There are, however, some regions in the world where frost is long-continued and occurs with great severity and where its action is more particularly pronounced and effective. These are (a) regions in high latitudes, and (b) mountain areas which rise above the snow line. Some of these regions—most of them in actual fact—suffered glaciation during the Ice Age and many of their physiographical features relate to, and are the result of, that glaciation. But whether or not they were affected in the past, certainly they are being affected at present by frost action.

The effectiveness of frost action is not everywhere alike for the simple reason that a number of variable factors, such as the frequency of freezing, the availability of water, the rock character, etc., are at play. But almost everywhere in these high latitude regions—one might say roughly poleward of the 60° line of latitude—the land surface is subjected to frost attack, often on a severe scale, and that exposed rock surfaces are, either quickly or more slowly, shattered by frost to produce a loose surface cover of rock debris. In many arctic areas the weathering action of frost is so rapid that striations and grooves cut by the former ice-sheets have been practically eliminated. However, it must be borne in mind that areas of permanent freezing do not suffer as much mechanical weathering as do those which are subjected to repeated freeze-thaw action.

The rock structure greatly helps or hinders the work of frost. If, for example, a rock possesses a well-developed joint system, this allows moisture to collect in, or seep through, the joints and this, in turn, allows frost wedging to take place; the water freezes, expands, and the blocks of rock are prized apart. There are many examples of areas littered by small and large angular boulders, the

237

relics of frost wedging; such rock-strewn areas are termed *felsen-meer* (literally a "sea of rocks").   Such boulders, weathered from

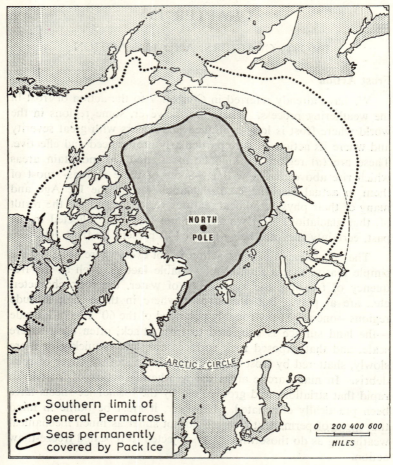

NORTH POLE

ARCTIC CIRCLE

····· Southern limit of
····· general Permafrost

Seas permanently
covered by Pack Ice

0   200 400 600
MILES

Fig. 93.   REGIONS OF PERMAFROST.

the bedrock, are of course, in turn, broken up and progressively
reduced in size through continued frost attack.

There are extensive areas suffering from the condition known as
permafrost, i.e. permanently frozen ground (Fig. 93).   Although the

upper or surface layers of the soil may thaw out seasonally, the sub-soil may remain permanently frozen. The presence of permafrost is likely to lead to the waterlogging of the surface layers, since the water resulting from the summer melt is unable to escape. Most of the boggy, marshy tracts of arctic regions are due to the permafrost condition. The waterlogging of the surface layers greatly assists mass wasting, especially solifluction or soil flowage since the saturated mantle is enabled to glide over the underlying frozen layer. Such soil flow is a common feature of high latitudes but it also

STONE POLYGONS AND STRIPES

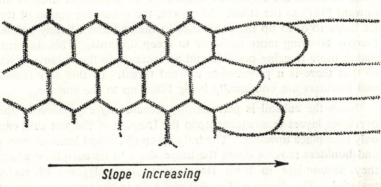

Slope increasing

Fig. 94

Stone polygons, nets, and stripes are thought to be due to freeze-thaw processes but there is no certainty about their exact mode of origin.

occurs in the alpine areas of middle and lower latitudes. Solifluction deposits can be seen draping many mountain slopes.

Physiographic Features

A variety of distinctive physiographic features result from frost action. Especially interesting are the remarkable polygonal structures and mounds which are to be seen in the tundra lands and the adjacent northern boreal regions. Both appear to be closely associated with frost action.

The unusual polygonal patterns (Fig. 94) appear to be formed as a result of the expansion and contraction which takes place consequent upon freezing and thawing. The details of the complex processes which produce these polygonal patterns are not fully understood. It is suggested that the structures are brought about in the following way. Where thawed-out mud or morainic debris lies cn top of permafrost conditions are suitable for the uplift and sorting of stones. Stones, as any gardener knows, have an annoying habit of working their way up to the surface. This is due to the differences between their thermal properties and those of the soil in which they are embedded. Now it appears that when freezing is in progress the under surface of a stone is chilled more rapidly than is the surrounding soil. Ice thus forms beneath the stone first and the expansion caused by ice formation imparts an upward "lift" to the stone. Moreover, the expansive action of the ice helps to open up the capillaries in the soil immediately below, thereby allowing more moisture to creep upwards. This, in turn, makes more freezing possible and an increase in the volume of ice so that there is a progressive upward thrust. In this way stones and boulders are continually being lifted up to the surface.

Since the subsoil is permanently frozen, any expansion of the overlying layers (consequent upon the freezing of the wet soil) can only take place upwards. The bulging-up of the soil leads to stones and boulders moving down the bulge slope to its periphery where they accumulate to form rings, or rather polygons, of rocky material. The diagram (Fig. 95) will help in the understanding of what happens. It is interesting to note that *stone polygons* of this kind may be observed in the English Lake District. In addition to the stone polygons there are also *mud polygons* which are found in areas of fine-grained soil.

The lifting up of the soil or debris cover through the freezing of moisture and its attendant expansion is known as frost-heaving. The lifting of lawns in winter as a result of the action of frost is a small-scale demonstration of this process. In tundra lands, however, quite large mounds, often termed "blisters", result from frost-heaving.

Another interesting surface feature found in the tundra lands is the *pingo*. Pingos are larger than the surface swelling we have just referred to: some of them are over 100 feet high and several hundreds of feet in diameter (Fig. 96). These features, sometimes technically referred to as *hydro-laccoliths,* appear to have been formed when ground water becomes trapped between an underlying

DIAGRAM ILLUSTRATING
FORMATION OF POLYGONS

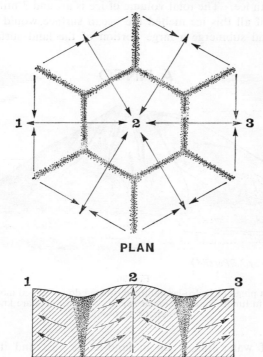

PLAN

ELEVATION

(After A. Holmes)

Fig. 95.

The diagrams (upper, plan; lower, elevation) illustrate the formation, in an idealised way, of stone polygons.

layer of permafrost and an overlying layer of frozen ground. When this trapped water freezes, it expands and lifts up the overlying frozen layer. Some of these pingos have crater-like summits and some even carry shallow lakes during the summer season in these summit depressions.

Ice Cover, Past and Present

Six million square miles of the earth's surface is permanently covered with ice. The total volume of ice is around 7 million cubic miles and if all this ice melted the ocean surface would rise some 150 feet and submerge a large portion of the land surface. The

(From a photo by A.E.Porsild)

Fig. 96.

A sketch of a pingo or hydro-laccolith, an isolated dome-shaped mound of earth often found in tundra lands. Similar smaller scale features are known as frost blisters or ice mounds.

amount of water locked up in land-ice is vast and it has been estimated that the melting of the Antarctic ice cap alone would provide sufficient water to maintain the flow of all the world's rivers for nearly a millenium. These facts indicate that the amount of water locked up in the earth's ice caps is large compared with that in the world's rivers. Fig. 97 shows the area in the northern hemisphere under ice at present and during the Ice Age.

Not so very long ago, geologically speaking, ice covered much larger areas of the earth's surface than it does to-day. Periodically throughout geological times there have been Ice Ages. The last, the Pleistocene, is estimated to have begun over one million years ago and is generally considered to have lasted until about 10,000 years ago.   Some would say we are at the tail-end of the last phase of the Great Ice Age and that the ice-sheets which linger in both hemispheres are the remnants of the former much more extensive ice caps.   The fact that the ice-sheets and glaciers are almost everywhere in retreat lends credence to this idea.

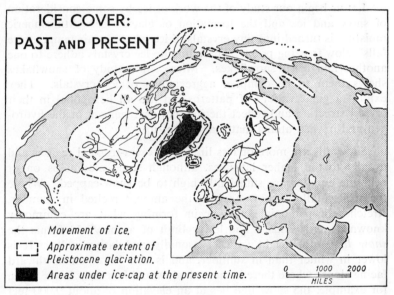

Fig. 97.

Extensive continental areas, mainly based on the ancient shield areas, were covered by ice during the Pleistocene age.   To-day, with the exception of Greenland and Antarctica, only a few small areas are under permanent ice.

We can only surmise what the earth was like during the Great Ice Age.   But by studying the present-day ice-sheets and the glaciers of mountainous regions we are able to gain a fairly complete picture of the character and behaviour of past glaciation.   The knowledge gained from such studies can be applied to those areas which we know to have been glaciated in the past and from this it is possible to reconstruct the conditions of the Ice Age, to work out the sequence of events, and to explain the topographic and drainage features which have resulted. There can be no doubt that the effects of glaciation on the landscape have been considerable; furthermore, the effects of ice action on human activities have been far-reaching.[1]

SNOW AND ICE

Let us begin our study of the work of ice by some consideration of snow and ice and the formation of glacier ice. Atmospheric moisture is turned into tiny crystals of ice when the air temperature falls below freezing point. These minute ice crystals adhere to one another and form snowflakes. Microscopic study of snowflakes shows them to be complex aggregations of ice crystals. They exhibit a great variety of patterns but are all hexagonal in their crystal structure and reflect the internal arrangement of the hydrogen and oxygen atoms that make them up.

Snowfalls are more or less limited to extra-tropical regions and usually to the higher latitudes, although some mountains on or near the equator are sufficiently high to be snow-capped. Where the winter fall of snow exceeds the amount melted in summer, stretches of perennial snow occur forming what are commonly known as *snowfields*. The lower limit of a snowfield forms the *snow line*. Its height varies seasonally and latitudinally. It is lower in winter than in summer, and is also lower on northward facing slopes where there is more shadow and less sun; in the Alps, for example, the snow line lies at an elevation of about 9,000 feet on the southern side with its sun-facing aspect, but at about 8,000 feet on the northern slopes. Some mountains in equatorial latitudes are of sufficient altitude to have snow on their summits, and in the case of the East African mountains, Kilimanjaro and Kenya, the snow line reaches down from about 18,000 to 16,000 feet. The highest snow lines occur in the tropical "dry" zones, *i.e.* between 20 and 30 degrees North and South of the equator; here they lie higher than 20,000 feet. As one proceeds polewards the snow line,

---

[1] It is worth noting that there is a school of thought which believes in the protective function of ice. It is argued that when the land was blanketed by ice, the surface was thereby protected from the normal processes of weathering and erosion. This idea, however, has never achieved wide support.

generally speaking, becomes lower and in polar regions it reaches down to sea level.

Fresh snow falls and accumulates as a light, fluffy, and easily moved mass, but after it has lain on the ground for some time it changes its physical character; it becomes compacted, heavier, and granular and in this state it is known as *névé* or *firn*. The transformation of snow into névé is the result of several processes—sublimation, compaction, melting, and re-freezing, etc. In the process of sublimation (the changing of solid material into its gaseous state without first becoming a liquid) molecules of water vapour escape from the edges of the snowflakes; some of these molecules attach themselves to the centre of the snowflakes with the result that the individual flakes begin to grow in size and to become more tightly packed together. This process is helped by the pressure which is exerted by new overlying falls of snow. The increasing pressure causes some of the ice particles to melt; the melt-water trickles downwards through the accumulated snow and then refreezes, so that the tiny ice granules become more closely welded together. In this state the ice is known as firn. Finally, continued pressure causes most of the air existing between the ice granules to be expelled so that the granules become even more closely locked together. When the ice has reached the stage where it has become changed into a true solid state composed of interlocking ice crystals, it is said to form glacier ice, which is normally opaque and of a blue-grey colour.

CLASSIFICATION OF GLACIER ICE

It is usual to classify masses of glacier ice into (i) valley glaciers, (ii) piedmont glaciers, and (iii) ice-sheets and caps.

(i) *Valley glaciers.* These are streams of ice and, as such, they behave in many respects like rivers of water. Originating in névé fields, the ice flows downslope by the easiest routes, which are along the valleys. Like rivers, glaciers vary in their width, depth, length, and speed of flow. Glaciers may be as much as 100 miles in length; the Jacobshavn Glacier in Greenland is 5 miles wide at its mouth. Normally, glaciers move only slowly, a matter of a few inches or a few feet a day, although under the rather exceptional conditions in

Greenland, glaciers there are known to move as much as 50 feet a day.[1] The rate of movement depends upon a variety of factors, including the steepness of the slope, the amount of friction presented by the channel, the constriction of the valley, the thickness and temperature of the ice, and the degree of pressure from the icefield above.

MALASPINA GLACIER

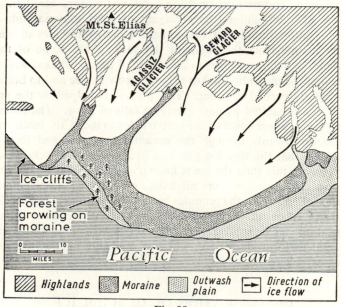

Fig. 98.

Malaspina Glacier is a piedmont glacier covering 800 square miles. Note the trees which have grown in the soil on the stagnant ice.

(ii) *Piedmont glaciers.* These are formed by the union of several valley glaciers. As the latter emerge from their valleys they spread out on to the lower ground and coalesce to form an apron of ice. Because piedmont glaciers cover a broad lowland, but are fed by valley glaciers, they move extremely slowly. Piedmont glaciers vary widely in size, but some are very extensive, such as the

[1] These glaciers are impelled along by the tremendous pressure exerted by the Greenland ice-sheet.

Malaspina Glacier in Alaska which is 70 miles across, about 1,000 feet thick, and covers an overall area of some 800 square miles. Its outer margin is so thickly covered with morainic debris that pine forests are growing above the glacier (Fig. 98).

(iii) *Ice-sheets.* These cover vaster areas; they may be defined as broad or extensive accumulations of glacier ice which tend to spread radially outwards under their own weight. The larger ice spreads, such as those covering Antarctica and Greenland, are usually termed continental ice-sheets; more localised sheets, such as occur in Iceland and Norway, are sometimes called ice caps. Vatnajokull in Iceland, which is the largest ice-sheet outside Greenland and the Polar Regions, is an ice cap of some 7,500 square miles in extent and about 750 feet thick. But this is puny beside the ice-sheet which covers the whole of Greenland apart from a narrow coastal fringe and which is at least 700,000 square miles in area and which, as seismic tests have shown, is in places as much as 8,000 feet in thickness.

CHARACTERISTICS OF VALLEY GLACIERS

A valley glacier is a slowly moving mass of ice which descends from a snowfield, its source of origin, downslope across the snow line to the point where, as a result of evaporation and melting, the tongue of the glacier can proceed no further. Broadly speaking, a glacier may be said to have three main sections: (i) an area of accumulation or nourishment; (ii) an area of transit; and (iii) an area of wastage or ablation.

The source of origin is the snowfield and icefield above the permanent snow line. The seat of accumulation is usually a semi-circular basin. As we have already noted, seasonal snows collect here and in time become consolidated into névé which, in turn, produces the glacier ice of which the glacier stream is composed. An interesting feature in these collecting grounds is the deep, vertical crack or crevasse which develops between the steep basin wall and the mass of snow-covered ice within the basin. This curving crevasse is known as the *bergschrund* (German) or, much less frequently, the *rimaye* (French). Its formation is probably due in part to the downstream flow and pull of the ice and in part to local melting at the point of contact with the rock face. In winter the

bergschrund is usually filled with snow but in summer it becomes
a yawning chasm which may be up to 200 feet deep (Fig. 99).

DETAIL OF BERGSCHRUND

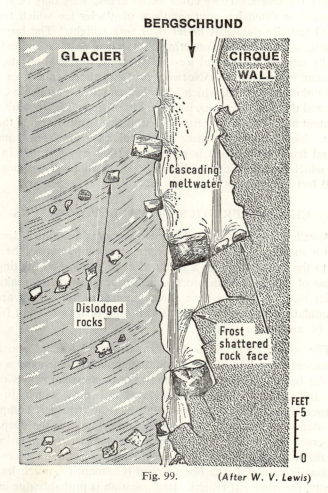

BERGSCHRUND

GLACIER

CIRQUE WALL

Cascading meltwater

Dislodged rocks

Frost shattered rock face

FEET
5

0

Fig. 99.   (*After W. V. Lewis*)

As the ice mass begins to move downslope its surface begins to
split and crack; such openings are called *crevasses*. These appear

to be due to differential movement within the ice which causes shearing and shattering of the upper part of the glacier. Crevasses may be transverse or longitudinal. The former develop wherever the bed steepens; the latter wherever the glacier widens. Crevasses also often develop along the margins of the glacier because of the difference in the rate of movement of the ice near to the valley wall and in the middle of the glacier. Crevasses are often divided by steep ridges of ice known as *seracs*. The combination of crevasses

LONG PROFILE OF A GLACIER

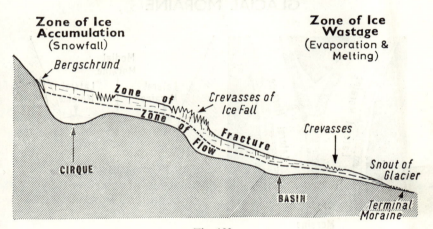

Fig. 100.

A glacier has many features comparable to those found along a river; the ice fall is the equivalent of the waterfall, broken crevassed sections are the equivalent of rapids.

and seracs makes the crossing of a glacier an extremely difficult and dangerous business. Just as waterfalls occur on streams where there is an abrupt change in slope, so *ice falls* are developed where there is a change in the steepness of the gradient followed by the glacier. Ice falls show a tangled mass of deep crevasses and sharp ice ridges or pinnacles. Another feature of glacier surfaces is the *moulin*, a pipe or kind of sink-hole worn out by surface melt-water swirling down cracks in the ice and fashioning a circular opening.

During its journey down the valley the glacier grinds, tears, and plucks at the bedrock with which it comes into contact. Rock fragments which split off the valley walls as a result of frost weathering roll on to the glacier and are carried along by it. All the material worn away by and collected by the ice is termed *moraine*. The glacier, especially along its flanks where it comes into contact with the valley walls, becomes heavily charged with rock fragments thereby discolouring the ice. Such lateral "stripes" are known as *lateral moraine*. When two valley glaciers coalesce, the inner lateral moraines unite and move along the centre axis of the glacier below the junction forming *medial moraines*. It may

GLACIAL MORAINE

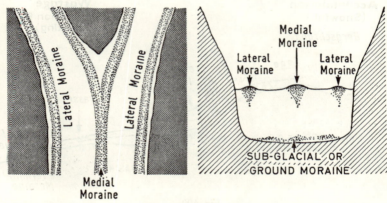

Fig. 101.

The left-hand diagram shows the stripes made by surface moraine on the glacier. The right-hand diagram is a cross-section of a glacier showing the disposition of moraine within the glacier.

happen that a trunk glacier receives many tributaries during its course in which case it will have many medial moraines. It should be noted that these morainic stripings are not just superficial but extend deeply into the glacier. Material swept along the valley floor by the moving ice is called *sub-glacial moraine* (Fig. 101).

Finally, there is a good deal of water circulating on, in, and under the ice. Streams on the surface are called *super-glacial streams,* those within the ice *englacial streams,* and those underneath the glacier *sub-glacial streams.*

When a glacier passes the snow line it enters its area or zone of wastage; in other words, it begins to waste away. Wastage occurs as a result of, first, evaporation and, second, melting; the combined process is sometimes referred to as *ablation*. Whether a glacier advances or retreats depends upon its rate of nourishment and wastage: if the former is the greater, then the ice front will advance; if wastage is greater than nourishment, the glacier will retreat. If the rate of nourishment balances the rate of wastage, a state of equilibrium will be achieved and, accordingly, the ice front will remain stationary. In practice glaciers seldom remain in a stable condition for a long time but if the ice front is stationary for a period a crescentic mound or *terminal moraine* will form at the glacier's end or *snout*. The general condition, the world over, is for glaciers to retreat. This retreat has been going on for a century but the rate of retreat appears to have been speeded up during the past three or four decades. Glaciers are useful indicators of climatic change.

CHARACTERISTICS OF CONTINENTAL GLACIERS

The great ice-sheets which cover Antarctica and Greenland are called continental ice-sheets because of their vast dimensions. The Antarctic ice-sheet covers some 5 million square miles; the Greenland ice-sheet, though much less in size, has an area of nearly 700,000 square miles or roughly ten times the area of England and Wales.

Eighty-five per cent. of Greenland's area is covered permanently with ice. Throughout the interior the ice is mostly over 6,000 feet thick, and in places recent seismic soundings suggest that the depth of the ice may be as much as 10,000 feet. The central part of Greenland appears to be depressed and to lie below sea level; it may well be that the land surface has sagged under the enormous weight of this huge mass of ice. Near the coasts, where the ice is thinner, there are mountain ranges. Their steep slopes and exposure to high winds keep parts of them free from permanent snow. Mountain summits which rise up amidst the encircling snows like islands in the sea are called *nunataks*. The ice-sheet spills through the rocky mountain rim and splits up into valley glaciers which descend very often directly to the sea, forming what are known as "tidewater glaciers". Except in the south-west, where nowadays most of the glaciers terminate before reaching the sea, Greenland's numerous glaciers calve icebergs in summer which are carried southwards into the North Atlantic by the Labrador and East Greenland currents. One of the most spectacular of Greenland's glaciers is the Humboldt Glacier in the north-west; it ends in a mighty rampart of 300-ft high cliffs which stretch for a distance of 40 miles (Fig. 102).

The Antarctic ice-sheet is the world's largest; it must bear some resemblance to the great ice-sheets which covered the Canadian and Fennoscandian Shields in former geological times (see p. 258). The greater part of the Antarctic continent[1] stands above the snow line and, apart from the higher areas of coastal mountains, the whole of it is buried under a vast accumulation of ice and snow. How long Antarctica has been under its mantle of snow and ice is unknown, but certainly it has not always been covered. The accumulated ice takes the form of a huge flattened dome. Fed annually by snows, the ice flows generally outwards, pieces breaking off at the edges to float away as icebergs in the Southern Ocean. "In the Ross Sea the main sheet is extended into the great ice platform of the Ross Barrier, which is at least partly afloat and rises and falls with the tide. The Barrier appears to be mainly self-nourished, largely no doubt by snowfall on its surface, but also perhaps in part by the freezing of sea water on to its base in winter. The occurrence of seafloor muds lying undisturbed on its surface, which have apparently worked their way up through the ice, suggests that this mechanism may make a major contribution to maintaining the Barrier. Seawards the Barrier terminates in huge ice-cliffs, from which fragments periodically break away as tabular icebergs."[2]

The polar plateau ascending to 9,000 feet has most of the features of the Greenland ice-sheet: nunataks, crevasses, and hard snow ridges, rucked-up by the winds, which are known as *sastrugi.*

[1] How far Antarctica comprises a single land mass is not known. Recent geophysical exploration suggests that Antarctica may consist of a series of mountain ridges with the intervening areas beneath sea level.

[2] R. F. Peel, *Physical Geography,* English Universities Press, 1952, p. 131.

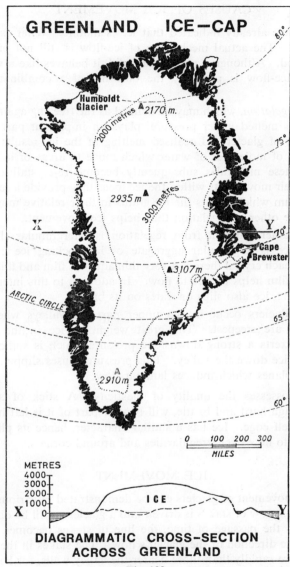

Fig. 102.

The map shows extent of Greenland which is under ice cover. The cross-section shows, in an approximate way, the profile and depth of the ice cover.

CAUSES OF ICE MOVEMENT

We have already indicated that ice is mobile. What causes it to move? The actual mechanism of ice-flow is still not properly understood. Although a crystalline solid, it behaves like a viscous liquid. Ice-flow is probably the outcome of a combination of factors.

(i) *Regelation,* which may be defined as the freezing again of ice which has melted under pressure, plays an important part in the behaviour of glaciers. Localised melting of the ice results in the liberation of molecules of water which move to areas of less pressure. These molecules subsequently become re-crystallised, but during their movements within the ice mass they provide a lubricating medium which assists the ice-grains in their relative movement one to the other. Regelation thus helps ice movement.

(ii) Rather different from regelation is intergranular slipping. Glacier ice is a granular aggregate of interlocking ice crystals. Between each crystal there is a very thin aqueous film and this intergranular film helps the ice to flow. In addition to this intergranular slipping, ice also slips or slides on its base.

(iii) Glaciers occur in the upper parts of valleys where the gradients are steepest. The great weight of ice in the higher reaches exerts a strong downslope pressure which is sufficient to push the ice down the valley. This pressure causes slipping along fracture planes which induces laminar flow.

Ice possesses the quality of plasticity. A stick of sealing-wax, though hard and brittle, will bend if part of it is left hanging over a shelf edge. Ice has a similar character, hence its plasticity helps ice to flow over irregularities and around corners.

ICE MOVEMENT

The movement of glaciers can be demonstrated in various ways. If a straight row of stakes is driven into a glacier it will be observed that, with the passage of time, the line of stakes becomes visibly bent in the direction of the glacier's flow. The stakes in the centre move more rapidly than those nearer the valley walls, for here friction between the ice and the valley side is greater. Fig. 103 shows the rate of movement of the Rhône glacier during the eight-year period 1874-82. The rock material carried by the ice also provides evidence of movement. If the rocks contained in the ice are examined, it may be found that they differ from those in the adjacent bedrock but can be matched up with those occurring in areas higher up the valley; since their only possible source lies up-stream, it can be concluded that they have been carried by the ice. A macabre bit of evidence of ice-flow was provided by the bodies of two Alpine climbers who fell to their deaths in the deep crevasses of the Bossons

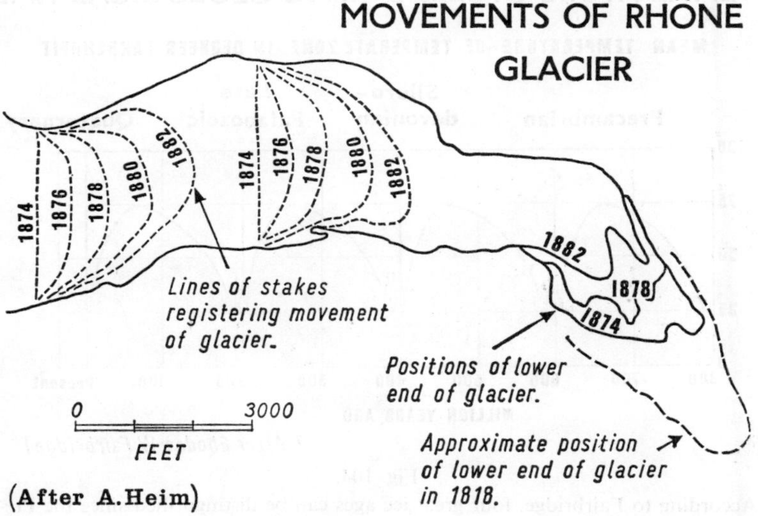
MOVEMENTS OF RHÔNE GLACIER
1874
1876
1878
1880
1882
1874
1876
1878
1880
1882
1882
1878
1874
Lines of stakes registering movement of glacier.
Positions of lower end of glacier.
0
3000
FEET
Approximate position of lower end of glacier in 1818.
(After A.Heim)

Fig. 103.

Glacier, and whose corpses were released forty-one years later at the snout of the glacier several miles down-valley. A further indication of ice movement is provided by the polished, scratched rock floor that is often exposed when a glacier retreats. It can be assumed that this smoothing and grooving of the bedrock was done by the ice as it moved over the valley floor using the rocks it has embedded in it as graving and polishing tools.

Not only does a glacier move but different parts of it move at different rates. We have already mentioned that due to friction with the valley walls, the centre of a glacier travels more quickly than its sides. In this respect a glacier behaves like a river of running water. In like manner, friction with the valley floor causes the surface ice to move more quickly than the bottom ice.

Glaciologists, who have studied the motion of glaciers, distinguish two main zones of movement within a glacier: (i) an upper zone which tends to break and shear and is, therefore, known as the *zone of fracture*, and (ii) a lower zone, which, due to the pressure

TEMPERATURE CYCLES DURING GEOLOGICAL TIME

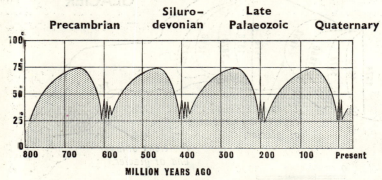

(After Rhodes W. Fairbridge)

Fig. 104.

According to Fairbridge, four great ice ages can be distinguished since the Pre-Cambrian period. Each ice age was separated by a prolonged period when temperatures were much higher and when often, as in Triassic times, dry hot desert conditions prevailed.

of the overlying ice, behaves more after the manner of a plastic substance and so is called the *zone of flow* (Fig. 100).

THE PLEISTOCENE ICE AGE

So far we have been describing the occurrence and characteristics of ice at the present day. Before we proceed to look at the work of ice, it is necessary to refer to the Ice Ages of the past, for these have been responsible for much of the work undertaken by

PLATE XIII

Above: A dry valley in the chalk, near Broad Chalke, Wiltshire. (*Eric Kay.*)

Below: The Aletsch Glacier, Switzerland. This river of ice is fed by the snows which fall on the mountains of the Jungfrau area. The dark marks on the glacier surface are moraine. (*Eric Kay.*)

PLATE XIV

Above: U-shaped valley, Videsaeter, Vestlandet, Norway. Glacial erosion deepens, widens, and straightens V-shaped river valleys to give a characteristic U-shape as in Hjelledal Valley shown here or in the famous Lauterbrunnen Valley in Switzerland. (*Eric Kay*.)

Below: Glaciated landscape, Molde, in Norway. Note the accordant summit levels of the peaks, the cirques, aretes, and hanging valleys, the waterfalls pitching down the steep slopes and the fan which is being built out into the fiord. (*Bergen Line*.)

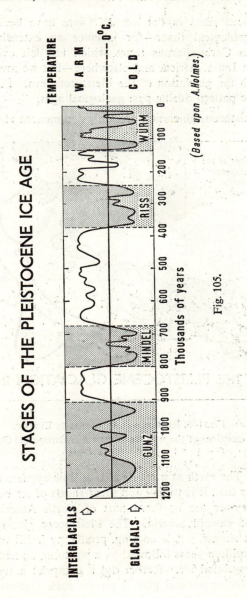

STAGES OF THE PLEISTOCENE ICE AGE

Fig. 105.

(Based upon A.Holmes.)

ice in various parts of the world. There have been several Ice Ages in geological times—for instance an extensive glaciation occurred in Carboniferous times which has left evidence of its presence in India, Africa, and elsewhere—but we are mainly concerned with the glaciation of the Pleistocene era. Fig. 104 shows the climatic pattern during past geological ages.

The Pleistocene glaciation probably commenced about 1,500,000

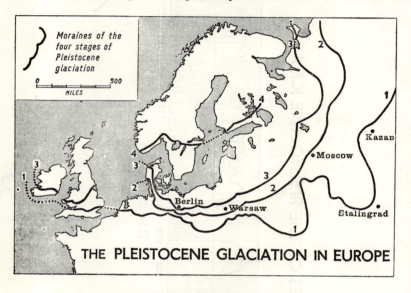

Fig. 106. RECESSIONAL MORAINES IN EUROPE.
The terminal moraines of the four ice advances in Europe: (1) Günz, (2) Mindel, (3) Würm, and (4) Riss.

years ago. The earth as a whole at that time appears to have been much cooler than it is to-day and great sheets of ice began to grow and spread over the northern part of North America, northern Europe, and eastern Siberia. The Pleistocene glaciation did not consist of a simple, single cooling, producing frigid conditions for nearly two million years followed by a warming up and the melting of the accumulated ice. Rather did it comprise a series of oscillations producing several glacial phases each separated by interglacial periods when the ice, due to ameliorating conditions, melted away and probably disappeared almost entirely except in the higher latitudes and higher altitudes.

In Europe, early research work was done in the Alps and here five separate glaciations have been distinguished and named the *Donau, Günz, Mindel, Riss,* and *Würm* (Fig. 105). In northern Europe only the last three have been discerned with any sureness but the Günz and Donau phases almost unquestionably occurred. The evidence of the earlier glaciations is very confused and the unravelling of it is not made easy by the fact that the ice moved over the same region time and time again, thereby destroying the "clues". The extent of the Pleistocene glaciation in Europe is indicated in Fig. 106. Similar glacial advances and retreats happened in North America and these can be roughly equated with the last four glacial phases of Europe. In North America each glacial phase is named after the state in which the deposits were first studied and where they are best preserved, *viz.* the Nebraskan, the Kansan, the Illinoian, and the Wisconsin. Table VI shows the correlation between the American and European glaciations.

TABLE VI

CORRELATION OF EUROPEAN AND AMERICAN PLEISTOCENE GLACIATIONS

EUROPE		NORTH AMERICA
Alpine Region	*Northern Europe*	
Würm	Weichsel	Wisconsin
Riss	Saale	Illinoian
Mindel	Elster	Kansan
Günz		Nebraskan
Donau		

CHAPTER 14

GLACIATED LANDSCAPES

GLACIAL EROSION AND RESULTING LANDFORMS

Before proceeding to look at the various landforms which result from glacial erosion, let us note the mechanics of erosion by ice. The main processes effecting glacial erosion are *nivation, abrasion,* and *plucking.* Alternate freezing and thawing of snow which is in contact with rock causes the latter to rot or disintegrate; this mechanical weathering is called nivation or sometimes "snow-patch erosion". Abrasion, *i.e.* the abrasive action of the ice itself, and more particularly of the rock debris which it carries, results in the scraping, scratching, and general grinding down of the rock with which the ice comes into contact. When ice moves across fractured or jointed bedrock it may actually freeze onto the rock and then tear off, or lift up, blocks of rocks; such action is termed plucking or, sometimes, quarrying. It may be noted also that frictional drag of ice may give rise to considerable disturbance of underlying strata; for example, some folding and thrusting in the chalk of Norfolk has been ascribed to this mechanism.

Ice erosion produces debris of varying kinds but, broadly, it is either finely ground rock, called *rock flour,* or fragmental material ranging in size from small chips to large boulders. *Glacial till,* which we shall describe shortly as a product of glacial deposition, is a mixture of rock flour and rock fragments of all shapes and sizes.

(i) *Glacial pavements.* As ice grips hold of rock fragments and drags them across the ground, the bedrock is cut away as though it were planed by a giant rasp or file. Not only is the bedrock abraded but the cutting tools are also abraded. It is this abrasion which gives rise to the polished surface of many rocks (and, incidentally, produces the rock flour referred to above). Abrasion also produces fine scratches on the smooth bedrock known as *striations* or *glacial striae.* Sometimes deeply-cut ruts are carved into the bedrock; these result from extensive abrasion where massive rocks have become locked in the ice and have gouged out great *grooves*. Such grooves may be one or two feet deep and two or three wide and in the Great Bear Lake district of Canada grooves of greater dimensions have been described. Both the grooves and striations observed on a rock surface indicate the direction of ice movement. A rock surface which has been stripped of its soil cover and ground down and smoothed is called a *glacial pavement*. Where such action has taken place on a large scale and continental ice-sheets have advanced over lowland plains an *ice-scoured plain* results; this consists of extensive areas stripped of its soil cover exposing wide sheets of bare abraded rock, dotted with lakes in the hollows and sometimes with patches of vegetation where there is a plastering of soil. Large areas of the Canadian Shield and of northern Finland provide good examples.

(ii) *Roches moutonnées.* These are glacially-moulded outcrops of rock. The front edge or upstream side exhibits a smooth, gently sloping, rounded shape, the result of abrasion by the oncoming ice, and a steeper and more ragged downstream side due to the plucking action of the moving ice. Such rock masses are called roches moutonnées—a French term—because of their fancied resemblance to the white wigs smoothed down with mutton grease which were in common use towards the end of the 18th century. They are common features in most glaciated areas; they are to be seen, for example, on many hillsides in the Highlands of Scotland and on the sides of Llanberis Pass in North Wales (Fig. 107).

(iii) *Cirques.* One of the most prominent of glacial landforms is the *cirque* (French), which also goes under a variety of other names, *e.g. cwm* (Welsh), *corrie* (Gaelic), and *combe* (in Cumberland). A cirque may be defined as a semi-circular or arm-chair shaped hollow eroded by glacial action. The hollow is surrounded on three sides by steep, and in some cases nearly vertical, walls. On the fourth side is a threshold over which a glacier may move (Fig. 108). When the ice disappears a small lake or tarn may occupy the hollow, as in the case of many of the small cirques in the Lake District. Cirques are thought to have originated from pre-glacial hollows which have become progressively enlarged by nivation, frost shattering, and ice abrasion. Frost action and the alternation of freezing and thawing of water which penetrates into cracks and crevices help to break up the rock. The eating back of the cirque wall by this constant freeze-thaw process is known as *basal sapping*; it helps to maintain the steepness of the cirque wall. Vertical joints in cirque walls also help to develop steep faces. The basin shape of the cirque floor is due to the great pressure and the rotary action of the moving ice. The abrasive and plucking action

FEATURES OF GLACIATION

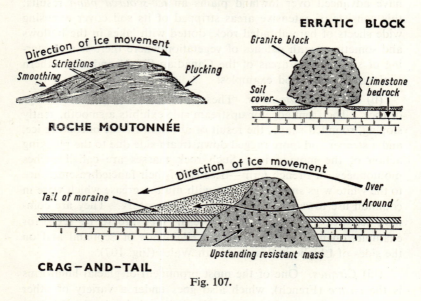

Fig. 107.

of the moving ice also assists in the general enlarging of the cirque. Some cirques such as the Cirque de Gavarnie in the Pyrenees and the Walcott Cirque in Antarctica have backwalls towering up several thousands of feet.

(iv) *Arêtes.* When two cirques are situated back to back the retreating walls of their rear faces will ultimately meet one another to produce a narrow, knife-edge ridge which is jagged and serrated. Similar sharp ridges are produced by glacial valleys lying side by side. These steep-sided ridges are known as *arêtes.* The term arête is a French one meaning a "fishbone" or "sharp edge". Striding Edge in the Lake District and Crib Goch on Snowdon are well-known examples of arêtes. The coalescence of the headwalls of two cirques often results in the formation of a gap in the intervening ridge called a *col*.

(v) *Horns.* The headward erosion of three or more cirques on the flanks of a mountain may result in the formation of a pyramidal peak. Such horn-shaped peaks with their radiating arêtes separated by cirques are characteristic and essential features of glaciated

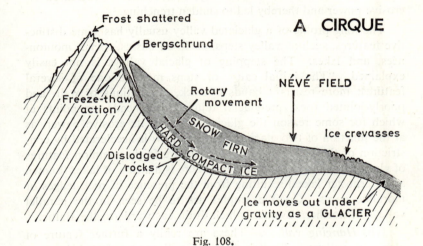

Fig. 108.

mountain landscapes. The Matterhorn in Switzerland is the type example of this striking landform. The names of many of the peaks in the Alps, *e.g.* the Dent (tooth) du Midi, Zugspitz (spike), are an obvious reflection of their ice-etched, sharpened forms.

(vi) *Glaciated valleys.* Glaciers, though following the courses of pre-existing valleys, considerably modify those valleys by their erosive effects. First, the cross-profile of a valley is usually broadened to become U-shaped, *i.e.* its floor is flattened and its sides are steepened. Secondly, as the glacier ploughs its way downstream it straightens the valley and planes off any projecting spurs to form *truncated spurs,* bluffs with cliff-like triangular faces. Sometimes the abrasion of a powerful glacier will shear off not only any pro-jecting spurs of land but the entire valley side. Thirdly, *alps* or *benches* are common features of glaciated valleys; they lie at the change of slope above the steep walls of the valley and mark the level to which the glacier filled the pre-glacial valley. Fourthly, many valleys which have suffered glaciation terminate at their heads in steep, wall-like faces known as *trough-ends*. It seems probable that these steep end walls resulted from the coalescence of several cirque glaciers above the valley head; the accumulated thickness and weight of the ice enormously, and suddenly, increased its erosive power and thereby led to sudden trenching.

The long profile of a glaciated valley usually has some distinc-tive features, such as valley steps, enclosed basins, roches mouton-nées, and lakes. The stepping of glacial valleys is not easily explained. "The initial cause of steps may be one of several features: more resistant bands of rock, alternations of well- and poorly-jointed rock, pre-glacial rejuvenation heads, or points at which for some reason the glacier increases its erosive power, as at the junction of two glaciers or where flow is accelerated by con-striction of the valley sides." [1]   Lakes are fairly common features of glaciated valleys; often, indeed, there is a string of lakes (known as paternoster lakes) resulting from the presence of rock ledges or morainic dams. Good examples are to be seen in the parallel valleys of northern Sweden which drain eastwards to the Baltic.

(vii) *Hanging valleys.* These are really a further feature of glaciated valleys. Though hanging valleys are found in non-glaciated areas (*e.g.* above a coastline), they are seen characteristic-ally in mountain areas which have suffered glaciation. Such hang-ing valleys which are tributary to, and lie above, the main valley are the troughs carved by tributary glaciers (see Fig. 109). But because their ice-streams were smaller than that of the main valley glacier, their erosive action was less and, accordingly, they did not cut so deeply. Hence, when the ice melted away, the tributary valleys were left "hanging" above the trunk valley. And, as a result, present day streams plunge from the high-level tributary valleys by means of a series of falls into the main valley below. The Lauterbrunnen Valley in Switzerland provides some good

[1] B. W. Sparks, *Geomorphology*, 1960, p. 276.

examples of hanging valleys with their associated cascading streams. See Plate XIV.

(viii) *Fiords.* The coasts of Norway, Greenland, Labrador, Alaska, British Columbia, South Chile, and South Island, New Zealand are deeply cut by narrow, penetrating arms of the sea called *fiords.* Such inlets owe many of their special and characteristic features to glaciation, although they cannot be explained in terms

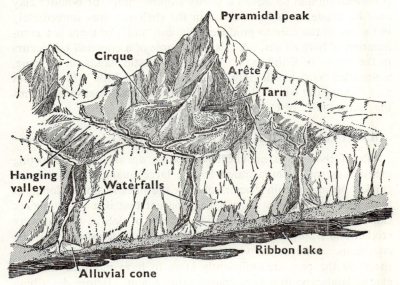

GLACIATED FEATURES OF AN ALPINE REGION

Fig. 109.

The sketch shows some of the typical features of a glaciated mountain area; horn-shaped peaks, cirques, aretes, hanging valleys, vertical valley walls, waterfalls, tarns, and ribbon lakes.

of glacial erosion alone. Their typical U-shape, the occurrence of hanging valleys, the scouring of the valley floors, and the presence of a bar or threshold near the mouth are all indicative of glacial erosion, but their rectilinear branching patterns are suggestive of pre-glacial valley systems which were subsequently modified by the passage of ice and then partially submerged. The sea-lochs of western Scotland are fiords.

(ix) *Crag and tail*. This feature is partly an erosional, partly
a depositional, landform. It is developed where an obstructive
mass of rock, the crag, lies in the path of advancing ice. As a result
of the obstruction, the oncoming ice is compelled to move over and
around the crag. The side facing the oncoming ice, known as the
stoss, is roughened and striated by the ice. The lee side, however,
is protected; either the crag protects the softer rocks in the lee
from erosion and so leaves a gently sloping "tail", or boulder clay
may be plastered and preserved in the sheltered area immediately
in the lee of the crag to produce a similar "tail", or there is a combination of both effects. A classic example of a crag and tail occurs
in the centre of Edinburgh. Edinburgh Castle stands on the crag,
a denuded hard basalt plug, while the "Royal Mile" (High Street
and Canongate) which slopes away from the rock eastwards, forms
the softer "tail" of Carboniferous limestone.

NOTES ON 266-73   IGNORE DIAGRAMS 268-70 ? 3

GLACIAL DEPOSITION AND RESULTING LANDFORMS

Proof that ice is an effective eroding agent and transporting
medium is well demonstrated by the large quantities of moraine
carried on and within glaciers and by the piles of debris found at
the snouts of glaciers. It will be apparent that if a valley glacier
can erode and carry a substantial amount of debris, the quantity
eroded and transported by the great continental ice-sheets must be
enormous. Indeed, the vast loads of debris dumped by the ice-
sheets of the past are sufficiently large to have modified the pre-
glacial landscape to a very considerable extent. Before describing
the landforms resulting from glacial deposition, let us note the
chief types of glacial deposit.

To all the various deposits that are laid down directly by ice
action, or are assorted and re-laid by streams, the general term *drift*
is applied. The piles of debris smeared across the landscape by
direct ice action are called *glacial till*. Such deposits of drift are
unsorted and unstratified. They are composed of rock fragments
of varying character and of all sizes, ranging from massive boulders
to tiny clay particles, mixed together at random; hence the alternative name to till of boulder clay.[1] Although some of the component

---

[1] Boulder clay is the traditional English term for deposits of glacial drift
but the American term till is, perhaps, preferable—especially since boulder
clay does not always contain boulders.

rock fragments may have been scratched, polished, or faceted as they were being carried along by the ice, most of them are sharply angular, or at best subrounded, and are quite unlike the smoothed and rounded pebbles and boulders commonly found in streams and beach deposits. Boulder clay is deposited by retreating ice in a wide variety of topographic forms, such as moraines, drumlins, eskers, etc.

Deposition results mainly from the melting ice which drops its load, but some of the finer material may be carried by the melt-waters, worked over and sorted and then re-laid. Selective sorting of this kind results not only in the grading of rock particles according to size but in the stratification of the re-deposited material. Drift carried and graded by glacial melt-water is designated *fluvio-glacial material*. Thus to the geographer and geologist drift may be divided into two broad categories: unstratified deposits dumped directly by receding glaciers and ice-sheets, and stratified fluvio-glacial deposits washed and sorted by melt-water.

Let us now turn our attention to the topographic forms resulting from glacial deposition.

(i) *Moraines.* Moraine is a general term used to describe the deposits of boulder clay directly deposited by the ice; it occurs either as spreads or in ridges. (The term is also used, as we have already noted, for the debris carried within or on an active glacier.) When an ice-sheet begins to melt, the steady and continuous withdrawal of the edge of the sheet results in a layer of drift or till being laid down over wide areas. This plaster of moraine which veneers the land surface is commonly called *ground moraine* or sometimes, *sheet deposition*. Ground moraine is the most widespread of the various glacial deposits left behind by continental ice-sheets. A *terminal* or *end moraine* is a hummocky ridge which marks the point of furthest ice advance. It is formed when the ice reaches a state of equilibrium, that is, when the rate of ice advance and the rate of ice melt are both steady; this condition causes the ice front to remain more or less stationary and this, in turn, leads to the piling up of moraine in approximately the same place. In this fashion great crescentic ridges, sometimes hundreds of feet high, are built up. Amelioration of the climatic conditions may result in the ice retreating for a while; then a further halt in the recession and stabilised conditions lead to the formation of another ridge. A whole series of ridges may mark phases in the intermittent retreat of the ice; such ridges are known as *recessional moraines* (Fig. 110).

Mounds of sand and gravel in the periglacial fringe, *i.e.* the area

THE PLEISTOCENE GLACIATION IN EUROPE

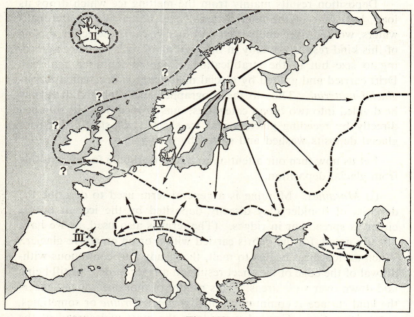

Fig. 110.

I is the main glaciation focused on the Fennoscandian Shield; II, III, IV, and V are the minor ice caps which developed over Iceland and in the mountainous areas of the Pyrenees, Alps, and Caucasus respectively.

bordering the edge of the ice-sheet, may as a result of the advancing ice be pushed into ridges. When such material is thrust into low ridges by ice-sheet movement a *push moraine* is formed. Good examples of these are found in the Veluwe area of the Netherlands and in front of the present-day glaciers in Spitzbergen.

(ii) *Erratics and perched blocks.* Examination of glacial boulders shows that most of them have come from local sources, but some, usually found in restricted localities, are foreign to the area. In other words, they occur far from the outcrop from which they were originally derived; for example, Shap granite is a unique type of granite occurring in a limited area in the Shap district, and yet boulders of it are to be found in glacial deposits in east York-shire. In like fashion pebbles of rhomb porphyry, a rock native to Norway, can be picked up on the east coast of northern England. In North America, boulders of red jasper have been found in Kentucky some 600 miles from the nearest solid rock of this type, which occurs to the north of Lake Superior. Such "foreign" rock frag-ments are known as *erratics* or erratic blocks, literally "wandering stones". It is difficult to conceive of any other explanation than carriage by ice to account for the distribution of erratics. By noting their occurrence it is possible to trace the direction of ice movement over long distances. Sometimes large erratics are to be found pre-cariously poised on other rocks, in which case they are called *perched blocks*. Fine examples of perched blocks are to be found on the Norber limestone plateau on the flanks of Ingleborough. These blocks, which are composed of Silurian grit, never outcrop so high up. They rest on bases of Carboniferous limestone some 12 to 18 inches high. This is a point of interest for it suggests that the blocks have protected the rock upon which they rest from erosion and that the entire plateau surface has been lowered by this amount since the end of the Ice Age.

(iii) *Drumlins*. These are smooth, rounded, elongated hills shaped like half an egg cut lengthwise. Asymmetrical in form, they have their blunt end pointing in the direction from which the ice advanced. They vary considerably in size ranging from a few yards long and high, up to a mile or more in length with heights of around 200 feet. Commonly occurring in clusters or "swarms", they give rise to what has been called "a basket of eggs topography". Although some drumlins have been found to have a core of bed-rock, mostly they are composed of boulder clay. Exactly how they have been formed and shaped is not perfectly clear. It seems reasonable to assume that they originated as masses of subglacial debris which have been shaped into streamlined forms. Probably they resulted from the ice-sheet becoming overloaded with drift so that some of it was left behind. Deposition may have been facili-tated by a slowing up of the speed of movement of the ice. Wide spreads of drumlins occur in the Midland Valley of Scotland, in the Solway Plain, in the Aire Gap, in Northern Ireland, and in the New England and Wisconsin areas of the United States.

(iv) *Eskers*. Another feature of glacial deposition is the *esker*, a long, winding ridge composed of sand and gravel, not boulder clay. The material composing them appears to be more sorted and more bedded than that making up drumlins. Again, they seem to

DRUMLINS IN THE VALE OF EDEN

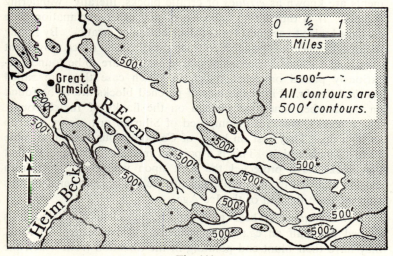

Fig. 111.

The 500-foot contour in this part of the Vale of Eden brings out clearly the occurrence of drumlins. Most are 100 to 200 feet high. Note their long axis lies in a W.N.W. to E.S.E. direction. The dots indicate spot heights—the highest point of each drumlin.

run across the land surface regardless of the topography. In Sweden and Finland, where they are known as *asar*, they are common and are aligned at right angles to the original ice fronts. Though less frequent in Britain, they are to be found in Scotland and northern England, and in Shropshire one runs from Wolverhampton to Newport. Eskers are of variable length ranging from under a mile to as much as 100 miles, but they are only narrow, often only a few yards or feet wide. Their sinuous character suggests a connection with stream deposition, and it is generally believed they were formed either by streams tunnelling beneath the ice and leaving behind their sandy and gravelly stream-beds after the ice melted, or by streams dumping their load as they emerged from the ice front to build up a "delta" which receded in step with the shrinkage of the ice front, thereby gradually building up an elongated ridge. So called *beaded eskers*—eskers which broaden out in places—probably formed when the ice made a temporary halt, causing increased deposition at that point.

(v) *Kames.* Low, relatively steep-sided mounds, usually of random shape with their longer axis usually at right angles to the direction of ice movement are known as *kames*. They differ from drumlins in the latter respect, and also in the fact that boulders, which are an ingredient of boulder clay composing drumlins, are usually absent; although the material making up kames tends to be unsorted. Kames may occur in isolation or in groups. Their origin poses something of a problem and several theories have been offered to explain their formation. It has been suggested that they are a type of alluvial cone or delta built up by streams issuing from an ice-sheet which, temporarily, was stationary. The beading of eskers lends support to this idea. Another suggestion is that they represent accumulations of material in cavities along the edge of a stagnant ice mass or even in crevasses, although kames tend to lack the linear arrangement normally discernible in crevasse fillings. The ridges at West Ayton in the Vale of Pickering, and at Carstairs in the Southern Uplands of Scotland, are usually classed as kames while Dury says that the so-called Irish eskers which curve across the Central Plain are really kames.[1] Features designated *kame terraces* are in all probability accumulations of sand and gravel deposited by streams flowing between a wasting glacier and the valley wall. After the glacier has melted away these marginal deposits stand in the form of terraces along the sides of the valley wall.

(vi) *Outwash plains.* When a glacier or ice-sheet melts, much water drains away, carrying with it some of the finer stuff of the terminal moraine. This material which is washed out of the

[1] *The Face of the Earth*, 1959, Penguin Book, p. 150.

moraine is called fluvio-glacial outwash. At the end of glaciers, outwash fans are built up by the re-depositing of this washed-out, sorted material. If the outwash fans from a series of glaciers coalesce they will give rise to the formation of an outwash plain. Ice-sheets, of course, will produce more extensive plains. For example, along the southern coast of Iceland there is a plain, some 10 miles wide, covered with outwash material, called *sandur,* which has been derived from the ice-sheets of Vatnajökull and Myrdalsjöku·l in Iceland (Fig. 113). Even more extensive are the outwash plai·s of the North European Plain; here melt-waters have laid down vast sheets of clays, sands, and gravels which completely mask the pre-existing topography. Often these outwash plains are pitted

SEQUENCE OF DEPOSITION AT THE EDGE OF AN ICE-SHEET

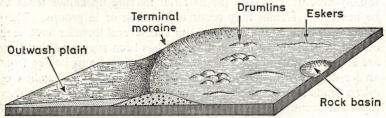

Fig. 112.

with depressions, large and small, which are known as *kettles* or *kettle holes.* Usually they are undrained and may contain a small lake. They are the result of detached blocks of ice becoming partially buried in outwash material; when the ice melted, a depression or kettle hole was left behind.

(vii) *Varves.* Lakes which developed as a result of glacial activity have left behind distinctive banded deposits known as *varves.* A varve consists of a pair of very finely bedded clays, one light in colour and coarser in texture, the other darker and finer. Each varve is taken as being the sedimentary deposit for a single year. The lighter layer represents the summer deposit. During this season, the period of the summer thaw, there would be much water in circulation and this would be capable of carrying much coarser

PLATE XV

Above: Vallone di Verra in the Breithorn-Monte Rosa area. The snow-covered peaks provided the supply of névé which fed the glacier which once ground its way down this valley. Here the magnificent moraines, left behind by the glacier which has all but disappeared, are clearly evident. (*Aerofilms.*)

Below: Muckle Roe, Shetlands. A peneplaned landscape, partly levelled and smoothed by ice action. Note the bare, barren aspect and the fact that the land surface has been largely denuded of soil; also the lakes in the rock-scoured hollows. (*Aerofilms.*)

PLATE XVI

Above: Terminal moraine at Malham, Yorkshire, now bisected by stream. Note the slump terracettes on its surface and the land slips above the moraine to the left. (*A. Potter*)

Below: Weathered blocks in current-bedded Millstone Grit, Brimham Rocks, Yorkshire. This outcrop of grit rocks has been carved into fantastic shapes partly by wind action, perhaps by strong winds carrying sharp grit particles at the end of the Ice Age, and partly by the action of frost and water. (*Eric Kay.*)

material. Some of this coarse sediment would settle, but the finer stuff would remain in suspension. In winter the lake water would freeze, the water movement would be stilled, and the finer particles would settle to the bottom to form a thinner layer of fine, dark coloured silt. Each varve consists usually of only a few millimetres of deposit, although thicknesses of up to two or three inches are known. The accumulated deposits of varve clay are seldom more than about 30 feet thick. Where, however, a series of lakes were formed marking the successive retreat of the ice it is sometimes

ICELAND — STRUCTURE

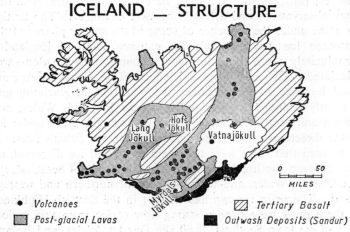

● Volcanoes   ▨ Tertiary Basalt
▦ Post-glacial Lavas   ■ Outwash Deposits (Sandur)

Fig. 113. SANDUR IN ICELAND.
Surrounding the interior plateau of Iceland are the coastal lowlands; these are mainly strandflat, partly covered by outwash material known as *sandur*. The sandur plains are best developed along the southern coast.

possible to match up accumulations of varves. Since each varve represents one year's deposit, it is possible, by counting up the number of varves, to arrive at the number of years involved in the making of the varve deposit; moreover, by matching up successive varves in different deposits it is possible, through their enumeration, to build up a rough time-scale of glacial retreat. This, in fact, was the system used by the Swedish scientist Baron G. de Geer who estimated that it took the Würm ice-sheet approximately 11,000 years to retreat from northern Germany to southern Sweden and some 3,500 years for it to reach Stockholm from Scania.　This indicated a period of rather slow retreat followed by a phase of accelerated movement.　Thus the study and correlation of varves affords a valuable method of glacial chronology.

THE ICE AGE IN THE BRITISH ISLES

It is impossible to recount in a paragraph or two the full story of the Ice Age in the British Isles; a large book would be needed to do full justice to it.　We must be content, therefore, with one or two observations and a few illustrative examples.　The British Isles came under the influence of some of the earlier phases of the Pleistocene Ice Age and only the extreme south of England—approximately south of a line from Gloucester to London—was unglaciated.　The chief observable effects of the Great Ice Age are related, however, to the last phase (the Würm) of the glaciation and are mostly confined to Scotland, northern England, Wales, and northern and central Ireland.　Fig. 114 shows the areas under ice and the directions of movement of the ice in the British Isles.　It will be seen that there were five main centres of ice dispersal, all of them occupying highland areas: the Highlands of Scotland, the Lake District, Wales, and the mountains of northern and western Ireland.　The main ice cap had its seat in the Scottish Highlands and there must have been a strong flow of ice from this region.　Lobes of ice from Scotland, the Lake District, Wales, and Ireland filled the Irish Sea and displaced that sea temporarily.　Ice-streams also penetrated the Lancashire and Cheshire Plain.　A similar movement of ice took place on the eastern side of Britain.　Scottish and north Pennine glaciers flowed eastwards towards the North Sea where they joined forces with the ice-flow from Scandinavia, thereby filling the northern part of the North Sea with ice and forcing its waters southwards.　One lobe of this ice, emanating from the Lake District and the northern Pennines, penetrated southwards into the Vale of York.　A bulge of the North Sea ice covered Holderness, eastern Lincolnshire, and the Wash.

The Ice Age in the British Isles has left its mark on the scenery of both the highlands and the lowlands.　In Scotland, where the ice-sheet covered the Highlands, the mountains had their outlines rounded. In some cases, as in the Cuillins of Skye, glaciers eroded corries and their associated arêtes. Glaciers excavated deep U-shaped valleys, and some of these form the sea lochs of the west.

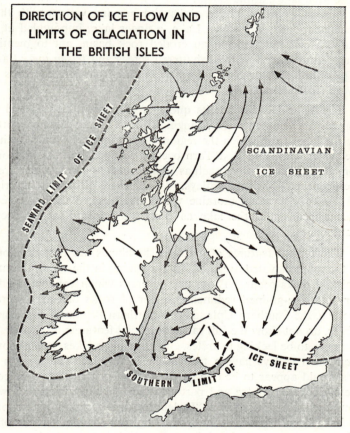

Fig. 114.

The ice was responsible for the ponding back of several lakes which later were drained, leaving only lake terraces as a witness of their previous existence, as in the case of the three terraces of the parallel roads of Glen Roy, in Inverness.

North Wales, especially in the Snowdonia and the Cader Idris areas, show similar glacial features. The Cader Idris area, though small, possesses a superb collection of glacial features and landforms. Here are a group of cirques, with precipitous headwalls and cirque lakes, a fine glacial trough in the Tal y llyn valley, with its straight, spurless, cliffed walls and hanging valleys with their spectacular falls, Tal y llyn Lake, a finger lake, impounded at its southern end but lying in an eroded rock basin, not to mention other features such as frost-shattered screes and *felsen meer* (large angular boulders or blocks formed *in situ* from jointed rocks by severe frost action).

The Lake District has its quota of arêtes and cirques and U-shaped valleys notched with hanging valleys. Especially noteworthy are the lakes from which the region takes its name. Some, such as Bleawater Tarn and Red Tarn occupy scooped hollows in mountain cirques, while others such as Windermere and Wastwater are in overdeepened U-shaped valleys. Windermere also owes its origin in part to a terminal moraine which has blocked the valley exit. Also appearing in the lake as islands are hump-backed roches moutonnées.

The typical features of glaciated highlands are best developed in the more elevated areas of Britain where, in the main, the most resistant rocks occur. Those upland areas which are composed of very old fine-grained sedimentaries, or of rocks of Carboniferous age, *e.g.* the Southern Uplands, the northern Pennines, and central Wales, do not show the full range of glacial features; they tend, for example, to be lacking in arêtes, cirques, ribbon lakes, etc., although their main valleys have a trough-like character. The reasons for this would appear to be due partly to the fact that they were completely covered by ice and partly to the rocks of which they were composed. As Dury says: "Ingleborough is certainly high enough to have been exposed to corrie-cutting, but the shaly rocks of its upper part seem to have been incapable of developing—or of preserving—the sheer faces of corrie headwalls".[1] Thus, although such areas in the field do not bear the impressive features of glaciation which one tends to expect in areas which have suffered from ice attack, careful study of the landscape shows plenty of

[1] *The Face of the Earth*, p. 142.

evidence of its former glaciation. By way of illustration, let us look at Swaledale.

The narrow, steep-sided valley of Swaledale cut in the dip-slope of the Askrigg Block, which forms the Central Pennines, shows few signs of ice erosion, although there is considerable evidence attesting glaciation. During the later Ice Age, glaciers extended down all the Yorkshire Dales, but the higher areas, roughly over 2,000 feet, remained free from ice. It would seem that Swaledale itself had its valley glacier, but that the watersheds to the north and south were clear of ice. The retreat of the Swaledale glacier left behind a series of four terminal moraines, which are well-marked features of the valley floor. Viewed from the upper valley slopes, the one at Grinton stands out impressively. Below Grinton there is a moraine at Ellerton; above Grinton there are two, both situated between the villages of Healaugh and Gunnerside. The three lower moraines acted for a while as natural dams, ponding up the melt-waters which formed glacial lakes. The sites of these lakes are clearly evident in the stretches of flat valley floor. Streams flowing from these glacial lakes have left their mark on the landscape in the form of marginal overflow channels. These lateral channels can be seen on either side of the valley in the vicinity of Grinton.

In the lowlands the legacy of the ice is most apparent in the morainic deposits, which cover large areas, and in the effects which glacial lakes had on the topography. Terminal moraines were left where the ice halted: for example, the Cromer Ridge in northern Norfolk marks the southernmost front of the last ice advance while the curving York Moraine across the Vale of York, upon which the city of York is sited, marks a halt in the tongue of ice which penetrated southwards through the Northallerton Gate between the Pennines and the Cleveland Hills. Extensive and often deep spreads of boulder clay were laid down; in East Anglia, for instance, the drift attains a depth of up to 300 feet. Fertile drift also covers much of the Vale of York, although to the north-east of York is a patch of infertile sands and gravels forming Strensall Common. Most of Ireland, too, is covered by glacial drift.

Of great interest are the glacial lakes which were formed by the ponding back of melt-water by the ice. Valleys and basins blocked by ice would fill up with water, and the lakes so formed would continue to rise in level until they found an escape point at the lowest part of the rim. Overflow at this point would result in the carving out of a channel, which would become large if the lake persisted for any length of time. Such escape routes form glacial overflow channels. Sometimes a whole series of overflow channels

Fig. 115. MORAINES ACROSS THE VALE OF YORK.

Two main moraines, the York and Escrick Moraines cross the centre of the Vale of York. To the north-east of York lies Strensall Common, an area of infertile sands and gravels.

developed where one lake led to another. When the ice eventually disappeared, many of the overflow channels naturally lost their supply of water and at the present time are dry; some contain small streams in large valleys giving "misfits" while yet others have continued to serve as major drainage lines.

GLACIERS, GLACIAL LAKES AND OVERFLOW CHANNELS

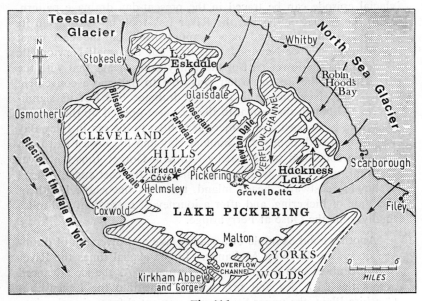

Fig. 116.

One of the most interesting examples of glacial lake development and overflow channel formation is to be found in Yorkshire. Here the North Sea ice-sheet moved along the east coast and penetrated up the Esk valley, thereby blocking the exit of the River Esk and causing it to pond up behind the ice barrier to form Lake Eskdale. The water eventually found an outlet to the south where it flowed into another lake, Lake Pickering, dammed up in the Vale of Pickering (Fig. 116). The deep, narrow, steep-sided valley of Newtondale marks the connecting link between these two lakes. Newtondale enters the Vale of Pickering at Pickering; the town grew up at this point where deltaic deposits were formed as a result of the overflowing waters entering the lake. The delta provided a dry site when the rest of the Vale floor was a sodden marsh. Lake Pickering itself drained at its lowest overflow point, which in this case was to the south-west; here, at Kirkham immediately to the south of Malton, the overflowing water cut a fine gorge before linking with yet another lake, Lake Humber. The results of this glacial episode can be traced in the present-day drainage pattern. With the retreat of the ice, the River Esk took up once again its pre-glacial direction and now empties itself on the east coast at Whitby. Upper Newtondale is dry, but the small Newtondale Beck drains the lower part of the valley; this means that with the departure of the ice the water was able to find more convenient outlets, and Newtondale as a major drainage line lost its significance. Although the retreat of the ice-sheet opened up the Vale of Pickering in the east, the former easy outlet to the sea in Filey Bay was choked with deposits of boulder clay and the lowest exit from the Vale continued to be that by Kirkham Gorge; thus the River Derwent, which rises within a few miles of the east coast, instead of flowing eastwards heads inland, traverses the whole length of the Vale of Pickering, and after a journey of more than 100 miles finally joins the Ouse at Ferrybridge.

Another good example of a glacial lake and diversion of drainage occurs in the West Midlands. In pre-glacial times the River Severn drained into the present Dee estuary. As the ice advanced across the Irish Sea and protruded a lobe into the Lancashire-Cheshire Plain, the upper Severn was prevented from escaping into the Irish Sea and its waters were ponded up to form Lake Lapworth (Fig. 117). The lake waters found an outlet to the south and cut the famous gorge of the Severn at Ironbridge. After the retreat of the ice, the newly cut gorge provided the lowest route and so the drainage continued to use it. The Severn's curious circuitous course can thus be explained in terms of this glacial interference.

The periglacial areas of southern England, though not directly affected by the ice were indirectly affected by it. A tundra-like type of climate must have prevailed and freezing and thawing must have been common.   This freeze-thaw process seems to have given rise to sludging for a number of sludge-deposits are recognised, *e.g.* the combe rock (a sandy chalk rubble) formed on chalk slopes as at Black Rock at Brighton.   Any compacted mass of rubble,

LAKE LAPWORTH

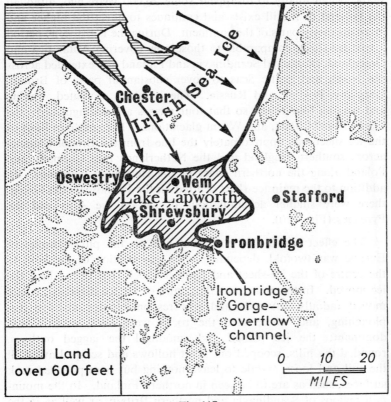

Fig. 117.

sand, and clay which was formed under periglacial conditions and originated as a product of solifluction is termed *head*.   It has also been suggested that the brick earths in England may be loess (see p. 304) and were laid down when a near-glacial climate prevailed.

THE GREAT ICE AGE IN EUROPE

Let us now look at a sample area which has suffered glacial erosion and deposition on a large scale: the northern part of the continent of Europe. The Great Ice Age of Quaternary times was the last great episode in the geological history of Europe. This period of glaciation, which as we have seen lasted for about 1,500,000 years, began finally to disappear some 20,000 years ago, although the tail-end of it still exists and continues to affect the higher and more northerly parts of the continent. During the Pleistocene period a vast ice-sheet, comparable to those now covering Antarctica and Greenland, smothered Scandinavia and Finland and extended across the North and Baltic Seas to cover substantial parts of Britain, Germany, Poland, and Russia. The ice-sheet oscillated, waxing and waning four times, so that four phases are distinguished: the Günz, Mindel, Riss, and Würm glaciations. The southern limit of the ice-sheet was approximately the line from the Bristol Channel across southern England and the Netherlands into Germany and Poland along the northern edges of the Hercynian highlands. In addition to the main ice-sheet centred on the Fennoscandian Shield, there were smaller accumulations of ice on the Alps and the Pyrenees (Fig. 110).

The effect which this glaciation had on the physiography of Europe was twofold, depending upon the relation of the land to the centre of the ice-sheet and upon the rock type over which the ice moved. In the areas near the centre of the ice dispersal, which moved radially outwards and was responsible for massive ice-ploughing, and where also the rocks were hard, erosion was dominant; the ice planed and smoothed the jagged outlines, rounded the hills, scooped out great hollows and scraped away all the soil and loose mantle to leave nothing but bare polished rock surfaces, such as are to be seen in northern Finland. In the mountain regions of Scandinavia and northern Britain, as well as in the Alps and Pyrenees, the moving ice ground its way down the pre-existing valleys and there, where thickest, effected pronounced vertical erosion, causing the valleys to be greatly deepened. The mountain tops and sides were chiselled and scoured by rasp-like action of rock fragments firmly embedded in the moving ice.

On the other hand, the areas which lay near the edge of the ice-sheet suffered deposition rather than erosion; hence the land surface has been plastered with accumulations of boulders, gravels, sands, and clays, *i.e.* ground moraine, and is often covered with ridges and hummocky deposits. Large areas of eastern Germany and Poland, as well as parts of England, were covered with boulder clay. Where the ice-sheet stood still for a while, allowing material to be dropped and to accumulate as the ice melted, terminal moraines were formed; these, to-day, are represented by the long lines of boulder clay hills that run roughly east-west across the North European Plain. The Pomeranian Heights and the Salpauselka Ridge of southern Finland mark the massive terminal moraines built along the ice during its successive stages of halt. On the inner or northern side of these roughly concentric hill ridges is a zone commonly strewn with drumlins, eskers, and other features of morainic deposition while on the outer or southern side is an apron of outwash sands and gravels.

Amongst the mountainous areas, where valley glaciers lingered, and still linger on, long after the ice-sheet had retreated and disappeared, evidence of ice action is to be seen in such features as pyramidal peaks, cirques, arêtes, U-shaped valleys, hanging valleys, truncated spurs, finger lakes, etc. In such elevated areas as the Alps, the Pyrenees, and the Scandinavian Highlands, remnants of the Ice Age are still present in small ice caps and valley glaciers but elsewhere even these glacial remnants have disappeared. None the less, the impress of glacial action in former times is clearly apparent as a visit to the English Lake District so readily shows.

Less spectacular but even more important from the human point of view are certain after-effects of the Ice Age. Both the topography and the soils of the areas invaded by and influenced by the ice-sheet have been modified. In places are piles of hummocky moraine, often with numerous lakes, as in the Masurian Heights and on the Finnish Plateau; elsewhere, as in the Luneburg Heath, the Veluwe or "badland" of Holland, and the Kempenland of eastern Belgium, stretches of infertile sands and gravels have been left behind; while in other places outwash plains of rock-flour have blanketed parts of the lowlands of northern and central Europe, as streams issuing from the hill masses of sodden morainic rubbish sorted out and laid down the finer material. Subsequently, when the land began to dry out, anticyclonic winds blowing outwards from the shrinking ice-sheet picked up the finer particles of glacial material and carried them southwards to deposit them upon the northern flanks of the Hercynian highlands. This accumulated wind-blown material, which is known as *loess* in Germany and

Fig. 118. Drainage, Finnish Plateau.

The Lake Plateau of Finland is a legacy of the Ice Age.   It is an area of largely indeterminate drainage.   The lakes are due in part to ice hollowing, in part to the hummocky terrain, and in part to the great moraines of the Salpauselka. Note how the general north-west to south-east trend of the lakes reflects the retreat of the ice north-westwards.

limon in France, extends in a belt across central Europe from northern France, through Belgium and Germany, to southern Poland and Ukraine. It occurs in layers of varying thickness at heights from near sea level to over 3,000 feet. It commonly produces a buff-coloured, fine-textured, friable, loamy soil of great fertility. Not surprisingly, therefore, the loess zone has come to be one of the most important agricultural regions of Europe.

Another important result of the Ice Age was the interference with the drainage pattern. Here we may note two interferences. In some areas, but especially well exemplified in central and southern Finland, the drainage is indeterminate (Fig. 118). Land and water are inextricably intermixed on the Finnish Plateau. A maze of streams links some 40,000 lakes together into an inter-connected water system. The region provides an excellent example of an immature drainage pattern. The three curving morainic ridges of the Salpauselka which rim the plateau in the south and south-east have impounded the drainage behind them, although a number of streams have succeeded in cutting their way across the ridges. Such streams have not yet had time to grade their beds, and so are broken by rapids which offer opportunities for hydro-electric power development. The "semi-aquatic environment" of the Finnish Plateau has both advantages and disadvantages: while the ubiquitousness of water greatly assists the timber industry, has allowed water transport to be developed, and provided a source of power, it has, on the other hand, made road and railway communication difficult and resulted in much waterlogging of the soils. Communications frequently thread their way across the plateau on the winding esker ridges. These upstanding ridges, though of no great height, provide well-drained, dry sites for communication and, also, for settlements.

A second interference has occurred on the North European Plain. East of the Rhine the rivers follow zigzag courses. The marked right-angled bends which they display are a legacy of the Ice Age. The proto-rivers of the present Weser, Elbe, Oder, etc., flowed from south to north, but as the ice-sheet crept southwards their northern outlets were blocked and the rivers were diverted westwards, carving out new great east-west valleys along the edge of the ice front. Each time the ice-sheet retreated the rivers

returned to their pre-glacial channels and then, once again, were
diverted westwards. Hence, at the present time, the rivers follow
their original courses in part and their Ice Age courses in part.
The melt-water channels, which run east-west and can be easily
traced on a good topographic map, often contain tributaries and
provide convenient routeways for canals which link up the tribu-

EXTENT OF ICE-SHEET, URSTROMTÄLER, AND LOESS ZONE.

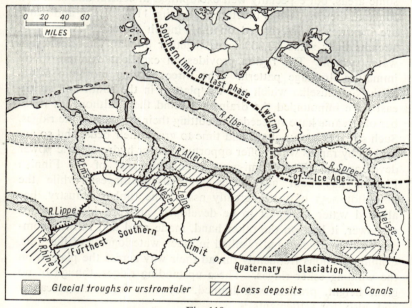

Fig. 119.

taries. These wide, but shallow, east-west valleys are known in
German as *urstromtäler* and in Polish as *pradoliny*. Fig. 120 shows
the detail of urstromtäler.

Another after-effect of the Ice Age of considerable importance
has been the readjustment in sea level. Two somewhat paradoxical
effects have resulted. In the first place, the enormous weight of
the ice-sheet depressed the Fennoscandian region; but, with the

disappearance of the ice, the land could swell upwards again: hence many parts of northern Europe are still gradually emerging from the sea. In the second place, however, the melting of the ice-sheet released enormous quantities of water which led to a rise in the sea level. This, in turn, modified the coastline resulting in the linkage

DETAIL OF URSTROMTÄLER

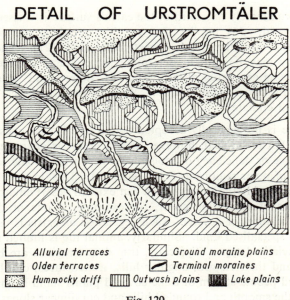

	Alluvial terraces		Ground moraine plains
	Older terraces		Terminal moraines
	Hummocky drift		Outwash plains		Lake plains

Fig. 120.

of the Baltic and North Seas and in the separation of Britain from the continent. Many changes in detail also occurred along the coasts: for example, many off-shore islands were created, glacial valleys were submerged to produce fiords and lochs, and river valleys were flooded to give rias and estuaries.

CHAPTER 15

WIND AND ARID LANDSCAPES

Approximately one-third of the earth's surface is classed as arid or semi-arid; this implies that roughly one-third has desert or semi-desert conditions and characteristics (Fig. 121). The degree of aridity may be said to determine the character of the desert. But in using geographical terms such as "desert" and "aridity" we are faced with certain difficulties. What is meant by desert? What is an arid climate?

There is no generally accepted definition of what constitutes a desert. It can be said, however, that a desert is characterised by an absence or deficiency of moisture (except where some folk refer to parts of polar regions as "cold deserts"). This, in turn, restricts the number of living things which can exist in desert environments. Scantiness of vegetation cover, for example, is one of the most obvious features of deserts. Such vegetation as exists is usually of a highly specialised kind. Similarly, animal life is limited and also of a specialised type. Typically, true desert regions are bare and barren and their rugged, angular hills, fretted faces, cliff-like canyons, and pebble-strewn or dune-covered plains stand in sharp contrast to the smooth and rounded hills and curvilinear slopes of more humid environments.

An arid climate may be defined as one in which all the rain that falls could be evaporated if it remained at the surface. It is important to note that aridity is not necessarily equated with low rainfall, although of course regions of low rainfall may be arid. But there are regions experiencing low rainfall that are not deserts or even semi-deserts. Evaporation may be said to be the crucial factor; in fact, all attempts at defining dry climates are based fundamentally on the relation between evaporation and rainfall. For convenience, however, it may be said that deserts are areas experiencing less than 10 inches of rainfall annually and, often, scarcely any or no moisture at all; semi-arid areas may be said to

PLATE XVII

Above: Wind erosion in Iran. The rocks of a denuded anticline have been scoured by wind action producing upstanding ridges. Note the sinuosity of the strata. Intermittent streams have helped to erode this plateau surface and by careful scrutiny one or two of their courses, in the foreground of the photograph, can be made out. (*Hunting Aero-surveys Ltd.*)

Below: Sand dunes in Death Valley, California, the deepest parts of which lie 280 ft below sea level. (*USIS.*)

PLATE XVIII

Above: Mesas and buttes in Monument Valley on the dry Colorado Plateau in Utah and Arizona. (*Spence Air Photos.*)

Below: Bryce Canyon, Utah, where the multi-coloured rocks have been sculptured into fantastic shapes by the action of wind and rain. (*Pan-American Airways.*)

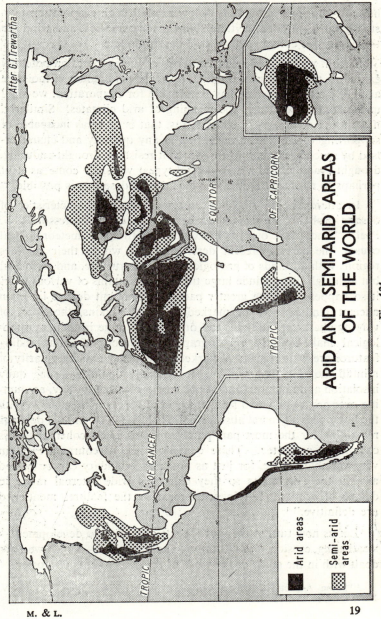

ARID AND SEMI-ARID AREAS
OF THE WORLD

Fig. 121.

After G.T.Trewartha

Arid areas

Semi-arid
areas

have 10-20 inches annually. A low rainfall, high evaporation rate, strong sunshine, high daytime summer temperatures, and wind are the distinctive components of true desert climate.

Thus if we think of aridity in terms of the evaporation potential exceeding the actual precipitation, or as the net amount of moisture available after allowance has been made for evaporation, we shall understand more clearly the meaning of arid climates. Similarly, if we think of deserts in biotic terms, that is of areas incapable of supporting vegetation or vegetation in any quantity and characterised by specialised plant forms (drought-resistant, drought-enduring, drought-evading, and water-storing types) we shall come as near perhaps to appreciating the real meaning of desert as is possible.

In attempting to elucidate the meaning and characteristics of deserts probably we cannot do better than quote Professor R. F. Peel: "Since they owe their existence entirely to meteorological causes, the earth's present deserts include within their confines regions with all kinds of geological history, structure, and tectonics; but although they include large tracts of mountains of various types it so happens that the greater part of the present deserts lie upon ancient land-surfaces of marked stability. Plains, therefore, of varying character, altitude, and origin, bulk large in their morphological make-up. In physiographic conditions the outstanding features are well known: a marked infrequency and irregularity of rainfall, both in time and place; typically dry air; strong daily insolation and nocturnal radiation; and a marked sparsity, amounting over great tracts to a total absence, of vegetational cover. With the latter goes a general absence of true soils, the superficial deposits remaining for the most part purely mineral and incoherent unless chemically cemented. These conditions are of course present in very variable degree, for just as no sharp boundary can be placed around the arid zones so they exhibit a wide internal range in degree of aridity. But in some measure the features mentioned are definitive." [1]

Let us now turn to the four aspects of landscape development— weathering, erosion, transportation, and deposition—which we have dealt with in the study of the work of the other agents of erosion.

[1] "Some Aspects of Desert Geomorphology", *Geography*, Vol. XLV, Nov. 1960, p. 243.

WEATHERING

Considerable doubt exists concerning the exact mechanism of weathering under desert conditions. Formerly it was generally held that desert weathering was the outcome purely and simply of temperature changes and wind action. Observers, impressed by the general absence of surface water and by the inchoate character of desert landscapes, sought to explain the sheets of sand, the piles of angular rock fragments and boulders, and the fantastically etched and sharply serrated mountains in terms of the sudden temperature changes experienced and the action of wind which frequently blew with great strength.

The argument ran on the following lines: because of the clear, cloudless skies and low relative humidity characteristic of desert regions, great diurnal variations of temperature were experienced which directly affected the surface rocks since these were not protected by any soil or vegetation cover which would shield them from insolation by day or radiation by night. Extremes of temperature, which not uncommonly range from $37.8°$ C. (*100° F.*) during the day to as much as $-11.1°$ C. (*20° F.*) of frost at night time, produced acute stresses and strains in the rocks as a result of the alternate rapid expansion, through heating, and equally rapid contraction, through cooling, of the surface layers. This, it was believed, induced mechanical disintegration: the surface layers would be prised away from the underlying rock where the temperature changes were considerably less and gradually the rock would break up and crumble away. Such disintegration was also assisted by the mineralogical composition of the rock. Rocks are usually made up of different minerals which expand and contract at different rates; such differential expansion and contraction would contribute to the shattering and break-up of the rock.

Futhermore, because of the dryness of the land surfaces and the absence of any protective vegetation cover, strong winds had fairly free play, and it was maintained that wind action was the dominant agency in fashioning the relief features. The wind picked up particles of rock waste, which in the process of transportation underwent attrition. Such particles, hurled against rock faces, gradually wore the rocks away: rock pedestals, fretted cliff faces, etc., all pointed to the erosive power of the wind. And the vast piles of sand in the sand deserts were a testimony to the destructive wear and tear of wind action.

Recently studies of desert landscapes and tests in the laboratory have cast considerable doubt upon this orthodox interpretation. For example, D. C. Barton, studying the ancient monuments in Egypt, observed that the weathering of the stonework was more pronounced in Lower than in Upper Egypt; also that the decay of the stonework on individual monuments was greatest on those parts which were constantly in shadow. These facts seemed to suggest that the moister atmospheric conditions in the Delta region induced more accelerated rock decay and that the effects of temperature contrasts were not as significant in causing rock shattering as had previously been thought. The latter conclusion was borne out by laboratory tests. D. T. Griggs exposed granite to alternate heating and cooling through a range of 111° C. (200° F.) which was greater than that experienced naturally in desert environments. Such extreme heating and cooling produced no observable or measurable damage to the rock. When, however, the experiment was repeated and the rock subjected to a cold-water spray it quickly disintegrated. This confirmed the inadequacy of purely thermal shattering. Confirmatory evidence of the effectiveness of moisture as a disintegrative factor is provided by Cleopatra's Needle which has suffered much more damage through weathering in its Thames embankment site since 1878 than it suffered during its three millenia in Egypt. The American geomorphologist, E. Blackwelder, carried out investigations in the arid lands of the United States and came to the conclusion that the thermal-shattering theory of desert weathering was mistaken and untenable, and that chemical weathering involving moisture was the real destroyer of rocks in desert environments just as it was in temperate humid regions.

The accumulated evidence now predisposes towards the acceptance of chemical processes of weathering being more effective than mechanical processes, but it acts in conjunction with mechanical processes. That mechanical weathering plays some part is suggested by the pistol-shot reports of cracking rocks that occasionally are to be heard, by the occurrence of pebbles split as if by frost action, and by the sharp angular shapes of many rock fragments.

Thus the efficacy of thermal-shattering and mechanical weathering cannot be entirely disposed of and ignored, but one can agree with Peel when he says, "It is difficult to conceive how the many tor-like forms, pedestal rocks, rock pinnacles, and arches, to say nothing of tafoni and rock cavities, could be formed by any purely mechanical process of weathering; and direct evidence of chemical decay is often to be found in the deep rotting of exposed rock surfaces especially of the plutonic igneous rocks".[1]

If, however, one subscribes to the belief in the greater import-ance of chemical processes in desert weathering, the question immediately arises: where does the moisture come from which is necessary for chemical weathering? There are many and large areas of desert which are, for all intents and purposes, rainless (one can think of Iquique in the Atacama Desert which had 1 inch of rain in five years and Calama which has never registered a single drop). But occasional showers are experienced in most desert areas and we know from the steep-sided valleys or *wadis* that severe rain-storms do sometimes occur. Passing showers and occasional storms are probably a contributing factor, but it seems more likely that night dews make a more significant contribution. Peel, for instance, found that relative humidity readings in the Libyan Desert showed increases of up to 60 to 70 per cent. by midnight after day minima of 10 per cent. or less. Moreover, Ritchie Calder noted excep-tionally heavy dews in the Negev Desert which were the equivalent of 4 to 5 inches of rainfall annually. It has also been demonstrated that pervious rocks which have undergone desiccation by day absorb water in the form of vapour during the night. Such a process is also linked with the drawing out of salts from the rock through evaporation and their encrustation on the surface, a condition which J. T. Jutson believed was a weathering agency. Jutson cited the crystallisation of salts as a potent factor in the eating away of the bases of rock pedestals.

It becomes clear that there is, in fact, much more moisture in arid areas than is apparent at first sight and, as Peel says, "The apparent total absence of surface water during the daylight hours may thus have misled observers as to the possibilities of water-motivated chemical weathering even in the driest locations".[2] But,

[1] *Op. cit.*, p. 247.   [2] *Op. cit.*, p. 248.

even allowing for this, weathering under arid conditions is an extremely slow business and another question poses itself: how could the present desert landscapes have developed under such a slow rate of weathering? Peel has brought forward the suggestion that the weathering which has been mainly responsible for the present landscape (strictly he is referring to the Sahara but his thesis is applicable to the other arid areas) may well have occurred in the past when the climatic conditions were much more humid. If desert weathering is interpreted in this way, it implies that the present desert landscape is essentially a relict one. There is a considerable body of evidence to indicate wetter phases in the more remote past and it must be admitted that cumulatively it strongly supports Peel's idea. For example, there is the presence of many old lake beds indicating the existence formerly of numerous lakes; there are old strand lines indicative of more extensive lakes than now exist in such depressions as Chad; there are ancient watercourses radiating from such mountain massifs as the Ahaggar; there are fossil soils, such as the fossil laterites in Libya; there are species of cypress and olive in the Tassili found nowhere else which must be looked upon as relic forms of vegetation; there are relic faunas such as tropical fish and dwarf crocodiles which are to be found in pools in Algeria and Tibesti respectively, not to mention historical records of elephants living in North Africa; there is evidence testifying to the occupation by man of areas now deserted by him; and there is the existence of pediments which, according to modern theories of their formation, are water-worn surfaces.

Clearly, there is much evidence to indicate wetter conditions in arid lands in earlier times, and for a long time now there have been advocates of climatic pulsations. But before we can safely theorise about the evolution of desert landscapes there must be more research into the whole problem. Enough has been said, however, to indicate that the orthodox interpretation of weathering in desert regions is questionable to say the least and we must grant a bigger role to the action of water in the weathering process.

WIND EROSION

Erosion by wind is accomplished through two processes: (i) deflation, the removal by lifting or rolling of loose ground material;

and (ii) abrasion, the sand-blast action of wind upon rock surfaces. Deflation is the work of air currents alone; abrasion requires wind-borne cutting tools.

Deflation

This is the erosive process by which wind carries away dry unconsolidated material. The power of the wind to remove material depends upon its velocity, but clearly there is a limit to the size and weight of rock fragments removable by the wind. Fine dust is easily picked up and blown away; heavier material, such as sand grains, can be swept along the ground by strong winds; while coarser material, such as small fragments of rock and pebbles, may be rolled or "jumped" along the ground during storms when eddies and turbulence give the wind extra motive power.

The action of wind is selective and as a result of its "winnowing" process the finer particles are removed to leave behind the coarser and heavier fragments. In places this residual rock litter is strewn with gravel fragments which lie quite flat and have the appearance of having been raked smooth. In other places pebbles and boulders have become firmly and closely fitted together as though the fragments have been deliberately laid and wedged despite their random character. Such sheets of rock fragments are called *desert pavements*. Sometimes the precipitation of salts at the surface, *e.g.* calcium carbonate, gypsum, due to the drawing of water out of the ground and its evaporation, has the effect of cementing the rock fragments together. Cementation of this kind provides effective protection against attrition and further deflation.

One of the principal landform features produced by deflation is the shallow depression termed a *blowout*. Where surface layers are soft or unconsolidated, the wind may scoop out hollows; these, though sometimes of large size—they may be miles long—are usually only a few feet deep. Blowouts are typical of arid plains regions. In the practically featureless High Plains region of North America there are hundreds of these wind-excavated hollows. Worcester quotes one of exceptional size, Big Hollow, in Wyoming, which is 9 miles long, 3 miles wide, and 300 feet deep; during the excavation of this blowout it is estimated that some 10,000 million tons of dust must have been removed by the wind. Some authorities believe that the Qattara Depression excavated in the limestone plateau of western Egypt, the floor of which lies 440 feet below sea level, is a product of wind erosion. Blowouts are to be found in all the arid and semi-arid areas of the world: in Texas, in the Kalahari, in Western Australia, and in Turkestan and Mongolia.

The inception of localised deflation, especially in areas of consolidated material, presents something of a problem. The broad, shallow depressions which have been scooped out of the sandstone rocks of eastern New Mexico and western Texas owe their origin in part to solution. It is thought that in wetter periods in the past downward-percolating water dissolved the calcium carbonate which bonded the sandstone particles together; this loosened the surface layers which allowed deflation to commence during the dry periods. Deflation may be initiated in resistant surface rocks if the strata have suffered displacement through minor faulting. Exposure of a less resistant layer may lead to its attack by the wind and the formation of a hollow. In fact, any dimple on the surface is likely to assist deflation, since wind-eddies are set up which gradually enlarge and deepen the hollow.

One of the most important results of deflation is soil erosion. Abnormal conditions of drought lead to the baking, cracking, and disintegration of the topsoil which can then be readily blown away by strong winds. Even in non-desert locations such as central North America and southern Russia, the ploughing of prairie soil for tillage, thus destroying the protective sod cover, or the overgrazing by animals of grasslands, preventing adequate regeneration of the vegetation, predispose towards soil erosion. For example, in the United States, during the early 'thirties, several years of accentuated drought led to devastating dust storms which removed vast quantities of soil creating the so-called "dust-bowl" of the American West.

Abrasion

This is the sand-blast action of wind upon rock surfaces. Very little mechanical abrasion is accomplished by light winds. Like running water, the wind must have cutting tools if it is to be an effective corrading agent. Strong winds, which are characteristic of deserts, pick up grains of sand and drive them with considerable force against exposed rock surfaces. A strong wind armed with a heavy load of quartz grains can be a powerful eroding agent. It should be borne in mind, however, that wind-driven sand seldom rises to heights of more than 3 or 4 feet above ground level and that most of the sand is concentrated in the 18 inches nearest to the ground. Hence the sand-blast effect is greatest near the surface, becoming increasingly less potent with increasing height.

One of the most common products of wind abrasion is the *ventifact,* a term derived from Latin words for "wind" and "made", in other words "made by the wind". Ventifacts, which may range in size from pebbles to boulders, have two characterising features:

VENTIFACTS

Fig. 122.

first, the surface is faceted and, secondly, it is polished. Pieces of rock, wedged in the ground or too heavy to be moved by the wind, are abraded on the windward side so that the surface is planed down (Fig. 122). The constant scouring of the surface gradually polishes it so that it eventually comes to have a sheen. Ventifacts may have only one face or facet, or several; some possess as many as a dozen. One kind, common in the Sahara, has three faces and is called a *dreikanter* (German: three faces). A question which naturally poses itself is: how does the wind manage to abrade more than one facet on a rock surface? If a rock fragment has been broken off by mechanical weathering it is likely to be angular and if this lies directly in the path of the wind the sharp edge will divide the air current so that some wind flows along one side and some along the other, thereby abrading two surfaces simultaneously.

Then, if the wind changes its prevailing direction or if the stone is moved, new faces will be presented to the air currents for abrasive action by moving sand or wind-borne dust. Constant shifting of position at long intervals will ultimately lead to the production of a multi-faceted ventifact.

Wind abrasion produces a variety of interesting features. Where, for instance, exposed rocks differ in their degree of hardness erosion will take place at different rates; also, if there are any joints or bedding-planes exposed, these will be a target for special attack. Selective and differential abrasion of this kind may produce quite fantastic forms exhibiting grooving, fluting, pitting, honeycombing, etc. Upstanding rocks frequently become "waisted" and pinnacled. The so-called *mushroom* or *pedestal rocks* are a typical feature of wind abrasion. As the wind swirls around the base of an upstanding rock, the portion near the base is subjected to abrasive action and under-cutting takes place. The under-cutting is more drastic a foot or so above ground level than at ground level because friction between the moving air currents and the ground surface reduces the speed of movement, and therefore the cutting action, of the rock particles carried by the wind. The grotesquely shaped forms of Brimham Rocks near Harrogate, though probably weathered in part by ground water, also show clearly the effect of etching, scouring, and under-cutting by wind.

Similar action tends to steepen the basal slopes of hills and something in the nature of cliff faces may be formed. Cliff faces may be undercut at their bases to produce recesses. Cliff faces may also be pitted and honeycombed by sand-blast action to produce rock lattices; these bear a resemblance to lace curtains rent by large holes. There are instances, as in Monument Valley, Arizona, where cavernous openings (similar to sea arches) are to be found; but whether these are entirely due to wind abrasion is disputed.

Where layers of rock of differing hardness are horizontally disposed, features known as *zeugen* are formed. If the hard capping rock becomes cracked or broken, wind abrasion will scour such points of weakness ultimately deepening them and cutting down into the softer underlying strata. Eventually tabular masses of the resistant capping rock are left perched upon the softer rocks beneath. Zeugen, rising up to heights of as much as 150 feet, stand up boldly above ground level. In the final stage they become completely under-cut and collapse. The flat-topped, steep-sided zeugen usually run in parallel sequence. They are common in the "badlands" areas of the United States.

Another striking landscape feature produced by wind corrasion is the *yardang,* a term used in the deserts of Central Asia where it was first described. Fantastically shaped rock ridges, rising up to heights of 20 feet, they are separated by wind-cut troughs; the latter are known as yardang troughs. The yardangs and their associated furrows show a roughly parallel alignment and run in the direction in which the wind customarily and steadily blows; hence there is little doubt that they owe their origin to wind erosion (Fig. 123).

WIND TRANSPORTATION

R. A. Bagnold[1] has shown that rock particles are moved by the wind in three ways: suspension, saltation, and surface creep. The mechanics of wind transportation are rather complex but the main points may be summarised as follows. Immediately above ground level there is a very shallow zone where there is no, or very little, air movement, irrespective of the velocity of the wind above it. This zone of no air movement depends upon the size of the particles covering the ground surface; it is approximately 1/30th of the average of the diameter of the particles. Hence, if the average diameter of the rock particles is 30 millimetres, the zone will be roughly 1 millimetre deep. Wind velocities above this "zone of no movement" increase rapidly with height; here is a parallel with running water whose speed of flow increases with height above the stream bed. Furthermore, just as running water moves with a turbulent flow, so does the wind: eddies and gusts swirling upwards, downwards, or sideways are superimposed on the general forward movement of the wind. It has been shown by experiment that near to the ground the average speed of upward motion of air eddies is roughly 1/5th of the average forward velocity (see Fig. 124). These factors have a considerable bearing on the ability of the wind to move material.

[1] *The Physics of Blown Sand and Desert Dunes,* Methuen, 1941.

FEATURES DUE TO WIND EROSION

ROCK LATTICE

Pitted surface

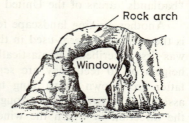

Rock arch

Window

WIND–EXCAVATED ARCH

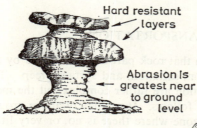

Hard resistant layers

Abrasion is greatest near to ground level

PEDESTAL ROCK

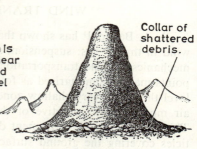

Collar of shattered debris.

INSELBERGE

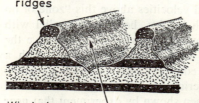

Hard rock gives rise to upstanding ridges

Wind abraded furrows in soft rock.

ZEUGENS

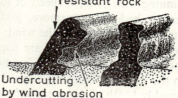

Upstanding ridges of resistant rock

Undercutting by wind abrasion

YARDANGS

Fig. 123.

An analysis of wind-blown material shows that it falls into two size groups: particles with diameters less than 0·06 millimetres, which are classified as dust, and those with diameters greater than 0·06 millimetres, which are classified as sand. Dust, very fine par-

WIND VELOCITY AND THE MOVEMENT OF PARTICLES

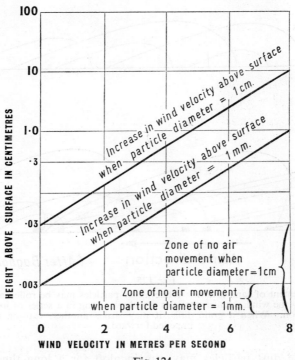

Fig. 124.

ticles of clay, mud, or silt, is picked up by the wind and carried in suspension; it is held aloft by eddies and in this way may be transported over very long distances—as much as 1,000 miles. Dust, too, can be lifted to great heights and Worcester quotes an example of a dust storm in the United States in November, 1933, which reached a height of 9,000 feet. Dust particles are buoyed up by the upward movement of turbulent air since the terminal velocity of the particle (*i.e.* the constant rate of fall attained by the particle when the acceleration due to gravity is balanced by the resistance of the air through which it is falling) is smaller than the velocity of the upward moving air.

SALTATION

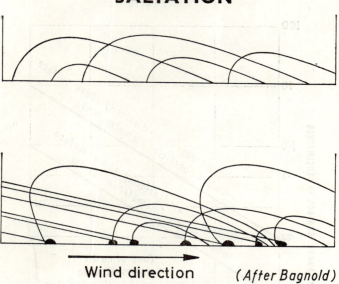

Wind direction   *(After Bagnold)*

Fig. 125.

The movement of sand grains. While larger particles may be rolled along the surface by the wind, smaller particles are blown along in a series of jumps, *i.e.* by saltation. When a grain falls, it may strike another, causing it to be impelled forward.

While dust particles may remain aloft for a long time, sand grains are usually too large to be held aloft for more than a very brief period. Grains of sand have terminal velocities which are greater than the upward moving currents of air, hence even when they are lifted into the air they fall back to the ground. How, then, if the upward moving air is incapable of supporting sand grains, do they become lifted into the air in the first place? The answer seems to be that the sand particles are ejected into the air as a result of impact with another particle. The wind is capable of rolling particles along the ground and when these suddenly come into sharp contact with other particles they bounce off into the air or, alternatively, cause the particles with which they have collided to be lifted into the air. Thus the sand particle is said to become airborne by *saltation*. Once in the air, a grain is carried forward by the wind but at the same time it is pulled towards the ground; it thus follows a parabolic path and strikes the ground at an angle varying between 10 and 16 degrees. When the grain hits the ground it may, if the surface is hard, rebound to almost its original height and follow a new trajectory. Impact and rebound may occur many times, and so lead to a particle being moved over a considerable distance. If when the grain hits the ground for the first time, it falls on a soft surface, such as loose sand, it may bury itself in the sand, but, as it does so, it may cause other grains to be thrown into the air through its impact. Thus if we could as it were put the desert surface under a microscope we should see millions of grains ricochetting off one another and the whole surface would appear to be dancing. Sand particles seldom rise more than 6 feet above ground level during transit, and the greater part of the movement occurs within a zone 18 inches from the ground.

Some of the larger grains of sand never become airborne even under the impact of other grains; they merely roll forward. Strong winds blowing over flat surfaces may, however, roll gravel fragments and pebbles up to 2-3 inches in diameter along the ground, though such large fragments do not move very far. Material which is pushed or rolled along the ground in this way is said to move by surface creep. It is generally believed that between one-fifth and one-quarter of the total weight of drifting sand travels by surface creep, the remainder being moved by saltation.

It is difficult, if not impossible, to estimate the quantity of material eroded and transported by the wind in any year, but there can be little doubt that it is extremely large. Worcester quotes some estimates of quantities of material deposited as a result of dust storms: one, which occurred in the Sahara and covered nearly 500,000 square miles, resulted in an estimated amount of nearly

2,000,000 tons being deposited over an area of 168,500 square miles which equalled a deposit of just over 12 tons of dust per square mile; another, a dust storm of short duration which happened in Nebraska during the "dust bowl" period of the early 'thirties, resulted in a deposit of 35 tons of dust per square mile. J. A. Udden, who made a careful examination of dust storms in the western part of the United States, estimated that in one year something of the order of 850,000,000 tons of dust was transported over a distance of nearly 1,500 miles.[1] Clearly, the amount of material transported by the winds annually must be enormous.

WIND DEPOSITION

The finer particles of dust which are carried in suspension by the wind, and the larger fragments such as sand grains or rock fragments which are transported by saltation or rolling, eventually are deposited as a result of the reduction in the wind's velocity. The two chief deposits are dust deposits generally known as *loess* and sand deposits which form dunes or sand-spreads.

Loess

Loess, a German name, is a deposit accumulated from wind-borne dust. Carried over long distances by strong, steady winds, the dust, originating in arid desert regions, eventually arrives in more humid areas where, washed out of the atmosphere by rain, it settles and accumulates. Loess was first studied by the German traveller-geologist, von Richthofen, in north-western China where it is spread over an extensive area. It is a fine-grained, coherent, friable, porous, non-stratified material, yellowish or buff in colour. Although it is not stratified—strong evidence of its aeolian origin—it has a columnar structure; this, it is believed, derives from the stems and roots of grasses which became buried as the loess accumulated. A vertical section of loess reveals numerous fine vertical tubes commonly lined with a deposit of calcium carbonate left by the decaying vegetable matter. These grass "casts" help to reinforce the loess and this explains why loess, though easily erodible, stands

[1] "Dust and Sand Storms in the West," *Pop. Science Monthly*, Vol. 49, 1896, pp. 655-64.

PLATE XIX

Above: View across Whitby Harbour. The sea has eroded a gap between the jetty and the cliff so that a bridge has had to be built to link the two together. Some of the shales in the upper part of the cliffs are slipping down over the harder beds beneath, resulting in the tilting of the houses on parts of the cliff.

Below: Stack and arch, Armed Knight and Enys Dodnan, near Land's End, Cornwall. (*Eric Kay.*)

PLATE XX

Above: Pebble storm beach at Newgale Sands, Pembrokeshire, Wales. Piles of pebbles such as this may be thrown up by wave action during storms. Others, such as the famous Chesil Bank, in Dorset, are similar storm beaches but alongshore drift has also helped in the case of the Chesil Bank, the Isle of Portland acting as a bulwark and helping to prevent the further movement of the deposited material. *(Eric Kay.)*

Below: Stair Hole, Dorset. The sea, penetrating the coastal cliffs, has found its way inland. Wave attack, first producing caves, then tunnels and finally breaching the narrow coastal band of limestones has led to the erosion of a circular bay in the softer clays and shales inland. The better known Lulworth Cove is a similar feature to the east of Stair Hole. Note the upfold of limestone. *(Eric Kay.)*

up in steep walls. The loess occurs in thicknesses of several hundreds of feet, smothering much of the pre-existing landscape so that only the higher hills rise, nunatak-like, above the loessic mantle. The fact that the loess climbs up hill slopes is another pointer to its aeolian origin. This fact, together with its lack of stratification, the presence of the vertical tubing, and the occurrence of shells of land

DISTRIBUTION OF LOESS IN NORTH CHINA

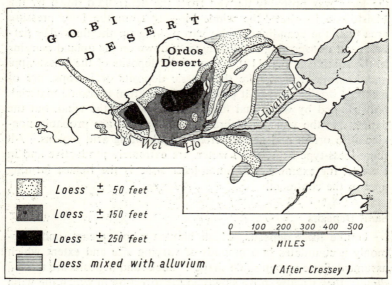

Fig. 126.

The extensive loess deposits of north-western China are probably derived from the Gobi Desert and may well be being added to at the present day for dust storms in winter are a feature of northern China. Much of the alluvium of the Great Plain of Northern China is really re-deposited loess; it is sometimes called secondary loess.

snails refutes the early suggestion that loess may have been of marine origin. The loess deposits of north-western China (Fig. 126) occur in an area of semi-arid climate or light rainfall, hence they have been deeply eroded in many areas and produce a so-called "badland" topography. Much of the alluvium that floors the Great Plain of Northern China is composed of loess carried down and re-deposited by the flooding Hwang-ho; this alluvium is sometimes termed "secondary loess".

Similar deposits occur in other parts of the world, *e.g.* on the North European Plain, in Asia Minor, in the central part of the United States, in Argentina, and in Australia. In Europe, the deposit forms a widespread, but discontinuous, belt stretching from the Paris Basin (where it is known as *limon*) across the Hercynian foreland in Germany and Poland into southern Russia. In Europe, the loess was probably derived from the debris laid down by the Pleistocene ice-sheet, the winds blowing from the high pressure area over the Scandinavian ice cap picking up the finer clay particles and transporting and laying them down on the upland margins to the south (see Fig. 119). The *adobe* deposits of the Mississippi and Missouri basins, like the loessic deposits of Europe, are of disputed origin; part of it probably comes from morainic material, redistributed by water and finally laid down by the wind, but the deposits in the west, in Nebraska and Kansas, are probably non-glacial in origin and derived from neighbouring arid regions. All these loess-type soils, given water, are extremely productive and in Europe, for example, the limon-loess zone is the richest farming area in the continent.

Sand Deposits

Unlike loess deposits, which blanket whole areas, sand commonly accumulates into mounds of varying size and extent which assume definite recognisable shapes. Such sand deposits are termed *dunes*; they usually move slowly in the direction in which the wind is blowing. An interesting feature of the dune is that, once formed, it tends to perpetuate itself. Dunes vary widely in size ranging from only a few feet in height and a few yards in length to as much as 700 feet in height with base widths of 2-3,000 feet; usually, however, they do not exceed about 100 feet in height. Sand dunes may occur singly, but more commonly they form "colonies" which cover large areas, often thousands of square miles.

Dunes are found along many stretches of coast in Britain and so it is possible for us to study them at first hand. They show certain of the characteristics of desert dunes, but they also possess differences in many particulars and it is wise not to confuse coast dunes with desert dunes. In coastal localities they usually occur on only a small scale, as there is only a limited supply of sand available for their formation. The Culbin Sands in Morayshire form the most extensive area of dunes in Britain. Another important difference is that coastal dunes are more readily anchored, since there is usually some vegetation which helps to fix them; only on exposed coasts open to strong prevailing winds, as in the Landes district of Biscayan France, is there chance of considerable move-

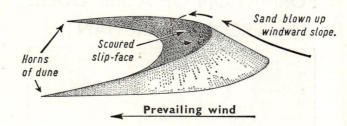

A BARCHAN

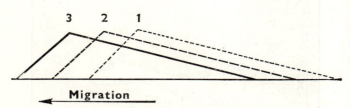

Fig. 127.

Barchans are crescentic in shape. They form where the wind direction remains more or less uniform throughout the year. Barchans migrate downwind and, generally speaking, the larger the barchan the slower it moves.

ment. In the latter area, in fact, conifer plantations had to be grown to halt the encroachment of the dunes into the fertile lands of Aquitaine.

Two chief types of dune may be distinguished: *barchans* which are crescent-shaped and have two horns pointing downwind; they possess a gentle convex slope on the windward side and a steep slope on the leeward side; they advance as a result of the wind

driving sand grains up the gentle windward slope to the crest of
the dune, where the sand then slides down the slip face of the lee
slope; and, secondly, *seifs*, long ridges of sand which may run for
miles; they get their name from their fancied resemblance to the

STAGES IN THE
FORMATION OF A SEIF DUNE
FROM A BARCHAN

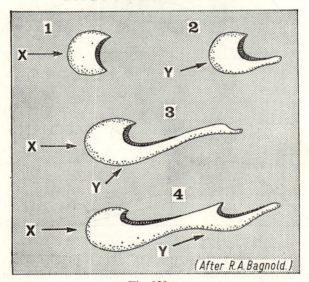

Fig. 128.

The formation of seif dunes is not completely understood but it is believed that
they originate from barchans.   If a cross-wind intervenes the barchan will tend
to swing round and one of the horns will become elongated.   If the wind from
the new direction persists the limb will continue to grow and the barchan will
become changed into a seif dune.

long, flat blade of an Arab sword; and, unlike the barchan which
always lies transverse to the prevailing wind direction, the seif
dune runs parallel to the prevailing wind, but is also subject to
cross-winds which, blowing alternately from quarter to quarter, are

responsible for its forward movement. Barchans may be transformed into seifs or seif-type dunes; Fig. 128 shows how this transformation may occur.

Dunes are developed in level areas. As mentioned above, they may occur singly, or in groups often disposed in regular series, or most commonly in vast colonies where the dune ridges are partially coalesced. In the latter form they give rise to the familiar sandseas, vast areas of seemingly chaotic, ever-changing dune ridges such as photographs of Saharan *erg* display.

Apart from dune deposits, there are extensive areas in desert regions covered with spreads of sand which lie level or are very gently undulating and whose surfaces are rippled. Although the surfaces of these sand sheets or spreads may be in constant motion, they preserve their general surface characteristics. This may be due to the fact that such sheets are nearly always strewn with pebbles: the wind seems to spread the loose sand evenly between them.

WATER EROSION IN ARID REGIONS

There are certain other landforms in arid areas which owe their origins and characteristic features to water, as distinct from wind, action. They exhibit the effects of both intermittent and regular erosion by running water both in the past and at present. Chief amongst these features are wadis and canyons, mesas and buttes, bajadas, playas, pediments, and inselberge.

Wadis and Canyons

Although there is little rainfall in arid regions, some does occur from time to time usually in the form of short, torrential downpours. The heavy rain swills off the surface collecting and carrying large quantities of the debris produced by desert weathering. If water is carrying a near maximum load it is able to use this load for active scour, then the torrents, mainly undertaking vertical erosion, quickly scour out deep, steep-sided valleys called *wadis*. Partly because of the high rate of evaporation and partly because there is so much loose solid matter available, such torrents rarely travel far; they quickly become choked with material, are converted into mudflows, and lose their momentum. The load is thus deposited as a mass of loose, unconsolidated material, spread out after the fashion of an alluvial fan. Once the fragmentary material has dried out, the wind can attack it, the finer particles gradually being winnowed out. The Hadhramaut coast of southern Arabia is scarred with craggy, deeply-cut, ravines providing some of the most spectacular wadis in the world. Sometimes wadis are to be found in areas which are extremely arid, and in which rain is so infrequent that present-day, or recent, fluvial erosion must be discounted. The presence of such wadis presents a problem. It is thought that they probably originated in pluvial periods during the Pleistocene glaciation since at that time the high pressure systems developed over the ice-sheet caused the southward displacement of the wind belts. If this be the explanation, then the northern part of the Sahara, for instance, would periodically come under the influence of the Westerly Winds, which would bring sufficient rain for the formation of streams and erosion by water.

In arid areas where rivers manage to maintain a regular flow (either by receiving water from mountain areas within the region, such as the rivers Colorado and Snake, or from rains outside the region, as in the case of the Nile) especially deep valleys have been carved out called *canyons*. The most spectacular of these is the Colorado Canyon in the west of the United States. The Grand Canyon is 200 miles long, 5-15 miles wide at the surface, and over 6,000 feet deep. The extraordinary excavation of the Rio Colorado has been assisted, however, by the fact that the plateau across which it runs has been slowly rising during the past several million years. The plateau is built up of horizontally-bedded rocks, including resistant limestones and sandstones, and softer shales. As a result, a succession of canyons has been formed, the harder and more resistant strata giving rise to vertical cliffs, the softer and more easily eroded beds producing more gentle slopes; the effect has been to produce an alternation of cliffs and benches on the canyon sides. The deep entrenched river gives rise to spectacular and fantastic scenery made even more wonderful by the colours of the rocks—grey, green, buff, purple, and brown—which have been preserved by the dryness of the climate. Though less spectacular, the Nile has carved a great "slot" in the surface of the African plateau which, in Egypt, varies in width from less than half a mile in the south, where it cuts through granitic rocks, to some 10 miles in the north where limestone prevails while the valley is bounded by cliff-like walls which rise in some places to over 1,000 feet above the river.

Mesas and Buttes

Plateau surfaces in arid lands, such as those referred to above, are scored by many deep valleys. Highly dissected areas form what is known as "badland" country, characterised by topographic features known as mesas and buttes. Where plateaus composed of

MESA, BUTTE AND CANYON

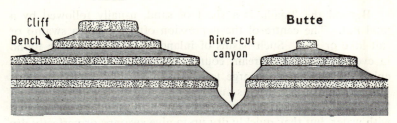

Fig. 129.

The diagram shows three characteristic landforms developed in semi-arid lands such as south-western United States.

horizontal rock layers are capped by resistant beds, which protect the strata beneath, tabular, steep-sided hills are produced as a result of erosion; such landforms are termed *mesas*, from the Spanish word for a table. *Buttes* are small, isolated remnants of mesas (Fig. 129). The "badlands" of South Dakota in the United States exhibit an intricate mass of steep-sided, fantastically etched mesas and buttes which are the residual remnants of flat beds of soft sandstone and clay overlain by gravels. The Colorado Plateau country is similarly diversified by mesas and buttes separated by deep ravines. See Plate XVIII.

Intermontane Basins

Intermontane basins and depressions in arid regions show distinctive features. Streams of regular or intermittent character may descend from the surrounding highlands into the depressions, which usually are more or less enclosed. These streams carry rock debris down into the basins. Around the periphery of these basins is to be found a piedmont fringe of water-borne deposits. Wherever a stream course opens into a depression an alluvial fan or scree cone tends to be built up as a result of the check in the speed of stream flow. Where depressions have been faulted and there are sudden changes in the gradient, large accumulations of scree, gravel, and other coarse material occur at the foot of the fault scarps. Sometimes a number of fans or cones coalesce along the margin of the depression producing a gently undulating inclined slope; such piedmont benches are termed *bahadas* or *bajadas*.

Beyond the bajada is a sheet of sand, usually followed by a mud flat. The centre of the depression often carries a swamp or salt lake or pan. Such basins of inland drainage are to be found in every arid area. Stream courses, carrying trickles of water or ephemeral streams, converge towards the centre of the depression where there is a pan. Pans may be defined as the temporary inland lakes of areas of arid climate. From time to time they are flooded with water, but they quickly dry up to give swamps or perfectly dry salt flats. Pans are known by a variety of names: *vlei* and *sebkha* in Africa, *playa* and *salina* in North America, and *salar* in South America. Sometimes these names are applied not only to the temporary lakes but to the depressions in which they lie.

Pediments

Pediments are features of many arid and semi-arid areas (and of the savanna lands also). They may be defined as gently sloping surfaces of rock which stretch away from the base of a plateau or hill mass. The lower parts of the pediments commonly slope upwards at an angle of about $\frac{1}{2}$ degree, the upper parts at approximately 5 degrees. Pediments are usually bare rock surfaces but sometimes there is a thin veneer of weathered fragmentary material. The lowest slopes, furthest away from the adjacent upland, may be smothered by weathered and transported debris. A striking feature

of pediments is that their upper limits are usually sharply defined
by a steep scarp slope leading up to the plateau or hill mass over-
looking them. "Pediments are superficially similar to bajadas,"

INTERMONTANE BASINS
IN ARID AREAS

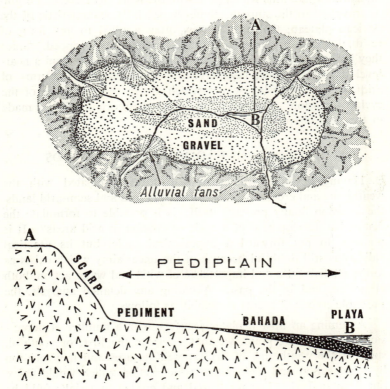

Fig. 130.

says Monkhouse, "but while the latter are undulating plains of
aggradation formed by the accumulation of debris, the pediments
are more level plains of degradation." [1]   The origin of these pediments will be discussed in the next chapter.

[1] *Principles of Physical Geography.*   University of London Press, p. 171.

Inselberge

In many arid areas steep-sided, round-topped hills with often a basal collar of fragmentary material rise up sharply from generally level surfaces. They are usually regarded as residual features, the final remnants of former level, higher plateau surfaces which have been weathered and eroded. The term *inselberge* was first used by the German geographer, Passarge, to describe the monadnock-like hills which he saw in the Kalahari Desert. Originally applied to the smooth, dome-shaped hills characteristic of the African plateau, the term is now often applied to any form of residual hill in arid regions—round-topped or flat-topped. Since they have been isolated by circumdenudation and rise from a near-level erosion surface, inselberge are characteristic landforms of arid and semi-arid landscapes which are in the late stage of the cycle of erosion. Further reference to their origin will be made in the next chapter.

THE CYCLE OF EROSION IN ARID LANDS

Having described the various features associated with the weathering and erosion of rock surfaces in arid and semi-arid lands, the question finally presents itself: is it possible to formulate the distinctive development of a cycle of erosion in arid areas? It is possible to put forward a hypothetical cycle, but its practical validity is still doubtful because of the uncertainty which exists as to the relative roles and importance of wind and water action, both at present and in the past. Avoiding any detailed analysis, the probable course of events is roughly as follows.

Assuming an upland plateau surface with a number of depressions as a starting point, we may envisage the first, or youthful, stage as the weathering of the exposed surfaces and their erosion by wind action and intermittent water action which would carve out deep ravines. The weathered and eroded material would be swept by wind and water action into the surface basins leading to their infilling and hence raising their floor levels. The Colorado Desert possibly represents this youthful stage.

Next, in the mature stage, the intervening ridges between the depressions become dissected and lowered and the basins begin to coalesce, as well as becoming filled up. The stream courses become enlarged as they cut backwards into the plateau and hence the pediments at the plateau base are extended. As this erosive work proceeds the higher land is reduced and extensive pediments, overlain by sand and gravel spreads and dunes, are produced. Parts of the Libyan and Afghanistan-Baluchistan Deserts are probably in the stage of senility.

Desert Landscapes

As a result of weathering, wind, and water action, deserts, whether torrid or temperate, show an astonishing variety of landscapes. Four main types of desert landscape are commonly distinguished, each showing fairly distinctive landforms and landscape features, although even within a relatively small area two or more of the "type features" may be represented.

(i) The sandy desert, in its typical form, consists of vast sheets of sand which may lie almost horizontal or which may be shaped into dunes. The so-called "sand seas" are undulating and monotonous. Libya contains two extensive areas of sand sea, the Calanscio Sand Sea in the north-east of the country and the Rebiana Sand Sea in the east-central region. Sandy deserts are found in two main parts of Arabia, in the Nefud in the north and in the Rub' al Khali or Empty Quarter in the south. Sandy deserts are called *erg* in the Sahara and *koum* in central Asia.

(ii) A second type of desert consists of extensive sheets of angular fragments or gravel; it is known as *reg* in the Algerian Sahara, as *serir* in Libya, and as *harras* in Arabia. In Egypt stretches of serir have a pebbly-like surface. The harras or stony desert of Arabia and Syria has been derived from the weathering of widespread surface flows of basalt. In places the surface comprises great rounded boulders. The stony deserts are usually very difficult to traverse.

(iii) Where deflation and abrasion have been dominant and the loose material has been transported away bare rock surfaces (sometimes with local patches of gravel or sand) are dominant. In aspect the *hamada* desert may present extensive wind-smoothed pavements or they may be etched by wind action to give a highly diversified surface of zeugen, yardangs, and the like. Such fantastically shaped deserts are common in certain parts of the Asiatic deserts—see, for example, Plate XVII. Baked clay plains, found in the western United States, may be said to fall into the hamada category. Hamada is bare, desolate, and sterile desert.

(iv) Finally, there are mountain deserts where erosion, probably by water action in periods of wetter climatic conditions, has dissected high plateaus into complex, grotesque, highly serrated forms. The Ahaggar and Tibesti massifs of the central Sahara, the peaks of Sinai, and the intensely dissected south-western edge of Arabia fall into this category. Wild and rugged with steep, craggy faces, deeply scored by ravines, and with their valley slopes littered with accumulations of rock waste, the mountain deserts offer harsh, but truly magnificent, scenery.

CHAPTER 16

TROPICAL HUMID AND SEMI-HUMID LANDSCAPES

We have noted that W. M. Davis treated the normal cycle of erosion as that of running water. In addition to the fluvial cycle, he recognised a glacial and an aeolian cycle for he saw that the work of ice and wind produced different landscapes. He recognised and emphasised a difference of "process" resulting from changes in the manner of weathering and in the medium of transportation. In Chapter 12 we studied the work undertaken by rivers and the results of fluvial erosion; but what was said in that chapter largely appertained to the events taking place under *humid temperate conditions.* The question raises itself: what happens under *humid* or *semi-humid tropical conditions?* Do streams work in the same way? Are landforms that are developed of the same kind? Are there any different factors at work? It must be admitted that though English geographers are familiar with the typical landforms that are developed under equatorial and savanna conditions, little work upon, or understanding of, the development of landforms in the humid or semi-humid tropics has so far been attempted. German and French geographers are much more familiar with the development of landscape features under these exotic conditions than we are.

In this chapter we shall attempt to show in a brief and simple way some of the differences in landforms that occur in humid or semi-humid tropical conditions and draw attention to some of the factors that are at play which are responsible for landscape differences. The two main factors responsible for landscape development are (*a*) temperature and humidity, and (*b*) the behaviour of soils. The equatorial forest lands and the tropical savanna lands have fairly contrasting sets of climatic conditions: the one is perennially hot and wet, the other hot but with marked wet and dry seasons; under these basically different climatic conditions we should expect different operations in the land-forming processes.

317

Rock Weathering and Soil Formation

Let us first turn our attention to weathering in these tropical regions. In tropical humid climates weathering is fairly uniform from place to place. It takes place under conditions of perpetual warmth and constant heavy torrential rains. There are no great fluctuations in heat and cold as may, and frequently do, occur in temperate latitudes; neither is there any frost action. Because of the great heat and abundant moisture, the weathering process is more emphatically chemical in character than mechanical. The warm rain water, well carbonated and charged with humic acid (derived from decaying vegetation) breaks down the silicates (especially felspar) which are common constituents of most rocks. The salts, derived from this breakdown, are easily leached away because their solubility is increased at higher temperatures, leaving the sesqui-oxides (alumina, iron) in the soil. Just as vegetable matter decays at an accelerated rate under hot, humid conditions, so weathering operates very rapidly; according to Miller, it is ten times as rapid as in arctic climates, and more than three times as fast as in temperate climates.[1]

This accelerated rate of weathering means that rocks rot very quickly and also very deeply. Although the thickness of the regolith or weathered mantle overlying the bedrock varies, it may be up to 100 feet thick in many places. This deep layer of regolith is maintained by progressive rock decay at depth.

Because there is an excess of rainfall over evaporation in tropical humid climates there is a steady percolation of rain water downwards which effects a steady and continuous removal of soluble salts in the soil, the process of leaching. Where a thick vegetation cover exists some replacement of the solubles occurs through humus renewal but where the forest has been removed and there is no humus to re-fortify the soil the soil undergoes progressive deterioration and increasing infertility results. Continuous cultivation of such soils quickly exhausts them and herein lies the explanation for the custom of shifting agriculture which is common in the inter-tropical belt. Where the organic content of the soil is low, ground water is enabled to break down complex aluminium silicates more speedily than other compounds; the silicates thus tend to be

[1] "Climate and the Geomorphic Cycle." *Geography,* 1961, p. 189.

removed leaving behind the clay elements and the iron oxides. This process, termed *laterisation*, leads to the production of a soil which is composed, in the main, of clays and iron compounds and which is distinctly red in colour (due to the oxides of iron). The end product of laterisation is laterite, a bright red soil of cellular structure which is porous, highly leached, and practically sterile. True laterite is of limited occurrence within the tropics but most soils betray, to a greater or lesser extent, laterisation.

In regions having semi-humid tropical conditions—the so-called savanna lands—high temperatures are experienced throughout the year but there is a distinctive alternation of wet and dry seasons. During the summer convective storms give rains that rival in intensity those of equatorial regions but in winter there are many weeks or even months of drought. During the rainy period there is much run off where there are slopes but where the terrain is level there is much percolation for the ground is thirsty. Percolation leads, as in equatorial regions, to heavy leaching; soluble salts and bases are removed from the soil which suffers a deterioration in its fertility. With the onset of the dry season, however, evaporation induces an upward movement of the ground water and solubles are drawn up into the topsoil. The accumulation of mineral matter in the upper layers leads to the development of a hardpan. On level surfaces this pan forms within a few feet of the surface but on slopelands, since the water drains downwards, the pan develops at the bottom of the slope. For example, on the Planalto Central of Brazil the sandy and gravelly soils, which have developed from the weathered sandstones, contain ferruginous residual matter which forms a pan, known as *canga*. This pan, often lying near the surface, tends to make the soil impervious and is so tough that steel ploughs drawn by tractors often make no impression on it.

These ferruginated layers act like a coat of armour and play an important role in the development of minor landforms, helping to preserve the flatness of the landscape. Where the horizontal stratified layers are broken through, the pan functions as a hard, resistant capping and helps to produce mesa-like hills.

In the tropics rainfall is the really important factor in weathering. In equatorial regions the perennial warmth and wetness results, as we have noted, in chemical weathering being predominant, although this is greatly helped by biological weathering. In the savanna, with their seasonal changes, we should expect a change in the manner of weathering according to the seasonal conditions; and this, in fact, is what we get. During the hot moist summer chemical weathering is predominant and proceeds at a rapid pace but in the dry winter season mechanical weathering takes precedence and the rate of weathering is reduced.

Soil Erosion

At this point we may make a brief reference to soil erosion since it is in these regions of tropical humid and semi-humid climates that it is especially pronounced and reaches serious proportions.

In tropical regions, since the parent rocks break down fairly rapidly, soils may attain a considerable depth if they are formed on an almost level surface; on anything but gentle slopes, however, they are easily eroded away, and this is especially the case if the vegetative cover is removed. There is, indeed, a very delicate balance between the vegetative cover and the soils.

The heavy torrential rains of equatorial thunderstorms on steep slopes play havoc with the soil if the vegetative cover has been removed and sheet erosion and gullying occur. Tropical forest shields the ground from the intensity of the rainfall while the ground "mat" and plant roots help to protect and hold the soil in place. If deforestation occurs for any reason, such as shifting agricultural practices, the soil becomes prone to erosion. All bare surfaces suffer from mechanical erosion and are rapidly gullied by rainfall of tropical intensity.

Soil erosion is much worse, however, in the savanna lands. Here, to begin with, there is much less protective vegetative cover; moreover, during the dry season the soil bakes hard and cracks so that when the torrential rains commence it easily succumbs to mechanical erosion. Large areas in Africa and South America have suffered seriously in this respect. Soil erosion has resulted as much from human misuse of the land, *e.g.* the firing of the grasslands to produce better pasture and the over-grazing of the pasturelands by animals, as from purely physical causes.

In some areas as, for example, in parts of Colombia and Ceara, in north-eastern Brazil, the land has been carved and fretted to produce a fantastically diversified surface such as that illustrated in Plate XVIII. Not all land which has suffered erosion is as badly eroded as this, of course, but the photograph well illustrates what may happen under certain conditions. Eroded land of this kind is clearly beyond redemption.

The Work of Streams

Because of the heavy and regular rainfall in equatorial regions there is continuous run-off. The abundant run-off has given rise to a drainage pattern of closely-spaced streams. Where the forest cover is intact, streams are often relatively clear, for the vegetation mat and plant roots act as a kind of filter of sediment; on the other hand, where there is no protective cover the streams are heavily charged with sediment. Since there is deep and rapid weathering, there is always an abundance of material awaiting removal. Rivers flow swiftly because of the volume of discharge and the rate of removal of material is fairly rapid, especially on steep slopes. On plains the rivers are frequently braided, that is the river splits up into an interlacing network of distributaries with shoals and shingle banks often forming low islands. Although braiding is not necessarily related to an excess of total load transported by the river, there can be little doubt that the heavily-laden waters predispose towards the braiding conditions. Tropical rivers lower the surfaces of their drainage basins much more quickly than do those of temperate latitudes; as a very rough generalisation it may be said that tropical rivers lower their basins ten times as fast as their temperate latitude counterparts.

In the savanna lands, where there is a seasonal distribution of rainfall, the rivers flow in spate during the summer rainy season and frequently flood but in the dry season they dwindle to dry courses punctuated with water holes. Many of the rivers on savanna plains flow in broad shallow hollows, rather than in valleys, flooding extensively in the wet season and often changing their courses. When the summer rains begin "the heavy rain runs off and overflows the banks of shallow dry watercourses and runs as sheet-floods over the floor between the dead tufts of tussock grass

Where this happens on a slope, sheet-floods first do their work, detrital fans are formed (some of the most fertile and well-drained areas of cultivation), and later gullies form and grow. Where the land is flat the river spreads and anastomoses over a wide area. There is no forest to confine the stream and small rivers may find themselves in new courses after the rains".[1]

Mass Wasting

Mass movement is especially pronounced in the tropics. The tendency to mass wasting is promoted by the frequently loosely consolidated and deeply weathered soil and mantle, by the frequent presence of steep slopes, and by, in savanna regions, the heavy saturating rains which follow long, dry spells and the frequent absence of any substantial cover of vegetation. All these factors assist downslope movement. Dobby, writing about equatorial regions, has said: "Because laterised soils are so wet and thick, the destructive processes of slumping and slipping assert themselves strongly. Soil creep on slopes operates relatively fast, particularly if an iron pan exists not far below the surface. Whole sections of a hillside may thus slump down into a valley leaving a scar which wild vegetation needs a long time to conceal. Road cuttings frequently slump at the sides as though huge spoons had been used upon them. Almost any ditch will show soil creep in the form of root-matted topsoil hanging well out over the side of the ditch." [2]

In January, 1967, the region around Rio de Janeiro, in eastern Brazil, following unusually heavy rains, suffered severe flooding and large-scale mass movement. Many villages and farms were destroyed or damaged and many killed through a series of landslips. This is a recurring feature of the region but in 1967 it proved to be more calamitous than usual.

Mudflows are a common feature on the slopes of volcanic cones in low latitudes, *e.g.* in Java where they are called *lahars*. The loose deposits of ash on the steep slopes of volcanoes form suitable material favourably placed for removal as mudflows when saturated by rain.

[1] A. Austin Miller, *op. cit.*, p. 195.

[2] *South-east Asia*, University of London Press, p. 81.

Thus landforms due to mass wasting are a common feature in tropical regions.

Sugar-loaves and Half-oranges

A feature of areas composed of granite, especially where there is high relief, is the upstanding dome-shaped hill. Features of this kind are commonly called "sugar-loaves" if they have pointed summits, and "half-oranges" if they have blunted, flattish tops. The best-known examples are those in the vicinity of Rio de Janeiro. Here, on the steep slopes of the Serra do Mar, they are of common occurrence. The peculiar shapes of these hills are due to the spheroidal weathering or exfoliation of the crystalline rocks of which they are composed.

Although these sugar-loaf forms are usually thought of as being the product of rather special processes of weathering and erosion peculiar to the rain-forest regions of low altitudes, it should be noted that some authorities deny this and claim that these crystalline domes are not peculiar to a specific climatic zone but have a world-wide occurrence and can be distinguished even in Arctic regions.

Savanna Landscapes

Over much of inter-tropical Africa and South America, especially where tropical semi-humid climates prevail but also in adjacent semi-arid areas, there is a distinctive type of landscape. The land surfaces, over extensive areas, are remarkably uniform; level surfaces often stretch as far as the eye can see with no hills to break the skyline. The general effect of this uniformity is to give an impression of great monotony. In some places, however, hills with steep slopes rise abruptly from the plateau surfaces; these residual masses, as we noted in the last chapter, are known as inselberge.

Although we often talk about the African Plateau and the Brazilian Plateau as though they formed single general plateau surfaces, there are in fact several plateau surfaces. We must try to visualise the African and Brazilian tablelands as consisting of a series of plateau surfaces, lying at varying elevations, which are terminated by, or separated from each other by, steep erosional scarps. Thus we can think of these plateaus as descending in a series of gigantic steps and of the landforms resulting from successive stages of denudation.

Level or flat-topped plateaus, steep scarp-like edges, and steep-sided hills rising abruptly from the plateaus are the outstanding landscape features. The plateau surfaces are unmistakably erosional in their character and in some ways resemble the forms of the peneplains which are recognisable in temperate latitudes, but so distinctive are these savanna landforms that some geomorphologists believe them to have a distinctive mode of origin.

Pediplanation

It will be recalled that in Chapter 9 we discussed the idea of erosion by means of hill slope retreat and in the last Chapter we referred to the formation of pediments. Denudation by scarp retreat and pedimentation is known as *pediplanation* and it is this process which is held, by many recent workers such as Lester King, to be responsible for the fashioning of savanna landscapes. In interpreting and explaining the origin of savanna landscapes by pediplanation, three questions present themselves: (i) how is the flattish form of the pediment developed, (ii) how is the scarp-slope separating two pediments at different levels maintained, and (iii) how are the steeply-sloping inselberge formed?

The origin of pediments is not understood with any certainty but it is generally believed that they are water-worn surfaces and that the dominant erosive action has been lateral rather than vertical. The general argument runs as follows: streams, emerging from the adjacent highlands, are heavily charged with detrital material, because rock weathering proceeds fairly rapidly under the tropical conditions of high temperatures and high humidities, and so tend to become choked, with the result that the streams continually change their courses; the streams are obliged to move sideways, or laterally, and in so doing undertake lateral corrasion. It has been pointed out that rivers on a developing savanna plain are not usually incised in it but flow in broad, shallow hollows; hence, the rivers flow over, or flood, the surface in the wet season in constantly shifting courses. Again, the heavy rains of the summer rainy season result in sheet flow, *i.e.* the water moves over the land surface as a thin sheet, and this, though it may sort out loose material, has very little erosive action. Finally, it has been pointed out that, under the very thorough weathering that occurs under tropical climatic conditions, there is very little coarse material available to act as a cutting tool: the products of weathering are very fine and even though these are swept along by flood water very little erosion of the bedrock is effected. The consensus of opinion seems to be

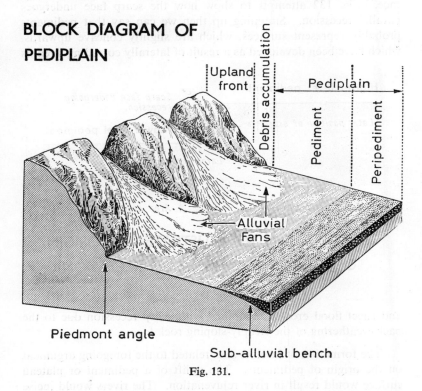

BLOCK DIAGRAM OF PEDIPLAIN

Fig. 131.

that erosion is carried out less by river action than by sheet wash that sweeps away the finer particles.

The scarp face is formed, it is alleged, by the process known as the *parallel recession* of slopes. The weathered, loosened rock on the steep scarp face is moved in part by gravity and in part by hill wash: in other words, there is a combined operation of mass wasting and water movement. Recession is probably helped by stream and flood water washing fine particles against the foot of the scarp and so probably doing a certain amount of undercutting. This, along with the removal of the fine rock waste at the foot of the scarp-slope by sheet flow, helps to preserve the sharp junction between the upper part of the pediment and the base of the scarp face. Fig. 132 attempts to show how the scarp face undergoes parallel recession. Summing up then we can say that pediments probably represent surfaces, which are slightly concave upwards, which have been developed as a result of laterally corrading streams

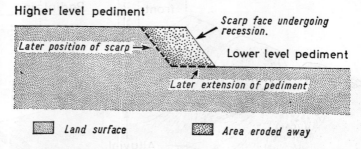

CROSS-SECTION TO ILLUSTRATE THE ORIGIN
OF PEDIMENTS AND SCARP RECESSION
(After Jarrett)

Fig. 132.

and sheet flood erosion combined with scarp recession due to the back-weathering of the steeply-sloping rock face.

The formation of inselberge is related to the foregoing argument on the origin of pediments. The uplift of a pediment or plateau surface would result in river rejuvenation. The rivers would incise themselves into the uplifted surface and applying the line of reasoning outlined above the various segments of the plateau separated by the rivers would undergo a slow process of shrinkage. The recession of the scarps bounding the upland mass would ultimately lead to its complete destruction, leaving behind mere residual stumps, or inselberge. Fig. 133 shows the development of pediments and inselberge.

The Problem in Arid and Humid Tropical Areas

In the previous chapter we referred to pedimentation in arid and semi-arid areas, and in many of these areas where pedimentation has taken place there is an almost total absence of flowing

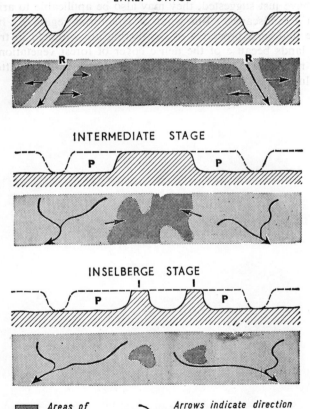

DEVELOPMENT OF PEDIMENTS
AND INSELBERGE

Fig. 133.

water: how, then, could pediments have been fashioned by fluvial action? The most reasonable suggestion seems to be that they were formed in earlier times when conditions were wetter. There is a fair amount of corroborative evidence indicating that in past ages the Sahara had a much moister climate than it has to-day and herein probably lies the answer to the occurrence of pediments and inselberge in the Sahara.

The possible sequence of events which we have outlined above are applied by many geomorphologists to savanna landscapes and, as we have just suggested, they may also be applicable to arid and semi-arid landscapes. But what of equatorial regions? It may well be that such processes of weathering are withheld in tropical humid lands because of the dense cover of forest vegetation; but we do not know: this is one of the problems awaiting attention and solution.

CHAPTER 17

MARINE EROSION AND DEPOSITION

The coast forms the zone of contact between the land and the sea. It is a zone of endless variety and tremendous fascination. Sometimes the coast is almost perfectly straight over long distances, at other times it possesses a sinuosity of bewildering complexity; sometimes the land meets the sea in awe-inspiring abruptness where cliffs, thousands of feet in height, plunge almost vertically into the sea; whereas at other times the land merges, almost imperceptibly, into the sea.

The configuration and character of any coast are the result of the interplay of five main factors:

(i) the nature of the rocks which form the land, *e.g.* whether they are hard or soft, homogeneous or varied, and their structural disposition;

(ii) the work of waves, tides, and currents, *i.e.* the action of the sea, together with other denuding, transporting, and constructing agencies, such as the wind;

(iii) the changes in the relative level of the land and the sea linked with, for example, isostatic readjustment or ice melt;

(iv) the special conditions which may operate in some coastal localities such as volcanic activity, the growth of coral, and the growth of mangroves;

(v) the interference of man who, by dyking and dredging, building groynes, constructing breakwaters and artificial harbours, has often greatly modified the natural coastline.

MARINE EROSION

The work of the sea as an agent of erosion, transportation, and deposition is the most important factor modifying any coastline. Unlike most of the other agents of erosion, the action of the sea is very localised and confined to a narrow zone margining the land. The upper limit of direct sea action is that point reached by the highest tides. Indirectly the action of the sea is exerted above and beyond this point for the under-cutting of cliffs may lead to the collapse of cliff faces well out of reach of direct sea attack. On the other hand, the lower limit of marine action lies some considerable distance below low water mark because of deep-water movements.

Three movements are associated with sea water: waves, tides, and currents. From the point of view of coastline modification, wave action is normally most important. When a wave enters shallow water its speed of movement is reduced, its crest becomes steeper and higher, then it curls over and breaks. The broken water advances up the beach as the *swash* and then retreats down the beach slope as the *backwash*. Waves are propagated by, and driven shorewards by, the wind, hence their height, and therefore their energy, are determined by the wind-strength and the fetch, or distance of uninterrupted water surface over which the wind has blown. Exposure of a coast to a prevailing wind and to the open sea, and therefore to the maximum length of fetch, is thus of great consequence. Such exposure means the coast is open to attack by waves having the greatest energy. Storm waves, which are high, travel fast, and follow in rapid succession, are usually destructive. When they break, they plunge almost vertically and this results in the backwash being more powerful than the swash; hence more beach material is moved downslope than upslope. It is said that 4,500,000 tons of shingle were removed from Chesil Beach during a great storm in 1852. In contrast to these destructive waves are the constructive waves, which are long in proportion to their height, and roll in much less frequently; their crests do not plunge as steeply and most of their energy is spent in running up the beach; moreover, the backwash from one wave has usually returned before the following wave breaks. Hence these waves tend to move material up the beach and so to build up the beach.

Waves usually approach a shore obliquely. If the coastline is straight and if the shore is gently shelving, the part of the advancing wave nearest to the coastline will be subjected to greater friction at its base than that part furthest away and, accordingly, will be held back. That part of the wave furthest from the coast, suffering less frictional drag, continues to move relatively freely shorewards until it, too, comes under the influence of increased friction with the sea bed and its progress is retarded. This "bending" of the wave so that finally it approaches almost parallel to the coast is known as *wave refraction*.

Where the coastline is irregular in its configuration, wave refraction is partly responsible for the erosion of coastal protruberances.

WAVE REFRACTION

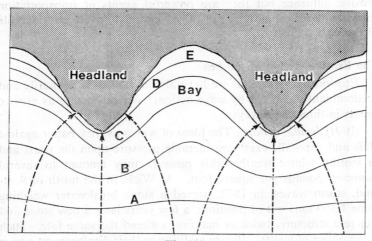

Fig. 134.

A shows the beginnings of sinuosity along the wave front as it enters the shallower water off the headland. *B* and *C* show a greater degree of refraction. *D* breaks on the point of the headland and also against its sides. Hence there is a concentration of erosion along the headlands which leads gradually to their elimination and the straightening of the coastline.

As Fig. 134 illustrates, waves directly approaching headlands turn inwards and concentrate their attack upon them, whereas the waves approaching the bays spread outwards and dissipate their energy. As a result of the wearing back of the headlands (and frequently the associated silting up of the bays), the embayments become less deep; these two conditions mean that more erosive wave energy is available for an attack on the bays. This oscillation in attack, first on the promontories, then on the embayments, means that a kind of equilibrium is established with the entire coastline retreating but retaining, in a general sort of way, the same outline.

Tides also play a significant role in coastal modification firstly because they are responsible for the raising and lowering of the plane of action of waves, and secondly because of the currents that may be associated with them. Strong tidal currents ebbing and flowing in estuaries churn up bottom material and, if they are reinforced by river currents, they may exert a scouring action, flushing material out to sea. Currents are normally too weak to have much erosive influence but they are powerful agents of transportation carrying large quantities of fine material over considerable distances.

The Erosive Action of the Sea

Erosion by the sea, as we have already noted, is primarily and predominantly effected by wave action. Waves operate as erosive agents in three main ways:

(i) *Hydraulic action.* The force of waves as they batter against cliffs and sea-walls exert considerable pressure upon the coast and in stormy winter weather this pressure may amount to several thousand pounds per square foot. At Wick, in the north of Scotland, storm waves, in 1872, moved a stone breakwater weighing some 1,350 tons out of position; a few years later a new stone and concrete structure, twice as massive, suffered the same fate. Such is the power of waves. But, in addition to their displacement power and their direct shattering effect as they pound rocks, waves also effect erosion in another way. When a breaker strikes a cliff face, the air in the cracks and crevices of the rock is imprisoned and compressed and the increased pressure acts like a wedge being driven into the rock and forcing it apart; as the wave retreats, the compressed air expands again and probably subjects the rock to further strain. The continual alternation of compression and expansion of the air in the cracks and fissures of the rock helps to weaken the rock and to enlarge any cavities in it.

(ii) *Corrasive action.* The erosive work of waves, like that of running water, will clearly be greater when they are provided with cutting tools. Waves, armed with sand and pebbles, are able to undertake their erosive work much more quickly and effectively.

In rough seas the hurling of shingle and beach boulders against the cliffs can be extremely destructive; but even under normal conditions the constant swirling of sand and shingle over and against the coast has an abrasive effect. Corrasive action at the base of a cliff leads to undercutting and finally an overhanging cliff is produced. Weathering by frost and rain action, structural weaknesses, together with the pull of gravity, may lead in time to the partial or complete collapse of the overhanging cliff. The fragments of beach material as they are thrown up against cliffs or sea-walls or as they are swirled up and down the beach by the swash and backwash of waves are constantly being shattered and ground up; this break-up and comminution is known as *attrition*.

(iii) *Solvent action.* Sea water contains dissolved chemicals, hence its solvent action is more effective than that of land water. Where rocks which are susceptible to solution, such as chalk and limestone, abut on the coast the chemical solvent action of sea water may have a pronounced effect. For example, "the intricate details of the Carboniferous limestone coast west of Tenby are by no means wholly the result of wave erosion, but to waves acting upon rocks already greatly affected by subaerial and subterranean denudation".[1] Sea water and spray penetrating cracks, joints, and fissures in limestone help to dissolve the rock and are partly responsible for the deep, narrow clefts which are found on the north-east coast of Yorkshire and along the coast of Pembrokeshire.

The Rate of Erosion

The rate at which marine erosion proceeds and also the shape which a coast assumes depend upon a variety of conditions or factors:

(i) The exposure of the coast to wave action and the power of the waves which, as we have already noted, are related to the depth of the sea and to the length of fetch. Inshore water may have shoals or protruding ledges which have a protective function, since they retard wave movement and break the force of the waves and, accordingly, reduce the rate of wave erosion.

(ii) The supply of beach material which the waves find suitable as tools with which to work. While hard rocks and boulder clay

[1] Lake, *Physical Geography*, 1949, p. 276.

usually provide an abundance of pebbles, fine-grained rocks yield mostly fine fragments which are less effective as erosive tools.

(iii) The hardness, resistance, and character of the coastal rocks affect the rate of erosion. Hard, tough rocks, especially if they are massive in character and have few joints and bedding planes, are much more resistant to erosive forces than soft, loosely compacted, or fissured rocks. The presence of cracks, joints, fissures, etc., helps to accelerate erosion.

(iv) The rock structure: massive rocks are usually more resistant than bedded rocks but the dip of bedded rocks is important.

STRUCTURE AND CLIFF PROFILES

  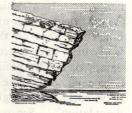

A. Vertical cliffs cut in strata which is horizontally bedded.

B. Stepped cliffs formed where the strata dip landwards.

C. Overhanging cliffs cut in strata dipping seawards.

N.B. The wave-cut notches which are developed at the base of cliffs are formed of hard, resistant rocks.

Fig. 135.

If the beds dip seawards, there is a tendency for the rock to slip downwards along the bedding planes, although tilt towards the sea can be protective. If the strata tilt towards the land, landslips cannot take place and the coast is fairly stable, although under-cutting of the cliff base by wave action facilitates the fall of the overhanging rock (Fig. 135).

(v) The degree and rate of subaerial weathering. This may not only assist coastal disintegration by wave attack, but have an important influence upon the cliff profile. The gentler the slope, the greater, generally speaking, the role of subaerial erosion in coast formation.

It is impossible to give any general figure for the rate of coastal erosion, since the speed with which the land is cut back is dependent upon the above-named variables. It might be thought that the western coasts of the British Isles, exposed to Atlantic storm waves, would be the ones most readily eroded, but strong wave attack is offset by the hard, tough, erosion-resistant rocks of which long stretches of these coasts are built. Erosion here is likely to be a matter of mere inches, perhaps even millimetres, a year. On the other hand, there are coastal stretches in the British Isles where erosion is taking place extremely rapidly, sometimes at the rate of several feet a year. Easily erodible rocks such as sands, gravels, and clays, like those in the boulder clay cliffs of Holderness and East Anglia, are being eaten away with startling rapidity.

The Yorkshire coast between Flamborough Head and Spurn Point is mainly composed of soft boulder clay and erosion is taking place here at a higher rate than anywhere else in the British Isles. The coast is receding with surprising uniformity by between 5 and 7 feet per year, and since Roman times a strip of land, approximately 1 to 2 miles in width, has been eroded away and numerous villages and towns which once existed along the coast of Holderness now lie beneath the waves (Fig. 136). Measurements along the coast south of Bridlington during the years 1952-57 showed a loss of 66 feet in this five-year period; this resulted in an annual loss of about 30 acres a year. The Lincolnshire coast, between Mablethorpe and Skegness, similarly is suffering acute erosion and it has been estimated that the coast has receded between one quarter and half a mile during the past 400 years. In the great storms of early 1953 this stretch of coast suffered especially and great loss and damage were sustained.

One of the most interesting and spectacular examples of coast erosion is provided by the island of Heligoland off the coast of Germany. It is made up of soft Cretaceous sandstone which is very susceptible to erosion and during the past millenium its size has shrunk at an astonishing rate. In A.D. 800 the coastline was 120 miles in length; by 1300 it had been reduced to 45 miles and in the 1930s it was only about 3 miles. To-day the island is 1 mile long, its greatest breadth is less than a third of a mile, and its area is 130 acres; had the Germans, who strongly fortified it, not built sea defences to halt the erosion the entire island would have soon disappeared.

EROSION of the YORKSHIRE COAST

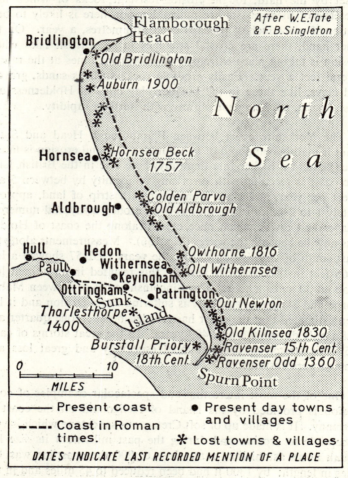

After W.E.Tate & F.B.Singleton

Bridlington
Flamborough Head
Old Bridlington
Auburn 1900

North Sea

Hornsea
Hornsea Beck 1757

Colden Parva
Old Aldbrough

Aldbrough

Hull
Hedon
Withernsea
Paull
Keyingham
Ottringham
Patrington
Tharlesthorpe 1400
Sunk Island
Burstall Priory 18th Cent.

Owthorne 1816
Old Withernsea

Out Newton

Old Kilnsea 1830
Ravenser 15th Cent.
Ravenser Odd 1360

Spurn Point

0   10
MILES

—— Present coast
---- Coast in Roman times.
● Present day towns and villages
✱ Lost towns & villages

DATES INDICATE LAST RECORDED MENTION OF A PLACE

Fig. 136.

The map shows the towns and villages along or near to the Holderness coast which since Roman times have disappeared as a result of coastal erosion.

PLATE XXI

Above: Wave-cut rock platform carved into nearly vertical beds of Old Red Sandstone, Manorbier Bay, Pembrokeshire. Similar rock platforms resulting from marine erosion occur around the coasts of Britain. They are well developed in the Flamborough Head area. (*Eric Kay.*)

Below: Terrace of glacial drift backed by Old Red Sandstone hills, Gower, South Wales. (*Eric Kay.*)

PLATE XXII

Above: Milford Haven, Pembrokeshire. A magnificent ria formed as a result of a rise in sea level (or subsidence of the land) flooding a former river valley. Note the branching limbs of the inlet, marking former tributary valleys. Milford Haven forms a fine, spacious, deep-water harbour and on this account has been developed as a tanker harbour: the oil storage installations can be seen in the middle distance. (*Aerofilms.*)

Below: North Cape, Norway, showing flat erosion surface. Note the steep cliffed coast, the deep cleft in the surface, and the fiord entrance. (*Bergen Line.*)

Topographic Features

A variety of topographic features result from marine erosion. These features fall into two broad, though not entirely unrelated, groups: those connected with the configuration of the coast and those developed as a result of coast recession.

Coastal configuration is primarily dependent upon geological structure. We have noted above the importance of the nature of rock, its hardness, toughness, and resistance, of the structural character of the rock, whether it is massive or bedded and the importance of the lie of the beds, and of the significance of the presence or absence of cracks, joints, and fissures in the rock. These features are largely responsible for the differential erosion that takes place along any stretch of coastline.

Many stretches of coast show an alternation of headlands and bays. These develop in areas where the rock strata differ in hardness and in their resistance to wave attack. A good example is provided by the Torquay area where two cliffed headlands enclose Tor Bay. North and south of Oddicombe, resistant Devonian limestone gives rise to cliffs, whereas Oddicombe Bay itself is composed of softer New Red Sandstone. At Anstey's Cove the limestones dip sharply to form steep cliffs. The rounded shoulder of Black Head is due to a resistant igneous intrusion while the projection of Hope's Nose and the offshore islands are the result of hard, resistant fragments of Devonian limestone. The deep embayment of Tor Bay has been eroded by the waves out of the softer New Red Sandstone and grits and slates. South of Tor Bay, the Devonian limestone reappears and gives rise to another bold promontory (Fig. 137).

Turning now to the features resulting from coast recession, such as caves, arches, sea stacks, etc., we find that they are all associated with the formation of cliffs or the modification of cliffs and the production of wave-cut platforms. In tracing and explaining the evolution of these various features of coastal erosion, it is useful to think in terms of a cycle of events. We can imagine an initial land surface of smoothly sloping character which begins to be attacked by wave action, and which in due course is eroded to produce a cliff face margined to seaward by a gently shelving platform. This is largely theoretical, especially the initial stage in the shore profile, where we assume the existence of an original surface

TOR BAY: INFLUENCE OF ROCKS

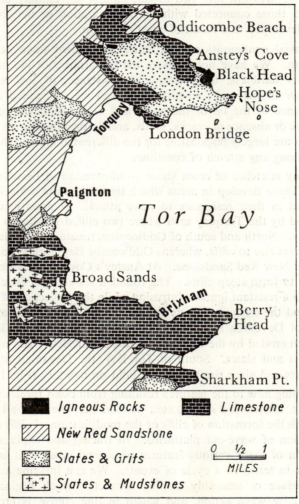

Oddicombe Beach

Anstey's Cove

Black Head

Hope's
Nose

London Bridge

Torquay

Tor Bay

Paignton

Broad Sands

Brixham

Berry
Head

Sharkham Pt.

■ Igneous Rocks   ▨ Limestone
▨ New Red Sandstone
▨ Slates & Grits
⊞ Slates & Mudstones

0   ½   1
MILES

Fig. 137.

Tor Bay illustrates the influence which rocks of differing resistance exert upon coastal configuration: hard, resistant limestone, and an igneous intrusion have resulted in cliffs and headlands while Oddicombe Bay and Tor Bay have been eroded out of the softer New Red Sandstone.

which is smooth and slopes uniformly below sea level; but it helps us to understand the development of coastal features.

The action of waves beating against a smoothly sloping land surface will lead to a notch being cut into the surface. Constant attack by marine erosion, *i.e.* battering by waves, the solvent action of sea water, the horizontal sawing action of swirling shore material, will result in the enlargement of the notch and the production of a cliff face. The eroded material will be carried downslope by wave action and deposited a little offshore. As time goes on the cliff face will retreat, the cliff will get higher, a rock platform (sometimes covered with beach deposits) will be left at the base of the retreating cliff, and an underwater offshore terrace, built up of eroded material, will be developed. Continued erosion and deposition will produce

WAVE-CUT PLATFORM

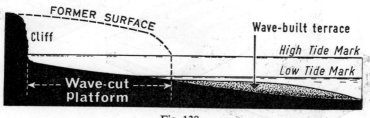

Fig. 138.

a broad wave-cut platform and a wave-built terrace, and also a lowering of the cliffs and a decrease in their steepness due to weathering and subaerial erosion. This sequence of events is illustrated in Fig. 138.

We have just referred to the effect of marine erosion on a smooth, gently-sloping land surface; what happens in the case of an abrupt or steep land surface such as occurs along a fractured coastline? Fig. 139 illustrates the sequence of events. In the initial stage (i) the fault-scarp face will be attacked by wave action and a narrow marine bench developed from the debris deposited at their bases. Moreover, any streams flowing on the land surface will be rejuvenated, because of the change in their base level, and the intensified fluvial action will assist in lowering the land surface.

A fault coast, therefore, frequently exhibits an alternating sequence of deeply cut valleys and spurs ending in abrupt cliff faces. (ii) Finally, the land surface will be reduced in height and the cliff faces lowered while increased marine deposition, provided it is not removed by longshore currents, will lead to the development of a narrow beach. A feature of such fault coasts is the straightness of the cliff line. The northern section of the east coast of South Island, New Zealand, and the western coast of the Indian Deccan are of this kind.

The outcome of the above process of erosion and deposition is to produce a shore profile of equilibrium (cf. the graded profile of

STAGES IN THE EROSION OF A FAULT COASTLINE

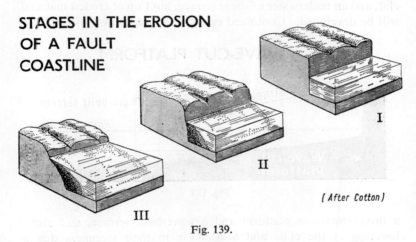

(After Cotton)

Fig. 139.

a river). Such a profile of equilibrium may be defined as a shore slope where the amount of deposition is more or less balanced by the quantity of material which is removed (Fig. 140). Such a condition of equilibrium is, of course, one of a very temporary nature for even a single storm can upset the balance, not to mention slow earth movements or fluctuations in sea level. A perfect idealised profile of equilibrium—a smooth, sweeping curve of concave form, steepest to landwards and flattening seawards—is probably nowhere to be found, although there are many coasts whose general average slopes approach the condition of equilibrium. That something in the nature of graded profiles do exist, and are not purely hypothetical, is shown by the profiles of former shores which in many places have been uplifted to form raised beaches.

Let us now look at some of the features which are developed during the process of shore profile evolution. Cliffs themselves, their height and steepness, depend largely upon the geological structure of the constituent rocks. The height of the land being eroded naturally will determine the height of the cliff, but, gener-

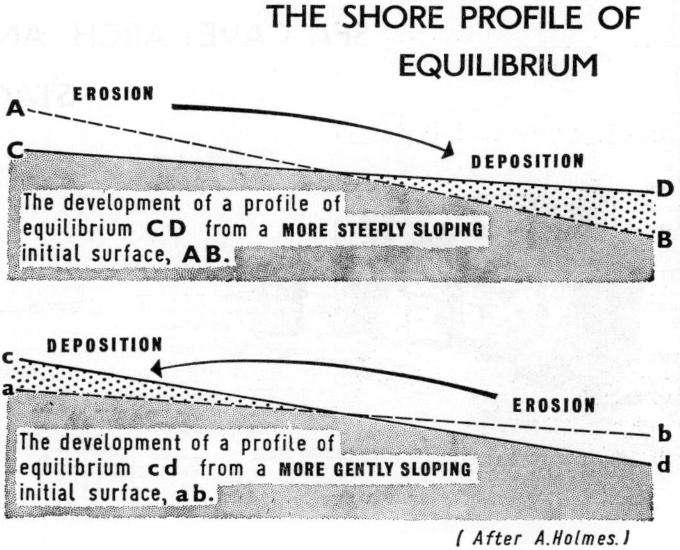
THE SHORE PROFILE OF EQUILIBRIUM
EROSION
A
C
DEPOSITION
D
B
The development of a profile of equilibrium CD from a MORE STEEPLY SLOPING initial surface, AB.
DEPOSITION
c
a
EROSION
b
d
The development of a profile of equilibrium cd from a MORE GENTLY SLOPING initial surface, ab.
(After A.Holmes.)

Fig. 140.

ally speaking, the harder and the tougher the rock, the steeper and the more resistant and durable will be the cliff face. Young rocks of sedimentary origin, which are often softer, will tend to form low cliffs with shelving faces such as those developed along the coast of East Anglia. The rate of erosion also influences the steepness of the cliff face: rapid erosion produces steep cliffs, whereas slow erosion, which allows subaerial denudation to contribute to the shaping, produces a gentler cliff.

Caves are common features along many coasts. They occur at weak points in the cliff face, as along joints or bedding planes.

Once a hole is produced in the cliff face the waves proceed to enlarge it by compression and erosion. Geos, long, narrow inlets penetrating inland from the cliff face, are at least in some cases due to the collapse of cave roofs. The term *geo* is of Scandinavian origin and comes from the Faroe Islands where geos are common coastal features. Huntsman's Leap in Pembrokeshire is a similar feature. Some caves suffer limited roof collapse and a chimney may lead up to the cliff top. In rough weather, waves breaking

SEA CAVE, ARCH AND STACK

Fig. 141.

inside the cave throw up spray through the chimney. These chimneys are also called blow-holes or gloups.

If two caves develop on opposite sides of a headland, ultimately their rear walls may break through to form an arch, *e.g.* Durdle Door, near Lulworth Cove, and the Needle Eye, near Wick. If the roof of the arch collapses, then large pillars of rock are left standing detached from the cliff face; such rock pinnacles are known as stacks and many examples occur around the coasts of Britain, *e.g.* Old Harry, off the Isle of Purbeck, the Needles, off the Isle of Wight, and the Old Man of Hoy in the Orkneys, which is 450 feet high.

The constant attack of cliff faces by wave action leads to the under-cutting and progressive retreat of the cliff face. At the base of the cliff a rocky bench or platform, covered at high tide but uncovered at low, is gradually formed. The platform itself is abraded by the waves rolling and sweeping sand and pebbles to and fro across its surface. These wave-cut platforms slope gently seawards: this is because the outer portion of the platform has suffered scouring action for a much longer period than the inner part. The scars and carrs off the north-east coast of Yorkshire are wave-cut platforms in embryo. Some wave-cut platforms extend out for considerable distances; one of the finest examples is the *strandflat* of north-western Norway which, in places, is up to 30 miles wide. It must be emphasised that the creation of a wave-cut platform is a very slow process, especially if the rocks in which it has been cut are massive and resistant. Moreover, with the extension of the platform, cliff recession is slowed down for the waves have farther to travel and in crossing the broad shallow shelf their energy is diminished; thus when at last they do reach the cliff face their destructive power is negligible.

COASTAL TRANSPORTATION AND DEPOSITION

Marine Transportation

The first point to emphasise with respect to the transporting action of the sea is that the larger proportion of the material moved is provided by rivers and that only a relatively small amount is derived from the direct erosion of coastal rocks. But all this material is modified by abrasion and sorting during its transportation by the sea.

Material is moved by suspension, by saltation, and by rolling as in the case of river transportation. The marine agents of transportation are waves and currents. Material is moved up and down the beach by the swash and backwash of the waves, but an along-shore drift of beach material may take place if the waves approach the shore obliquely. When this happens the swash runs obliquely up the shore carrying material with it. The backwash returns immediately and directly downslope, but the next wave carries the beach material a little further along the shore; hence a progressive movement is maintained. This longshore drift is particularly well demonstrated in southern England where there is a pronounced drift of material from west to east along the Channel coast; here both the dominant waves and the prevailing winds are from the south-west. Waves also contribute to the transportation process by churning up material in readiness to be carried away by coastal currents.

BEACH DRIFTING

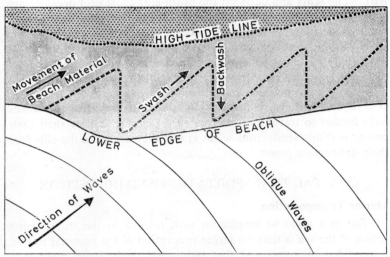

Fig. 142.

Longshore drift or beach drift is the gradual movement of material along the coast. Waves normally approach a shore obliquely and so the swash runs obliquely up the shore. The backwash returns directly downslope. The next wave carries the beach material a little further along the shore. Hence a progressive alongshore movement is maintained unless halted by some obstruction such as groynes.

Currents, both tidal and longshore, undertake much movement of material. The undertow associated with tidal oscillations moves large amounts of fine material, usually in a saltatory fashion, which has been disturbed and stirred up by waves. Tidal currents running in constricted channels, and especially if they are reinforced by river currents, help to "flush out" material. Longshore currents carry fine material in suspension and are often largely responsible for the formation of bars and spits.

Lastly, we should note that wind, though not a marine agent of transportation, frequently assists in the movement of beach material. Dry unconsolidated beach material lies exposed to wind action and strong winds may lead to the piling up of sand to form coastal dunes. Strong onshore winds may result in sand encroaching landwards, as along the Biscayan coast of France, until the dunes were anchored and halted.

Marine Deposition

If, along any coast, some obstruction interferes with the transporting power of waves or currents, some deposition will occur. Obstructions may take the form of strong head-winds, debouching rivers, conflicting currents, or coastal projections. A variety of depositional forms are developed as a result of these obstructions, *e.g.* beaches at the heads of bays, bars across the mouths of rivers, spits across bays, etc.

Marine deposition is normally a slow and steady process, but over a prolonged period major depositional features may be built up. Although the process of deposition is in general a gradual one, actual deposition may be irregular in its character due to the fact that the power of waves and currents constantly varies. Old maps are often helpful in indicating rates of deposition, and Fig. 147 shows the growth of the shingle spit of Orford Ness during the past three hundred years. Deposition at Southport on the Lancashire coast has led to the sea retreating by more than half a mile since the middle of the 18th century.

The more important constructional features are large sand and shingle formations: the chief features may be enumerated as follows: (*a*) beaches and beach ridges; (*b*) offshore bars; (*c*) spits; (*d*) cuspate forelands; (*e*) marshes; (*f*) sand dunes. Let us look first at these constructional features in general and then study one or two specific examples.

TOPOGRAPHIC FEATURES RESULTING FROM MARINE DEPOSITION

Beaches and Beach Ridges

The term beach refers to the accumulation of shore material lying between the low water mark and the highest point reached by storm waves. The amount of beach material present on any shore is variable: upland, cliffed coasts may exhibit little in the way of beach material apart from some boulders and shingle littering the cliff base, but if such a coast is punctuated by headlands, accumulations of sand may occur at the heads of the intervening coves, as in the case of the bay-head beaches along the coast of southern Pembrokeshire or the Gower coast; on the other hand, a gently sloping lowland coast usually gives a wide expanse of sand, as along much of the Lancashire and Lincolnshire coasts. Beaches often show minor features such as shingle cusps, cuspate accumulations of shingle several feet high pointing downslope and separated by embayments of finer shingle and sand, and beach ridges running roughly parallel with the coast and built up by constructive waves.

Offshore Bars

Bars are ridges of sand and/or shingle built up parallel to the shore or across inlets. They are found at the mouths of most of the East Anglian rivers, and in South-west England at the mouths of the Exe, Teign, and Loe (Fig. 144). Although the exact details of bar formation are not quite clear, it seems that they result mainly from wave excavation. Where shores are gently sloping, the breakers break long before they reach the coast and their rotating action excavates material from the sea-bed and a bar is built up offshore. Such a submarine bar may ultimately rise above sea level to enclose a lagoon, as in the Cape Hatteras area of the United States, or link the headlands enclosing a bay to produce *baymouth bars*. A bar which connects an erstwhile island to the mainland is known as a *tombolo*. There is a tendency for offshore bars to move inland as the waves erode the material from the outside of the bar. The lagoon behind the bar gradually silts up and is converted into marsh.

Spits

Spits differ from bars in two main ways: they are attached to, and spring from, the coast, and they are built up by shore drift and not by material from the sea-bed. There are two principal types of spit: those running parallel with the coast and those trending away from the coast at a considerable angle. Their formation is to be explained in part by wave action and in part by alongshore currents. The alongshore drift of marine material frequently augmented by deposits of fluviatile origin coupled with the action of dominant winds and waves are responsible for most spits and when we come to discuss Hurst Castle Spit we shall see the roles played by these

HAFFS AND NEHRUNGS

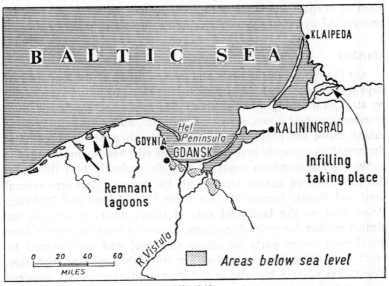

Fig. 143.

The spits or nehrungs grow out and enclose estuaries or bays, as the Hel Peninsula is doing. The lagoons so formed, called haffs, eventually become silted up and disappear. The figure shows nehrungs in various stages of formation, the infilling of a lagoon, and a series of remnant lagoons which will degenerate into marsh and ultimately disappear.

causative factors. Once a spit begins to form it is built up and extended by the accumulation of longshore drift; such growth continues until the water becomes so deep that destructive wave action prevents further extension. Some of the finest examples of spits occur along the southern shore of the Baltic, as illustrated in Fig. 143.

Cuspate Forelands

These are depositional features of great interest but of considerable complexity; good examples are provided by Dungeness, the Darss on the Polish Pomeranian coast, and Cape Kennedy in Florida. They form cusp-shaped forelands built up of shingle ridges with dunes and backed by marshes. In origin they would appear to have developed from a single spit which has undergone deformation at the hands of powerful wave attack. The development of cuspate forelands is so complicated that they can best be understood by reference to a specific example (see p. 353).

Marshes

On the inner sides of spits and bars, infilling of the lagoons and bays proceeds through deposition by the tides, by storm waves, and by streams draining into the area. Sea sands and muds and river alluvium are laid down, slowly accumulate, and eventually become raised above sea level. Marsh vegetation then begins to colonise the mudflats, spreads and helps to trap silt, and so builds up the surface. The northern coast of Norfolk probably best illustrates the formation of marsh land in all its stages. Here are several sand and shingle formations, *e.g.* Scolt Head Island and Blakeney Point, and on the landward side of these, where conditions are almost perfect for quiet deposition, extensive tracts of marsh have developed; some parts lie above sea level and are covered by vegetation while other stretches are still submerged at high tide. Vegetation plays a big role in the formation of marshes; seaweed and salt-loving plants (halophytes) assist the growth of salt marshes. See Plate XXIII.

Sand Dunes

A stage beyond marsh formation is to be seen where sand dunes have developed. For dunes to develop, the land must be built up sufficiently above sea level, there must be plentiful supplies of sand, and plants to colonise and trap the sand. Marram grass, with its deeply-penetrating and branching root system, is particularly effective as an anchoring agent and is often deliberately planted to halt the encroachment of moving dunes. A case in point is the Lancashire coast between the Ribble and the Mersey especially around

Formby; here accumulating sand put an end to Formby's career as a port and threatened to overwhelm the town itself, which was saved only by fixing the dunes with marram grass. Other notable stretches of dune coast are the Culbin Sands of the Moray Firth, Morecambe Bay, and Cardigan Bay in Britain, while on the Continent there is a much more highly developed dune coast in the Landes region of France, along the coast of the Low Countries, and along the southern shore of the Baltic. See Plate XXIII.

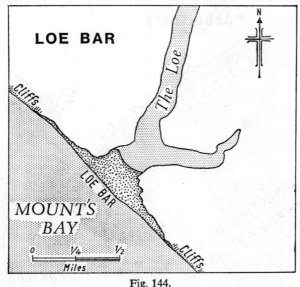

Fig. 144.

SOME NOTABLE DEPOSITIONAL FEATURES

Loe Bar

Loe Bar on the south coast of Cornwall may be said to be a representative example of a baymouth bar. It consists of a shingle ridge about a quarter of a mile long and some 200 yards wide which completely encloses the Loe or the Pool, the water escaping through an artificial tunnel. The bar has been built up by wave action, which has thrown up this great ridge, now appreciably above the level reached by the highest tides. Much of its material must

have been derived from the cliffs further west and carried eastwards by longshore drift (Fig. 144).

Chesil Beach

One of the finest examples of a spit is Chesil Beach which forms

CHESIL BEACH

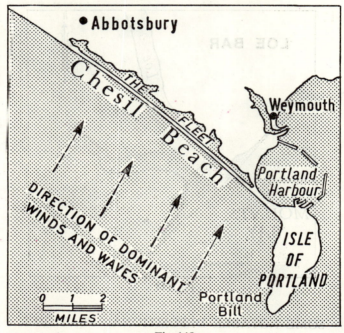

Fig. 145.

Chesil Beach or Bank is a fine example of a tombolo, *i.e.* an island tied to the
land by a spit. The Beach is built up of shingle. Its precise origin presents
something of a problem: it is not certain whether it started off as a spit or as an
offshore bar.

an unbroken stretch of shingle, some 16 miles long, running along
the Dorset coast from Bridport to the Isle of Portland (Fig. 145).
This shingle ridge, 20 to 43 feet high, has been built up by wave
action and longshore drift, the latter being held up by the Isle of

Portland. The dominant winds and waves are from the south-west and these are probably responsible for the longshore drift towards Portland and also, perhaps, for the peculiar grading of the shingle which ranges from pea size in the west to the size of a cricket ball near Portland. A study of the pebbles indicates that many of them have come from far to the west. The Bank itself hugs the coast

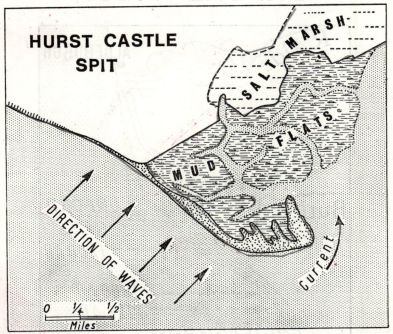

Fig. 146.

for the first few miles and then encloses a lagoon known as the Fleet, a long narrow stretch of tidal water.

Hurst Castle Spit

Situated on the solent coast of Hampshire, Hurst Castle Spit forms a good example of the divergent form of spit which springs off the coast at a marked angle (Fig. 146). It is a shingle spit, about 1½ miles in length, which at its terminal, or distal, end has three recurved ridges. Dominant south-westerly winds have resulted in an eastward longshore drift of beach material which has been built up into a ridge by dominant wave action, which is also from the south-west. The recurring eastern end is due to the fact that this

ORFORD NESS

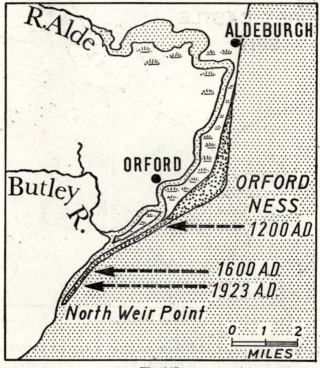

Fig. 147.

part of the spit comes under the influence of north-easterly winds which, in turn, affect the wave direction. Spurn Point has developed a similar hook at its end as a result of the sweeping round of the dominant waves there.

PLATE XXIII

Above: Sand-flats and sand dunes with marram grass (low tide), Goswick, Northumberland. (*Eric Kay.*)

Below: Salt marshes and "emergent coast" with old cliffs, near Silverdale, Lancashire. (*Eric Kay.*)

Orford Ness

Orford Ness on the Suffolk coast is a shingle spit which grew first across the mouth of the River Alde and then extended southwards and grew across the mouth of the River Butley. The long tapering spit has deflected and diverted southwards the water from both these rivers. The main factors involved in the creation of Orford Ness are: alluvium carried down by the rivers, longshore drift moving southwards, the sea current flowing southwards, and dominant winds and waves from the east. Note the growth of the spit since A.D. 1200 or thereabouts, at which time Orford was a seaport facing the open sea (Fig. 147).

Dungeness

This is the best English example of a cuspate foreland. At one time a bay existed between Winchelsea and Hythe and the old cliff line can still be discerned, particularly at Appledore which is now 15 miles inland. Dungeness probably originated as a simple shingle spit developing just south of Winchelsea which was extended across the embayment now occupied by Romney Marsh. It is thought that after this early stage the spit was breached at its western end and, robbed of its supply of eastward-moving shingle, began to move round to face the dominant waves, *i.e.* those from the south-west. Shingle then began to be transported eastwards and to be moved round the Ness itself to build up new shingle ridges on the eastward-facing side, where the dominant waves come from the east. This explanation gives the bare bones of an exceedingly complex, but fascinating evolution. The vast shingle spreads growing eastwards have cut off the bay, which has become filled in with marine muds and sands, and alluvium deposited by the Rother and other streams, which emptied themselves into the bay. Romney Marsh which grew up behind the shingle ridges as a result of this infilling has now, of course, been reclaimed (Fig. 148).

PLATE XXIV

Above: Tropical gully erosion, near Agulu (Udi Plateau), Eastern Region, Nigeria. Torrential rains may carve up the land surface in this fashion and render the land completely useless. The soil is particularly prone to erosion where the natural vegetation has been removed. (*Eric Kay.*)

Below: Wase Rock, 100 miles south-east of Jos, Nigeria, is a volcanic plug, the final residual remnant of a former large volcano. Pelicans use the top of the plug for a breeding ground during the period November to April; the white marking on the summit is due to accumulations of bird-lime. Note the collar of waste material around the base of the plug and the semi-arid bush landscape. (*Aerofilms.*)

The Coast of Norfolk: an Example

To conclude this chapter let us examine a stretch of coast. The coast of Norfolk has been chosen because it presents a variety of interesting coastal features including two which are unique in Britain, viz. marshland areas which are more fully developed than elsewhere and a range of barrier beaches in various stages of formation. Four types of coastal formation—cliffs, shingle beaches and

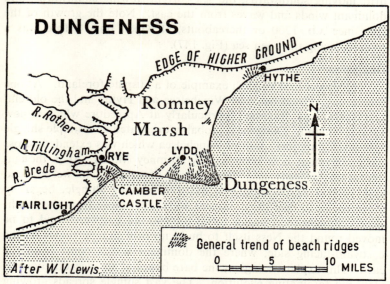

Fig. 148.

There is still considerable doubt about the exact origin of Dungeness which is made up of a series of old beach ridges. The foreland has advanced into the sea by more than one mile during the past four hundred years.

spits, salt marshes, and sand dunes—are to be found along the Norfolk coast and there are good examples of both coastal erosion and coastal accretion. The coast of Norfolk is, therefore, much more varied than its generally smooth outline suggests; moreover, it is a stretch of coast that has undergone, and continues to undergo, constant modification, sometimes through losses by wave attack and sometimes by additions from marine deposition. It provides, therefore, an excellent stretch of coast for the study of many of the processes in coastal formation.

Cliffs abut the shore in three main places: around Hunstanton, between Weybourne and Happisburgh, and a few miles to the north and south of Great Yarmouth. The cliffs, which are quite spectacularly developed at Hunstanton where the chalk hills reach the sea, are composed of the Carstone (Lower Greensand), which forms the base and outcrops on the foreshore, the Red Rock (Gault), an iron-rich pebbly limestone, and the capping layer of Lower Chalk. The Carstone, a coarse sandstone, forms a fine rock platform and a study of this basal platform and the cliffs above it illustrate well the relationship of structure and erosion in a sequence of not very resistant rocks. The beds dip to the east so that at Old Hunstanton the cliff at the back of the beach is no longer present.

Cliffs also extend from Weybourne to Happisburgh where the Cromer Ridge, a conspicuous glacial frontal moraine, reaches the sea. This stretch of coast, at mid-point along the Norfolk coast, is attacked by waves having the longest fetch, *i.e.* the greatest stretch of open sea over which the wind blows. The only winds which travel far enough over uninterrupted stretches of open water and so are capable of building up really big sea-waves are those from a northerly quarter. Since the fetch helps to determine the height and energy of waves, and therefore their erosive force, wave attack upon this particular stretch of coast is emphasised and cliffs have been produced. The cliffs range from sandy, gravelly material in the west, near Sheringham and Cromer, to strong clays with few pebbles in the vicinity of Happisburgh. In the latter area of cliffs, the bedding is simple and the layers lie more or less horizontally with the upper layers exhibiting slumping. The cliffs are eroded after the manner of those in a normal sedimentary series. In contrast, at the western end of the cliffed coast the beds are contorted and twisted and they have resulted in numerous face slips, the formation of gullies, and short-lived sea-stacks. At Sheringham a wave-cut platform has been cut in the chalk.

The third stretch of cliffs, of a more intermittent extent, occur just north and south of Hemsby and to the south of Great Yarmouth. The cliffs along this east coast tend to be low and easily destroyed.

The impingement of the big waves on the north-eastern section of the coast has led to a westerly longshore drift towards the Wash and a south-easterly drift towards Great Yarmouth, with Cromer marking approximately the point of divergence. Flints, derived from the chalk, and pebbles from glacial material have produced shingle beaches. The shingle, together with sand, is transported

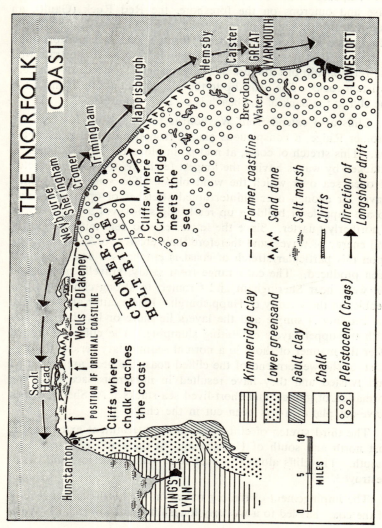

Fig. 149.

alongshore by wave action and accumulations of it have given rise to the spits of Blakeney Point and Yarmouth Spit. Blakeney Point composed more particularly of shingle, which is plentiful at this point, appears to be a spit rather than an offshore bar, although it has been suggested that it may have originated as a bar which has been driven so far inshore that it became attached to the coast.

South of Caister coastal erosion gives way to coastal accretion and longshore drifting has produced Yarmouth Spit. This originated as a sandbank which was thrown up by wave action across Breydon Water, the former wide estuary of the Rivers Yare, Bure, and Waveney. At one time, near Caister, there was an opening but this has become silted up. The southern end of the bank was extended by drift accumulation to form a spit which in medieval times continued much further southwards, almost to Corton. Note

SCOLT HEAD ISLAND

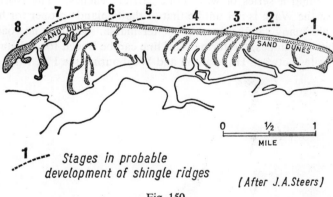

1 Stages in probable development of shingle ridges

(After J.A.Steers)

Fig. 150.

that whereas Yarmouth Spit points southwards, Blakeney Point has developed in the opposite direction, westwards.

Some 10 miles or more west of Blakeney Point is Scolt Head Island. This, basically, is a low ridge of shingle and sand; it is the most fully developed offshore bar along the Norfolk coast. It appears to have been built as a result of the formation of a progressive series of shingle ridges of arcuate form. Each arc suffered

erosion at its eastern end, since it came under the attack of dominant north-east winds, but the western end was extended by longshore
drifting. A series of re-curving lateral shingle ridges in the island
mark the stages in its growth. Fig. 150 will help to make this clear.

East of Scolt Head Island, approximately as far as Wells, is a
series of sand dunes, now largely planted with conifers, although the
dunes are prograding, that is are gradually growing seawards, and
the foreshore is wide and sandy and slopes extremely gently to the
sea. A single line of dunes also fringes the coast between Eccles
and Horsey, a stretch of coast which is now largely protected by a
sea-wall. North of Lowestoft is another stretch of sand dunes. On
exposed coasts sand, unless anchored by marram grass or other
vegetation, is apt to drift and become a menace; for instance,
during the 19th century, the church at Eccles was temporarily
buried prior to it being destroyed by the sea.

Finally, between Wells and Blakeney Point and west of Scolt
Head Island as far as Old Hunstanton are stretches of marsh usually
lying behind a series of wave-built barrier beaches. The Norfolk
coast of the Wash is not unlike that of the Fenlands proper for here
there are many sandbanks that shelter marsh. Behind the coastal
marshes and dunes, the former cliff line can be traced for a distance
of 25 miles between Hunstanton and Weybourne (see Fig. 149).

CHAPTER 18

COASTS, SHORELINES, AND ISLANDS

The terms "coast" and "shore", and "coastline" and "shore-line", are often used interchangeably, but it is useful to draw a distinction between them. Strictly speaking, the coast is the configuration of the margin of the land where it fronts the sea while the coastline is delineated by the cliff line or, if this is absent, by the line reached by storm waves. The shore is the zone of variable width between low water mark and the base of the cliffs, or their equivalent, where the action of the sea is operative. The term "beach" refers to the accumulations of rock debris, *i.e.* sand, shingle, boulders, which lie in the shore zone and rest on the wave-cut bench.

In the last chapter we dealt with the work of the sea as an agent of erosion, transportation, and deposition and noted the various topographic features which resulted from marine action. These features were largely related to coastal and shoreline details. Now we turn our attention to stretches of coast and the types of shoreline which have been developed along them.

COASTS

Coastlines, interpreted as boundaries of the land against the sea, depend for their principal distinguishing features upon the general structural character of the land areas which they demarcate; in other words, their configuration (*i.e.* whether they are generally straight or greatly indented) and their character (*i.e.* whether they are high and cliffed or low, shelving coasts) depend upon the geological origins of the land, whether they are due to mountain-building or to continental uplift or depression.

Long ago the Austrian geologist Suess drew a distinction between coasts of the "Pacific type" and those of the "Atlantic type". The former ran parallel with the structural trend of the

young fold-mountain ranges and were generally disposed longitudin-
ally; the Atlantic type were independent of, and generally ran
across the structural grain of, the margins of the continents. This
fundamental distinction has been generally recognised, but it is
probably more usual nowadays to refer to them either as longitudinal and transverse, or as concordant and discordant coasts,
respectively (Fig. 151).

Other coast types have been added to these, and now five main
types are commonly recognised:

ATLANTIC AND PACIFIC COAST TYPES

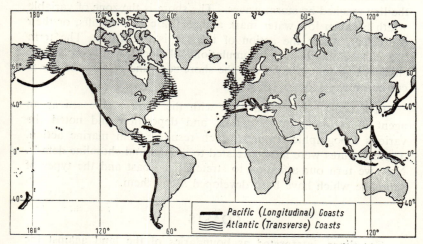

Fig. 151.

 (i) longitudinal or concordant coasts which run parallel with,
     and reflect, the structural grain: the so-called "Pacific type";
 (ii) transverse or discordant coasts which cut across the general
     structural grain: the so-called "Atlantic type";
(iii) fault-block coasts edging the ancient stable plateau blocks
     of Africa, Arabia, India, and Brazil;
(iv) fractured coasts of the margins of foundered basins associated
     with fold mountains, *e.g.* the western Mediterranean basin,
     the Sea of Japan;

(v) alluvial coasts built up of recent sedimentary deposits, *e.g.* the south-east coast of the United States.

Coasts may exert some control over the nature and details of shorelines; this control is particularly well illustrated in the rias of south-western Ireland with its transverse coast, and in the *canali* of the eastern Adriatic coast with its longitudinal structure.

SHORELINES

A wide variety of shorelines exists, and it is possible to attempt a classification of them in various ways. For instance, it is possible to classify them numerically, which is an expression of the degree of their indentation; or to classify them on a descriptive or morphological basis; or to divide them topographically into flat shorelines or steep shorelines; or to divide them according to whether the shore is retreating or advancing; or to classify them genetically, that is by their origin.

The most commonly adopted classification is the simple and useful genetic grouping put forward by D. W. Johnson, who recognised four main categories: submergent shorelines, emergent shorelines, neutral shorelines, and compound shorelines. Even this apparently straightforward grouping is fraught with difficulties for, as a result of the oscillations in sea level during the Pleistocene period, shorelines frequently show signs of both submergence and emergence; the best that can be done is to grade them according to their most strongly marked characteristics.

(i) *Shorelines of submergence.* These are due either to the depression of the land or to a rise in sea level. Three principal subgroups are distinguishable according to the topography:

(a) submerged lowland regions giving rise to estuarine coasts having broad, shallow indentations, usually narrowing inland, and often winding, exposing expanses of mud-flats at low tide and possessing many creeks, *e.g.* the shores of eastern England and northern Germany;

(b) submerged highland regions producing *rias*, funnel-shaped, branching inlets, decreasing in depth and breadth inland, such as characterise south-western Ireland, the south coast of Cornwall and Devon, and Galicia in north-western Spain, or, where these have been glaciated, *fiords* such as are found

TYPES OF COAST

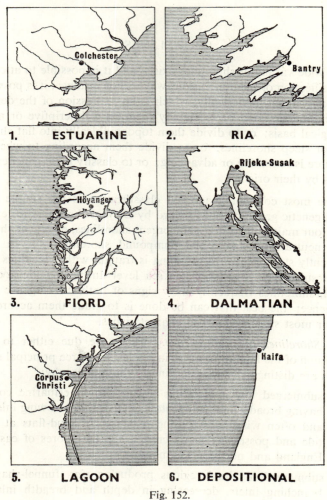

1. **ESTUARINE**   2. **RIA**

3. **FIORD**   4. **DALMATIAN**

5. **LAGOON**   6. **DEPOSITIONAL**

Fig. 152.

in Norway, western Scotland, and along the western coast of South Island, New Zealand;

(c) submerged mountain ranges which are disposed parallel with the coast, giving "Dalmatian type" shorelines, which are characterised by elongated offshore islands, peninsulas, and gulfs (called *canali* and *valloni*), e.g. the Dalmatian shore in the Adriatic, the Arakan coast of Burma.

(ii) *Shorelines of emergence.* Resulting from either the uplift

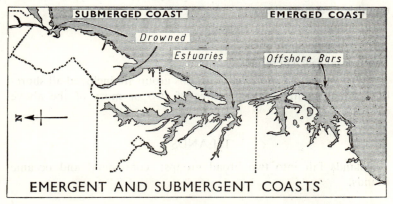

EMERGENT AND SUBMERGENT COASTS

Fig. 153.

Approximately south of Chesapeake Bay to the tip of Florida the Atlantic coast of the United States is emergent. Two raised beaches inland from the coast testify to this uplift: the lower or Suffolk shoreline lies twenty-five feet above sea level, the upper or Surrey shoreline is 100 feet above the present sea level. A wonderful series of offshore bars and lagoons fringe the whole of this emergent coast.

of the land or a fall in sea level, emergent shorelines are less common than those suffering submergence. Two sub-groups, again related to topography, may be distinguished:

(a) a coastal plain shoreline giving in general a smooth, gently-shelving, even shoreline; although such coasts, due to rapid deposition in the shallow waters, tend to build up offshore bars, spits, lagoons, etc. The best example is the shoreline of south-eastern U.S.A., but the Bothnian coasts of both Sweden and Finland fall into this category;

(b) an emerged upland shore resulting from the uplift of a hilly or highland coast; these steeply-sloping shores often exhibit raised beaches, or cliff lines inland and at a higher elevation than the present shore; examples of this type occur in eastern Scotland, north Wales, Crete.

(iii) *Neutral shorelines.* These are to be found in areas where there has been no recent change between the level of the sea and the land margin against which it abuts; in other words, the form of the shore is due neither to submergence nor emergence, but to new materials being built seawards. Again several sub-types are distinguished, among them:

(a) alluvial and delta shorelines;

(b) volcanic shorelines;

(c) coral-reef shorelines.

(iv) *Compound shorelines.* In this group are included all shorelines which combine the features of two or more of the above classes.

ISLANDS

Islands fall into two broad groups: continental and oceanic islands.

Continental Islands

These may be defined as islands which formerly had a connection with the neighbouring continent. This implies that they are usually structural continuations of the adjacent land areas. Typically they arise from the continental shelves. Two sub-groups are frequently distinguished:

(i) those which have been separated from the adjacent mainland in recent geological times, either as a result of subsidence or of erosion; such islands are situated on the shallow continental shelves, are usually built up of the same rocks as their parent continents, and have the same flora and fauna, *e.g.* the British Isles, Ceylon, Newfoundland, Tasmania;

(ii) those which were parted from their mainlands in remote geological times and rise out of deep water; although possessing geological structures which bear strong resemblances to the nearby land masses they show, as a result of their prolonged isolation, peculiar and sometimes unique forms of plant and animal life, *e.g.* Madagascar and New Zealand, which are often described as "old continental islands" to indicate their ancient and complete separation.

Oceanic Islands

Oceanic islands lie in the open ocean, rise out of deep water, are far removed from the continents, and share none of the geological characteristics of the latter, except fortuitously. Oceanic islands may be formed in three different ways: by earth folding, by volcanic action, and by coral growth. New Caledonia and South Georgia are above-water summits of submarine ridges; St Helena and the Hawaiian Islands are volcanic peaks rising from the ocean bed; the Gilbert, and Ellice, and Marshall Islands are coral islands. The factors giving rise to these three types of oceanic island are not mutually exclusive, however, for volcanic activity is often intimately bound up with earth movements, while coral growth frequently occurs around the base of volcanoes or upon submerged platforms.

Topographically, the oceanic islands may also be divided into "high" islands, if they are of tectonic origin, and "low" islands if they are coralline. Many of the volcanic islands have sprouted from the bed of the ocean and tower up massively to great heights. The volcanic peak of Mauna Loa, in Hawaii, built up of successive lava flows, measures a height of 32,000 feet from its base level, the ocean floor (cf. Everest 29,000 feet). An interesting feature in some parts of the world is the tectonic conjuring trick of appearing and disappearing islands.

Island Patterns

Islands conform to one or other of three patterns:

(i) individual, isolated islands such as Easter Island, Bouvet Island;

(ii) archipelagos; irregularly clustered groups of islands of different sizes, *e.g.* the Bahamas, the British Isles, the Aegean Islands;

(iii) island arcs or festoons of islands which mark a partially submerged ridge, *e.g.* the Aleutian Islands, the Antilles.

The patterns which islands take are, in general, linked with their origin. Isolated islands are commonly residual or relic land areas, *e.g.* Jan Mayen, Ceylon, or volcanic islands rising up from submarine platforms or the deep ocean bed itself. Arcs of islands are inescapably linked up with the earth's mobile belts and reflect lines of crustal weakness where submarine ridges with associated vulcanism occur. The arcuate strings of islands are also closely associated with ocean deeps or trenches which parallel them. Archipelagos usually, though by no means always, comprise either foundered platforms, *e.g.* the Cyclades, Faroes, or constructive growths on submarine platforms, *e.g.* coral islands such as the Carolines and Bahamas, and volcanic islands such as the Canaries and Galapagos Islands.

Coral Islands and Reefs

Corals are small marine organisms which have skeletons of calcium carbonate. What actually happens is that corals absorb from sea water soluble calcium salts which they convert into their own calcium carbonate skeletons. Some of them live solitarily, but others dwell in colonies. Along with other organisms such as nullipores, calcareous algae, they build up coralline (limestone) structures. Corals have restricted habitats, thriving only under specific conditions; these are:

(*a*) in waters which are uniformly above 20° C. (*68° F.*);

(*b*) in saline water, for they cannot flourish in fresh water;

(*c*) in clear, clean water which is free from sediment;

(*d*) in water which is not deeper than about 40 fathoms;

(*e*) in water which is well supplied with oxygen and plankton.

Corals are to be found within a zone approximately 30° north and south of the equator, and flourish more particularly in the western parts of the oceans where the westerly equatorial currents have become warmed and agitated and abundantly supplied with oxygen and food. Corals are absent, or few, in sea areas adjacent to debouching rivers which yield sediment and fresh water. They grow most luxuriantly near the sea surface where there is plenty of sunlight. The coral polyp is a fixed organism, for it attaches itself to a resting place. When it dies another coral grows on its surface.

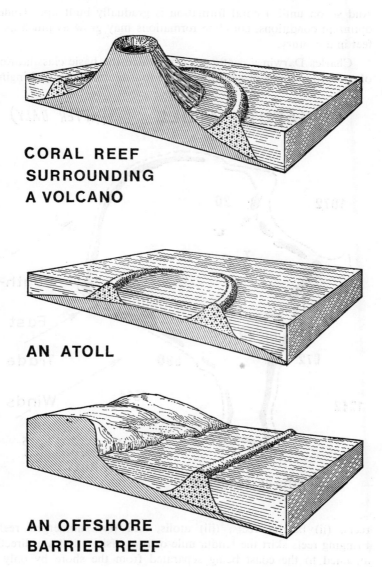

**CORAL REEF
SURROUNDING
A VOLCANO**

AN ATOLL

**AN OFFSHORE
BARRIER REEF**

Fig. 154.

And so on until a coral formation is gradually built up. Under optimum conditions, coralline formations may grow as much as 6 feet in a century.

Charles Darwin a century ago provided the basic classification of coral formations of which there are four main types: (i) fringing

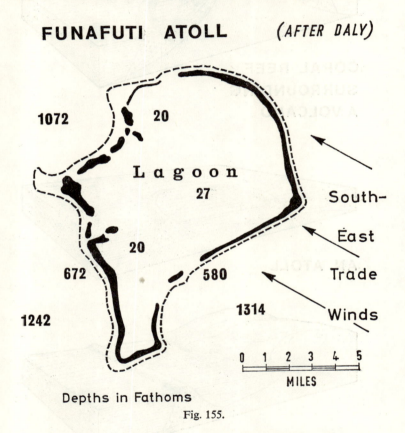

FUNAFUTI ATOLL *(AFTER DALY)*

1072   20

L a g o o n

27

South-

East

Trade

Winds

20

672   580

1242   1314

0 1 2 3 4 5
MILES

Depths in Fathoms

Fig. 155.

reefs, (ii) barrier reefs, (iii) atolls, and (iv) submerged reefs. Fringing reefs skirt the land a mile or two offshore but are directly attached to the coast being separated from the shore by only a shallow lagoon. Fringing reefs grow out seawards or, in other words, where the food supply for the corals exists. Fringing reefs occur around many of the volcanic islands in the Caribbean, the Pacific, and along the coast of East Africa. Barrier reefs are built on the continental shelf but are separated from the mainland by wide and deep channels. The Great Barrier Reef of Australia provides the classic example of this kind of formation; it runs for about 1,200 miles at a distance of around 20 to 100 miles off the coast of Queensland. The Brazilian coast has similar reefs. There is a general tendency for a gently shelving shore to develop a barrier reef and for a steep shore to have a fringing reef. Atolls are roughly circular in shape enclosing a central lagoon of no great depth; their floors are usually flat; and the reef is usually breached in a number of places, but the main passage connecting the lagoon with the open sea is generally on the leeward side. Suvadiva in the Maldives with dimensions of 42 by 32 miles is the largest atoll in the world. Submerged reefs found on submerged banks are not uncommon and these, of course, can be especially dangerous to shipping.

The Origin of Coral Formations

The origin of coral reefs has presented a problem for over a century; the matter is still disputed and remains unsolved. Three main theories have been advanced associated with the ideas of subsidence, submarine platforms, and changes in sea level.

(i) The subsidence theory, put forward by Darwin in 1842 and supported by W. M. Davis, argued that fringing, barrier, and atoll reefs formed successive stages in coral growth around slowly subsiding areas; the slowness with which the sinking took place enabled coral-building to keep pace with the subsidence. For instance, according to Darwin's theory, a volcanic island would first develop a fringing reef which would become a barrier reef with submergence and, ultimately, following on the complete submergence of the island, an atoll.

(ii) The submarine platform theory, proposed by Sir John Murray, the oceanographer, in 1880, argued that reefs were built on subsurface structures which were raised to the critical depth at which corals lived, thus allowing reef-building to take place. The necessary height for coral growth—about 40 fathoms—was achieved either by the marine abrasion of volcanic islands or by the building up of submarine banks by volcanic activity or by submarine plateaus accumulating pelagic deposits.

(ii) The glacial-control theory advanced by R. A. Daly explains reefs in terms of changes in sea level which occurred during the Pleistocene Ice Age. During that period the sea level was lowered as a result of large volumes of water becoming locked up in the ice-sheets. When the sea surface was at its lowest, some 40 or 50 fathoms below the present level, oceanic islands gradually had their summits planed off by wave action. Then, as the ice-sheets melted and the sea level rose and also as the water became warmer, the corals began to re-colonise the newly-cut platforms and in their building were able to keep pace with the rising sea level.

Each of these theories has its drawbacks and poses problems. Darwin's hypothesis requires widespread subsidence which cannot be clearly substantiated although there is more and more evidence to suggest that volcanic piles subside.   A major weakness in Murray's antecedent platform theory is that it demands the occurrence of large numbers of underwater platforms at the required height for reef building; moreover, as Beckinsale says, "to postulate pelagic accumulation in the one instance and wave erosion in the other is rather contradictory". Daly's theory was an attempt to overcome the chief problems encountered in the earlier theories, although Daly's theory itself poses difficulties with respect to coral re-colonisation.

The merits of the various theories can only be satisfactorily attested by deep-water borings. Several borings have indeed been carried out, e.g. at Funafuti, in the Great Barrier Reef, and in the Bikini atoll. The evidence revealed by these experiments is, however, in no way conclusive although it tends to favour the subsidence and glacial control theories. On the whole, it would seem that a combination of these two ideas may best explain atoll formation. Certainly in their simple form, none of the theories appear sufficient to explain the complete range of coral reef phenomena.

CHAPTER 19

LAKES: THEIR ORIGINS AND CLASSIFICATION

Water is a major element in the landscape. One of the forms which the water component takes is the lake. To ask the question "What is a lake?" may seem superfluous; most people can conjure up a clear mental image of a lake. But the question is worth a little careful thought. Let us consider for a moment Lake Victoria, in central Africa, and the Aral Sea, in central Asia: both are extensive sheets of water yet one is termed a lake, the other a sea; wherein lies the difference? Is it because one consists of fresh water and the other of salt water? But why, if this should be the reason, the Dead Sea and the Great Salt Lake, Utah? Obviously, the term lake is not readily nor easily definable. Neither is it a question of mere size: some lakes are larger than so-called seas; for example, Victoria Nyanza is many times the size of the Dead Sea. Moreover, English lakes are mere ponds when measured alongside some of the lakes in the world. Nor is it a question of shape, for some lakes are very regular in shape, such as Lough Neagh in Northern Ireland and Lake Tana in Abyssinia, while others are highly irregular, such as Lake Sungari in Manchuria and the Great Slave Lake in Canada. Considering these points, it becomes clear that the matter of definition is one of considerable complexity.

The study of lakes is known as *limnology*. Broadly speaking, an initial twofold division of lakes can be made: they are either natural or artificial, the latter being man-made reservoirs built for drinking-water, industrial use, irrigation, or hydro-electricity. Natural lakes are accumulations of water in either valleys or depressions. If such bodies of water are drained by rivers, their waters are fresh; if they have no such outlet to the sea, they are salty.

Lakes are temporary features of the earth's surface. Though some lakes may have a long life, such as the Aral and Caspian Seas, which are really relic seas resulting from the uplift of the Eurasiatic platform, lakes in general are relatively short-lived.

Lakes are essentially ephemeral features, since they are the agents of their own destruction. Inflowing streams bring sediment into the lake and, as a consequence of the check in velocity of water-flow, the material held in suspension is deposited on the lake bed. In due time, the lake floor will be raised and the lake reduced in size. That lakes function as "traps for sediment" is well illustrated by the River Rhône: when it enters Lake Geneva its waters are turbid and milky, but when it leaves the lake its waters are crystal clear. Study of a photograph of a lake will very often reveal a lake delta at the point of entry of an inflowing stream, evidence of the infilling process which ultimately will extinguish the lake. Outflowing streams, on the other hand, cut downwards and eventually the lake level is lowered and finally drained. All lakes, no matter what their origin or size, have a common fate. Low-lying lakes are doomed to disappear through the process of in-filling alone; in many cases though they are only partially silted up, they ultimately disappear because of the lowering of their outlet.

Lakes may contain water permanently or seasonally. Under semi-arid conditions especially, but sometimes also under seasonal rainfall regimes, lakes show great variations in size. Tonle Sap in Cambodia, for example, increases its area threefold during the summer monsoon season. In semi-arid climes, lakes may for a time dry up completely; Lake Eyre in Australia provides a good instance of this. In some years, and often for two or three years together, it dries up completely, becoming nothing more than a salt flat. In the summer of 1949 the streams feeding the dry lake bed brought flood waters which led to the inundation of 3,000 square miles and the lake reached a depth of about 12 feet at its maximum. But by the end of 1952 all the water had disappeared by evaporation and the lake-bed was dry once again.

Summing up this brief discussion on lakes, it may be said that they may be: artificial or natural; permanent or seasonal; large or small; deep or shallow; freshwater or saline; and regular or irregular in shape. The innumerable permutations upon these characteristics illustrates the difficulty in defining the term lake other than in broad general terms, such as the accumulation of water in a hollow on the earth's surface.

THE CLASSIFICATION OF LAKES

Lakes may be classified in various ways, but a classification by mode of origin is a convenient and rational method. Collet in his book *Les Lacs,* published in 1925, quotes several suggested classifications, but proposed a grouping by origin as follows: (i) Lakes due to glacial erosion; (ii) barrier lakes; (iii) crater lakes; (iv) lakes of tectonic origin; (v) lakes due to solution in calcareous rocks; (vi) lakes in or on ice; (vii) lakes in hollows intersecting a water-bearing bed; and (viii) organic lakes.

Here it is proposed to adopt a broad, simple, threefold classification based on origin, viz. tectonic or earth movements, erosion, and deposition. It should be borne in mind, however, that some lakes may be due to a combination of causes; for example, a lake may occupy an erosion hollow but at the same time be impounded by a depositional barrier. In addition to natural lakes there are, of course, innumerable lakes, large and small, which are man-made.

Tectonic

(i) Folding. Regions which have undergone folding may give rise to lakes of structural origin. For example, the Lac de Joux in the Jura Mountains has been dammed by an upfold which runs obliquely across a synclinal valley situated between two parallel ridges.

(ii) Warping, that is the twisting and depressing of the land surface, consequent upon earth movements, may produce hollows in which water accumulates, *e.g.* the Caspian and Aral Seas, Lake Balaton in Hungary, and Victoria Nyanza. The Great Lakes of North America are, in part, the outcome of surface warping.

(iii) Faulting producing steep-sided, linear rifts, as in East Africa, provides good sites for lake formation. Lake Tanganyika, Lake Baikal, Lake Torrens, and the Dead Sea are examples of rift valley lakes. Such lakes tend to be long and narrow and deep, with their floors often lying well below sea level.

(iv) Crater lakes are lakes which have formed in the craters of volcanoes, more usually in collapsed calderas or in explosion hollows which have been blasted out of solid rock, such as the *maaren* in the Eifel district of Germany, rather than in ash accumulations, which are not normally water-holding. Well-known examples of crater lakes are Crater Lake in Oregon, U.S.A., and Lake Avernus, near Naples. Lake Toba in Sumatra occupies a vast caldera. Crater lakes are characteristically circular in shape.

(v) Subsidence of the surface may produce hollows in which water may collect. Lough Neagh in Northern Ireland, for instance, resulted from the sagging of the crust after the effusion of lava. Lake Pontchartrain, in the Mississippi delta, is believed to be due to the depressing of the crust by the accumulated weight of deltaic deposits. Rather different are the small, shallow lakes, or meres, of Cheshire which have resulted from local subsidence of the land following upon the removal of underground beds of salt.

Erosion

(i) The erosive action of valley-glaciers and ice-sheets may scoop out hollows in the rock surface, in which water may accumulate. Broadly, two varieties may be distinguished: (*a*) those lakes which are due almost solely to erosive action such as cirque tarns, *e.g.* the tarns of the English Lake District, and (*b*) those which, although occupying ice-scoured depression, are also impounded by morainic deposits, such as the numerous lakes of the Lake Plateau of Finland or the Canadian Shield.

(ii) The deflating action of wind on the land surface may excavate hollows, which reach the water-table and give rise to shallow lakes or swamps. Some of the lakes in central Australia undoubtedly result from wind action which has moved surface sand leading to the formation of shallow lake-pans. Many authorities believe the Qattara depression in western Egypt, with its floor swamps, is at least in part a wind-excavated hollow. Many oases, of course, originate in this way.

(iii) Running water passing over soluble rocks, such as limestone, may give rise to solution hollows. The Shannon lakes of central Ireland, Loughs Derg and Ree, etc., developed through the widening, by solution, of the channel of the Shannon. Lake Scutari (Skadar) on the Albanian-Yugoslavian boundary may be said to fall into this category, since it occupies the bed of a polje, a karst depression, owing its origin, at least in part, to solution. Lake Okeechobee, in Florida, is another example. Another interesting case is the Jura lake, the Lac de Chaillexon; here a former subterranean lake has been exposed by the collapse of the limestone roof which originally covered it.

Deposition

Many lakes owe their origin to an obstruction formed by the deposition of material; lakes in this category are frequently termed "barrier lakes". Such lakes are commonly of a more temporary character, since the impounding barrier is usually easily and relatively quickly removed or pierced.

(i) Fluviatile deposition is a common cause of lake formation. Reference has already been made to the origin of oxbows, or meander cut-offs, which are common features of many river floodplains. Again, a tributary stream may build up an alluvial fan where it enters the main valley, and, in due course, create a blockage which may lead to impounding; this is well illustrated in the case of the Sail Beck, whose extended deltaic fan has led to Bassenthwaite being cut off from Derwentwater. Yet, again, natural river levees may prevent flood waters from flowing back into the river channel, thereby producing temporary lakes such as the *billabongs* along the River Murray in Australia.

(ii) Sand or shingle moved alongshore by currents or piled up by storms or sea-surf across or against a river mouth or bay may lead to the formation of lagoons such as the *fleets* behind Chesil Bank, the haffs of the southern shore of the Baltic, the lagoons of the Malabar coast of India, or the lagoons of the Gulf of Mexico. Here we may note in passing that the Norfolk Broads, originally ascribed to estuarine deposition, are now believed to have been created, at least in part, by man as a result of peat-cutting.

(iii) Morainic deposition by ice-sheets and glaciers has been responsible for the formation of innumerable lakes. The uneven deposits of ground moraine provide hollows in which water can collect, and the low plateaus of Mecklenburg and Pomerania are peppered with hundreds of small lakes. Similarly, the lakes of the Finnish Plateau, in part due to the irregular dumping of ground

SOME TYPES OF LAKES

1. Glacial moraine-dammed lakes   **2.** The broads: man-made lakes

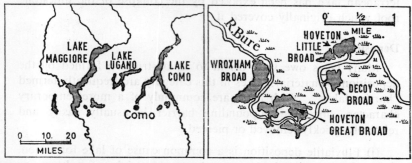

3. Lakes due to crustal warping   **4.** Volcanic crater lakes

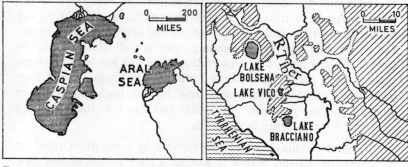

5. Lake caused by glacier dam   **6.** Oxbow lake

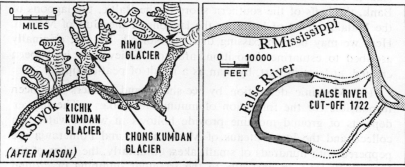

Fig. 156.

moraine and in part to the great terminal moraine of the Salpau-selka, as well as to a measure of ice-scooping, form a maze of oddly-shaped lakes and waterways. Not for nothing is this region called "the land of 40,000 lakes". Sometimes glaciers themselves may create barriers and result in the formation of lakes: the Märjelensee in Switzerland and Lake Valnsdalur in Iceland are ice-barrier lakes.

(iv) Barriers created by lava-flows may give rise to lakes. A flow may block a valley and so, in effect, create a basin for a lake. One such flow has been responsible for the damming-up of the Sea of Galilee in the Jordan Valley. Snag Lake in California is of like origin. Some of the lava-flows which occurred in Iceland in 1783 interfered with the drainage of the Skaptar and its tributaries and formed lakes.

(v) A landslip or rockfall may block up a mountain valley and so impede the drainage to form lakes. Such lakes are usually of a very temporary character since the obstruction is soon cut through. Landslip lakes are not uncommon in Alpine regions. A good British example is Lake Gormire in the Hambleton Hills of Yorkshire which lies cradled in the hollow of a great landslip. In the United States a great earth-flow in Slumgullion Gulch, in the San Juan Mountains of Colorado, led to the damming-up of a river and the creation of Lake San Cristobal.

The Value of Lakes

Lakes have many uses and are of great value to man. Lakes help to regulate the flow of rivers, check flooding, and maintain river level. Flood waters, for example, are spread out over the surface of the lake instead of being concentrated in the narrow river channel, and so help to retard flooding; the lakes hold back the flood waters, as it were, so that the rise in the river level is comparatively small. The lakes on the Yangtse serve a useful function in this respect.

Lakes act as natural reservoirs and so serve as important suppliers of water. Since water is needed in ever-increasing quantities these days for a wide variety of purposes, lakes are valuable assets to man. Thirlmere has long supplied the city of Manchester with much of its water and that city has recently been able to secure Ullswater to meet its additional growing demands for water. Many Welsh lakes (natural and man-made) serve the Merseyside and West Midlands areas.

Lakes also assist hydro-electric power development. One can think of the natural lakes of the Alps, Scandinavia, and Scotland which have been utilised in the generation of power; while, more recently, vast man-made lakes, such as Lakes Kariba and Volta in Africa, and Volga Lakes (*e.g.* Rybinsk) in Russia, have been created for the same purpose.

Where lakes are of large size, they can be used for transportation. The Great Lakes of North America have long offered invaluable transport facilities for the movement of heavy, bulky goods and provide the finest internal water highway in the world. The larger lakes in Africa have lake steamer services.

Lakes often provide valuable sources of fish food. Perhaps the finest example of a lake fishery in the world is Tonle Sap in Cambodia; but most lakes throughout the monsoon lands of Asia are assiduously fished. In an attempt to provide additional supplies of food, and especially protein food in East Africa, fish have been introduced into Lake Victoria and into the new artificial lake of Kariba; both these lakes are likely to develop into important fisheries.

Since lakes are frequently situated in hilly or mountainous country, they enhance the beauty of the scenery, and help to attract the tourist and to stimulate the tourist industry; the most obvious examples are the Lake District and the Trossachs in Britain and the Swiss and Italian lakes. Lakes, then, have an aesthetic value which, in turn, may bring economic dividends.

Lakes, if they are large enough, may exert slight climatic effects by ameliorating the local climatic conditions. The most striking example of this is provided by the Great Lakes of North America; both the Lake Peninsula and the eastern shores of Lake Michigan have more equable conditions than they would have if there were no lake waters to mitigate the low temperatures of winter. Lake Nyasa, too, exerts a noticeable effect on the local climatic conditions, bringing pronounced humidity to the lakeside lowlands of Malawi.

If lakes are strongly saline their waters may be treated to yield the chemicals in them. The best example in this connection is, of course, the Dead Sea whose abnormal salinity makes it economically feasible to evaporate its waters for potash.

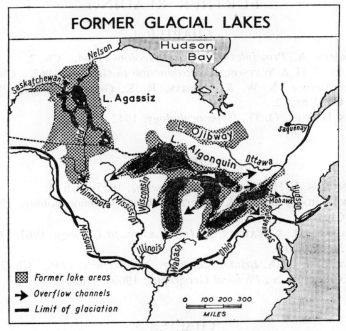

FORMER GLACIAL LAKES

Former lake areas
Overflow channels
Limit of glaciation

0   100 200 300
MILES

Fig. 157.

Finally, it may be noted that old lake beds provide deep, rich, stoneless, alluvial soils of great value for agriculture. Examples of such are the Vale of Pickering in Yorkshire, the Vale of Nepal, and the Red River valley, south of Winnipeg, which was the site of the former Lake Agassiz.

FURTHER READING

CHAPTER 1

HOLMES, A., *Principles of Physical Geology*, 1964. Ch. 2.
READ, H. H. & WATSON, J., *Introduction to Geology*, 1962. Ch. 2.
WOOLDRIDGE, S. W. & MORGAN, R. S., *Geomorphology*, 1959. Ch. 1 and 2.
VON ENGELN, O. D., *Geomorphology*, 1942. Ch. 2.

CHAPTER 2

EDMUNDS, F. H., *Geology and Ourselves*, 1955. Ch. 3.
WOOLDRIDGE, S. W. & MORGAN, R. S. *Geomorphology*, 1959. Ch. 10.
READ, H. H. & WATSON, J., *Introduction to Geology*, 1962. Ch. 3, 5, 7, and 9.
STAMP, SIR L. D., *Britain's Structure and Scenery*, 1946. Ch. 7.
STRAHLER, A. N., *Physical Geography*. 1960. Ch. 19.

CHAPTER 3

SHAND, S. J., *Earth-lore*, 1933. Ch. 2 and 14.
STEERS, J. A., *The Unstable Earth*, 1932. Ch. 4.
HOLMES, A., *Principles of Physical Geology*, 1964. Ch. 2, 26, and 31.
DIETZ, R. S,. "Continent and Ocean Basin Evolution by Spreading of the Ocean Floor." *Nature*, 1961. Pp. 854-7.
HEEZEN, B. C., "The Rift in the Ocean Floor." *Scientific American*, 1960. Pp. 99-111.
CREER, K. M., "Tracking the earth's continents." *Discovery*, 1965. Pp. 34-9.
BULLARD, E. C., "Continental Drift." *Quarterly Journal Geological Society*, 1964. Pp. 1-33.

CHAPTER 4

HOLMES, A., *Principles of Physical Geology*, 1964. Ch. 9 and 11.
WOOLDRIDGE, S. W. & MORGAN, R. S., *Geomorphology*, 1959. Ch. 6.
COLE, A. J. G., *The Geological Growth of Europe*, 1928.

CHAPTER 5

COTTON, C. A., *Volcanoes as Landscape Forms*, 1944.
HOLMES, A., *Principles of Physical Geology*, 1964. Ch. 12.
VON ENGELN, O. D., *Geomorphology*, 1942. Ch. 23.
FOSHAG, W. F., "The Life and Death of a Volcano." *Geogr. Mag.*, 1954.
STRAHLER, A. N., *Physical Geography*, 1960. Ch. 31.

CHAPTER 6

DAVIS, W. M., "The geographical cycle." *Geogr. Journal*, 1899.
WALTON, K., "The Unity of the Physical Environment." *Scottish Geogr. Mag.*, 1968. Pp. 5-14.
SPARKS, W. B., *Geomorphology*, 1960. Ch. 2.
CHORLEY, R. J. & HAGGETT, P., ed. *Frontiers in Geographical Teaching*, 1965. Ch. 2.
BIROT, P., *The cycle of erosion in different climates*, 1968.

CHAPTER 7

LINTON, D. L., "The problem of Tors." *Geogr. Journal*, 1955. Pp. 470-87.
SPARKS, W. B., *Geomorphology*, 1960. Ch. 3.
HOLMES, A., *Principles of Physical Geology*, 1964. Ch. 14.
READ, H. H. & WATSON, J., *Introduction to Geology*, 1962. Ch. 4, pp. 126-36.
MILLER, A. A., "Climate and the geomorphic cycle." *Geography*, 1961. Pp. 185-97.

CHAPTER 8

MEINZER, O. E., *Hydrology*, 1942. Ch. 10.

KUENEN, P. H., *Realms of Water*, 1955. Ch. 5.

SANDERS, E. M., "The Cycle of Erosion in a Karst Region." *Geogr. Review*, 1921. Pp. 593-604.

SWEETING, M. M., "Erosion cycles and limestone caverns in the Ingleborough District." *Geogr. Journal*, 1950. Pp. 63-78.

SPARKS, W. B., *Geomorphology*, 1960. Ch. 7.

STRAHLER, A. N., *Physical Geography*, 1960. Ch. 21.

CHAPTER 9

WARD, W. H., "The stability of natural slopes." *Geogr. Journal*, 1945. Pp. 170-91.

YOUNG, A., "Some field observations of slope form and regolith and their relation to slope development." *Inst. Brit. Geographers*, 1963. Pp. 1-29.

KING, C. A. M., *Techniques in Geomorphology*, 1966. Ch. 2, pp. 51-60.

SPARKS, B. W., *Geomorphology*, 1960. Ch. 4.

COTTON, C. A., "The erosional grading of convex and concave slopes." *Geogr. Journal*, 1952. Pp. 197-204.

CHAPTER 10

SHARPE, C. F. S., *Landslides and Related Phenomena*. 1938.

GIFFORD, J., "Landslides on Exmoor caused by the storm of 15th August, 1952." *Geography*, 1953. Pp. 9-17.

KING, C. A. M., *Techniques in Geomorphology*, 1966. Ch. 3. Pp. 117-30.

HOLMES, A., *Principles of Physical Geology*, 1964. Ch. 17.

DURY, G. H., *The Face of the Earth*, 1959. Ch. 2.

WILLIAMS, P. J., "Some investigations into solifluction features in Norway." *Geogr. Journal*, 1957. P. 42.

CHAPTER 11

LINTON, D. L., "Some Scottish River-captures re-examined." *Scottish Geogr. Mag.*, 1949.

LEBON, J. H., "On the Watershed Migration of the Lowther Hills." *Scottish Geogr. Mag.*, 1935.

LINTON, D. L., "The origin of the Wessex rivers." *Scottish Geogr. Mag.*, 1932. Pp. 162-75.

DURY, G. H., *The Face of the Earth*, 1959. Ch. 3 and 4.

BECKINSALE, R. P., *Land, Air and Ocean*, 1956. Ch. 21.

SPARKS, W. B., *Geomorphology*, 1960. Ch. 6.

KING, C. A. M., *Techniques in Geomorphology*, 1966. Ch. 3. Pp. 81-92.

KUENEN, P. H., *Realms of Water*, 1955. Ch. 6.

CHAPTER 12

MILLER, A. A., "The Entrenched Meanders of the Herefordshire Wye." *Geogr. Journal*, 1935.

LEWIS, W. V., "Nick points and the curve of water erosion." *Geogr. Mag.*, 1945. Pp. 256-66.

DURY, G. H., "Rivers in Geographical Teaching." *Geography*, 1963. Pp. 18-30.

LEIGHLY, J., "Turbulence and the transportation of rock debris by streams." *Geogr. Review*, 1934. Pp. 453-64.

HOLMES, A., *Principles of Physical Geography*, 1964. Ch. 23.

SPARKS, W. B., *Geomorphology*, 1960. Ch. 5.

CHAPTER 13

TABER, S., "Frost heaving." *Journal of Geology*, 1929. Pp. 428-61.

LEWIS, W. V., "Valley steps and glacial valley erosion." *Inst. Brit. Geographers*, 1947. Pp. 19-44.

WRIGHT, W. B., *The Quaternary Ice Age*, 1936.

COTTON, C. A., *Climatic Accidents in Landscape-making*, 1942.

KING, C. A. M., *Techniques in Geomorphology*, 1966. Ch. 3. Pp. 92-107.

DURY, G. H., *The Face of the Earth*, 1959. Ch. 12 to 15.

HOLMES, A., *Principles of Physical Geology*, 1964. Ch. 20.

WORDIE, J. M., "Ice in Greenland." *Geogr. Mag.*, 1955. Pp. 613-20.

CHAPTER 14

BROWN, E. H., "Glacial and Periglacial Landscapes in Poland." *Geography*, 1965. Pp. 31-44.

DURY, G. H., *The Face of the Earth*, 1959. Ch. 12 to 15.

SPARKS, W. B., *Geomorphology*, 1960. Ch. 12, 13.

STRAHLER, A. N., *Physical Geography*, 1960. Ch. 26.

CHAPTER 15

BAGNOLD, R. A., *The Physics of Blown Sand and Desert Dunes*, 1941.

BAGNOLD, R. A., "Movement of Desert Sand." *Geogr. Journal*, 1935.

BAGNOLD, R. A., "Sand formation in Southern Arabia." *Geogr. Journal*, 1951. Pp. 78-86.

STEERS, J. A., "The Culbin Sands." *Geogr. Journal*, 1937.

BARBOUR, G. B., "Recent observations in the loess of North China." *Geogr. Journal*, 1935.

STRAHLER, A. N., *Physical Geography*, 1960. Ch. 28.

DURY, G. H., *The Face of the Earth*, 1959. Ch. 16.

PEEL, R. F., "Some aspects of Desert Geomorphology." *Geography*, 1960. P. 243.

CHAPTER 16

COTTON, C. A., "The theory of savanna planation." *Geography*, 1960. Pp. 89-101.

MILLER, A. A., "Climate and the geomorphic cycle." *Geography*, 1961. Pp. 185-97.

DOBBY, E. H., *Southeast Asia*, 1958. Ch. 3 and 4.

DURY, G. H., *The Face of the Earth*, 1959. Ch. 6.

HOLMES, A., *Principles of Physical Geology*, 1964. Ch. 17.

SPARKS, B. W., *Geomorphology*, 1960. Ch. 11.

KING, L. C., "A theory of bornhardts." *Geogr. Journal*, 1948. Pp. 83-6.

MABBUT, J. A., "Pediment landforms in Little Namaqualand." *Geogr. Journal*, 1955. Pp. 77-85.

CHAPTER 17

LEWIS, W. V., "The formation of Dungeness Foreland." *Geogr. Journal*, 1932.

STEERS, J. A., "The East Anglian Coast." *Geogr. Journal*, 1927.

KING, C. A. M. & WILLIAMS, W. W., "The formation and movement of sand bars by wave action." *Geogr. Journal*, 1949. Pp. 70-85.

GRESSWELL, R. K., *Sandy shores in South Lancashire*, 1953.

SPARKS, B. W., *Geomorphology*, 1960. Ch. 8.

STEERS, J. A., *The Coastline of England and Wales*, 1946.

DURY, G. H., *The Face of the Earth*, 1959. Ch. 9.

CHAPTER 18

JOHNSON, D. W., *Shore processes and shore-line development*, 1919.

SPARKS, B. W., *Geomorphology*, 1960. Ch. 8.

STEERS, J. A., "The coral islands of the Great Barrier Reef." *Geogr. Journal*, 1937.

COTTON, C. A., "Fault coasts in New Zealand." *Geogr. Review*, 1916. Pp. 20-47.

STRAHLER, A. N., *Physical Geography*, 1960. Ch. 27.

HOLMES, A., *Principles of Physical Geography*, 1964. Ch. 23.

LADD, H. S. & TRACEY, J. L., "Coral Reefs in Colour." *Geogr. Mag.*, 1951. Pp. 373-83.

CHAPTER 19

COLLET, A., "Alpine lakes." *Scottish Geogr. Mag.*, 1922. Pp. 73-101.

BECKINSALE, R. P., *Land, Air and Ocean*, 1956. Ch. 22.

LOWE-MCCONNELL, R. H., ed. *Man-made Lakes*, 1966.

INDEX

PRINTED IN GREAT BRITAIN BY UNIVERSITY TUTORIAL PRESS LTD, FOXTON
NEAR CAMBRIDGE